Buenos Aires: 400 Years

Buenos Aires: 400 Years

Edited by Stanley R. Ross and Thomas F. McGann

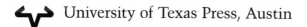 University of Texas Press, Austin

Copyright © 1982 by the University of Texas Press
All rights reserved
Printed in the United States of America

First Edition, 1982

Requests for permission to reproduce material from this work
should be sent to Permissions, University of Texas Press, Box 7819,
Austin, Texas 78712.

Library of Congress Cataloging in Publication Data

Main entry under title:
Buenos Aires, 400 years.

   Includes index.
   1. Buenos Aires (Argentina)—Addresses, essays, lectures.
I. Ross, Stanley Robert, 1921–   . II. McGann, Thomas Francis,
1920–   . III. Title: Buenos Aires, four hundred years.
F3001.B98393   982'.11   82-6903
ISBN 0-292-70738-X   AACR2

The editors dedicate this volume to the memory of James R. Scobie, whose extraordinary contributions to the historiography of Argentina and of Buenos Aires were noted at this conference.

Contents

Foreword

It gave me special pleasure to welcome the participants in this conference to the Library of Congress, not only because of the significance of the subject of the symposium, but because this kind of gathering is prototypical of what the Library of Congress should be doing. We are doubly grateful to those who founded the city of Buenos Aires about 400 years ago for inciting so modular a scheme for enlisting the Library of Congress in the community of scholars.

Henry David Thoreau, who hated cities, once described a city as the place where millions of people are lonesome together. He might have used that as a way of describing what libraries sometimes can be, a place where people work on their own subjects and often are not even aware of the community that they have with other scholars. This occasion, bringing together the scholars of several countries and of several disciplines, attests to the concern of the Library of Congress to become a more active community of scholars, a gathering place where scholars do not need to be lonesome by themselves but can be lonesome in community. I am especially grateful, and we all should be, to the staff of the Library who made this possible, and I want to add my word of thanks to Dr. Broderick, who is the assistant librarian for Research Services, and Bill Carter, Georgette Dorn, John Hébert, and the many others on our staff as well as to those on the staff of the Embassy of Argentina. For leadership in developing this symposium, I especially wish to thank the University of Texas at Austin and Stanley Ross, director of the Office of Mexican Studies of that university. It was he who planned the program and recruited the participants.

The city, especially in the New World, has a significance which awakens us to the meaning of cities everywhere but which is not so visible elsewhere. We can celebrate the 400th anniversary of the founding of Buenos Aires. We can celebrate the founding of many North American cities in a way in which it is difficult for the people of London, or of Paris, or of Rome to celebrate their founding, which is hidden in the mist of prehistory. But, here in the New World, the city is one of our most self-conscious artifacts. The celebration here today of the antiquity and recency of one of the world's largest cities is testimony to our awareness both of our debt to the past and of our power over our future.

We sometimes forget that, in the perspective of the history of our planet, the Spanish language itself is a relatively recent achievement, having been developed only within the last millennium. Many of our greatest cities, too, can trace their lineage in recent history. To paraphrase one of our New England forebears, "All cities are as civilization upon a hill." We are here today to discover our urban inheritance, to see what it brings us, and to find our power and opportunities to shape it together. The city is the most visible, the most graspable, and also the most elusive and the most dissectable of modern communities.

We were especially honored to have the presence of His Excellency, Jorge Aja Espil, ambassador of Argentina, with us because his career embodies most of the dimensions that are explored in these essays. He has explored the world of law and technology and economics, all of which will be seen converging in the papers that were presented to us and are here made available to a larger audience. So his presence was a source of great pleasure for us. We hope that this will be only the first of a continuing series of exchanges on ways of building the community which we all feel and which scholars should always celebrate.

Washington, D.C.

DANIEL J. BOORSTIN
Librarian of Congress

Prologue

I was honored to greet the distinguished group gathered at the Library of Congress to discuss a matter close to the heart of every Argentine. Our magnificent city, Buenos Aires, is 400 years old this year, and the celebration of its birth means so much to us.

It was a great pleasure to see there my friend the distinguished librarian and American historian Dr. Daniel Boorstin, as well as Dr. William Carter, chief of the Hispanic Division of the Library of Congress. In particular, I would like to say thank you to Dr. Stanley Ross, professor of history at the University of Texas in Austin, who has been the moving spirit behind this symposium, and was so responsible for making it a reality.

Dr. Boorstin is in the great tradition of scholarly administrators who often head the world's national libraries. As a justice of your Supreme Court once said, "There must be people who *read* books, *make* books, and *love* books."

Some, like Dr. Boorstin, are noted historians. Others have been well-known poets, like Archibald MacLeish, who occupied the chair that Dr. Boorstin now occupies. Argentina's greatest living poet and writer, Jorge Luis Borges, once directed our national library.

Borges wrote a notable book, *Fervor de Buenos Aires*, which is not well known in this country. The best sense of the title in English perhaps is *Passion for Buenos Aires*. However, it is a passage from another volume, *Cuaderno de San Martín* (A San Martín Notebook), that best expresses how we feel about our city. "To me it is a fairy tale," Borges wrote, "that Buenos Aires was ever created. It is as eternal as the water, as the air."

Buenos Aires was not very eternal during its first years. What has it become? What will it be like in the future? These are questions that occupy the contributors to this volume. I think Borges would like to concede that the eternal must have had a beginning, even though it may have no ending.

As if to assure its grasp on eternity, Buenos Aires did not have one beginning but two. The first, in 1536, was filled with noble hopes but came to an ignoble ending. The founder, Don Pedro de Mendoza, had an eloquent scenario for the drama he tried to stage, but not much plot or many characters. He said he came, and I quote, "to conquer for my Lord, and to proclaim the glory of the name of Him who, though born in a stable, is higher than all kings."

Don Pedro's city was nothing more than a collection of miserable mud huts. Its name, "Our Holy Lady Mary of the Fair Wind," reflected hope, not reality. The settlement soon vanished.

The second founding of Buenos Aires, by Juan de Garay in 1580, is the one we commemorate. De Garay brought less passion and more pragmatism to his task. A Creole, not a Spanish grandee, his ambition was to create a lasting city that amounted to something. The Buenos Aires we know testifies to his success. The people of Buenos Aires wanted to turn to good use the vast River Plate Grant, which they correctly believed was a region of extraordinary potential wealth.

One need only look at Buenos Aires and at Argentina today to see how sound their prophecy was.

This brings me to a point I have made often since I have been ambassador to this country. Our two nations have much more in common than most people realize. Certainly much more than that which sets them apart. Consider our great cities.

Boston is 350 years old this year. Buenos Aires is 400. Over such distance of time and history, the difference in age means nothing. What is significant is the way so many cities in this hemisphere began—Boston as well as Buenos Aires. We can hardly understand today the courage and determination of our early settlers. They came together for protection—and trade—in tiny communities far from what was then the civilized world. Vast, unknown continents stretched beyond, filled with dangers and opportunities they could not even imagine.

Their backs were to the seas they had crossed. In one sense, these people were not only adventurers, but also pioneers who would spread the word of God at the same time they conquered a new world. We know how well they succeeded. The cities from which they started—Boston, Buenos Aires, New York—remain as their monuments, and, of course, have become more than that.

One hears a great deal today about the growth and the importance of Buenos Aires. In the few moments of the program I have been asked to occupy, let me leave you with an impression, no more.

What is Buenos Aires like today? Does it project an image of the whole nation of Argentina? I believe it does. Like the legendary phoenix, it was born, died, and then was born again. My country shows a similar resiliency.

Argentines have a sharp sense of self-criticism that at times seems to become self-inflicted punishment. No matter what problem or condition exists at a particular time, an Argentine will say to a foreign visitor, "This whole situation in my country is a disaster. Nobody, not even the government, has the slightest idea of what they are doing. I see only trouble ahead." Fine for a member of the Argentine family to say! But if the foreigner agreed, and added observations along the same lines, an Argentine would draw himself up proudly. "You are attacking my country unreasonably. We don't have to put up with criticism from misinformed people like you." We have a great deal of national pride, you see.

So it is with Buenos Aires. Like any large city, especially any very old large city, it has problems and drawbacks, as does the nation which reflects its image. We know this is within the family that is Argentina, but we prefer to keep these matters within the family. Buenos Aires, after all, is the paradigm of Argentina.

I should say more about the family that is Argentina. Like yours, it is not merely a single tribe that has grown larger and larger. It is a melting pot of tribes from all over the world. A distinguished Frenchman once described my compatriots. Being French he thought of us in terms of food, and wondered what sort of recipe might have produced such a breed of people.

"Take an Indian woman with large haunches," he began. "Add two Spanish cavaliers, three gauchos well seasoned, an English traveler, a pinch of Basque shepherd, a soupçon of African slave, and simmer for three centuries.

"Before serving, stir in briskly five peasants from southern Italy, a Polish, German, or Russian Jew, a Spanish farmer, three quarts of Lebanese merchant, and a whole French cocotte. Do not let sit longer than fifty years before serving."

Thus, our two countries have a great deal in common. One thing we do not have in common is Buenos Aires, which we believe is the greatest city in the world. I am sorry you cannot have it, except as the topic for a symposium such as this. But we Argentines are not selfish. We will share Buenos Aires with anyone who comes there, as we have for 400 years.

Buenos Aires is more than the gateway to the Pampas. It stands on the Pampas. Before Buenos Aires, the Pampas were nothing but grass and sky, sky and grass, and then more grass and still more sky. Today, they are a rich sea of alternating wheat, corn, and sorghum; a sea filled not with fish but with vast herds of fat cattle.

The Pampas, in other words, are the golden dream, the magic fountain, that first brought Pedro de Mendoza, Juan de Garay, and also our Buenos Aires to Argentina. Borges said that Buenos Aires is as eternal as the water, as the air. So are the Pampas. So is Argentina.

Washington, D.C.   JORGE AJA ESPIL
                                              Ambassador of Argentina
                                               to the United States

Introduction

Multiple-centennial celebrations are occasions for explosions of patriotic pride, with drums beating, bands playing, and flags flying. Not inappropriately, it frequently falls to the academic community to provide a substantive element to the celebration. The 400th anniversary of the founding of Buenos Aires became the occasion for a number of intellectual endeavors.

Just as the Argentine Academy of History dedicated the Sixth International Congress of the History of America in October 1980 to the anniversary celebration, so Latin Americanists at the University of Texas at Austin believed it to be appropriate to organize a symposium similarly dedicated. The event proved to be a national and international undertaking. Organized at the University of Texas at Austin and including scholars from all parts of the United States, the conference was held in September 1980 at the Library of Congress in Washington, D.C. Like the Sixth International Congress in Buenos Aires, the Washington gathering was sponsored by the Municipality of Buenos Aires.

Buenos Aires has always been one of the most interesting, dynamic, and attractive cities of the Americas. One senses its spell and extraordinary appeal whether one first views from sea or air the vast, white mass of the city spread upon the endless green pampas. A year or so ago we were contemplating a series of studies of half a dozen Latin American cities for the *Texas Quarterly*. The decision to discontinue that publication ended the project; but when, in preparation for the undertaking, we surveyed a substantial number of people for suggestions for our list of six cities, only two—Buenos Aires and Mexico City—appeared on every list. Thus, it is particularly appropriate and significant to quote the distinguished Mexican writer Carlos Fuentes, who describes Buenos Aires as the city which he has known best and loved most.

It is a city with a rich history, rewarding to those who are privileged to search its past. The settlement of 1580 grew little during the colonial centuries, from its beginning as a tiny palisaded outpost on the most remote rim of the Spanish Empire. The inhabitants chased cattle, fought off the pampas Indians, and prayed for the discovery of gold and silver mines, none of which existed in their land. By the year 1810, when the movement for independence began, in what was by then somewhat pretentiously named the Viceroyalty of the Río de la Plata, Buenos Aires had only some sixty thousand inhabitants, who still chased cattle and fought off Indians but now also traded large quantities of hides and dried beef abroad.

All that had changed dramatically one hundred years later. Buenos Aires had become a city of 500,000 people, a world trade center for enormous amounts of agricultural and ranch exports, and the magnet for hundreds of thousands of European immigrants each year. One of the world's largest (at its fourth centennial, Buenos Aires had about eleven million inhabitants) and more sophisticated cities, the metropolis exercises a peculiar fascination over all who know it. Part of its attraction—mixed often with hostility and aversion, it must be admitted—may lie in the fact that it is a thwarted city, highly Europeanized and "Americanized," yet remote from the power centers of the world and frustrated by unrealized dreams of continental and world leadership. Then, too, internal political strife has marred the city in recent years, but this may also be considered evidence of the degree to which Buenos Aires shares in the contemporary ills of all dynamic nations.

One point is clear: Buenos Aires, with 40 percent of Argentina's population, leads the nation despite the resistance of many people in the provinces. Whether in industrial production or in opera and poetry the *porteños* (the people of *the* port) deserve good historical study and continued world focus.

In preparing to organize the conference, we reviewed the contributions to the written history of Buenos Aires and of Argentina during the past decade. We gained a sense of the direction of our compatriots' scholarship, of the important new sources they have begun to examine, and of the significant role being played by those chosen to participate in this symposium. Both monographic literature and articles appearing in the scholarly journals reveal a focus on geography and urban growth and on social and economic history. Studies emphasizing the more recent period evidence a similar concern with socioeconomic issues, the evolution and growth of the metropolis, the role of ethnic subdivisions, and the political development of the nation as well as the pivotal place of the federal capital.

The initial section of the volume (like the first part of the conference) is dedicated to the historical city, and it consists of three essays and a commentary. All four scholars have been in the forefront of the recent scholarly emphasis on economic and social history and on the use of new sources in an effort to illuminate and to place in a fresh perspective pivotal periods in Buenos Aires' past. It is our purpose here to describe briefly the contributions of each of the conference participants.

Jonathan C. Brown was responsible for the presentation on the colonial city. He tells how Buenos Aires grew from incredibly humble beginnings—from modest settlement and outpost—to a major colonial city. And he stresses that it was trade and commerce which effected the conversion. After detailing the importance of smuggling and contraband and the succession of illicit trading partners against whom Spanish authorities found it impossible to maintain commercial exclusivity, Brown details how the liberalization which resulted from Buenos Aires becoming the capital of the viceroyalty of the Río de la Plata ironically led to the triumph of protectionism and Spanish domination as a trading partner. However, viceregal prosperity was not without its price, as wartime disruptions, foreign invasion, and exhaustion of the Bolivian silver mines brought division to the city's merchant community and contributed to Spain's eventual loss of its wealthy port.

As a device for examining Buenos Aires in the period of independence, Susan M. Socolow employs the theoretical framework of José Luis Romero, specifically his theory of growth stages, in explaining the urban development of Latin America. The focus is on the transition from the *ciudad criolla*, which increasingly reflected mercantile power, interests, and zeal for progress and which reached its apogee at the time of the Bourbon reforms of the latter half of eighteenth century, to the *ciudad patricia* of the independent Latin America, in which the bourgeoisie governed but had to share power with the countryside.

Socolow chose to analyze the changes that occurred in urban ecology between the viceregal city and that of the early days of independence. Examining population and physical structure from 1740 to 1830, she describes conditions at the beginning of the period, documents new developments, and analyzes the nature and extent of change. She finds that the transition did not occur suddenly, nor did all types of change occur at the same rate. Both the physical growth of the city and population growth continue and are not markedly different in the early years after independence from the lines established during the colonial era. However, there is strong evidence that this growth slowed in the decades following 1810. She does find a shift in the racial balance, as the city began the "whitening process" which would continue through the century. In many ways the independent city does not depart much from the earlier colonial city until somewhat later. "Rather than physical or population changes, the major shift would be in a new psychology of the port city, now free to determine its own economic and political future."

The distinguished senior scholar James R. Scobie, for whom this major contribution is quite unhappily posthumous, began his essay by raising two questions: why does Buenos Aires above all other Argentine cities emerge and flourish during the nineteenth century, and what is the pull, the power, the magic that Buenos Aires exerts over individuals and over other Argentine cities? Noting the recent increase in works of economic and social history and the use of techniques for ordering large amounts of personal data through collective biographies, and for recording and organizing data through the use of computers, he urges that three pivotal eras—the 1810s, the 1830s and 1840s, and the 1860s and 1870s—be studied by these methods. While much has been accomplished, much remains to be done if we are to understand the effect of independence in stimulating the city's economic and demographic growth, the manner in which the Rosas era made Buenos Aires viable as the region's political capital, and the importance of the first two decades in the development of the city and the nation. Suggestively, he lists five aspects which contribute to the city's magnetism: the development of the transportation system; the concentration of profits from new products and new technologies; Buenos Aires' imposition of a state of dependency on the provincial cities; the changing social and cultural environment of the provincial cities; and the political centralization that seemed to confirm *porteño* (the inhabitant of the port: Buenos Aires) power over the nation. Scobie concludes: "The Argentine capital changed enormously during the nineteenth century. But more important than mere growth and development are changes in its relationship with Argentina."

The commentator, Mark D. Szuchman, underscores the magnetism of the port city as well as its key role in the political, economic, and intellectual life of the nation. He notes further that rarely have historians, as historians, played such a fundamental role in the formation of the political ideology of a nation as in Argentina. While recognizing the divisions and the differences, he insists that Buenos Aires has had much in common with the rest of the country. He remarks on the emphasis on growth and development in the presentations, but stresses the process of selective modernization. In that regard, he recommends that topics such as those of Brown and Socolow be considered in the comparative context suggested by Scobie. Finally, he recommends that research stress the manner in which *porteños* related their developing institutional forms, including law, the state, the school, and the family.

Only two issues arose during the brief period of public discussion following the morning presentation. Those who spoke during this period divided fairly evenly on the issue of whether the relationship between the provinces and Buenos Aires was friendly or rooted in antagonism and resentment. A common view seemed to develop that while historically and, perhaps, inevitably there would be tension arising from the preeminence and dominance of the capital, there were also strong ties, both economic and emotional, which provide the basis for a more favorable provincial view of Buenos Aires.

Not unrelated was the challenge to James Scobie's statement that Juan Manuel de Rosas represented Argentine reality. Luis Arocena observed that Rosas surely was a part of that reality, but not all of it. Scobie did not disagree, but stressed that he was endeavoring to show that it was Rosas who, in the political realm, had been able to project Buenos Aires as a capital and to enable it to assert its national role.

During the discussion on the historical city, tribute was paid to the influential nature of Scobie's contributions to the history of Buenos Aires and of Argentina. Therefore, it was not surprising that Richard J. Walter, initiating the session on the contemporary city, should take Scobie's work as his point of departure. Referring to Scobie's book entitled *Buenos Aires: Plaza to Suburb, 1870–1910,* Walter notes that he not only described the basic characteristics of the city's growth within the model of the "commercial-bureaucratic" city, but also suggested that many of the patterns and characteristics of Buenos Aires at the turn of the century persisted into the 1970s. In his paper tracing the socioeconomic growth of Buenos Aires from 1910 to 1980, Walter is concerned with both continuities and changes from the pattern described by Scobie. He does this by considering as principal themes the general demographic patterns, the impact of industrialization, the social structure, the social and ethnic ecology of the city, transportation, and the general features of everyday life. As supporting data he draws heavily on national and municipal censuses.

This scholarly evidence leads him to three conclusions. First, he confirms Scobie's suggestion that many characteristics of the city at

the start of the century and specifically of the commercial-bureaucratic model have continued to the present. Indeed, he concludes that the capital seems more "commercial-bureaucratic" than
ever. However, he cautions that such continuity should not obscure
changes which have occurred: massive migration from the interior,
the increasingly important role of women, the growth of industry,
the expansion of the suburbs, and the increased importance of politics. Second, he remarks that the history of Buenos Aires provides
challenges and opportunities for scholars, because relatively little is
known about the history of the city and its environs since World
War I. Finally, Walter sees the growth of Buenos Aires as posing important challenges today for the nation's leadership. He concludes
with the question: "In sum, will the future greatness of Buenos
Aires be measured only by size and by numbers or instead by the
improved quality of life of each and every one of its inhabitants?"

The difficult task of discussing the intellectual and cultural life
of Buenos Aires fell to Merlin H. Forster. Sensitive to the complexity
and richness of the city's intellectual life and conscious of the relative lack of organized material on the subject, Forster recognizes
that his task is a formidable one. He does adduce evidence which
conveys the centrality as well as the magnitude and intricacy of the
cultural life of the great metropolis. He reaches the conclusion that
"Buenos Aires in the twentieth century has a cultural and intellectual life unrivaled by any Latin American city, and indeed by few cities in the world."

Turning to the field of poetry as his principal illustration, Forster remarks on the effort by some modern Argentine poets to create
an ancient lineage and appropriate mythology for their beloved city.
He analyzes in detail Jorge Luis Borges' poem "La fundación mítica
de Buenos Aires," concluding that for Borges, Buenos Aires indeed
did not have a beginning point; that it "is really as eternal as the elements." With further illustrative material, Forster suggests the variety and richness of the city's cultural life as well as the responses
from some of the city's most sensitive and committed interpreters.

While several of the speakers in this session had touched upon
the contemporaneous condition of the city, and even remarked on
key questions about its future, it fell to Roberto Etcheparreborda to
examine the present and future of his nation's capital. He is fully
aware of the rocky terrain he must traverse with only extrapolation
and presentiment available as tools with which to work. Rejecting
any futurologist pretensions, the distinguished scholar–public official opts for extrapolating some present indicators and perceived tendencies in an effort to define what might occur.

Etchepareborda concludes that the future of Buenos Aires rests on how the city and its inhabitants come to grips with a number of problems: its disordered, uncontrolled, and even irrational development; the dangers of a gigantic city crisscrossed by superhighways; and the deficient location of industry forming a strangulating ring threatening the city and its environment. Culturally and socially, the urban conglomerate has achieved a homogeneous expression and a more defined character. In the political realm the writer stresses the need for autonomy as a municipality for the national capital and for "a democratic feeling" which "pervades the entire society with a sense of rejuvenation" as the only basis on which true progress will be possible.

Joseph S. Tulchin proved once again that last is not least. The commentator for the afternoon session began his remarks by noting that two Argentines who are resident in the United States and a North American have shaped the thinking of North American scholars and the writings about Argentine history in the United States. The North American to whom he referred is James Scobie.

In his remarks Tulchin stresses the sense of neighborhood which both historically and more recently differentiates Buenos Aires from other cities. He believes that one perceives this sense of neighborhood by walking through the city or even by riding through it using the famous *colectivo* (small public bus). What one finds is the persistence of the world of the small town in one of the truly great cities of the world.

Finally, three other Argentine presentations illuminated the conference, and they are included in this volume. His Excellency, Ambassador Aja Espil, set a high tone for the proceedings with his remarks of welcome, which comprise the Foreword to this book. Two distinguished Argentines living abroad offer perspectives from afar. Christián García-Godoy evokes an image of his nation's capital from the viewpoint of the provinces, while Luis A. Arocena has contributed an evocative view of Buenos Aires by a *porteño*. The latter two presentations compose the third and final section of the volume.

A successful conference implies the cooperation of many individuals. We are indebted to the former cultural attaché of the Argentine Embassy, Sr. Pedro Pico, with whom the concept of the symposium was first discussed, and to his successor, Sr. Alberto Carrí, who did superb work serving as intermediary between Austin and Washington and between Austin and Buenos Aires. Special thanks are due to the Municipality of Buenos Aires, which provided the financial support for the event, and to the Library of Congress, which afforded a most appropriate setting for commemorating in this country's capital city the 400th anniversary of the founding of another great capital in this hemisphere. Specifically, appreciation is due to Dr. Daniel J. Boorstin, the Librarian of Congress, and to the outstanding personnel of the Hispanic Division of the Library of Congress: William Carter, chief of the division; John Hébert, assistant chief of the division; and Mrs. Georgette Dorn.

Finally, we wish to acknowledge the invaluable assistance of Warren McKesson, graduate student at the University of Texas at Austin, in the preparation of the manuscript for this book. It is our hope that these pages will illuminate in ever greater clarity that exceptional city known as Buenos Aires, and in so doing will be a substantial contribution to the celebration of the 400th anniversary of its founding.

Austin, Texas   STANLEY R. ROSS
                                                                    THOMAS F. McGANN

I. THE HISTORICAL CITY

1. Outpost to Entrepôt: Trade and Commerce at Colonial Buenos Aires

Jonathan C. Brown

What we know today as Buenos Aires—largest city in the southern cone of South America, the cultural center, Argentina's national capital, and the great commercial hub—rose from incredibly humble beginnings. Early sixteenth century attempts at a truly grand settlement failed. In 1541, the last remnants of Don Pedro de Mendoza's thousand-man expedition of 1536 abandoned the original settlement amid hunger, hostile Indians, and internal discord. Juan de Garay returned from Paraguay thirty-nine years later with only sixty-four Spaniards and Creoles. His modest settlement persisted, not as the administrative center of Spanish dominion in the region, but as an outpost.

The last of the sixteenth-century towns to be established in the Río de la Plata region, Buenos Aires held no exalted place in the original colonial blueprint. It certainly was not intended to be a future viceregal capital. The settlement's particular advantage lay in its position relative to Peru, which contained the colonial world's most productive silver mines, and on the shores of the South Atlantic, whence ship routes could lead to Europe. Consequently, trade and commerce made an important colonial city of the estuary village called Ciudad de la Santísima Trinidad y Puerto de Santa María de los Buenos Ayres.

Throughout its colonial existence, Buenos Aires struggled against Spain's protectionist, mercantilist economic policies. While official trade flowed through Lima and Panama, this modest outpost on the bank of the Río de la Plata gradually prospered on contraband and smuggling. Its experience as a cosmopolitan port began early. In the seventeenth and eighteenth centuries, residents carried on commerce with a succession of foreigners—Portuguese, Dutch, English, French, and North Americans, in addition to Spaniards. Officialdom acknowledged its failure at protectionism with fitful concessions allowing freer legal exchange at the port, but each concession served only to embolden smugglers. Illegal trading proved exceedingly flexible for this outpost, so much so that the decline of any single trading partner—even Spain itself—did not result in economic collapse for Buenos Aires.

In 1776, having more or less on its own become a leading commercial and urban center, the Spanish crown created the viceroyalty of the Río de la Plata, and Buenos Aires was named its capital. This new status resulted in triumph for the protectionist policies of the empire, for Spain now became the leading trading partner of Buenos Aires, to the near exclusion of unauthorized foreigners. The city increased its population, and its merchants grew wealthy importing Spanish and European goods for the entire region. Although silver led all exports, the secondary trade in pastoral products stimulated a growing cattle industry. The city prospered.

Viceregal prosperity carried a price. Wartime trade disruptions, foreign invasion, and exhaustion of Peru's silver mines split the city's merchant community according to the divergent political tendencies of its colonial trade. One group favored freedom of commercial exchange; the other sought to safeguard and protect the port's trade for Spain. If commerce had made Buenos Aires a valuable city in the empire, then commercial rupture contributed to Spain's eventual loss of its wealthy port. As Argentine historian Juan Agustín García wrote, "Buenos Aires was commercially oriented from its beginnings."[1]

The humble village of 1580 was to grow and nurture itself on illegal commerce for one and a half centuries until it had become, quite without imperial sanction, one of the great commercial centers of Spanish America. Shortly after the port's establishment, cartmen from Córdoba and Tucumán brought native cotton textiles and wheat to the estuary for embarkation on ships bound for Brazil. In exchange, merchants secured the European goods they considered vital to the maintenance of civilization in the Indies. Numbering no more than 500 in 1600, the port's residents consumed little of the interior's products and few of the Portuguese and Castilian imports and owned none of the slaves.[2] This was to be a trading people, often *contrabandistas*, at that.

Spanish policy had forbidden direct trade at Buenos Aires because the crown lacked sufficient maritime power to manage it. Official trade in silver from the mining town of Potosí (now Bolivia) descended the Andes Mountains to Lima, went by ship to Panama, transferred across the isthmus to the Portobelo trade fair, and passed aboard Spanish galleons to Sevilla and Cádiz. Thus, Spanish officials were able to protect the passage of bullion and merchandise from pirates and from national enemies while collecting taxes along the way. On the fringes of empire, meanwhile, scarcity and high prices led to smuggling on a grand scale.[3] Buenos Aires was just such an outpost.

Early *porteños*, residents of the port of Buenos Aires, expressed the need for increased trade in their town. Deprived of European goods that they called "necessities," residents complained that Lima's merchants infrequently sent cargoes overland. When European clothing, wine, oil, and weapons did arrive from Peru, their prices were prohibitive and the quality poor. Woolen cloth that cost two and a half pesos in Spain brought twenty pesos in Buenos Aires. Moreover, townspeople lamented having to export their hides and dried meat over the Andes, when direct shipments of native products to Brazil brought twice their original cost.[4] In letters to crown officials, *porteños* pointed out the advantages of Buenos Aires' harbor, including the fact that brigantines of seventy tons burden could come to anchor under the protecting guns of the nearby fort, where they could be loaded with Cordoban wheat for Brazil and cattlehides for Sevilla. The residents suggested a stop at Angola for a shipment of slaves on the return trip.[5] Clearly, these complaints concealed the intention of *porteños* to sell rather than to consume most items of their expanded trade, for the markets of Córdoba, Tucumán, and Potosí at the time were larger.

Royal authorities, under the influence of Sevilla and Lima commercial interest, preferred to respond by permitting only a few registered ships into the harbor. At first, *porteño* merchants were permitted to trade with Brazil and Spain, if they exported no silver bullion. The activity of these "permission" ships persisted into the mid-seventeenth century. Authorities also recognized the right of vessels "in distress" to put in at Buenos Aires for repairs, but their seamen were forbidden to trade.[6] Lacking merchant vessels, the crown also granted slave-trading contracts to foreign companies, beginning with the Portuguese. *Porteño* merchants and their international trading partners abused each of these concessions.

In the end, the crown proved unable to halt contraband. The Council of Trade was located many months away in Sevilla, and the coastlines of the estuary and of the Paraná River system were impossible to patrol. Local officials often chose to participate in the illegal trade, freely granting permission to foreign and unlicensed ships to stop at Buenos Aires. Without proper figures for clandestine commerce, population growth instead may reveal its importance to this commercial city. In 1615, Buenos Aires had approximately 1,000 inhabitants; in 1674, 4,607; in 1720, 8,908; and in 1770, 22,551.[7] The port city, allowed to receive from two to four official ships annually, nonetheless had a population that doubled once every thirty-one years.

The Portuguese were the first of a long line of foreigners who traded at and were absorbed by Buenos Aires. Portuguese merchants passed through as early as 1586, selling their products in Santiago del Estero. Their favored commercial line consisted of African slaves from the Guinea coast. In 1595, the royal grant of the *asiento* (the exclusive contract to sell slaves in the colonies) aided Portuguese traders in both their legal and illegal dealings. They were to exchange slaves for flour, cloths, beef jerky, hides, and tallow, but silver smuggling consumed much of their effort. In the first years of the seventeenth century, their ships appeared with increasing frequency in the waters off Buenos Aires. Portuguese traders even settled permanently in the city, intermarrying with families of the king's worthiest town councillors. By 1650, the older Portuguese merchant families counted themselves among the most loyal of Spanish subjects.[8]

Indeed, Portuguese merchants and local officials collaborated amicably at this Spanish colonial port. City authorities regularly confiscated unlicensed imports of merchandise and slaves, only to sell them back to the original owners at a mock auction. This deception provided importers with the proper documentation to transport otherwise illegal cargoes to the interior.[9] Between 1606 and 1625, approximately 450 slaves annually passed through Buenos Aires, and 9 of 10 lacked the necessary prior licensing. Most slaves sent to the interior worked as household servants, artisans, farmers, herdsmen, and miners. The ships that brought in Africans in irons then departed with illegal silver mixed in with wheat and dried beef for delivery to Portugal.[10] Clergymen had a hand in smuggling, too. Portuguese novitiates would travel to Buenos Aires ostensibly for ordination, then leave with silver bullion in their baggage. Such methods apparently were so successful that lay merchants used Jesuit buildings as warehouses for their merchandise and silver.[11]

In the early seventeenth century, silver and slaves were the principal items of this clandestine commerce. Córdoba and Tucumán merchants added hides, wheat, dried meats, tallow, and domestic woolen and cotton cloths for export. For their part, Portuguese traders brought wines, iron products, sugar, Castilian and Dutch woolens, dried fish, and quince preserves.[12] Between 1606 and 1615, the port annually took in approximately 837,000 pesos' worth of slaves and merchandise and sent out an average of 144,000 pesos' worth of domestic products.[13] Presumably, the difference represents the average yearly export of 693,000 pesos of illegal silver.

By the mid-seventeenth century, Portuguese traders had relinquished their commercial hegemony at the port of Buenos Aires to Dutch traders. Portugal and Brazil had broken away from the control of the Castilian crown, while Spain in the meantime was warring against the British. Under these circumstances, Dutch shippers found ready acceptance for their merchandise, including slaves, among patriotic officials in Buenos Aires. A royal permission ship that arrived at Buenos Aires in 1657 had to share anchorage with twenty-two Dutch and two British ships. Cattle hides were also becoming an increasingly valuable trade item at Buenos Aires. In addition to silver, each Dutch ship carried away several thousand hides, bought at the equivalent of one peso per hide and sold in Europe for six pesos.[14] Foreign traders had found a weak point in Spain's mercantile system.

Like their Portuguese predecessors, the Dutch and other foreigners proved to be capable practitioners of clandestine trade. They landed their richest merchandise along the coastline below Buenos Aires before coming to anchor in the port and paying customs dues on the less valuable items. These Protestant merchants even traded with the brethren of the Jesuit college, who were reputed to have the largest storehouse of illegal silver from Alto Perú. In addition, ships officially registered with the Spanish Council of Trade abused their privileges on a grand scale. Against regulations, a French trader aboard a permission ship in 1657 traveled to Potosí himself to supervise the cartage of illegal silver back to Buenos Aires. At the port, he loaded the bullion *after* his final customs inspection. Then he did not even bother to return to Spain but steered his ship straight to France and Holland.[15] Carlos II, the Castilian monarch, knew of such contraband at Buenos Aires and warned its citizens that illegal trade with foreigners weakened Spain and aided its enemies. He chastised *porteño* officials who enriched themselves on contraband and also merchants in the interior who preferred the cheaper commodities landed at the Atlantic port instead of those dispatched for Lima.[16] Despite the crown's displeasure, smuggling at Buenos Aires continued unabated into the eighteenth century.

British traders gained commercial supremacy in the Río de la Plata at the beginning of the eighteenth century. The Treaty of Utrecht, ending the War of Spanish Succession, awarded to the British South Sea Company the exclusive right to bring slaves into the Spanish dominions. The company established a warehouse in Buenos Aires that supplied the human cargoes to be sold in markets as far away as Potosí and Chile. Between 1715 and 1739, British slave ships delivered to the port some 18,400 Africans from the Guinea coast.[17] The *asiento* stipulated imports of slaves but not of merchandise and the export of native products but not of Spanish silver. The South Sea Company did not keep the bargain. British factors imported merchandise as "company provisions" or simply sold goods to *porteños* aboard ship and left it to them to put the goods ashore without paying customs duties.[18] Fake leaks in their ships afforded the English the opportunity to land illegal cargoes while the vessels were being "refitted." To gain sanction for this illegal trade, they shared their illicit profits with local officials.[19] The market, not the treaty, determined British trade.

Meanwhile, increased shipping in the estuary stimulated growth of the local cattle industry, as exports of bulky hides complemented that of silver bullion in the holds of foreign ships. From such hides, Europeans manufactured the leather utilized in clothing, harnesses, coaches, furniture, baggage, and containers of all sorts. The number of cattle hides leaving Buenos Aires increased from 45,000 in 1716 to 60,000 in 1724. Country residents near the port city acquired sun-dried hides from the *vaquería*, the name for a party of horsemen hunting among the herds of wild livestock that existed on the frontiers of the pampa south of Buenos Aires.[20] Ranchers of the interior also sent hides, tallow, and dried beef to the port via oxcarts, pack-mules, and river boats. As yet, few settled cattle-breeding estates in the vicinity of Buenos Aires provided pastoral exports in large amounts.

The war between Spain and Great Britain in 1739 terminated the British *asiento*, although English smuggling continued across the estuary at Colônia do Sacramento. Established on the Banda Oriental (today Uruguay) in 1680, the Portuguese trading outpost added yet another irritant to Spain's inability to control commerce in the Río de la Plata. Colônia served as outlet for the cattle industry of the Uruguayan prairies, and sailing barks easily transshipped illegal cargoes to and from the Spanish port. British ships, excluded from Buenos Aires, merely put in across the estuary. A Spanish military raid on Colônia in 1762 surprised twenty-seven English vessels in the port.[21] With this military action, the Spanish crown recognized that, against imperial wishes, trade had made Buenos Aires one of the most important commercial centers of Spanish America. It had to be protected for Spain.

In 1776, therefore, Spain established the viceroyalty of the Río de la Plata in order to consolidate its political control of the southern fringe of the empire. The Bourbon monarchy undertook economic reforms with the intention of reorganizing commerce within the colonies. For Buenos Aires, designated viceregal capital and principal port of Spanish trade in the region, a new era of commercial growth began.

Actually, the Bourbon reforms represented the most successful imperial effort yet to regulate commercial exchange in the estuary. *Potosino* silver now was to be exported legally through Buenos Aires, not Lima, because the viceroyalty included within its borders most of the mining centers of Alto Perú. Free trade at the port pertained only to ships of Spanish registry passing between ports within the empire. The new *consulado*, a regulatory chamber of merchants, was intended further to protect Spain's commercial interests in the estuary. Most of all, the new Spanish customshouse was to collect duties on the expanded and now legal trade.

Porteño merchants no longer needed to resort to large-scale contraband and illegal commercial practices, as long as official trade flourished. For a while, it did. Spain became the chief trading partner of Buenos Aires for the first time in the port's two centuries of existence. Annually, about sixty ships from Spain arrived at the port, and in a good year such as 1796, as many as seventy-three vessels of Spanish registry entered.[22] Roughly half of the city's Iberian trade passed to and from the port of Cádiz, followed by Barcelona, Málaga, Coruña, and the colonial port of Havana. The dominance of Cádiz, Spain's international port, meant that many of the goods loaded there were transshipped from Northern Europe. Merchant vessels proceeding from Cádiz carried at least 60 percent foreign goods in their holds.[23] *Porteño* consumers, therefore, were legally receiving the foreign goods to which they long had been accustomed.

Colonial silver, European merchandise, and African slaves continued to dominate trade at Buenos Aires, while incidental exports of pastoral products further developed the cattle-breeding industry. As during contraband times, the textiles of Spain, England, and France dominated import manifests, and Vizcayan iron and general European luxury items also found markets in Buenos Aires. Yearly imports of Spanish mercury, carried by oxcart and packmule to the mines of Alto Perú, reached 273 metric tons in 1790.[24] During the viceregal period, silver production at Potosí averaged 3.6 million pesos per year, and approximately two-thirds of it headed toward the Río de la Plata. Available sources estimate the value of silver as 50 to 80 percent of all freight leaving Buenos Aires and Montevideo.[25] Farm and ranch products comprised up to one-third the value of all exports. Annual exports of dried and salted beef for the Cuban slave population jumped from 158 metric tons in 1787 to 1,785 tons within ten years. The hide trade alone increased nearly sixfold in eighteen years, from 150,000 hides in 1778 to 874,594 in 1796.[26] River boats delivered cattle products from the riverine provinces and the Banda Oriental, where the traveler still found the largest livestock estates. The Estancia de las Vacas near Colônia, for instance, ran more than 40,000 head of livestock and employed nearly forty permanent workers in the 1790s.[27] Cattle-breeding was developing rapidly in another area as well.

Rural residents on the pampa south and east of Buenos Aires gradually began to breed and domesticate livestock in order to supply expanding export markets. Inefficient cattle hunts no longer sufficed to meet the demand for pastoral products and actually threatened depletion of cattle on the prairies. Thus, frontier areas like Chascomús and Rojas attracted settlers who began to duplicate the more sophisticated production systems of the interior provinces and of the Banda Oriental. The colonial *hacendado* lived on his estate and worked the cattle with his sons, hired hands, and one or two slaves.[28] Experienced workers came from elsewhere in the region, and rapid population growth in the area between Buenos Aires and the Río Salado reflected the extent of migration within the viceroyalty. The district of Luján, for instance, had increased its population from 464 persons in 1781 to 2,000 in 1798.[29] Accomplishing most of the slaughtering, hide preparation, and tallow extraction right on their estates, ranchers dispatched products to the port aboard oxcarts.[30] In this fashion, the area south of Buenos Aires began to provide an increasing volume of cattle products for the city's warehouses.

The port of Buenos Aires, it appears, supported a favorable balance of foreign trade during the viceregal period. For the years 1794 to 1808, exports totaled 30,521,186 pesos, while imports reached 25,726,723 pesos. Customs receipts also depict the general trend of foreign trade at the port, for revenues increased from 20,000 pesos in 1777 to 400,000 pesos in 1790 and to 1 million pesos by 1804.[31] These conclusions reflect official trade and presume a negligible amount of smuggling. Such may not have been the case.

Contraband did not disappear, for the Bourbon trade reforms had neither eliminated high customs duties nor ended certain monopolies, nor had they permitted unrestricted foreign shipping in the estuary. Foreign shipmasters engaged in short-manifesting of their cargoes, while their *porteño* buyers brought goods ashore under cover of darkness. Wandering salesmen sold illegal Brazilian tobacco throughout the city and countryside, openly violating the prerogatives of the tobacco monopoly.[32] Occasionally, authorities did punish large-scale abuses, and raids on merchant warehouses uncovered foreign cottons, linens, woolens, and silks for which customs duties had not been paid.[33] Officials were aware that silver was being exported in much the same clandestine fashion. Contraband goods turned out to be cheaper for consumers, and the profits for the merchant were higher.

Population growth, administrative importance, and commercial wealth now combined to make Buenos Aires the largest consuming market in the entire region. Urban residents increased in number from approximately 24,000 persons in 1776 to 42,000 in 1809.[34] The viceregal government expended more revenue on improvements and bureaucratic salaries in the capital than in any other jurisdiction of the viceroyalty. In 1790, for instance, it spent 3 million pesos in the capital yet collected only 2.3 million pesos there in revenues and taxes.[35] Import merchants saved their quality merchandise for customers in the capital, while sending the unsalable and shoddy goods to the interior. In 1802, only a third of the 4 million pesos' worth of imported goods was passed on to markets in cities of the interior.[36] More than most traders, *porteños* now were the region's most important consumers.

The importance of foreign trade at the port engendered a social system in which the most respected members were wealthy merchants engaged in the import-export sector. Whether Creole like Juan M. de Pueyrredón or Basque like Gaspar de Santa Coloma, the richest businessmen easily moved among the ranks of the viceroyalty's Spanish-born administrators. Numbering about 178, the import-export wholesalers, or *comerciantes*, conducted all trade from the port, controlled most capital resources, and arranged freighting of goods to interior markets. The largest merchants maintained contacts in the ports of Spain as well as with correspondents in interior cities like Potosí, Mendoza, and Córdoba. They invested in auxiliary economic activities, such as retail sales, coastal and river shipping, and meat-salting plants, but rarely in rural land. As yet, ranching did not produce the sort of wealth that attracted the *porteño* businessman.[37] Below this group of commercial moguls existed a large network of warehousemen and retailers. *Porteño* retailers of cloths and imported goods numbered about 600, and an additional 700 *pulperías* (general stores) were located throughout the city for the sale of wines, spirits, candles, salt, bread, kindling, and other consumer items.[38] The commercial structure of the city had matured greatly since the days of contraband trade.

Indeed, for the colonial port, these were the best of times as well as the worst, because interruptions and uncertainties of international trade during the viceregal era tarnished this record of prosperity. After 1797, the Napoleonic conflicts of Europe brought Buenos Aires a decade of poor trade, added two foreign invasions by British troops, produced a sudden glut of foreign imports on domestic markets, and concluded with the unrelated collapse of Potosí's silver production. Spain, allied to France at the beginning of the European wars, suffered the displeasure of the greatest sea power of the age, Great Britain. A British naval blockade against the Spanish mainland reduced Spain's trade with its colonies. Buenos Aires' exports fell from a level of 5 million pesos in 1796 to less than one-half million pesos the following year.[39] In retaliation, Spain closed its ports to British merchandise, much to the consternation of *porteño* merchants who had been prospering on the sale of transshipped goods from Bristol and Liverpool.[40]

The European conflicts caused Spain to relinquish its brief commercial leadership at Buenos Aires to the merchantmen of other trading nations, who now returned to the port without Spanish intermediation. Portuguese shipping from Brazil revived, while for the first time, North American vessels began to call in the estuary. In 1800, forty-three United States ships arrived from Boston, New York, and Philadelphia with slaves from Mozambique and with re-exported European goods.[41] Meanwhile, Great Britain was feeling the same pain of wartime trade disruption that troubled Spain and its American ports. British merchantmen no longer were sailing into the estuary, nor were they dealing with Spanish American *contrabandistas*. After a decade of commercial frustration, one British military leader sought singlehandedly to re-open old markets in the Río de la Plata.

Sir Home Riggs Popham, leading naval and land force from the Cape of Good Hope, captured Montevideo and Buenos Aires in 1806. Although Sir Home had acted without the authority of his own government, the invasion excited the commercial imagination of British businessmen, who fitted out 100 ships for Buenos Aires. The resulting surfeit of foreign merchandise at the port collapsed consumer prices, and both British and *porteño* merchants suffered losses.[42] English trade, nevertheless, had returned to Buenos Aires permanently. By 1808, the Spanish and the English were allied against the French, and in the following year, British mariners unloaded more than 1 million pounds sterling of cargo at Buenos Aires.[43] French-occupied Spain was powerless to protect its colonial trade.

Such commercial turmoil divided the influential *porteño* merchant community and contributed to the city's dramatic political events of 1810. One party, of which the *contrabandistas* of the seventeenth century had been precursors, favored trade at the port with ships of all nations and encouraged the sale of products in the quality and quantity determined by the marketplace. Free trade, argued Creoles Mariano Moreno and Manuel Belgrano, reduced the price of goods to the domestic consumer and enlarged export markets for the region's ranch products.[44] The opposite interest preferred trade stability, Spanish commercial contacts, and the sanction of the crown. *Porteño* merchants with strong ties to Spain, like Spanish-born Martín de Alzaga, longed for a return to the golden age of viceregal commerce, when ships from Cádiz had dominated Buenos Aires trade.[45] The latter position, having been legitimized by the silver-rich commercial prosperity of the late eighteenth century, ultimately was undermined by an economic event beyond anyone's control. By 1810, the silver mines of Alto Perú had played out. Henceforward, the free traders would benefit from the port's carefully nurtured ability to shift the export line from silver to hides and from its historic penchant to deal freely with non-Spanish shippers.

Many of these commercial trends that are evident in the colonial experience of the port of Buenos Aires continued into the nineteenth century, albeit with important changes. Foreign trade increased dramatically. Sailing vessels from many nations, which formerly had called at the port for silver, now came for the hides, tallow, and also raw wool demanded by the North Atlantic countries then undergoing industrial revolution. Foreign merchants settled in the city in order to organize the import-export business, much as had the Portuguese and English slave traders of previous centuries. Cart trains and river boats continued to arrive from the provinces with export and consumer items and to return with imported goods.

Between 1810 and mid-century, the export trade consisted of those pastoral commodities previously disdained by the wealthy viceregal merchants. To fill the city's warehouses with export products, stockyards and slaughterhouses in the suburbs processed cattle on-the-hoof, while marketplaces gathered sheep's wool and dried hides directly from *estancias*. The largest Argentine landowners, many of whom were sons of colonial merchant families, now became the city's wealthiest citizens, as cattlemen and sheepmen settled the virgin prairies beyond the colonial frontier of the Río Salado. After all, colonial commerce at the port gradually had brought the livestock industry from an incidental pursuit to the principal activity of the economy. Buenos Aires, the outpost of empire, long since had become Buenos Aires, the commercial entrepôt.

Notes

1. Juan Agustín García, *La ciudad indiana: Buenos Aires desde 1600 hasta mediados del siglo XVIII* (Buenos Aires, 1955), p. 104. García's study first appeared in 1900.

2. Manuel E. Gondra Manuscript Collection at the University of Texas Library, document number 1828 (hereafter cited as MG 1828), Manuel de Frías, "Justificación del . . . procurador general del Río de la Plata y Paraguay . . . ," copy (n.p., 1614?), p. 7; MG 1260, Pedro Sotelo Narváez, "Relación de las provincias del Tucumán . . . ," copy (n.p., 1582), pp. 24–25; and Enrique de Gandía, *Francisco de Alfaro y la condición social de los indios, Río de la Plata, Paraguay, Tucumán y Perú, siglos XVI y XVII* (Buenos Aires, 1939), p. 477.

3. For the theory and practice of Spanish trade with the colonies, see C. H. Haring, *Trade and Navigation between Spain and the Indies in the Times of the Hapsburgs* (Cambridge, Mass., 1918).

4. MG 1262, Cabildo de Buenos Aires, "Memorial y instrucción para nuestro procurador general . . . ," copy (Buenos Aires, 1614), pp. 3–6, 9; MG 549e, Manuel de Frías, "Carta a S. M. sobre que se prorrogue y amplíe la merced . . . ," copy (n.p., 1618?), pp. 79–80; and MG 1205, Pedro Baygorri Irruez, "Informe extenso a S. M. sobre la provincia," copy (Buenos Aires, 6 December 1653), pp. 3–6.

5. From 1580 to 1640, Portugal, Brazil, and Angola formed part of the Spanish Hapsburg empire. For various trading schemes out of Buenos Aires, see MG 1205, Baygorri Irruez, pp. 8–10; ibid., pp. 11–12; and MG 32a, Manuel de Frías, [Viaje de Cádiz al Río de la Plata . . .], copy (Buenos Aires, 30 April 1621), p. 9.

6. For trade restrictions, see MG 1828, Frías, p. 4; MG 1410, Felipe III [Real Cédula deliberando y reglamentando el comercio . . .], copy (Madrid, 10 December 1618), pp. 1–3; and MG 549e, Frías, pp. 76–78. Also consult Ricardo Zorraquín Becú, "Orígenes del comercio rioplatense (1580–1620)," *Anuario de Historia Argentina*, vol. 5 (1943–1945), 71–105; and Ruth Tiscornia, *Hernandarias estadista: La política económica rioplatense de principios del siglo XVII* (Buenos Aires, 1973), p. 47.

7. Jorge Comadrán Ruiz, *Evolución demográfica argentina durante el período hispano (1535–1810)* (Buenos Aires, 1969), pp. 43–44. These figures were derived from travelers' estimates as well as from city censuses. Revised and more complete population figures appear in Susan M. Socolow's essay which follows.

8. For the economic penetration of the Río de la Plata by Portuguese traders, see MG 32c, Manuel de Frías, [Semillas introducidas en las provincias del Río de la Plata y Paraguay], copy (Buenos Aires, 21 May 1621), pp. 17–18; MG 1482, Martín Ignacio de Loyola, [Carta a S. M. sobre algunas cosas ...], copy (Buenos Aires, 13 February 1603); MG 1205, Baygorri Irruez, p. 10; and MG 32a, Frías, pp. 4–5. Also see Alice Piffer Canabrava, *O comércio português no Rio da Prata, 1580–1640* (São Paulo, 1944).

9. MG 1812g, Mateo Sánchez [Verdadero testimonio sacado de los libros Reales de los derechos . . .], copy (Buenos Aires, 18 May 1599), pp. 94–100.

10. Magnus Mörner, *The Political and Economic Activities of the Jesuits in the La Plata Region, Hapsburg Era*, trans. by Albert Read (Stockholm, 1953), p. 51; Gandía, *Francisco de Alfaro*, pp. 478–479; and Elena Fanny Scheuss de Studer, *La trata de Negros en el Río de la Plata* (Buenos Aires, 1958), pp. 91, 102.

11. Mörner, *Political and Economic Activities*, p. 118n. For other information on seventeenth-century contraband, see Zorraquín Becú, "Orígenes del comercio"; and Mario Rodríguez, "The Genesis of Economic Attitudes in the Río de la Plata," *Hispanic American Historical Review*, 36, no. 2 (May 1956), 179n.

12. MG 1812h, Sánchez, p. 99

13. Laura Randall, *A Comparative Economic History of Latin America, 1500–1914*, vol. 2, *Argentina* (Ann Arbor, 1977), p. 167.

14. Acarete du Biscay, *Account of a Voyage up the River de la Plata and Thence Overland to Peru* (London, 1698 [Reprint: New Haven, Conn., 1968]), pp. 3–5, 13, 20–21.

15. Mörner, *Political and Economic Activities*, p. 167; and the French merchant's report in Acarete du Biscay, *Account of a Voyage up the River de la Plata*.

16. MG 318, Carlos II, "Resumen de las consultas en que su magestad resolvió fundar y extinguir la Audiencia de Buenos Aires . . .," copy (n.p., 1672?), pp. 1–6.

17. Arthur S. Aiton, "The Asiento Treaty as Reflected in the Papers of Lord Shelburne," *Hispanic American Historical Review*, 8, no. 2 (May 1928), 167–168; Judith Blow Williams, "The Establishment of British Commerce with Argentina," *Hispanic American Historical Review*, 15, no. 1 (February 1935), 44; George H. Nelson, "Contraband Trade under the Asiento, 1730–1739," *American Historical Review*, 51, no. 1 (October 1945), 60–61; and Sergio R. Villalobos, *Comercio y contrabando en el Río de la Plata y Chile, 1700–1811* (Buenos Aires, 1965), p. 32.

18. Jean Olivia McLachlan, *Trade and Peace with Old Spain, 1667–1750* (Cambridge, Eng., 1940), p. 82; and Vera Lee Brown, "The South Sea Company and Contraband Trade," *American Historical Review*, 31, no. 4 (July 1926), 666–668, 672.

19. J. Campbell, *The Spanish Empire in America, by an English Merchant* (London, 1747), pp. 318–319.

20. On the export of hides, see Rodríguez, "Genesis of Economic Attitudes," p. 179n; and Aiton, "The Asiento Treaty," p. 175. For the *vaquería*, consult Martin Dobritzhoffer, *An Account of the Abipones, an Equestrial People of Paraguay*, trans. from the Latin, 3 vols. (London, 1822), vol. 1, p. 221; and the seminal work of Emilio Coni, *Historia de las vaquerías del Río de la Plata (1555–1750)* (Madrid, 1930).

21. Villalobos, *Comercio y contrabando*, pp. 21–22; and Dauril Alden,

"The Undeclared War of 1773–1777: Climax of Luso-Spanish Platine Rivalry," *Hispanic American Historical Review*, 41, no. 4 (February 1961), 55–74.

22. Villalobos, *Comercio y contrabando*, pp. 56–57; and Anthony Z. Helms, *Travels from Buenos Ayres, by Potosí, to Lima*, trans. from the German (London, 1807), p. 44.

23. Félix de Azara, *Descripción e historia del Paraguay y del Río de la Plata*, trans. from the French, 2 vols. (Madrid, 1847), vol. 1, p. 357.

24. Manfred Kossok, *El Virreinato del Río de la Plata, su estructura económica-social*, trans. from the German (Buenos Aires, 1972), p. 76.

25. See the estimates of Lamberto de Sierra, treasurer of Potosí, in *Colección de documentos inéditos para la historia de España*, 10 vols. (Madrid, 1842–1895), vol. 5, pp. 170–184; Vicente Pazos, *Letters on the United Provinces of South America*, trans. by Platt H. Crosby (New York and London, 1819), pp. 136–138; and Herbert S. Klein, "Structure and Profitability of Royal Finance in the Viceroyalty of the Río de la Plata in 1790," *Hispanic American Historical Review*, 52, no. 3 (August 1973), 444–445.

26. For the Cuban trade, see Alejandro Malaspina, *Viaje al Río de la Plata en el siglo XVIII* (Buenos Aires, 1938), p. 309; and MG 16b, Pedro Melo de Portugal, [Carta a Diego de Gardogni dando cuenta del estado de la renta de S. M.], copy (Buenos Aires, 12 November 1795). For hide exports, see Villalobos, *Comercio y contrabando*, pp. 56, 97; John Lynch, *Spanish Colonial Administration, 1782–1810; The Intendant System in the Viceroyalty of the Río de la Plata* (London, 1958), p. 169; and Helms, *Travels from Buenos Ayres*, p. 44.

27. John Mawe, *Travels in the Interior of Brazil*, 2nd ed. (London, 1823), pp. 49–51; Archivo General de la Nación, Buenos Aires (hereafter referred to as AGN), Sala IX 37-5-4, *Cuentas de la Estancia de las Vacas en la Banda Oriental, 1790–1800* (E. 19), "Expediente sobre propuesta del administrador . . ." (Vacas, 1799); and ibid. (E. 1), "Cuenta de cargo y data hecha por el administrador . . ." (Vacas, 1792).

28. AGN, Sala IX 3-10-4 (E. 249), "Bando publicado prohibiendo el uso de las carretas grandes . . ." (Buenos Aires, 23 December 1783); and AGN, Colección Biblioteca Nacional 187 (1800), "Los comandantes de Chascomús, y los Ranchos, no permitirán que Don Antonio Obligado haga establecimiento de corrales . . ." (Buenos Aires, 3 November 1797).

29. Comadrán Ruiz, *Evolución demográfica argentina*, p. 99.

30. AGN, Sala XIII 15-4-3 (libro 3), *Estancia San Miguel del Monte de la familia Roca, 1809–1812.*

31. Germán O. E. Tjarks, unpub. ms. on government income and foreign trade during the viceroyalty, as quoted by Randall, *A Comparative Economic History*, vol. 2, pp. 179–180; and Lynch, *Spanish Colonial Administration*, pp. 121–122.

32. AGN, Sala IX 33-5-2 (1179), "Hacienda. Causa sobre la aprehensión echa en la campaña . . ." (n.p., 1788); and Sala IX 33-4-1 (940), "Hacienda. Autos obrados con motivo de haver aprehendido . . ." (n.p., 1786).

33. AGN, Sala IX 34-2-6 (2515), "Contrabando sobre remate de los efec-

tos aprehendidos . . ." (n.p., 1800); and Germán O. E. Tjarks and Alicia Vidaurreta, *El comercio inglés y el contrabando: Nuevos aspectos en el estudio de la política económica en el Río de la Plata, 1807–1810* (Buenos Aires, 1962), p. 10.

34. Comadrán Ruiz, *Evolución demográfica argentina*, pp. 80, 115.

35. MG 1055, Ignacio Flores, [Carta a José de Gálvez exponiendo su opinión sobre la erección de virreynatos . . .], copy (n.p., March 1783), p. 5; and Herbert Klein, "Las finanzas del Virreinato del Río de la Plata en 1790," *Desarrollo Económico*, 13 (July 1973), 388.

36. Susan Migden Socolow, "Economic Activities of the Porteño Merchants: The Viceregal Period," *Hispanic American Historical Review*, 55, no. 1 (February 1973), 5n; and Germán O. E. Tjarks, *El consulado de Buenos Aires, y sus proyecciones en la historia del Río de la Plata*, 2 vols. (Buenos Aires, 1962), vol. 1, p. 315.

37. For a comprehensive treatment of the import merchants of the period, see Susan Migden Socolow, *The Merchants of Buenos Aires, 1778–1810* (London and New York, 1978).

38. Mawe, *Travels in the Interior of Brazil*, pp. 49–51.

39. John Lynch, *The Spanish American Revolutions, 1808–1826* (New York, 1973), pp. 46–47.

40. John Constanse Davie, *Letters from Paraguay; Describing the Settlements of Montevideo and Buenos Aires* (London, 1805), p. 87; and also Mawe, *Travels in the Interior of Brazil*. Mawe was a British merchant engaged in the legal trade between Cádiz and Spanish America when the war broke out. In 1797, he was seized in Montevideo.

41. For information on early U.S. trading in the Río de la Plata, see Charles Lyon Chandler, "United States Merchant Ships in the Río de la Plata (1801–1808), as Shown by Early Newspapers," *Hispanic American Historical Review*, 2, no. 1 (February 1919), 27, 29; and Arthur P. Whitaker, "Early Commercial Relations between the United States and Spanish America," in R. A. Humphreys and John Lynch, *The Origins of the Latin American Revolutions, 1808–1826* (New York, 1965), pp. 92–93.

42. R. A. Humphreys, *Liberation in South America, 1806–1827: The Career of James Paroissien* (London, 1952), p. 1; Mawe, *Travels in the Interior of Brazil*, pp. 14–15; and Williams, "The Establishment of British Commerce," pp. 46–47.

43. A figure of 1.2 million pounds sterling between 1 November 1808 and 1 November 1809 is most often quoted. See Lynch, *Spanish American Revolutions*, p. 47. Tjarks and Vidaurreta, *Comercio inglés y el contrabando*, p. 21, place the figure at 1.6 million pounds sterling.

44. See Diego Luis Molinari, *La representacíon de los hacendados de Mariano Moreno*, 2nd ed. (Buenos Aires, 1939), pp. 280–377; and Tulio Halperín Donghi, *Revolución y guerra: Formación de una élite dirigente en la Argentina criolla* (Buenos Aires, 1972), pp. 130–137.

45. Socolow, *The Merchants of Buenos Aires*, pp. 163–168.

2. Buenos Aires at the Time of Independence

Susan M. Socolow

José Luis Romero in his book *Latinoamérica: Las ciudades y las ideas*[1] describes a series of chronological growth stages which he believes best explain the urban development of Latin America. After passing through the first stage—that of *ciudad hidalga de Indias*, when the Baroque city of the sixteenth and seventeenth century was controlled by an American nobility—Latin America's urban units entered a second stage—that of *ciudad criolla*. The *ciudad criolla* was a city which increasingly reflected mercantile power, interests, and zeal for progress; its apogee coincided with eighteenth-century Bourbon reforms. In turn, the *ciudad criolla* gave way to the *ciudad patricia*, that of independent Latin America, a city governed by a bourgeoisie but forced to share power with the countryside. According to Romero, the crucial date in the transformation of the city from *criolla* to *patricia*, from Bourbon to independent, was 1810, a date not surprising in light of the momentous political events which included a certain *cabildo abierto* meeting in May of that year in the city of Buenos Aires.

In Buenos Aires the Revolution of 1810 unleashed a period of tumultuous political life covering the next twenty years. A series of different political factions each made a bid for power, in turn eventually giving way to other factions. Not only were a variety of political forms attempted, with the supreme director replacing the triumvirate which in turn had replaced the junta, but the balance of power and prestige of different sectors of the government shifted greatly.[2] But what of the city itself? What changes, if any, occurred in the urban ecology between the viceregal city and that of the early days of independence? To examine this larger question, this study will focus on two aspects of urban ecology—population and physical structure—from 1740 to 1830, first describing these components and then determining the extent of continuity and of change as the city moved from one stage to another.

Founded initially in 1536 and resettled again in 1580, Buenos Aires grew slowly during the seventeenth century. Only in the eighteenth century, the time of the *ciudad criolla*, did the city begin to prosper, first as the result of illegal trade and after 1776 as an official port of the Spanish commercial empire. In 1580, at the time of the second founding, the city's original site was shifted slightly, so that the Santa María de los Buenos Ayres which survived lay on the banks of the Río de la Plata, a broad, shallow estuary of the Paraná River, at the point where the lower reaches of the Matanza River, the Riachuelo, entered the larger waterway.[3] The city's site had two natural geographical advantages: relatively high ground provided by the low *meseta* which came almost to the shoreline, and a deep estuary anchorage provided by the Riachuelo. It also had several disadvantages including two *zanjas* or streams which flooded during heavy rains, shallow waters along the Río de la Plata coast, a lack of firewood, and no lack of hostile Indians.

The original plan of the city, that of the founder, Juan de Garay, divided the area into 231 *solares* or plots. According to Garay's *repartimiento*, the city was to cover an area of approximately two kilometers running north to south along the river, by one kilometer running east to west, toward the interior (230 hectares). The total space encompassed by this *repartimiento* was 9 by 15 square blocks; each block measured 150 *varas* squared.[4] But more than half of the 133 square blocks included in the original plan were not effectively inhabited, consisting instead of land at the future disposal of the founders and their families. Garay's plan was overly ambitious given the city's original population, but the general outlines drawn by the founder were to remain the same during the seventeenth and eighteenth centuries.

The few maps extant from the first half of the eighteenth century show essentially the same configuration as the original Garay plan.[5] In these maps the city runs 9½ blocks from east to west, that is, from the shore inland (the half block is the area below the *meseta* [the *bajo del río*]) and sixteen blocks from north to south. All of the major civil and ecclesiastical establishments except one (the exception being the Concepción parish church) are within 3½ blocks from the coast, suggesting that the areas farther from the shoreline were sparsely inhabited.

By 1744, the year of the first more or less complete census of the city, the city proper covered an area of 14½ by 26 square blocks. By 1778, the urban plants had only grown to 15 by 27 square blocks, and by 1810, the city was 15½ by 28 square blocks. Clearly, although the late colonial period was one of economic growth of the Río de la

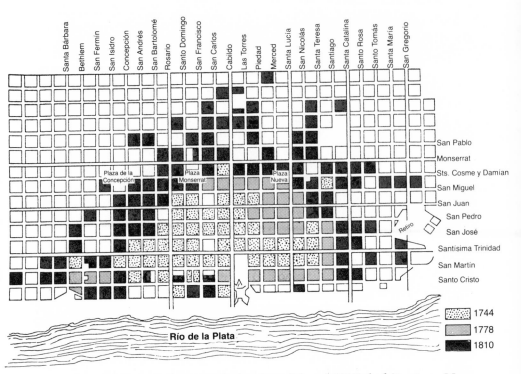

Map 1. *Blocks with Population Densities of 100 Inhabitants or More*

Plata area, it was not reflected in the physical size of the major city.

Not all of the area considered to be within the city was inhabited, and among those blocks which were, population density varied widely. Mapping those blocks with population densities of 100 inhabitants or more in 1744, 1778, and 1810, we can see that while the physical size of the city increased only slightly, the area of dense population expanded, more than doubling over the 66-year period. Although density expanded in all directions, there was a slight tendency for the southern sectors of the city to be more populous (see map 1).

As early as 1744 the area covered by the city of Buenos Aires was beginning to be differentiated into specialized zones. The major sections of the city consisted of a center, the area surrounding the central plaza where governmental, ecclesiastical, and commercial power was concentrated; the outskirts to the north and south of the

Table 1. *Population of Buenos Aires*

Year	Census total	Revised total
1744	10,056	11,620*
1778	24,083	29,920*
1810	42,540	61,160*
1822	56,416	68,896**

*Lyman L. Johnson, "Estimaciones de la población de Buenos Aires en 1744, 1778, y 1810," *Desarrollo Económico*, 19, 73 (April–June 1979), 107–119.
**Vicente López y Planes, *Registro Estadístico* (Buenos Aires?, 1822).

city, artisan, semiurban districts separated from the center of the city by the aforementioned *zanjas*; and the more distant *quintas*, a ring of summer homes and farms which surrounded the city. In 1778 and 1810 the same pattern is repeated; the center of the city has grown slightly, artisan districts to the north and south are somewhat better defined, and the *quintas* still surround the city. The only major difference is in the geographical spread of *quintas* to areas more distant from the center, and the gradual transformation of these *quintas* closest to the semiurban zones into parts of this area.

Although most of the city lay along a slight *meseta*, the elevation fell 15 feet within a few hundred yards of the river. The area which lay below the *barranca* was on the flood plain of the River Plate and as such was a relatively unattractive place to live. Although close to the central plaza, houses along the *bajo del río* were poor, inhabited chiefly by free coloreds. Along the edge of the *barranca*, but above the water-line, several important hide merchants had constructed warehouses for their goods.

These changes in the physical dimensions of the city reflect far greater changes in the population density of the area. In 1744, there were approximately 11,600 inhabitants in the city; by 1810 this number had increased between four- and sixfold. Population figures suggest that during the later part of the eighteenth century, Buenos Aires was numerically the fastest growing city in Spanish America. Several different estimates of the actual number of people in the city have been made by demographers and historians. Table 1 contains the published totals of the four major city censuses taken between 1744 and 1822, and the best estimated upward revisions. Table 2, which calculates annual growth rates based on both sets of figures, demonstrates some similarities between the two growth patterns.

Table 2. *Annual Population Growth Rates: Buenos Aires, 1744–1822*

Dates	Rate based on census totals	Rate based on revised totals
1744–1778	2.6	2.8
1778–1810	1.8	2.3
1810–1822	2.1	1.0
1744–1810	2.2	2.5
1744–1822	2.2	2.3

Growth between 1744 and 1778 for both figures was greater than that for any other period, slowing somewhat after the creation of the viceroyalty (the dramatic decline in growth evidenced by the official census figures, a decline *not* supported by any other evidence, presents a convincing argument for undercounting in the 1810 census). It is highly probable that growth slowed somewhat between 1810 and 1822, although overall growth for either the late colonial period (1744–1810) or the entire period (1744–1822) was high. Although the use of average figures can be somewhat misleading, between 1744 and 1822, Buenos Aires was growing at an average annual rate of at least 2.2 percent per year.[6]

Late colonial population growth resulted from a combination of natural increase and in-migration. The latter movement, more important than the former in increasing the city's numbers, had several sources: European immigrants, overwhelmingly Spaniards, attracted by the new prosperity of the region, Africans brought to Buenos Aires in a forced migration as slaves, and inhabitants from the interior of the viceroyalty, chiefly from the northwestern regions of Salta, Jujuy, and the north-central cities of Córdoba and Santa Fe who were also attracted by Buenos Aires' growing prosperity.

Independence initially upset some of these migration patterns. First, although a variety of Europeans continued to migrate to the area after 1810, the large current of Spanish immigration stopped completely. In theory the forced migration of slaves was also ended shortly after independence, for although the province of Buenos Aires did not formally end slavery until 1861, the slave trade was supposedly abolished in 1813.[7] In addition, the chaotic political and economic conditions which marked the first decade of independence did little to encourage the continuation of internal movement

Table 3. *Population Distribution by Sex*

Year	Male	Female	Male:female ratio
1744	4,003	3,577	1.12:1
1778	11,758	12,325	.95:1
1810	12,155	11,236	1.08:1
1822	26,447	28,969	.91:1
1827	16,542	21,766	.76:1

from the interior to the port city. Continued warfare was also draining off a sizable segment of the male lower-class population. The city, entering into the first decade of existence as a *ciudad patricia*, continued to grow, but the rate probably slowed appreciably.

Population growth from 1744 to 1822 was not uniform, and the sex distribution of this population also shifted over this period. Although the following table (table 3) is based on incomplete data, and must therefore be treated with some skepticism, the male predominance in 1744 and 1810 is not inconsistent with the profile which would be presented by a city receiving a continuous flow of male immigrants. What is striking is the radical shift in sex ratio which occurs in the 1822 census. The predominance of females after independence is consistent with slowdown of European and internal migration, and the male mortality occasioned by the wars of independence. Sex ratios calculated from the partial census returns of 1822 and 1827 indicate the continuing female predominance of the *porteño* population.

Although the data are incomplete, masculinity indices (i.e., the number of males per 100 females) for the principal racial groups in the city can be constructed from existing information. Table 4, which presents indices for both the entire racial group and the adult segment of the group, shows that while women tended to predominate in both racial groups, the whites generally enjoyed a more even sexual balance than blacks and mulattoes. Only data from the 1744 census show a greater number of males than females in the black population, and these early figures are most incomplete. The masculinity index for the nonwhite population of the city declined markedly from 1778 on, caused in part by the colonial preference for female domestic slaves, and later by the toll of the independence wars among the city's black male population.

Table 4. *Masculinity Index of Principal Racial Groups*

	White		Black	
Year	All	Adult	All	Adult
1744	96.6		115.2	
1778	99.0	100.0	88.0	86.0
1810	103.4	97.0	74.9	72.0
1822	98.0		75.0	
1827	90.3	74.9	58.5	40.5

SOURCES: José Luis Moreno, "La estructura social y demográfica de la ciudad de Buenos Aires en el año 1778," *Anuario*, 8 (1965), 151–170; Marta B. Goldberg, "La población negra y mulata de la ciudad de Buenos Aires, 1810–1840," *Desarrollo Económico*, 16, 61 (April–June 1976), 75–99; George Reid Andrews, "Forgotten But Not Gone: The Afro-Argentines of Buenos Aires, 1800–1900," Ph.D. dissertation, University of Wisconsin, 1978.

Immigration also affected the racial characteristics of the urban population. Although whites always clearly dominated the city's racial structure, the black and mulatto population grew during the late colonial period. Both in actual numbers and in total percentage of the population, blacks increased dramatically; one out of every six residents of Buenos Aires in 1744 was black or mulatto; by 1778 this ratio had increased to one out of every 3.5. While the black population continued to grow numerically, the racial balance seems to have shifted toward whites shortly before independence, the result of nonblack immigration, miscegenation, and changing racial perceptions.[8] Between 1810 and 1822, although their numbers had increased from about 8,900 to about 14,700, blacks and mulattoes fell from two-sevenths to about one-fourth of the city's population. This decline continued throughout the nineteenth century.

The source for the increased numbers of coloreds in the city was the slave trade. In fact while the numbers of both free colored and slaves increased from 1744 to 1810, the slave increase outstripped that of the free colored population. The latter experienced a 2.8-fold growth (from 425 free mulattoes and blacks in 1744 to 1,224 in 1810) while the former increased six-fold (from 1,276 slaves in 1744 to 7,719 in 1810). Free coloreds comprised one-fourth of the total black/mulatto population in 1744, but less than 14 percent in 1810. Only after independence did the numbers of free coloreds begin to approach those of slaves.

Although the free colored population was about 48 percent of

Table 5. *Population Distribution by Race, Buenos Aires*

Race	1744 N	%	1778 N	%	1810 N	%	1822 N	%	1827 N	%
White	8,068	80.2	16,097	66.8	23,066**	71.5	40,616	72.0	29,964*	78.2
Black/ Mulatto	1,701	16.9	6,835	28.4	8,943*	27.7	14,685	26.0	7,802*	20.4
Indian/ Mestizo	287	2.9	1,151	4.8	270*	.8	1,115	2.0	542*	1.4
Total	10,056	100.0	24,083	100.0	32,279*	100.0	56,416	100.0	38,308*	100.0

*These figures reflect those cases for which information is complete, hence the disparity between these numbers and the official census totals.

**Included in this number are 5,210 individuals with no racial classification who are presumed to be white.

the total colored population by 1822, these figures are striking, for they show that although the Laws of Free Womb had greatly increased both the numbers and proportions of free people within the colored population, the majority of coloreds in Buenos Aires were still slaves. Clearly laws which freed only children born from 1813 on had not abolished slavery within nine years. A rough approximation of the pace at which slavery was being eliminated under the Law of Free Womb of 1813 is provided by the fact that of the 7,074 free blacks, 2,540 (more than one-third of the group) were listed as *libertos*, children between the ages of birth and 14 who were serving the legally required apprenticeship before receiving their freedom. These *libertos*, although included in the free colored population, were legally still in bondage, although slated for eventual freedom.[9]

In addition to the ratio of free coloreds to slaves, the growth of the black and mulatto group during the twelve-year period between 1810 and 1822 is astonishing. The growth of the total colored population and the virtual preservation of the total numbers of slaves during this period are even more striking when we remember that from 1813 to 1816 the government of Buenos Aires passed a series of decrees creating military units of slaves who were to be free when they completed military service. These battalions, drawn solely from the slave population, totaled more than 2,000 individuals, males between the ages of 13 and 60.[10] In the face of dangerous military action in the wars of independence, in the face of the legal abolition of the slave trade, the colored population of Buenos Aires increased by 69 percent, a growth of 4.2 percent per year, over this

Table 6. *Legal Status of the Colored Population*

	1744		1778		1810		1822	
	N	%	N	%	N	%	N	%
Free	425	25.0	1,170	18.6	1,224	13.7	7,074	48.2
Slave	1,276	75.0	5,125	81.4	7,719	86.3	7,611	51.8
Total	1,701	100.0	6,295	100.0	8,943	100.0	14,685	100.0

period. Although military service did eventually allow a number of former black slaves to achieve their freedom, it is clear that the 1813 abolition of the slave trade remained a dead letter for several years. As early as 1814, the government of the province modified its own legislation concerning freedom for all entering blacks, by decreeing that all slaves who entered the country in the domestic service of their owners would not automatically be freed. In addition, the revolutionary governments of the decade were more than willing to issue special permits allowing individuals to import slaves for their personal use.[11] Both of these actions invited widespread abuse, and they help to explain the fact that while military service and the Law of Free Womb drained off approximately 4,500 individuals from the slave population, the numbers of slaves in the city remained constant.

The impact of this large group of people of African descent on the port city becomes clear when one considers the occupational structure of late colonial and early independent Buenos Aires. Although the city had prospered primarily because of trade, from 1778 onward the administrative sector of the city had also grown greatly. With increased numbers involved in trade (wholesalers, retailers, *pulperos* or barroom/store owners) and religious and civil administration (clergy, public employees, lawyers), the local demand for a variety of services was also increased. By 1778 Buenos Aires had developed a sizable artisan class; in fact artisans engaged in skilled and unskilled labor comprised 27.9 percent of the economically active male population.[12] Added to this artisan sector was a large group of domestic servants, predominantly female although with a sizable male proportion, who provided personal service to the *porteño* upper and middle groups. It was the colored population of the city which increasingly filled positions in these two crucial economic sectors.

As early as 1744, of a total of 303 artisans engaged in 34 different

Table 7. *Black Male Population as a Percentage of Total Male Population and Total Nonelite Labor Force*

Year	% of male pop.	% of nonelite labor force
1744	18.7	14.7
1778	28.5	—
1810	24.6	18.5
1822	23.8	—
1827	16.8	22.3

occupations enumerated by the census takers, 21.78 percent were black or mulatto. In 1780 a *matrícula* (listing) of the most prestigious and skilled artisan trades included 12.2 percent in these racial categories (4.7 percent free blacks and mulattoes; 7.5 percent black and mulatto slaves).[13] Considering the nonwhite artisans in this *matrícula* by guild rank, we can see that although there were fairly small overall numbers of blacks in the sample within the skilled artisan group, they had a disproportionate influence at the level of journeymen and apprentices. While only 5.8 percent of the master artisans were people of color, their numbers rose to 15.7 percent on the journeyman level, and comprised 21.4 percent of all apprentices. Blacks were especially predominant in tailoring (11.5 percent of the total number of tailors), barbering (16.3 percent of all *barberos*) and masonry (10.7 percent of all masons), while they were totally absent from occupations such as ship's carpenters, caulkers, and the leather trades.

In 1780, *porteños* and *peninsulares* (Spaniards) dominated the skilled trades, but gradually through the period under study black males became a sizable proportion of the lower levels of the skilled trades and the unskilled trades as well. In 1744, 14.7 percent of male residents with occupational classifications of skilled artisan or less were black or mulatto. By 1810, 18.5 percent of those employed as artisans, skilled, semiskilled, or unskilled, were free coloreds or slaves. (Only four of every ten whites with a known occupation were employed as skilled or semiskilled laborers; for free coloreds the proportion jumps to eight out of ten, approximately the same proportion as for colored slaves: 37.7 percent of the whites; 77.8 percent of the free coloreds; 83.3 percent of the slaves.)[14] By 1827, the proportion of blacks in the artisan, semiskilled, and unskilled groups had risen to 22.3 percent. Paradoxically, as their percentage of the male

Table 8. *Workforce by Race*

	White		1810 Free blacks		Slaves		Total
	N	%	N	%	N	%	
Artisans	560	(74.1)	154	(20.4)	42	(5.6)	756
Semiskilled	602	(89.6)	42	(6.3)	28	(4.2)	672
Unskilled	224	(82.1)	42	(15.4)	7	(2.6)	273
Total	1,386	(81.5)	238	(14.0)	77	(4.5)	1,701

NOTE: This table is based on sample data contained in George Reid Andrews, "Forgotten But Not Gone: The Afro-Argentines of Buenos Aires, 1800–1900," 85–86; Andrews' samples have been reconstituted by multiplying his totals by the sampling factor used for each racial group; the numbers of cases obtained are therefore synthetic rather than absolute.

population declined, black males came to play a greater role in the city's nonelite work force. Nevertheless there is a strong suggestion in these data that blacks were increasingly concentrated in semi-skilled and unskilled positions, while artisan groups became whiter between 1810 and 1827 (table 8).

Among unskilled occupations in which many blacks were employed were street vendors, water sellers, and *changadores* (load carriers). Large numbers of blacks were also employed by the city's bakeries and furniture factories. In addition, black women often worked as washerwomen. Blacks also monopolized domestic service. In spite of liberal pronouncements like those of 1813, Buenos Aires, by the first decade of independence, still dependent on colored labor, both slave and free. Masters and mistresses who lived off the wages which their slaves earned working for hire, and families whose continued physical well-being depended on numerous servants, were therefore opposed to any legislation which threatened to free their slaves while drying up a source to replenish this labor.

What were the physical attributes of this dynamic city at the time of independence? Like many colonial cities in Hispanic America, Buenos Aires was organized around a central plaza. In the traditional pattern, the plaza was flanked by the city's cathedral, and the municipal *cabildo* (town hall). Nevertheless, the central plaza was distinctive because of two peculiarities. First, instead of being square, the plaza was rectangular, running one city block from north to south, but two blocks from west to east. Second, the easternmost

White		Free blacks		Slaves		Total
		1827				
N	%	N	%	N	%	
1,840	(82.7)	272	(12.2)	112	(5.0)	2,224
980	(81.9)	136	(11.4)	80	(6.7)	1,196
520	(59.1)	264	(30.0)	96	(10.9)	880
3,340	(77.7)	672	(15.6)	288	(6.7)	4,300

flank of the plaza bordered on the largest building in the city, the fort, which served as both the major defensive installation and the residence and offices of the central government. In addition, the maritime nature of the city was underlined by the fact that the main square, instead of being located at some point in the geographical center of the city, lay within view of the River Plate.

By 1810, Buenos Aires was served by eight churches in addition to the main cathedral. The cathedral itself was in the throes of its fifth remodeling; work on the entire building, which had collapsed in 1752, was still being carried out. Within ten years, a new, less "colonial" style would be undertaken by the revolutionary government, and the façade would eventually emerge in a neoclassic design.

The city's five other parish churches had been founded during the eighteenth century,[15] and their placement reflects the gradual growth of the area of dense population from a small area around the central plaza to an ever enlarging arc. The parish churches of Concepción, Monserrat, and San Nicolás had all been placed on secondary plazas, which competed with the central commercial zones by the coming of independence. These new plazas ran along an imaginary line nine blocks west of the riverfront, and in turn served as nuclei for areas of increasing density. Two other parishes, La Piedad and Socorro, lay outside of the original *traza* (plat) of the city, serving the poor semiurban populations on the city's edges (see map 2).

In addition to parish churches, the city had at the time of independence six convents, two nunneries, two hospitals, one spiritual

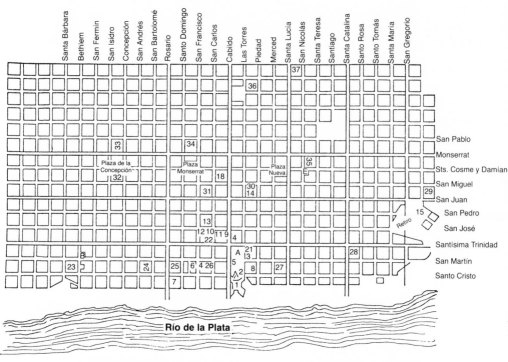

1—Fuerte, R^l Audiencia y Cajas Reales
2—Piquete de Caballería
3—Casa Episcopal
4—Casas Capitulares
5—Casilla del Fiel Executor
6—Adm^{ción} Gral. de Tabacos
7—R^l Aduana
8—R^l Consulado
9—Adm^{ción} de Correos
10—Escuelas Públicas y R^l Proto Medicato
11—Casa de Expósitos
12—Adm^{ción} de los Pueblos de Misiones
13—Cuartel de Soldados
14—Hospital de Mugeres
15—Retiro: Plaza de Toros y Cuartel de Artillería
*16—Guardia del Riachuelo
*17—Entrada al mismo
18—Presidio
*19—Casa de la Pólvora
*20—Cuerpo de Guardia
21—Catedral-Parroquia
22—San I. Colegio de S^n Carlos
23—Residencia; Casa de Depositadas
24—Hospital de Betlemitas
25—Convento de S^{to} Domingo

26—Convento de S^n Francisco y Capilla de Franc^o
27—Convento de Mercedarios
28—Monjas Catalinas
29—Nuestra Señora del Socorro-Parroquia
30—San Miguel, Casa de Huérfanas
31—Monasterio de Capuchinas
32—N^{tra} S^{ra} de la Concep^{ón}, Parroquia
33—Capilla y Casa de Exercicios
34—N^{tra} S^{ra} de Monserrat, Parroquia
35—S^n Nicolás, Parroquia
36—La Piedad, Parroquia
37—Sta Lucía, Capilla
*38—Recolección Franciscana
*39—Hospicio de Misioneros
 A—Plaza mayor
 B—Plaza de la Residencia
*C—Plaza de Monserrat
 D—Plaza nueva
 E—Plaza de S^n Nicolás
*F—Hueco de d^a Gracia

*These locations are off the map
 after its reduction to present dimensions.

Map 2. *Buenos Aires, 1778*

retreat house, one orphanage, and one home for "wayward" women. Several of these institutions had been founded after 1760, reflecting a growing need for religious social services. These institutions continued to function after independence, albeit with some modification.[16] Other institutions grew out of seeds planted during the viceroyalty. The Sociedad de la Beneficencia, founded in 1823, for example, had its roots in the list of the "ladies who, with great charity, have taken charge of providing beds . . . to be used by the sick poor" organized by the Hermandad de Caridad in 1798.[17]

Colonial education had been provided to a limited clientele by ten primary church schools and one secondary school, the Colegio de San Carlos.[18] The church schools continued to function after independence (ten such schools are listed in the 1826 *Almanac* of the city),[19] while San Carlos was converted into a university preparatory school and a university. In addition, private schools headed by recent arrivals to the city were set up to teach English and French.[20]

To the north of the city lay a large empty area known as the Retiro. From 1718 to 1739 during the British slave *asiento*, Retiro had served as the major slave market of the city. It was later converted into a general open ground where the city's urban militia was drilled. From 1801 until bullfighting was outlawed in 1822, Retiro served as the city's principal bullfighting ring.[21] In 1791, the viceregal government established a new slave market near Retiro but within the royal *aduana* compound. Although many of the local residents of the area objected to this placement of the slave market and offered several petitions to move the market out of the center of town, the depot remained there until after independence.[22] To the south of the city, on the far side of the Zanja del Hospital, lay the Matadero (slaughterhouse) de Santo Domingo.

Although the streets of the city were theoretically to bisect each other at ninety-degree angles, with houses neatly aligned along them, the reality was somewhat less perfect. Especially outside the more densely inhabited central zone which covered approximately half the city, streets were somewhat irregular. Many streets in the city were not paved until well into the nineteenth century,[23] and the heavy oxcarts which regularly crossed the city bringing in hides and other goods wore deep ruts along the major thoroughfares. During the rainy season, the rutted, unpaved streets quickly became impassable, a difficulty noted by travelers and residents alike.[24] In part to stop the continued destruction of the city's streets, a viceregal order of January 1784 limited *carreta* traffic to the Plaza de Monserrat in the city's western section and the Plaza Nueva to the north.[25]

Although the entire bureaucratic apparatus of a viceregal capital was located in Buenos Aires after 1776, and a royal *audiencia* (court) was established five years later, little new building was undertaken to house the expanded bureaucracy either at the time of the founding of the viceroyalty or after independence. Rather, existing structures were rented or purchased, and modified to serve new ends. Such is the case of the Casa del Asiento, a large building located along the river to the north of the city, so named because it had originally served as the headquarters for the English *asiento* (slave import monopoly). This property, rented from the heirs of a local merchant, was used after 1785 to house the *aduana*. Likewise the royal tobacco monopoly first rented quarters and then purchased an already existing structure for its offices.[26] Indeed, few new government buildings were constructed during either the viceregal or early independence periods.

The quality of construction for private housing varied greatly from the center of the city to the outskirts. In general, houses within five or six blocks of the main plaza, except for those along the *bajo del río*, were constructed of adobe and brick. The wealthier residences featured tile roofs, *rejas* (grilled windows) overlooking the main street, and massive walls. These homes tended to follow a uniform pattern of construction which consisted of an entrance hall or *zaguán* leading to a large patio from which the living room, dining room, and bedrooms were approached. A second and even third patio followed, again with surrounding rooms, the province of children and servants. Even the most elegant residences often had corner rooms facing the streets, the ubiquitous *esquinas* which could be rented out for some sort of commercial activity. The majority of houses in the center of the city had been one-story constructions before the founding of the viceroyalty, but increasingly the growing affluence of a sector of the city's inhabitants led to the construction of some two-story manses. As one moved farther from the center of the city and along the *bajo del río*, a poor type of construction appeared. Here along with modest houses were small dwellings with straw roofs (*casitas con techo de paja*), and huts.

Houses in the central city, in addition to being larger and better constructed, often contained one or more apartments in addition to the main living quarters. Other buildings were divided into two equal-sized quarters, *media casas*, and still others consisted of multiple small apartments, the colonial equivalent of the modern-day *conventillo* (tenement). Many of the more prosperous citizens of Buenos Aires invested in these income-producing properties. In addition, a goodly number of upper- and middle-group widows supplemented their inheritance with incomes derived from renting out apartments in their homes, combined with day wages (*jornales*) of slaves. On the outskirts of the city, homes large enough to be subdivided were rare, and the single-family dwelling was most prevalent.

As early as 1772, under Governor Vértiz, there had been some attempt made to improve the city's cleanliness and safety.[27] Under the intendency system the improvements in sanitation and physical surroundings were continued by imposing a building code; cleaning, leveling, and paving some of the streets near the central plaza; constructing an *alameda* (public walkway); and installing public street lighting.[28] All of these reforms did remedy problems and beautified at least the heart of the city. Nevertheless, well past 1810, Buenos Aires had poor sanitation and drinking-water facilities. Although a few houses had *aljibes* (cisterns), the majority of the population depended on water vendors who filled their leather vats with water drawn from the shallows of the River Plate. Since the same river was also used for washing clothing, bathing, and sewerage, this solution was less than ideal. Poor water supply was a factor influencing the periodic epidemics which visited the city.

Another important landmark running along the south side of the plaza central, between the fort and the Cabildo, was the Recova, or public food market. This construction had first been suggested to the town council as early as 1756 in an effort to improve the appearance of the central plaza and produce additional revenue for the council, but actual construction was not begun until 1802.[29] Although the Recova provided forty-eight stalls for retail vendors of clothing and foodstuffs, outdoor stands selling meat, produce, and eggs could be found in all the city's plazas, including the central plaza, and ambulatory notion vendors (*bandoleros*) continued to provide their services.[30] The Recova also served as a meeting ground for the astonishing number of beggars found in the city after independence. The Recova, the last colonial structure put up in Buenos Aires, stood until 1884.

Although Buenos Aires had developed because it was an important interoceanic port, throughout the colonial period, and in the first decades after independence, the city had notoriously poor port facilities. A mole of rough stone had been constructed during the viceregal period of building material brought over from Colônia on the other side of the Río de la Plata, but it had never served as an effective landing place because of shallow water. Instead, both passengers and cargo had to be ferried back and forth from ships which moored in the outer roads (an area less sheltered than the harbor where ships may ride at anchor), first in sailing lighters and then from the smaller vessels in horse-drawn carts which served as mobile piers.[31] Not until the 1830s were two long, sturdy wharves constructed, and even then ships could not anchor alongside the city docks. Because of this combination of shoal waters and unimproved port facilities, ships could spend from 30 to 150 days in loading time,[32] a paradoxical situation for a growing port.

Cultural life and entertainment, although they had improved during the viceregal period, were still somewhat limited. Two or three theaters had had rather ephemeral lives before the establishment of the Ranchería in 1783 under the sponsorship of Viceroy Vértiz. The theater presented classical Spanish plays until one fateful night in 1792 when it was destroyed by fire. Eleven years later, a local café owner was given permission to build a temporary new theater, the Colisea Provisional, which opened in 1804. Construction of a more permanent facility was begun in 1805, but discontinued the year before independence because of prohibitive costs.[33] The city also had one printing press (founded in 1780), and during the first decade of the nineteenth century, cultural life quickened with the appearance of three newspapers (*El Telégrafo Mercantil*, 1801–1802; *El Semanario de Agricultura, Industria, y Comercio*, 1802–1807; and *El Correo de Comercio*, 1810–1811). The same decade also saw the first appearance of public cafés in the capital city.

In general, both Spanish and foreign visitors were pleased with the frequently pleasant aspects of Buenos Aires, but not overly impressed. This evaluation of the city changed little from 1770 to 1820. The traveler Concolorcorvo noted in 1773 that "this city is well situated and planned in the modern way, divided into uniform blocks and with streets of the same regulation width."[34] About forty years later, an anonymous English traveler noted: "The city of Buenos Aires, observed from the outer anchorage at about eight miles distance, has an imposing appearance. The public buildings and the cupolas of the numerous churches give it a certain air of grandeur which vanishes when we draw near."[35]

Throughout the period, houses were repeatedly described as being adequate, although the general impression was not of great luxury.[36] The entrance of several foreign, especially British, merchants into Buenos Aires after independence did affect residential patterns somewhat, for some of the larger homes in the center of the city were either rented or sold to these foreigners and turned over entirely to commerce.[37]

Independence would bring an increase in public diversions available in the city, especially public meeting places such as cafés and bars. This growth reflected an increased foreign population of both residents and transients, and the city's postindependence attempt to become a more cosmopolitan center. By 1824 the city could boast five cafés, one of which, the "Café de la Victoria," was judged by an English resident to be superior to any in London, although not quite as fine as some found in Paris.[38] Bars and bordellos had grown up along the *bajo del río*, providing entertainment for the growing numbers of sailors who visited the port as a result of postindependence free trade.[39] By the middle of the second decade after independence, the city also contained at least three hotels (two British-owned; one run by a North American widow), two *pensiones* (boarding houses), and one restaurant, all serving a middle- and upper-class clientele.[40] In 1827, the first public park combining a botanical garden, exotic animals, a French-owned hotel, and a small summer theater was opened to the public.[41]

A political event of far-reaching consequence occurred in 1810—the beginning of the struggle for independence—but for the next twenty years the bureaucratic organization of provincial government, as well as the physical plant occupied by government branches, underwent only slight modification. An independent executive (which itself underwent several internal modifications during the postindependence period) had replaced viceregal authority, but the seat of government remained in the city's fort. The *consulado*, founded in 1794, continued to function in the same quarters, but was now rechristened *tribunal de comercio*; the same was true of the *protomedicato*, which was known as the *tribunal de medicina* after independence. When the royal *audiencia* was disbanded, a *tribunal de la cámara de justicia* was set up, and met in the same quarters which had served its predecessor. The police department and jail continued to be located in the Cabildo building, even after the council was shorn of responsibilities and then totally dissolved in 1821. *Correos, aduana*, the treasury, and *hacienda* all displayed a great degree of organizational and physical continuity with the viceregal institutions that had preceded them, as did the local military. Although the balance of power shifted dramatically after independence, with government bureaucrats losing power and prestige to the military, form often remained constant.

This is not to say that independence did not produce new bureaucratic organizations. Buenos Aires was the capital city of a sovereign province and as such boasted a national-level ministry, which included departments of External Relations, Interior Relations, and a General Archive. A provincial legislature had been created in 1823, and a new House of Representatives building was built during the

1820s. A national bank (1822), a public library (1812), and a university (1821) were also set up. Nevertheless, there was a high degree of continuity, which provided a much needed underlying stability during a time of political chaos.

The transition from *ciudad criolla* to *ciudad patricia* did not occur suddenly, nor did all types of change proceed at the same rate. Physically the city continued to grow in the same directions that had been established in the late colonial period; neither in area nor in physical plant were the first years after independence markedly different from those that had preceded them. Population growth also continued along parameters established during the colonial era, and there is a strong indication that this growth actually slowed in the decades following 1810. The racial balance of the city did shift, as Buenos Aires began a "whitening process" which would continue throughout the century. In addition, the black and mulatto population were increasingly freed, but this change was not as rapid as government pronouncement would lead one to believe. In many ways the *porteña ciudad patricia* would not depart radically from the earlier *ciudad criolla* until the Rosas years. Rather than physical or population changes, the major shift would be in a new psychology of the port city, now free to determine its own economic and political future.

Notes

1. José Luis Romero, *Latinoamérica: Las ciudades y las ideas* (Buenos Aires, 1976).

2. Tulio Halperín Donghi, *Politics, Economics and Society in Argentina in the Revolutionary Period* (London, 1975).

3. Lyman L. Johnson and Susan Migden Socolow, "Population and Space in Eighteenth Century Buenos Aires," in David J. Robinson (ed.), *Social Fabric and Spatial Structure in Colonial Latin America* (Ann Arbor, 1979), pp. 339–368.

4. Guy Bourdé, *Urbanisation et immigration en Amérique latine: Buenos Aires* (Paris, 1974), p. 15.

5. The Garay plan as well as two early eighteenth century maps are reproduced in Javier Aguilera Rojas, *Urbanismo española en América: Selección de planos y textos* (Madrid, 1973).

6. A variety of possible population figures for the city have been suggested over the years. For other population estimates, see Alberto B. Martínez, "Historia demográfica de Buenos Aires," in Dirección General de Estadística Municipal, *Censo general de población . . .* (Buenos Aires, 1910), vol. 3, pp. 261–367; Nicolás Besio Moreno, *Buenos Aires, puerto del Río de la Plata, capital de la Argentina, estudio crítico de su población, 1536–*

1936 (Buenos Aires, 1939); César A. García Belsunce et al., *Buenos Aires, su gente 1800–1830* (Buenos Aires, 1976); Emilio Ravignani, "Crecimiento de la población en Buenos Aires y su campaña (1726–1810)," in Facultad de Ciencias Económicas, *Anales*, vol. 1 (1919), 405–416; Angel Rosenblat, *La población indígena y el mestizaje en América* (Buenos Aires, 1954), vol. 2, pp. 205–211, 231–238, 263–265. Official census figures are taken from the 1744 census, Facultad de Filosofía y Letras, *Documentos para la historia argentina*, vol. 10, *Padrones de la ciudad y campaña de Buenos Aires* (Buenos Aires, 1919); the 1778 census is in vol. II, *Territorio y población* (Buenos Aires, 1919); total population for the 1810 census in García Belsunce et al., *Buenos Aires*, p. 62; and 1822 totals in Martínez, "Historia demográfica," pp. 288–290. For a discussion of the growth of the national population in the years between independence and the first national census, see Ernesto J. A. Maeder, *Evolución demográfica argentina desde 1810 a 1869* (Buenos Aires, 1969).

7. The slave trade was officially ended in 1812, and in the following year a modified "Law of Free Womb" was passed by the Asamblea General Constituyente. In addition all slaves brought into Buenos Aires were to be free, although a series of regulations limited this freedom. See Marta B. Goldberg de Flichman and Laura Beatriz Jany, "Algunos problemas referentes a la situación del esclavo en el Río de La Plata," in Academia Nacional de la Historia, *Cuarto Congreso Internacional de Historia de América* (Buenos Aires, 1966), vol. 6, pp. 61–75.

8. Racial classification used in all the censuses was a phenotypic designation based on the census taker's assessment of an individual's race.

Although a certain amount of error is introduced into the data because of the perception of individual numerators, racial categories were applied with some consistency in each of the censuses. Nevertheless, foreign visitors often perceived the *porteño* population as being darker than did the census takers. Alexander Gillespie, writing in 1807, described the *porteño* population as only one-fifth white, a view essentially in agreement with that of the Robertson brothers. Alexander Gillespie, *Buenos Aires y el Interior* (Buenos Aires, 1921), p. 65; J. P. and G. P. Robertson, "Cartas de sud-America," in José Luis Busaniche (ed.), *Episodios históricos, vida y costumbres de Buenos Aires* (Buenos Aires, 1950), vol.2, 184. See also Marta B. Goldberg, "La población negra y mulata de la ciudad de Buenos Aires, 1810–1840," *Desarrollo Económico*, 16, 61 (April–June 1976), 75–79.

9. George Reid Andrews, "Forgotten But Not Gone: The Afro-Argentines of Buenos Aires, 1800–1900," Ph.D. dissertation, University of Wisconsin, 1978, p. 115.

10. Goldberg and Jany, "Algunos problemas," pp. 5–10.

11. Andrews, "Forgotten But Not Gone," p. 121.

12. José Luis Moreno, "La estructura social y demográfica de la ciudad de Buenos Aires en el año 1778," *Anuario*, 8 (1965), Instituto de Investigaciones Históricas, Facultad de Filosofía y Letras, Universidad Nacional del Litoral, Rosario, 151–170.

13. Lyman L. Johnson, "The Artisans of Buenos Aires during the Vice-royalty, 1776–1810," Ph.D. dissertation, University of Connecticut, 1974, p. 249.

14. Andrews, "Forgotten But Not Gone," p. 83.

15. José Luis Trenti Rocamora, *La cultura en Buenos Aires hasta 1810* (Buenos Aires, 1948), pp. 60–69.

16. The most important change in the city's religious structure was the suppression of most of the monasteries in 1822. See José Antonio Wilde, *Buenos Aires desde 70 años atras (1810–1880)* (Buenos Aires, 1966), p. 90.

17. Alberto Meyer Arana, *La caridad en Buenos Aires* (Buenos Aires, 1911), vol. 2, and Susan Migden Socolow, *The Merchants of Buenos Aires 1778–1810: Family and Commerce* (Cambridge, 1978), pp. 95–100.

18. Trenti Rocamora, *La cultura*, p. 13.

19. *Almanaque politico y de comercio de la ciudad de Buenos Ayres para el año de 1826* (Facsimile edition, Buenos Aires, 1968), p. 65.

20. Wilde, *Buenos Aires*, pp. 87–88.

21. Antonio Pillado, *Buenos Aires colonial* (Buenos Aires, 1910), pp. 241–345; Wilde, *Buenos Aires*, pp. 69–70.

22. Andrews, "Forgotten But Not Gone," pp. 58–61.

23. Un Inglés, *Cinco años en Buenos Aires, 1820–1825* (Buenos Aires, 1962), p. 34.

24. "During the rainy season the streets of Buenos Aires are impassable . . . people often must go without hearing mass when they have to cross a street to get to church," Concolorcorvo, *El lazarillo de ciegos caminantes* (Buenos Aires, 1942), p. 46. "This past Easter Sunday, when everybody knows the great amount of mud there was in the streets, we put one of the two horses . . . to the small coach in order to go to church," Archivo General de la Nación Argentina, Sucesiones 8821, Testamentaria de Don Ambrosio de Zamudio, 1798.

25. Pillado, *Buenos Aires colonial*, p. 47.

26. Municipalidad de la Capital, *Documentos y planos relativos al período edilicio colonial de la ciudad de Buenos Aires* (Buenos Aires, 1910), vol. 3, pp. 49–69 and 71–161.

27. Archivo General de la Nación Argentina, Bandos, Libro 3, 1763–1777, IX-8-10-3.

28. In 1792 public lighting was changed from *velas de sebo* (candles of animal fat) to *grasa de potro* (lamps of horse grease), a move heralded as a major advancement for the city, Pillado, *Buenos Aires colonial*, p. 51.

29. Ibid., pp. 29–145.

30. Wilde describes the following wares sold by *bandoleros* in the main plaza: "combs, garment pins, women's and tailor's thimbles, rosaries, holy figures, rings, pendants and necklaces of glass or with artificial stones, and an infinity of costume jewelry, all of little value," *Buenos Aires*, p. 38.

31. Jonathan C. Brown, *A Socioeconomic History of Argentina, 1776–1860* (Cambridge, 1979), pp. 70–71; E. E. Vidal, *Picturesque Illustrations of Buenos Aires and Montevideo* (London, 1830), p. 15.

32. Brown, *A Socioeconomic History*, p. 71.

33. Trenti Rocamora, *La cultura*, p. 110.

34. Concolorcorvo, *El lazarillo*, pp. 45–46.

35. Un Inglés, *Cinco años*, p. 17.

36. Concolorcorvo, *El lazarillo*, p. 39; Un Inglés, *Cinco años*, pp. 35–36; Wilde, *Buenos Aires*, p. 20.

37. Un Inglés, *Cinco años*, p. 36.

38. Ibid., p. 29.

39. Ibid., pp. 26–27.

40. Ibid., pp. 28, 30.

41. Wilde, *Buenos Aires*, pp. 90–92.

3. The Argentine Capital in the Nineteenth Century

James R. Scobie

All of us who have lived in or passed through Buenos Aires have experienced the captivation and the attraction of one of the world's
great cities. In this essay we are concerned with the years up to 1900.
This is the historical background that the visitor or tourist to Buenos Aires misses completely and of which the *porteño*, the inhabitant of that city, is usually only vaguely aware.

For the last five or six years, I have been involved in research and
analysis quite distant from Buenos Aires—in the cities of Corrientes, Salta, and Mendoza, in an effort to compare and contrast their
patterns of growth and development during the second half of the
nineteenth century. But constantly hanging over me—and not only
because of a telephone call from Stanley Ross last March asking me
to prepare this paper on nineteenth-century Buenos Aires—has been
the question: Why Buenos Aires? Why does this city above all others
in Argentina blossom and flourish during the nineteenth century?
What is the pull, the power, the magic that Buenos Aires exerts over
individuals and over other Argentine cities?

Each generation of historians develops new questions, new insights, new tools and techniques. As you well know, until the 1950s,
Argentine historiography largely stopped with 1860. In addition,
many who wrote on Argentine developments tended to limit themselves to political figures and events and often used history as a vehi-
cle to advance their own political prejudices and positions. In recent
decades, we have witnessed an increasing interest in economic and
social history and an awareness by both Argentines and foreigners of
the need to explore broad issues, to use new methods, and to avoid
political rhetoric.

I propose that we continue this trend by examining the nineteenth-century capital of Argentina to see what approaches might
yield more insights on its extraordinary growth and attraction. Since
1960 the techniques of ordering large amounts of personal data in

the form of collective biographies and the use of the computer to record and organize data have become very useful tools for historical analysis. Historians studying Buenos Aires need to increase their use of these methods significantly. I suggest that they first be used to reexamine three critical periods in the city's growth—the 1810s, the 1830s and 1840s, and the 1860s and 1870s.

Let us then place ourselves in nineteenth-century Buenos Aires, effective capital of the Argentine area since 1776. The first major leap forward in Buenos Aires' status and importance came with independence from Spain. Perhaps no period of Argentine national history has been so carefully scrutinized as this initial decade, which brought increasing wealth and prosperity to a port that now handled a world trade no longer dominated and regulated by Spain's interests. Napoleon's expanding authority in Spain in 1810 temporarily cut the lines of crown power, especially in the outlying ports of the empire. The merchant elite in these newer commercial centers of Buenos Aires, Caracas, Valparaiso, or Montevideo were not as powerful or as closely tied to Spanish credit and trade as their colleagues in Lima or Mexico City. It is not difficult to imagine ourselves in the narrow cobblestoned streets or in the salon or formal patio of a one-story mudbrick home near the main plaza of Buenos Aires in May 1810. An English ship has just brought news of the abdication of Spain's monarch. What does this mean for Buenos Aires?

With hindsight we can, of course, see how the city benefited from the series of steps, some decisively planned and executed, others accidentally or even unwittingly brought about, that led to the assembling of a carefully selected body of leading citizens on 25 May. The cautious assumption of political authority by those who planned that assembly gradually led the city toward local autonomy within the empire and then by 1816 to outright independence. The end result was to stimulate the city's economic and demographic growth through increasing the region's trade connections with Europe and with the world's maritime power, England.

Although we may know much about the final effect of independence on Argentina and on Buenos Aires and are able to reconstruct minutely the often chaotic events as well as the activities of the principal actors, we can take comfort as historians that there is still a great deal to investigate. Research—such as Susan Socolow's recent study of merchant families, or Lyman Johnson's work on artisan groups, or Reid Andrew's study of blacks, or José M. Mariluz Urquijo's examination of early industrial efforts—tells us how little we know about significant groups—their composition, their attitudes, and their interests. Much still can be done, even with spotty

census, property, and court records, to re-create the city of the 1810s
and make us more aware that this was not just the domain of an Al-
vear or a Pueyrredón but of a total society, and that, in addition to a
25 May and a 9 July, there were many other days critical to this city's
evolution. Furthermore, despite the volume of political histories
written about this decade, we are left with the impression that economics, not politics, primarily determined Buenos Aires' expansion
during the first decade of independence. But we need to know better
what the political objectives of various groups were, how they were
expressed, and how they were achieved or frustrated. What institutions and interests supported, for example, the repeated efforts made
from Buenos Aires during these years to maintain hegemony and
control over the area of the former viceroyalty? Or again, although
much has been written about the intellectual climate in Buenos
Aires, we might benefit from content analysis and comparison of the
contemporary broadsides, pamphlets, and newspapers with the writings of French and Spanish authors who popularized enlightenment
or romantic philosophies. Such probing into the decade of 1810 in
Buenos Aires may not reverse our conclusion about the period's importance or the judgment that the city flourished primarily for commercial reasons, but it will enrich our comprehension of how uncer-
tain those directions appeared to *porteños* at the time and how
complex and rich was the social and political fabric of this port.

The next moment of major importance to *porteño* development
was that of Rosas. An audience of your knowledge and culture immediately bristles. "But what of Rivadavia?" you say. How can one
leap over the 1820s and settle instead on what many of us have been
taught to view as Argentina's "Dark Ages"? Before I outrage too
many of you, let me stress that we are searching for the important
elements that will explain the tremendous attraction which Buenos
Aires acquired during the course of the nineteenth century. Rosas,
not Rivadavia, best reflected and expressed Argentine political realities in the first half of the nineteenth century and thus enabled the
city of Buenos Aires to regain its political dominance.

Buenos Aires had embarked on the nineteenth century with
three factors in its favor—status as a major port, largest city, and regional capital. But any or all of these could have been lost. Independence accentuated the first of these, the one that would have been
hardest to take away from the *porteños*. Buenos Aires became Argentina's only door to the world at the very moment when this region, in response to outside markets, began to develop two major
products—salted meat and wool—to add to its long-standing export
of hides. Land and animals gained enormously in value, and Buenos

Aires, as the exchange point for this expanding export market, bene-fited accordingly. Its virtual monopoly of Atlantic and, therefore, Eu-ropean commerce continued to fuel its population growth, but failed to resolve Buenos Aires' political dilemma: how to legitimize and make acceptable to all of Argentina a political authority acquired by royal fiat in 1776 and reimposed by local *porteño* activism in 1810. In this context, the 1820s and the modernization schemes of Rivadavia continued the thrust of the independence era—to expand and develop the port and its immediate area but without reference to or integration with other Argentine provinces and cities. To mix metaphors, the door became an appendage without attachment to the Argentine body politic.

The major contribution of the Rosas era, therefore, was that it made Buenos Aires viable as the region's political capital. Although Buenos Aires as viceregal capital had aroused little resistance—as far as we know—from interior population and cities, the moment Spanish rule ended, each subregion aspired to the same autonomy and sense of self-importance that the *porteños* had demanded. Para-guay, Uruguay, and Bolivia each broke away as separate nations. One surmises that, had not the threat of Spanish reconquest from Chile and Peru initially seemed a worse fate to large areas of Argentina's interior than did *porteño* domination, a veritable Central America of small, divided nations might have emerged, or at least republics, such as Mendoza, Córdoba, Tucumán, and Salta. As it was, these subregions served as buffer zones that prevented Spanish attempts at reconquest from reaching down from the empire's heartland in Peru toward Buenos Aires. Tucumán and especially Salta turned back several royalist invasions, and Mendoza served as staging area for San Martín's march across the Andes to Chile and his eventual vic-torious strike at Lima in 1821.

Once the Spanish menace had been laid to rest, however, these outlying regions had second thoughts about accepting *porteño* rule over the remains of the former viceroyalty. In 1819–1820 and again in 1826–1827—in the latter years in direct repudiation of Rivada-via—the provinces formally rejected control by those whom they considered to be virtual foreigners. In the haste to modernize and de-velop the city, the Anglophile Rivadavia, minister of government, or effectively the prime minister, for the province of Buenos Aires, had moved beyond what most Argentines outside of Buenos Aires found acceptable religiously, politically, and socially. His attacks on the church, especially on its role in education, and on monasteries and convents; his apparent acceptance and even favoring of Protestants; his welcoming of British capital and loans; his advocacy of strong central authority vested in a government ostensibly located in Buenos Aires and controlled by *porteños*; his design to restructure Argentine population and values through substantial European immigration, all aroused fear, resentment, or scorn among many provincial chieftains and *caudillos*. So strong and unanimous was that opposition that Rivadavia proved unable to survive even a year as head of the United Provinces of the Río de la Plata. By 1827, despite its port and population, Buenos Aires seemed to be rapidly losing ground in its bid to remain the nominal capital of the Argentine area. The provincial government of Buenos Aires, by virtue of its location where European subjects, ships, and trade first entered Argentina, possessed limited responsibilities for a larger area, but all efforts to formalize and define that hinterland as a nation had been frustrated by the repeated rejection of Buenos Aires by the provinces.

Into that troubled arena came Rosas, a *porteño*, but cut from much different cloth than Rivadavia. A landowner, indeed eventually the largest in Argentina, a cattleman who had made much of his wealth by salting meat, Rosas represented native Argentine interests and forces, where Rivadavia had stood for much that was foreign to the Argentine environment. Yet Rosas was not anti-European and certainly not anti-British. The cattle interests he epitomized thrived on European products and markets. When he was finally driven from power in Argentina, he sought refuge aboard a British ship and then lived out his life in exile in Southampton. But the key to his political success, perhaps not so much in Buenos Aires but certainly outside the city, in my opinion, was that he represented dominant Argentine values and attitudes. The story of more than two decades, from 1829 to 1852, of his political domination over Argentina is far too well known to require review here. For us, the significant feature is that Rosas restored Buenos Aires to its role of political influence over the rest of Argentina. Foreign commerce and representatives viewed Buenos Aires as Argentina's capital; provincial governors accepted direction and leadership from Buenos Aires; and Argentines of all persuasions and classes began to consider the city as a national capital.

Yet this Rosas era, as any student of Argentine history will tell you, is the least-known period of the nineteenth century. Our ignorance does not spring from a lack of study, for the bibliography is voluminous. It is caused rather by two elements that have always wreaked havoc with historical studies: political bias and lack of perspective. The first sprang from the bitterness that built up within the city and within Argentina over the personality and methods of

Rosas. Those intellectuals whom he persecuted and exiled ultimately returned to write his history. Not until near the end of the
century were voices raised to balance the score, to view Rosas as the
product of his time. But then, and even today, few people have been
able to examine the Rosas period with equanimity or to take any but
a polemical approach to the man. Without probing into the historiography of Rosas, the sorry state of historical studies of the 1830s
can be judged from the fact that no first-rate biography of Rosas exists; certainly none that is definitive or dispassionate, but not even
one that is honest and readable, from either his apologists or detrac-
tors. The lack of perspective has handicapped even those studies
which might try to escape the overbearing influence of Rosas by
dealing with broader topics or thematic questions. One immediately
thinks of Miron Burgin's classic study of Argentine federalism; and
Burgin does not apply the same scrutiny or analysis to the 1830s and
1840s that he uses on earlier decades. The great compiler of consti-
tutional documents Emilio Ravignani, in a brief essay, suggested
that he might attempt a broad analysis of political thought, but political and personal considerations interfered. More recently Enrique
Barba's series of essays on Rosas as well as the work of a small group
of economic and social historians under the direction of César
García Belsunce have cast new light on both the personality of Rosas
and the complexity of the era. One searches almost in vain, however,
for detailed analyses of economic trends, of demography, of urban developments. Little use has been made by quantitative or social historians of the relatively rich materials available in notarial and parish
archives, or of land records and manuscript censuses.

Rosas placed in stark and often in damning context the actual
and potential conflicts between local and outside values, and, largely
for that reason, he continues to be a significant symbol for Argentines today, either to stone or to admire and emulate. It may be,
however, that enough time has passed to enable some scholars to acquire sufficient perspective to evaluate and analyze the Rosas phenomenon. The application of new methodologies and techniques of
analysis as well as the utilization of neglected sources also can provide us with assessments less dominated by Rosas' personality. Only
then will we be able to understand better what was happening
within the city of Buenos Aires. How did the groups that emerged
during the early independence years fare? What happened to the cattlemen, the merchants, the artisans, the blacks, the foreigners?
What really occurred in the intellectual environment of the city?
What of wages, prices, and profits, or of life expectancy, migration
and immigration, and housing? Most relevant to the ideas that I have

suggested—the restoration of Buenos Aires' viability as a national capital—will be the study of how the city regained credibility with the provinces. Melodramatic as is the Quiroga-Reinafé liquidation—that combination of assassination and execution so often credited to Rosas' machinations—we can hardly rely on explanations such as those to explain *porteño* political resurgence. What economic bonds—in credit, markets, facilities—did the *porteños* forge with merchants and producers in the interior? Who came to Buenos Aires from the interior cities and who returned? How did the perception of Argentina's major port by those in Tucumán, or La Rioja, or Corrientes change? Once the answers to such questions begin to flow from historians of Argentina, we will start to understand those enigmatic decades of the 1830s and 1840s and develop new awareness for the role of the city of Buenos Aires in what appears to be a critical readjustment of its position within the nation.

Our next leap carries us to the 1860s and 1870s, equally critical decades for the city's and the nation's development, yet badly underrepresented in both *porteño* and national historiography. The troubled era of the State of Buenos Aires and the Argentine Confederation from 1852 to 1861 suggests that neither half could survive without the other. Rosas had fallen, but the politically dominant role for Buenos Aires, which he had helped to resuscitate and revitalize, not only lived on but also began to flourish. By intuition, one feels that this is the time when Buenos Aires started to develop its magnetism and pull. But why? And how?

Traditionally, because of the economic loom of the 1880s, we have settled for a formula of sudden takeoff in an agricultural export economy producing sufficient profits to create that attraction. The definition of the federal district in 1880 provides a convenient political event that seems to consolidate *porteño* dominance. The contract in 1884 to build new port works at Buenos Aires, and its implementation from 1887 to 1898, ensured the continuance of *porteño* commercial monopoly. And Buenos Aires' demographic supremacy now appeared irreversible: in the 1850s its population passed the 100,000 mark and by 1870 had reached 180,000 inhabitants. Its closest rivals in that year, Córdoba and Rosario, had 29,000 and 23,000 inhabitants, respectively.

But what was going on in Buenos Aires to prepare for the finality of the political and economic success in the 1880s? And are we witnessing merely the conclusion of a process of commercial, demographic, and political dominance which started in the colonial period—or has something new been added? We just do not have the answers. At the national and international level, Argentine and foreign scholars have assiduously investigated the origins and course of the Paraguayan War in the 1860s, but the following decade is largely a blank. Despite the unusual number and quality of the leaders and intellectuals during these decades, we find few biographies and fewer studies of trends and influences. Three notable figures occupied the Argentine presidency: Mitre still has eluded the grasp of a first-rate biographer; Sarmiento, the most brilliant of the three, has received much attention, but most of it focused on his pre-1868 activities; and Avellaneda probably ranks as the most unknown of major nineteenth-century political leaders. The same oversight applies to the economic and social bibliography. A number of works, including those by two of us on this platform today, start in the 1870s, but their real contribution and emphasis fall on the 1880s and ensuing decades.

Lack of information cannot rob us, however, of the pleasure of speculating about the attractions developed by Buenos Aires during these two decades. I will, therefore, launch five suggestions that you can reject, replace, or applaud, and thereby draw to a close my thoughts on the Argentine capital of the nineteenth century.

One process that seems fairly obvious is the linking together of the country. Transportation and communication technology, embodied in the railroad and the telegraph, now made it possible to move products, people, and information quickly and cheaply. While the full outline of the dual network finally emerged in the 1890s, by the 1870s, the backbone was in place. The Rosario-to-Córdoba Central Railroad was completed in 1870. Its extension to Tucumán was finished in 1876, and work started on another branch westward toward San Luis. Construction also began in the 1870s on the Buenos Aires and Rosario Railroad, although that line did not reach Rosario until 1886. Finally, from Buenos Aires came the western and southern lines toward Mendoza and Bahía Blanca. Telegraph lines accompanied or in some cases preceded the railroads. Now the advantages that Buenos Aires had already fashioned brought rich dividends and made it the unquestioned primate city of Argentina. Buenos Aires by its gains in the 1810s and in the 1830s and 1840s stood at the forefront of Argentine cities. Its success in capturing control of the transportation-communication network, amplified still further in 1889, when mergers and added construction placed Buenos Aires at the hub of a national railroad system, made the city master of Argentina and ushered in the prodigious urban growth of the 1880s and the 1900s.

The story of *porteño* growth, as with the Rosas era, is familiar to you. But a second process, in addition to the transport system, should be underlined here, namely, the concentration at Buenos Aires of profits and benefits generated by the development of new products and technologies throughout Argentina. Refrigeration of meat, first as frozen carcasses and then by 1910 as chilled meat; the simultaneous improvement of stock with new breeds, fences, and alfalfa pastures; the spread of sheep-raising toward Patagonia; the cultivation of wide expanses of the pampas north of Buenos Aires with corn and flax, and westward with wheat; and eventually the growth of a tobacco industry in Salta, a sugar industry in Tucumán, and wine and fruit industries in Mendoza, all added enormously to Argentina's consumption and export capabilities. These earnings translated themselves into a rising tide of imported consumer goods as *porteños* of all social levels improved their standard of living. Buenos Aires' merchants, landowners, bureaucrats, capitalists, and professionals—along with increasing numbers of shopkeepers, clerks, servants, mechanics, tailors, carpenters, and day laborers who served them—were the ones who reaped the most profits from Argentina's new-found ability to produce vast amounts of products needed by local and world markets.

For the *porteños* of the late nineteenth century, this process seemed highly beneficial. Buenos Aires now monopolized national earnings and profits in much the same fashion as it had monopolized national revenues under Rosas through control of the customshouse. But along with that monopoly of benefits, *porteños* during the 1860s and 1870s made decisions that facilitated what later generations would call economic dependency and would label evil. The building of the railroad system was wholly the work of foreign capitalists and engineers. Even the pick-and-shovel men usually were immigrants. With the increasing volume of commerce, local merchants turned more and more to European credit, banking, and trade facilities. For the introduction and operation of the myriad technological innovations—telephones, electric lights, motors, streetcars—the *porteños* looked to foreign capital, managers, and workers. The success of the 1860s and 1870s in attracting foreign capital and foreign immigrants to the city was accelerated in the 1880s and 1900s and each new influx stimulated more growth and necessitated additional injections from abroad. Success at Buenos Aires, based on ever greater yields of agricultural products in return for consumer goods, robbed the country of the possibility of diversifying its economic production, building other major commercial centers that might share prosperity with Buenos Aires, or developing industries to manufacture consumer goods locally. Later critics could see that

Argentina as a whole had become locked into dependency on outside markets as well as on constant supplies of foreign capital and immigrants. But at the same time, Buenos Aires had imposed a similar state of dependency on the Argentine provinces. Salta or Tucumán or Santiago del Estero could prosper and progress insofar as they produced goods for export to the coast or beyond and received consumer goods and capital from Buenos Aires.

With these first three processes—transportation, concentration, and dependency—we are talking about economic developments, generally associated with their fruition at the end of the century. I suggest, however, that by pushing investigation of these phenomena backward into the 1860s and 1870s we may well uncover significant approaches, attitudes, and decisions. What were the relationships between foreign and *porteño* merchants or between European creditors and Argentine debtors? Why did not the tools, skills, and capital that European artisans brought into Buenos Aires generate some support for industrialization? How did the attitudes of politicians and leaders evolve and change during these decades, in monetary, immigration, and tariff policies? How did *porteño* capitalists and merchants adjust their relations with colleagues in provincial cities? The list of questions could go on indefinitely, but there seems to be a rich field for inquiry here—one that can be probed effectively with existing as well as new techniques and methodologies.

The last two processes that I want to suggest deal with the social and political arenas. Mastery of these areas will enable us to comprehend the sometimes subtle but always powerful influences acquired by Buenos Aires over the nation in the 1860s and 1870s.

I suggest that the provinces became increasingly linked to Buenos Aires in those decades not only by the railroad, centralization, and dependency but also by the movement of people between interior cities and the coast, the penetration of outside ideas into provincial centers, and acceptance of the idea that those at Buenos Aires set the style or mode in matters of dress, education, and culture in general. To suggest such a hypothesis is easy. Researching it will prove more difficult. Sources exist, however, and their exploitation will depend on the historians' imagination. One time-consuming task that might yield results would be an examination of the manuscript booklets from the 1869 national census to identify *porteños* located in provincial cities as well as persons of provincial origins in Buenos Aires. To search out the connections and position of all such individuals doubtless would prove impossible, but from the data in the census itself one can compile information on sex, age, occupation, size of family, residential location, and literacy. A further dimension could be added by a similar examination of the 1895 census booklets. The compilation of collective biographies affords yet another rich technique to explore the movement of groups and individuals to and from Buenos Aires.

The changing cultural and social environment in provincial cities has not yet received much attention in Argentine historiography, yet such studies may reveal a change in attitudes that was as decisive and important as the obvious economic predominance achieved by Buenos Aires. Newspapers, often maligned as unreliable sources and even more disparaged because of the tremendous amount of time required for their perusal, can provide voluminous data. The advertisements alone, systematically reviewed and analyzed, speak eloquently of outside influences on products, styles, and occupations. Sections on local events and announcements as well as occasional editorial comment give further insights into direct and indirect influences from Buenos Aires and abroad. What did people wear? What did they do for amusement? What did they read and eat? Perhaps content analysis, applied to editorials or to writings of local authors, will pinpoint the arrival and acceptance of new vocabulary and concepts. Admittedly, not only does the review of newspapers take time but it also means locating collections, often several issues or a few years scattered between a number of repositories in a provincial city or available only in some private home. But with patience and effort, a rich harvest can be garnered that will tell us about the environment of another Argentina which gradually came to resemble that of Buenos Aires.

The fifth and final process is the political centralization that seemed to confirm *porteño* power over the nation. Implicitly today we are also commemorating the centennial of the federalization of Buenos Aires, the events leading to a brief civil war between the province of Buenos Aires and the national government in June 1880 and the law of September 1880 that transformed the municipality of Buenos Aires into a federal district. I have saved this political process to the last, since, despite the interest and ink already expended on political history, we still have much to learn about how and why this climax occurred and what its impact was. Arturo B. Carranza's five volumes on the "capital question" afford an excellent illustration of what I mean. (*La cuestión capital de la república, 1826 a 1887*, 5 vols. [Buenos Aires, 1926–1932].) Collected in those pages are documents and narrative from 1826 to 1887, but we discover virtually nothing about how the political process works.

What are we witnessing in mid-February 1880 when provincial guardsmen and police, gathered under the arches of the Cabildo, threaten to open fire on hastily assembled cavalry and infantry units ranged around the Casa Rosada on the other side of the Plaza de Mayo? Why does the Buenos Aires governor, after losing the presidential election of 1880 to a native of Tucumán and hero of the recent Indian campaigns, Julio Roca, threaten a repetition of the standoff between Buenos Aires and the provinces that lasted from 1852 to 1861? Why is he able to force the president to abandon the Casa Rosada and set up a temporary capital five miles away in the northern suburb of Belgrano? These questions are all the more puzzling if we recall that Mitre, the *porteño* governor who ascended to the presidency in 1862, had carefully engineered an accord that made Buenos Aires the residence for the national government as well as for the authorities of the province of Buenos Aires. Furthermore, his successors, one from San Juan and the other from Tucumán, had steadfastly refused to consider any other national capital but Buenos Aires and had repeatedly vetoed congressional measures to build a new federal capital outside Buenos Aires. At stake seemed to be the tremendous economic power, the human resources, and the political influence of the city. But the question remains: Who won? Did federalization capture that predominance and primacy for the nation? Or did the city emerge figuratively and practically in control of the nation?

The year 1880, in the political context, can be viewed both as the climax of processes which I have suggested developed during the 1860s and 1870s, or, as has been more common, as the solution that preceded the overwhelming economic growth of the 1880s and 1900s. But regardless of one's vantage point, much research and analysis needs to be undertaken to grasp the city's political role. As I mentioned earlier, we have few authoritative studies of national figures or political trends for the earlier period, and we face similar blanks after 1880. What happened to provincial politicians who came to Buenos Aires? Was it national or *porteño* influence that reached out to provincial centers? Where were federal monies expended?

The Argentine capital changed enormously during the nineteenth century. But more important than mere growth and development are the changes in its relationship with Argentina. In 1800, Buenos Aires was the area's major port, largest city, and seat of government. By 1900, Buenos Aires had absorbed the nation. Although we know some of the broad outlines and many of the details of this history, many intriguing questions and concerns remain. I have pointed to three chronological periods in the nineteenth century where our ignorance may prevent us from understanding the legacy that this modern megalopolis has received from the nineteenth century. Only through the use of new techniques to examine the 1810s, the 1820s and 1840s, and the 1860s and 1870s can those questions, which are conjectures or hypotheses today, be answered.

4. Continuity and Conflict in Buenos Aires: Comments on the Historical City

Mark D. Szuchman

The preceding papers show the ample variety of themes that urban history is capable of touching. The study of Buenos Aires is particularly important. The port city was crucial in the course of political events for many areas of South America during the independence era. From Buenos Aires, Argentine *pensadores* (intellectuals) have illuminated Latin American thought and ideas; and because of its commercial strength and economic linkages with Europe, Buenos Aires figures among the major financial centers of the world. In addition, the city projects a magnetism felt by visitors and residents alike.

Porteños comprise, even by Latin American standards, an extremely complex society. And that social complexity is reflected by histories of the city, and even of the country as a whole. Indeed, it is most difficult to differentiate myth from reality in much of Argentine historiography. Traditionally, Argentine historians have been biased in favor of certain issues and personalities, causing them to excoriate ideals not their own. *Revisionism* in North American history refers to the studies that take a second look into the accepted truths of the past in order to re-test them with newly found evidence or modern techniques. *Revisionismo* in Argentina, however, identifies itself clearly with political tenets such as nationalism, nativism, and the redemption of Rosas, who is thus identified as the quintessential defender of authentic Argentine interests. In opposition to liberals and internationalists whose intent was to impose alien material values and forms of development, Rosas is supposed to have been the promoter of an authentically Argentine mode of development stressing continued exploitation of resources for the export market but without undermining traditional—some say colonial—values. The importance of this debate in Argentina, indeed in Latin America, is felt well beyond the world of academics and archivists.

Seldom have historians *qua* historians played such a fundamental role in shaping a nation's political ideology as in Argentina.

Thus, various fields of historical investigation have been prevented from reaching full development by the excessively polemical nature of Argentine historiography. In sum, writes Tulio Halperín Donghi,

> the search for a social clue to the ideological-political conflict has not yet resulted in totally satisfactory conclusions; either social contentions are cast yet again along ideological-political lines, or else the linkages between the two become even less clear. As soon as the researcher's inquiry begins, he has already formed an image of that conflict, one that will not be altered to fit any discoveries which may emanate from researching the conflict's social aspects. . . . It is thus a fact that socioeconomic history has remained subordinate to political history even in the cases of researchers who look to the former for solutions to the latter.[1]

Yet I would insist that we should be able to view the passage of time in Buenos Aires without such polemics, and see both historical distinctions and similarities between the city and much of the rest of the nation. The great divisive issue is, of course, that which treats the organizational principle for the country under the well-known headings of centralism and federalism. These conceptual implications lead us to think in terms of a fragmented country: Buenos Aires at one pole; the interior at the other. The *porteños'* disdain for the *provincianos* was based on some vaguely articulated standard of cultural achievement which Buenos Aires was supposed to have attained. At the same time, *provincianos* smirked at the mention of Buenos Aires or of *porteños*, as symbols of their objection to having a part of Argentine territory "occupied" by cultural hybrids—no longer kindred spirits—and much too well endowed materially.

But as we see in one of the papers, and as I will argue later on, Buenos Aires had much in common with the rest of the country. Buenos Aires did, ultimately, surpass the rest of the nation, and it did so, at least initially, as Dr. Brown's paper illustrates, through subterfuge. Before and after the enactment of the Bourbon reforms, clandestine trade was responsible for promoting much of the welfare of certain groups of *porteños*. Brown's paper serves to remind us that if, politically, Buenos Aires gained prominence at the start of the nineteenth century, it was also responsible for integrating a relatively large zone of the country into a rational mode of exchange. Thus, we can see that ranchers of the interior joined those of the littoral in the mushrooming export of hides. Buenos Aires' role as commercial entrepôt was, therefore, not necessarily an exclusionary or divisive element in the process of nation building. Other regions could participate in exports as long as they followed the city's lead in satisfying the European demand for pastoral goods. Success was a function of adaptation to the emerging southern Atlantic economic order.

As important as the process of economic reorientation away from Andean production toward pampean activities was, the human links between city and countryside took new forms essential to future development. Commerce and ranching joined to make possible the extension of *porteño* urban families into lucrative rural settings. Moreover, expanding pastoral production linked the pampas demographically to other regions as never before; here we can point to the dramatic growth of population as a consequence of migration to the new southern frontier; the town of Luján illustrates this phenomenon.

However, while Brown does present an economic scenario in which an enlarging territorial arc of production joined the port city's commercial and distributive powers of exports, he avoids discussion of the distribution of returns. In terms of profits or of material acquisitions, was the distribution of income derived from the import-export model proportionate among the regional merchants? Did merchants from Córdoba, Rosario, Corrientes, or the newly emergent pampean towns acquire the wealth (as distinguished from the local status) that *porteño* merchants amassed? In other words, did the unfair distribution of silver and customs receipts in favor of the city represent inequitable earnings among the participants in production and trade? If so, could we not investigate this differential and add it to the growing list of resentments among *provincianos* in the early nineteenth century?

Brown's investigations, and to a large extent Socolow's, are discussions of growth and development. Buenos Aires was modernizing, albeit slowly, and this modernization was reflected in an urban construction program which symbolized the growing divergence between the traditional and the modern social sectors. Urban growth became perhaps the most overt expression of the social stratification that transformed the once-tranquil city into an area of tension. While conflict among residents of Buenos Aires in the first half of the nineteenth century reflected militant political wings, it also found expression in class- and occupation-based antipathies.

The gradual loss of patronage by urban liberal elites over lower social groups culminated with the Rosas era. It was not the case of plebeians running amuck, creating anarchy; it was only a shift in their allegiance and deference to other elites. The growth and building program of Buenos Aires manifested the physical location of those whom the liberals disdained as the ignorant savages who maintained *rosista* (pro-Rosas) leaders in positions of privilege.

I recently had the opportunity to read a paper presented by Richard Morse in 1968 at a conference at SUNY Stony Brook which was addressed to the problems of training Latin Americanists. He urged that we sublimate our North American tendency to observe society in Latin America with what he labeled the "American Eye"—antiseptic and prone to see matters in utilitarian fashion. Instead, he called for the recovery of the "Innocent Eye" of childhood, which observes and internalizes, among other things, the oft-found passions, ironies of action, and recalcitrance of society. One way of achieving this metamorphosis in observational attitudes, suggested Morse, is to immerse oneself in literature.[2] Even one not versed in Latin American letters can recognize the poignant sentiments of Latin American, and particularly Argentine, authors when they write about strife. It is to one such author that I wish to turn in order to illustrate some of the urban consequences of growth in the nineteenth century.

One of the finest examples of the visions and ideals held by liberals about their enemies, the "underworld" which supported Rosas, can be found in Esteban Echeverría's "El matadero."[3] In this short story, written between 1838 and 1840, we can see the state of enmity that existed between *la clase culta* (the cultivated class) and the rabble which Echeverría described as belonging to the traditional, antimodern sector of Argentine society, allowed and urged to follow their animalistic instincts in defense of self-serving functionaries. The story is familiar enough to those who have reviewed the history of the clash between *unitarios* and *federales*. A well-dressed young man riding a horse (the man atop an English saddle, of course) is taunted, accosted, and brought down by a small band of workers and hangers-on at a slaughterhouse in the southern suburbs of Buenos Aires, on the road to Barracas. In the end, the young man, tied and about to be stripped in preparation for a whipping, wills himself to death, in a romantic expression of challenge and macabre victory over his captors.

Echeverría, the *pensador* who founded Joven Argentina (Young Argentina), a club of liberal opponents of the dictator Rosas, who wrote the essentially human *Dogma socialista*, and who, together with Alberdi and Gutiérrez, formed the cornerstone of Argentine liberalism, was not capable of viewing the ignorance and anomie among lower social groups in Buenos Aires as expressions or symptoms of the manner of development in the nineteenth century. Instead of sympathy for the plebeians' own plight, he scorned them and accused them of being largely responsible for the Rosas regime.

In the final passage of the story we see two elements which depict urban society during and after Echeverría's lifetime. I wish to discuss one now, briefly, and to save the second for later. The first is the summary judgment equating *rosismo* with the lower classes. Echeverría wrote,

> In those days the butchers of the slaughterhouse were the apostles who propagated the *rosista* federation at the point of a dagger, and it is not difficult to imagine what type of federation would result from their heads and their blades. In accordance with the gibberish invented by the Restorer, mentor of that fraternity, they labeled as savage unitarian anyone who was not a decapitator, a butcher, a savage, or a thief; anyone who was a decent man, with his heart in the right place, any enlightened patriot who promoted knowledge and freedom; and by what just occurred it can be clearly seen that the source of the federation could be found in the slaughterhouse itself.[4]

This and many other slaughterhouses, stockyards, and warehouses were on the increase in the city's suburbs after 1810, serving to maintain the growth of the export trade. The economic upswing after the Bourbon reforms was responsible for the growth of a laboring suburban population which would not remain orderly or subservient and which would be impossible to administer along the old colonial lines of status hierarchies.

In Socolow's paper we can observe the spatial consequences of the growth of the import-export trade. Buenos Aires displayed classic Hispanic urban patterns, not only in the grid layout of its streets, but also in the spatial allocation of its wealthy and well-born. The Buenos Aires of the late colonial period began to have a sense of the need for corporate urban planning. We can see this interest in the attempts of the authorities to allocate space and function to corporate entities, such as the *audiencia* and the *aduana*, even to routing carts to specific areas designated as local markets.

Socolow correctly points to the scant building program for governmental institutions. The authorities continued to rely on rented quarters well into the second half of the nineteenth century, to house public and semipublic offices. However, the construction of buildings for use as private homes and businesses did continue to ac-

commodate the growing population. In the process, despite the meteoric rise in municipal ordinances, the authorities after 1810 found
it increasingly difficult to enforce regulations governing everything
from sanitation and fairness in business operations to public
behavior.[5]

This expanding society retained some small-town cultural
forms which facilitated the integration of many new entrants. For
example, despite the distribution of street names and numbers to locate people, residents retained the informal mode of referring to the
location of their peers in terms that assumed a universal knowledge
of the local society; hence police reports refer simply to the "Panadería de Dn José López" with no further indication of locale.[6]

Again, growth in the population resulted largely from the migratory currents of lower social strata, particularly by arrivals of humble workers from the interior, and of African slaves, all of whom
were engaged in daily urban activities and contacts. Their style of
life was described by Echeverría in the first pages of "El matadero":
the men were raucous, spoke loudly of intimate parts of both steers
and women; in sum, they formed a microcosm of the male subcul-
ture in which bravado and dexterity with knives could earn one a
reputation for leadership. The women were hangers-on, Africans or
Afro-Argentines who awaited the butchers' less-than-charitable toss
of the entrails which would allay their hunger. And everyone was
surrounded by the poorly clad children, always taunting and blindly
following the example of the crowd's leader in speech and manner.

These suburban streets bred much of the antisocial behavior so
bitterly decried by urban liberals. In fact, in some sections of Buenos
Aires, as on the pampas whence many migrants began their journey
into the city, the social setting demanded cunning and bravado for
survival. In several parishes, the proportion of orphaned and abandoned children was symbolic of this state of affairs. In the parish of
Montserrat, 6.1 percent of white and 2.9 percent of colored children
baptized in 1840 had been abandoned; in the parish of Concepción,
19.2 percent of the baptized white children were reported without
parents. In Catedral al Norte, the figure stood at 15.5 percent for
whites and 31.3 percent for *pardos* and *morenos*, while in 1846 the
parish of Chascomús witnessed 45.9 percent of births—nearly all
whites—involving abandoned children.[7] It is clear that despite economic growth, the corresponding benefits accrued differently to different sections of the *porteño* population.

We see, therefore, a society which was in the process of selective modernization; that is, not only was the port city leaving behind

other cities of the interior in terms of accumulated wealth, but the distribution of income among its own residents was resulting in larger socioeconomic gaps than ever before. Yet, the increasing prevalence of a surrounding zone characterized by plebeian behavior on the part of humble suburbanites was not the political design of *rosista* authorities. On the contrary, perhaps the clearest element of continuity threading through the pre-Rosas liberal era of the 1810s and 1820s, the federalist period itself, and the post-Rosas generations of '37 and '80 was the quest for the reestablishment of order and the social hierarchies that would safeguard everyone's place in society.

The gauchos, so scorned by post-1852 liberals for their support of Rosas and his agents, were in fact persecuted by Rosas, the *Restaurador* as much as by his predecessors or heirs. During the 1830s and 1840s a wide range of decrees set severe limits on freedom of movement and access to weapons. Decrees also limited the numbers and types of general stores and taverns, or *pulperías*. Finally, the judiciary lost some of its jurisdiction to the chiefs of police, who now had greater freedom to dispense justice to prisoners charged with criminal, civil, or political offenses.[8]

Justice continued to be meted out selectively, depending upon the circumstances and personalities of each case. Here we can point to a case of two young boys who ran away from home in 1840, with the aid of a Portuguese and an Englishman. The two adults were captured and sent to prison. The boy claimed by his father was returned to him; the second boy, claimed by his *patrón* (employer/protector), was instead sent to the nearest military encampment at the disposition of the commanding officer, to be treated as a deserter.[9]

The budget allocated to the police department of Buenos Aires in the 1830s was sizable indeed. In 1837 the police received over 490,000 pesos. In the city alone, there were sixty mounted policemen and forty-five walking the beat.[10] The constricted budgets of the 1840s drastically reduced the allocations to public safety personnel. And then, the liberal State of Buenos Aires, also aware of the need to maintain law and order, increased the budget for the rural police to 190,000 pesos.[11]

It appears to me that one of the central features of the history of Buenos Aires, which subsumes political differences across time, is the search for and application of means of social control, but without the mass alienation of political clients. Thus, the same man who had been flogged publicly in the streets of Buenos Aires on various occasions would only be severely reprimanded for horse-stealing and perjury, solely on the basis of his participation as a federalist soldier in Rosas' army.[12] By the same token, one who belonged to opposition groups would receive harsher punishment.[13]

No great differences appear in the drive by authorities to maintain social stability in the Buenos Aires of Rivadavia, Rosas, or Mitre. If Rosas' police incarcerated Nicolás Durán in 1835 because he had been caught sleeping armed with a pistol and a knife, Rivadavia's security officers had sent Norberto Cuello to jail in 1826 for having been seen sharpening a knife.[14] If Echeverría and his colleagues lamented the poor's loss of deference to authority, Rosas would sentence his own military officers to years of forced frontier duty as punishment for insulting municipal functionaries. After Rosas, the prescription for punishment would be maintained—but the number of years of forced service would be increased![15] In sum, the great intent of *caudillos* and civilians to limit the freedom of action and movement of rural dwellers in an Argentine countryside racked by revolutions and rebellions in the nineteenth century had its urban counterpart in Buenos Aires.[16]

The weight of the law did not diminish; on the contrary, it showed a tendency toward increased incursion by state authorities into private matters. In turn, *porteños* came to rely on the authority of the state to resolve familial disputes or to punish members of the household, particularly children, for repeated minor infractions. It was thus not unusual to find the police of Buenos Aires arresting children. Such was the case of Marcelino Salcedo, whose mother requested police intervention in 1835, for being "disobedient and for not wanting to disassociate himself from harmful friends."[17] In addition, officials came to rely on public awareness to deter civil offenses, family indelicacies, and infractions of corporate regulations. For example, in a case that was resolved in 1836 after eighteen months of deliberation, a nineteen-year-old woman from San Vicente and her husband were sentenced for having eloped. The *juez de paz* (justice of the peace) subsequently discovered that the couple had, in fact, been properly married by the church, and he so informed the government. What then should be done about the young man's jail sentence and lady's forced retention at the Casa de Ejercicios? The local prosecutor advised that the sentences be rescinded and that the couple should be free to live together. But the government's *asesor general* (attorney general) handed down a different and binding decision:

> With the subsequent matrimony contracted by Juan Neira and Josefa Ornós, the crime still remains to be purged; and for

various reasons of morality adduced by said *asesor*, he deter-
mines that the Government must order the *juez de paz* of San
Vicente to deliver Juan Neira and Josefa Ornós as prisoners, he
to serve for one month in the General Hospital for Men . . .
and she to be used as a servant in the Casa de Ejercicios for the
same length of time as punishment for her misconduct. . . . In
addition, it is also determined that, in order to satisfy and clarify dutifully all elements involved in this case, the *juez de
paz* involved should be ordered to stand at the door of the
church after Mass during the next three holidays to read aloud
the Government's resolution of the case before the townspeople. . . .[18]

The generation of '37 continued the policy of publicly embar-
rassing men and women who had engaged in misconduct. Thus, the
names of students of the University of Buenos Aires found absent
from classes were published for the information of the general public and in particular to bring their delinquency to the attention of
their peers.[19]

The intensification of laws governing moral and social conduct
is an important element that binds together the various periods of
the history of Buenos Aires. If nineteenth-century political and territorial fragmentation could threaten the coherence of the River
Plate's economy, anomic behavior by *porteños* would challenge officials to take increasingly sterner measures to keep the city an attractive place of residence for foreign entrepreneurs. This search for
formulas of control meant that the cultural form of colonial legal-
ism was retained and strengthened. At this point I wish to return to
Echeverría's story to bring to bear the second element in order to illustrate the concept of legal continuity. Upon seeing our young hero
lying dead in a pool of blood, the rabble—who earlier urged his inde-
cent punishment—now gaze in amazement and stand silent. In the
end, the *juez del matadero* keeps a bizarre adherence to legal form.
The official, who failed to prevent the young hero's capture and who
directed the preparations for his whipping, proclaims in words that
are difficult to translate: "Pobre diablo, queríamos únicamente di-
vertirnos con él y tomó la cosa demasiado a lo serio. . . . Es preciso
dar parte. . . ."[20]

The attempts at channeling public and private behavior to fit
definitions of morality determined during the colonial experience
(and even earlier) lead me to alter—or rather complement—Scobie's
hypothesis that—in addition to the railroad, centralization, dependency, and population mobility—the provinces became increasingly

linked to Buenos Aires by "the penetration of outside ideas into provincial centers, and acceptance of the idea that those in Buenos Aires set the style or mode in matters of dress, education, and culture in general." It is true that the port city set the pace in economic production and gradual modernization of the processing of primary goods, but for most of the nineteenth century it did so within a Hispanic, indeed interior, cultural mode. Buenos Aires challenged the rest of Argentina for primacy in the material sphere; success was facilitated by its wealth and its geographic position, which favored exchanges with Europe, and by the fact that it operated within an Argentine model of normative values.

I submit, therefore, that we study the growth and modernization of *porteño* society—the themes discussed by Brown and Socolow—in the comparative context suggested by Scobie. Furthermore, to Scobie's list of topics for investigation I would add that the research should be conducted along lines and from sources that would highlight the manner in which *porteños* of all social ranks related to their evolving institutional forms, including law (customary, civil, and criminal), the state, the school, and the family.

Notes

1. Tulio Halperín Donghi, *El revisionismo histórico argentino* (Buenos Aires, 1971), p. 71.

2. Richard M. Morse, "The Care and Grooming of Historians or: Stop the Computers, I Want to Get Off," in Stanley R. Ross (ed.), *Latin America in Transition: Problems in Training and Research* (Albany, 1970), pp. 27–40.

3. Esteban Echeverría, *La cautiva. El matadero*, 2nd ed. (Buenos Aires, 1965).

4. Ibid., p. 91.

5. Archivo General de la Nación (hereafter, AGN), Sala X, 36-2-13, Policía, 1830, fs. 17, 20, 21, 28, 2227.

6. AGN, División Gobierno Nacional, Censos, 1813–1861, Sala X, 42-8-5.

7. AGN, Sala X, 17-2-7, Registros Parroquiales, 1840; and Sala X, 16-10-7, Defunciones y Matrimonios en Buenos Aires.

8. AGN, Sala X, 17-2-7, Registros Parroquiales, 1840.

9. Ibid.

10. AGN, Sala X, 31-9-3, Ajuses de Comisarías, Rifas de muebles e inmuebles, 1822–1852.

11. AGN, Sala X, 43-8-9, Juzgados y Comisarías de Campaña, 1855–1863, 1890.

12. AGN, Sala X, 43-8-8, Comisarías de Campaña, 1826–1848.

13. AGN, Sala X, 43-7-5, Policía, 1830–1838, 1850–1859, Serenos.

14. AGN, Sala X, 31-9-4, Policía, 1825–1831.

15. AGN, Sala X, 43-7-5, Policía, 1830–1838, 1850–1859, Serenos.

16. Tulio Halperín Donghi, *Revolución y guerra* (Buenos Aires, 1972); Richard Slatta, "Rural Criminality and Social Conflict in Nineteenth Century Buenos Aires Province," *Hispanic American Historical Review*, 60 (August 1980), 450–472.

17. AGN, Sala X, 31-9-4, Policía, 1825–1831.

18. AGN, Sala X, 43-8-8, Comisarías de Campaña, 1826–1848.

19. AGN, Sala X, 28-11-4, Expediente 13992 (1857–1858).

20. Echeverría, *La cautiva. El matadero*, p. 91.

II. THE CONTEMPORARY CITY

5. The Socioeconomic Growth of Buenos Aires in the Twentieth Century

Richard J. Walter

In the early 1970s, James Scobie wrote a pioneering book about the emergence of Buenos Aires as a major world metropolis. In this work, which concentrated on the period from 1870 to 1910, Scobie not only described the basic characteristics of the city's growth, but also placed this growth within the model of the "commercial-bureaucratic" city. This model, according to Scobie, describes a city ". . . in which urban economic activity remains concentrated in commerce and government or in closely related subordinated fields."[1] Scobie also suggested that many of the patterns and characteristics of turn-of-the-century Buenos Aires resulting from the "commercial-bureaucratic" model persisted into the 1970s.

In this paper[2] I shall attempt to trace in broad strokes the major outlines of the socioeconomic growth of Buenos Aires (the city and the outlying suburbs) from roughly 1910 to 1980. I shall be particularly concerned with the continuities and change from the pattern described by Scobie and the applicability of his model for the post-1910 period. Practical limitations prohibit a comprehensive treatment of all aspects of Buenos Aires' development over a seventy-year period. Therefore, the principal themes considered will include general demographic patterns, the impact of industrialization, social structure, the social and ethnic ecology of the city, transportation, and general features of everyday life. A concluding section will deal with current problems and the future of the metropolitan area. This review will draw heavily from national and municipal censuses. Frequent statistical references will be a necessary evil, with more complete information provided in appended tables.

Between the first national census of 1869 and the third national census of 1914, the population of the city of Buenos Aires increased ninefold, from 177,787 persons to 1,576,597. This phenomenal demographic growth has continued to characterize the metropolitan area. Between 1914 and 1936, the population of the city, or federal

Table 1. *Population of the City of Buenos Aires, Greater Buenos Aires, and the Metropolitan Area: Sex and Nationality (Absolute, Percentage, and Percentage of National Totals): 1914*

| | National totals | % | City of Buenos Aires | | |
			Absolute	%	% of nation
Argentine males	2,753,214	34.9	394,463	25.0	14.3
Argentine females	2,774,071	35.2	403,506	25.6	14.5
Foreign males	1,473,809	18.7	455,507	28.9	30.9
Foreign females	884,143	11.2	323,338	20.5	36.6
Total males	4,227,023	53.6	849,970	53.9	20.1
Total females	3,658,214	46.4	726,844	46.1	19.9
Total Argentines	5,527,285	70.1	797,969	50.6	14.4
Total foreigners	2,357,952	29.9	778,845	49.4	33.0
TOTAL	7,885,237		1,576,814		20.0

SOURCE: República Argentina, *Tercer censo nacional*, vol. 2, pp. 3 (city), 3–37 (G.B.A.), and 109 (national).

capital, grew by almost a million to 2,413,829 persons. In the next decade another half million were added, for a total of 2,982,580 by 1947. Since that date the population of the federal capital has stabilized at almost 3 million, with a slight decline registered in 1960. The nineteen counties of the province of Buenos Aires, or Greater Buenos Aires, which surround the capital have experienced even more marked growth than the city itself—a population increase from 458,217 persons in 1914 to 5,380,447 in 1970.[3] Combined, the population of the city and surrounding counties—the metropolitan area—has grown fourfold between 1914 and 1970, from 2,035,031 persons to 8,352,900 (see tables 1–5).

For much of this period the metropolitan area of Buenos Aires represented the leading urban center by population in Latin America and one of the ten or fifteen most populous urban regions in the world. Today that position for Latin America is being challenged and perhaps surpassed by São Paulo and Mexico City. What sets Buenos Aires apart from these competitors, however, is the percent of the total national population concentrated in and around the capital city. This process was already well advanced by 1914, when almost 26 percent of all Argentines lived in and around the capital. By 1970,

Greater Buenos Aires			Metropolitan area		
Absolute	%	% of nation	Absolute	%	% of nation
133,203	29.1	4.8	527,666	25.9	19.2
133,041	29.0	4.8	536,547	26.4	19.3
112,524	24.6	7.6	·568,031	27.9	38.5
79,449	17.3	9.0	402,787	19.8	45.6
245,727	53.6	5.8	1,095,697	53.8	25.9
212,490	46.4	5.8	939,334	46.2	25.7
266,244	58.1	4.8	1,064,213	52.3	19.3
191,973	41.9	8.1	970,818	47.7	41.2
458,217		5.8	2,035,031		25.8

almost 36 percent of the national population could be found in the Buenos Aires agglomeration (see tables 1 and 5).

The geographic patterns of this population growth followed the general trend which Scobie described for the early twentieth century; that is, a steady expansion outward from the central core of the city. The capital's densely inhabited southern and central districts (2–4, 8–14, 20) showed only slight increases in population after 1914, with two (4 and 8) actually registering slight declines over time. Outlying districts (1, 5–7, 15–19), on the other hand, experienced marked increases. Particularly notable was the growth of large districts such as Vélez Sarsfield (1), San Bernardo (15), and Belgrano (16), the population of which grew by four and five times between 1914 and 1970 (see table 6 and maps 1–9).

In the surrounding counties of Greater Buenos Aires, the pattern was different. Counties in the northern and southern areas grew rapidly at first, with population later reaching out to the west. The overall growth in the suburbs produced counties whose numbers rivaled that of Argentina's largest cities (after Buenos Aires). For example, by 1970 the population of Lomas de Zamora was 659,193; that of Morón, 485,983; that of La Matanza, 449,824. All counties experienced rates of growth which saw the populations of most of them increase tenfold between 1914 and 1970 (see table 7 and maps 10–16).[4]

Certain demographic features of this massive growth remained relatively constant during this period. For example, reflecting larger hemispheric trends, literacy rates in the city of Buenos Aires were high throughout this period and consistently higher than for the republic as a whole (see table 8).[5] Also reflecting larger trends, the population of the city became progressively older than the national average, family size smaller, and life expectancy somewhat greater.[6] Other features, however, showed distinctive changes. In 1914, almost 50 percent of the city's population and 48 percent of that of the metropolitan area were foreign-born, reflective of the heavy European immigration which characterized the 1880–1910 period. After 1914, the proportion of foreigners showed a progressive and steady decline, until by 1970 only 17.8 percent of the city's population and 15.6 percent of the metropolitan area were foreign-born. Another important change occurred with regard to sex ratios. In 1914, males, in both the city and the metropolitan area, predominated numerically over females by a substantial margin. This was due primarily to the greater number of foreign males as opposed to foreign females. Among native-born Argentines in the metropolitan area, females predominated slightly. As with nationality, these ratios changed steadily over time. By 1970, the percentage ratio of women to men in the capital was the reverse of what it had been in 1914, and the ratio for the metropolitan area was also favorable to women (see tables 1–5).

Changes in nationality and sex ratios were directly related to the major demographic shift of this period. Although foreigners continued to contribute to the Buenos Aires population throughout these decades, the major additions to the metropolitan area came through the internal migration of native-born Argentines from the interior provinces.[7] This movement, paralleling the experience of much of Latin America, began in earnest in the 1930s. A combination of factors, including restrictions on foreign immigration, the "push" of changes in agricultural production and the decline of economic opportunities in the countryside, the "pull" of employment opportunities in Buenos Aires, and improved communication and transportation facilities stimulated this rush to the cities.

Migrants moving to Buenos Aires by the hundreds of thousands after the mid-1930s accounted for almost half of the rate of growth of the metropolitan area.[8] Most migrants in the 1930s and 1940s were persons of rural backgrounds and from small towns and vil-

Table 2. *Population of the City of Buenos Aires: Sex and Nationality (Absolute and Percentage): 1936*

	City of Buenos Aires	
	Absolute	%
Argentine males	726,524	30.1
Argentine females	816,583	33.8
Foreign males	476,522	19.7
Foreign females	394,200	16.3
Total males	1,203,046	49.8
Total females	1,210,783	50.2
Total Argentines	1,543,107	63.9
Total foreigners	870,722	36.1
TOTAL	2,413,829	

SOURCE: Municipalidad de la Ciudad de Buenos Aires, *Cuarto censo general, 1936* (Buenos Aires, 1939), vol. 2, p. 36.

lages of some of the most distant and least developed provinces and territories.[9] After World War II, migrants continued to come from small towns, but from all provinces and territories, most of which lost population to Buenos Aires in these years. Also, after World War II, the majority settled in the suburbs surrounding the city rather than in the capital itself. Finally, again reflecting general trends for Latin America, women predominated in the movement from the countryside, contributing substantially to the reversal of the sex ratio in the metropolitan area during these years.[10]

The major attraction of Buenos Aires for most migrants was the rapid growth of industry and the employment opportunities this growth produced. Stimulated by the consequences of the world depression and more favorable government policies in the 1930s, the number of industrial establishments in the republic doubled between 1935 and 1946, from 40,613 to 86,440. This growth continued apace after 1946, reaching 151,828 establishments in 1954 and 190,892 by 1964 (see table 9).

Even before the spurt of the 1930s, industry in the republic, like almost everything else, tended to concentrate in and around the city of Buenos Aires. In 1914, the capital contained 21 percent of all Argentina's industries and 36 percent of all persons employed in industrial activity. By 1935, the city had 33 percent of all establishments and 46 percent of all personnel. These proportions held reasonably

Table 3. *Population of the City of Buenos Aires, Greater Buenos Aires, and the Metropolitan Area: Sex and Nationality (Absolute, Percentage, and Percentage of National Totals): 1947*

	National totals	%	City of Buenos Aires		
			Absolute	%	% of nation
Argentine males	6,730,739	42.3	1,005,206	33.7	14.9
Argentine females	6,727,161	42.3	1,156,756	38.8	17.2
Foreign males	1,414,436	8.9	444,200	14.9	31.4
Foreign females	1,021,491	6.4	376,418	12.6	36.8
Total males	8,145,175	51.2	1,449,406	48.6	17.8
Total females	7,748,652	48.8	1,533,174	51.4	19.8
Total Argentines	13,457,900	84.7	2,161,962	72.5	16.1
Total foreigners	2,435,927	15.3	820,618	27.5	33.7
TOTAL	15,893,827		2,982,580		18.8

SOURCE: República Argentina, *Cuarto censo general de la nación, 1947* (Bueno Aires, 1947), vol. 1, pp. 12 (city and national) and 90–103 (G.B.A.).

Table 4. *Population of the City of Buenos Aires, Greater Buenos Aires, and the Metropolitan Area: Sex and Nationality (Absolute, Percentage, and Percentage of National Totals): 1960*

	National totals	%	City of Buenos Aires		
			Absolute	%	% of nation
Argentine males	8,585,974	42.9	1,040,511	35.1	12.1
Argentine females	8,820,118	44.1	1,246,268	42.0	14.1
Foreign males	1,419,923	7.1	344,993	11.6	24.3
Foreign females	1,184,524	5.9	334,862	11.3	28.3
Total males	10,005,897	50.0	1,385,504	46.7	13.8
Total females	10,004,642	50.0	1,581,130	53.3	15.8
Total Argentines	17,406,092	87.0	2,286,779	77.1	13.1
Total foreigners	2,604,447	13.0	679,855	22.9	26.1
TOTAL	20,010,539		2,966,634		14.8

SOURCE: República Argentina, *Censo nacional de población, 1960* (Buenos Aires 1965), vol. 1, p. 8 (national), vol. 2, p. 110 (city), vol. 2, p. 245 (G.B.A.).

Greater Buenos Aires			Metropolitan area		
Absolute	*%*	*% of nation*	*Absolute*	*%*	*% of nation*
696,032	38.3	10.3	1,701,238	35.5	25.3
689,211	37.9	10.2	1,845,967	38.5	27.4
243,277	13.4	17.2	687,477	14.3	48.6
187,660	10.3	18.4	564,078	11.8	55.2
939,309	51.7	11.5	2,388,715	49.8	29.3
876,871	48.3	11.3	2,410,045	50.2	31.1
1,385,243	76.3	10.3	3,547,205	73.9	26.4
430,937	23.7	17.7	1,251,555	26.1	51.4
1,816,180		11.4	4,798,760		30.2

Greater Buenos Aires			Metropolitan area		
Absolute	*%*	*% of nation*	*Absolute*	*%*	*% of nation*
1,470,561	39.0	17.1	2,511,072	37.3	29.2
1,508,551	40.0	17.1	2,754,819	40.9	31.2
418,244	11.1	29.5	763,237	11.3	53.8
375,055	9.9	31.7	709,917	10.5	59.9
1,888,805	50.1	18.9	3,274,309	48.6	32.7
1,883,606	49.9	18.8	3,464,736	51.4	34.6
2,979,112	79.0	17.1	5,265,891	78.1	30.3
793,299	21.0	30.5	1,473,154	21.9	56.6
3,772,411		18.9	6,739,045		33.7

Table 5. *Population of the City of Buenos Aires, Greater Buenos Aires and the Metropolitan Area: Sex and Nationality (Absolute, Percentage, and Percentage of National Totals): 1970*

			City of Buenos Aires		
	National totals	%	Absolute	%	% of nation
Total males	11,602,438	49.7	1,370,562	46.1	11.8
Total females	11,761,993	50.3	1,601,891	53.9	13.6
Total Argentines	21,183,513	90.7	2,444,009	82.2	11.5
Total foreigners	2,180,918	9.3	528,444	17.8	24.2
TOTAL	23,364,431		2,972,453		12.7

SOURCE: República Argentina, *Censo nacional de población, familias, y vivier das—1970; Resultados provisionales* (Buenos Aires, 1970), vol. 1, p. 53 (national p. 9 (city), and p. 57 (G.B.A.).

steady until 1946, when they began to decline, showing a substantial drop to 19 percent of establishments and 26 percent of personnel by 1964. As with population, beginning in the 1930s, industry began to grow substantially in the counties of Greater Buenos Aires, which between 1935 and 1964 saw their national share of establishments grow from 8 percent to 19 percent and of personnel from 12 percent to 27 percent. Combined, the metropolitan area from the 1930s to the 1960s included on the average about 40 percent of all industrial establishments and about 55 percent of all industrial personnel (see table 9).

The locational pattern of industrial growth was essentially the same as for population. Within the city, the largest numbers of industries and most rapid expansion occurred in outlying districts such as Vélez Sarsfield (1), Flores (5), San Bernardo (15), and Belgrano (16). Combined, these four districts contained almost 58 percent of all the city's industries in 1964. A substantial number of establishments could still be found in more central districts by the 1960s, but several of these (10, 12–14, 19–20) experienced a marked decline in numbers between 1946 and 1964, indicating a general movement outward from the center (see table 10).

All of the counties of Greater Buenos Aires, with the exception of San Fernando, experienced a dramatic growth in industry during this period. As with the city, this development generally paralleled the pattern of population expansion. By the 1930s, industry in the

Greater Buenos Aires			Metropolitan area		
Absolute	%	% of nation	Absolute	%	% of nation
682,821	49.9	23.1	4,053,383	48.5	34.9
697,626	50.1	22.9	4,299,517	51.5	36.6
502,864	85.5	21.7	7,046,873	84.4	33.3
777,583	14.5	35.7	1,306,027	15.6	59.9
380,447		23.0	8,352,900		35.8

suburbs was concentrated in the southern counties of Avellaneda and Quilmes. By the 1940s, however, it had spread north and west to La Matanza, Morón, and General San Martín. By 1964, these five counties, plus Lanús, carved from Avellaneda in 1944, included 58 percent of all industries in Greater Buenos Aires (see table 11). These counties, too, seem to have attracted the greatest number of internal migrants to the metropolitan area in the postwar era.[11]

Although the industrial sector grew significantly in size and importance in these years, certain characteristics, at least for the city of Buenos Aires, remained generally constant. First, industry in the capital was relatively diversified, with no single branch of activity clearly dominating over all others. Among the main categories, there was a marked decline between 1914 and 1954 in the proportion of those establishments devoted to the processing of foodstuffs and a slight decline in those dealing with wood products, printing and publishing, and clothing. These losses were balanced by gains in textiles, metals, paper and cardboard, rubber products, leather products, vehicles and machinery, and electrical machinery and appliances (see table 12). Second, most industrial establishments, in terms of number of personnel, remained very small-scale. The average number of industrial workers and employees per establishment for the city declined from 14.5 in 1914 to 9.8 in 1964 (see table 9). The 1935 industrial census recorded that 64 percent of all establishments in the city employed 10 or fewer workers.[12] A similar count in

Table 6. *Population Growth and Density (Per Hectare) in the City of Buenos Aires, by Circunscripción (Voting District): 1914–1970*

Circunscripción	Population 1914(a)	1936(b)	1947(c)	1960(d)	1970(e)	Density 1914(a)	1936(b)	1947(c)	1960(d)	1970(e)
1 Vélez Sarsfield	103,358	330,848	444,719	515,241	499,535	19.8	63.4	85.2	98.7	95.7
2 San Cristóbal Sud	70,628	88,947	101,620	88,399	83,850	80.7	101.7	116.1	101.0	95.8
3 Santa Lucía	104,188	103,168	118,288	107,495	89,510	172.2	170.5	195.5	177.7	148.0
4 San Juan Evangelista	76,024	73,586	76,088	68,462	61,694	194.9	188.7	195.1	175.5	158.2
5 Flores	79,660	123,339	149,663	152,233	150,755	99.0	153.2	185.9	189.1	187.3
6 San Carlos Sud	77,705	105,808	118,190	114,467	116,529	165.3	225.1	251.5	243.5	247.9
7 San Carlos Norte	67,007	78,311	92,440	96,204	112,643	159.5	186.5	220.1	229.1	268.2
8 San Cristóbal Norte	82,095	72,634	79,921	70,106	64,304	328.4	290.5	319.7	280.4	257.2
9 Balvanera Oeste	83,252	84,639	97,322	88,412	87,305	287.1	291.9	335.6	304.9	301.1
10 Balvanera Sud	42,293	44,226	52,367	45,816	46,478	352.4	368.5	436.4	381.8	387.3
11 Balvanera Norte	43,530	51,783	63,602	54,706	57,982	334.8	398.3	489.2	420.8	446.0
12 Concepción	73,165	74,855	95,819	74,826	70,785	348.4	356.5	456.3	356.3	356.3
13 Monserrat	75,064	81,214	100,312	77,829	69,855	227.5	246.1	304.0	235.8	211.7
14 San Nicolás	62,598	74,807	83,165	64,021	58,034	231.8	277.1	308.0	237.0	214.9
15 San Bernardo	106,716	396,097	497,913	516,721	459,403	30.8	114.5	143.9	149.3	132.8
16 Belgrano	89,866	228,826	306,799	325,051	318,078	38.2	97.4	130.6	138.3	135.4
17 Palermo	76,182	115,514	136,597	140,887	169,216	69.9	106.0	125.3	129.3	155.2
18 Las Heras	111,939	123,002	149,847	146,500	167,575	139.9	153.8	187.3	183.1	209.5
19 Pilar	86,968	99,394	137,123	137,142	174,951	193.3	220.9	304.7	304.8	388.8
20 Socorro	49,748	62,831	76,234	82,116	113,931	187.7	237.1	287.7	309.9	429.9
TOTAL	1,561,986	2,413,829	2,978,029	2,966,634	2,972,413	83.1	128.4	158.4	157.8	158.1

SOURCES: (a) *Tercer censo nacional*, vol. 2, pp. 129–149.
(b) *Cuarto censo general de la ciudad de Buenos Aires*, vol. 2, pp. 12–129.
(c) *Cuarto censo general de la nación*, vol. 1, p. 47.
(d) *Censo nacional de poblacion, 1960*, vol. 1, p. 106.
(e) *Censo nacional de población, familias, y viviendas—1970*, vol. 1, p. 9.

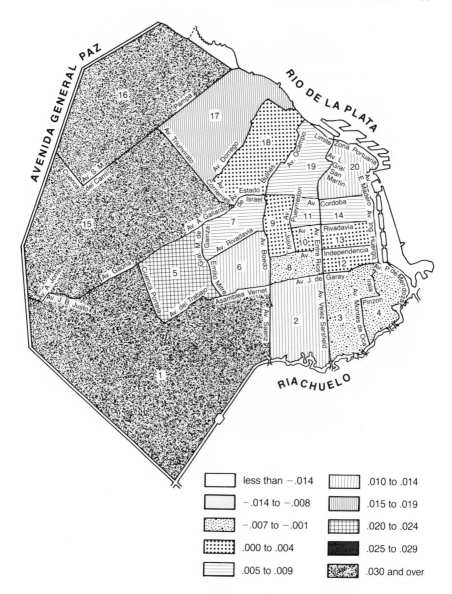

	less than −.014		.010 to .014
	−.014 to −.008		.015 to .019
	−.007 to −.001		.020 to .024
	.000 to .004		.025 to .029
	.005 to .009		.030 and over

Map 1. *Estimated Annual Growth Rates: 1914–1936*

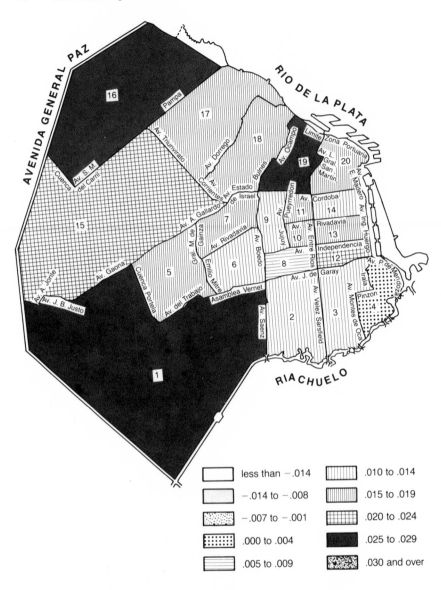

less than −.014		.010 to .014	
−.014 to −.008		.015 to .019	
−.007 to −.001		.020 to .024	
.000 to .004		.025 to .029	
.005 to .009		.030 and over	

Map 2. *Estimated Annual Growth Rates: 1936–1947*

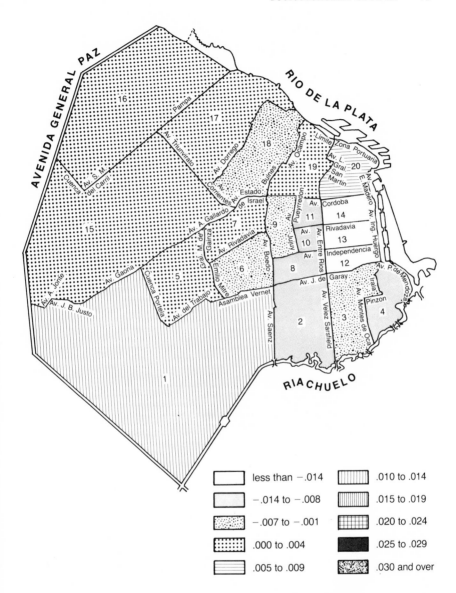

Map 3. Estimated Annual Growth Rates: 1947–1960

Legend:

- less than −.014
- −.014 to −.008
- −.007 to −.001
- .000 to .004
- .005 to .009
- .010 to .014
- .015 to .019
- .020 to .024
- .025 to .029
- .030 and over

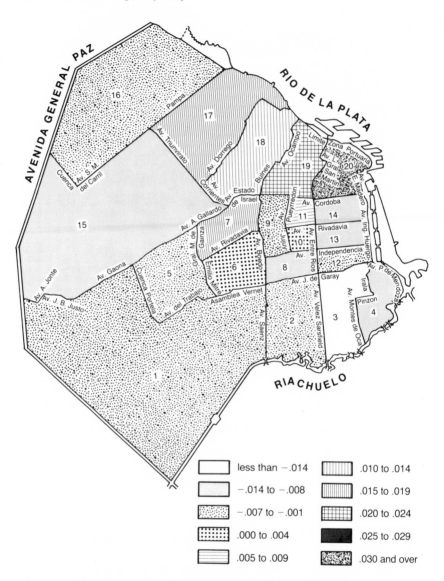

Map 4. Estimated Annual Growth Rates: 1960–1970

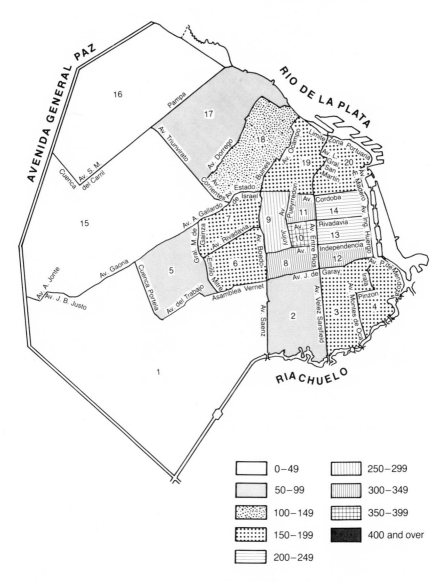

Map 5. *Population Density by Hectare: 1914*

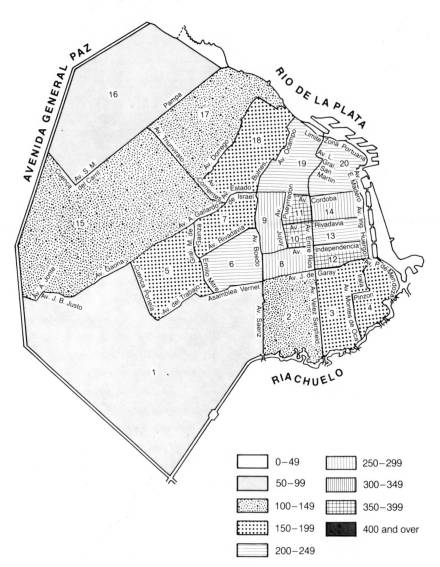

Map 6. Population Density by Hectare: 1936

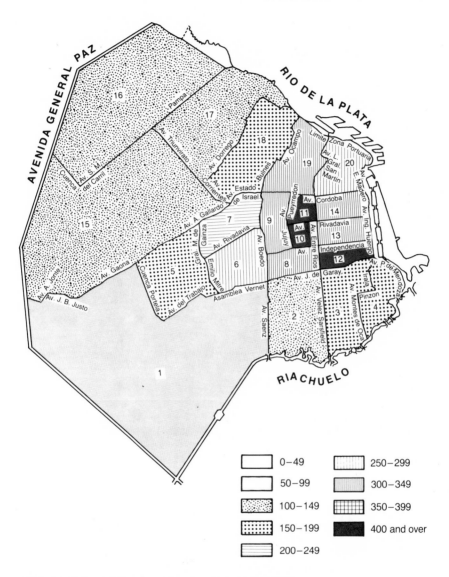

Map 7. Population Density by Hectare: 1947

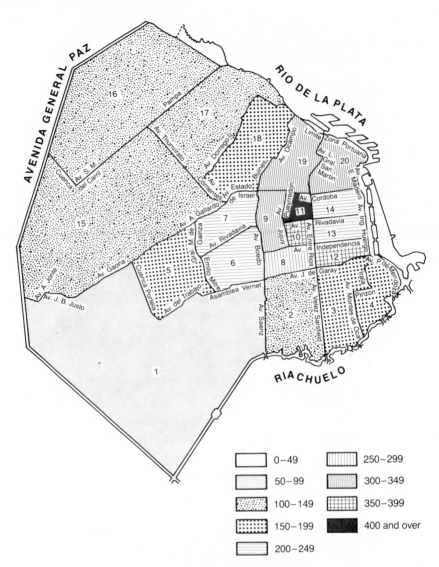

Map 8. *Population Density by Hectare: 1960*

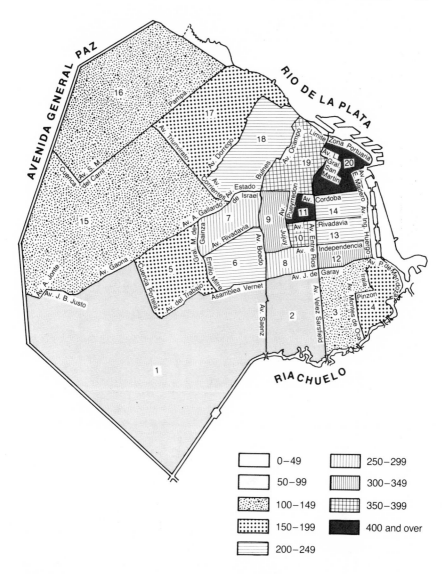

	0–49		250–299
	50–99		300–349
	100–149		350–399
	150–199		400 and over
	200–249		

Map 9. *Population Density by Hectare: 1970*

Table 7. *Population Growth and Density (Per Square Kilometer) in Greater Buenos Aires, by County: 1914–1970*

County	Population				Density			
	1914(a)	*1947(b)*	*1960(c)*	*1970(d)*	*1914(a)*	*1947(b)*	*1960(c)*	*1970(d)*
Almirante Brown	14,094	39,700	136,924	245,017	129.3	364.2	1,122.3	2,008.3
Avellaneda	144,739	348,676	326,531	337,538	1,539.8	6,705.3	5,936.9	6,137.1
Berazategui				127,740				NA
Esteban Echeverría	5,047	19,068	69,730	111,150	12.8	48.4	185.0	294.8
Florencio Varela	5,174	10,480	41,707	98,446	25.4	51.4	202.5	477.9
General San Martín	50,852	269,514	278,751	360,573	518.9	2,750.1	4,977.7	6,438.8
General Sarmiento	12,726	46,413	167,160	315,457	65.3	238.0	852.9	1,609.5
La Matanza	17,935	98,471	401,738	449,824	53.1	291.3	1,243.8	1,392.6
Lanús		244,473	375,428	410,806		5,820.8	8,342.8	9,129.0
Lomas de Zamora	59,874	127,880	272,116	659,193	604.8	1,291.7	3,057.5	7,406.7
Merlo	6,990	19,865	100,146	188,868	41.1	116.9	589.1	1,111.0
Morena	4,836	15,101	59,338	114,041	26.3	82.1	329.7	633.6
Morón	24,624	110,349	341,920	485,983	190.9	855.4	2,610.1	3,709.8
Quilmes	38,783	123,132	317,783	355,265	120.1	381.2	1,015.3	1,135.0
San Fernando	24,660	44,666	92,302	119,565	1,072.2	1,942.0	99.9	129.4
San Isidro	19,092	90,086	188,065	250,008	353.6	1,668.3	3,918.0	5,208.5
Tigre	16,691	58,348	91,725	152,335	48.2	168.6	254.8	423.2
Tres de Febrero			263,391	313,460			5,725.9	6,814.3
Vicente López	12,100	149,958	247,656	285,178	355.9	4,410.5	6,350.2	7,312.3
TOTAL	458,217	1,816,180	3,772,411	5,380,447	164.0	650.0	1,025.1	1,462.1

SOURCES: (a) *Tercer censo nacional*, vol. 2, pp. 3–37.
(b) *Cuarto censo general de la nación*, vol. 1, pp. 69–71.
(c) *Censo nacional de población, 1960*, vol. 1, p. 241.
(d) *Censo nacional de población, familias, y viviendas—1970*, vol. 1, pp. 59–61.

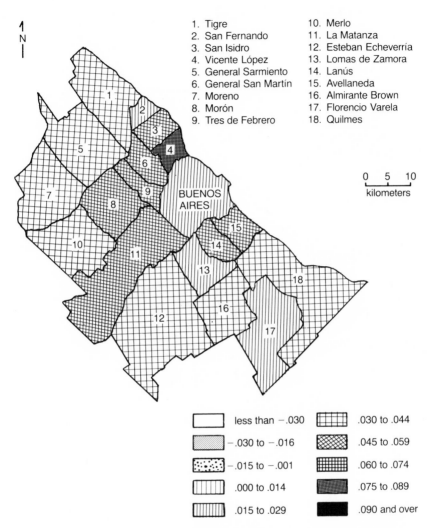

1. Tigre
2. San Fernando
3. San Isidro
4. Vicente López
5. General Sarmiento
6. General San Martín
7. Moreno
8. Morón
9. Tres de Febrero
10. Merlo
11. La Matanza
12. Esteban Echeverría
13. Lomas de Zamora
14. Lanús
15. Avellaneda
16. Almirante Brown
17. Florencio Varela
18. Quilmes

less than −.030	.030 to .044
−.030 to −.016	.045 to .059
−.015 to −.001	.060 to .074
.000 to .014	.075 to .089
.015 to .029	.090 and over

SOURCE: Sargent, *The Spatial Evolution of Greater Buenos Aires*, p. xix.

Map 10. *Estimated Annual Growth Rates: 1914–1947*

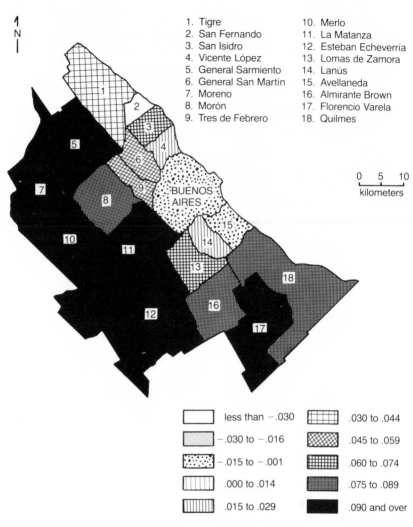

1. Tigre
2. San Fernando
3. San Isidro
4. Vicente López
5. General Sarmiento
6. General San Martín
7. Moreno
8. Morón
9. Tres de Febrero

10. Merlo
11. La Matanza
12. Esteban Echeverría
13. Lomas de Zamora
14. Lanús
15. Avellaneda
16. Almirante Brown
17. Florencio Varela
18. Quilmes

0   5   10
kilometers

less than −.030		.030 to .044
−.030 to −.016		.045 to .059
−.015 to −.001		.060 to .074
.000 to .014		.075 to .089
.015 to .029		.090 and over

SOURCE: Sargent, *The Spatial Evolution of Greater Buenos Aires,* p. xix.

Map 11. *Estimated Annual Growth Rates: 1947–1960*

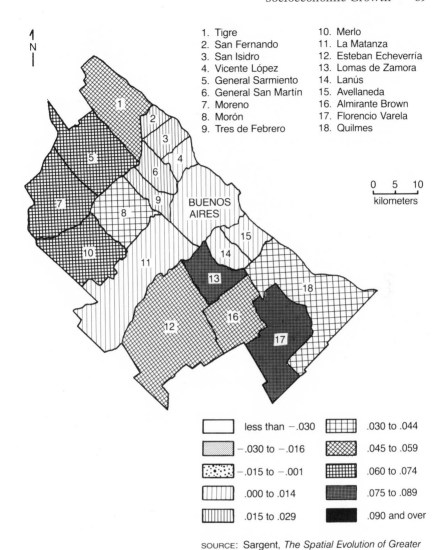

1. Tigre
2. San Fernando
3. San Isidro
4. Vicente López
5. General Sarmiento
6. General San Martín
7. Moreno
8. Morón
9. Tres de Febrero

10. Merlo
11. La Matanza
12. Esteban Echeverría
13. Lomas de Zamora
14. Lanús
15. Avellaneda
16. Almirante Brown
17. Florencio Varela
18. Quilmes

less than −.030		.030 to .044
−.030 to −.016		.045 to .059
−.015 to −.001		.060 to .074
.000 to .014		.075 to .089
.015 to .029		.090 and over

SOURCE: Sargent, *The Spatial Evolution of Greater Buenos Aires*, p. xix.

Map 12. *Estimated Annual Growth Rates: 1960–1970*

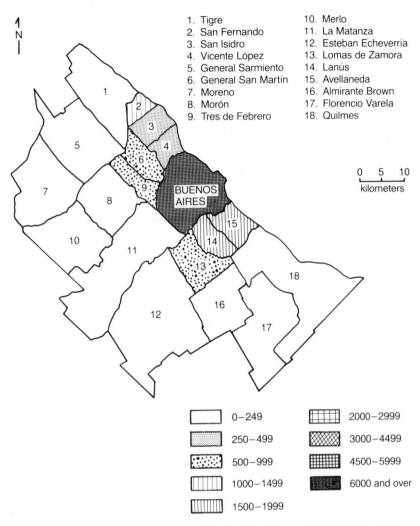

1. Tigre
2. San Fernando
3. San Isidro
4. Vicente López
5. General Sarmiento
6. General San Martín
7. Moreno
8. Morón
9. Tres de Febrero

10. Merlo
11. La Matanza
12. Esteban Echeverría
13. Lomas de Zamora
14. Lanús
15. Avellaneda
16. Almirante Brown
17. Florencio Varela
18. Quilmes

0   5   10
kilometers

0–249	2000–2999
250–499	3000–4499
500–999	4500–5999
1000–1499	6000 and over
1500–1999	

SOURCE: Sargent, *The Spatial Evolution of Greater Buenos Aires*, p. xix.

Map 13. *Population Density by Square Kilometer: 1914*

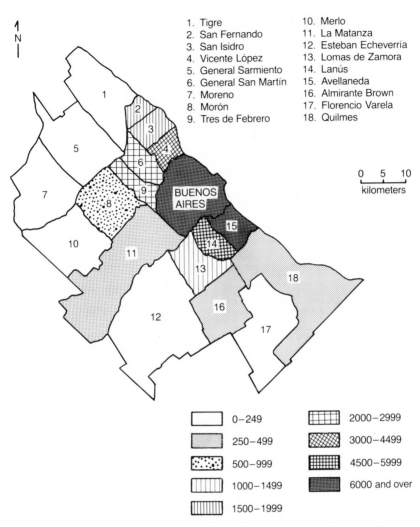

1. Tigre
2. San Fernando
3. San Isidro
4. Vicente López
5. General Sarmiento
6. General San Martín
7. Moreno
8. Morón
9. Tres de Febrero
10. Merlo
11. La Matanza
12. Esteban Echeverría
13. Lomas de Zamora
14. Lanús
15. Avellaneda
16. Almirante Brown
17. Florencio Varela
18. Quilmes

0   5   10
kilometers

0–249	2000–2999
250–499	3000–4499
500–999	4500–5999
1000–1499	6000 and over
1500–1999	

SOURCE: Sargent, *The Spatial Evolution of Greater Buenos Aires*, p. xix.

Map 14. *Population Density by Square Kilometer: 1947*

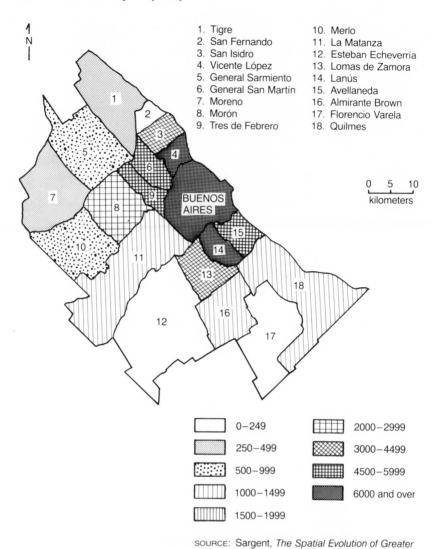

1. Tigre
2. San Fernando
3. San Isidro
4. Vicente López
5. General Sarmiento
6. General San Martín
7. Moreno
8. Morón
9. Tres de Febrero
10. Merlo
11. La Matanza
12. Esteban Echeverría
13. Lomas de Zamora
14. Lanús
15. Avellaneda
16. Almirante Brown
17. Florencio Varela
18. Quilmes

0   5   10
kilometers

	0–249		2000–2999
	250–499		3000–4499
	500–999		4500–5999
	1000–1499		6000 and over
	1500–1999		

SOURCE: Sargent, *The Spatial Evolution of Greater Buenos Aires*, p. xix.

Map 15. *Population Density by Square Kilometer: 1960*

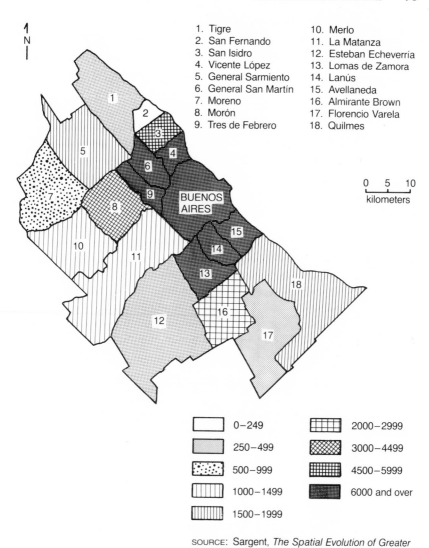

1. Tigre
2. San Fernando
3. San Isidro
4. Vicente López
5. General Sarmiento
6. General San Martín
7. Moreno
8. Morón
9. Tres de Febrero

10. Merlo
11. La Matanza
12. Esteban Echeverría
13. Lomas de Zamora
14. Lanús
15. Avellaneda
16. Almirante Brown
17. Florencio Varela
18. Quilmes

N

0　5　10
kilometers

BUENOS AIRES

☐ 0–249	▦ 2000–2999
▨ 250–499	▧ 3000–4499
⋯ 500–999	▦ 4500–5999
▥ 1000–1499	■ 6000 and over
▥ 1500–1999	

SOURCE: Sargent, *The Spatial Evolution of Greater Buenos Aires*, p. xix.

Map 16. *Population Density by Square Kilometer: 1970*

Table 8. Literacy for City of Buenos Aires and Republic, by Sex (Absolute and Percentage): 1914–1960*

	1914(a)		1936(b)		1960(c)	
	City	Republic	City	Republic	City	Republic
Literate males	604,410	2,232,046	1,025,621	NA	1,095,539	6,524,539
%	83.3	65.2	94.9	NA	97.0	92.1
Literate females	459,081	1,683,903	993,150	NA	1,260,648	6,425,570
%	75.9	58.5	91.0	NA	95.0	89.9
Total literate	1,063,491	3,915,949	2,018,771	NA	2,356,187	12,950,109
%	79.9	62.1	92.9	NA	95.9	91.0

*Figures for 1914 and 1936 are for persons seven years of age and older; figures for 1960 are for persons fourteen years of age and older.

SOURCES: (a) *Tercer censo nacional*, vol. 3, pp. 321 (city) and 329 (republic).
     (b) *Cuarto censo general de la ciudad de Buenos Aires*, vol. 2, pp. 175–181.
     (c) *Censo nacional de población, 1960*, vol. 1, pp. 26–27 (republic) and vol. 2, pp. 134–135 (city).

Table 9. Industrial Growth in the City of Buenos Aires, Greater Buenos Aires, the Metropolitan Area, and the Argentine Republic: 1914–1964

	Number of establishments					Number of personnel employed				
	1914(a)	1935(b)	1946(c)	1954(d)	1964(e)	1914(a)	1935(b)	1946(c)	1954(d)	1964(c)
City of Buenos Aires	10,275	13,440	25,156	40,080	36,573	149,289	244,231	437,249	406,922	356,944
% of republic	21.5	33.1	29.1	26.4	19.2	36.4	46.4	40.7	33.3	26.0
Avg workers per establishment						14.5	18.2	17.4	10.2	9.8
Greater Buenos Aires	NA	3,257	8,497	24,485	36,813	NA	63,587	191,367	293,492	369,495
% of republic		8.0	9.8	16.1	19.3		12.1	17.8	24.0	27.0
Avg workers per establishment							19.5	22.5	12.0	10.0
Metropolitan area	NA	16,697	33,653	64,565	73,386	NA	307,818	628,616	700,414	726,439
% of republic		41.1	38.9	42.5	38.4		58.5	58.5	57.3	53.0
Avg workers per establishment							18.4	18.7	10.9	9.9
Argentine Republic	47,779	40,613	86,440	151,828	190,892	410,201	526,495	1,073,871	1,222,476	1,370,483
Avg workers per establishment						8.4	13.0	12.4	8.1	7.2

SOURCES: (a) *Tercer censo nacional*, vol. 7, pp. 320 and 403.
(b) República Argentina, *Censo industrial de 1935*, pp. 43, 183, and 195–196.
(c) República Argentina, *Cuarto censo general de la nación: Censo industrial de 1946*, pp. 18–19 and 68–69.
(d) República Argentina, *Censo industrial de 1954* (Buenos Aires, 1960), pp. 14–15 and 53–56.
(e) República Argentina, *Censo nacional económico: Industria manufacturera* (Buenos Aires, 1968), pp. 5–6.

Table 10. *Industrial Growth in the City of Buenos Aires, by Circunscripción: 1935–1964*

Circunscripción	Number of establishments			Number of personnel employed		
	1935(a)	1946(b)	1964(c)	1935(a)	1946(b)	1964(c)
1	1,034	3,828	7,132	17,877	46,056	63,908
2	571	961	1,446	22,197	33,414	25,835
3	616	832	886	21,222	33,475	17,577
4	369	442	545	14,833	19,760	14,428
5	488	1,063	1,452	8,077	15,512	13,214
6	768	1,314	1,403	12,037	20,666	12,405
7	563	940	1,116	10,510	21,167	14,779
8	464	806	904	5,978	9,448	7,890
9	541	941	1,014	9,947	17,006	10,965
10	261	437	417	3,992	6,750	3,604
11	476	792	951	5,284	8,942	6,892
12	461	643	634	7,264	11,540	9,336
13	825	1,096	703	17,724	20,013	9,961
14	1,242	1,464	810	16,941	20,548	8,504
15	1,772	4,402	9,215	19,705	55,786	65,658
16	684	1,702	3,373	13,399	28,398	29,248
17	627	1,137	1,469	10,493	25,774	15,081
18	792	1,576	1,822	10,363	20,105	12,054
19	387	719	642	4,041	8,249	3,814
20	495	1,057	611	12,335	18,345	9,382
Isla Martín García	4	4	25	12	34	2,409
TOTAL	13,440	26,156	36,570	244,231	440,988	356,944

SOURCES: (a) *Censo industrial de 1935*, p. 183.
(b) *Censo industrial de 1946*, pp. 66–67.
(c) *Censo nacional económico: Industria manufacturera*, p. 5.

Table 11. Industrial Growth in Greater Buenos Aires, by County: 1935–1964

County	Number of establishments				Number of personnel employed			
	1935(a)	1946(b)	1954(c)	1964(d)	1935(a)	1946(b)	1954(c)	1964(d)
Almirante Brown	73	185	413	706	405	1,336	1,707	3,163
Avellaneda	1,366	1,741	3,231	3,926	36,237	71,593	63,288	50,387
Berazategui	—	—	—	579	—	—	—	12,007
Esteban Echeverría	33	83	303	628	174	1,032	2,615	7,114
Florencio Varela	24	42	183	313	302	811	2,899	4,610
General San Martín	291	1,673	5,169	4,662	3,457	22,643	40,682	41,782
General Sarmiento	49	140	403	842	762	2,025	3,081	5,925
Lanús	—	—	3,497	4,511	—	—	37,923	40,817
Lomas de Zamora	349	662	1,407	2,066	6,079	10,738	13,204	17,418
Matanza	136	507	1,638	3,285	1,190	11,646	24,325	36,662
Merlo	34	84	257	554	345	651	1,344	5,929
Moreno	23	45	182	370	278	448	771	2,626
Morón	NA	489	1,457	2,494	NA	13,444	17,459	25,563
Quilmes	252	705	1,768	2,538	7,787	24,279	35,723	24,433
San Fernando	158	441	768	767	1,529	3,975	3,379	5,500
San Isidro	77	443	991	1,524	803	7,194	16,791	21,214
Tigre/Las Conchas	178	339	622	802	1,877	4,629	5,186	10,733
Tres de Febrero	—	—	—	3,457	—	—	—	20,725
Vicente López	214	918	2,196	2,789	2,362	14,923	23,115	32,887
TOTAL	3,257	8,497	24,485	36,813	63,587	191,367	293,492	369,495

SOURCES: (a) *Censo industrial de 1935*, pp. 195–196.
(b) *Censo industrial de 1946*, pp. 68–69.
(c) *Censo industrial de 1954*, pp. 53–56.
(d) *Censo nacional económico: Industria manufacturera*, pp. 5–6.

Table 12. Industries by Category, City of Buenos Aires (Absolute and Percent): 1914–1954

Category	Number of establishments				Percent of national total			
	1914(a)	1935(b)	1946(c)	1954(d)	1914(a)	1935(b)	1946(c)	1954(d)
Foodstuffs, beverages, tobacco	1,548(15.1)	1,966(14.6)	2,460 (9.8)	2,680 (6.7)	8.2	17.0	13.4	11.7
Clothing	2,459(23.9)	2,782(20.7)*	5,128(20.4)	7,961(19.9)	34.7	58.9	49.3	51.7
Textiles	157 (1.5)		943 (3.7)	1,834 (4.6)	6.4		45.8	30.7
Construction	2,067(20.1)	495 (3.7)			24.1	31.9		
Wood products (furniture, etc.)	1,497(14.6)	1,420(10.6)	2,659(10.6)	3,540 (8.8)	33.7	35.7	26.4	17.8
Decoration	295 (2.9)				29.6			
Metals	1,321(12.9)	1,751(13.0)	3,690(14.7)	6,457(16.1)	40.3	46.8	41.1	35.2
Chemicals	159 (1.5)	412 (3.1)	863 (3.4)	929 (2.3)	28.0	44.3	41.0	34.3
Printing and publishing	511 (5.0)	923 (6.9)	1,312 (5.2)	1,579 (3.9)	35.5	42.1	42.9	42.8
Paper and cardboard		152 (1.1)	360 (1.4)	615 (1.5)		71.0	68.7	64.6
Petroleum refining		23 (0.2)	13 (0.1)	12 (0.03)		41.1	27.7	17.7
Rubber products		29 (0.2)	73 (0.3)	275 (0.7)		63.0	55.7	52.4
Leather products		611 (4.6)	1,982 (7.9)	3,763 (9.4)		56.2	45.4	46.7
Stone, glass, and ceramics		507 (3.8)	775 (3.1)	957 (2.4)		22.4	12.2	7.8
Vehicles and machinery		1,322 (9.8)	2,120 (8.4)	4,577(11.4)		26.2	17.3	18.0
Electrical machinery and appliances			702 (2.8)	1,576 (3.9)			39.8	35.2
Electricity and gas		9 (0.1)	6 (0.02)	5 (0.01)		1.0	0.6	0.6
Various	261 (2.5)	1,038 (7.7)	2,070 (8.2)	3,320 (8.3)	27.3	49.6	48.0	43.5
TOTAL	10,275	13,440	25,156	40,080				

*Includes textiles.

SOURCES: (a) *Tercer censo nacional*, vol. 7, pp. 120 and 192.
(b) *Censo industrial de 1935*, pp. 44 and 183–184.
(c) *Censo industrial de 1946*, pp. 26–31 and 66.
(d) *Censo industrial de 1954*, pp. 12 and 51.

1946 found that number somewhat reduced but still a substantial 53 percent.[13] On the other side of the coin, both censuses also discovered that large-scale enterprises employing over a hundred workers made up less than 3 percent of the total number of industries, but employed almost half of the total personnel.

Some significant changes occurred in the sex and nationality of industrial personnel, changes which reflected the major demographic shifts previously noted. In 1914, foreigners outnumbered Argentines employed in industry in the capital by a ratio of 3 to 2 overall and by 2 to 1 among males. Among females, who at that time represented almost 16 percent of the industrial work force, Argentines predominated over foreigners by a ratio of almost 3 to 2. Women were best represented in the textile, clothing, and chemical industries (see table 13). By 1946, Argentines outnumbered foreign personnel in industry 2 to 1, with Argentine males enjoying a 3 to 2 edge and Argentine females a 4 to 1 advantage. Also by 1946, females had come to represent 28 percent of the industrial work force, almost doubling their 1914 proportions, and composed 61 percent of the workers in clothing, 47 percent in textiles, 29 percent in chemicals, and 22 percent in printing and publishing (see table 14).[14]

The description of the growth and changes in the overall population and in industry rests on a reasonably secure statistical base. Data for a discussion of social structure, and particularly of the impact of population and industrial growth on the class composition of Buenos Aires, are more problematic and less secure. However, occupational information from the 1914, 1947, and 1960 censuses, plus a rather liberal interpretation of occupational categories, provides a picture of rather significant social change over time. The three main categories I shall use are blue-collar, white-collar, and professional. Reference will also be made to smaller and more specific groups.[15]

In 1914, Buenos Aires was essentially a blue-collar city, its occupational structure dominated by the working class, which made up 67.4 percent of the total economically active population. The white-collar category included 28.3 percent of the total and professionals 4.3. With regard to nationality, foreigners predominated among the blue-collars, making up 72.5 percent of the total. Foreigners also made up 58.5 percent of the white-collar group, their representation being particularly high among merchants. Argentines predominated among professionals, with 68.5 percent of the total, reflecting the native hold on elite-status occupations. With regard to sex, women made up 30 percent of the blue-collar category, with heavy concentrations in the menial and semiskilled groups. Foreign-

Table 13. *Personnel Employed in Industry by Category and Sex and Nationali* *(Absolute and Row Percentages), City of Buenos Aires: 1914*

		Totals			Male
Category	General	Argentine	Foreign	Total	Argentine
Foodstuffs	21,021	7,263(34.6)	13,758(65.4)	19,612(93.3)	6,428(32.8)
Clothing	34,813	13,226(38.0)	21,587(62.0)	24,305(69.8)	7,129(29.3)
Construction	23,526	9,263(39.4)	14,263(60.6)	23,440(99.6)	9,215(39.3)
Furniture	13,576	5,842(43.0)	7,734(57.0)	13,116(96.6)	5,556(42.4)
Decoration	2,102	869(41.3)	1,233(58.7)	1,972(93.8)	778(39.5)
Metals	15,614	6,792(43.5)	8,822(56.5)	15,291(97.9)	6,598(43.1)
Chemicals	2,787	1,109(39.8)	1,678(60.2)	2,210(79.3)	736(33.3)
Printing	6,951	3,778(54.4)	3,173(45.6)	6,404(92.1)	3,464(54.1)
Textiles	8,881	4,769(53.7)	4,112(46.3)	4,143(46.7)	1,779(42.9)
Various	15,176	5,502(36.3)	9,674(63.7)	11,266(74.2)	3,428(30.4)
TOTAL	144,447	58,413(40.4)	86,034(59.6)	121,759(84.3)	45,111(37.0)

SOURCE: *Tercer censo nacional,* vol. 7, p. 320.

Table 14. *Personnel Employed in Industry by Category and by Sex and Nationality (Absolute and Row Percentages), City of Buenos Aires: 1946*

		Totals	
Category	General	Argentine	Foreign
Foodstuffs	57,826	39,006(67.5)	18,820(32.6)
Clothing	123,136	80,134(65.1)	43,002(34.9)
Construction	69,712	35,772(51.3)	33,940(48.7)
Electricity, gas and water	9,868	6,320(64.0)	3,548(36.0)
Printing and paper	40,007	30,997(77.5)	9,010(22.5)
Wood products	36,207	19,474(53.8)	16,733(46.2)
Metals	91,032	64,035(70.3)	26,997(29.7)
Chemicals	38,818	28,713(74.0)	10,105(26.0)
Textiles	56,249	40,952(72.8)	15,297(27.2)
Various	5,434	4,109(75.6)	1,325(24.4)
Unspecified	41,739	30,448(73.0)	11,291(27.1)
TOTAL	570,028	379,960(66.7)	190,068(33.3)

SOURCE: *Cuarto censo general,* vol. 1, p. 67.

Foreign	Total	Female Argentine	Foreign
,184(67.2)	1,409 (6.7)	835(59.3)	574(40.7)
,176(70.7)	10,508(30.2)	6,097(58.0)	4,411(42.0)
,225(60.7)	86 (0.4)	48(55.8)	38(44.2)
,560(57.6)	460 (3.4)	286(62.2)	174(37.8)
,194(60.5)	130 (6.2)	91(70.0)	39(30.0)
,693(56.9)	323 (2.1)	194(60.1)	129(39.9)
,474(66.7)	577(20.7)	373(64.6)	204(35.4)
,940(45.9)	547(7.9)	314(57.4)	233(42.6)
,364(57.1)	4,738(53.3)	2,990(63.1)	1,748(36.9)
,838(69.6)	3,910(25.8)	2,074(53.0)	1,836(47.0)
,648(63.0)	22,688(15.7)	13,302(58.6)	9,386(41.4)

Total	Male Argentine	Foreign	Total	Female Argentine	Foreign
46,847(81.0)	29,859(63.7)	16,988(36.3)	10,979(19.0)	9,147(83.3)	1,832(16.7)
48,164(39.1)	22,327(46.4)	25,837(53.6)	74,972(60.9)	57,807(77.1)	17,165(22.9)
68,592(98.4)	34,864(50.8)	33,728(49.2)	1,120 (1.6)	908(81.1)	212(18.9)
9,319(94.4)	5,844(62.7)	3,475(37.3)	549 (5.6)	476(86.7)	73(13.3)
31,124(77.8)	23,030(74.0)	8,094(26.0)	8,883(22.2)	7,967(89.7)	916(10.3)
34,481(95.2)	18,057(52.4)	16,424(47.6)	1,726 (4.8)	1,417(82.1)	309(17.9)
33,224(91.4)	57,138(68.7)	26,086(31.3)	7,808 (8.6)	6,897(88.3)	911(11.7)
27,428(70.7)	18,564(67.7)	8,864(32.3)	11,390(29.3)	10,149(89.1)	1,241(10.9)
29,976(53.3)	19,328(64.5)	10,648(35.5)	26,273(46.7)	21,624(82.3)	4,649(17.7)
3,373(62.1)	2,284(67.7)	1,089(32.3)	2,061(37.9)	1,825(88.5)	236(11.5)
30,237(72.4)	20,430(67.6)	9,807(32.4)	11,502(27.6)	10,018(87.1)	1,484(12.9)
12,765(72.4)	251,725(61.0)	161,040(39.0)	157,263(27.6)	128,235(81.5)	29,028(18.5)

Table 15. *Social Structure of the City of Buenos Aires by Sex and Nationality (Absolute and Row Percentages): 1914*

| | | Argentine | |
Category	Male	Female	Total
1. Menial	7,792 (5.3)	17,046(11.6)	24,838(16.9)
2. Semiskilled service	18,312(11.9)	37,573(24.4)	55,885(36.3)
3. Rural semiskilled	106(57.9)	0	106(57.9)
4. Skilled	50,615(25.3)	6,863 (3.4)	57,478(28.7)
5. Rural skilled	1,391(22.2)	4 (0.1)	1,395(22.3)
6. Low nonmanual	56,164(42.7)	8,684 (6.6)	64,848(49.3)
7. Middle nonmanual	15,796(25.0)	504 (0.8)	16,300(25.8)
8. High nonmanual	6,451(35.8)	616 (3.4)	7,067(39.2)
9. Low professional	8,628(34.9)	7,906(32.0)	16,534(66.9)
10. High professional	5,693(73.2)	56 (0.7)	5,749(73.9)
11. Misc. and students	27,042 (7.1)	129,797(34.1)	156,839(41.2)
TOTAL	197,990(17.5)	209,049(18.4)	407,039(35.9)
Blue-collar (1−5)	78,216(15.4)	61,486(12 1)	139,702(27.5)
White-collar (6−8)	78,411(36.8)	9,804 (4.6)	88,215(41.4)
Professional (9−10)	14,321(44.0)	7,962(24.5)	22,283(68.5)

| | | Foreign | |
Category	Male	Female	Total
1. Menial	80,062(54.6)	41,809(28.5)	121,871(83.1)
2. Semiskilled service	58,565(38.1)	39,418(25.6)	97,983(63.7)
3. Rural semiskilled	77(42.1)	0	77(42.1)
4. Skilled	133,059(66.7)	9,174 (4.6)	142,233(71.3)
5. Rural skilled	4,810(76.8)	62 (0.9)	4,872(77.7)
6. Low nonmanual	62,122(47.2)	4,590 (3.5)	66,712(50.7)
7. Middle nonmanual	43,956(69.5)	2,979 (4.7)	46,935(74.2)
8. High nonmanual	9,316(51.7)	1,651 (9.1)	10,967(60.8)
9. Low professional	5,009(20.2)	3,198(12.9)	8,207(33.1)
10. High professional	1,966(25.3)	64 (0.8)	2,030(26.1)
11. Misc. and students	29,929 (7.9)	193,497(50.9)	223,426(58.8)
TOTAL	428,871(37.9)	296,442(26.2)	725,313(64.1)
Blue-collar (1−5)	276,573(54.6)	90,463(17.9)	367,036(72.4)
White-collar (6−8)	115,394(54.2)	9,220 (4.3)	124,614(58.6)
Professional (9−10)	6,975(21.4)	3,262(10.0)	10,237(31.5)

Table 15, *continued*

Category	Male	General Total Female	Total	%
1. Menial	87,854 (59.9)	58,885(40.1)	146,709?	13.0
2. Semiskilled service	76,877 (50.0)	76,991(50.0)	153,868	13.6
3. Rural semiskilled	183(100.0)	0	183	0
4. Skilled	183,674 (92.0)	16,037 (8.0)	199,711	17.6
5. Rural skilled	6,201 (99.0)	66 (1.0)	6,267	0.6
6. Low nonmanual	118,286 (89.9)	13,274(10.1)	131,560	11.6
7. Middle nonmanual	59,752 (94.5)	3,483 (5.5)	63,235	5.6
8. High nonmanual	15,767 (87.5)	2,267(12.5)	18,034	1.6
9. Low professional	13,637 (55.1)	11,104(44.9)	24,741	2.2
10. High professional	7,659 (98.5)	120 (1.5)	7,779	0.7
11. Misc. and students	56,971 (15.0)	323,294(85.0)	380,265	33.6
TOTAL	626,861 (55.4)	505,521(44.6)	1,132,382	
Blue-collar (1–5)	354,789 (70.0)	151,949(30.0)	506,738	67.4
White-collar (6–8)	193,805 (91.0)	19,024 (8.9)	212,829	28.3
Professional (9–10)	21,296 (65.4)	11,224(34.5)	32,520	4.3

SOURCE: Compiled from *Tercer censo nacional,* vol. 4, pp. 201–212. See also note 14.

born females outnumbered Argentines by more than 2 to 1 in menial occupations, but the two groups were about even in semiskilled and skilled blue-collar occupations. Females made up only 8.9 percent of the white-collar categories, but, surprisingly, 34.5 percent of the professionals. Within the white-collar group, Argentine and foreign females were almost evenly represented, while among professionals native-born women enjoyed a better than 2 to 1 edge over their foreign-born sisters (see table 15).

Unfortunately, the next national census, that for 1947, does not provide the same detailed occupational breakdown as that of 1914. The census does, however, divide the economically active population of the capital into those engaged in basic production (0.7 percent), secondary or industrial production (40.2 percent), and services (56.2 percent). The changes among those engaged in industrial activities have already been described. Many of those same changes with regard to nationality and sex can also be discerned in the service categories. Overall, natives outnumbered foreigners by more than 2 to 1. Among particular categories, foreigners held the edge only in occupations related to the hotel business. Natives held sway most no-

Table 16. *Personnel in the Service Sector in the City of Buenos Aires, by Sex and Nationality (Absolute and Row Percentages): 1947*

Category	General	Totals Argentine	Foreign
Commerce	282,192	173,608(61.5)	108,584(38.5)
Communications	7,451	6,146(82.5)	1,305(17.5)
Entertainment	14,843	9,805(66.1)	5,038(33.9)
Hotels	37,009	15,744(42.5)	21,265(57.5)
Liberal professions	44,434	34,348(77.3)	10,086(22.7)
Health services	23,105	12,059(52.2)	11,046(47.8)
Air-maritime transportation	13,804	8,462(61.5)	5,302(38.5)
Land transportation	66,897	40,355(60.3)	26,542(39.7)
Various	4,072	2,031(49.9)	2,041(50.1)
Government	170,005	149,124(87.7)	20,881(12.3)
Sanitary services	17,350	11,538(66.5)	5,812(33.5)
Domestic services	114,781	82,503(71.9)	32,278(28.1)
TOTAL	795,903	545,723(68.6)	250,180(31.4)

Category	Total	Male Argentine	Foreign
Commerce	237,766(84.3)	138,724(58.3)	99,042(41.7)
Communications	5,010(67.2)	3,894(77.7)	1,116(22.3)
Entertainment	11,889(80.1)	7,614(64.0)	4,275(36.0)
Hotels	31,624(85.4)	12,496(39.5)	19,128(60.5)
Liberal professions	28,484(64.1)	21,658(76.0)	6,826(24.0)
Health services	15,808(68.4)	6,586(41.7)	9,222(58.3)
Air-maritime transportation	13,381(96.9)	8,115(60.6)	5,266(39.4)
Land transportation	65,926(98.5)	39,570(60.0)	26,356(40.0)
Various	1,819(44.7)	654(36.0)	1,165(64.0)
Government	134,661(79.2)	116,121(86.2)	18,540(13.8)
Sanitary services	6,330(36.5)	3,698(58.4)	2,632(41.6)
Domestic services	15,099(13.2)	4,821(31.9)	10,278(68.1)
TOTAL	567,757(71.3)	363,951(64.1)	203,846(35.9)

Table 16, *continued*

Category	Total	Female Argentine	Foreign
Commerce	44,426(15.7)	34,884(78.5)	9,542(21.5)
Communications	2,441(32.8)	2,252(92.3)	189 (7.7)
Entertainment	2,954(19.9)	2,191(74.2)	763(25.8)
Hotels	5,385(14.6)	3,248(60.3)	2,137(39.7)
Liberal professions	15,950(35.9)	12,690(79.6)	3,260(20.4)
Health services	7,297(31.6)	5,473(75.0)	1,824(25.0)
Air-maritime transportation	423 (3.1)	347(82.0)	76(18.0)
Land transportation	971 (1.5)	785(80.8)	186(19.2)
Various	2,253(55.3)	1,377(61.1)	876(38.9)
Government	35,344(20.8)	33,003(93.4)	2,341 (6.6)
Sanitary services	11,020(63.5)	7,840(71.1)	3,180(28.9)
Domestic services	99,682(86.8)	77,682(77.9)	22,000(22.1)
TOTAL	228,146(28.7)	181,772(79.7)	46,374(20.3)

SOURCE: *Cuarto censo general,* vol. 1, p. 67.

tably in government employment (87.7 percent), communications (82.5 percent), liberal professions (77.3 percent), and domestic services (71.9 percent). Women made up 28.7 percent of those in services. They were fairly well represented in communications (32.8 percent), liberal professions (35.9 percent), and health services (31.6 percent), but most markedly in sanitary services (63.5 percent) and domestic services (86.9 percent). Within the domestic services category, native-born women predominated over foreign-born females by a 4 to 1 margin, sharply reversing the situation among menials in 1914 and suggesting the importance of these occupations for the many female migrants of the period (see table 16).

The fifth national census (1960) also has occupational data for the capital, although the categories are again different from preceding censuses, and this census does not discriminate between foreigners and native-born Argentines. Nevertheless, rough calculations provide some interesting results.

First, despite the growth of industry, the blue-collar percentage of the economically active population in 1960 represented only about half of the total (49.7 percent), a decline of almost 18 points from 1914.[16] The white-collar sector, on the other hand, represented 35.1 percent of the total, and professionals 15.2 percent, increases of

Table 17. *Social Structure of the City of Buenos Aires, by Sex (Absolute and Row Percentages): 1960*

Category	Male	Female	Total	% Total
1. Service workers	50,806 (33.0)	103,375(67.0)	154,181	12.4
2. Day laborers	23,116 (91.1)	2,265 (8.9)	25,381	2.0
3. Other artisans	41,666 (69.7)	18,091(30.3)	59,757	4.8
4. Artisans	204,675 (75.1)	68,017(24.9)	272,692	21.9
5. Transportation	47,538 (98.3)	820 (1.7)	48,358	3.9
6. Miners	382(100.0)	0	382	0.03
7. Agriculturists	5,993 (91.9)	531 (8.1)	6,524	0.5
8. Merchants	140,164 (82.8)	29,043(17.2)	169,207	13.6
9. Office employees	147,897 (64.0)	83,159(36.0)	231,056	18.5
10. Administrators	53,568 (91.5)	4,987 (8.5)	58,555	4.7
11. Professionals	57,801 (50.5)	56,712(49.5)	114,513	9.2
12. Miscellaneous	75,044 (70.7)	31,137(29.3)	106,181	8.5
TOTAL	848,650 (68.1)	398,137(31.9)	1,246,787	
Blue-collar (1–7)	374,176 (66.0)	193,099(34.0)	567,275	49.7
White-collar (8–9)	288,061 (72.0)	112,202(28.0)	400,263	35.1
Professional (10–11)	111,369 (64.3)	61,699(35.7)	173,068	15.2

SOURCE: *Censo nacional de población, 1960,* vol. 2, pp. 196–201.

almost 7 percent and 11 percent, respectively (see table 17). These findings seem to support the widely accepted proposition that the socioeconomic structure of Buenos Aires afforded many opportunities for mobility up the social ladder.[17] They also suggest the continued commercial-bureaucratic nature of the city. While industry expanded greatly in the decades after 1930, so did commercial and governmental activities, many of which were spinoffs of industrial growth. Commercial expansion and concentration can be seen by again referring to census data. In 1914, the city of Buenos Aires contained 27,761 commercial establishments, 30.6 percent of the national total, employing 116,813 persons, 36.6 percent of the national total.[18] In 1954, the capital had 92,877 commercial establishments, 23.8 percent of the national total, which employed 246,918 persons, 38.9 percent of the national total.[19] With regard to government employees, the 1914 census listed 49,438 persons, while the 1947 census numbered 170,005 as engaged in "activities of the national, provincial, and municipal government."[20]

Second, a comparison between 1914 and 1960 reveals the important changes in the role of women in the capital. Although the proportion of women in the total work force remained about the same, as did proportions in the blue-collar and professional categories, their absolute and proportionate increases in the white-collar category represented a remarkable shift. In 1914, the absolute number of women in this category was only 19,024, representing just 8.9 percent of the total. By 1960, the absolute number was 112,202, a better than fivefold increase representing 28 percent of the total. Looking at specific groups, women registered their greatest gains as skilled workers, merchants, office employees, and professionals. On the other hand, in 1960 they were only slightly represented (under 10 percent) among day laborers, administrators, and persons engaged in transportation. It should also be noted that in 1960 the largest numbers and highest proportion of women in any particular category were among service workers, presumably domestic servants (see table 17). Although mobility allowed women to move into the middle and upper levels of society in ever-increasing numbers, many also remained at the bottom engaged in the most menial occupations.

The 1960 census, unlike its predecessors, does allow for some comparisons of occupational groups in the city and the suburbs. Overall, according to the census, Greater Buenos Aires had a significantly greater proportion of blue-collars (67.8 percent) than the capital and a correspondingly smaller number of white-collars (24.3 percent) and professionals (7.9 percent). This difference would appear to reflect the rapid growth of industry in Greater Buenos Aires and the gradual decline of such activity in the city after the 1950s. Women were a smaller percentage of the work force: 21.6 percent as compared with 31.9 percent in the city. Females made up a significantly smaller proportion of the blue-collars (19.5 percent as compared with 34 percent), slightly smaller among white-collars (22.7 percent as compared with 28 percent), and about the same (35.6 percent as compared with 35.7 percent) among professionals (see table 18). Looking at smaller categories, females in the suburbs reflected the general occupational pattern of their sisters in the capital. Women were well represented among office employees (26.7 percent) and professionals (52.1 percent) and poorly among day laborers, administrators, and persons engaged in transportation. Unlike the city, the greatest absolute numbers of women were in the skilled worker category, again reflecting the growth of industry in the suburbs. Female service workers represented the second largest category in absolute terms, although the total was substantially below that for the city (see table 18).

In his study of Buenos Aires, Scobie argues that by the 1970s, settlement patterns in the capital had changed little from 1910.[21] Al-

Table 18. *Social Structure of Greater Buenos Aires, by Sex (Absolute and Row Percentages): 1960*

Category	Male	Female	Total	% Total
1. Service workers	54,473 (47.0)	61,311(53.0)	115,784	8.0
2. Day laborers	60,642 (96.5)	2,213 (3.5)	62,855	4.3
3. Other artisans	107,396 (81.3)	24,687(18.7)	132,083	9.1
4. Artisans	414,588 (82.5)	87,655(17.5)	502,243	34.6
5. Transportation	72,716 (98.9)	817 (1.1)	73,533	5.1
6. Miners	380(100.0)	0	380	0.03
7. Agriculturists	25,101 (96.3)	961 (3.7)	26,062	1.8
8. Merchants	113,879 (82.9)	23,567(17.1)	137,446	9.5
9. Office employees	139,579 (73.3)	50,756(26.7)	190,335	13.1
10. Administrators	35,499 (95.0)	1,854 (5.0)	37,353	2.6
11. Professionals	33,257 (47.9)	36,176(52.1)	69,433	4.8
12. Miscellaneous	81,001 (77.7)	23,276(22.3)	104,277	7.2
TOTAL	1,138,511 (78.4)	313,273(21.6)	1,451,784	
Blue-collar (1–7)	735,296 (80.5)	177,644(19.5)	912,940	67.8
White-collar (8–9)	253,458 (77.3)	74,323(22.7)	327,781	24.3
Professional (10–11)	68,756 (64.4)	38,030(35.6)	106,786	7.9

SOURCE: *Censo nacional de población, 1960*, vol. 2, pp. 328–333.

though the evidence to support this assertion is often scattered and imprecise, most observers agree that the ecology of the city, in terms of the location of social and ethnic groups, has remained remarkably constant.[22] Most of the information I have been able to gather supports this assumption.

It has been noted, for example, that—unlike most North American cities—the central downtown core of Buenos Aires continues as the heart of the city, in which most of the Republic's important commercial, cultural, financial, and governmental establishments can be found. The center and its near northern neighborhoods, particularly the *barrio norte* (the northern ward), also continue as attractive residential areas for the upper middle class and the elite.[23] Scobie and others have already described the development of oligarchical residences in this area at the beginning of the twentieth century.[24] Another piece of evidence is a comparison of a list of the twenty-five leading landowning families in the province of Buenos Aires, all of whom had one or more homes in the capital, with their addresses in the city as of 1918. This shows a strong concentration in the center and the *barrio norte*, with a pronounced grouping along Calle Flor-

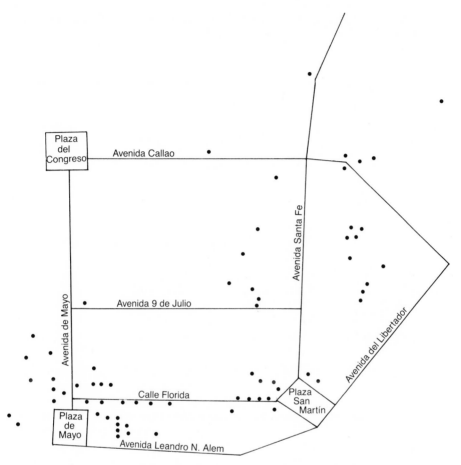

Map 17. *Location of Elite Residences in the Federal Capital: 1918*

ida (Florida Street) (see map 17 and table 19). Although strictly similar data were not available for a comparison over time, José Luis de
Imaz, in his systematic study of *La clase alta de Buenos Aires*,
found the majority of the upper-class families in his survey still located in the *centro* and the *barrio norte* as of 1965.[25]

Other districts of the city also retained many of their social
characteristics despite the massive demographic changes from 1910
to 1980. A comparison of information previously compiled for a
study of voting in the city for 1918, along with data from the 1960

Table 19. *1918 City Addresses for the Twenty-Five Leading Landowning Families of the Province of Buenos Aires.*

Family name	Capital addresses
1. Luro	Victoria 618, Sante Fe 2363
2. Pereyra Iraola	Esmeralda 1212, Florida 888
3. Alzaga Unzué	Rivadavia 1352, Av. Alvear 1329, Santa Fe 1676, Maipú 66, Av. Alvear 1345, Av. Alvear 2502
4. Anchorena	Florida 161, Sucre 3302, Maipú 262, Reconquista 268, Arenales 761, Maipú 1210, Echeverría 1837
5. Pradere	Belgrano 802
6. Guerrero	Córdoba 753, Venezuela 637, Paraguay 1132, Venezuela 637, San Martín 186, Maipú 1230, Av. Alvear 1419
7. Leloir	Florida 770
8. Graciarena	Maipú 268, Uruguay 747, Rodríguez Peña 1384, Maipú 863
9. Santamarina	Victoria 864
10. Duggan	Florida 329, Cangallo 456
11. Pereda	Tacuarí 371
12. Duhau	Juncal 1248, Talcahuano 893
13. Herrera Vegas	Florida 832, Florida 846, Juncal 848
14. Zuberbühler	Viamonte 550, Montevideo 1575, Paraguay 1850, Guido 1633
15. Martínez de Hoz	Belgrano 554, Paraguay 577, Parera 78, Florida 862
16. Estrugamou	Basavilbaso 1251, Av. de Mayo 622, Salta 1007
17. Díaz Vélez	Paraguay 1535
18. Casares	Sarmiento 357, Melo 1826, Florida 470, Uruguay 1396, San Martín 233, Av. Alvear 1372, Carlos Calvo 948, Florida 271, Uruguay 1400, Sarmiento 357, Juncal 1759
19. Atucha	Cangallo 454
20. Drysdale	Perú 84, Perú 440
21. Cobo	Bartolomé Mitre 519
22. Bosch	Lavalle 349, Rivadavia 1425, Maipú 1263, Bartolomé Mitre 1094, Paraguay 1207
23. Drabble	Chacabuco 332, Florida 32, Chacabuco 73
24. Bunge	Maipú 134, Cangallo 328
25. Pueyrredón	Bartolomé Mitre 836, Callao 1247, Juncal 1045, Suipacha 1379

SOURCES: The names of the largest landowning families were taken from Jacinto Oddone, *La burguesía terrateniente argentina*, 3rd ed. (Buenos Aires, 1967), p. 185. The addresses were derived from "Nómina de socios," *Anales de la Sociedad Rural Argentina*, 52 (Buenos Aires: February 1918), 116–134.

census, suggests strong continuities over time. For example, in 1918, southern districts (1–4, 6–8), especially La Boca and Barracas, and certain western districts (15–16), were predominantly working class. White-collars and professionals could be found in high proportions in central and northern districts (5, 8–14, 19 and 20) (see table 20).[26] The data for 1960 show significant continued concentrations of blue-collars in southern and western districts (1–4, 15–16). White-collars, as in 1918, were well represented in central districts (5–13) and professionals in northern districts (19 and 20).[27] It should also be noted that in 1960, as in 1918, no districts in the city were completely "pure" in terms of class composition. Significant representatives of all three categories could be found scattered throughout most of the city's neighborhoods.

Relatively little is known about the important ethnic neighborhoods. Available evidence does seem to confirm a consistent pattern of particular foreign-born groups settling in close proximity to one another and developing a distinct character and flavor in particular *barrios*. Well-known neighborhoods which seem to have retained their special ethnic traits include La Boca, with its large Italian population, Once, the heart of the city's Jewish community, and the Avenida de Mayo and its near southern areas, favorite locales for the Spanish immigrant population.[28] An examination of census information reinforces the picture of continuity, showing that those districts with large foreign populations generally retained their relative positions in this regard between 1914 and 1960 (see table 21). Census information from 1914 and 1936, however, shows that while certain ethnic areas kept their particular character, substantial dispersion occurred throughout the city. Significant numbers and proportions of foreign groups, especially Italians, could be found in almost every part of the capital (see tables 22 and 23). One study has noted that the Jewish population, in the 1930s and 1940s, spread out from Once west into Villa Crespo and other districts.[29]

Information on the location of social groups in the counties of Greater Buenos Aires is available only for 1960. It shows a substantial proportion (over 50 percent) of blue-collars in every county, with particular concentrations in most of the southern, western, and far northern counties. The counties with the largest proportions of white-collars and professionals were Lomas de Zamora, San Isidro, and Vicente López (see table 24). Information from the 1914, 1947, and 1960 censuses reveals much the same pattern of foreign settlement in the suburbs as in the city. Counties which attracted significant numbers (over 40 percent of total population) of immigrants by 1914 (Avellaneda, General San Martín, La Matanza, Quilmes, San Is-

Table 20. *Percent of Blue-Collars, White-Collars, and Professionals in the City of Buenos Aires, by Circunscripción: 1918 and 1960*

Circunscripción	1918 Blue-collar %	Rank	1918 White-collar %	Rank	1918 Professional %	Rank	1960 Blue-collar %	Rank	1960 White-collar %	Rank	1960 Professional %	Rank
1	49.7	4	42.6	14	2.8	18	53.5	1	28.3	18	8.6	19
2	52.4	3	41.5	17	2.3	19	51.5	4	30.0	17	9.1	18
3	42.5	8	47.0	8	2.9	17	45.2	7	33.3	10	12.3	16
4	60.3	1	34.6	20	1.3	20	51.7	3	33.2	11	7.3	20
5	30.0	14	53.6	4	5.6	10	37.2	20	36.9	1	18.5	3
6	44.2	6	43.9	13	3.9	15	38.2	18	36.5	3	17.7	7
7	39.5	10	46.5	11	4.5	14	38.4	16	34.5	8	18.3	4
8	40.0	9	46.8	10	5.0	13	41.7	11	35.8	4	13.2	14
9	31.7	13	50.1	7	6.2	7	41.5	12	35.8	5	13.3	13
10	29.3	16	51.6	5	6.6	6	40.0	15	35.7	6	14.8	11
11	21.6	17	47.0	9	10.5	3	38.4	17	34.1	9	18.2	5
12	29.8	15	53.8	3	5.0	11	40.6	13	36.9	2	13.4	12
13	19.5	19	56.1	2	8.7	5	40.2	14	35.7	7	14.8	10
14	15.2	20	57.1	1	12.1	2	37.4	19	32.5	12	18.0	6
15	55.6	2	36.7	19	2.9	16	48.0	5	33.1	13	12.0	17
16	35.9	11	51.0	6	5.0	12	45.7	6	33.1	14	13.2	15
17	45.6	5	40.4	18	5.9	8	42.5	10	31.4	16	15.9	9
18	43.3	7	41.5	16	5.7	9	43.6	8	31.9	15	17.0	8
19	31.7	12	42.1	15	8.8	4	43.4	9	26.9	19	21.9	1
20	21.6	18	46.4	12	13.2	1	52.4	2	20.6	20	19.5	2

SOURCES: For 1918, see note 25. For 1960, see *Censo nacional de población, 1960*, vol. 2, pp. 196–201.

Table 21. *Percent and Ranking of Foreign-Born Residents in the City of Buenos Aires, by* Circunscripción: *1914 - 1960*

Circunscrip-ción	1914(a) %	1914(a) Rank	1936(b) %	1936(b) Rank	1947(c) %	1947(c) Rank	1960(d) %	1960(d) Rank
1	43.5	18	32.5	17	25.6	15	22.5	12
2	46.2	13	34.4	15	26.2	14	22.1	13
3	51.4	8	37.3	8	27.7	10	23.6	9
4	47.6	10	36.1	11	25.5	16	21.3	15
5	39.9	20	28.7	20	22.1	20	18.1	20
6	42.8	19	31.4	19	24.1	19	19.2	19
7	45.7	14	34.4	14	26.2	13	20.7	16
8	49.2	9	34.5	13	26.3	12	21.8	14
9	52.9	7	41.3	5	31.1	5	25.8	5
10	55.2	5	40.1	6	30.1	6	25.9	4
11	56.9	4	43.6	4	31.3	4	26.4	3
12	53.7	6	39.5	7	28.0	9	25.3	6
13	62.4	2	47.2	1	32.5	2	28.9	1
14	65.2	1	46.8	2	34.7	1	28.8	2
15	47.2	11	37.0	9	29.6	7	24.8	7
16	45.4	15	34.6	12	27.5	11	22.7	11
17	44.0	17	32.2	18	24.4	18	19.6	18
18	45.0	16	36.2	10	28.3	8	22.9	10
19	46.8	12	34.3	16	24.9	17	20.4	17
20	58.2	3	43.9	3	32.2	3	24.1	8

SOURCES: (a) *Tercer censo nacional*, vol. 2, pp. 129–149.
    (b) *Cuarto censo general de la ciudad de Buenos Aires*, vol. 2, pp. 130–159.
    (c) *Cuarto censo general de la nación*, vol. 1, pp. 54–57.
    (d) *Censo nacional de población, 1960*, vol. 2, pp. 110–120.

idro, Las Conchas/Tigre, and Vicente López) generally continued to have the highest proportions of foreign-born by 1960 (see table 25).

The dispersion of the urban population out from the center of the capital toward the periphery of the city and beyond to the suburbs has been intimately connected with developments in public transportation. The introduction of the streetcar at the turn of the century permitted *porteños*, particularly upwardly mobile working- and middle-class *porteños*, to buy land and to build houses in cheaper outlying areas and still have access to places of employment downtown.[30] South America's first major subway system, opened in 1914 and completed in 1944, provided rapid transit for the immediate downtown area and connections with the main southern, northern, and western rail terminals. Gradually, buses of various types be-

Table 22. Percentages of Population by Nationality in the City of Buenos Aires: 1914

Circunscripción	Total population	Argentine	Italian	Spanish	French	Russian	American	Other
					Percentages by nationality			
1	103,358	56.5	20.5	15.6	1.1	1.1	2.6	2.5
2	70,628	53.8	18.7	21.1	1.0	0.8	2.3	2.4
3	104,188	48.6	17.7	25.3	1.5	0.5	2.4	4.0
4	76,024	52.4	29.2	10.5	0.5	1.3	2.2	4.0
5	79,660	60.1	14.8	16.8	0.4	1.9	2.9	2.2
6	77,705	57.2	21.4	15.6	1.4	0.4	2.4	1.6
7	67,007	54.4	21.9	15.5	1.6	2.0	2.5	2.1
8	82,095	50.8	25.4	16.1	1.1	0.8	2.5	3.2
9	83,252	47.2	23.1	17.8	1.6	5.9	2.4	2.0
10	42,293	44.8	27.6	20.0	1.6	1.6	2.0	2.9
11	43,530	43.1	15.2	17.5	2.5	14.1	2.4	5.2
12	73,165	46.3	14.3	32.2	0.9	0.5	2.8	3.1
13	75,064	57.6(?)	8.5(?)	44.3(?)	2.4(?)	0.5(?)	2.9(?)	3.7(?)
14	62,598	34.8	14.8	31.2	5.9	2.4	3.3	7.4
15	106,716	52.8	23.6	13.3	1.2	3.4	2.3	3.4
16	89,866	54.6	18.8	16.3	1.9	0.5	2.9	4.9
17	76,182	56.0	21.7	13.6	1.3	0.6	2.6	4.2
18	111,939	55.0	21.1	13.4	1.4	1.1	2.3	5.7
19	86,968	53.2	19.9	18.0	1.9	1.5	2.5	2.9
20	49,748	41.8	15.4	26.2	4.6	0.8	2.3	9.0
Total federal capital	1,561,986	50.9	19.8	19.5	1.7	1.8	2.5	3.8
National totals	7,885,237	70.1	11.8	10.5	1.0	1.2	2.7	2.7

SOURCE: *Tercer censo nacional*, vol. 2, pp. 129–149.

Table 23. Percentages of Population by Nationality in the City of Buenos Aires: 1936

Circunscripción	Total population	Percentages by nationality						
		Argentine	Italian	Spanish	French	Russian	American	Other
1	330,848	67.5	14.1	12.0	0.4	0.7	1.5	3.9
2	88,947	65.6	11.1	15.5	0.4	0.7	1.4	5.4
3	103,168	62.7	11.0	17.8	0.5	0.5	1.9	5.6
4	73,586	63.9	19.3	7.7	0.2	0.5	2.5	6.0
5	123,339	71.3	9.2	11.6	0.6	1.4	2.2	4.0
6	105,808	68.6	12.8	12.3	0.7	0.8	1.9	2.8
7	78,311	65.6	12.4	11.1	0.7	2.3	2.0	5.8
8	72,634	65.5	15.3	12.8	0.5	0.8	1.8	3.3
9	84,639	58.7	13.6	12.7	0.6	3.6	1.9	9.0
10	44,226	59.9	15.6	16.8	0.7	1.1	2.2	3.7
11	51,783	56.4	6.0	11.6	0.9	6.5	2.2	16.4
12	74,855	60.5	8.7	22.7	0.5	0.4	2.3	4.9
13	81,214	52.8	5.3	31.4	0.8	0.5	3.1	6.1
14	74,807	53.2	8.3	20.8	2.0	1.2	4.1	10.4
15	396,097	63.0	15.2	10.5	0.4	2.1	1.4	7.4
16	228,826	65.5	13.4	11.2	0.6	0.5	1.8	7.1
17	115,514	67.8	12.6	9.9	0.6	0.7	1.9	6.5
18	123,002	63.9	11.1	10.4	0.7	2.1	1.8	10.1
19	99,394	65.7	8.9	16.1	1.0	0.8	2.3	5.1
20	62,831	56.1	7.0	19.9	2.0	0.8	3.4	10.8
Total federal capital	2,413,829	63.9	12.4	13.4	0.6	1.3	1.9	6.4

SOURCE: *Cuarto censo general de la ciudad de Buenos Aires*, vol. 2, pp. 130–159.

Table 24. Occupational Structure of Greater Buenos Aires, by County (Absolute and Percentages): 1960

County	Blue-collar	White-collar	Professional	Miscellaneous	Total
Almirante Brown	29,283(60.1)	11,358(23.3)	3,971 (8.2)	4,073(8.4)	48,685
Avellaneda	82,080(62.3)	30,676(23.3)	8,078 (6.1)	10,933(8.3)	131,767
Esteban Echeverría	17,357(68.9)	4,891(19.4)	1,544 (6.1)	1,393(5.5)	25,185
Florencio Varela	11,373(72.2)	2,299(14.6)	690 (4.4)	1,391(8.8)	15,753
General San Martín	71,922(64.7)	22,975(20.7)	7,126 (6.4)	9,122(8.2)	111,145
General Sarmiento	42,502(65.7)	12,618(19.5)	3,281 (5.1)	6,267(9.7)	64,668
La Matanza	107,022(69.4)	27,862(18.1)	7,902 (5.1)	11,354(7.4)	154,140
Lanús	94,364(65.0)	33,781(23.3)	8,400 (5.8)	8,590(5.9)	145,135
Lomas de Zamora	57,136(56.8)	25,890(25.7)	9,657 (9.6)	7,931(7.9)	100,614
Merlo	23,603(65.2)	8,185(22.6)	1,949 (5.4)	2,487(6.9)	36,224
Moreno	14,434(66.7)	4,341(20.1)	1,269 (5.9)	1,591(7.4)	21,635
Morón	75,819(59.3)	33,881(26.5)	11,115 (8.7)	6,977(5.5)	127,792
Quilmes	80,677(66.4)	22,935(18.9)	8,584 (7.1)	9,334(7.7)	121,530
San Fernando	23,947(64.9)	8,233(22.3)	2,800 (7.6)	1,943(5.3)	36,923
San Isidro	43,613(57.7)	19,263(25.5)	8,738(11.6)	4,027(5.3)	75,641
Tigre	25,276(71.7)	6,286(17.8)	1,806 (5.1)	1,896(5.4)	35,264
Tres de Febrero	63,163(62.4)	23,817(23.5)	6,765 (6.7)	7,397(7.3)	101,142
Vicente López	49,369(50.2)	28,310(28.8)	13,111(13.3)	7,571(7.7)	98,361
TOTAL	912,940(62.9)	327,601(22.6)	106,786 (7.4)	104,277(7.2)	1,451,784

SOURCE: *Censo nacional de población, 1960*, vol. 2, pp. 328–333.

Table 25. *Percent and Ranking of Foreign-Born Residents in Greater Buenos Aires, by County: 1914–1960*

County	1914(a) %	1914(a) Rank	1947(b) %	1947(b) Rank	1960(c) %	1960(c) Rank
Almirante Brown	36.3	11	23.1	7	17.5	14
Avellaneda	46.1	2	21.5	11	22.7	5
Esteban Echeverría	37.3	10	23.0	8	18.9	11
Florencio Varela	30.1	16	21.4	12	19.8	10
General San Martín	43.0	3	24.8	2	22.8	4
General Sarmiento	36.1	12	15.3	16	14.1	18
La Matanza	40.8	6	23.7	4	22.6	6
Lanús					23.8	2
Lomas de Zamora	39.7	8	22.8	9	20.0	9
Merlo	34.0	14	22.3	10	17.5	13
Moreno	31.5	15	21.0	13	16.0	15
Morón	35.9	13	20.8	14	18.8	12
Quilmes	42.0	4	24.5	3	21.1	8
San Fernando	38.9	9	19.5	15	15.0	16
San Isidro	40.4	7	23.4	5	21.9	7
Tigre	41.3	5	23.2	6	15.0	17
Tres de Febrero					23.1	3
Vicente López	49.0	1	29.0	1	26.1	1

SOURCES: (a) *Tercer censo nacional*, vol. 2, pp. 3–37.
(b) *Cuarto censo general de la nación*, vol. 1, pp. 90–103.
(c) *Censo nacional de población*, vol. 2, pp. 245–254.

gan to replace the streetcar, which, as in so many cities, had almost disappeared by the 1960s. In the metropolitan area, railroads and subways continued as important means of public transport in the 1950s and 1960s, although generally declining in numbers of passengers carried over these years. The most popular and most utilized public conveyance was the *colectivo* or microbus, which, according to one source, by the 1960s daily realized almost three-fourths of all motorized journeys in Buenos Aires.[31] Attractive because of its low cost, flexibility, and frequency—if not its comfort, particularly for persons over six feet in height—the *colectivo* played an important role in opening up the outskirts of the city and the suburbs to the population.[32] Finally, despite the general high quality and varied and extensive nature of the area's public transportation system, *porteños* in recent years have relied more and more on the private automobile for movement within the city and for commuting from the suburbs to downtown.[33]

So far this paper has focused on broad developments involving large-scale trends and numbers. The emphasis has been on groups rather than particular individuals. One important question to be asked is: to what degree have the enormous and rapid social, economic, and political changes of the twentieth century affected the basic pattern of the urban dweller's daily life? What impact, for example, have they had on attitudes and behavior in respect to such forces as religion, family relations, education, politics, and government? In this regard our knowledge of Buenos Aires, or of any Latin American city, seems particularly deficient.[34]

In this paper I cannot attempt to answer this question. Rather, I present it as an important area for future research and would like to suggest some possible avenues by which the problem might be approached. One path is to search out and use primary documentation more extensively, particularly census manuscripts, statistical series, and parish records. Mark Szuchman and Samuel Baily have already used these kinds of materials to great effect to study marriage patterns and ethnic assimilation in Córdoba and Buenos Aires, respectively.[35] Another useful source is the rich fictional literature of twentieth-century Argentina. Writers such as Roberto Arlt, Jorge Luis Borges, Julio Cortázar, Manuel Gálvez, Eduardo Mallea, Ezequiel Martínez Estrada, Ernesto Sábato, and Raúl Scalabrini Ortiz, to mention some of the most prominent, have provided intimate and compelling pictures of the customs, mores, and lives of *porteños* from all walks of life. A wide variety of newspapers, readily available and heavily consumed by the highly literate urban populace, provide further information. An examination of newspapers, for example, can tell us much about the entertainment preferences of *porteños* over time, ranging from notices of opera, theater, and cinema performances, to radio and television programming, to athletic events.

Other published sources include the many popular magazines of the period. *Caras y Caretas*, the Argentine *Punch*, for example, was one of the most successful weeklies of the first half of the twentieth century. A sample issue from February 1925 supplies information on politics, usually in cartoon form, literary selections, social news related to the celebration of carnival and the summer season at Mar del Plata, and articles on fashion and child-care. In addition, *Caras y Caretas* was an important source of advertising for the expanding urban consumer market. Two features of the advertisements in the sample issue stand out. One is the prominent number of items publicizing products made in the United States. These included Johnson and Johnson baby powder, Westinghouse electrical appliances, Ford, General Motors, and Dodge automobiles, and Colt revolvers, "El arma de la ley y del orden" (the weapon of law and order). Second, a substantial proportion of the advertisements were specifically directed to women. Household items (food and appliances) and products for health and child-care appealed to the female's traditional role as wife and mother. Most ads, however, were aimed at the woman as woman and urged her to buy perfumes, soaps, skin lotions, fashionable shoes and dresses, and flattering undergarments.[36] These advertisements, then, reflect two important larger trends: the growth of imports from the United States, gradually edging out European competition, and the emerging and changing role of women as independent consumers.

The general buying habits of the urban population offer another useful area of investigation into the daily life of the *porteño*. Scobie noted the strong sense of materialism and the importance of acquiring goods at the beginning of the century.[37] The continued emphasis on fashionable dress, the numerous shops with luxury items along Calle Florida and Avenida Santa Fe, and the images diffused over the electronic media indicate that little has changed in this regard over the past seventy years. What has changed dramatically is the ability of the average urban dweller to purchase the items so tantalizingly displayed. Beginning in the mid-1940s, the cost of living in the capital rose dramatically, and by the late 1970s, Buenos Aires was one of the most expensive cities in the world.

Another characteristic of the urban population which many have sought to examine is what might be called the *porteño* character. An important aspect of this character, noted by observers from Scalabrini Ortiz to Martínez Estrada to Juan José Sebreli, is the isolation and alienation felt by the individual in the large and impersonal urban environment of Buenos Aires.[38] Whether this sense of aloneness is greater in Buenos Aires than in other large cities is open to question. However, one way by which individuals in the twentieth century have overcome their feelings of isolation and powerlessness has been to demand and achieve a greater voice in the decisions which directly affect their lives. Usually this has meant active involvement in politics, either as partisan militants or simply as regular and conscientious voters. In this regard the citizens of Buenos Aires have etched a rather remarkable record. Beginning with national electoral reform in 1912 and municipal reform in 1918, *porteños* have gone to the polls to elect their chosen representatives with greater frequency and in higher numbers than in any other region in the country and, one would suspect, in generally greater numbers than in most comparable urban areas in the western hemisphere.[39] In addition to the act of voting, political activity has also provided a sense of social integration through regularized party activities, which have been particularly intense in the capital.

It could not be argued that active participation in party and electoral activities serves to overcome all sense of alienation and powerlessness. Indeed, frustration and disappointment at the ultimate results of such activity might on occasion increase these feelings.[40] But the continued high levels of participation, even in the face of the disappointments and difficulties of the recent past, indicate that politics and elections have held a high priority for *porteños* and have been important ingredients in their daily lives for much of the twentieth century.

The rapid growth of Buenos Aires in the twentieth century has created many new problems and intensified several of long-standing. Taken separately, they are similar in many respects to those experienced by urban areas throughout the world. In the aggregate, however, they may be unique. In the words of Jorge Hardoy, in Argentina ". . . we run the risk of constructing an urban society with all the inconveniences of the cities of developed economies and many of the problems of the cities of developing economies."[41]

A major concern is the lack of sufficient and adequate housing. According to the 1960 census, there were in the metropolitan area only 1,600,000 residential units for some 2,000,000 families.[42] Furthermore, much of the housing which does exist is old, dilapidated, and deteriorating. These conditions are particularly notable in the southern districts of the city and in the southern and western industrial suburbs of Avellaneda, Lanús, La Matanza, Tres de Febrero, and General San Martín.[43] Government public-housing programs, initiated in 1915, have generally been sporadic, ineffective, and insufficient to meet growing demands.[44] Future housing construction, whether public or private, because of inflation, land scarcity, and speculation, will be increasingly expensive.[45]

The most dramatic feature of the housing picture in Buenos Aires is the *villa miseria*. Although considerable controversy has arisen over the name (*villa miseria* or *villa de emergencia*) and the total number of persons living in these shantytowns (from 200,000 to 800,000), there is little disagreement as to the miserable living conditions which characterize them. Established primarily by migrants from the interior and neighboring countries, they are located mainly on the fringes of the city and in the suburbs. Generally composed of shacks constructed with whatever material is available and lacking in public services, the *villas miserias* have replaced the turn-of-the-century *conventillos* (tenements) as breeding grounds for disease, crime, and social unrest.[46] Although the *villas* have received considerable publicity and attention, efforts to find or to build more suitable housing for their residents, at least into the early 1970s, have produced few satisfactory results.[47]

Rapid growth has also strained general public services and utilities, particularly those which supply electricity, gas, and water. In addition, Buenos Aires in recent years has been increasingly plagued by the environmental ills so familiar to the city dweller of the United States: traffic congestion, noise, water, and air pollution, and difficulties related to the disposal of garbage and human wastes. Of particular concern to several observers has been the increasing separation of the *porteño* from the natural environment. Although Buenos Aires contains many lovely parks and plazas, the areas within the metropolis set aside for "green spaces" are considerably smaller in total size than for comparable world capitals. Moreover, opportunities for outdoor recreation are limited. A trip into the surrounding countryside is often complicated by massive weekend traffic jams. Nearby rivers are becoming increasingly polluted and unfit for swimming.[48]

Almost all observers agree, too, that most of these problems— and others—have been exacerbated by a lack of planning for orderly urban growth. Although a number of "city plans" have been prepared, beginning in 1906, they have generally been unconnected, ineffective, and ignored. A low level of public interest in urban matters, political instability, and a lack of continuity have complicated planning. Inadequate funds, weak and fluctuating government support, and external interference have hampered the activities of persons and institutions concerned with urban development. Jurisdictional disputes, in the case of Buenos Aires involving national, provincial, and municipal governments, have further hindered effective planning.[49]

Jorge Hardoy, an eloquent spokesperson for the necessity of urban planning, argues that the structured growth of Buenos Aires is a national problem requiring decision making at the national level and within a broad national context. Certainly the expansion of Buenos Aires has had important consequences for the rest of the nation. The concentration of population in the metropolitan area and the corresponding losses in the interior have already been described. Although attempts have been made to disperse industry to other regions and urban areas, much of it still locates in Buenos Aires.[50] The city's port still handles about 80 to 90 percent of the nation's imports and 30 to 40 percent of its exports. Most railroads and highways still lead to the capital, which continues to dominate the republic's political, social, and cultural life.[51] Most forecasts indicate that these trends will persist. Estimates of the total population of the metropolitan area by the year 2000 vary from 13,000,000 to 25,000,000, the latter figure based on the rate of growth for the decade of the 1960s.[52] Whichever figure is used, continued population growth and continued concentration will serve to intensify further the problems briefly sketched above.

Three main conclusions emerge from this review of the socioeconomic growth of Buenos Aires in the twentieth century. First, many of the characteristics of the city at the start of the century and of the "commercial-bureaucratic" model suggested by Scobie have continued to the present day. Indeed, the capital itself seems more commercial-bureaucratic than ever. Nevertheless, the continuities should not obscure the important changes which have taken place: the massive migration from the interior, serving in Guy Bourdé's term to "nationalize" urban society;[53] the increasingly important role of women in all aspects of urban life; the growth of industry; the expansion of the suburbs, forcing attention not just on the capital but on a large and varied metropolitan region; and the increased importance of politics, particularly the crucial role played by parties and elections in twentieth-century urban life.

Second, just as Buenos Aires has offered many challenges and opportunities for both native-born and foreign newcomers, so too does its history provide challenges and opportunities for scholars. Despite its importance and despite the fact that most studies of Argentina have focused on the capital, relatively little is known about the history of the city and its suburbs from World War I to the present. I would hazard a guess that much more has been written about the twentieth-century history of most major United States cities than has been written about Buenos Aires. In this review I have suggested some areas for future investigation; undoubtedly many others exist which might be fruitfully explored.

Third, the growth of Buenos Aires poses important challenges for the nation's leadership. A prime test for any government will be how it responds to the consequences of urban growth. Will the capital and its suburban area continue to drain the population and resources of the interior, becoming an urban island surrounded by an increasingly weakened and barren hinterland? Or will Buenos Aires symbolize the development of a prosperous, balanced, and progressive nation in which population and resources are equitably distributed? Within the metropolitan area itself, will the deficiencies of housing, public services, and general urban amenities continue to fester and worsen? Or will resources, attention, and independent and continuous planning be directed to remedy these ills? In sum, will the future greatness of Buenos Aires be measured only by size and by numbers or instead by the improved quality of life of each and every one of its inhabitants?

Notes

1. James R. Scobie, *Buenos Aires: Plaza to Suburb, 1870–1910* (New York, 1974), p. 250. See also Scobie's "Buenos Aires as a Commercial-Bureaucratic City, 1880–1910: Characteristics of a City's Orientation," *American Historical Review*, 77, 4 (October 1972), 1035–1073.

2. The author wishes to acknowledge his deep appreciation for the assistance provided by Mr. Scott Graczyk of Washington University in the compilation and preparation of the statistical material for this paper and the work of Mrs. Dora L. Arky of the department of history in typing the appended tables.

3. The counties which make up Greater Buenos Aires are listed in table 7. Their boundaries remained relatively stable over the course of the twentieth century, although in 1944 Lanús was created from Avellaneda, in 1959 Tres de Febrero from General San Martín, and in 1960 Berazategui from Quilmes.

4. See Charles S. Sargent, *The Spatial Evolution of Greater Buenos Aires, Argentina, 1870–1930* (Tempe, Arizona, 1974), pp. 102–105.

5. For general information on the relationship between literacy and urbanization in Latin America, see Philip M. Hauser (ed.), *Urbanization in Latin America* (New York, 1961), pp. 112–113.

6. Gino Germani, *Estructura social de la Argentina: Análisis estadístico* (Buenos Aires, 1955), pp. 21–32, and Zulma L. Recchini de Lattes, *La población de Buenos Aires: Componentes demográficos del crecimiento entre 1855 y 1960* (Buenos Aires, 1971), p. 79.

7. Throughout this period most foreign immigrants settled primarily in and around Buenos Aires. Substantial numbers of European immigrants arrived in the 1920s and after World War II. Increasingly in the postwar era, however, immigrants tended to come primarily from neighboring Bolivia, Paraguay, and Uruguay. Zulma Recchini de Lattes and Alfredo E. Lattes, *La población de Argentina* (Buenos Aires, 1975), pp. 64–66.

8. Ibid., pp. 130–134.

9. Gino Germani, "El surgimiento del peronismo: El rol de los obreros y de los migrantes internos," *Desarrollo Económico*, 13, 51 (October–December 1973), 446–457.

10. For Latin America, see Hauser (ed.), *Urbanization*, pp. 100–102. For Argentina, see Recchini de Lattes, *La población de Buenos Aires*, pp. 116–128. For more information on internal migration, see Germani, *Estructura social*, pp. 74–78; Mario Margulis, *Migración y marginalidad en la sociedad argentina* (Buenos Aires, 1978); and Zulma L. Recchini de Lattes and Alfredo E. Lattes, *Migraciones en la Argentina: Estudio de las migraciones internas e internacionales, basado en datos censales, 1869–1960* (Buenos Aires, 1969).

11. José Victor D'Angelo, "La conurbación de Buenos Aires," in Francisco de Aparicio and Horacio A. Difrieri (eds.), *La Argentina: Suma de geografía* (Buenos Aires, 1963), vol. 9, pp. 168–169.

12. República Argentina, *Censo industrial de 1935* (Buenos Aires, 1938), p. 101.

13. República Argentina, *Cuarto censo general de la nación: Censo industrial de 1946* (Buenos Aires, 1952), pp. 50–51.

14. For more information on the general characteristics of industrialization in Argentina, see Carlos F. Díaz Alejandro, *Essays on the Economic History of the Argentine Republic* (New Haven, 1970), pp. 208–276.

15. The information for 1914 comes from occupational data for the city's population found in the third national census. Separate occupations have been ordered in the categories suggested in Mark D. Szuchman and Eugene F. Sofer, "The State of Occupational Stratification Studies in Argentina," *Latin American Research Review*, 11, 1 (1976), 159–172. For 1960, I have used the separate categories provided by the fifth national census and have grouped them by blue-collar, white-collar, and professional—for comparative purposes—as indicated in table 17. In both instances I have determined the economically active population by subtracting the miscellaneous and students (1914) and miscellaneous (1960) categories from the total.

16. Another source, published in 1968, found an even greater decrease in the blue-collar population of the city. It argued that ". . . the present working-class population is 33.5 percent of the total (around 30 percent less than in 1947); employees represent 39.5 percent and owners and self-employed 27 percent, the latter two showing strong increases in relation to 1947. There has been, then, a sharp decline in the working-class population, which means that the federal capital can be called, besides an industrial center, also a service center," Municipalidad de la Ciudad de Buenos Aires, Organización del Plan Regulador, *Informe preliminar, etapa 1959–1960* (Buenos Aires, 1968), p. 114.

17. See, in particular, Germani, *Estructura social*, pp. 194–225.

18. República Argentina, *Tercer censo nacional (1914)* (Buenos Aires, 1916), vol. 8, pp. 145 and 216.

19. República Argentina, *Censo de comercio, 1954* (Buenos Aires, 1959), vol. 1, p.38.

20. República Argentina, *Tercer censo nacional*, vol. 4, p. 209, and República Argentina, *Cuarto censo nacional*, vol. 1, p. 67.

21. Scobie, *Buenos Aires*, p. 255.

22. See, for example, Guy Bourdé, *Urbanisation et immigration en Amérique Latine: Buenos Aires (XIXᵉ et XXᵉ siécles)* (Paris, 1974), pp. 274–275, and Martha Schteingart and Horacio Torres, "Procesos sociales y estructuración metropolitana en América Latina: Estudio de casos," *Desarrollo Económico*, 12, 48 (January–March 1973), 725–760.

23. Horacio Torres, "Evolución de los procesos de estructuración espacial urbana: El caso de Buenos Aires," *Desarrollo Económico*, 15, 58 (July–September 1975), 301.

24. Scobie, *Buenos Aires*, pp. 130–135. See also Francis Korn, et al., *Buenos Aires: Los huéspedes del 20* (Buenos Aires, 1974), pp. 31–76.

25. José Luis de Imaz, *La clase alta de Buenos Aires* (Buenos Aires, 1965), p. 15.

26. Richard J. Walter, "Elections in the City of Buenos Aires during the First Yrigoyen Administration: Social Class and Political Preferences," *Hispanic American Historical Review*, 58, 4 (November 1978), 595–624.

27. It should be noted that the data for 1918 are based on Argentine males over the age of 18 and registered to vote, whereas figures for 1960 include all males and females in the economically active population.

28. D'Angelo, "La conurbación de Buenos Aires," p. 165.

29. Eugene F. Sofer, *Invisible Walls: Jewish Residential Patterns in Gran Buenos Aires: 1890–1947* (New York, 1977), pp. 22–23.

30. Scobie, *Buenos Aires*, pp. 160–191, and Sarent, *Spatial Evolution*, pp. 66–83.

31. República Argentina, Oficina Regional de Desarrollo Area Metropolitana, *Organización del espacio de la región metropolitana de Buenos Aires: Esquema director año 2000* (Buenos Aires, 1969), p. 55 and *cuadro* 33.

32. Torres, "Evolución de los procesos de estructuración espacial urbana," pp. 296–297.

33. República Argentina, *Organización del espacio*, p. 56.

34. This gap is referred to in a recent review of the literature on urban growth in Latin America. See M. R. Wolfe, "The Growth of Cities," *Latin American Research Review*, 15, 1 (1980), 189–197.

35. Mark D. Szuchman, "The Limits of the Melting Pot in Urban Argentina: Marriage and Integration in Córdoba, 1869–1909," *Hispanic American Historical Review*, 57, 1 (February 1977), 24–50, and Samuel L. Baily, "Marriage Patterns and Immigrant Assimilation in Buenos Aires, 1883–1923," *Hispanic American Historical Review*, 60, 1 (February 1980), 32–48.

36. *Caras y Caretas*, 28, 1378 (Buenos Aires: 28 February 1925).

37. Scobie, *Buenos Aires*, pp. 232–235.

38. Raúl Scalabrini Ortiz, *El hombre que está y espera* (Buenos Aires, 1931); Ezequiel Martínez Estrada, *La cabeza de Goliath: Microscopía de Buenos Aires* (Buenos Aires, 1940); and Juan José Sebreli, *Buenos Aires: Vida cotidiana y alienación*, 6th ed. (Buenos Aires, 1965).

39. For information on election turnout in the city of Buenos Aires as compared with the rest of the republic, see Darió Cantón, *Materiales para el estudio de la sociología política en la Argentina* (Buenos Aires, 1968), vol. 1, pp. 81–254.

40. Some of the attitudes of Argentines toward parties, politics, and politicians in the 1950s and 1960s are reviewed in Peter G. Snow, *Political Forces in Argentina* (Boston, 1971), pp. 46–51.

41. Jorge E. Hardoy, *Las ciudades en América Latina: Seis ensayos sobre la urbanización contemporánea* (Buenos Aires, 1972), p. 203.

42. República Argentina, *Organización del espacio*, p. 39.

43. Ibid., and D'Angelo, "La conurbación de Buenos Aires," pp. 208–209.

44. Martha Schteingart and Beatriz Broide, "Procesos sociales, política de vivienda y desarrollo metropolitana: El caso de Buenos Aires," in Manuel Castells (ed.), *Estructura de clases y política urbana en América Latina* (Buenos Aires, 1974), pp. 235–286.

45. Hardoy, *Las ciudades*, p. 184.

46. For studies of two *villas miserias*, see Margulis, *Migración y marginalidad*, and Gino Germani, "Inquiry into the Social Effects of Urbanization in a Working-Class Sector of Greater Buenos Aires," in Hauser (ed.), *Urbanization*, pp. 206–233.

47. See, for example, Carlos Tobar, "The Argentine National Plan for Eradicating *Villas de Emergencia*," in Francine F. Rabinovitz and Felicity M. Trueblood (eds.), *Latin American Urban Research* (Beverly Hills, Calif., 1972), vol. 2, pp. 221–228.

48. D'Angelo, "La conurbación de Buenos Aires," pp. 203–207; Municipalidad de la Ciudad de Buenos Aires, Organización del Plan Regulador, *Informe preliminar*, pp. 31–35; and República Argentina, *Organización del espacio*, pp. 50–51.

49. Hardoy, *Las ciudades, passim.*

50. Mario Brodersohn, *Regional Development and Industrial Location Policy in Argentina* (Buenos Aires, 1967).

51. A good summary of the various features of Buenos Aires' national predominance can be found in D'Angelo, "La conurbación de Buenos Aires," pp. 92–105.

52. República Argentina, *Organización del espacio*, pp. 85–86.

53. Bourdé, *Urbanisation et immigration*, p. 281.

6. Buenos Aires: Culture and Poetry in the Modern City

Merlin H. Forster

I consider it an honor to be a part of this observance. However, I find the task assigned to me to be a formidable one. I am not a stranger to contemporary Buenos Aires, having spent most of 1971 there under the auspices of a Fulbright Research Grant. If anything, that acquaintance with the city increases my sense of concern about this assignment, since I am more aware than a casual visitor might be of the complexity and richness of the city's intellectual life.

A contributing problem is the relative lack of organized materials on the subject. I am aware of James R. Scobie's excellent study on Buenos Aires from 1870 through the beginning decade of the twentieth century,[1] but cultural life is not one of the factors which he considers in depth, nor does his chronological frame extend far enough toward the present time to be directly applicable to this presentation. A doctoral dissertation in history by Jesús Méndez, at the University of Texas, deals with Argentine twentieth-century intellectual life, but only up to 1943.[2] One can turn with profit and considerable illumination, however, to a series of personal meditations on Buenos Aires. Ezequiel Martínez Estrada, for example, in 1946 published *La cabeza de Goliat: Microscopia de Buenos Aires* (The Head of Goliath: Microscopic Views of Buenos Aires), in which he applies to the city the critical and narrative techniques used in his earlier masterwork *Radiografía de la pampa* (X-Ray of the Pampa, 1933). Alberto Mario Salas' *Relación parcial de Buenos Aires* (A Fragmentary Account of Buenos Aires), which appeared initially in 1955 and in its second edition has an epistolary prologue by Victoria Ocampo, is a subjective testimonial to the city in its historical and contemporary dimensions. Abelardo Arias moves through the city from section to section in his *Intensión de Buenos Aires* (Intensity of Buenos Aires, 1974), and with nostalgic eye measures the current spatial and human dimensions against what the city has been. *La*

noche de mi ciudad (Night in My City), published in 1979 by
Ulises Petit de Murat, uses the nocturnal world of Buenos Aires as
the main focus of a fascinating and idiosyncratic account of cultural
and literary life during the past several decades. *Letra e imagen de
Buenos Aires* (Buenos Aires in Words and Images, 1977), combining
texts by Manuel Mujica Láinez and photographs by Aldo Cessa, is a
brilliant *paseo* through and into the essence of the contemporary
city. *Rostros de Buenos Aires* (The Faces of Buenos Aires, 1978),
published by the Municipality of Buenos Aires as the first of a number of volumes having to do with the quadricentennial observance,
presents a kaleidoscopic vision of the city and its activities, combining photographs and texts from earlier periods with present-day
names, places, and patterns.

Against the general background that is available in works such
as those I have mentioned, let me now attempt to sketch for you
some of the individual and often interrelated facets of cultural and
intellectual life in the modern city. To begin, one must keep in mind
that although in cultural terms Sarmiento's "civilización y barbarie"
polarity is perhaps not as pronounced as it was in the nineteenth
century, Buenos Aires is by all odds the center of the country. As Edwin R. Harvey points out clearly in his documentation on cultural
organization and policy in Argentina, in most cases the lion's share
and in some cases virtually all of the public and private infrastruc-
ture dealing with culture is located in and controlled from the metropolitan Buenos Aires area.[3]

Having made the point of the centrality of Buenos Aires, it is
important to present some statistics which I trust will convey a
sense of complexity and magnitude.[4] There are some 70 museums of
different kinds and some 130 art galleries in the city, and some 2,000
expositions of different kinds are mounted in any given year.
Abelardo Arias makes the claim that Buenos Aires is one of the cities in which most public lectures are presented, "perhaps because of
a typical desire to clarify and explain and interpret."[5] The latest figures I have indicate that somewhere between five and six thousand
lectures on all topics are presented annually. The city is also the
center for an intense musical and theatrical life. One of the focal
points of these activities is the venerable Teatro Colón, which opened
at its current location in 1908 and is one of the most important opera
houses in the world. In addition to a full-length season of grand opera,
the building also houses the Buenos Aires Philharmonic Orchestra
and is the setting for a number of ballet performances, concerts, and
individual recitals. There are some 45 functioning theaters in the city,
ranging in size of locale and program from the Teatro Nacional de

Comedia, under the auspices of the National Commission of Culture, and the San Martín Municipal Theater, under the direction of the municipal Under-Secretariat of Culture, to a number of small independent theaters. It is estimated that somewhere between eight and nine thousand theatrical presentations occur annually in the city. Also, account should be taken of some 250 movie houses, together with 4 television channels and 13 radio stations. The urban concentration of the area, together with a very high level of literacy and education, has made Buenos Aires the second or third major publishing and journalistic center of the Spanish-speaking world. There are currently 6 Spanish-language daily newspapers which appear in the metropolitan area, including the internationally known *La Nación* and *La Prensa*, plus some 20 newspapers in other languages. Also, more than 50 magazines and journals, covering a large number of subject areas, currently appear. Some of the best-known publishing houses in the Hispanic world are located in Buenos Aires, and a large number of literary and technical works are published each year. Harvey documents a national production of 6,674 literary works for 1976, representing a total printing of some 35 million copies, of which the largest share pertains to Buenos Aires.[6] The city boasts some 800 book stores, which supply local needs as well as national and international orders. The National Library is located in the metropolitan area, and an extensive expansion of its facilities, planned by the architect Clorindo Testa, is now under construction. There are as well some 150 other, smaller public libraries within the city. Finally, one should mention the important role played by the 8 public and private universities located in the metropolitan area, the most important of which is the world-renowned University of Buenos Aires. One could go on with such facts, but it seems to me that these statistics are sufficient to suggest that Buenos Aires in the twentieth century has a cultural and intellectual life unrivaled by any Latin American city, and indeed by few cities in the world.[7]

A principal effect of this present-day richness—and we must keep in mind that it is a rather recent development within the 400-year span being commemorated in these sessions—has been to develop discriminatory capacities in a growing consuming public, and to give creators, in particular artists, writers, and musicians, a heightened sense of tradition and on-going process. I make no attempt to consider in any detail artistic creation in music and the plastic arts, but I would like to examine further one dimension of a literary expression which finds its natural center in Buenos Aires, which very frequently takes the city itself as a focus for literary creation, and which in turn enriches the cultural life on which it depends. Here again, I do not intend a complete survey. There are many works from all genres which center on Buenos Aires as a place and as a complex of cultural values. One could mention the *grotescos* of Armando Discépolo, which portrayed in theatrical form life in the *conventillos* of La Boca, Eduardo Mallea's *La ciudad junto al río inmóvil* (The City beside the Unmoving River, 1936), Leopoldo Marechal's *Adán Buenosayres* (Adam Buenosayres, 1948), Manuel Mujica Láinez' *La casa* (1954), or perhaps even the intricate interfacings of Paris and Buenos Aires in Julio Cortázar's *Rayuela* (Hopscotch, 1963). I wish to take my illustrative examples, however, from twentieth-century Argentine poetry.[8]

In his introductory vision of a nocturnal Buenos Aires, Ulises Petit de Murat speculates on the effects of prior millennia of advanced non-European culture on present-day Mexico City.[9] By comparison, Buenos Aires has a relatively short past, and a number of modern Argentine poets have felt it necessary to formulate an ancient lineage and an appropriate mythology for their beloved city. Probably the most important among them is Jorge Luis Borges, who early and often has declared his devotion for Buenos Aires:

> Esta ciudad que yo creí mi pasado
> es mi porvenir, mi presente;
> los años que he vivido en Europa son ilusorios,
> yo estaba siempre (y estaré) en Buenos Aires.

> This city that I believed to be my past
> Is my future, my present.
> The years I have lived in Europe are illusory;
> I have always been (and will be) in Buenos Aires.[10]

One of Borges' masterpieces is a poem which he published in his 1929 collection *Cuaderno San Martín* (A San Martín Notebook) with the original title "La fundación mitológica de Buenos Aires" (The Mythological Founding of Buenos Aires). Borges later revised the title to its present-day form: "La fundación mítica de Buenos Aires" (The Mythic Founding of Buenos Aires). The poem is an excellent illustration of my point, and I want to look more closely at the text.[11] The first three stanzas are as follows:

> ¿Y fue por este río de sueñera y de barro
> que las proas vinieron a fundarme la patria?
> Irían a los tumbos los barquitos pintados
> entre los camalotes de la corriente zaina.

Pensando bien la cosa supondremos que el río
era azulejo entonces como oriundo del cielo
con su estrellita roja para marcar el sitio
en que ayunó Juan Díaz y los indios comieron.

Lo cierto es que mil hombres y otros mil arribaron
por un mar que tenía cinco lunas de anchura
y aun estaba repleto de sirenas y endriagos
y de piedras imanes que enloquecen la brújula.

And was it along this torpid muddy river
that the prows came to found my native city?
The little painted boats must have suffered the steep surf
among the root-clumps of the horse brown current.

Pondering well, let us suppose that the river
was blue then like an extension of the sky,
with a small red star inset to mark the spot
where Juan Díaz fasted and the Indians dined.

But for sure a thousand men and other thousands
arrived across a sea that was five moons wide,
still infested with mermaids and sea serpents
and magnetic boulders which sent the compass wild.

Borges begins the poem with an interrogative sentence, and he can thus assert his own truth about the mythical founders and their activities. The prows of the toylike boats of the discoverers touch the shores of the sacred river, whose waters are chestnut-colored with clay but seem relatively calm after a long sea journey threatened by sirens and dragons. In the second stanza the estuary of the river is portrayed in a maplike vision with the water now bluish in tone and with a mark in red at the place where one of the founders was eaten by Indians.

Stanzas 4 and 5 expand even further Borges' creative mythology:

Prendieron unos ranchos trémulos en la costa,
durmieron extrañados. Dicen que en el Riachuelo,
pero son embelecos fraguados en la Boca.
Fue una manzana entera y en mi barrio: Palermo.

Una manzana entera pero en mitá del campo
presenciada de auroras y lluvias y suestadas.
La manzana pareja que persiste en mi barrio:
Guatemala, Serrano, Paraguay, Gurruchaga.

On the coast they put up a few ramshackle huts
and slept uneasily. This, they claim, in the Riachuelo,
but that is a story dreamed up in the Boca.
It was really a city block in my district—Palermo.

A whole square block, but set down in open country,
attended by dawns and rains and hard southeasters,
identical to that block which still stands in my neighborhood:
Guatemala—Serrano—Paraguay—Gurruchaga.

The fragile initial settlements were not in the Riachuelo, as has been asserted by inhabitants of La Boca, but rather a single one-block area in Palermo. The *manzana* (city block) appeared miraculously in the middle of the countryside, accompanied by the natural processes of nature, and has come down to the present day in its ancient form, circumscribed by our streets.

The next three stanzas express, in a compressed and miraculous fashion, the vision of the *manzana*, which does not extend beyond the encircling streets but which contains in miniature all of the elements of *porteño* life. Colors, names, the sound of a tango, all of these things make up what Borges calls "un pasado ilusorio" (an illusory past):

Un almacén rosado como revés de naipe
brilló y en la trastienda conversaron un truco;
el almacén rosado floreció en un compadre
ya patrón de la esquina, ya resentido y duro.

El primer organito salvaba el horizonte
con su achacoso porte, su habanera y su gringo.
El corralón seguro ya opinaba: Yrigoyen;
algún piano mandaba tangos de Saborido.

Una cigarrería sahumó como una rosa
el desierto. La tarde se había ahondado en ayeres,
los hombres compartieron un pasado ilusorio.
Sólo faltó una cosa: la vereda de enfrente.

A general store pink as the back of a playing card
shone bright; in the back there was poker talk.
The corner bar flowered into life as a local bully,
already cock of his walk, resentful, tough.

The first barrel organ teetered over the horizon
with its clumsy progress, its *habaneras*, its wop.

The cart-shed wall was unanimous for YRIGOYEN.
Some piano was banging out tangos by Saborido.

A cigar store perfumed the desert like a rose.
The afternoon had established its yesterdays,
and men took on together an illusory past.
Only one thing was missing—the street had no other side.

The eight full stanzas of the poem have prepared us for Borges'
final statement, which appears in the closing couplet of the text. In
spite of everything, Buenos Aires does not really have a beginning
point. Such accounts are stories or myths, and Buenos Aires is really
as eternal as the elements:

A mí se me hace cuento que empezó Buenos Aires:
La juzgo tan eterna como el agua y el aire.

Hard thing to believe Buenos Aires had any beginning.
I feel it to be as eternal as air and water.

Borges has continued to use Buenos Aires as a thematic focus, as
Zunilda Gertel points out in her excellent article on the subject,[12]
and the nebulous, dreamlike quality of his vision of the city is constant. For example, in the poem "Elogio de la sombra" (In Praise of
Darkness), the title poem of a collection of the same name published
in 1969, Borges says:

Buenos Aires
que antes se desgarraba en arrabales
hacia la llanura incesante,
ha vuelto a ser la Recoleta, el Retiro,
las borrosas calles del Once.

Buenos Aires,
which once broke up in a tatter of slums and open lots
out toward the endless plain,
is now again the graveyard of the Recoleta, the Retiro square,
the shabby streets of the old Westside.[13]

We might look briefly at some other examples of created mythology. "Es Todaniebla" (All Is Fog) of Leopoldo Marechal is sugges-
tive of ritual baptisms in the homeland, Buenos Aires, near the river,
so that the seasons of the year can be observed properly:

Todaniebla quería levantar cuatro barrios
en Buenos Aires, junto al río:
Uno donde habitara sin adioses
la movediza primavera,
     y uno en que para siempre
     desmontase el invierno
     de su yegua mojada,
y éste para el otoño y aquél para el estío.

Todaniebla wanted to build four neighborhoods
in Buenos Aires, next to the river:
One in which the shifting spring
might live without goodbyes,
     and one in which winter
     might dismount forever
     from its moisture-covered mare,
and this one for the fall and that one for the summer.[14]

In her poem "Buenos Aires," Silvina Ocampo imagines a pre-history for the city, expressed in nebulous and ambiguous terms, against which she portrays a clearly expressed vision of present-day realities:

Mucho antes de Solís y de Mendoza,
como una delirante nebulosa,
muchos te imaginaron desde lejos,
caminando en la arena o en cortejos.
Sin saber que existías te inventaron
entre ambiguas llanuras te anhelaron
sin fiebres, sin tirano, sin serpientes,
con tus soles de ahora, tus relentes.

Y yo, Silvina Ocampo, en tu presencia
abstracta he visto tu posible ausencia,
he visto perdurar sólo tus puertas
con la insistencia de las manos muertas.
Entre piedras y latas y cementos,
debajo de alterados firmamentos,
como en gran desierto me traspasan
diarios soles y vio como pasan
dejándote basuras exultantes
el Puente Alsina y lo que queda de antes:
el monumento atroz que persevera,
tus seccionadas casas, la severa

nostalgias de jardines ya baldíos,
los amputados árboles sombríos
y los últimos patios, las señoras
saludando la tarde en mecedoras,
tus palmas teñidas y tus flores
y tus confiterías, tus olores.

Long before Solís and Mendoza,
like a delirious fogginess,
many imagined you from afar,
walking on the sand or in courtship.
Without knowing you existed they invented you;
between ambiguous plains they longed for you
without fevers, without tyrant, without serpents,
with your suns of now, your evening mists.

And I, Silvina Ocampo, in your presence
abstractly I have seen your possible absence,
I have seen perdure only your gates
with the insistence of dead hands.
Between stones and tin cans and cement,
beneath changed firmaments,
as if in a great desert, passing over me,
daily suns, and the Alsina Bridge saw how
exultant garbage passes by leaving you
what remains from before:
the atrocious monument that perseveres,
your sectionalized houses, the severe
nostalgias of now-vacant gardens,
the amputated somber trees
and the back patios, the ladies
greeting the afternoon in rocking chairs,
your dyed pigeons and your flowers
and your confectioners' shops, your scents.[15]

Expanding on the second aspect of Ocampo's poem, there are a number of other writers who have attempted to portray in verse form what they feel is the essence of the modern city. For example, in a *letra de tango*, Florencio Escardó wonders about the geographic and personal complexities of the city:

En qué esquina te encuentro
Buenos Aires.

En Callao y Quintana, mundo ajeno,
tal vez en Mataderos,
en la esquina
adonde junta leguas el resero
o cerca de la estatua de Florencio
o rumbo del abasto por Salguero,
donde anduvo Gardel silbando tangos
que aguantaron el tiempo,
y algunos que no oí
porque murieron.

En qué esquina te encuentro
Buenos Aires.
¿En qué esquina te encuentro?
En la esquina de Sábato y Pichuco
o en la esquina de Borges y Carriego.
Estás en todas, todas las esquinas
del arrabal y el centro,
y estrás en las riberas del Riachuelo
cuyas aguas oscuras van diciendo
Juan de Dios Filiberto.

On which corner do I find you
Buenos Aires.
At Callao and Quintana, alien world,
perhaps in Mataderos,
on the corner
where the cowpuncher gathers the miles
or near the statue of Florencio
or on the way to the store by way of Salguero,
where Gardel walked whistling tangos
that withstand time,
and some that I did not hear
because they died.

On which corner do I find you
Buenos Aires.
On which corner do I find you?
At the corner of Sábato and Pichuco
or at the corner of Borges and Carriego.
You are on all of them, all the corners
of the suburb and of downtown,
and you are on the banks of the Riachuelo
whose dark waters flow by saying
Juan de Dios Filiberto.[16]

In his "Canto a Buenos Aires" (Song to Buenos Aires), Manuel Mujica Láinez expresses the sounds, movements, and crowds of what he terms the "infinita ciudad" (infinite city). This fragment of a much longer poem portrays the differences in living space within the present-day city, and therefore the corresponding differences of life style among the city's inhabitants:

> Ciudad de hoy. Ciudad de los petit-hotels
> (vanidad de mansardas y de puertas canceles);
> de los departamentos lisos, que cuadriculan
> las idénticas vidas que allí dentro pululan;
> y de los conventillos de miseria y de broncas,
> con llantos afilados y palabrotas roncas;
> de las casas solemnes con balcones cerrados
> en que, tras el portero de botones dorados
> —prodigioso almidón de indiferente calma—
> se adivina un jardín en el que no hay un alma;
> de las casas del sur con patios y con reja
> que encierran una vid o una palmera vieja
> y cuyo solo ornato, sobre el muro desnudo,
> es una chapa nueva, con laureles y escudo,
> contra cuya inscripción: *Aquí vivió . . .* rebota
> de los chicos del barrio la insolente pelota.

> City of today. City of the petit-hotels
> (vanity of mansard roofs and of screened doors);
> of bare apartments which box in
> the identical lives which abound therein;
> and of the tenements of misery and
> filled with shrill cries and growling vulgarities;
> of the solemn houses with closed-in balconies
> in which, behind the gold-buttoned doorman
> —prodigious starch of an indifferent calm—
> one makes out a garden in which not a soul exists;
> of the houses on the south side,
> with patios and grillwork
> that enclose a vine or an old palm tree
> and whose sole ornament, on the naked wall,
> is a new plaque, with laurels and a coat of arms,
> against whose inscription: "Here lived . . ." bounces
> the insolent ball of the neighborhood kids.[17]

The sense of isolation which Mujica Láinez expresses in a general way becomes for Alfonsina Storni a reason for personal anguish.

Her sonnet "Versos a la tristeza de Buenos Aires" (Verses to the Sadness of Buenos Aires) centers on the grayness and monotony of an impersonal city, and on the corresponding state being felt by the poet herself. The quatrains of the poem are as follows:

> Tristes calles derechas, agrisadas e iguales,
> por donde asoma a veces un pedazo de cielo.
> Sus fachadas oscuras y el asfalto del suelo,
> me apagaron los tibios sueños primaverales.
>
> Cuánto vagué por ellas, distraída, empapada
> en el vaho grisáceo, lento que las decora.
> De su monotonía mi alma padece ahora.
> —¡Alfonsina!—No llames. Ya no respondo a nada.

> Sad straight streets, gray and identical,
> whence a piece of sky occasionally looms.
> Their dark façades and the asphalt covering the ground,
> extinguished my tepid springtime dreams.
>
> How I roamed them, distracted, absorbed
> in the lingering gray vapor that adorns them.
> My soul now suffers from their monotony.
> Alfonsina! Don't call me. I no longer respond to anything.[18]

Oswaldo Rossler maintains a nostalgic and openly affectionate tone in his poem "Buenos Aires." He loves his native city in all its forms and moments, and at the same time is sharply aware of its shortcomings:

> Amo, ciudad, la luz que te ofrecen los días,
> la cabellera extensa que derraman tus noches
> otorgando una dulce gravedad a las formas.
> Amo, ciudad, el río que bate en tus orillas.
>
> Amo también las lluvias que te concede el año,
> la crueldad de tu invierno castigándome el cuerpo,
> los estrados vacíos de tus amaneceres
> volcándome hacia el llanto como quien clama un pecho.
>
> Sé que en tu cuerpo caben la lujuria y el crimen,
> la soledad de muchos, la suciedad de todos.
> Somos tus derrotados, tus lobos permanentes.
> Hemos hecho tu vida con nuestras mismas vidas.

I love, city, the light the days offer to you,
the long, long hair that your nights spill forth
granting a sweet seriousness to your forms.
I love, city, the river that pounds against your shores.

I also love the rains that the year concedes to you,
the cruelty of your winter punishing my body,
the empty drawing rooms of your dawns
turning me toward sobs like an infant who cries out for a
    breast.

I know that your body shelters lewdness and crime,
the solitude of many, the filth of all.
We are your defeated ones, your ever-present wolves.
We have made your life with our very own lives.[19]

One could add many more examples, but it is perhaps not necessary. I have attempted, and I hope with reasonable clarity, to suggest the variety and richness of the cultural life of Buenos Aires, and to examine briefly varied responses to that life from some of the city's most sensitive and committed interpreters. Let me close now by using the last lines from José Isaacson's *Oda a Buenos Aires*. After wandering as a pedestrian through the well-known streets of his city, identifying people and places with parts of the city which have characteristic smells and sounds, Isaacson's *despedida* (farewell) expresses with affectionate familiarity a recognition of both greatness and problems to be overcome:

Para despedirme te digo:
cuando seamos tu intendente
te desembotaremos de embotados botarates
y curarermos amorosamente
todos tus baches.

Cada hombre tendrá un andamio
y un lápiz
y elevará cantando la pared
y constuirá cantando la canción.

Nada más que eso, y eso será
Buenos Aires.

In saying goodbye I want to say:
when we become mayor
we will disconnect you from debilitating drifters

and lovingly take care of
all your potholes.

Each man will have a scaffold
and a pencil
and will build the wall singing
and will construct, singing the song.

Nothing more than that, and that will be
Buenos Aires.[20]

Notes

1. James R. Scobie, *Buenos Aires: From Plaza to Suburb, 1870–1910* (New York, 1974).

2. Jesús Mendéz, "Argentine Intellectuals in the Twentieth Century, 1900–1943," Ph.D. dissertation, University of Texas at Austin, 1980.

3. Edwin R. Harvey, *Cultural Policy in Argentina* (Paris, 1979).

4. My figures come from the two most recent sources available to me, namely Harvey, *Cultural Policy in Argentina*, and *Rostros de Buenos Aires* (Buenos Aires, 1978).

5. Abelardo Arias, *Intensión de Buenos Aires* (Buenos Aires, 1974), p. 23.

6. Harvey, *Cultural Policy*, p. 70.

7. Ibid., pp. 5, 9–61.

8. The most complete study of Buenos Aires as a theme in modern Argentine poetry is that of Angel Mazzei, *La poesía de Buenos Aires* (Buenos Aires, 1962). For an anthology of texts, see *He nacido en Buenos Aires: Poemas de la ciudad* (Buenos Aires, 1971).

9. Ulises Petit de Murat, *La noche de mi ciudad* (Buenos Aires, 1979), pp. 10–11.

10. These lines come from "Arrabal," published originally in *Fervor de Buenos Aires* (1923) and in a final version in *Poemas, 1922–1943* (Buenos Aires, 1943). The English translation is mine.

11. I take the text in Spanish from *Obra poética, 1923–1967* (Buenos Aires, 1967), pp. 101–102. The English translation is by Alistair Reid and is included in *Jorge Luis Borges: Selected Poems 1923–1967*, edited by Norman Thomas di Giovanni (New York, 1972), pp. 48–51.

12. Zunilda Gertel, "La visión de Buenos Aires en cincuenta años de poesía borgiana," *Anales de Literatura Hispánica*, 4 (1977), 133–148.

13. *Elogio de la sombra* (Buenos Aires, 1969), p. 155. The English translation is by Norman Thomas di Giovanni, included in *Jorge Luis Borges: In Praise of Darkness* (New York, 1974), p. 125.

14. *La rosa en la balanza* (Buenos Aires, 1944), p. 19. The English translations for this and the following texts are mine.

15. *Enumeración de la patria y otros poemas* (Buenos Aires, 1942), pp. 15–18.

16. Included in *He nacido en Buenos Aires*, p. 126.
17. *Obras completas* (Buenos Aires, 1978), pp. 473–474.
18. *Obras completas* (Buenos Aires, 1976), p. 255.
19. *Buenos Aires* (Buenos Aires, 1964), pp. 23–24.
20. *Oda a Buenos Aires* (Buenos Aires, 1966), pp. 69–70.

7. Buenos Aires: Today and Tomorrow

Roberto Etchepareborda

Despite their complexity, very special circumstances lead me to undertake the topic of present-day Buenos Aires.[1] Though I was not born a *porteño*, my deepest life experiences are intimately related to the city by the Plata.

I spent thirty years of my life in its hospitable environment. The people of Buenos Aires elected me as their representative on three occasions, and I was proud to serve them for nearly half a decade either as an appointee of the legislative power or as head of the executive branch. In spite of my present distance and the time that has elapsed, I hope to be able to share some observations and experiences which may help to illustrate and grasp the subject which has called us together here.

We are on more treacherous ground, however, as far as the future of Buenos Aires and my skill in lighting the way are concerned. In the end, we must agree that there are only two ways to become a historian of the future: scientific induction and the interpretation of dreams and prophecies. In other words: extrapolation and presentiment. Neither of these is precise and it may well be that the second produces better results than the first. Futurologists, planners, poets, and essayists are equally inexact because they can only begin with the present and proceed by analogy with the past.

Thus, it is best to abandon prophetic pretension. If inference becomes necessary, then it should be done from a position of strict humility and deep respect for a reality which often roguishly surpasses all our expectations. So, with no pretense of futurology, but simply by extrapolation of a few indicators from the present and certain trends from the past, and with full knowledge that we can taint the future exclusively with shades of our present mood, and being unable to say what will happen, I will attempt to define what should happen.

There are too many predictions of the future of Argentina for us not to realize which tendencies would lead to interesting extrapolations. The future of Argentina has a great potential which cannot be ignored but which is too often subjected to chronic frustrations. It is there now, moving along positive paths, but its attainment depends entirely on inner peace, the full consensus of its people, and the audacity required of its rulers to change the direction of a long history of mishaps and disappointments.

The history of Buenos Aires, beginning four centuries ago with its second founding, has been brilliantly and knowledgeably told and analyzed by several other participants. However, the concern for what the city has become and the uneasiness for what is "to be or not to be" in the city are much more recent. The old port of Santa María de los Buenos Aires developed through those centuries according to the historical models of different periods: the "Indian City," the viceroyalty's capital, the agro-exportation port. During the 1930s, industrial sites multiplied, and they were accentuated during World War II as a result of the forced substitution for imported goods. This period was marked by spectacular growth of the city beyond its jurisdictional limits. It overran the borders of the neighboring province of Buenos Aires thanks to the dynamism produced by the presence of massive numbers of immigrants from the interior, who increased their numbers from 16 percent in the municipal census of 1936 to 37 percent in the national census of 1947. The presence of a unique method of public transportation, the *colectivo*, and the promotion of redistributive legislation increased suburbanization. This resulted in a large increase in small properties from 26.8 percent in 1947 to 58.1 percent in 1960. This phenomenon was admirably captured by the pen of Borges when he referred to it as an "epic civilian time of the brick oven and monthly payments." A social process that had started during the first decades of the century had taken shape. "By 1960," states Gino Germani, "half of those born of working parents had become part of the middle class and the other 40 percent had gone from unskilled occupations to skilled occupations."

Our story, then, goes back to more recent times, the decade of the forties, when the Municipality of Buenos Aires hired the eminent French urban planner Le Corbusier to design a master plan for the development of the city. Finally, in the early sixties, a Regulating Plan was approved, establishing some of the lines of development undertaken today, and the "regional" concept was introduced, since it had become necessary to shuffle terms such as "Greater Buenos

Aires," "Conurbation," "Buenos Aires Conglomerate," and, most recently, "Metropolitan Area."

A growth pattern which had a spectacular character—keep in mind that the city had multiplied its population eightfold from the national census of 1869 to that of 1914—became vertiginous. Some indices are very illustrative of the accelerated growth of present-day Buenos Aires. In 1947, there were 4,660,635 inhabitants in the metropolitan area; in 1960, 6,737,170 (a 43 percent increase in thirteen years); in 1970, 8,323,372 (19 percent in only ten years). The next national census, in October 1982, will show whether the projected figure of 11 million is far from reality.[2]

It is fair to say that this was a very disorderly, uncontrolled, and even irrational growth which was only partially mitigated by unconnected sectorial measures instituted by the various political jurisdictions involved, the capital and nineteen Buenos Aires municipalities.[3] Its inhabitants suffered the unfavorable consequences of a spontaneous urbanization which the aforementioned Le Corbusier had predicted when he called Buenos Aires the city "without hope" because its inhabitants could not keep even the illusion of "pure and harmonious days." But, he added, "a magnificent destiny awaits it, yes, fortress of its strength; Buenos Aires, react and act!"

In Buenos Aires' response to that challenge in the march toward its present, several memorable events can be pointed out. Twenty-six years elapsed from the conception of the project to the approval of the present Avenida Nueve de Julio, from the time of the centennial (1910) to the commemoration of the Fourth Centennial of the First Founding of Buenos Aires in 1936; but the plan's execution took only 128 days, in spite of its magnitude. In 1960, the city's Regulating Plan tried to organize the city into a new reality: active utilization of trash, new green areas, highway design, building code, industrial zoning. Recently, on the 400th anniversary of its second founding, the city has been adding a new element to its urban features: superhighways.

Keep in mind that, in the last twenty-five years, the number of automobiles multiplied tenfold, totaling more than 1½ million units, while the highway network of 1,560 miles remained practically unchanged.

The first two express highways, which were started in 1978 and scheduled for completion late in 1981, are the Perito Moreno and 25 de Mayo. They cover ten miles with four lanes in each direction. Four more expressways will be added to these: the Central, Transversal, Nueve de Julio (started in May 1981), and Occidental highways. This will form a 46-mile network. These highways are being built without any capital expenditure from the state, since it only guarantees the credits sought by the concessionaires.

There is presently a great dispute between those who favor the completion of the highway plan and those who prefer decentralization, based on satellite cities and the effective transfer of industries. The future is full of questions in view of this opening up of issues, which modifies the existing balance. Will Buenos Aires retain its unique features? It will certainly not become like Caracas, which is nothing more than a series of isolated districts connected by an intricate network of highways. Will it instead become a gigantic city, crisscrossed by expressways? Much will depend on the reaction of *porteños* themselves, since a city is shaped by its people, from the bottom up. The inhabitants go on creating the city, which in some ways is their living expression.

Although chaotic at times, Buenos Aires is a beautiful city. More precisely, it is as beautiful as a city deprived of natural beauty can be, since everything in it is owed to human hands. It has the enchantment of its personality, its quaint corners, and its people. Until only a decade ago, it also had its own river and its creek, the Riachuelo. It has gradually lost these so conclusively that it has become, in fact, a Mediterranean city which, in spite of being laid out on the banks of the Río de la Plata, now lives with its back to the river.

During recent years, one could appreciate just how counterproductive it has become to locate industries along a narrow belt which squeezes to the point of strangulation a city avid for air.

It should be noted that, according to the 1974 National Economic Census, there are as many industrial establishments in the capital city (26,448) as there are in nineteen provinces, and that they represent 20 percent of the shops and factories and employ onefourth of the entire number of industrial workers in the country. Their production value surpasses that of all other provincial states, with the exception of the province of Buenos Aires. In addition, Buenos Aires houses 5,236 wholesale business establishments and 80,261 retail establishments. As a result, the city began to be besieged by thick layers of contaminated air. The siege extended to water, whose density reached unheard-of levels as a result of waste plants. The extensive open-air dumps completed a circle which at a certain point became very difficult to break through.

In 1977, an agreement between the Municipality of Buenos Aires and the authorities of the province effected the creation of a state society, the Metropolitan Area Ecological Belt (Cinturón Ecológico del Area Metropolitana). This step seems to be the jumping-off place for a new era. The city is determined to break the barrier which threatens it; it only remains to be seen whether ten years will be enough to restore its forgotten characteristics to the city.[4]

The eradication of factories and the implementation of new norms will be a positive step toward the removal of the principal sources of contamination for the city and its riverbank. The riverbank will also gain greenbelts when the recovery of 40,000 hectares is achieved through the project known as the Ecological Belt (Cinturón Ecológico) initiated in December 1977. It includes the creation of a system of recreational parks, with the recovery and eventual forestation of flood land by using as fill tons of waste discarded daily in the metropolitan area.[5] At the same time, this will eliminate the obsolete open-air incinerators which loosed eighty tons of soot daily into the atmosphere. These will be replaced by recycling plants where the waste will be compacted and later shipped to places for final disposal.[6] This project has eliminated an estimated 60 percent of the soot that shrouds the city. Other measures include the construction of new parks, thus increasing the city's 10-percent greenbelt area. The city's southwest side, once occupied by an immense dump, now has a park (Parque Almirante Brown) which day by day becomes a powerful oxygen factory.[7]

Predicting what will happen in the metropolitan area in twenty to fifty years is a task subject to possible error. Problems related to traffic, transportation, scarcity of parks, air and water pollution, waste disposal, noise and increased population, and the geographic distribution and characteristics of the population will depend on the government's orientation and its ability or inability to promote the growth of the economy, since the organization of great human concentrations is above all a political process.

In order to confront the imbalance between the hypertrophy of the metropolitan area and the weak development of the rest of the Argentinean territory, policies of "decongestion" must be established to allow effective decentralization of economic activities and the reversal of migratory flows, going from a process of minimally controlled urbanization to the regulation and orientation of urban growth; from the excessive predominance of activities related to the industrial front in certain areas to the regionalization of industrial growth; from a monopoly of tertiary activity to the decentralization of services.

Having described its physical characteristics, I would now like to examine a few of the human and cultural aspects of Buenos Aires. This vast conglomeration of people, over 10 million inhabitants, has achieved a homogeneous character in spite of the multiplicity of yarns in its mesh. The diverse ethnic groups of which it is composed have managed to conserve their native cultural expressions while uniting under a common denominator their own symbols. This process has best been defined by José Luis Romero. He states: "Argentinean culture stopped being entirely Hispanic in order to become just that, only better: a Mediterranean culture, both Spanish and Italian at the same time . . . with everything this entails in keeping an open mind toward a world of creation, . . . which is characterized by a prudent exercise of a critical sense. This characteristic is evident in life styles, in the current system of norms and values, and even in the dress and speech of the people."

It has recently been noted that nearly half the population of the metropolitan area is of Italian descent, 20 percent is of Spanish descent, 20 percent is of Creole descent, and the remaining 10 percent is divided mainly among Slavic, Jewish, and Arabic ethnic groups—a veritable melting pot of races and nationalities.

There is also a gamut of religious groups. A great part (84.3 percent) of the population of Buenos Aires professes the Roman Catholic faith and practices it in 210 churches; 152 houses of worship of various Protestant denominations serve 2.3 percent of the population; and the Jewish community (6.6 percent) gathers at 83 synagogues.

Argentinean society has acquired an increasingly definite character, and Buenos Aires is one of its most legitimate expressions. Even some of the traumatic attitudes of other times and circumstances have been noticeably overcome. We Argentines will stop being on the defensive, as Ortega put it. We will lose some of our formula approach to life, derived from a deep-rooted preoccupation with the way we believe we should look. The *porteños*, still deeply rooted in their soil, seem to have freed themselves from the feeling of insecurity brought on by their urge to affect greatness. They have even changed their common speech, their clothing, and even their old "fatalistic sense," not because there are fewer problems today, but because today's problems are new and different. The maturity acquired through so many changes in the recent past will give rise to social cohesiveness and surpass the individual's frame of reference, contrary to the interests of society as a whole. In the end, common objectives will prevail over narrower individual interests, and we may even take a hopeful glimpse at a future in which individual behavior will be inspired in a spirit of peaceful cohabitation, tolerance, and constructive dialogue. An epoch of sensuality and egoism seems to be followed by one of self-discipline, and greater concern for the spiritual values, and for the best interests of the nation.

It has been perceptively noted that certain tendencies of the *porteños'* way of thinking have intensified. If the *porteños* have not reached maturity, while being subjected to contradictory and passing influence from all directions, it is because their physical and spiritual development have not yet ended. I would venture to guess that the *porteño* of the year 2000 will be vastly different from today's *porteño*, although there will always be a certain familiarity between them, like the one that exists between the *porteño* of yesterday and the *porteño* of today.

Buenos Aires has an old, deeply rooted cultural tradition. The most diverse cultural expressions flourish in its midst, and all indications are that these tendencies will continue to flourish, especially with the continued affirmation of Argentina's own culture and its acquisition of a more definite and spontaneous character and a greater national character.

The list of the city's cultural arsenal is impressive: 45 theaters with more than 8,000 presentations per year; 250 movie theaters which are patronized by 32 million spectators; 141 public libraries and 17 principal museums; 800 bookstores; 130 art galleries; 6,000 conferences and recitals. Physical culture itself has 17 stadiums and 182 athletic clubs.[8]

The city government has a rich tradition in the area of cultural policy which extends into the most diverse fields, from the Teatro Colón to sports. I recall that in the sixties, tent theaters flourished in the plazas, and the municipality even passed tax relief ordinances to promote construction of entertainment centers.

In the political arena, Buenos Aires has exhibited several noteworthy features in the recent past. The constant represented by the *variable* response of *porteño* voters from the time of the sanction of the Sáenz Peña Law in 1912 to use the rise of *peronismo* is not unknown. They have at times been inclined to support radicalism, either on an upward move or in power, but they have most often turned in favor of the opposition socialists, who only thus can enrich their roots. There was also an "independent" group of voters representing a sector of the population which refused to accept an ironclad option. This attitude would continue through the age of *peronismo*, when the city repeatedly had the highest percentages of opposition in successive elections in the entire country. This independent attitude continued to thrive in 1961, giving the victory to Alfredo L. Palacios, in a Castro-type landslide repeating his triumph of 1904, when he was elected the first socialist congressman in Latin America; or as it did in 1962, when it gave a resounding victory to the ailing government of Arturo Frondizi over *peronismo* and radicalism. In 1965, facing the return of *peronismo* and with the strong support of the women's vote, it tipped the scale in favor of the people's radicalism. Finally, in the the fateful year 1973, after the victory of the justicialist coalition on 11 March, it defeated the coalition's senatorial candidate in the runoff election and elected his radical opponent. These independent attitudes, throughout time, signal a response different from the rest of the country. A similar difference could be seen in the less exacerbated and turbulent attitudes found in other regions during the "terrible years," following 1969; but nothing compared to uprisings such as that in Córdoba—the *cordobazo*. This behavior is somehow reflected daily in the low crime rate and the absolute security of the city's environment. In view of its recent history, it can be concluded that the inhabitants of the city have known how to demonstrate an independence and a balance that permit one to augur a beneficial future if their institutional possibilities are extended.

Various measures recently adopted by the national authorities, such as broadening the functions of communal Buenos Aires, foretell positive steps toward the implementation of true and effective municipal autonomy. The return of jurisdiction and the transfer of educational institutions to the communal level (the 476 schools which have sprung up under the Laínez Law) more clearly configure the elements of authentic municipal power. Moreover, if we consider the fact that the community budget for 1979 was 1,136,200 million pesos compared to a national budget of 20,481,821 million (which includes funding for national defense, security, and public works), we realize the abundance of possibilities and the weight of the federal district in the national picture.[9] By gross comparison, the municipality spends almost six times more than the nation's health allocation and an amount equal to the nation's educational and cultural allocation.

I would like to point something out in the way of a testimonial. In 1958, after nearly two decades of dissolution, the people of Buenos Aires regained their representation in municipal government. The proportional electoral system of the time allowed ample representation. Five political factions ranging from various shades of radicalism to communism (except *peronismo*, which was outlawed) had to get along together. Since no one was in the majority, the factions worked together, ironing out differences and shaping their own hopes and dreams to the common consensus. The result was ample and positive legislation for the benefit of the city. That was all a vital experience that deserves to be taken into consideration, as a subject of political significance, especially in reference to open discussion about the influence of the electoral system and its impact on the political stability of the country.

Buenos Aires was a city and had its own government long before its territory was federalized. It has a historical right to rule itself independently from the central power. It is unfair to deprive the city's residents of the right that other communities have to establish community institutions and to rule themselves. The National Constitution should be amended in reference to the government of Buenos Aires, establishing the autonomy of that municipality.

The Constitution of 1949, going to the other pole, established another system, granting all power over the federal district to the president of the republic, along with the authority to delegate the governing functions. Real progress can only be achieved if a democratic feeling pervades the entire society with a sense of rejuvenation.

There is also another political-jurisdictional problem which requires prompt attention. The city technically overflows the municipality, thus surpassing its political boundaries. Buenos Aires is, then, in the urbanistic sense, governed by a handful of municipalities that should merge their functions. Indeed, reasons exist that demand the rationalization and coordination of functions in the near future. Something is being done, but much remains to be done. The current tendency is to view cities as part of a whole that covers entire regions and forms large systems. In other words, the community system of the twenty-first century cannot be the same as that of colonial times.

A series of steps could lead to the optimal solution of this situation. First there should be established a body for the Coordination of Municipal Governments. Then, with a broader scope, a decision should be made as to the transfer of the federal capital. If this is approved, the present municipality should be granted the status of provincial state. Finally, in the same process, consideration should be given to the possibility of incorporating into the new state the municipalities forming the greater metropolitan area of the existing province of Buenos Aires. This undertaking, utopian as it may appear today, would avoid duplication, overlapping, and jurisdictional conflicts and would solve as many institutional problems as administrative and urban ones.

In order to do this, we need only be conscious of the meaning of a well-structured country attuned to all its possibilities, so that

Buenos Aires can be the great city which has called to its soil all the races on earth and the most diverse expressions of universal culture.

Notes

1. The preliminary English translation of this paper was made by Esther Bailey; Professor Thomas F. McGann prepared the final text [editors' note].

2. The results of the Seventh National Census conducted 22 October 1980 showed 2,908,000 in the federal capital and a total of 6,769,200 in the surrounding districts, giving a grand total of 9,677,200 and representing an increase of 25.8 percent. The federal district showed a decline of some 5,000 inhabitants, but one must take into account the elimination of the slum districts containing some 200,000 inhabitants.

3. This growth took place within little more than 2,300 square miles.

4. Buenos Aires has approximately 300,000 trees. Since 1977, some 200,000 new trees have been planted, and another 100,000 were planted during 1980. Forty-nine plazas were remodeled; 70 hectares of greenbelts were added and an additional 639 hectares are currently being created.

5. It is estimated that the city's annual waste totals nearly 1 million tons.

6. Where factories were, model elementary schools have been constructed (fourteen elementary classrooms, four pre-elementary rooms, a multiple-use classroom, a library, a recreation facility, workshops, laboratories, a dining room, etc.).

7. The entire area is being remodeled. Other projects in the industrial sector include: the President Roca Park; the San Lorenzo Sports Country Club; a golf course; six hectares for a supermarket; a private-use sector to be opened for public bidding; three schools; a commercial center; and the necessary community services.

8. The Sixth Exhibition of the International Fair of the Book of Buenos Aires—entitled "The Meeting of Two Worlds, or the Spanish Epic Achievement in America in the Sixteenth Century"—held in 1980 was attended by more than 800,000 persons.

9. The Municipal Budget amounted to 2.3 billion dollars in 1980.

8. How to Know the City

Joseph S. Tulchin

There is one point I'd like to make before beginning the comments I had prepared on these three excellent papers, a comment that first occurred to me as I sat listening to the three papers delivered during the morning session and was reinforced by my experience during the afternoon session. The North American scholars who have spoken to you today all owe an intellectual debt to the three scholars of Argentine history. The debt is largely unconscious, though the notes to the papers reveal the extent of the conscious debt. Two Argentines and one North American clearly have shaped the thinking of all of our North American speakers today—and I would include myself as well—shaped our thinking about the city of Buenos Aires. Two of the scholars are Argentines who are not with us today, Tulio Halperín Donghi and Jorge Enrique Hardoy. One, however, is a North American who is with us, and I'd like to take this moment to bow toward Jim Scobie, whose work really has shaped writings about Argentine history in the United States, as can be appreciated by reading the *conjunto* of papers contained in this volume.

I want to begin my comments on the papers on the contemporary city with some words Professor Arocena offered us at lunch. In talking in a very evocative manner about the city of Buenos Aires, Arocena referred over and over again to several features of the *porteños'* perception of their city which I want to seize upon in organizing my own thoughts about these papers. Specifically, I want to point to the experience of walking in the city of Buenos Aires and, probably as a result of walking through the city, the sense of *barrio*, the sense of neighborhood which one has if one lives in that city for any length of time.

Walking in a city, any city, is probably the best way to get a sense of life there, of how people actually live. It is one way to give greater meaning to the census data which Walter and Socolow have used and explained so intelligently and with such great imagination. It is a dimension in understanding a city which I would suggest is indispensable to the scholar's activity. On one of my first visits to Buenos Aires, I had occasion to chat one afternoon, in his office at the National Library, with Jorge Luis Borges. We were talking not about literature, a field in which I'm remarkably ignorant, but rather about the city, which fascinated me. We were talking about days gone by, and he described one afternoon in particular. He said it was one of many such experiences when he would leave his office and walk arm in arm with the Argentine painter Xul Solar, through the southern part of the city, across the Avenida de Mayo, along the Calle Florida and then up Santa Fe and out to the suburbs to the house of Victoria Ocampo in San Isidro for tea. Now, for those of you who know Buenos Aires, you might appreciate that is some *paseo*! But, if you know Borges and if you know anything about Xul Solar, it is not at all difficult to imagine these two walking oblivious to the noise and effervescence of the city, focusing on those elements of their surroundings that caught their attention, and arriving, perhaps an hour or two later, at the Ocampo house. As they walked, they talked about their city. They talked about the neighborhoods through which they passed. They started in the southern section, very near where the old National Library building is on Calle Mexico, a neighborhood of small factories and modest *petits hotels*, walking along, crossing the Avenida de Mayo, with its Spanish hotels and *confiterías*, walking along Florida, which, of course, as you know, no longer houses those residences of the elite. Today, there are commercial houses, where tourists tend to walk. The walk continued up the length of Santa Fe, where there are now seemingly limitless rows of skyscrapers, all residences, and equally elegant shops which did not exist for the most part when Xul Solar and Borges walked.

Aside from the energy and activity, the principal feature of the city which Borges conveyed in describing his walk was the changes in life style along the route, those changes as you go from one neighborhood to another. This is a peculiar characteristic of Buenos Aires, which distinguishes it from other major capitals in the western hemisphere. The quality of neighborhood life, lacking in most other large cities, is, I believe, very important for an understanding of contemporary Buenos Aires. But I'll get back to that in a moment. First, some comments about the *barrios* themselves. The neighborhoods of Buenos Aires today, as fifty years ago, are defined in a variety of ways. We can begin with the census data that Dr. Walter described for us: ethnic composition, demographic density, and so on. They're also described in a manner which Jim Scobie explained so clearly for the late nineteenth century city. His explanation holds with some very few changes well up to the present, near the end of the twentieth century. The elements that create a sense of belonging include the local *boliche*, the *mercado*, the *panadería*, the *farmacia de turno*, which is *your farmacia*, and so on. Even with the introduction of supermarket chains, there still is the sense in Buenos Aires today of the neighborhood *mercado*. It may be called *DISCO* and it's a little less personal perhaps than Don Juan in the *mercado* may have been, but there's a marvelous schizophrenia in the neighborhoods of Buenos Aires today. Even with a *DISCO* there is a *mercado municipal* close by where Don Juan the *carnicero* still picks out the best cuts for his regular clients, even providing them credit, and which offers the kind of interpersonal relations characteristic of that neighborhood 100 years ago. The *boliche* is perhaps the most vibrant sign of neighborhood in the city. The role and popularity of the *boliche*, where one would go to eat informally, are extremely important for understanding the contemporary city. It's a restaurant, as you know, a restaurant of no particular distinction, of no particular socioeconomic level. It tends to be less expensive than more formal restaurants, but it's clearly a place where members of your family can go, relax, and eat. It has what in the United States we call "family atmosphere." The term *morfar* might characterize the experience in any of these restaurants better than the term *comer*. But that is not a criticism. Indeed North American friends of ours would refer to *boliches* like that with affection as *morferías*. We would seek out such restaurants, because they had a true sense of place in the social and geographical sense.

How, then, are we to account for the persistence of this sense of neighborhood from the nineteenth into the twentieth century, a very unusual characteristic for modern cities, if we think of the United States. I would suggest that we begin by looking at the extraordinary network of public transportation in the city of Buenos Aires. Transportation in that city, as in others, serves to tie the urban units together. If you have taken one of the walking tours of the city that I recommend, you get an impression, I'm certain, of an omnipresent and varied system of transportation that's available to anybody who chooses to use the city. There are taxis, the subway, and there is the famous *colectivo*. Indeed, I suggest for those who don't know the city well, if you're too tired, or not interested in walking across the city, that one way to get to know it and palpably experience the change from neighborhood to neighborhood is to take a *colectivo*. A good one might be No. 60, starting out in Constitución and ending up at the Tigre Hotel. Or, better yet, on a Saturday, start out at Retiro on the 108 and wind up in Liniers, getting off there to see what happens at Liniers, a place which your reading of Esteban Echeverría would help explain. But, all in all, as a layperson I would say that the network of urban transportation in Buenos Aires is probably unequaled in the world.

Colectivo today has taken on characteristics which point to changes in the city over the past fifty years and to some of the problems to which Walter and Etchepareborda referred in their papers. Who takes the 59 from the center of town at six or seven in the evening out to the suburbs? While I haven't taken a comprehensive survey, I've taken that route many times, and I'm confident it is not, principally, the middle-class and professional groups that tend to live in the suburbs. You'll notice that most of the *colectivos* which go out to the northern suburbs of the city stick fairly close to Libertador *y por arriba*. There are few, if any, that service the area between Libertador and the river. The reason for this is that most of those elegant middle-class residential areas don't really care to have *colectivos* barreling through their streets. Although they claim to have cleaned up their act, *colectivos* still put out a lot of *hollín*. But, more significantly, the *colectivo* is no longer the principal mode of transportation for the rising middle class in Argentina. I'm speaking generally and impressionistically; obviously there are many exceptions. I'm sure, if you think about it, all of you who know Argentina can come up with specific examples of friends in the professions who might say, or have indeed said, "I don't take *colectivos*." They much prefer to take a taxi or take a car, despite the expense.

The rise in the use of the automobile to which both Etchepareborda and Walter have referred is a function as much of social changes in the city as of technological progress. Certainly the technology has enabled people to use the car. But the social symbolism of the car, as opposed to the *colectivo* or the subway, is obvious. Most people wish to take a car from their home, let us say, in San Isidro or Martínez to their office in the center, rather than the *colectivo*, in part because the trip would take two and a half hours in the morning. While a laborer, who cannot afford to buy a car and go to work in it, may undergo that trip, a good middle-management executive or professional whose time is now worth something is certainly not going to spend that amount of time on the trip. Don't forget, it's even uncomfortable for people under six feet tall to get into the 59 during rush hour, much less stand up for more than an hour as the machine burps along potholed streets, stopping at every other corner, unless they have to.

The availability of transportation ties a city together, and it ties Buenos Aires together in a way that is important for an understanding of the city today. The *colectivo* allows the neighborhoods to participate in the life of the city and to take advantage of that curious phenomenon known as *el centro*. After all, we're talking about a metropolis of anywhere from 10 to 11 million people in Gran Buenos Aires, but there persists a sense of a center which is available for the use of all people who live there. There still is in Buenos Aires, almost unique among great cities of the world, the sense of a small town. For the middle class, if you walk along Florida, if you have a coffee in Florida Gardens—a few years ago, it would have been Augustus, but tastes change—you will see friends. You can't help but see friends. If you go to the latest "in" restaurant near Recoleta there is the feeling of community in the *barrio norte* that belies the size of the city. The *centro* focuses that same feeling of community for those who wish to eat out or go to the movies. Lavalle and Corrientes are jammed on weekends, even during the worst of economic slowdowns.

As I have spoken, I have referred implicitly on several occasions to another phenomenon which has contributed to maintaining both the sense of neighborhood that is so peculiar to Buenos Aires and the idea of a center of Buenos Aires, which all feel is theirs and can enjoy so easily: the growth of the suburbs—*la provincia*, the nineteen municipalities in the province of Buenos Aires which are correctly understood as part of the metropolitan area. But what are the characteristics of those suburbs? I've already mentioned what we call in North America the "bedroom suburbs" along the northern rim of the city. But if you look to the west, if you look to the south, the socioeconomic configuration of those suburbs is markedly different. Now, let us look at the statistics which Roberto Etchepareborda cited about industrial establishments within the *capital federal*. These indicate extensive industrial activity. If you look more closely at those statistics, as some recent studies have done, you will discover that, while the number of industrial units has remained high, the total amount of industrial production within the federal capital has gone down. Where there were small factories, now there are offices. The production facilities have moved out of town. The counterpart of that decline has been the extraordinary growth of industrial activity outside the federal capital. So, what has been occurring, with some important exceptions, is the creation of an industrial ring around the federal capital, with its corresponding working-class residential zones, reinforcing the bureaucratic-commercial character of the center of the federal capital and concentrating ever more of the economy and the government of the country in the center of Buenos Aires. In human terms, this phenomenon has preserved that city which is evoked in such a nostalgic manner by several of the contributors to this volume. You can still go to the *centro*, to the theater, the movies, a restaurant, and find it more or less as it was ten or fifteen or even thirty years ago. The reason you can is the extraordinary growth of what is called *la provincia*.

As the city or, more properly, the *porteños*, particularly the middle-class and upper middle class *porteños*, turn themselves over to the car, and as increasing energy and resources are devoted to building highways through the city, there is the very grave danger that the new automotive transportation network will divide and isolate sections of the city rather than tie them together, as the public transportation network has done in the past. As Francisco Bullrich pointed out in the mid-1960s, roads not only allow cars to go from one place to the other, but, if they are of a certain size, they serve with incredible effect to separate people on one side of the road from the people on the other. Think of the Nueve de Julio, as an example, or the General Paz. There are studies now of urban developers in the United States and Japan which have proven Bullrich's point over and over. Indeed, now it is almost a cardinal test of urban developers in northern countries to avoid the kind of road network which characterizes the city of Caracas. Roberto Etchepareborda and I were in Caracas together recently and we shared exactly the same feeling coming out of our hotel. The first thing you see is an eight-lane highway in front of you. Well, from one point of view that highway takes you where you want to go. But if you are a pedestrian trying to figure out where to go, it's a terribly frightening experience: cars going back and forth at great speed, and the powerful sensation that you can't possibly cross to the other side. And, as Bullrich pointed out for Buenos Aires more than ten years ago, the new *autopistas* may well have the same sociological impact on the city. It seems to me that this is a real problem which *porteños* have to keep in mind. The new roads may move cars around quickly, but at the expense of destroying the traditional notion of community.

The impact of the city, the role of the city in national affairs, has been mentioned over and over again. Perhaps the dominant characteristic of the city through its history in the last 100 years has been the extraordinary centripetal force that it has exerted on economic, cultural, and social activity within the country, sucking activity outside into its orbit. I had a conversation once with an executive vice-president of Sudamtex, and I commented to him about what I thought was the peculiar quality of his advertising campaign for an article of clothing. I said, "It seems to me, that while this might catch the flavor of the *porteño* market, it certainly would not appeal in the same manner to the market in the interior." He laughed and said, "In categorizing or in setting up our national advertising campaign we do not pay attention to the interior." I asked, "Why is that?" He said, "Eighty percent of the market is in Gran Buenos Aires." So, while the city dominates the interior in a demographic fashion that is obvious from the census data, it dominates the countryside in an economic fashion that planners and policy makers too often do not understand.

Roberto Etchepareborda referred to the question of politics in organizing or planning for city development. I would add to that the notion of the market in determining the evolution of how a city's space is used and what functions occur within it, as well as the relationship of the city to its hinterland. It seems to me that we have to take into account the functioning of the market to understand the evolution of Buenos Aires. It was not until the city put a halt to certain kinds of construction in the *barrio norte* by legislation that construction began—I should say the eruption of construction began in Belgrano and in the Sud, which is only a ten- or fifteen-year-old phenomenon. We must understand that the desire to invest funds in residential housing in a certain area, with an objective of short-term speculative return in an era of high inflation rather than long-term investment dictated by the long-run planned needs of urban policy, is more characteristic of a city like Buenos Aires—or of Rio, or Mexico City for that matter—than one would like to contemplate. We have here a mix of market forces and political forces, and in determining the Buenos Aires of the future we must take both into account. It is impossible to imagine Buenos Aires in the year 2000 without some intervention of planners, of government, of policy making. But it is impossible, also, to imagine Buenos Aires in the year 2000 organized along the lines of even the most intelligent and imaginative city planners. Jorge Enrique Hardoy and his team of researchers at the Centro de Estudios Urbanos y Regionales (CEUR) pointed out these problems over fifteen years ago, but no one in the power structure cared to listen. Indeed, what is required, if it is at all possible for any city in the world, much less for Buenos Aires, is a combination of factors in which the socioeconomic requirements of the entire country are taken into account. Because the end result, over a hundred-year period, of those centripetal forces to which I have referred is the interaction, the unavoidable interaction, of Gran Buenos Aires with the nation as a whole in economic and in political terms. In other words, the need is for a national policy to determine the future of Buenos Aires. Whether it will be by the imposition of government decree, as has been done in a number of countries around the world, or by market incentives to establish demographic balance or establish industrial activity far away from the city, it will be necessary to play with those same market forces which are themselves partly responsible for the creation of the urban monster. Another option might be to try the Brazilian mode, or the North American mode, and arbitrarily set up a bureaucratic governmental center that is separate from the commercial and social center, *à la* Brasilia or Washington, D.C. My guess is that the latter is impossible for Argentina today, in political terms, but those are two options open to a society confronted with this kind of dizzying centripetal force of its capital city, such as is the case with Argentina.

The model of urban development which has had greatest echo among students of Argentina and students of urban development, generally, has been that of Jorge Enrique Hardoy and his colleagues at CEUR. The principal attraction of that model is that Hardoy seeks to combine attention to systemic factors such as the market and politics, to which I've alluded, with factors which take into account the needs and aspirations of individuals. Urban progress is more than making the trains run on time and building miles of superhighways that move large numbers of expensive cars to their destinations in an efficient manner; it means enhancing the quality of life for those who live in the city or, in this case, preserving the quality of life that represents Buenos Aires. The very kinds of aspirations and needs to which Roberto Etchepareborda and Luis Arocena draw our attention with such elegance and grace combine the models of the social scientist with the intuitive understanding of the tango singer, the poet, and the humanist critic of society, all of whom understand that attraction and the magic of the city we all know, the magic of the city whose 400th anniversary we are celebrating.

III. TWO FINAL PERCEPTIONS

9. A View from the Provinces

Christián García-Godoy

One of the surprises presented by the course of time is to find one-self doing something totally unexpected. Because never could I have imagined that I, a Mendocinian—a native of Mendoza—of old pro-vincial stock, would have nothing less than the honor of speaking at a conference in Washington, D.C.—that is to say, the capital of the western world—in celebration of four centuries since the second founding of Buenos Aires.

In the presence of such distinguished colleagues, accompanied by scholars of both Americas, surrounded by friends, my voice could appear the least appropriate to be heard on such a unique occasion. Perhaps there is, however, a certain symbolism in that—though it be by precarious means—the interior of our republic is represented at a remembrance of Buenos Aires, one of the "cities of destiny" which Toynbee forgot in his masterly work.

As an intellectual counterpoint to the theme that Luis Antonio Arocena will develop today, I would like to mention briefly one Mendocinian among many who went to Buenos Aires and loved it intensely. Without giving his complete history, I can say to you that he was an interesting figure of the society, culture, and politics of his time in his native province before establishing himself as a man for all seasons in the business, political, and social life of Buenos Aires at the beginning of this century. I refer to Benito Villanueva, who was born in Mendoza, obtained his bachelor's degree in Santa Fe, and was a lawyer in Buenos Aires. A national representative and sen-ator from his province and president of both chambers, he temporar-ily occupied the presidency of the nation. Singularly, he was also a national representative and senator for the federal capital. A power-ful landholder, associated with the Martínez de Hoz family in the founding and exploitation of the horse farm "Chapadmalal," he was twice the president of the Jockey Club of Buenos Aires. In addition, he presided over the Círculo de Armas (Fencing Club) and the

Círculo del Progreso, the latter the organization that generated the idea and raised funds for the construction of the monument to San Martín now standing at the corner of Virginia Avenue and Twentieth Street in the city of Washington.

Villanueva's personality—remembered with gratitude, a certain satiric humor, and solicitous respect by the famous Ramón Columba, and his history (not yet written) project in some measure another of the extraordinary dimensions of Buenos Aires: the city open toward the exterior, the city dazzling to many from the provinces, in which intelligence and elegance, knowledge and beauty, value and talent, integrity and sacrifice, enterprise and ability are gladly received from wherever they come in a tradition of equality of opportunity. Benito Villanueva was, thus, an example of a successful provincial who was not blinded by the lights of the city.

I could remember other Mendocinians—for example, the enterprising don Emilio Civit, national representative and senator from Mendoza, minister of public works of President Julio A. Roca; or the urbane Abelardo Arias, the contemporary writer who in *Alamos talados* (Trimmed Poplars) reconstructed with a certain imaginative liberty the life of his native province as seen from the perspective of life in the capital, but who in *Intensión de Buenos Aires* gathered and ordered impressions of forty years regarding neighborhoods, characters of everyday life, corners, monuments, and museums, in a sort of counter-melody for the city which he loves, the city which "has soul," according to his passionate words.

But it is not my intention to limit myself to one province, but rather to give examples. Perhaps it is good to remember that Leopoldo Lugones came to Buenos Aires and was received by Rubén Darío with statements of admiration which he included in his *Autobiography*: "One day Lugones appeared, audacious, young, strong and fierce, as a *hecatónquero*." He was born in Villa María del Río Seco, in that centuries-old province of Córdoba which he would never forget. Notwithstanding, he became the center of a literary renovation prompted from Buenos Aires. The author of *Odas seculares*, written to celebrate the national centennial, he would later be the first president of the Argentine Society of Writers, the famous SADE, which still exists.

Another provincial who went to Buenos Aires, studied it intensely until he understood it, and was an important figure there is Joaquín V. González, who has been called the link between the generations of 1880 and 1900. A perceptive humanist, he was born in La Rioja, graduated in Córdoba, presided over the University of La Plata, which he founded in 1906, collaborated with *La Prensa* and *La*

Nación (newspapers now more than a hundred years old), and was minister of the interior (that is to say, the guiding force behind national politics no less than President Julio A. Roca), and minister of justice and education under President Manuel Quintana.

I am going to cite Sarmiento, the formidable man from San Juan, for a phrase which is the synthesis of my thought in this 400-year celebration: "Provincial in Buenos Aires, *porteño* in the provinces." And Juan Pablo Echagüe, also from San Juan, a fine writer of delicate prose, the personality with the broad-brimmed hat whom I saw many afternoons on Florida Street in the area of the San Martín Plaza. Wenceslao Escalante, born in Santa Fe, educated in Rosario, graduated in Buenos Aires, professor and creative philosopher who established the philosophy chair in the university where he studied, teacher of several generations, was also a cabinet member under presidents Luis Sáenz Peña, José Evaristo Uriburu, and Julio A. Roca. I could continue naming the positions which many other provincials achieved and the influence which they exercised in Buenos Aires. But that would take me away from my purpose. For this reason, I am going to try to complete this remembrance with a view of Buenos Aires from the provinces.

There is no doubt that the provinces, many of whose capitals were founded before Buenos Aires, progressed in their visualization of Buenos Aires: from the city to the capital of the viceroyalty, but always as the port, and later—much later—as the legal capital of the unified nation. Thus, Buenos Aires was slowly converted into the "head of Goliath," and being a port, was the antechamber of the exit to Europe and the world. But it was also the port of entrance of intellectual contagion, social style, institutional novelty, political happenings, scientific advance, economic progress. It may be concluded that if Buenos Aires influenced the provinces, they in turn decisively influenced Buenos Aires. This type of mutual cross-fertilization would contribute to create what Miguel Angel Cárcano has called the "Argentine style of life," which is personified in Paz, Mansilla, González, Roca, Figueroa Alcorta, and Sáenz Peña. It could be added that José Hernández with *Martín Fierro* and Ricardo Güiraldes with his *Don Segundo Sombra*, Lugones with his *Guerra gaucha*, and A. J. Pérez Amuchástegui with his *Mentalidades argentinas* have amplified the above-mentioned vision.

My remembrance of Buenos Aires in 1934, the first time I knew it, is indelibly associated with the International Eucharistic Congress and the ascetic figure of Cardinal Pacelli, who became pope; later, with the visits of the presidents Franklin D. Roosevelt and Getulio Vargas. But also with the *popular olla* (people's stew) in

Puerto Nuevo; the streetcars on the corner of Callao and Santa Fe; the Confitería Ideal, meeting place of the provincials, who during each visit to Buenos Aires were found drinking tea at five in the afternoon, with biscuits, marmalade, and fine pastries. The *porteños* of society went to the Confitería París after a function in the Colón theater; the politicians to the Confitería Molino, located across the street from the palace of the National Congress; the residents of the northern section to the Confitería del Aguila. On my last visit to Buenos Aires, only El Molino (the Mill) remained, disguised as a *pizzería*. The París was, by then, an imposing apartment building; the Aguila (the Eagle), a store with fine quality crystal. The streetcars had given way to trolley-buses; and these, to a renovated *colectivo* created 52 years ago; and by now, thanks to electronic gadgetry, to modernized taxis of compact size and distinctive colors.

The provinces have been evolving in their vision of Buenos Aires, and what they admire least is its centralist politics. On the other hand, they love its theater, enjoy its restaurants, frequent its academies, museums, and libraries, use its historical archives, and are proud of its architecture. They recognize that it is the financial center on which convenient credit decisively depends, and they tolerate it as the omnipotent administrative seat to which our modern airlines take them "for the day" to accomplish missions that are best done personally.

Buenos Aires is the accelerated life, the pulsing rhythm. It is popular talent; it is the *fileteado* (filigreed designs) on its buses and *colectivos*; it is Carlitos Gardel, who every day sings better; and it is, also, the classic concert in the Mozarteum Argentino.

Luis Antonio Arocena, who in the following essay defines how a *porteño* looks at his city, has abundant academic credentials which mark him as a historian and humanist of rare and subtle ability of observation, synthesis, and foresight, ideal for re-creating on this occasion that city in its antithetical dimension of the good and the elevated, the doubtful and the vulgar; that city which, being the first, is not the oldest among the historical cities of our America; that city which has come to be the most awesome and difficult political-cultural problem that the republic must resolve in these remaining two decades which, far from providing distance, are flinging us with growing historical acceleration into the twenty-first century of science and technology.

To you, Buenos Aires of the hunger and the tragedy of Pedro de Mendoza; of the predestined founder, Juan de Garay; of Santiago de Liniers and the exciting times of defense and reconquest.

To you, Buenos Aires of the May Revolution which the genius

of San Martín converted into the American Cause with the liberty of Chile and the independence of Peru; of the Assembly of the Year XIII, which abolished slavery forever.

To you, Buenos Aires of the brave struggle and immediate recovery from yellow fever; of immigration and productive sacrifice; of the thousand corners of expectation; of the ten thousand neighborhood cafes; and of the man who is still alone and hopes.

To you, Buenos Aires of intelligence and refined culture; of scientific research and artistic creation; of the International Eucharistic Congress and of Nobel prizes.

To you, Buenos Aires of the hundred theaters and the million books, which gathers the most illustrious, the most classic, the most current thought of humanity in its intermingling of easterners and westerners.

To you, Buenos Aires of the Argentinian who is inside and feels restive; of the Argentinian who is far away and remembers you; of the stranger who knew you once and will never forget you.

10. A *Porteño*'s View of His City

Luis A. Arocena

Since I am to assume the role of the *porteño*, although most briefly, allow me first to claim a right which is essential to the Buenos Aires native: the right to pass the blame. Thus, I will not be held responsible for disrupting amiable table conversation. Also, the attempt to characterize how *porteños* feel about their city was not my idea. The only one responsible for both of these imminent misfortunes is my friend and colleague, Dr. Stanley Ross. I am, thus, totally innocent and hold his charming, yet stern organizational efficiency fully responsible for this.

One needs not be a determinist of whatever stripe to know that a great city necessarily creates unique ways of life. Among the many disciplines concerned with people and humankind, not one has failed to study in some way the cultural conditioning resulting from urban cohabitation. Everything that has been said about the rootlessness and other consequences of mass urban society, including lack of unity and anonymity, alienation, gregariousness, technological manipulation of the collective will and sensitivity, as well as many other consequences of living in the large urban conglomerations of our time, almost escapes our cognitive or contemplative ability.

A more accessible subject, on the other hand, is the study of the relationship between people and city which is manifested ostensibly by people's feelings for their city and the value they place on their city; the value citizens place on the environment in which they live, or which lives in them. This unifying attitude turns out to be no less important than the unfavorable consequences of living in large urban concentrations. Every city, to some degree or another, in more or less open manifestations, turns into the lively object of emotional and intellectual attributions. A city is felt or thought of as native or foreign, protective or hostile, beneficial or harmful. Once personified, it becomes the object of love and hate, happiness and sadness, hopes and fears, dreams of success and reminders of failures.

Buenos Aires is indeed no exception to the objective results of the obviously dual relationship between people and their urban environment. More noticeable yet is the city's stern way of imposing itself, which has shaped and continues to shape the character of *porteños*—of being *porteños*—with unquestionably unique habits, attitudes, and feelings. No less notorious, on the other hand, is the zeal with which the people of Buenos Aires project a profusely warm and cordial feeling toward their city, with all the elements of intimacy, and not always in subtle or surreptitious ways. When Borges confesses in one of his poems:

> Las calles de Buenos Aires
> ya son la entraña de mi alma
>
> The streets of Buenos Aires
> are the roots of my soul [1]

he expresses a feeling which no *porteño* would consider excessive.

In any attempt to characterize the nature of the existential ties between Buenos Aires and its inhabitants, one must keep in mind, methodologically, that the elements of this relationship are far from static or unchanging through time. The city has a history of profound changes, and *porteños* have experienced and lived that history from a position of equally changing emotions. The present megalopolis obviously has little in common with the turn-of-the-century *gran aldea* (the Big Village), as little as the native *porteño* with traditional ancestry has in common with the immigrant who arrived in the years when there were dreams and promises of easy land. In order to avoid making unsubstantiated generalizations, one should refer to specific and well-defined times in the history of these feelings of affinity whose reality in day-to-day living I would like to highlight. This, of course, only as long as the enumeration of these changes occurs without canceling out something that remains as a background for the change itself. In that case, it may be wise to point out these consistencies.

One of these, and certainly the most notorious for its unwavering presence, is the exalted feeling which *porteños* have for their city. This superlative esteem is evident even in the mid–eighteenth-century text. In reference to the attitude of the Buenos Aires native, Father Domingo de Neyra writes, "The love for their country is so certain that there is not a man, however useless he may be, who wouldn't offer himself or defend his country from insults and proclaim its good qualities, and even if it had none, his passion would surely help him find them."[2]

The love that makes Buenos Aires the standard by which everything else is judged is not only the most deeply ingrained instinct among *porteños*, it is also, by far, the most widely known and aggressive. Carlos Guido Spano voices this feeling in several lines destined to become part of the national heritage for that very reason:

> He nacido en Buenos Aires
> No me importan los desaires
> Con que me trate la suerte.
> Argentino hasta la muerte,
> He nacido en Buenos Aires.

> In Buenos Aires I was born
> I care not if fortune frowns upon me.
> I am Argentinean until death,
> In Buenos Aires I was born.[3]

This deep-rooted and tenacious feeling of attachment to their city shows itself in different ways in the native *porteños*. Perhaps the most meaningful of these is the one which causes the people of Buenos Aires to feel existentially linked to it. City and personal life constitute an inseparable whole in the *porteños'* experience. The city is not just a physical environment for the events of city life; it is more, much more. It is felt as part of life; it is life itself in the expression of its efforts, achievements, and failures. This communion between *porteños* and their Buenos Aires has been offered up, and is offered up, as a constant in many fine examples of Argentine poetry:

> Buenos Aires resume el universo
> y en su barro, en su asfalto o en su piedra
> es surtido mi renovado verso
> y yo humedo y fiel como la hiedra
> con mi canción a cuestas testarudo
> que de mi sangre y de la tuya medra.

> Buenos Aires encapsulates the universe
> and in its clay, its asphalt, or its stone
> my renewed verse is nurtured;
> and I remain as faithful as ivy,
> with a song on my back, convinced
> that it thrives on your blood and mine.[4]

We will not go into the profound psychological motivations behind such an urge to experience the city, to feel it a part of oneself and constituting an important factor in the determination of one's values and attitudes. A more pressing concern, with greater possibilities for verification, is the discovery of some of the various forms of expression assumed by the aforementioned identification.

It may be affirmed, with considerable certainty, that affective factors in the feeling for Buenos Aires reach their climax in their role as reminders of the distance and the change which result from the passage of time. Nothing inspires the sensibilities of *porteños* more easily than the mention of their distant city, experiencing it from afar. That is when distance hurts like a mutilation of the spirit, like an unbearable amputation. Even the first generation of Argentinean romanticists managed to enhance with pathetic forms the feelings aroused by their physical distance.

"Buenos Aires," exclaims José Mármol in the dedication of his *Cantos del Peregrino*,

> my eyes first opened to the light of your beautiful sky; and as deserving child of your past glory, they will perhaps close under the sky of a foreign land. But in my exile, your holy memory is mingled with the memory of my mother's first kisses; and if, in my greed for glory, I have sought the poet's wreath through the inspirations of my soul, it was only to deposit it at your feet, because you, my beloved homeland, are the magnet of those inspirations . . . Farewell, Buenos Aires: though proud of my birth, I shall die in exile if I cannot someday breathe the fresh air of liberty in your bosom; but my last word will be your name, and my last thought, your image.[5]

Homesickness may be thought of as a "malady" characteristic of the Romantic sensibility. But then, we must add, as proven fact, the persistence with which *porteños* have maintained their faithfulness to their romantic attitude. And just as for the *porteño* there is no feeling more painful than separation, the possibility of reunion, of return to the city ardently longed for, is a joy that motivates boundless and warmhearted outpourings:

> Hoy que la suerte quiere que te vuelva a ver
> ciudad porteña de mi único querer,
> y oiga la queja de tu bandoneón
> dentro del pecho pide rienda el corazón.

Today, when fortune has decreed that I may see you again,
oh city of my only love,
and I hear the lament of a concertina,
my heart demands a free rein within my breast.

Thus goes a popular song which expresses, with accurate simplicity, the reign of an emotion widely shared.

The bond between the city and life's experiences provides *porteños* with another emotion which does not require physical distance in order to assume the character of painful longing. It so happens that the city permeates the existence of Buenos Aires natives at definite periods of their life. These are the years of childhood and adolescence; the years of youthful adventure, and those of the inevitable entrance into the first stages of maturity. The city is thus destined to remain emotionally tied to those stages of life. Buenos Aires thus becomes the street which was both world and mystery to the child; the places of adolescent wonderment; the locale which is conquered by youthful daring; the true face of things that is slowly revealed to the maturing youth. But this city, thus instilled during well-defined stages of life, is the one that slips away from *porteños* just as life itself slips away. There is no possible return to that intimate Buenos Aires. Its recovery is left up to memory; reliving it is left up to nostalgia. This idealized return which every *porteño* ardently makes, is well reflected in the discreet poetic melancholy of Fernández Moreno:

Mira que te soy fiel: ¡oh ciudad mía!
otra vez en la calle como antes,
silenciosos los pasos o sonantes
conforme a mi tristeza o alegría.

Bajo el sol empolvado de tu día,
bajo los crudos focos centelleantes,
entre el bullicio de tus habitantes
estoy buscando algo todavía.

Look how faithful I am, o dear city!
I am once again in the streets as before
with a light or heavy step
according to my happiness or sadness.

Under the dusty sun of your day,
under the crude shining lights,

among the bustle of your people
I still search for something.[6]

It's not that all *porteños* are constantly at the point of bursting
out into a nostalgic *ubi sunt*. But undoubtedly, the time of their urban emotion is the past. The present or future Buenos Aires is not
the object of their most intimate emotional echoes. It is the Buenos
Aires of yesterday, the one that was frozen forever in that part of
their lives that has already been lived and assigned to the past.

A dual process has been accomplished in the public and social
history of Buenos Aires which is destined to have profound effects
on the feelings of *porteños*. First, the progressive development of urban centers with sufficiently different characteristics to grant them
distinct personalities, that is, the sprouting and spreading of the so-
called *barrios* of the city. Second, the gradual disappearance of all
physical and human singularities as a result of the impact of all that
tends toward the uniformity of depersonalizing urban mass society.
This has resulted in the tendency toward the disappearance of one of
the most pronounced elements of the spiritual geography of Buenos
Aires: the feeling of belonging to the *barrio* in which one lives. As if
the entire city had become inaccessible for life experiences, *porteños* have felt the physical and social immediacy of the *barrio* as
their habitual environment; its physical appearance and prestige, its
history and its legends are measures of true worth. Thus, in a poem
by Ulises Petit de Murat, we hear:

Belgrano: único barrio que he conocido.
Yo calmé mi sed urbana de claridad
en la represa musical de tus astros.
Engarcé mis ojos con tus estrellas
para saciar mi hambre de universo.

Belgrano: only barrio I've ever known.
I quenched my city thirst for clarity
in the musical fountain of your stars.
I linked my eyes to your stars
to satiate my hunger for the universe.[7]

Now that the unique characteristics of *porteño* barrios are disappearing, now that so many things precipitate rootlessness and the
rigors of a lack of solidarity, the natives of Buenos Aires have yet another reason for renewed nostalgia:

Nostalgia de las cosas que han pasado,
arena que la vida se llevó
pesadumbre del barrio que ha cambiado
y amargura del sueño que murió.

Nostalgia for the things that have happened,
sand that life carried off,
grief for the barrio that has changed
and bitterness for the dream that has died.[8]

The emotional reactions and expressions aroused by Buenos Aires in its people have served as repeated themes of Argentine literature from the beginning. Journalistic outpourings, civic orations, didactic prose, history, novels, theater, and essays—all have considered urban themes at length. But poetry has undoubtedly been the favorite medium for the expression of the feelings that bond *porteños* to their city. Patriotic verses attribute to Buenos Aires the revolutionary fervor of the generation of 1810. Romantic poets identify it with their bold ideals, their dreams, their struggles, and their sadness during their days of failure and exile. Bartolomé Mitre provides this example:

¡Oh patria! ¡Oh Buenos Aires! ¡Oh sueño de mi vida!
Como inmortal recuerdo reinas en mi memoria,
Recorriendo los días de dicha promisoria
Que en tu seno amoroso, Buenos Aires, pasé.

Oh homeland! Oh Buenos Aires! Oh dream of my life!
You reign in my memory as an undying feeling,
As a memory of the promise of happy days
That in your loving arms, Buenos Aires, I lived.[9]

The generation of 1880, less lyrically effusive than its romantic predecessors, expresses its love for Buenos Aires, nevertheless, in the steadfast persistence of Carlos Guido Spano, the grandiloquence of Olegario V. Andrade, the deep and decorous patriotism of Rafael Obligado, and the first tirades of Almafuerte. Modernism, in turn, registered, in the midst of its formal audacity and verbal fireworks, the transition from the *Gran Aldea* to a metropolitan exuberance in the *carmina secularia* of Leopoldo Lugones and Rubén Darío:

¡Buenos Aires! Es tu fiesta.
Sentada estás en el solio;
el himno, desde la floresta

hasta el colosal Capitolio
tiende sus mil plumas de aurora.
Flora propia te decora
Mirada universal te mira.
En tu homenaje pasar veo
a Mercurio y su caduceo,
al rey Apolo y la lira.

Buenos Aires! This is your feast.
There you sit on the throne;
from the meadows to the colossal Capitol
a hymn spreads its thousand wings of dawn.
Fitting flowers adorn you,
The eyes of the universe are upon you.
In your homage I see
Mercury and his caduceus,
King Apollo and his lyre as they pass.[10]

From that city, now cosmopolitan metropolis where Mercury's caduceus begins to count much more than Apollo's lyre, Evaristo Carriego decided to preserve poetically a handful of municipal feelings, of humble things and destinies, of emotions and happenings confirming the soul of the suburban *barrio*. He did this in such a way that, as Borges suspected, "I believe that some of his pages will deeply touch many future Argentinean generations." Among them—and why not?—is that picture of the old organ-grinder passing through dusky streets, leaving memories and sadness deep in the poor and suffering souls with his well-known melodies:

Has vuelto organillo. La gente
modesta te mira
pasar melancólicamente.
Pianito que cruzas la calle cansado
moliendo el eterno
familiar motivo que el año pasado
gemía a la luna de invierno,
con tu voz gangosa dirás en la esquina
la canción ingenua, la de siempre, acaso
esa preferida de nuestra vecina
la costurerita que dió aquél mal paso.

You've returned, organ-grinder.
The poor people watch you
melancholically pass by.

Little organ that crosses through the streets,
tired of grinding the same familiar melody
that only last year cried at the winter moon.
With your whining voice,
you will sing your candid little song at the corner,
the usual one, perhaps our neighbor's favorite,
the little seamstress who made
just one mistake.[11]

Jorge Luis Borges himself belongs to a poetic generation which, with deliberate insistence, tried to make Buenos Aires the object of literary accomplishments, both intimate and factual. In fact, between the 1920s and the 1940s, the best efforts of Argentinean lyricism dealt with the rediscovery of the city, whose spirit they hoped to decipher through the interpretation of its emotional signs and symbols. Borges himself, in a neat and calculated mythology of suburbs, of streets softened by trees and sunsets, by more or less mercenary, knife-wielding young bullies, ends up glimpsing its possible eternity:

A mi se me hace cuento que empezó
Buenos Aires: la juzgo tan eterna
como el agua y el aire.

I think it is a fairy tale that
Buenos Aires ever began:
I believe it is as eternal as water and air.[12]

The profound yet simple Baldomero Fernández Moreno takes lyrical possession of the city by walking through it. Everyday things, even the simplest and lowliest, reveal their unsuspected beauty and emotion to the faithful and attentive steps of the poet: the old general store, a well-worn threshold, the ragged ends of a vine, a hedge of *cinacina*, a rain-soaked brick wall . . . And after those nocturnal walks, he was left with the disquieting suspicion that those cordial messages were being lost in a monumental and pragmatic city:

Setenta balcones hay en esta casa
setenta balcones y ninguna flor . . .
¿A sus habitantes, Señor, que les pasa?
¿Odian el perfume, odian el color?

Si no aman las plantas, no amarán el ave,
no sabrán de música, de risas, de amor.

Nunca se oirá un beso, jamás se oirá un clave.
¡Setenta balcones y ninguna flor!

Seventy balconies there are in this house
seventy balconies but not one flower . . .
What is wrong with its dwellers, Lord?
Do they hate perfume; do they hate color?

If they love not plants, they will love not birds;
they know not music, laughter, and love.
Never a kiss shall be heard, never a clavichord shall be heard.
Seventy balconies and not one flower![13]

The tidal wave of immigration at the end of the last century and the beginning of this one precipitated the physical and social change of Buenos Aires. In spite of it all, the city demonstrated an extraordinary power of assimilation and, without painful twists, knew how to incorporate its Galicians, its gringos, its Russians, or its Turks into its fundamental way of life. Nicolás Olivari, among the audacities of his *Musa de la mala pata,* alludes to the manner of such assimilation when he poetically substantiates the memory of his Italian mother struggling with the beat of a *porteño* tango:

Buenos Aires, loma del diablo, Buenos Aires patria del mundo.
Buenos Aires, ancha y larga y grande,
Como aquélla primer palabra en Argentino que le oí a mi
    madre:
    'Yo soy la morocha,
    la mas agraciada . . .'
¡Buenos Aires, morocha de río, de hierro y de asfalto!
Buenos Aires: Seguís siendo la más agraciada de las
    poblaciones!

Buenos Aires, hill of the devil, Buenos Aires, homeland of the
    world.
Buenos Aires, wide, long, and great,
Like that first Argentine word I heard my mother speak:
    I am the *morocha*—the dark beauty—
    the fairest of them all . . .
Buenos Aires, *morocha* of river, steel, and asphalt
Buenos Aires: You are still the fairest of all towns![14]

Furthermore, when the frown and the clenched hand of misery and proletarian resentment start to grow in the city, it finds a way so that the protest will not conflict with adherence to its affective offerings. The poetry of José Portogalo, so precise in its description of rebelliousness, confirms this:

> No sé qué es lo vivido, pero tengo en un sueño
> la mañana que anduvo con un aire de fiesta;
> mil novecientos diez, un coche, calles, plazas
> y una lágrima oscura que humedece la fecha.

> I don't know which part was lived, but I remember in a dream
> a morning that bore an air of festivity,
> nineteen hundred and ten, a car, streets, plazas
> and a dark tear that dampens the date.[15]

And a final testimony. During the same years when poets of the literary vanguard were converting the symbols of Buenos Aires into elements of refined lyricism, the tango song flourished as the deepest expression of the soul of the *porteño*. This coincidence does not lack significance. The new poetry and the lyrics of the new tango allude to the same things. They may, of course, differ in their literary uses and their aesthetic achievements, but the reality alluded to is the same. It is Buenos Aires becoming one with the *porteños'* soul and the *porteños'* sensitivity flowing back in generous torrents over Buenos Aires—and doing so without losing sight of the fact that, more than once, the tango has stirred up a poetic experience, as in Ricardo Güiraldes:

> Tango severo y triste,
> tango de amenaza.
> Tango en que cada nota cae pesada
> y como a despecho, bajo la mano más
> bien destinada para abrazar un cabo de cuchillo.
> . . . .
> Tango fatal, soberbio y bruto.
> Notas arrastradas, perezosamente en un teclado gangoso.
> Tango severo y triste.
> Tango de amenaza.
> Baile de amor y muerte.

> Grave and sad tango,
> threatening tango.
> Tango in which each note looms heavily
> and unwillingly under the hand

more suited to grabbing the hilt of a knife.
. . . .
Tragic, arrogant, rough tango.
Notes slowly drawn from twangy keyboard.
Grave and sad tango.
Threatening tango.
Dance of love and death.[16]

At other times, *lunfardo*, the language of the outskirts, slang, challenges the limits of poetic reach. Thus, in this poem by Carlos de la Púa, so aptly entitled *Los bueyes* (The Oxen), the painter's lyric strokes of the *porteño* watercolor point up sad human experience and a bitter symbol of social reality:

Vinieron de Italia, tenían veinte años,
con un bagayito por toda fortuna
y, sin aliviadas, entre desengaños,
llegaron a viejos sin ventaja alguna.

Mas nunca a sus labios los abrió el reproche:
siempre consecuentes, siempre laburando,
pasaron los días, pasaban las noches,
el viejo en la fragua, la vieja lavando.

Vinieron los hijos, ¡Todos malandrinos!
Vinieron las hijas, ¡Todas engrupidas!
Ellos son borrachos, chorros, asesinos,
y ellas, las mujeres, están en la vida.

Y los pobres viejos, siempre trabajando,
nunca para el yugo se encontraron flojos;
pero a veces, sola, cuando está lavando,
a la vieja el llanto le quema los ojos.

They came from Italy, they were twenty years old,
with a bundle of clothes as their only possession
and, with no relief, through cruel disappointments,
they reached old age with nothing gained.

But their lips never parted to voice a complaint
always diligent, always working,
the days and nights went by,
with the old man at the forge, and the woman washing.

Then sons came: They were all scoundrels!
Then daughters came: They were all falsely vain!

The sons are drunks, thieves, murderers,
and they, the daughters, lead bad lives.

And the poor old people, always working,
never too lazy to bear the yoke;
but sometimes, when she's alone washing,
tears burn the old woman's eyes.[17]

What are these *porteños* like, whose existences are so intertwined with the city in which they live? What does Buenos Aires make of the *porteños*? Much has been written about the sum of faults and virtues which seem to characterize them. But if one definite and persistent trait were to be chosen as the constituent of this unique way of being, it would undoubtedly be the uplifted and satisfied knowledge of their urban rootlessness. An anecdote seems appropriate. It is written by Jerónimo Espejo somewhere in his *Recuerdos históricos* (Historical Remembrances):

—¿De qué país es usted? [preguntó Bolívar al argentino,
   Coronel Manuel Rojas, en Quito, en un banquete].
—Tengo el honor de ser de Buenos Aires.
—Bien se conoce por el aire altanero que representa.
—Es un aire propio de hombres libres—[respondió el argentino
   inclinándose].

—What country are you from? [asked Bolívar of the
   Argentinean Colonel Manuel Rojas at a banquet in Quito].
—I have the honor to be from Buenos Aires.
—It shows in your arrogant manner.
—It is a manner befitting free men—[answered the
   Argentinean with a bow].[18]

Notes

1. Jorge Luis Borges, "Las calles," in *Fervor de Buenos Aires* (1923). See *Obras completas* (Buenos Aires, 1974), p. 17.

2. Padre Domingo de Neyra, *Ordenanzas, Actas primeras de la moderna provincia de San Agustín de Buenos Ayres, Tucumán y Paraguay* (1742?). Ed. facs., Biblioteca Argentina de Libros Raros Americanos, Buenos Aires, Facultad de Filosofía y Letras (1927), vol. 5, p. 1.

3. Carlos Guido Spano, "Trova," in *Poesías; ecos lejanos* (Buenos Aires, 1895), p. 17.

4. Baldomero Fernández Moreno, "Buenos Aires," quoted in César Fernández Moreno, *Introducción a Baldomero Fernández Moreno* (Buenos Aires, 1956), p. 161.

5. José Mármol, "A mi patria," in *Cantos del Peregrino. Prólogo y edición crítica de Rafael Alberto Arrieta* (Buenos Aires, 1953), p. 3.

6. Baldomero Fernández Moreno, "Fidelidad," in *Ciudad* (1915–1949) (Buenos Aires, 1949), pp. 37–38.

7. Ulises Petit de Murat, *Aprendizaje de la Soledad* (Buenos Aires), p. 21.

8. Homero Manzi, "Sur (Tango)," in *Antología; selección y prólogo de Horacio Salas* (Buenos Aires, 1968), p. 136.

9. Bartolomé Mitre, "Recuerdos de Buenos Aires," in *Rimas* (Buenos Aires, 1916), p. 3.

10. Rubén Darío, "Canto a la Argentina (1910)," in *Obras completas* (Madrid, 1953), vol. 5, pp. 1094–1095.

11. Evaristo Carriego, "Has vuelto," in *La canción del barrio, poesías completas* (Buenos Aires, 1917), p. 196.

12. Jorge Luis Borges, "Fundación mítica de Buenos Aires," in *Cuaderno San Martín* (1929), in *Obras completas*, p. 81.

13. Baldomero Fernández Moreno, "Setenta balcones y ninguna flor," in *Ciudad* (1915–1949), pp. 37–38.

14. Nicolás Olivari, "Antiguo almacén 'A la Ciudad de Géneva,'" in *La Musa de la mala pata* (Buenos Aires, 1926), p. 63.

15. José Portogalo, *Poemas (1933–1955)* (1961), p. 196.

16. Ricardo Güiraldes, "Tango," in *El cencerro de cristal* (1915), in *Obras completas* (Buenos Aires, 1962), p. 63.

17. Carlos de la Púa, *La crencha engrasada. Poemas bajos*, 3d ed. (Buenos Aires, 1971), p. 21.

18. Jerónimo Espejo, *Recuerdos históricos. San Martín y Bolívar. Entrevista de Guayaquil (1822)* (Buenos Aires, 1873), p. 71.

Contributors

Educated in Buenos Aires and in Madrid, **Luis A. Arocena** is professor of Spanish and Portuguese at the University of Texas at Austin. He is the author and editor of a dozen books, including studies of El Inca Garcilaso de la Vega, Machiavelli, and Unamuno. His writings have earned the Conde de Cartagena Prize from the Spanish Royal Academy (1957), the National Prize for History from the Argentine government (1962–1965), and the Silver Pen award from the Pen Club of Buenos Aires (1979).

Jonathan C. Brown received his doctorate in history from the University of Texas at Austin. The recipient of a Fulbright-Hays Fellowship, he has been a visiting professor at the University of California at Los Angeles and Santa Barbara. Cambridge University Press published his book entitled *A Socioeconomic History of Argentina, 1776–1860* in 1979.

The acting director for cultural affairs of the Organization of American States, **Dr. Roberto Etchepareborda** of Argentina has had a distinguished career as a historian, university professor and administrator, and public official. He is a member of his nation's National Academy of History and is a corresponding member of the Royal Academy of History of Madrid. Among the most recent contributions on the list of a dozen books which he has published are the following: *Historia de las relaciones internacionales argentinas* (1978), *Rosas; controvertida historiografía* (1972), and *¿Qué fue el carlotismo?* (1971). While in the United States he has been a Fellow of the Woodrow Wilson International Center for Scholars and has served as a visiting professor at the University of North Carolina at Chapel Hill and at the School for International Studies of the Johns Hopkins University in Washington, D.C.

Currently professor and chairman of the department of Spanish and Portuguese at the University of Texas at Austin, **Merlin H. Forster** taught previously at the University of Illinois, where he directed the Center for Latin American and Caribbean Studies. His recent publications include *Tradition and Renewal: Essays in Twentieth Century Latin American Literature and Culture* (1975), *Fire and Ice: The Poetry of Xavier Villaurrutia* (1976), and *Historia de la poesía hispanoamericana* (1980).

A native of Mendoza, **Dr. Christián García-Godoy** received advanced degrees in business and law from the University of Buenos Aires. He has served his government in various technical positions, taught business administration at the University of Buenos Aires, and written on commerce, banking, and the Liberator San Martín. Prime mover and president of the San Martín Society of Washington, Dr. García-Godoy resides in Washington, D.C., where he serves as special advisor for the executive secretary for education, science, and culture of the Organization of American States.

James R. Scobie was professor of history at the University of California at San Diego when he died in 1981, having taught previously at the University of California at Berkeley and at Indiana University. He was the recipient of Doherty, Social Science Research Council, O.A.S., and Guggenheim fellowships. His published books include *Revolution on the Pampas; A Social History of Argentine Wheat, 1860–1910* (1964), *Argentina: A City and a Nation* (2nd ed., 1971), and *Buenos Aires: Plaza to Suburb, 1870–1910* (1974). His books twice earned him honorable mention for the Bolton Prize, and he won the Faja de Honor of the Argentine Society of History, the "Todo es Historia" Prize in 1976, and election as a corresponding member of the Argentine National Academy of History.

Trained at Columbia University, **Susan M. Socolow** is a member of the faculty of Emory University. She has also taught at the State University of New York at Plattsburgh. She has been awarded fellowships by the Tinker Foundation, the National Endowment for the Humanities/NDEA TITLE VI, and the Fulbright program. Her book *The Merchants of Viceregal Buenos Aires: Family and Commerce, 1778–1810* was published by Cambridge University Press in 1978 and received honorable mention for the Bolton Prize.

Mark D. Szuchman is a member of the faculty of Florida International University, where he is the associate director of the Latin

American and Caribbean Center. He received his doctorate in history from the University of Texas at Austin and has been the recipient of grants from the Social Science Research Council and the Department of State. He has also received Doherty and NDEA TITLE VI fellowships. He is the author of a book entitled *Mobility and Integration in Urban Argentina: Córdoba in the Liberal Era*, published in 1980 by the University of Texas Press.

A member of the faculty at the University of North Carolina, **Joseph S. Tulchin** received his doctorate from Harvard University. He has also taught at Yale University and served as Fulbright Lecturer at the National University of Buenos Aires. Professor Tulchin's monographic and edited work includes: *The Aftermath of War: The Latin American Policy of the United States, 1918–1925* (1971), *Latin America in the Year 2000* (1975), and *Hemispheric Perspectives on the United States. Papers from the New World Conference* (1978).

Since completing his graduate studies at Stanford University, **Richard J. Walter** has taught at Washington University in St. Louis, where he is currently professor and chairman of the department of history. Recipient of a fellowship from the Doherty Foundation and a research grant from the Social Science Research Council, Dr. Walter has published two books: *Student Politics in Argentina: The University Reform and Its Effects* (1968) and *The Socialist Party of Argentina, 1890–1930* (1977).

Stanley R. Ross is a professor in the history department at the University of Texas at Austin. He is also the director of the Border Studies Project and of the Office of Mexican Studies at the same institution. He is the author of numerous books and articles.

Thomas F. McGann is a professor in the history department at the University of Texas at Austin. He is the author of numerous books and articles on Latin American history. His most recent publication was a translation of José L. Romero's *A History of Argentine Political Thought*, Stanford University Press.

Index

TABLE OF CONTENTS

RED SOX — TRIUMPHS
AND TRAGEDIES

Two seasons have passed since "This Date In Boston Red Sox History" made its appearance in early April 1978. Many things of importance to Red Sox fans have occurred during those years. Players came to Fenway Park, some stayed, some left. History of a good nature was made and history of a bad nature was endured. In this first section you will find those entries under the appropriate date. Here is the meat of this book, a section which was enthusiastically received by all when "This Date In Boston Red Sox History" was published. In addition to those items of recent interest, I have added many new facts relating to years past. In the original volume I attempted to find an item for every day in the year. While I have not attempted this in *Red Sox Triumphs and Tragedies*, you will find a good cross section and I hope that that special date to you is one of them. If not, you are still sure to find many items that will interest you. All of this adds to the mini history of our beloved Red Sox. Facts are listed in chronological order by month and day. In the listings where a player's name appears followed by the letter B, this indicates the date he was born. The year or years are the period he played for Boston, followed by his position. A single listing of a year followed by a dash indicates he is still with the team. You may wish to keep updated by writing in the year he departs when that event occurs.

So let's start our second trip down through the years. I, again, hope your trip is an enjoyable one.

JANUARY 1

1960 — The Boston baseball club organized under the laws of the State of Maine and known as The Boston American League Baseball Company is officially liquidated.

January 3

1950 — Jim Dwyer — B   1979   OF

January 5

1934 — During the overhaul of Fenway Park, a four alarm fire destroys much of the new bleacher section. It took more than five hours to control the fire.

January 6

1963 — In a press conference at Fenway Park, Vice President Dick O'Connell of the Sox and President Bill Sullivan of the football Boston Patriots announce that the Patriots will play their 1963 and 1964 home games at Fenway Park. It is believed former Sox outfielder Dom DiMaggio (one of the Patriots ten owners) helped swing the deal. Red Sox owner, Tom Yawkey, had discontinued football at Fenway in 1956. Pro football was once played at Fenway Park by the Boston Redskins (now Washington) and the former Boston Yanks. It was also the site for many home football games of Boston College and Boston University.

January 7

1933 — Red Sox sign infielder Barney Friberg and trade first baseman Al Van Camp to Louisville for catcher Merv Shea.

January 8

1979 — Outfielder Jim Rice signs a seven year contract for an estimated $5.2 to $6 million. The contract made Rice the highest paid player in total salary in baseball. The contract reportedly includes an up front bonus of more than $1 million. Of course it also makes him the highest paid player in Red Sox history.

January 9

1904 — The Boston American League Club secures a seven year lease of the Huntington Avenue Grounds.

1941 — Ted Williams named as the right fielder on The Sporting News All Star Team.

January 13

1934 — Outfielders Mel Almada, George Stumpf and pitcher Jud McLaughlin optioned to Kansas City. Pitcher Curt Fullerton and third baseman Urbane Pickering released to the same club.

January 19

1979 — Free agent right handed pitcher Steve Renko signed to a one year contract for an estimated $100,000.

January 20

1934 — The Red Sox sign pitcher Herb Pennock who had been released by the New York Yankees on January 5.

January 23

1954 — Garry Hancock — B   1978   OF

January 27

1936 — First baseman Babe Dahlgren optioned to Syracuse.

January 29

1941 — Third baseman Marv Owen released.

January 30

1978 — Infielder Steve Dillard traded to the Detroit Tigers for cash and pitchers Mike Burns and Frank Harris, who were assigned to the minor leagues.

January 31

1940 — Catcher Moe Berg retired as a player is named as a Red Sox coach. Pitcher Mickey Harris purchased from Little Rock.

1949 — Fred Kendall — B   1978   C

FEBRUARY 2

1954 — John Tudor — B   1979   P

February 4

1955 — Gary Allenson — B   1979   C

February 6

1920 — Outfielder Joe Wilhoit sold to Toledo. In 1919 at Wichita, Kansas of the Western League he hit in 69 consecutive games. During his streak he went to bat 299 times, making 151 hits for a .505 batting average. He had 5 home runs, 8 triples, 23 doubles and 115 singles. (June 14 to Aug. 19)

February 7

1917 — Boston's beloved sports writer Tim Murnane dies suddenly.

February 11

1918 — Edward G. Barrow named Red Sox manager after resigning the International League presidency.

1920 — Red Sox increase ticket prices to 50¢ for bleachers, 75¢ for pavilion, $1.00 for grandstand plus war tax.

February 12

1979 — Infielder-outfielder Dave Coleman traded to the Minnesota Twins for third baseman Larry Wolfe. Coleman, on the Pawtucket roster, was assigned to Toledo.

February 17

1937 — First baseman Ellsworth Dahlgren sold to the New York Yankees.

1938 — Catcher George Dickey optioned to Portland of the Pacific Coast League.

1978 — The Red Sox sign free agent relief pitcher Tom Burgmeier.

February 18

1939 — Catcher George Dickey sold to Oklahoma City and pitcher Ted Olson sold to Louisville.

February 19

1962 — Sneak thieves break into the Red Sox minor league clubhouse at Ocala, Florida and steal $2,000 worth of shoes, caps, gloves, jackets and personal equipment causing the players to practice in an odd assortment of equipment.

February 20

1904 — Carl M. Green appointed Business Manager.

1934 — First baseman Dale Alexander traded to Jersey City for pitchers Spike Merena and Jim McCloskey.

February 22

1941 — Pitcher Yank Terry optioned to San Diego.

MARCH 5

1902 — Ticket prices for the coming season are announced as 25¢ general admission, 50¢ for the pavilion and 75¢ for the grandstand. The rationale for the price increase is that the American League has more star players and plays better baseball than the National League.

March 8

1954 — Win Remmerswaal — B   1979   P

March 10

1979 — Red Sox decided to open their clubhouse in Winter Haven to all members of the media, regardless of sex. At 10:01 A.M. well known authoress Doris Kearns Goodwin becomes the first woman to enter the Sox clubhouse. At the time all the players were on the field.

March 12

1963 — A bill is introduced into the Massachusetts State Legislature to make it illegal to use profanity at professional sports events in that state. Anyone convicted would be subject to a $50.00 fine. The bill was inspired by the loud and vulgar barrage directed at Cleveland Indian Jim Piersall at Fenway Park in 1961.

March 13

1941 — First baseman Tony Lupien optioned to Louisville.

March 15

1960 — Manager Billy Jurges reports he is impressed by a rookie second baseman who is the talk of the Scottsdale, Arizona spring training camp. He says if the rookie were an outfielder he would make the team now. The rookie's name—Carl Yastrzemski.

1979 — Outfielder Jim Dwyer acquired from the San Francisco Giants for a player to be named later.

Utility player Mike Easler traded to the Pittsburgh Pirates for minor leaguers outfielder George Hill and pitcher Martin Rivas (who were assigned to Pawtucket) and an unspecified amount of cash. Easler had been obtained from Pittsburgh on October 28, 1978. Hill was later dropped from the deal.

March 16

1920 — Boston's first spring training game upon return to the former Hot Springs, Arkansas training site is a 4 to 3 victory over Pittsburgh.

March 19

1920 — Outfielder Armando Marsans purchased from the New York Yankees.

March 21

1938 — Outfielder Ted Williams optioned to Minneapolis.

March 22

1941 — Pitcher Bill Butland optioned to Louisville; pitcher Alex Mustaikes given outright release and pitcher Bill Sayles sold outright to Louisville.

March 23

1960 — Red Sox manager Billy Jurges acknowledges a young catcher in the spring training camp may have won the regular catching job over veteran Sammy White. His name—Haywood Sullivan.

1978 — Pitcher Rick Kreuger traded to the Cleveland Indians for infielder Frank Duffy.

March 26

1909 — Boston makes a triple play during a spring training game at Memphis, Tennessee. Amby McConnell catching a line drive and relaying the ball to Heinie Wagner at second who relayed it to Jake Stahl at first to complete the

March 26 (continued)

play. By an odd coincidence these same three players were later (July 19) the victims in the major league's first unassisted triple play by Neal Ball of Cleveland.

1978 — Infielder Tommy Helms released.

March 27

1939 — Pitcher Monty Weaver purchased from Washington for less than the waiver price — $5,000.

March 28

1978 — Second baseman Denny Doyle is released.

March 30

1955 — Pitcher Sid Hudson released and named as a Red Sox scout.

1978 — Pitchers Rick Wise and Mike Paxton, infielder Ted Cox and catcher Bo Diaz traded to the Cleveland Indians for pitcher Dennis Eckersley and catcher Fred Kendall.

Pitcher Jim Burton traded to the New York Mets for infielder Leo Foster who was assigned to Pawtucket. Burton was assigned to Tidewater.

March 31

1936 — Pitcher Alex Mustaikis and outfielder Skinny Graham sent to Little Rock.

APRIL 1

1936 — Infielder Dib Williams optioned to Syracuse.

April 2

1938 — Pitcher Jim Henry and third baseman Jim Tabor optioned to Minneapolis.

April 4

1919 — Red Sox defeat the New York Giants 5 to 3 in the first game at their new spring training site in Tampa, Florida.

1922 — Second baseman Del Pratt named Red Sox team captain.

April 5

1934 — Injuring his arm in an exhibition game at Orlando Florida, pitcher Lefty Grove threatens to quit baseball for good.

1978 — Pitcher Jim Willoughby sold to the Chicago White Sox.

Shortstop Ramon Aviles sold to the Philadelphia Phillies.

April 7

1908 — Playing at Ft. Wayne, Indiana the entire Boston team, led by President John I. Taylor, visited Chick Stahl's grave and decorated it with flowers.

April 7 (continued)

1978 — The Red Sox lose to the Chicago White Sox 6 to 5 before 50,754 fans a record opening day crowd for Chicago's Comiskey Park.

April 8

1927 — Red Sox manager Bill Carrigan, entering his second term as the Sox field boss catches the last two innings of an exhibition game with the Boston Braves.

April 9

1960 — The Cleveland Indian—Boston Red Sox exhibition game at City Park Stadium in New Orleans, La. marks the first time blacks were permitted to sit among whites in the grandstand at that ball park.

April 10

1946 — Bob Watson — B   1979   1B-DH

1960 — In an exhibition game at New Orleans, La. Ted Williams becomes the first batter to hit a ball completely out of City Park Stadium.

April 11

1961 — Carl Yastrzemski strokes his first major league hit, a single against Ray Herbert of the Kansas City A's on Opening Day at Fenway Park.

April 12

1909 — Boston loses 8 to 1 to the Philadelphia A's in the first game ever played in Philadelphia's Shibe Park.

1911 — Boston loses 8 to 5 to the Washington Senators in the first game ever played in Washington's Griffith Stadium.

April 13

1926 — New York first baseman Lou Gehrig working a double steal in the first inning with Babe Ruth steals home against the Sox.

1963 — Pitcher Dave Morehead, in his first major league start, shuts out the Washington Senators 3 to 0. The first Red Sox rookie to break in with a shutout since Dave Ferriss in 1945.

April 14

1938 — The Red Sox lose an exhibition game to Holy Cross College 3 to 2. Could this be a sign of things to come?

1940 — Pitcher Ted Olson sold to Baltimore.

1953 — The season opening series with Washington is postponed by Fenway Park's first snow out since 1933.

1956 — Bob Sprowl — B   1978   P

1969 — 35,343 fans fill Fenway Park for a record opening day crowd as the Red Sox play Baltimore.

April 15

1931 — An eighth inning double steal by New York Yankees Lou Gehrig and Tony Lazzeri finds Gehrig stealing home against the Sox.

1935 — Catcher Gordie Hinkle optioned to Syracuse.

1937 — Infielder John Kroner sold to the Cleveland Indians.

1939 — Pitcher Bill Kersieck sent to Louisville.

1945 — Ted Sizemore — B   1979   2B-C

April 16

1935 — Free agent catcher Moe Berg signed. He had been released by the Cleveland Indians after the 1934 season.

1941 — First baseman Paul Campbell optioned to Montreal.

1960 — Outfielder Jerry Mallett sold to Indianapolis.

1967 — In an 18 inning game against New York, Carl Yastrzemski and Tony Conigliaro each have five hits.

1978 — Texas Ranger pitcher Len Barker uncorks a wild pitch which lands part way up the screen behind home plate. It was one of the wildest pitches ever seen at Fenway Park.

April 18

1960 — Washington Senator pitcher Camilo Pascual strikes out 15 Red Sox, to set a Washington club record, on his way to a 10 to 1 victory on Opening Day at Washington.

1978 — Pitcher Reggie Cleveland sold to the Texas Rangers.

1979 — Carl Yastrzemski plays his 2000th game in the outfield for Boston. Boston vs Milwaukee at Fenway Park.

April 19

1902 — 15,000 jam the Huntington Avenue Grounds for opening day as Boston defeats Baltimore 7 to 6.

1904 — Better than 28,000 fans see the two games with Washington at the Huntington Avenue Grounds.

1960 — Red Sox catcher Haywood Sullivan makes his first major league hit, a single to left center off New York Yankee pitcher Jim Coates. It took him five years and 16 at bats to make his first hit. He first went to bat for Boston in 1955.

April 20

1922 — The Red Sox hit six home runs against Philadelphia, including two by first baseman George Burns.

1951 — The Red Sox lose to the Philadelphia A's at Fenway Park for the first time since 1948.

April 20 (continued)

1954 — Mike O'Berry — B   1979   C

1978 — Carl Yastrzemski's fourth inning double vs the Milwaukee Brewers is the 2,735th hit of his career.

April 22

1913 — Steve Yerkes' single off Washington pitcher Bert Gallia scores three men.

1961 — Pumpsie Green's 11th inning home run gives the Bosox a 7 to 6 victory at Chicago, snapping a 13 game losing streak at Chicago dating back to August 26, 1959.

1978 — 36,005 fans jam Fenway Park for the fourth largest crowd in the Park's history as the Cleveland Indians defeat the Sox 13 to 4, ending an eight game Boston winning streak.

April 23

1919 — Before the largest American League crowd on record for New York the Red Sox defeat the Yankees 10-0 at the Polo Grounds.

1966 — The Red Sox make a triple play against Cleveland. Max Alvis hit a ball to second baseman George Smith who threw to shortstop Rico Petrocelli covering second to retire Vic Davalillo with Petrocelli throwing on to George Scott at first base to get Alvis. Gary Bell on third base broke for home and was out at the plate—Scott to catcher Bob Tillman.

1978 — 36,388 fans show up for a doubleheader at Fenway Park with the Cleveland Indians. This is the second largest crowd in Fenway history to-date.

Butch Hobson became the 15th player in major league history to drive in one or more runs in ten consecutive games. Cleveland and Boston split the doubleheader with Cleveland getting 19 hits in the second game.

April 24

1906 — Boston makes 20 hits in a game at Washington, winning 19 to 2.

1942 — At Fenway Park the Sox lead the Yankees 5 to 1 in the ninth. Six hits, including a Joe Gordon home run and doubles by Frank Crosetti and Buddy Rosar result in seven runs and an 8 to 5 Yank win.

1946 — Ted Williams hits into three double plays as New York defeats the Sox 12 to 5 at Fenway Park.

1977 — Pitcher Ferguson Jenkins and the Red Sox defeat the Toronto Blue Jays 9 to 0 at Toronto for the first ever shut out game at Toronto's Exhibition Stadium.

April 25

1940 — Catcher Joe Glenn purchased from the St. Louis Browns for just over the waiver price.

1960 — Reports emanate from Boston that there is considerable discontent among Red Sox players who are openly ridiculing manager Billy Jurges.

April 25 (continued)

1961 — Exactly two weeks after helping Boston Celtics win the world's basketball championship Gene Conley wins his first American League game for the Red Sox, a 6 to 1 win over Washington at Fenway Park.

April 26

1920 — Everett Scott plays in his 534th consecutive game, a streak which started June 20, 1916. This set a major league record. Fred Luderus of the Philadelphia Phillies (N.L.) had played in 533 consecutive games.

1935 — Shortstop Joe Cronin commits three errors in one game.

1937 — Second baseman Bobby Doerr hit on the head by a pitch. He was hospitalized with a slight concussion. Theory—this may have led to the headaches which plagued him later in his career.

1939 — Outfielder Fabian Gaffke optioned to Louisville.

April 28

1922 — Third baseman Joe Dugan, second baseman Del Pratt and first baseman George Burns make a triple play against New York.

1941 — Pitcher Woody Rich released to Louisville.

1944 — Outfielder Woody Wheaton of Philadelphia broke up a 16 inning game with a hit to give the A's a 7 to 5 win over the Red Sox. It was Wheaton's only hit in eight at bats in the game.

1978 — Boston city building commissioner sets Fenway Park crowd capacity for baseball at 36,005. Actual seats 33,505 and 2500 standing room.

Pitcher Louis Tiant's three strikeouts of Texas Ranger batters moves him ahead of Bill Monbouquette into third place on the all time Red Sox list of strikeouts. He now has 972 as a Red Sox and only Joe Wood and Cy Young are ahead of him on the all time list. He is 29th on the major league all time list.

April 29

1903 — In a 9 to 5 defeat at the hands of Washington, Boston pitcher Norwood Gibson walks nine and has eight bases stolen against him.

1970 — By striking out five times Oakland A's outfielder Rick Monday completes a string of striking out nine consecutive times against Boston pitching. He had four strike outs on April 28.

1972 — In a nine inning game against the Texas Rangers, Red Sox pitchers issue twelve walks.

April 30

1906 — Boston makes 23 hits in a game at New York, winning 13 to 4.

1936 — Slugger Jimmie Foxx strikes out four times.

April 30 (continued)

1979 — In the 4th inning of a game at Oakland Carl Yastrzemski grounds out in his 10,000th major league at bat.

MAY 1

1906 — An 8 to 0 loss at New York starts a string of 20 consecutive losses through May 24th.

1929 — Eleven Red Sox players have one or more assists in a game against the Philadelphia Athletics.

Boston and Philadelphia use 35 players in a game, an American League record at the time. (Boston 21, Philadelphia 14).

1935 — Infielder Dib Williams purchased from the Philadelphia Athletics.

Boston and Philadelphia tie their record of using 35 players in a game set May 1, 1929 (Boston 20, Philadelphia 15).

1944 — Washington second baseman George Myatt had a big day against the Sox when he paced a 20 hit Senator attack with five singles and a double in six at bats.

May 2

1901 — Boston scores ten runs in the third inning against Philadelphia and wins the game 23 to 12.

1904 — Boston Judge Emmons announces extra police will be assigned to the Boston ball parks to stop the gambling there.

1938 — Third baseman Pinky Higgins equals the modern major league record by making four errors in one game.

1953 — Larry Wolfe — B   1979   3B

1960 — The courts approved the dissolution of the Boston American League Baseball Company and approved the new name, the Boston Red Sox. Since there is no corporate set up, it is assumed Tom Yawkey is running the Red Sox as a personal investment.

1971 — Boston pitchers walk 13 Minnesota Twins batters in a nine inning game.

May 3

1922 — Second baseman Del Pratt accepts 13 chances against Washington.

May 4

1918 — In a game against the New York Yankees at Boston pitcher Babe Ruth is the victim of 8 sacrifices (6 bunts, 2 flies) a major league record.

1952 — A nine inning Cleveland Indian—Red Sox game takes 3 hours and 32 minutes to play, setting a record for the longest American League nine inning game.

1962 — The Chicago White Sox use 5 pitchers against the Red Sox in the fifth inning.

May 5

1909 — New York pitcher Lew Brockett has nine assists in a 2 to 0 victory over Boston.

1925 — Outfielder Bobby Veach and pitcher Alex Ferguson traded to the New York Yankees for pitcher Ray Francis and $8,000.

1967 — Carl Yastrzemski hits the 100th home run of his major league career. It came off Baltimore Oriole pitcher Eddie Fisher in a game at Fenway Park.

May 6

1911 — The first triple play in New York Yankee history is made against the Red Sox in a game at New York won by the Yankees 6 to 3.

1934 — The Red Sox make four triples in an inning against Detroit. The inning developed as follows: Roy Johnson grounded out to Charlie Gehringer. Carl Reynolds tripled to center. Moose Solters tripled to right center, scoring Reynolds. Rick Ferrell, after two strikes, tripled to right center, scoring Solters. Bucky Walters tripled to left center, scoring Ferrell. Chief Hogsett relieved Firpo Marberry. Rube Walberg sent a low fly over third baseman Marv Owen's head for a single, scoring Walters. Max Bishop bunted, but Owen made a two base throwing error, Walberg scoring. Billy Werber singled, scoring Bishop. Eddie Morgan fouled out to catcher Mickey Cochrane. Roy Johnson doubled to right, scoring Werber. Reynolds singled, Johnson stopping at third base. Solters singled, scoring Johnson, Reynolds went to 3rd. Steve Larkin relieved Hogsett. Ferrell walked to load the bases. Walters, after two strikes, doubled scoring Reynolds and Solters with Ferrell going to third. Walberg singled, scoring Ferrell and Walters. Bishop hit to shortstop Billy Rogell forcing Walberg for the final out. That was 12 runs scored for Boston.

1966 — Boston pitchers strike out 17 Minnesota Twins batters in nine innings.

1970 — Milwaukee pitcher Bob Bolin strikes out eleven Red Sox batters.

1977 — California Angel pitcher Nolan Ryan strikes out fifteen Red Sox on the way to an 8 to 4 win at Boston.

1978 — In the first game of a doubleheader against the Chicago White Sox at Fenway Park, Carl Yastrzemski gets his 2,750th major league hit. His four total bases in the twin bill give him a career total of 4,475, moving him past Hall of Famers Paul Waner and Nap Lajoie among the all time leaders

Rookie pitcher Jim Wright pitches a 3 to 0 shut out over Chicago in his first major league start, becoming the first Red Sox rookie to pitch a shut out in his first start since Billy Rohr did it in 1967.

In the first game of the doubleheader Jim Rice gets his 600th major league hit.

May 7

1903 — The start of great baseball rivalry as Bill Dineen defeats the New York Highlanders (now Yankees) at the Huntington Avenue Grounds 6 to 2 behind Hobe Ferris' home run.

May 7 (continued)

1918 — Babe Ruth hits a home run for the third consecutive game.

1961 — First baseman Vic Wertz hits the 250th home run of his career at Minneapolis off Camilo Pascual of the Minnesota Twins.

May 8

1918 — Washington scores eight runs in the fifth inning and five in the sixth against the Red Sox.

1941 — Pitcher Tex Hughson released to Louisville.

1946 — Pitcher Mickey Harris gives up 17 hits in 8-2/3 innings as the Red Sox defeat the Chicago White Sox 14 to 10 as the Red Sox set a club record to that date for consecutive wins at 13, a streak which continued to 15 games.

1976 — The Texas Rangers make 27 hits and score 18 runs (9 of which were scored in one inning) in a doubleheader against Boston.

1978 — Kansas City Royal manager Whitey Herzog employs a shift against Red Sox slugger Jim Rice in the third inning, by putting four men in the outfield leaving a hole at second base. Rice lined out but got a hit against the shift his next time up. This was a night game at Fenway Park.

May 9

1903 — Umpire Caruthers calls a ball on New York pitcher Tannehill as he starts to pitch and Stahl hits it for a double. The New York players storm the plate with Tannehill and second baseman Williams being put out of the game. Boston won 12 to 5 at Boston.

1918 — Babe Ruth hits three doubles, a triple and a single in five at bats as Boston loses to Washington.

1922 — Harry Heilmann of Detroit hit a home run that cleared the left field wall at Fenway Park for one of the longest hits ever seen at the ball park up until this date.

1940 — Pitcher Woody Rich optioned to Louisville.

1941 — Red Sox complete the purchase of pitcher Dick Newsome.

1961 — Carl Yastrzemski hits his first major league home run. The pitcher was former Red Sox Jerry Casale of the Los Angeles Angels. The game was at Chavez Ravine ball park.

May 10

1930 — Tom Oliver's 18 game hitting streak ends.

1953 — Del Wilber's pinch hit home run is his second consecutive homer in a pinch hitting role. The first occurred on May 6.

In a game with the New York Yankees Jim Piersall restrains Billy Goodman from challenging umpire Duffy so forcibly that Goodman is out for three weeks with bruised ribs.

1960 — First baseman Vic Wertz' grand slam home run off Chicago White Sox pitcher Early Wynn allows him to pass 1000 life time RBI's.

May 10 (continued)

1979 — Carl Yastrzemski's eighth inning single against the California Angels at Fenway Park was the 2900th hit of his career. Red Sox make a triple play against the California Angels at Fenway park. Remy caught Joe Rudi's pop up in short right and threw to Burleson to double Rod Carew at second, and Burleson relayed to first to Scott to nip Don Baylor trying to get back.

May 11

1903 — In a game at Cleveland, seven of Cleveland's twelve hits are doubles or better. Score, Cleveland 6, Boston 5.

1904 — Pitcher Cy Young completes 25-1/3 hitless innings, retiring 76 batters without giving up a hit—a string which started on April 25th.

1919 — John E. Stanton elected Red Sox Vice President.

1976 — As the Red Sox were losing 10 straight games a Boston radio station invited a modern day Salem witch to help break the slump. Perhaps it worked as on May 12th they defeated the Cleveland Indians at Cleveland 6 to 4 in 12 innings.

1978 — Left handed Red Sox pitcher Bill Lee makes his 300th major league appearance, becoming only the fifth Red Sox pitcher in their history to appear that often. The game was at Baltimore with the Sox and Lee winning 5 to 4. It was Lee's fifth victory of the season against no losses.

May 12

1938 — Pitcher Byron Humphrey sold to San Diego of the Pacific Coast League.

1946 — Following Mickey Harris's 3 to 1 victory over the New York Yankees before 63,193 at Yankee Stadium, the New York writers for the first time say, "The Red Sox will win the pennant".

May 13

1901 — Second baseman Hobe Ferris has 10 put outs vs. Washington.

1909 — In an 8 to 1 victory at Cleveland, Boston belts former teammate Cy Young for 17 hits, Harry Hooper collecting four of them.

1911 — In a game at Detroit the Red Sox trailed 10 to 1 after 5 innings, but went on to win 13 to 11 in 10 innings. Boston out hit Detroit 20 to 14. Ty Cobb had a third inning grand slam homer and Duffy Lewis had one in the ninth for Boston.

1913 — Boston hits 4 sacrifice flies against the Tigers, in a 6 to 1 victory at Detroit.

1914 — Catcher Les Nunamaker sold to the New York Yankees.

May 14

1932 — Pitcher Pete Donohue given an unconditional release. He later signed with Jersey City.

May 14 (continued)

1934 — First baseman Joe Judge unconditionally released setting off a controversy as to why he was not retained as a coach instead of Bibb Falk. The Red Sox said they had to get within the player limit and that in the spring Judge had a choice of two contracts, either as a coach or a player. He chose the latter.

1938 — Pitcher Dick Midkiff optioned to Minneapolis.

1941 — Pitcher Herb Hash optioned to Louisville.

1942 — Tony Perez — B   1980   1B

1946 — Sox pitcher Dave Ferriss uses only 78 pitches scoring a 3 to 0 two hit win over the Chicago White Sox.

1951 — Stan Papi — B   1979   IF

1961 — In the ninth inning against Washington, Boston pitchers walk three pinch hitters.

The Red Sox go scoreless in 27 consecutive innings against the Washington Senators, including 10-1/3 hitless at one point during the series which started May 12.

1966 — The Red Sox play before 42,655 fans at the California Angels Anaheim Stadium, a day game record for that field.

May 15

1903 — Detroit defeats Boston 8 to 6 at Detroit making five triples and two home runs. Boston outfielder Pat Dougherty misjudged many long hits.

1917 — A 6 to 5 win at Cleveland gives Babe Ruth his eighth consecutive win since the start of the season.

1921 — Dud Lee, St. Louis Brown second baseman, accepts 16 chances against the Red Sox in a ten inning game.

1934 — Infielder Fred Muller and $20,000 sent to the New York Yankees for infielder Lyn Lary. Muller was optioned to Newark.

1935 — Second baseman Eddie "Doc" Farrell is released.

1960 — A Fenway Park home run wins a bear cub for utility man Bobby Thomson. The cub was awarded by the State of Maine. Thomson presented it to a local zoo. The zoo did not need to hit a home run to win the prize.

1961 — Carl Yastrzemski hits his first home run at Fenway Park.

1977 — For the second day in a row the Red Sox play before one of the largest baseball crowds in Seattle's Kingdome—47,353. On May 14 attendance was 52,485.

May 16

1903 — Despite six errors, Boston beats Detroit 9 to 6.

1947 — The Red Sox play the New York Yankees before a crowd of 74,747, the largest to attend a single night game at Yankee Stadium.

1968 — Pitcher John Wyatt sold to the New York Yankees.

May 17

1909 — Red Sox catcher Bill Carrigan and Detroit infielder George Moriarty are suspended by league President Ban Johnson for fighting during a game at Detroit. Carrigan had to be escorted from the park by the police.

1921 — Shortstop Everett Scott plays in his 700th consecutive game.

1922 — Boston defeats St. Louis 4 to 3 scoring 4 runs in the ninth inning on two errors, a walk, single, bunt and a sacrifice fly.

May 18

1921 — The Detroit Tigers make a triple play against the Red Sox (Young to Bush) Everett Scott lined to second baseman Ralph Young, who tagged Stuffy McInnis and threw to shortstop Donie Bush who tagged out Tim Hendryx.

1937 — Catcher Rick Ferrell suffers a fractured right hand.

1946 — A 18 to 8 Boston win at St. Louis gives pitcher Mickey Harris his seventh straight victory since the start of the season.

1950 — Pitcher Joe Dobson pitches his 100th major league win a 6 to 1 victory over the Detroit Tigers.

1961 — Pitcher Don Schwall recalled from Seattle.

May 19

1903 — Boston beats Detroit 3 to 2 at Detroit. Nineteen players struck out in this game.

May 20

1903 — In losing to St. Louis 4 to 3, Boston breaks St. Louis pitcher Willie Sudhoff's three consecutive game shut out streak.

1910 — Infielder Charlie French sold to the Chicago White Sox.

1918 — Sox pitcher Carl Mays beans Cleveland's Tris Speaker in a game at Fenway Park causing words to be exchanged. Mays claimed he didn't mean it. Speaker replied he had worked on the same team with Mays long enough to know differently.

1977 — The Milwaukee Brewers make 33 total bases at Fenway Park.

1978 — Jim Rice's third inning home run at Detroit is his 100th career home run.

May 21

1921 — Pitcher Allen Sothoron purchased from the St. Louis Browns.

1936 — Pitcher Johnny Welch sent to San Diego. (Supposedly he did not keep in shape).

1942 — Ted Williams hits the 100th home run of his career during a game at League Park, Cleveland.

May 21 (continued)

1961 — Rookie pitcher Don Schwall wins his first major league start 2 to 1 over the Chicago White Sox.

1979 — Infielder Frank Duffy placed on the designated for assignment list for the purpose of dealing him away. No longer on the active roster the Sox have 10 days in which to deal him.

May 22

1977 — Pitcher Mike Paxton recalled from Pawtucket.

May 23

1951 — Pitcher Mel Parnell makes four hits and allows the same while shutting out the St. Louis Browns.

1978 — American League owners, meeting in Chicago, give unanimous approval of the sale of the Red Sox to a group headed by Mrs. Jean Yawkey, Haywood Sullivan and Buddy LeRoux for a possible record professional sports sale price of $20.5 million.

May 24

1903 — Defeating the Chicago White Sox at Chicago 7 to 0, Boston makes 14 hits.

1952 — New York Yankee Bill Martin and Boston's Jim Piersall trade punches under the stands before a Yankee—Red Sox game.

May 25

1939 — Cleveland Indians third baseman Ken Keltner hits three consecutive home runs in a single game against the Red Sox.

1977 — The Minnesota Twins make 24 hits against the Red Sox as both clubs have a combined total of 36 hits.

May 27

1914 — Pitcher Guy Cooper sent to Boston from the New York Yankees as part of consideration for catcher Les Nunamaker going to New York on May 13.

1920 — 45 runners were left on base in a Boston—New York doubleheader.

1960 — A season long dusting duel between the Red Sox and the Washington Senators erupts into a free for all between the clubs touched off by close pitches by Senator Camilo Pascual to Pete Runnels. The game took place at Washington.

1961 — Red Sox complete 98-1/3 innings without making an error tying the American League record, (including 9 games in a row). In the ninth inning, with 2 out, at Baltimore centerfielder Gary Geiger drops an easy fly ball to end the string.

May 28

1914 — Shortstop Everett Scott's error against Cleveland lets in two runs and ends George Foster's string of 42-2/3 scoreless innings.

1918 — Boston defeats Chicago 1 to 0 on Joe Bush's one hitter. Bush also knocked in the Red Sox run.

1941 — Pitcher Oscar Judd optioned to Louisville.

May 29

1909 — Home Run Baker's drive was the first ever over the right field wall in Philadelphia's Shibe Park. It came off Boston pitcher Frank Arellanes. Ten Boston batters struck out in this game.

1912 — The Red Sox behind pitcher Joe Wood defeat the Washington Senators at Fenway Park 21 to 8.

1972 — Milwaukee Brewer outfielder Billy Conigliaro ties a Milwaukee team record of 11 total bases by hitting two home runs and a triple at Fenway park.

1979 — First baseman George Scott upset over being benched demands that the Red Sox trade him.

May 30

1908 — Cy Young pitches a one hitter against Washington. Third baseman Harry Lord led the Boston attack with four hits in five at bats.

1916 — Washington leaves 15 men on base against Boston.

1922 — Boston manager Hugh Duffy celebrated his 35th anniversary in baseball.

1933 — First baseman Dale Alexander twists his knee in a game at Philadelphia, an injury which led to a conclusion of his baseball career. A then new method of treatment, diathermy, led to third degree burns and a gangrene infection which almost cost him the loss of the leg and eventually did cost him his career.

1939 — After his retirement Ted Williams says a home run he hit on this date at Fenway Park off New York Yankee Red Ruffing was the hardest home run he ever hit.

1943 — Third baseman Jim Tabor hits the first Red Sox home run at Fenway Park this season. It was the Sox 33rd game of the year. Leon Culberson had hit the first of the season at Detroit on May 23rd and Bobby Doerr had an inside the park homer at Washington in their 15th game. The reason it took so long was the war time ball in use in the majors was reminiscent of the dead ball era. The ball was known as the Balata ball.

1946 — A doubleheader sweep of the Washington Senators at Fenway Park gives the Red Sox a 21-6 record for the month of May and a 32-9 record overall.

1977 — Outfielder Dave Coleman optioned to Pawtucket, recalled on June 23 and returned to Pawtucket again on July 8.

May 31

1917 — Carl Mays 5 to 1 victory over Cleveland at Boston is the Sox 10th consecutive win.

May 31 (continued)

1946 — Red Sox owner Tom Yawkey announced the signing of manager Joe Cronin to a $50,000 per year three year contract.

1960 — Red Sox owner Tom Yawkey, upset at statements against his team in the Boston press, issues an implied threat to move the Red Sox out of Boston unless press relations improve.

1961 — Carroll Hardy pinch hits for rookie Carl Yastrzemski in the eight inning becoming the only player to pinch hit for both Yaz and Ted Williams. (see September 21, 1960).

1976 — 35,939 fans jam Fenway park for a night game with the New York Yankees.

JUNE 1

1906 — Pitcher Norwood Gibson released. He was chronically ill for the past two seasons.

1909 — In a doubleheader at Philadelphia shortstop Heinie Wagner accepts 20 chances.

1910 — Catcher Red Kleinow and outfielder Clyde Engle acquired from the New York Highlanders.

1951 — The Red Sox have made 32 double plays in the last twenty games (since May 7th).

1963 — Pitcher Ike Delock released. Pitcher Wilbur Wood recalled from Seattle.

June 2

1935 — Pitcher George Pipgras unconditionally released.

The New York Yankees hit six solo home runs in defeating the Red Sox at Yankee Stadium 7 to 2. This set the record for most home runs with no one on base. The Sox two runs were the result of Mel Almeda's two run homer in the eighth.

June 3

1913 — Tris Speaker hits in his twenty second consecutive game.

1956 — Pitcher Willard Nixon helps Chicago White Sox catcher Sherm Lollar tie a major league record when he hits him three times with pitched balls in the same game.

June 4

1913 — Pitcher Ed Cicotte of Chicago stops Tris Speaker's batting streak at 22 games.

1936 — Pitcher Johnny Welch sold to the Pittsburgh Pirates.

June 5

1929 — The Red Sox make 9 straight hits after two were out. Russ Scarritt singled, Bill Barrett doubled, Bob Barrett doubled, Phil Todt doubled, Grant Gillis

June 5 (continued)

doubled, Charlie Berry singled, Danny MacFayden singled, Bill Narleski doubled (the 13th consecutive game he hit in) and Jack Rothrock singled. This equalled the American League record at the time.

1961 — Rookie second baseman Chuck Schilling completes 33 games and 171 chances before making an error.

June 6

1903 — Boston wins their 25th game of the season, beating Chicago 10 to 2, marking the third day in a row they have scored 10 runs. Special ground rules were in effect as a crowd of 10,000 jam the ball park in Boston.

In their last six games the Pilgrims have scored 56 runs.

1908 — Outfielder Denny Sullivan has five hits in five at bats in a game against Detroit.

1940 — Outfielder Red Nonnenkamp optioned to Louisville and outfielder Stan Spence recalled from the same club.

June 7

1918 — The Cleveland Indians steal seven bases against Boston catcher Wally Schang.

June 8

1902 — A 7 to 1 victory at St. Louis gives pitcher Cy Young ten straight wins and an overall 13-1 record.

1903 — A 6 to 1 win over Detroit at Boston is marked by Boston pitcher Tom Hughes four consecutive base on balls. This game was a 5-1/2 inning affair and was Boston's eleventh consecutive victory.

1958 — In the first game of a doubleheader at Fenway Park, the Chicago White Sox made 19 hits to the Red Sox 5, but Boston won the game 6 to 5. Four of Boston's hits were home runs.

1960 — Coach Del Baker is announced as interim manager due to the ill health of manager Billy Jurges.

1961 — The Red Sox and Los Angeles Angels play a 4 to 4 tie game at Fenway Park called due to rain in the 11th inning at 1:15 A.M. The Angels took a 4 to 3 lead in the top of the 11th, but Gary Geiger tripled home the tying run in the bottom of the 11th. Geiger, thinking his hit had won the game, started walking to the dugout and was tagged out. Since the game was called due to rain, it was replayed in its entirety at a later date.

June 9

1912 — Tris Speaker hits for the cycle.

1914 — Infielder Hal Janvrin hits two doubles in the 6th inning at Cleveland.

1934 — In the 8th inning the Washington Senators hit six doubles off pitcher Lefty Grove.

June 10

1912 — The Red Sox go into first place where they remain for the rest of the season.

1921 — The St. Louis Browns make a triple play against Boston, Ellerbe to Lamb to Sisler.

1978 — Carl Yastrzemski's double in a game at Seattle ties him with Ted Williams on the Red Sox list of all time doubles leaders at 525.

June 11

1934 — Pitcher George Pipgras put on the voluntary retired list.

1962 — With the bases loaded with Cleveland Indians, Tito Francona on first shouts "Hold it, Earl" as Red Sox pitcher Earl Wilson was about to deliver a pitch. Obliging Wilson held the ball, stumbled off the mound and balked home a run.

1976 — Catcher Carlton Fisk and manager Darrell Johnson have words in the dugout at Minnesota with Fisk winding up throwing his batting helmet in Johnson's direction. A couple of days later the manager and his catcher smooth things over.

June 12

1961 — The Minnesota Twins leave 17 men on base in a game against Boston.

1978 — Carl Yastrzemski's fourth inning double off the centerfield wall at Fenway Park against the California Angels is the 526th double of his career, moving him past Ted Williams and into first place on the all time Red Sox list of doubles hitters.

1979 — At Kansas City after a tough loss to the Royals due to outfield mistakes by Jim Rice and Fred Lynn, pitcher Dick Drago on his way to the clubhouse questions whether they are allergic to fly balls. Manager Zimmer overhearing the remarks raged at the reliever leading to a shouting match. A meeting between the two next day to clear the air hopefully ended the incident.

June 13

1962 — Humiliated by the Cleveland Indians during five games at Fenway Park the Sox were glad to see them leave town in the wake of 80 hits, 51 runs, and 13 homers.

1979 — First baseman George Scott traded to the Kansas City Royals for outfielder Tom Poquette. After being benched on May 25th Scott had issued a play-me-or-trade-me edict.

First baseman Bob Watson obtained from the Houston Astros for minor league (Bristol) right handed pitcher Peter Ladd, a player to be named later, and a cash consideration. The player named later was pitcher Bobby Sprowl.

June 14

1963 — Pitcher Bob Heffner recalled from Seattle.

June 15

1912 — Tris Speaker hits in his twentieth consecutive game.

1978 — Outfielder Bernie Carbo sold to the Cleveland Indians for an undisclosed amount of cash.

1979 — Pitcher Andy Hassler sold to the New York Mets.

June 16

1908 — In a game against Boston the St. Louis team makes 9 errors. Boston made nine runs on just six hits.

1910 — Outfielder Harry Niles sold to Cleveland.

1914 — For the fourth time this season Boston pitchers throw back to back shutouts, this time Foster blanking St. Louis 2 to 0 following Woods 2 to 0 win on June 15.

1978 — Outfielder Sam Bowen recalled from Pawtucket.

Pitcher Bill Lee cleans out his locker and leaves Fenway Park stating he is retiring from baseball. Lee, boasting a 7-3 record, has been beset by arm problems in his last few starts and has been hurt by unearned runs scored against him (10 in the last two games). It is also known that Bernie Carbo, who was sold to Cleveland on June 15, was a good friend of Lee's.

1979 — Carl Yastrzemski's fifth inning double at Chicago is his 1000th career extra base hit. He becomes the 15th player in major league history to reach that mark. Shortstop Rick Burleson had an inside-the-park home run in Boston's 11-5 victory over the White Sox.

June 17

1915 — St. Louis Brown outfielder Burt Shotton is walked twice in the 8th inning in a game with Boston.

1920 — Pitcher Joe Bush starts three double plays against Detroit.

1933 — Catcher Lou Legett purchased from Albany.

1978 — Pitcher Bill Lee ends a one day walk out on the Red Sox in protest over the sale of outfielder Bernie Carbo to the Cleveland Indians.

June 18

1921 — Boston wins a series with Detroit during which they stole seven bases.

1977 — New York Yankee manager Billy Martin and his right fielder Reggie Jackson must be restrained from a near fight in their dugout at Fenway Park as a result of Martin's removal of Jackson from the game for lack of hustle.

1979 — Pitcher Bobby Sprowl sent to Houston to complete the Watson Deal (see June 13).

June 19

1932 — Marty McManus named as Red Sox manager.

June 20

1951 — Cleveland Indian infielder Bob Avila hits three home runs in a game against the Red Sox.

1954 — In the third inning Boston pitchers hit three New York Yankee batters.

1959 — Ted Williams' double at Municipal Stadium in Cleveland is his 2,500th major league hit.

June 21

1903 — A game with Cleveland is transferred to and played in Canton, Ohio. Boston behind Hughes wins 12 to 7. Outfielder Buck Freeman hits for the cycle.

1918 — Carl Mays pitches his second one hitter of the year against Philadelphia having allowed them only one safety on April 16.

1919 — Babe Ruth going 1 for 4 in a tie game with St. Louis hits in his 20th consecutive game.

1927 — A doubleheader loss 7 to 3 and 7 to 1 at Fenway Park to the New York Yankees starts a 15 game losing streak extending through the first game of a July 4th doubleheader with the Philadelphia A's.

1940 — Outfielder Red Nonnenkamp recalled from Louisville and optioned to Newark. The Red Sox had obtained outfielder Jimmy Shilling from Newark and sent him to Louisville.

1942 — Pitcher Ted Lyons of Chicago defeats the Red Sox for his 250th major league victory.

1977 — Luis Taint's two hitter completes back to back two hit victories over the Orioles at Baltimore. Rick Wise pitched a 4 to 0 two hitter on June 20. Tiant's was a 7 to 0 win.

June 22

1912 — The Red Sox complete a five game sweep of the New York Yankees at New York by the scores of 5 to 2, 15 to 8, 12 to 3, 13 to 2 and 10 to 3.

1962 — Pitcher Don Schwall gives up a long (469') home run to Baltimore Oriole Boog Powell over left center field hedge at Baltimore's Memorial Stadium.

1977 — In his last two games against the Red Sox, Baltimore pitcher Jim Palmer has been touched for nine home runs in 17 innings of pitching. (His other game was on June 9).

June 23

1903 — Boston gains first place and never drops out of it for the remainder of the season.

1909 — Boston makes 21 hits and New York 13 at the Huntington Avenue Grounds with Boston winning 14 to 5. Doyle and Chesbro pitched for New York, Steele for Boston.

1927 — New York Yankee slugger Lou Gehrig hits three home runs at Fenway Park in a Yankees 11 to 4 win.

June 24

1962 — Catcher Bob Tillman's home run in the ninth inning off Baltimore's Wes Stock ends a long drought against relief pitchers. It was the first earned run off an enemy reliever in 39-2/3 innings.

1963 — Three Sox players hit home runs giving the Red Sox a record 30 home runs in their last 15 games.

1970 — Milwaukee pitcher Jim Lonborg strikes out eleven Red Sox batters.

June 25

1970 — Boston and Baltimore combine for 39 hits in a 14 inning game at Boston. Orioles 21 hits, Red Sox 18 hits.

June 26

1918 — After 35 successive innings without being scored upon Red Sox pitcher Carl Mays allows 2 runs.

1922 — Baseball Commissioner Landis talks with the Boston players about their deportment on and off the field.

June 27

1916 — Third baseman Larry Gardner is caught stealing 3 times vs. Philadelphia.

1950 — The Red Sox have made 12 double plays in the last three games (since June 25th).

1960 — Red Sox owner Tom Yawkey denies statements made by Leo Durocher that the Red Sox are for sale.

June 28

1902 — Boston wins a game by forfeit from Baltimore.

1903 — Estimated attendance for a doubleheader at St. Louis is 20,000 as Boston wins 1 to 0, Cy Young over Red Donahue, and 3 to 0, Tom Hughes over Jack Powell. In each game St. Louis had only five hits. By shutting out St. Louis in both ends of the doubleheader at St. Louis, the Pilgrims complete their third consecutive shut out. They have also shut out St. Louis in five of their last six meetings, with St. Louis scoring only one run in the six games.

1961 — Pitcher Arnold Earley obtained from Seattle and pitcher Wilbur Wood obtained from Winston-Salem.

June 29

1912 — A doubleheader sweep of New York at Fenway Park, 13 to 6 and 6 to 0, gives the Red Sox a 21 win, 8 loss month of June.

In the second inning of the second game of this doubleheader catcher Hick Cady had two safe hits in one time at bat. Larry Gardner triples; Jake Stahl doubled; Heinie Wagner sacrificed; Cady hit safely and Stahl ran home. Umpire Frank O'Loughlin ruled that Stahl had scored on a balk and sent Cady back to bat. Cady then doubled.

June 29 (continued)

1928 — The New York Yankees work a double steal, Meusel and Gehrig, with Gehrig stealing home against the Sox.

1979 — Catcher Mike O'Berry sent to Pawtucket.

June 30

1903 — In a game at Chicago, the White Sox score eight runs in the first inning on three walks, a triple, and six singles, all off Nick Altrock who pitches the complete game (his only one ever for Boston). Final score Chicago 10, Boston 3.

JULY 1

1912 — The Red Sox defeat New York 4 to 1 at Boston behind Sea Lion Hall for their 14th consecutive win of the year over the Yankees, and the fifth straight in a six game series.

1935 — Pitcher Joe Cascarella called up from Syracuse and pitchers Hank Johnson and Hy Vandenberg sent to Syracuse.

1979 — The New York Yankees defeat the Red Sox 6 to 5 at New York hitting 5 home runs off Dennis Eckersley, one short of the major league record.

July 2

1902 — Setting a long standing record for the most at bats by both teams in a game Philadelphia has 54, Boston 32. Philadelphia also set a record of 27 hits for one game and the most hits in one inning 12 in the 6th.

1903 — Pitcher Nick Altrock sold to the Chicago Americans.

1906 — Washington shortstop Dave Altizer scores five runs against Boston.

1922 — Boston by scoring on Washington's Walter Johnson breaks his string of 30 scoreless innings.

1933 — Third baseman Buckey Walters purchased from the San Francisco Missions.

Second baseman Fred Muller and outfielder Mel Almada purchased for approximately $40,000 from Seattle of the Pacific Coast League.

1946 — 68,617 at Yankee Stadium see Yankee Spud Chandler out duel Mickey Harris 2 to 1. Chandler yielded 2 hits, Harris 5.

1979 — The Red Sox and the New York Yankees conclude a four game series at Yankee Stadium where they drew 206,016 fans for the four games—an American League record. The series was split, two games each.

July 3

1918 — Mystery man Harvey Fred Bluhm pinch hits for the Red Sox. Some box scores showed him as the hitter, others did not. The American League office showed no record. Some 40 years later this came to light and evidence was brought forward to prove he actually did bat.

July 3 (continued)

1934 — Two New York Yankees have two doubles each in the 6th inning against Boston.

1943 — Leon Culberson hits for the cycle.

1978 — Carl Yastrzemski's third inning double against the New York Yankees at Fenway Park is the 2,800th hit of his career.

July 4

1933 — Infielder Barney Friberg sent to San Francisco.

1940 — Pitchers Mickey Harris and Bill Butland optioned to Sacramento.

When the Red Sox defeated Philadelphia 19 to 5 they scored 14 runs in the 7th inning tying the modern major league for runs scored in an inning. The A's also scored twice making 16 runs for the inning setting a new American League record. Ted Williams was the only Red Sox not to get a hit in the game, yet he set a modern major league record by facing rival pitchers three times in one inning. He was first up in that 7th inning, walked twice, then grounded out to end the inning. Williams and Bobby Doerr tied a major league record by drawing two base on balls in one inning.

July 5

1906 — Boston makes nine errors in an 8 to 3 loss to New York at the Huntington Avenue Grounds.

1917 — The Sox complete their third doubleheader in three days against Philadelphia at Fenway Park. They split the games of July 3 and won both ends on the 4th and 5th.

1932 — Sandlotters Ed Gallagher and Larry Boerner, both pitchers, signed.

July 6

1979 — Jim Rice's two home runs at Seattle are the Red Sox's 100th and 101st of the season and marked the 34th consecutive year the Sox have hit at least 100 home runs, a major league record.

July 7

1939 — Pitcher Jim Bagby optioned to Little Rock and pitcher Bill Sayles is recalled from the same club.

1942 — Ted Williams, Bobby Doerr, and Tex Hughson compete with a team of American League All Stars vs a Service All Star team at Cleveland.

July 8

1902 — Philadelphia defeated Boston 22 to 9, not 27 to 18 as previously reported. This was a game in which there were 45 hits, including 12 by Philadelphia in the sixth inning against Sox pitcher Merle Adkins, who faced 16 batters.

July 8 (continued)

1978 — Catcher Carlton Fisk's first inning home run at Cleveland in the first game of a doubleheader was the Red Sox 100th homer of the season, marking the 33rd consecutive year the Sox have hit 100 or more home runs. Boston won the game 12 to 5. Carl Yastrzemski's home run in the same game was the 375th of his career.

July 9

1902 — Boston's Bill Dineen and Philadelphia's Rube Waddell duel in a 17 inning game at Boston, the A's winning 4 to 2.

1912 — The Red Sox defeat the St. Louis Browns 3 to 2 behind Buck O'Brien at Boston for their 10th consecutive win of the year over the Browns.

1961 — The Red Sox steal 5 bases in the second game of a doubleheader at Yankee Stadium, the most by a Boston team in years.

1979 — The Red Sox make history of a sort as Jim Rice, Fred Lynn and Carl Yastrzemski are named as the starting outfield for the American League All Star team in a game to be played later this month. Acutally, "Yaz" has spent more playing time at first base and as the designated hitter this season.

July 10

1908 — First baseman Garland "Jake" Stahl purchased from the New York Highlanders.

1940 — Pitcher Earl Johnson recalled from Rocky Mount.

1941 — Pitcher Tex Hughson recalled from Louisville and pitchers Emerson Dickman and Bill Fleming optioned to Louisville.

1948 — For the sixth time in this season Vern Stephens and Bobby Doerr hit successive home runs.

July 11

1909 — At Chicago shortstop Lee Tannehill and first baseman Frank Isabell make a triple play against Boston.

1918 — The Red Sox play their 27th consecutive inning without being scored upon.

1939 — Pitcher Dick Midkiff recalled from Minneapolis and pitcher Charlie Wagner sent to the same club.

1969 — In the second game of a doubleheader at Baltimore the Red Sox make twenty two hits.

July 12

1918 — Babe Ruth doubles in the second, triples in the fourth and sixth innings in four at bats scoring each time.

1919 — Boston has 17 hits for 28 total bases in Chicago. Among the hits was Babe Ruth's 11th home run of the season.

1939 — Pitcher Monte Weaver sent to Louisville.

July 12 (continued)

1951 — 52,592 fans turn out for a twi-night doubleheader between Boston and the Chicago White Sox at Comiskey Park in Chicago, a record for that ball park. The second game goes 17 innings. Boston wins each game 3 to 2 and 5 to 4.

July 14

1916 — Sox play a seventeen inning 0-0 tie with the St. Louis Browns at Fenway Park.

1954 — Chuck Rainey — B   1979   P

July 15

1916 — Boston defeats St. Louis 17 to 4 in the second game of a doubleheader at Fenway Park.

July 16

1901 — Pitcher Cy Young wins his 12th consecutive game. A 10 to 8 win, at Cleveland.

1903 — Four of Boston's seven runs in the first inning scored after the umpire disallowed a third out because he turned to the bench to demand new baseballs. The game at Boston resulted in a 11 to 4 victory over Cleveland.

1904 — Boston makes 19 hits in defeating Cleveland 13 to 3 at the Huntington Avenue Grounds.

1912 — Tris Speaker runs his hitting streak to thirty games.

1918 — Last of the ninth score tied 1-1 with the St. Louis Browns, winning run on first, Babe Ruth at bat. Ruth blasts one of pitcher "Lefty" Leifield's pitches out of the park FOR A TRIPLE. In those days the game was over as soon as the winning run scored and the Babe could not be credited with a home run or a run scored.

1924 — Pitcher Bill Piercy is fined $100 for alleged indifferent pitching in the second game of a doubleheader against Detroit. Eight runs were scored off him in the first inning as the Tigers won the game 11 to 3.

1978 — After being ejected from a ball game at Fenway Park for arguing about a pick off play at first base, Minnesota Twins manager Gene Mauch returns to his dugout and throws more than a dozen bats out on the field.

July 17

1909 — In a game at Cleveland pitcher Joe Wood, in relief, strikes out 10 Cleveland batters in four innings to save a 6 to 4 Boston win.

1922 — The Red Sox ask for waivers on shortstop Chick Maynard.

1971 — Milwaukee Brewers hit five home runs at Fenway Park.

1978 — The Red Sox 3 to 2 win over the Minnesota Twins at Fenway Park represents Manager Don Zimmer's 200th win as Bosox pilot.

July 18

1919 — Babe Ruth with two home runs bats in six runs against Cleveland.

1947 — Ted Williams has five hits in five at bats for the first time in his career. Included were two home runs, the tenth time in his career he had hit two homers in one game.

1970 — Milwaukee Brewer player Ted Kubiak has seven RBI's against Boston at Fenway Park.

July 19

1919 — Red Sox players issue a statement that they are not a dissatisfied team.

July 20

1914 — Dutch Leonard pitches 8 hitless innings in relief against Detroit.

1975 — The Texas Rangers steal six bases against Boston in a nine inning game.

July 21

1915 — Pitcher Babe Ruth holds the St. Louis Browns to 5 hits while making four himself, including a home run, two doubles and a single while scoring two runs and knocking in two.

1919 — Babe Ruth's batted ball over the right field fence at Detroit is the longest hit ever made in that ball park.

July 22

1902 — A 4 to 1 victory over Chicago at Boston is pitcher Cy Young's twentieth win of the season.

1909 — Detroit right fielder Ty Cobb steals four bases at Detroit against Boston catcher Pat Donohue.

1912 — Outfielder Tris Speaker is caught stealing base 3 times vs. New York.

Pitcher Ed Cicotte sold to the Chicago White Sox for the waiver price.

July 23

1903 — Boston gains their 50th victory of the season by defeating New York in the first game of a doubleheader at New York 6 to 1 behind Cy Young. It was an interesting twin bill, as the first game lasted only one hour and thirty five minutes, and the second game lasted only one hour and twenty five minutes. New York won the second game 4 to 2.

1912 — Pitcher Joe Wood gains a 6 to 3 win over the Cleveland Indians at Boston for his 20th win of the season. He has lost only 4 games.

1940 — Baseball Commissioner Landis fines the Red Sox $500 for failing to report the contract of pitcher Larry Jansen and makes Jansen a free agent. (He later starred with the New York Giants).

July 23 (continued)

1979 — The Red Sox make a triple play against the California Angels. Shortstop Rick Burleson takes a line drive (with runners on first and second) touches second and fires to first before the runner could return.

July 24

1903 — In beating the Highlanders at New York 7 to 5, Boston batters hit seven doubles. Freeman and Parent two each and Dougherty, Collins and Ferris one each.

1960 — While Cleveland Indian manager Joe Gordon changed pitchers his center-fielder Jim Piersall sought some shade by sitting behind the centerfield flag pole at Fenway Park.

1978 — Pitcher Allen Ripley sent to Pawtucket. Pitcher Andy Hassler acquired from the Kansas City Royals in exchange for a minor league player to be named later.

Carl Yastrzemski's sixth inning single at Minnesota drives in Fred Lynn with Yastrzemski's 1500th career RBI. He becomes the 21st player in major league history to achieve this milestone.

1979 — Carl Yastrzemski's seventh inning home run against the Oakland A's pitcher Mike Morgan at Fenway park is the 400th of his career.

July 25

1922 — The St. Louis Chamber of Commerce sent a letter of protest to American League President Ban Johnson regarding the Boston-New York trade which saw Dugan and Smith going to New York in exchange for Fewster, Miller and Mitchell. St. Louis and New York were battling for first place.

1961 — Pitcher Wilbur Wood sent to Johnstown of the Eastern League.

1974 — Carl Yastrzemski hits the 300th home run of his major league career. It comes off Mickey Lolich of the Detroit Tigers in a game at Detroit.

1979 — Pitcher Joel Finch becomes the first Red Sox pitcher to become a batter since Luis Tiant struck out on July 5, 1976. Finch flied to right field in this game against Oakland at Fenway Park. Finch became the fourth sox pitcher to bat since the DH rule went into effect in 1973. He joins Tiant, Jim Willoughby and Dick Pole.

July 27

1901 — Third baseman Jimmy Collins hits in his 14th consecutive game.

1946 — First baseman Rudy York matches a major league record by batting in 10 runs in a 13 to 6 over the St. Louis Browns.

1977 — The Milwaukee Brewers make twenty hits at Fenway Park.

July 28

1948 — Detroit Tiger pitcher Dizzy Trout shuts out the Red Sox at Detroit ending the Sox 13 game winning streak.

July 28 (continued)

1978 — Outfielder Sam Bowen sent to Pawtucket.

1979 — A triple play, started by second baseman Jack Brohamer on a blooper into short right field and going to second with shortstop Burleson covering and back to first baseman Bob Watson, is the Red Sox third triple play of the year and ties the American League record and Red Sox team record set in 1924.

July 29

1903 — New York defeats Boston 15 to 14 at Boston. The game lasted two hours and ten minutes with Cy Young pitching all the way for Boston. Boston made eight errors and New York three.

1909 — Shortstop Heinie Wagner accepts 11 chances without an error in a game against St. Louis at Boston.

1940 — Pitcher Yank Terry recalled from Louisville and pitcher Charlie Wagner optioned to the same club.

1967 — 35,469 fans fill Fenway Park for a twi-night doubleheader against the Minnesota Twins, a record crowd at the time for a Fenway Park twi-nighter.

July 30

1921 — Outfielder Ping Bodie purchased from the New York Yankees.

Outfielder Tim Hendryx transferred to St. Paul.

1948 — An 8 to 7 win over the Indians at Cleveland is the Sox 25th win of the month. The most wins in one month by any Red Sox club.

July 31

1912 — A 4 to 1 win at St. Louis gives the Red Sox a 21 win, 9 loss record for the month of July.

1915 — By defeating the Detroit Tigers 4 to 1 at Boston the Red Sox end the month's play having won 22 games while losing only 10.

1916 — Babe Ruth's 6 to 0 shutout of the Tigers at Detroit gives Boston a 20-10 record for July.

1918 — Bullet Joe Bush wins 8 to 4 at St. Louis giving Boston a 20 and 9 record for July. Pitcher Bush also had two doubles and two singles in four at bats.

1946 — A 4 to 1 loss at Cleveland leaves the Sox with a 20 and 10 record for the month of July.

AUGUST 1

1907 — Boston makes 23 hits against Cleveland in Boston winning 14 to 1.

1938 — Pitcher Joe Heving purchased from Milwaukee and pitcher Joe Gonzales is optioned to Milwaukee from Hazleton.

August 1 (continued)

1954 — Manager Lou Boudreau bats Ted Williams second in the order from now until the end of the season, in hopes that he may get enough at bats to lead the league in hitting.

August 2

1901 — An easy 16 to 0 victory at Philadelphia gives pitcher Cy Young his twentieth victory of the season.

1938 — Pitcher Bill Harris purchased from Buffalo for $20,000 and an option on pitcher Footsie Marcum.

Due to third baseman Pinky Higgins' bad leg, Jim Tabor joins the Red Sox on "loan" from Minneapolis.

Outfielder Fabian Gaffke sent to Minneapolis.

1940 — Shortstop Joe Cronin hits for the cycle in a game at Detroit.

1943 — Tom Burgmeier — B   1978   P

1979 — Pitcher Win Remmerswaal recalled from Pawtucket.

August 3

1936 — Pitcher Jim Henry sent to Minneapolis and outfielder Buster Mills purchased from Rochester.

1974 — Setting a day game record for the New York Yankees stay at Shea Stadium, 50,828 fans show up for a game against the Red Sox.

1978 — The Red Sox complete a 17 inning 7 to 5 victory over the New York Yankees at New York. The game actually was suspended from August 2 when the two teams played to a 14 inning 5 to 5 tie.

August 4

1936 — Catcher George Dickey optioned to Minneapolis. There are rumors that the option of Dickey and Henry (Aug. 3) will give the Sox an option on the purchase of a Minneapolis player probably to be outfielder Fabian Gaffke.

1937 — Outfielder Fabian Gaffke optioned to Minneapolis.

1938 — Pitcher Al Baker brought up from Little Rock who had obtained him from Dallas where he had pitched for five years.

1946 — Bobby Doerr has seven RBI's in a 9 to 4 Boston win at Detroit.

August 5

1951 — Catcher Aaron Robinson purchased from the Detroit Tigers.

1962 — Rumors circulate that Washington Senator general manager and former Red Sox director of public relations, Ed Doherty might return to the Red Sox to direct a major shake up of the organization.

During the eight day period from July 29 Red Sox reliever Dick Radatz worked a total of eight innings in four games in relief against the Washing-

August 5 (continued)

ton Senators and struck out 17 batters. The record for strikeouts in a 9 inning game at the time was 18.

Sleepy time prevailed during the second game of a twin bill with Washington at Fenway Park. In the 4th inning the Senators had the bases loaded and attempted a squeeze play. Hal Kolstad's pitch was low and catcher Bob Tillman caught it and stayed on his haunches staring at the ground. As he dozed Ed Brinkman came sliding across the plate to steal home. Pitcher Benny Daniels, on second, moved to third for a stolen base, but Jim Piersall on first was sleeping with Tillman as he never made a move to second. No one present could remember ever seeing such a colossal boo boo.

1979 — Hard up for starting pitchers Sox manager Zimmer uses a rare three pitcher three innings each pitching sequence at Milwaukee. Using relief pitchers Dick Drago, Win Remmerswaal and Tom Burgmeier (who was relieved by Bill Campbell) to defeat the Brewers 19-5 with Remmerswaal getting his first major league win. The Sox became the first team in 30 years to score in 8 innings of a game. In the doubleheader (7-2 first game Sox win) the Red Sox had 37 hits (a total of 133 in their last 13 games). The 27 hits in the second game (2 homers, 4 doubles, a triple and 20 singles) came within one of tying the team high of 28 set in 1950. The only inning the Sox failed to score was the fourth when they put the first two batters on base, but failed to score them.

August 6

1903 — A game at Philadelphia is called after eight innings because it became very cloudy. 9,661 attended and manager Collins protested the call. The A's won 4 to 3.

August 7

1908 — The Chicago White Sox make only six hits but score seven runs to defeat Boston 7-0.

August 8

1921 — Everett Scott hits an inside-the-park home run at Fenway Park.

1922 — Cleveland manager-outfielder Tris Speaker hits two home runs over the right field wall at Boston. The Red Sox make 21 hits in this game.

1939 — As a result of his first display of temperament, rookie outfielder Ted Williams is "spanked" publicly by manager Joe Cronin. Lou Finney was inserted as a runner in a game against the Detroit Tigers as Williams showed a lack of hustle in running out hits.

August 9

1914 — Pitcher Dutch Leonard defeats Tigers at Detroit for his 12th consecutive win.

1921 — By sweeping a doubleheader from the Detroit Tigers, it marks the 10th successive win over the Tigers by the Red Sox. Detroit breaks the string the next day.

August 9 (continued)

1971 — The Detroit Tigers hit six home runs in a game against the Red Sox at Fenway Park but lose 12 to 11.

August 10

1902 — A 5 to 4 win in 11 innings at Chicago gives Cy Young twenty five wins.

1960 — Ted Williams hits lifetime home runs 512 and 513 to become the all time number 3 home run hitter in baseball history.

1965 — The Red Sox score twelve runs in one inning against Baltimore at Fenway Park.

1978 — Third baseman Butch Hobson scores the tying run in the 13th inning of a Sox 6 to 5, 13 inning win over the Cleveland Indians by going all the way around the bases on a pop fly to second base.

1979 — Pitcher John Tudor recalled from Pawtucket.

August 11

1903 — One of the largest regular season crowds, 10,600 in Boston see the Pilgrims and Tom Hughes defeat the A's and Rube Waddell 5 to 1.

1922 — Boston makes a triple play against Washington—catcher Muddy Ruel to third baseman Pinky Pittenger to George Burns at first base.

1948 — Ted Williams home run into the left field stand at Yankee Stadium is the first he has ever hit to left at that ball park.

1962 — Former second baseman Bobby Doerr's appearance at Fenway Park with owner Tom Yawkey led to speculation of his part in Yawkey's reported plans for a club shake up.

1968 — The Detroit Tigers hit two pinch hit home runs during a 14 inning game against Boston.

1979 — Jim Rice hits his 30th home run of the season in a game at Fenway Park against the Milwaukee Brewers. He becomes only the third Boston player to hit 30 home runs in three consecutive seasons. Jimmie Foxx did it in five straight years and Ted Williams in four.

August 12

1938 — Pitcher Lee Rogers sold to the Brooklyn Dodgers for the waiver price of $7,500.

1939 — Pitcher Bill Butland purchased from Minneapolis.

1940 — Pitcher Bill Fleming purchased from Hollywood.

August 13

1946 — Pitcher Dave Ferriss picks up a 7 to 5 win over Philadelphia at Shibe Park for his 20th win of the season.

1914 — Pitcher Dutch Leonard loses to New York 1 to 0, ending his 12 game winning streak.

August 14

1903 — Pitcher Cy Young wins a 6 to 3 game at Detroit for his 20th win of the season.

1912 — Tris Speaker completes a 20 consecutive game hitting streak.

An 8 to 0 shutout of St. Louis in the second game of a doubleheader at Fenway Park gives Joe Wood his 25th victory of the year.

1919 — The Red Sox make 20 hits in defeating the Chicago White Sox 15 to 6 at Chicago, against White Sox pitchers Cicotti, Kerr and Sullivan.

1922 — A team of All Stars defeated the Red Sox 3 to 2 at Boston in a benefit game for the family of Tommy McCarthy a famous Boston outfielder who had recently died (August 5). More than $5,000 was raised. McCarthy played in the National League from 1884 to 1896 of which six seasons were in Boston.

1951 — Billy Goodman starts a triple play against Philadelphia catching Majeski's bases filled line drive, he steps on second and throws to Walt Dropo at first.

August 15

1922 — Infielder-catcher Eddie Foster sold to the St. Louis Browns.

The Chicago White Sox make 25 hits against the Red Sox.

August 16

1946 — A crowd of 29,226 for a game with New York at Fenway Park pushed the paid Fenway Park attendance to 1,015,425 an all time Red Sox record to that time.

1978 — Pitcher Luis Tiant defeats the California Angels 4 to 2 at Anaheim for his 200th major league victory.

August 17

1908 — Until the ninth inning of a game with Detroit, pitcher Elmer Steele had pitched 25 innings (in three games) without being scored upon.

1919 — Boston and St. Louis combine for 11 doubles in a doubleheader.

1946 — Skip Lockwood — B 1980   P

1979 — Infielder Ted Sizemore purchased from the Chicago Cubs for cash and a player to be named later. (Catcher Mike O'Berry).

August 18

1937 — Pitcher Charlie Wagner purchased from Minneapolis for cash and two players to be named later.

August 19

1934 — The Detroit Tigers and the Red Sox play before 46,995 fans, the largest crowd in Red Sox history. Julius Solters hits for the cycle in this game.

1970 — The Red Sox use 5 pitchers against the Chicago White Sox in the ninth inning.

August 20

1903 — Buck Freeman breaks a field record at Chicago by hitting the first ball ever over the right field scoreboard. Boston wins 9 to 5.

1956 — Joel Finch — B   1979   P

1961 — Boston and Detroit tie a major league record by grounding into 8 double plays in nine innings. Boston 5, Detroit 3.

1977 — A crowd of 40,502 turns out at Royal's Stadium in Kansas City for a Saturday night game with the Red Sox. This establishes a record for the stadium for attendance at a single game and a night game.

August 21

1903 — Chicago left fielder Ducky Holmes sets a record with four outfield assists, despite Boston's 11 to 3 victory.

1913 — Heinie Wagner's single off Cleveland pitcher Lefty James scores three men.

1914 — Second baseman Steve Yerkes unconditionally released.

1933 — Pitcher Curt Fullerton signed by the Red Sox.

1961 — Behind Warren Spahn the Milwaukee Braves made their first return to Boston to defeat the Red Sox 4 to 1 in an exhibition game for the benefit of the Jimmy Fund.

August 22

1936 — Shortstop Eric McNair has no assists in a 13 inning game.

1973 — The Texas Rangers make nine hits in one inning against the Red Sox.

1976 — Oakland A's Bert Campaneris steals five bases at Fenway Park.

August 23

1903 — In the second game of a double header at St. Louis, Boston makes a triple play. Boston swept the games 5 to 3 and 4 to 2 before 21,300, an extremely large crowd for the time.

1919 — Babe Ruth hits his fourth grand slam home run of the season. He had previously done it on May 20, June 30 (1st game) and July 18.

1937 — In one of the largest rookie recalls in their history the Red Sox bring up Jim Henry, George Dickey, John Peacock, Fabian Gaffke, Emerson Dickman, Dick Midkiff, Lee Rogers, Jinx Poindexter, Jim Tabor, and F. Lindsay Deal from Little Rock and Bob Daughters from Rocky Mount.

1974 — Luis Tiant shuts out Oakland at Fenway Park and gains his 20th win of the year.

August 24

1961 — Red Sox publicist Bill Crowley, in an unusual statement, announces that Boston management will not pay outfielder Jackie Jensen for any games he misses. Jensen was missing games due to his fear of flying.

August 24 (continued)

1977 — The longest night in Boston baseball history as the Red Sox lose two games to the Texas Rangers 3 to 0 and 6 to 3. The first game started at 6:00 P.M. and the second game ended at 2:26 A.M. on August 25. There were two hours and 22 minutes of rain and eighteen innings of baseball.

August 25

1911 — A 3 to 2 win at St. Louis is also the 20th win of the season for pitcher Joe Wood.

1946 — In beating the Cleveland Indians 2 to 1 at Boston, Dave Ferriss wins his 13th game of the year at Fenway Park. He had lost none. This became his final regular season record at home.

1963 — First baseman Dick Stuart, by striking out six times in a doubleheader in Cleveland, runs his season total to 123 topping Jimmie Foxx's Boston record of 119 set in 1936.

In the doubleheader Bill Monboquette fans 11 Indians in the first game and Bob Heffner 12 in the second game.

1968 — A game at Baltimore takes five hours and twenty seven minutes to play, 18 innings. Orioles 3, Sox 2.

1978 — Amateur umpires fill in for striking major league umpires at a game at Fenway Park as the Sox defeat the California Angels 6-0.

August 26

1938 — In a big Ladies Day crush at Fenway Park, 12,000 were admitted while many others milled around outside. Chaos was created inside with spectators trying to get into the grandstand.

1939 — Pitcher Al Brazle purchased from Little Rock.

1945 — A 4 to 3 win over the Philadelphia Athletics gives Dave "Boo" Ferriss his 20th win of the season.

1949 — An 11 to 4 victory at Chicago over the White Sox is Mel Parnell's 20th season victory.

1954 — The Red Sox hit eight doubles in a game against Baltimore at Fenway Park.

1966 — The Baltimore Orioles hit two pinch hit home runs in the twelfth inning against Boston.

August 27

1901 — A 15 inning 2 to 1 win over Detroit at Boston is Cy Young's twenty fifth victory of the year.

1905 — The Pilgrims complete six consecutive doubleheaders and their eighth on ten playing dates. Aug. 10 Detroit; Aug. 14 Chicago; Aug. 21 at Detroit; Aug. 23 and 24 at Cleveland; Aug. 25, 26, 27 at Chicago. They won one, lost three and split four of the eight.

1918 — Joe Bush strikes out 13 Detroit Tigers but loses the game 2 to 1.

August 27 (continued)

1978 — The Red Sox and California Angels tie the American League record for the most intentional base on balls in an extra inning game at 6. Boston - 4 California - 2.

August 28

1907 — Cy Young wins his 20th game of the season, 5 to 3 at New York.

1908 — Pitcher Joe Wood purchased from Kansas City.

1921 — Sad Sam Jones is the victor 6 to 5 in 11 innings at Chicago. It is his 20th win of the year.

1926 — In a doubleheader with Cleveland only one batter strikes out in the two games and he played for Cleveland.

1937 — The Red Sox purchase pitchers Jim Bagby and Bill Humphrey, infielder Al Niemiec and outfielder Red Nonnenkamp from Little Rock (Nonnenkamp was MVP in the Southern League, Bagby MVP in the New York Pennsylvania League with Hazelton where Little Rock had optioned him).

1941 — American League president Will Harridge announces that the game August 15 with the Washington Senators has been forfeited to the Red Sox.

1952 — Philadelphia A's third baseman Billy Hitchcock and Red Sox catcher Sammy White stage a grand fight during a game at Shibe Park. It was no sooner over than A's coach Tom Oliver and Sox pitcher Willard Nixon squared off.

August 29

1915 — A 1 to 0 shutout of the Indians at Cleveland ends the month of August with a 21 and 6 record for Boston 79-39 overall.

1916 — St. Louis pitcher Bob Groom strikes out twice in the 7th inning against Boston.

1935 — Pitcher Wes Ferrell wins his 20th game of the year, a 6 to 2 win at Philadelphia.

August 30

1904 — Boston makes 18 hits in defeating Detroit 13 to 0 at the Huntington Avenue Grounds.

1918 — By winning both ends of a doubleheader from Philadelphia at Boston pitcher Carl Mays wins his 20th and 21st victories of the year.

1928 — Proving starting pitchers can also be relievers Ed Morris comes in to snuff out a Philadelphia A's 9th inning rally by striking out Joe Hauser, Tris Speaker and Eddie Collins in succession.

August 31

1917 — A 5 to 3 win over Philadelphia in the first game of a doubleheader at Fenway Park is Babe Ruth's 20th win of the season.

August 31 (continued)

1932 — So far as is known a first was established for unusual reasons for rescheduling a game on this date. Boston baseball went into an eclipse along with the sun on this afternoon. Sox owner Bob Quinn, not wishing to have his team caught in the dark (fellow researcher Bob Lindsay says he thought they had been in the dark all season anyway) had rescheduled the game with the Cleveland Indians for an earlier date. Astronomers had figured in advance that the sun would be 90% obscured with Boston being in almost total darkness for about 20 minutes. Such a game today might be billed as a day-night-day game with owners foreseeing a bonanza at the concession stands.

1946 — By defeating Philadelphia 4 to 2 the Red Sox run their August record to 21 and 11.

SEPTEMBER 1

1976 — Pitcher Ferguson Jenkins suffers a torn Achilles tendon while covering first base in a game against the Texas Rangers. Going for his 13th win, the injury occured in the 5th inning.

1978 — Pitcher Bob Sprowl called up from Pawtucket.

September 2

1912 — By defeating the Yankees in a doubleheader 2 to 1 and 1 to 0 the Red Sox complete 10 straight wins over New York at New York this season.

1921 — Shortstop Everett Scott plays in his 800th consecutive game.

1946 — The Red Sox defeat the Yankees in a doubleheader at New York 5 to 2 and 3 to 1 for their 14th doubleheader win of the year. They lost no twinbills during the season and split 13.

Pitcher Dave Ferriss by winning the first game completes a 12 game winning streak.

September 3

1903 — Pitcher Cy Young wins his 25th game of the year, a 6 to 5 victory over Philadelphia at Boston in twelve innings.

1939 — Umpire Cal Hubbard forfeits a game with New York at Fenway Park to the Yankees when the fans litter the field making play impossible. The Sox protest the decision which is upheld by league president Harridge who orders the game replayed.

September 4

1905 — A 9 to 4 victory at New York gives Jesse Tannehill his 20th win of the season.

1908 — Frank Arellanes pitches a one hitter against Philadelphia Athletics. Boston won 10 to 1 making 13 hits.

1918 — Rain washes out first game of the World Series at Chicago.

September 4 (continued)

1936 — Catcher Gene Desautels purchased from San Diego. In December minor league pitcher Manny Salvo was sent to San Diego to complete the deal.

1974 — By beating the Red Sox 6 to 0, the Baltimore Orioles complete their third consecutive shutout of the Sox. On September 2, they defeated the Red Sox 1 to 0 in both games of a doubleheader. The Sox managed only eight hits in the three games, getting three in the first and third games and two in the second.

September 5

1903 — In a Boston 12 to 1, 8 inning win over Philadelphia at Boston, Pat Dougherty in five at bats has three triples and two singles.

1919 — The Red Sox make 25 hits in defeating the Philadelphia Athletics 15 to 7 in Philadelphia against pitchers Noyes and Geary.

1921 — In the second game of a doubleheader against Boston the New York Yankee outfield makes five assists.

1922 — The Red Sox defeat the New York Yankees 4 to 3 and 6 to 5 in the Yanks final games at New York's Polo Grounds where they were tennants of the New York Giants. Babe Ruth hit a long home run off Sox pitcher Herb Pennock. Pennock also gave up the Babe's first homer as a Yankee.

1927 — With Red Ruffing pitching 15 innings the Red Sox defeat the Yankees 12 to 11 in eighteen innings at Fenway Park in the first game of a doubleheader.

1936 — The Red Sox make a triple play against the New York Yankees in the second game of a doubleheader which darkness ended in a 7 to 7 tie.

1940 — Pitcher Mike Ryba purchased from Rochester.

Arrangements are made to send two players to Baltimore for infielder Skeeter Newsome.

September 6

1902 — A 6 to 5 win in St. Louis is pitcher Cy Young's thirtieth win of the season.

1904 — By defeating Washington 4 to 1 in the first game of a doubleheader Boston completes 16 consecutive wins over them this season and 22 consecutive over two seasons. The streak which began in 1903 ended in the second game when Boston lost by a score of 6 to 3.

1912 — A 1 to 0 shutout of Washington at Fenway Park gives Joe Wood a 30 and 4 record for the year.

1919 — Boston makes 21 hits against Johnson, Geary and Adams of Philadelphia.

1927 — New York Yankee Babe Ruth hits a ball off Sox pitcher Tony Welzer over the centerfield fence at Fenway Park that was referred to as "the longest hit ever at Fenway Park".

1953 — Pitcher Ellis Kinder's 62nd relief appearance to break the Red Sox record he set in 1951.

September 7

1912 — A 5 to 1 loss to the Washington Senators at Fenway Park ends a ten game Boston winning streak.

1920 — Infielder Hub Hiller strikes out twice in the 7th inning against Detroit.

1938 — Pitcher Woody Rich and outfielder Paul Campbell purchased from Little Rock.

1958 — At Baltimore the Orioles use twenty four players against the Red Sox in a ten inning game.

September 8

1904 — Pitcher Jesse Tannehill defeats Washington 3 to 1 at Washington for his 20th win of the season.

Boston completes their fourth doubleheader in four days, all with Washington, winning two and splitting two.

1908 — A 3 to 1 victory at Washington gives Cy Young his 20th win of the season.

1919 — Babe Ruth's 26th home run of the season made in New York breaks Buck Freeman's American League record of 25 homers.

1936 — Outfielder Fabian Gaffke and pitcher Archie McKain purchased from Minneapolis. In December outfielders Dusty Cooke, Dom Dallesandro catcher George Dickey and pitcher Mike Meola were released to Minneapolis to complete the deal.

1938 — Partnership in Louisville club was forced upon Red Sox owner Tom Yawkey by necessity. He changes his policy toward farm clubs in order to complete with rival clubs who were developing talent at the minor league level.

1940 — Pitcher Dick "Heber" Newsome purchased from San Diego.

September 9

1901 — Buck Freeman hits his 12th home run of the season. Quite a record for the dead ball era. The game was played in Chicago.

1940 — Pitcher Al Brazle sent to Rochester to complete the Ryba deal (See Sept. 5, 1940). Red Sox buy three players from the Louisville roster pitcher Tex Hughson: pitcher Brown (from Rocky Mount) and first baseman Al Flair (from Scranton) for cash and players to be named later. Infielder Skeeter Newsome obtained from Baltimore.

1951 — Ellis Kinder establishes a new Red Sox record for pitching appearances— 55. His two appearances in a doubleheader put him past Wilcy Moore, who held the Sox record with 53 in 1932.

1962 — Outfielder Lou Clinton hit a home run, a triple and a single to go along with four eye-popping catches in the outfield to lead the Sox over the New York Yankees 9 to 3 at Yankee Stadium. Relieving Hal Kolstad, pitcher Dick Radatz pitches nine innings in relief before being removed in the 16th inning for a pinch hitter.

September 9 (continued)

1969 — Carl Yastrzemski hits the 200th home run of his major league career. It came off Mel Stottlemyre during a game at Fenway Park.

1978 — New York Yankee pitcher Ron Guidry shuts out the Red Sox in Fenway Park 7 to 0 to become the first left hander to do so since Ken Holtzman of Oakland did it on August 5, 1974. Attendance at Fenway Park passed the 2 million mark for the second year in a row.

September 10

1953 — Pitcher Ellis Kinder sets an American League record with his 64th relief appearance.

1978 — The Red Sox conclude a vital four game series loss to the New York Yankees losing 7 to 4. The series saw the Sox lose four straight 15-3, 13-2, 7-0, 7-4. This moved New York into a first place tie with Boston. The amazing statistics for the series were: Runs — New York 42, Sox 9; Hits — New York 67, Sox 20; Errors — New York 5, Sox 12. The last Yankee 5 game sweep at Fenway Park was in 1943.

September 11

1919 — The Red Sox complete their third shutout in a row by taking a doubleheader from St. Louis at Fenway Park 4 to 0 and 6 to 0 behind Herb Pennock and Allen Russell. On Sept. 8 Waite Hoyt had shutout the Yankees in New York 3 to 0.

1940 — Outfielder Leo "Red" Nonnenkamp sold to Newark.

1978 — A crowd of 28,575 at Fenway Park for a game with the Baltimore Orioles (won by Boston 5 to 4) sets a club season attendance record of 2,074,549 for Fenway Park.

September 12

1903 — Long Tom Hughes' 10 to 1 victory over New York at Boston is his 20th win of the year.

1907 — A 7 to 1 loss at Philadelphia starts Boston on a 16 game losing streak. In addition during the streak Boston plays two tie games.

1909 — Former Red Sox pitching ace Bill Dineen joins the American League umpiring staff.

1913 — Red Sox defeat Detroit at Fenway Park 18 to 5 after losing to the Tigers the day before 15 to 2.

1967 — A 3 to 1 win at Fenway Park over Kansas City gives Jim Lonborg his 20th win of the season.

1979 — Carl Yastrzemski's eighth inning single through the infield to right field off New York Yankee pitcher Jim Beattie is his 3000th major league hit. It made him the first American League hitter in history to have 3000 hits and 400 home runs.

September 13

1955 — Ted Williams' two singles against Philadelphia broke Bobby Doerr's record of hits by a Red Sox player, which stood at 2,042.

September 14

1901 — Winning 12 to 1 over Washington at Boston, pitcher Cy Young raises his record to 30 and 9.

1917 — A 6 to 5 victory over the New York Yankees in New York gives Carl Mays his 20th victory of the season.

1949 — Ellis Kinder shuts out the Detroit Tigers at Fenway Park 1 to 0 for his 20th season win.

1959 — Red Sox officials sign papers to liquidate the corporation known as the Boston American League Baseball Company.

1963 — A 6 to 4 win over the Kansas City Athletics at K.C. gives Bill Monbouquette 20 wins.

September 15

1912 — The Red Sox win their 30th victory by a one run margin beating St. Louis 2 to 1 at St. Louis behind Joe Wood.

1946 — Pitcher Dave Ferriss defeats the White Sox at Chicago 4 to 1 in the first game of a doubleheader for his 24th win of the season.

1947 — Twelve double plays are made in a twin bill with Chicago, 7 by the Red Sox, 5 by the White Sox.

1962 — Sox first base coach Rudy York and scout Bobby Doerr are presented with plaques by American League President Joe Cronin, on being placed into the new 200 homer club established this year at Baseball's Hall of Fame.

1979 — First baseman Bob Watson hits for the cycle in a game at Baltimore.

September 16

1903 — Boston makes 23 hits in a game against Cleveland at Boston.

1904 — Cy Young pitches Boston to a 4 to 2 victory over New York at Boston in the second game of two for his 20th win.

1961 — Rookie pitcher Don Schwall loses his first game at Fenway Park. He had won 10 in a row there before the Baltimore Orioles beat him 5 to 4.

September 17

1916 — Babe Ruth wins his 20th game of the season defeating Chicago 6 to 2 in Chicago.

1920 — In a twelve inning game Detroit Tiger outfielder Bobby Veach hits for the cycle against Boston.

1921 — First baseman Stuffy McInnis plays his 100th game without making an error. Boston fans present Chicago White Sox outfielder Harry Hooper (formerly a Red Sox) with a watch, chain and guard.

September 17 (continued)

1942 — Pitcher Tex Hughson wins his 20th game of the season with a 5 to 1 win over the St. Louis Browns in St. Louis.

1945 — The Chicago White Sox have 18 infield assists and Boston has 17 in the second game of a doubleheader.

1953 — Pitcher Ellis Kinder pitches in his 67th game to break Ed Walsh's (Chicago White Sox) American League record set in 1908.

September 18

1903 — Defeating Cleveland at Boston 7 to 6 pitcher Bill Dineen wins his 20th game of the season.

1919 — The Detroit Tigers defeat Boston 8 to 2 at Fenway Park as Sad Sam Jones loses his 20th game of the season.

1938 — A season filled with hope for Sox fans ends as rain cancels a doubleheader with Chicago allowing the New York Yankees to clinch the pennant. The Yanks actually lost a doubleheader to St. Louis, but rain outs were not made up and the Bosox were out of the race.

1977 — The largest crowd ever to watch a regular season game at Baltimore's Memorial Stadium, 51,798 turn out for "Thanks, Brooks" Day as the Red Sox defeated the Orioles 10 to 4 while long time Baltimore favorite Brooks Robinson is honored.

September 19

1903 — Defeating Chicago at the Huntington Avenue Grounds 13-3 Cy Young wins his 28th game of the season. The Pilgrims have scored 72 runs in their last seven games.

1923 — Pitcher Howard Ehmke wins his 20th game of the season by defeating the Chicago White Sox 2 to 1 at Fenway Park.

1936 — Pitcher Wes Ferrell, by defeating the Philadelphia Athletics at Shibe Park 5 to 1, gains his 20th win of the season.

1953 — Mel Parnell's 3 to 0 shutout of the New York Yankees at Fenway Park is his 20th win of the season.

September 21

1946 — The Red Sox defeat the Washington Senators 7 to 5 in 11 innings at Washington to record their 100th win of the season. The winning pitcher is Bill Zuber.

1956 — New York leaves 20 men on base in a game against Boston.

1960 — Outfielder Carroll Hardy becomes the only man to pitch hit for Ted Williams. In the first inning of a game in Baltimore, Williams fouled a ball off his ankle and Manager Higgins sent in Hardy to hit. He hit into a double play. (See May 31, 1961).

1967 — The Cleveland Indians make four pinch hits against Boston.

September 21 (continued)

1976 — A 7 to 1 victory at Fenway Park in the first game of a doubleheader is Luis Tiant's 20th win of the season.

September 22

1902 — A 5 to 1 win in the first game of a doubleheader at Philadelphia gives Bill Dineen twenty wins.

1906 — Second baseman Hobe Ferris coming off the field swings on the dugout roof and kicks outfielder Jack Hayden in the face.

1948 — A crowd of 76,722 packs Cleveland's Municipal Stadium for a night game between the Red Sox and Indians.

1955 — The Throneberry brothers face each other for the first time in a major league game. Faye for the Red Sox, Marv for the New York Yankees.

September 23

1902 — A 14 to 1 victory at Washington gives pitcher Cy Young a 32-11 season's record.

1921 — After nine successive victories pitcher Joe Bush is defeated by St. Louis.

September 24

1916 — Cleveland infielder Marty Kavanaugh batting for pitcher Joe Boehling in the 5th inning against the Red Sox hits the American League's first pinch hit grand slam home run.

1919 — By hitting his 28th home run of the year Babe Ruth breaks the record made by Ed Williamson of the Chicago National League team in 1883.

1928 — Only 404 fans show up at Navin Field in Detroit for a game with the Red Sox.

1935 — Pitcher Lefty Grove wins his 20th game of the year by topping Philadelphia at Fenway Park 8 to 2.

1950 — 66,924 jam Yankee Stadium as New York defeats Boston 9 to 5.

September 25

1901 — Pitcher Cy Young wins his thirty third game of the season, beating Chicago 5 to 2 at Boston.

1912 — The Red Sox win their 100th game of the season.

1915 — The Red Sox have received more than 30,000 applications for World Series tickets and announce it will be necessary to reserve some of the bleacher seats.

1935 — A 7 to 2 win over Philadelphia at Fenway Park gives pitcher Wes Ferrell his 25th victory of the year.

1949 — Mel Parnell's 4 to 1 win over the New York Yankees at Fenway Park is his 25th of the year.

September 25 (continued)

1953 — Pitcher Mel Parnell shuts out the New York Yankees for the fourth time this season. The shut outs were July 1, 4 to 0; July 9, 4 to 0; September 19, 3 to 0; and September 25, 5 to 0.

September 26

1912 — In a game at Boston, the Red Sox trailed New York 12 to 3 after 5-1/2 innings, but went on to win 15 to 12 in eight innings when the game was called because of darkness. Boston had 14 hits to New York's 16.

1926 — Detroit Tiger outfielder Bob Fothergill hits for the cycle against Boston.

1948 — 69,755 fans set a Yankee Stadium day game attendance record as the Yankees play the Red Sox.

1979 — Red Sox announce manager Don Zimmer will return in 1980 but release pitching coach Al Jackson and will replace him with John Podres and hire Tommy Harper as a coach for the 1980 season. In a game against the Toronto Blue Jays, Jim Rice's first inning single gives him 200 hits for the third consecutive season to become the 17th player in baseball history to accomplish this feat. Last American Leaguer to do it was John Pesky in 1947.

The Red Sox set a season attendance record for Fenway Park surpassing last season's previous high by 11,617 for a total of 2,342,260.

September 27

1905 — Chicago defeats Boston 15 to 1 at Boston.

1914 — Pitcher Ray Collins gets the decision in an 8 to 6 win at Chicago for his 20th victory of the season.

1915 — A 8 to 4 win over the St. Louis Browns at Boston gives Boston a 20-7 record for September and the third month in a row in which they have won 20 games.

1946 — A 5 to 4 win over the Washington Senators at Fenway Park is the Red Sox 104th win of the year and pitcher Tex Hughson's 20th win of the season.

September 28

1903 — Defeating St. Louis 6 to 0 at Boston marks the 20th shutout of the season by Boston pitchers.

1914 — A 5 to 2 win over Chicago in the Windy City gives Boston a 21-9 record for September.

1915 — Dividing into two teams for practice at Braves Field for the upcoming World Series the Forrest Cady team wins 2 to 1. Del Gainor hits an inside the park home run, the first ever at Braves Field.

1936 — Outfielder Bing Miller released and signed as a coach. Coach Al Schacht released.

1963 — Rookie pitcher Pete Smith starts a Red Sox triple play against the Los Angeles Angels at Fenway Park. The play, on a ball Smith was told by

September 28 (continued)

shortstop Ed Bressoud to let drop, went from pitcher to third to second to first.

1965 — Pitcher Dave Morehead loses his tenth consecutive game to the California Angels, a string which started in July 28, 1963.

1973 — An 11 to 2 victory in the first game of a doubleheader with Milwaukee at Fenway Park is Luis Tiant's 20th win of the year.

September 29

1902 — Boston defeats Baltimore 9 to 5 in the final game played at Oriole Park in Baltimore.

1917 — An 11 to 0 shutout of St. Louis in the second game of a doubleheader is Babe Ruth's 24th victory of the year. The Sox also won the opener 13 to 5.

1957 — Ted Williams goes 2 for 2 (double, single) ending the season batting .388 and capturing his fifth batting title. At 39 he becomes the oldest player to win a batting crown.

1963 — Infielder Billy Gardner and pitcher Chet Nichols are released. Pitchers Billy MacLeod and Dave Busby and outfielder Pete Jernigan are sold to Seattle. Pitching coach Harry Dorish is fired. The Sox recall rookies Tony Conigliaro (OF), Tony Horton (1B), John Boyle (P), Archie Skeen (C), Dave Gray (P), and Pete Charton (P).

1978 — Jim Rice's second inning single at Fenway Park makes him the first American League player in 41 years to reach 400 total bases in one season. Joe DiMaggio of New York was the last in 1937.

September 30

1905 — The Pilgrims play their 11th doubleheader of the month. At one point, all the games on five consecutive playing dates were doubleheaders. The twin bills for the month were Sept. 4 at New York; Sept. 11, Washington; Sept. 15 at Philadelphia; Sept. 18 and 19 at Washington; Sept. 22 and 23, St. Louis; Sept. 25, 26, 27, Chicago and these two games with Detroit. They won 2, lost 2 and split 7.

1916 — Shuting out New York 3 to 0 at Fenway Park Babe Ruth wins his 23rd game of the season.

1978 — Pitcher Dennis Eckersley defeats the Toronto Blue Jays 5 to 1 at Boston for his 20th win of the season.

OCTOBER 1

1904 — Pitcher Bill Dineen wins his 20th game of the season beating the Browns 6 to 1 in St. Louis.

1912 — Pitcher Hugh Bedient wins his 20th game of the season 12 to 3 at Washington in a game which saw Tris Speaker walked five times.

October 1 (continued)

1940 — Catcher Joe Glenn sold to Louisville and pitcher Oscar Judd drafted from Sacramento.

1946 — The Red Sox defeat a team of American League All Stars behind Tex Hughson 2 to 0.

1978 — A 5 to 0 victory over the Toronto Blue Jays at Boston ties the Sox with the New York Yankees, who were losing to the Cleveland Indians 9 to 2 in New York, for first place in the American League East with identical 99-63 records. The tie, on the last game of the regular season, forces a one game play off for the championship.

October 2

1917 — Duffy Lewis' single off Washington pitcher Harry Harper scores three men.

1907 — A 4 to 2 loss to St. Louis at the Huntington Avenue Grounds marks Boston's 16th consecutive loss. A steak which began September 12.

1922 — Pitcher Lefty O'Doul obtained from the New York Yankees.

1946 — The Red Sox lose to a team of American League All Stars 4 to 2. Mickey Harris takes the loss.

1962 — A bill introduced in the Massachusetts Legislature which would subject abusive spectators at sporting events to a $50.00 fine.

1978 — The Red Sox lose the second ever play off for the American League championship to the New York Yankees 5 to 4 at Fenway Park.

October 3

1907 — A 1 to 0 victory over St. Louis at Boston ends a 16 game losing streak.

1908 — Boston plays a doubleheader vs the Philadelphia A's losing opener 8 to 7, winning the night cap 5 to 0. These were the final two games ever played in Philadelphia's Columbia Park.

1912 — Pitcher Smokey Joe Wood wins his 34th game of the year defeating Philadelphia at Shibe Park 17 to 5 in a game also highlighted by a Duffy Lewis home run.

1946 — The Red Sox defeat a team of American League All Stars behind Jim Bagby 4 to 1.

1954 — Dennis Eckersley — B   1978   P

1961 — Pitcher Dave Hillman and infielder Billy Harrell sold to Seattle. Released outright to Seattle were pitchers Bob Heffner and Darrell Massey. Pitcher Bob Carlson was sent to Johnstown.

October 4

1913 — The Washington Senators use 5 pitchers against the Red Sox in the ninth inning, and a total of 8 pitchers in a single game against Boston, winning 10-9, as Fred Anderson went the distance for Boston. The eight were A.

October 4 (continued)

Williams, Bentley, Griffith, Engel, Johnson, Schaefer, Ainsmith, and Gedeon.

1937 — Pitchers Rube Walberg and Tommy Thomas released.

October 5

1912 — A 3 to 0 win at Philadelphia gives the Red Sox a 48-27 road record for the season and their 105th win of the season.

1915 — Rain postpones the Red Sox game with the New York Yankees at New York marking the 22nd rain out of the year for Boston.

1978 — Red Sox outfielder Jim Rice is named co-winner, along with New York Yankee pitcher Ron Guidry, of the American League's Joe Cronin award for Distinguished Achievement. This is the first time in history that dual winners have been named and Rice is the first Sox to be honored with this award.

October 6

1915 — The Red Sox defeat the New York Yankees 2 to 0 at New York behind Dutch Leonard to win their 100th game of the season.

Contrary to the usual custom Manager Carrigan will not permit any of his Red Sox players to carry any rabbits feet in the World Series for good luck. He also barred charmed coins.

1979 — According to a published report the Red Sox may start their own airline company. Owners Buddy LeRoux and Rodger Badgitt have received FAA approval to start an airline to carry sports teams and other charter groups.

October 7

1908 — Catcher Lou Criger operated on in a private Boston hospital for the removal of a growth in the groin. Criger had complained all season of a troubled left leg.

October 8

1904 — Cy Young's 1 to 0 shutout in seven innings over New York in the second game of a doubleheader at Boston is his 26th win of the season. The game marked the 21st shutout of the year by Boston pitching.

October 10

1938 — Pitcher Bill Kerksieck drafted from Little Rock.

October 12

1933 — Pitcher Lloyd Brown traded to Cleveland for infielder Bill Cissell.

1960 — Pitcher Mike Fornieles is named by "The Sporting News" as the first American League Winner of their new "Annual Fireman of The Year" award. The award to be given annually to the top relief pitcher.

October 13

1907 — In a three way trade the New York Yankees obtain first baseman Jake Stahl from the Chicago White Sox and send infielder Frank LaPorte to the Red Sox who in turn send shortstop Fred Parent to the Chicago White Sox.

October 14

1909 — In a post season series of third place finishers the Red Sox complete the defeat of New York Giants 4 games to 1.

1946 — Frank Duffy — B   1978   IF

October 15

1962 — In his first act as Boson manager John Pesky announces the retention of coach Billy Herman, but releases coaches Sal Maglie, Rudy York and Len Okrie. Former manager Pinky Higgins, now elevated to executive Vice President, had recommended Herman's retention. Could he have known something? Ironically, it was Herman who replaced Pesky as manager two years later.

October 17

1962 — First baseman Don Gile sold to Seattle (Pacific Coast League). On this same day five first year bonus rookies were placed on the Sox roster. Recognize any of them? Pitcher Jerry Stephenson, infielder Rico Petrocelli, first baseman Jim Russin, outfielder Jim Gosger, and first baseman Gage Naudain.

October 18

1951 — Andy Hassler — B   1978-79   P

1952 — Allen Ripley — B   1978   P

October 19

1960 — John Pesky named manager of the newly acquired Red Sox Seattle farm club.

October 23

1962 — Manager Johnny Pesky names new coaching staff Harry Dorish (pitching), Harry Malmberg (first base), and Al Lakeman (bull pen).

1979 — Catcher Mike O'Berry sent to the Chicago Cubs to complete the Ted Sizemore deal. Pitcher Jim Wright assigned to Pawtucket.

October 25

1951 — John LaRose — B   1978   P

October 30

1933 — Second baseman Johnny Hodapp released to Rochester.

1951 — Tom Poquette — B   1979   OF

October 30 (continued)

1979 — Carl Yastrzemski gets new shoes specially fitted to ease painfully injured Achilles tendons. He will wear these for the 1980 season.

October 31

1933 — Outfielder Tom Oliver released to Baltimore in part payment for outfielder Moose Solters.

NOVEMBER 1

1909 — Fred Lake resigns as Red Sox manager and owner Taylor announces former Brooklyn National's manager Pat Donovan has been signed as Boston's manager for 1910.

November 3

1908 — Fred Lake, who had relieved James McGuire as manager during the 1908 season, is rehired for 1909.

November 6

1979 — Free agent first baseman Bob Watson signs with the New York Yankees.

November 7

1978 — Outfielder Jim Rice is named the American League's most valuable player.

November 11

1903 — Manager-captain Jimmy Collins signs a new three year contract.

November 13

1978 — Pitcher Luis Tiant, who early this month had declared his free agency, signs a two year playing and ten year scouting contract with the New York Yankees.

November 15

1934 — "The Sporting News" proclaims that the Red Sox "Play Boys" won't fool manager Cronin. He knows who they are and they'll be among the missing. This statement reflected back to a fracas that occurred in Baltimore on the way north in 1933 that caused a broken arm and in another case a quick trip to the minors, a story which got a lot of publicity everywhere but in Boston.

1955 — Manager Pinky Higgins voted American League "Manager of the Year" by the Associated Press.

November 16

1908 — Mrs. Julia Stahl, widow of Chick Stahl, the Boston manager who had committed suicide in Indiana while on a training trip in the spring of 1907, was found dead in the doorway of a South Boston tenement house.

1979 — Red Sox sign free agent first baseman Tony Perez.

November 22

1935 — Pitcher Mike Meola sold to the St. Louis Browns.

November 23

1934 — First baseman Eddie Morgan sent to Rochester for option on infielder James R. Brown.

November 26

1936 — Infielder Dib Williams sent to Rochester to complete the Buster Mills deal (Aug. 3, 1936).

November 27

1979 — Free Agent Pitcher Skip Lockwood signed.

November 28

1960 — Infielder Billy Harrell drafted from Buffalo.

November 29

1936 — Catcher John Peacock given a $10,000 bonus for signing with the Red Sox. Peacock had been made a free agent from the Cincinnati organization by Baseball Commissioner Judge Landis.

DECEMBER 6

1938 — Pitcher Footsie Marcum traded to the St. Louis Browns for infielder Tom Carey.

December 7

1941 — After a day of hunting at Tom Yawkey's game preserve pitcher Lefty Grove announces his retirement.

1978 — Pitcher Bill Lee traded to the Montreal Expos for utility infielder Stan Papi.

December 8

1921 — Utility man Ossie Vitt sold to the Cincinnati Reds for the waiver price.

December 10

1939 — Outfielder Dom DiMaggio purchased from San Francisco for cash estimated at $40,000 and two players to be named later.

1941 — Pitcher Lefty Grove announces his retirement from baseball after 17 years and 300 major league wins during regular season competition.

1944 — Steve Renko — B   1979   P

December 11

1924 — Infielder Howard Shanks traded to the New York Yankees for infielder Mike McNally, who was sent to Washington.

1934 — The Red Sox buy the Charlotte franchise in the Piedmont League.

Outfielder George Stumpf sold to Kansas City.

December 12

1904 — Outfielder Jesse Burkett obtained from St. Louis for cash and outfielder George Stone.

1924 — Catcher Steve O'Neill sold to the New York Yankees on waivers.

December 13

1939 — Outfielder Larry Powell purchased from San Francisco. This was part of the December 10 DiMaggio deal and only DiMaggio would report to the Red Sox in 1940.

December 14

1933 — Catcher Gordie Hinkle purchased from the St. Louis Cardinals for $10,000.

December 16

1920 — Former St. Louis Brown manager Jimmy Burke appointed Red Sox coach.

December 20

1954 — Joe McKenney named Red Sox public relations director.

December 21

1940 — Outfielder John Barrett (on option with San Franciso) purchased from Louisville for pitcher Alex Mustaikis.

1950 — Jim Wright — B   1978   P

December 28

1940 — Infielder Charley Gelbert released to Louisville.

December 29

1919 — Outfielder Braggo Roth and second baseman Red Shannon traded to Washington for pitcher Harry Harper, outfielder Mike Menoskey and third baseman Eddie Foster.

1962 — The Red Sox announce they will play a record number 32 night games in 1963. It was believed the sharp drop in attendance in 1962 was a key factor in the decision.

BOSTON YEARLY RECORDS

Presented in this section on a year to year basis are the more important of the batting and pitching records of the Boston American League team. The batting records include: runs scored (runs), opponent's runs (runs against), hits (H), doubles (2B), triples (3B), home runs (HR), walks (BB), stolen bases (SB) and team batting average (BA). The pitching records include: complete games pitched (CG), innings pitched (IP), hits allowed (H), walks issued (BB), strike outs (SO), shut outs (SHO) and earned run average (ERA). In the case of innings pitched where the final figures showed 2/3 of inning the last figure has been increased (1463-2/3 shown as 1464) and where 1/3 of an inning was recorded the 1/3 has been dropped (1463-1/3 shown as 1463).

These records make an interesting comparison of the various teams. Look up your favorite and compare it to others. You may be surprised!

BOSTON HOME-AWAY WON-LOST RECORDS 1901-1979

Year	Home	Pct.	Away	Pct.	Yearly Total	Pct.
1901	49-20	.710	30-37	.448	79-57	.581
1902	43-27	.614	34-33	.507	77-60	.562
1903	49-20	.710	42-27	.600	91-47	.659
1904	49-30	.620	46-29	.613	95-59	.617
1905	44-32	.579	34-42	.447	78-74	.513
1906	22-54	.289	27-51	.346	49-105	.318
1907	34-41	.453	25-49	.338	59-90	.396
1908	37-40	.481	38-39	.494	75-79	.487
1909	47-28	.627	41-35	.539	88-63	.583
1910	51-28	.646	30-44	.405	81-72	.529
1911	39-37	.513	39-38	.506	78-75	.510
1912	57-20	.740	48-27	.640	105-47	.691
1913	41-34	.539	38-37	.585	79-71	.527
1914	44-31	.579	47-31	.603	91-62	.595
1915	55-20	.733	46-30	.605	101-50	.669
1916	49-28	.653	42-35	.545	91-63	.591
1917	45-33	.577	45-29	.608	90-62	.592
1918	49-21	.700	26-30	.462	75-51	.595
1919	35-31	.522	31-40	.437	66-71	.482
1920	41-35	.539	31-46	.403	72-81	.471
1921	41-36	.532	34-43	.442	75-79	.487
1922	31-42	.425	30-51	.370	61-93	.396
1923	38-40	.487	23-51	.311	61-91	.401
1924	42-36	.538	25-51	.329	67-87	.435
1925	28-47	.373	19-58	.247	47-105	.309
1926	25-51	.329	21-56	.273	46-107	.301
1927	29-49	.372	22-54	.289	51-103	.331
1928	26-47	.356	31-49	.388	57-96	.373
1929	32-45	.416	26-51	.338	58-96	.377
1930	30-46	.395	22-56	.282	52-102	.338
1931	39-40	.494	23-50	.315	62-90	.408
1932	27-50	.351	16-61	.208	43-111	.279
1933	32-40	.444	31-46	.403	63-86	.423
1934	42-35	.545	34-41	.453	76-76	.500
1935	41-37	.526	37-38	.493	78-75	.510
1936	47-29	.618	27-51	.346	74-80	.481
1937	44-29	.603	36-43	.456	80-72	.526
1938	52-23	.693	36-38	.486	88-61	.591
1939	42-32	.568	47-30	.610	89-62	.589
1940	45-34	.570	37-38	.493	82-72	.532

Boston Home-Away Won-Lost Records 1901-1979 (continued)

Year	Home	Pct.	Away	Pct.	Yearly Total	Pct.
1941	47-30	.610	37-40	.481	84-70	.545
1942	53-24	.688	40-35	.533	93-59	.612
1943	39-36	.520	29-48	.377	68-84	.447
1944	47-30	.610	30-47	.390	77-77	.500
1945	42-35	.545	29-48	.387	71-83	.461
1946	61-16	.792	43-34	.558	104-50	.675
1947	49-30	.620	34-41	.453	83-71	.539
1948	55-23	.705	41-36	.532	96-59	.619
1949	61-16	.792	35-42	.455	96-58	.623
1950	55-22	.714	39-38	.506	94-60	.610
1951	50-25	.667	37-42	.468	87-67	.565
1952	50-27	.649	26-51	.338	76-78	.494
1953	38-38	.500	46-31	.597	84-69	.549
1954	38-39	.494	31-46	.403	69-85	.448
1955	47-31	.603	37-39	.487	84-70	.545
1956	43-34	.558	41-36	.532	84-70	.545
1957	44-33	.571	38-39	.494	82-72	.532
1958	49-28	.636	30-47	.390	79-75	.513
1959	43-34	.558	32-45	.416	75-79	.487
1960	36-41	.468	29-48	.377	65-89	.442
1961	50-31	.617	26-55	.321	76-86	.469
1962	39-40	.494	37-44	.457	76-84	.475
1963	44-36	.550	32-49	.395	76-85	.472
1964	45-36	.556	27-54	.333	72-90	.444
1965	34-47	.420	28-53	.346	62-100	.383
1966	40-41	.494	32-49	.395	72-90	.444
1967	49-32	.605	43-38	.531	92-70	.568
1968	46-35	.568	40-41	.494	86-76	.531
1969	46-35	.568	41-40	.506	87-75	.537
1970	52-29	.642	35-46	.432	87-75	.537
1971	47-33	.588	38-44	.463	85-77	.525
1972	52-26	.667	33-44	.429	85-70	.548
1973	48-33	.593	41-40	.506	89-73	.549
1974	46-35	.568	38-43	.469	84-78	.519
1975	47-34	.580	48-31	.608	95-65	.594
1976	46-35	.568	37-44	.457	83-79	.512
1977	51-29	.638	46-35	.568	97-64	.602
1978	59-23	.720	40-41	.494	99-64	.607
1979	51-29	.638	40-40	.500	91-69	.569

BOSTON RED SOX MONTHLY RECORDS

Year	APRIL	MAY	JUNE	JULY	AUGUST	SEPT.	OCT.
1901	1-3	10-11	20-5	16-12	17-14	15-12	
1902	3-4	16-10	13-12	14-12	16-9	15-13	
1903	4-6	15-9	19-7	16-9	18-9	19-7	
1904	10-2	15-8	12-11	15-12	17-10	18-14	8-2
1905	3-10	12-9	10-9	14-15	17-11	15-20	7-0
1906	6-7	4-22	6-17	9-22	13-13	9-21	2-3
1907	5-9	7-17	10-13	13-14	17-16	6-18	1-3
1908	7-7	8-17	14-13	14-13	13-12	14-14	5-3
1909	7-5	12-11	16-12	19-15	19-7	13-12	2-1
1910	7-6	12-10	13-11	23-10	17-12	8-17	1-6
1911	6-7	16-10	12-14	15-16	13-11	10-17	6-0
1912	9-4	16-9	21-8	21-9	20-7	15-9	3-1
1913	6-8	10-14	18-8	12-18	13-13	19-8	1-2
1914	4-6	13-13	18-13	19-9	13-8	21-9	3-4
1915	5-6	12-9	19-8	22-10	21-6	20-7	2-4
1916	9-6	12-12	13-12	20-10	17-12	19-9	1-2
1917	9-4	18-6	14-14	18-11	16-12	14-12	1-3
1918	11-2	14-12	14-14	20-9	15-13	1-1	
1919	4-1	8-14	12-16	15-17	14-14	13-9	
1920	10-2	12-12	8-17	10-21	19-12	13-17	
1921	5-5	11-14	16-14	10-19	16-10	17-14	0-3
1922	6-8	11-15	13-16	9-20	9-16	13-18	
1923	4-7	9-14	10-14	11-23	12-13	14-17	1-3
1924	4-7	17-7	11-18	10-22	16-14	9-19	
1925	2-10	12-17	9-18	6-24	7-19	9-17	2-0
1926	5-11	7-19	8-18	11-20	11-21	4-18	
1927	3-11	8-16	4-24	14-18	10-16	12-16	0-2
1928	4-10	11-12	12-14	11-24	8-23	11-13	
1929	4-5	7-22	11-21	7-20	15-14	12-14	2-0
1930	5-8	7-20	14-14	9-23	9-18	8-19	
1931	3-7	11-18	12-13	12-21	11-16	13-15	
1932	3-11	4-21	5-23	14-18	11-19	6-19	
1933	4-11	9-14	15-16	16-10	11-22	8-12	0-1
1934	5-6	12-15	18-11	17-15	13-15	11-14	
1935	7-5	12-12	13-16	17-11	14-18	15-13	
1936	11-5	15-13	12-14	16-14	10-19	10-15	
1937	3-2	13-13	15-10	18-12	15-15	15-18	1-2
1938	6-5	13-12	16-10	16-8	18-15	18-10	1-1
1939	5-3	16-9	12-12	23-10	18-14	15-14	
1940	7-4	15-6	14-16	14-18	19-14	13-14	
1941	7-6	12-13	17-11	14-16	18-17	16-7	
1942	9-6	14-14	19-7	14-17	23-9	14-6	
1943	2-5	15-14	15-12	13-16	14-20	9-15	0-2
1944	5-5	13-16	18-10	16-14	16-15	8-16	1-1
1945	3-8	13-11	16-8	14-16	13-23	12-17	
1946	11-3	21-6	18-10	20-10	21-11	13-10	

Boston Red Sox Monthly Records (continued)

Year	APRIL	MAY	JUNE	JULY	AUGUST	SEPT.	OCT.
1947	6-6	13-13	15-11	18-13	17-13	14-15	
1948	3-6	11-17	18-6	25-9	19-10	18-10	2-1
1949	5-6	15-10	15-15	18-12	24-8	19-5	0-2
1950	7-6	17-12	16-13	14-12	24-6	15-11	1-0
1951	7-4	17-9	16-14	17-12	18-12	12-16	
1952	10-2	12-15	15-14	16-13	16-14	7-20	
1953	6-6	15-15	17-13	19-11	15-15	12-9	
1954	4-8	9-13	12-21	15-16	16-14	13-13	
1955	8-8	11-18	20-9	21-8	14-13	10-14	
1956	4-5	16-14	15-12	18-13	15-14	16-12	
1957	8-4	13-17	17-12	16-12	14-15	14-12	
1958	4-10	16-12	15-12	14-14	17-13	13-14	
1959	6-7	13-17	12-16	13-17	18-12	13-10	
1960	5-6	9-15	10-22	15-12	16-16	10-16	0-2
1961	7-7	10-16	21-13	9-22	17-14	12-13	0-1
1962	7-9	11-17	17-14	11-16	17-15	13-13	
1963	9-6	13-14	18-13	13-18	11-20	12-14	
1964	5-7	16-14	15-17	16-14	7-22	10-16	3-0
1965	5-5	16-16	8-21	9-21	13-20	11-15	0-2
1966	3-7	14-19	10-21	18-14	15-17	12-12	
1967	8-6	14-14	15-14	19-10	20-15	15-11	1-0
1968	8-8	14-15	12-15	19-10	20-16	13-12	
1969	11-9	18-7	14-15	14-15	13-15	17-13	0-1
1970	11-8	9-17	14-11	18-13	16-14	19-12	
1971	12-7	17-11	14-13	16-14	11-19	15-13	
1972	4-7	11-12	12-15	20-12	17-12	20-9	1-3
1973	7-10	13-13	15-12	19-14	18-13	17-11	
1974	10-12	15-10	16-10	14-15	17-12	11-18	1-1
1975	7-9	16-9	18-13	22-11	16-12	16-11	
1976	6-7	13-15	15-13	12-19	16-14	18-11	3-0
1977	9-9	15-12	17-10	17-12	17-12	22-8	0-1
1978	11-9	23-7	18-7	13-15	19-10	14-15	1-1
1979	13-7	14-12	20-8	15-13	16-13	13-16	

BOSTON YEARLY BATTING RECORDS

Year	Runs	Runs Against	H	2B	3B	HR	BB	SB	BA
1901	759	608	1353	183	104	37	331	157	.278
1902	664	600	1356	195	95	42	275	132	.278
1903	708	504	1336	222	113	48	262	141	.272
1904	608	466	1294	194	105	26	347	101	.247
1905	579	565	1177	165	69	29	486	131	.234
1906	463	706	1223	160	76	12	298	99	.239
1907	466	558	1223	152	47	15	305	124	.234

Boston Yearly Batting Records (continued)

Year	Runs	Runs Against	H	2B	3B	HR	BB	SB	BA
1908	564	513	1243	116	88	14	289	168	.246
1909	601	549	1306	151	68	20	348	215	.263
1910	641	564	1350	175	87	43	430	194	.259
1911	679	643	1379	203	66	35	506	190	.274
1912	800	544	1404	269	84	29	565	185	.277
1913	631	610	1334	220	101	17	466	189	.269
1914	588	509	1278	226	85	18	397	177	.250
1915	669	499	1308	202	77	13	527	118	.260
1916	550	480	1245	196	56	14	464	129	.248
1917	555	455	1243	198	64	14	466	105	.246
1918	474	380	990	159	53	16	406	110	.249
1919	564	552	1188	181	49	33	471	108	.261
1920	650	699	1397	216	71	22	533	98	.269
1921	668	696	1440	248	69	17	428	83	.277
1922	598	769	1392	250	55	45	366	60	.263
1923	584	809	1354	253	54	34	391	77	.261
1924	725	801	1481	300	61	30	604	79	.277
1925	639	921	1375	257	64	41	513	42	.266
1926	562	835	1325	249	54	32	465	48	.256
1927	597	856	1348	271	78	28	430	82	.259
1928	589	770	1356	260	62	38	389	99	.264
1929	605	803	1377	285	69	28	413	85	.267
1930	612	814	1393	257	68	47	358	42	.264
1931	625	800	1409	289	34	37	405	42	.262
1932	566	915	1331	253	57	53	469	46	.251
1933	700	758	1407	294	56	50	519	62	.271
1934	820	775	1465	287	70	51	610	116	.274
1935	718	732	1458	281	63	69	609	89	.276
1936	775	764	1485	288	62	86	584	54	.276
1937	821	775	1506	269	64	100	601	79	.281
1938	902	751	1566	298	56	98	650	55	.299
1939	890	795	1543	287	57	124	591	42	.291
1940	872	825	1566	301	80	145	590	55	.286
1941	865	750	1517	304	55	124	683	67	.283
1942	761	594	1451	244	55	103	591	68	.276
1943	563	607	1314	223	42	57	486	86	.244
1944	739	676	1456	277	56	69	522	60	.270
1945	599	674	1393	255	44	50	541	72	.260
1946	792	594	1441	268	50	109	687	45	.271
1947	720	669	1412	206	54	103	666	41	.265
1948	907	720	1471	277	40	121	823	38	.274
1949	896	667	1500	272	36	131	835	43	.282
1950	1027	804	1665	287	61	161	719	32	.302
1951	804	725	1428	233	32	127	756	20	.266
1952	668	658	1338	233	34	113	542	59	.255
1953	656	632	1385	255	37	101	496	33	.264

Boston Yearly Batting Records (continued)

Year	Runs	Runs Against	H	2B	3B	HR	BB	SB	BA
1954	700	728	1436	244	41	123	654	51	.266
1955	755	652	1392	241	39	137	707	43	.264
1956	780	751	1473	261	45	139	727	28	.275
1957	721	668	1380	231	32	153	624	29	.262
1958	697	691	1335	229	30	155	638	29	.256
1959	726	696	1335	248	28	125	626	68	.256
1960	658	775	1359	234	32	124	570	34	.261
1961	729	792	1401	251	37	112	647	56	.254
1962	707	756	1429	257	53	146	525	39	.258
1963	666	704	1493	247	34	171	475	27	.252
1964	688	793	1425	253	29	186	504	18	.258
1965	669	791	1378	244	40	165	607	47	.251
1966	655	731	1318	228	44	145	542	35	.240
1967	722	614	1394	216	39	158	522	68	.255
1968	614	611	1253	207	17	125	582	76	.236
1969	743	736	1381	234	37	197	658	41	.251
1970	786	722	1450	252	28	203	594	50	.262
1971	691	667	1360	246	28	161	552	51	.252
1972	640	620	1289	229	34	124	522	66	.248
1973	738	647	1472	235	30	147	581	114	.267
1974	696	661	1449	236	31	109	569	104	.264
1975	796	709	1500	284	44	134	565	66	.275
1976	716	660	1448	257	53	134	500	95	.263
1977	859	712	1551	258	56	213	528	66	.281
1978	796	657	1493	270	46	172	582	74	.267
1979	841	711	1567	310	34	194	512	60	.283

BOSTON YEARLY PITCHING RECORDS

Year	CG	IP	H	BB	SO	SHO	ERA
1901	123	1217	1178	294	396	7	3.04
1902	123	1238	1217	326	431	6	3.02
1903	123	1255	1142	269	579	20	2.54
1904	148	1406	1208	233	612	21	2.12
1905	125	1356	1198	292	652	15	2.84
1906	124	1382	1360	285	549	6	3.41
1907	100	1414	1222	337	517	17	2.45
1908	102	1381	1200	366	624	12	2.28
1909	75	1358	1214	384	555	11	2.60
1910	100	1429	1236	414	670	11	2.46
1911	87	1364	1314	475	713	10	2.73
1912	110	1362	1243	385	712	18	2.76
1913	83	1355	1318	441	709	12	2.94
1914	88	1434	1212	397	605	24	2.35
1915	82	1397	1164	446	634	19	2.39

Boston Yearly Pitching Records (continued)

Year	CG	IP	H	BB	SO	SHO	ERA
1916	76	1411	1221	463	584	24	2.48
1917	115	1421	1197	413	509	15	2.20
1918	105	1120	931	380	392	26	2.31
1919	85	1222	1251	420	380	15	3.30
1920	91	1395	1481	461	481	11	3.82
1921	88	1364	1521	452	446	9	3.98
1922	71	1373	1508	503	359	10	4.30
1923	78	1372	1534	520	412	3	4.20
1924	73	1391	1563	519	414	8	4.36
1925	68	1327	1615	510	310	6	4.97
1926	53	1362	1520	546	336	6	4.72
1927	63	1376	1603	558	381	6	4.68
1928	70	1352	1492	452	407	5	4.39
1929	84	1366	1537	496	416	9	4.43
1930	78	1360	1505	488	356	4	4.70
1931	61	1367	1559	473	365	5	4.60
1932	42	1362	1574	612	365	2	5.02
1933	60	1328	1396	591	473	4	4.35
1934	68	1361	1527	543	538	8	4.32
1935	82	1376	1520	520	470	6	4.05
1936	78	1373	1501	552	584	11	4.39
1937	74	1366	1520	597	682	6	4.48
1938	67	1316	1472	528	484	10	4.46
1939	52	1351	1533	543	539	4	4.56
1940	51	1380	1568	625	613	4	4.89
1941	70	1372	1453	611	574	8	4.19
1942	84	1359	1260	553	500	11	3.44
1943	62	1426	1369	615	513	13	3.45
1944	58	1394	1404	592	524	5	3.82
1945	71	1391	1389	656	490	15	3.80
1946	79	1397	1359	501	667	15	3.38
1947	64	1392	1383	575	586	13	3.81
1948	70	1379	1445	592	513	11	4.20
1949	84	1377	1375	661	598	10	3.97
1950	66	1362	1413	748	630	6	4.88
1951	46	1399	1413	599	658	7	4.14
1952	53	1372	1332	623	624	7	3.80
1953	41	1373	1333	584	642	14	3.59
1954	41	1412	1434	612	707	9	4.01
1955	44	1384	1333	582	674	9	3.72
1956	50	1398	1354	668	712	8	4.17
1957	55	1377	1391	498	692	9	3.88
1958	44	1380	1396	521	695	5	3.92
1959	38	1364	1386	589	724	9	4.17
1960	34	1361	1440	580	767	6	4.62
1961	35	1443	1472	679	831	6	4.29
1962	34	1438	1416	632	923	10	4.22

Boston Yearly Pitching Records (continued)

Year	CG	IP	H	BB	SO	SHO	ERA
1963	29	1450	1367	539	1009	6	3.97
1964	21	1422	1464	571	1094	9	4.50
1965	33	1439	1443	543	993	9	4.24
1966	32	1464	1402	577	977	10	3.92
1967	41	1459	1307	477	1010	9	3.36
1968	55	1447	1303	523	972	17	3.33
1969	30	1467	1423	685	935	7	3.92
1970	38	1446	1391	594	1003	8	3.87
1971	44	1443	1424	535	871	11	3.80
1972	48	1383	1309	512	918	20	3.47
1973	67	1440	1417	499	808	10	3.65
1974	71	1455	1462	463	751	12	3.72
1975	62	1437	1463	490	720	11	3.98
1976	49	1458	1495	409	673	13	3.52
1977	40	1428	1555	378	758	13	4.11
1978	57	1473	1530	464	706	15	3.54
1979	47	1431	1487	463	731	11	4.03

RED SOX BEST MONTHLY RECORDS

MOST WINS			BEST PCT.		
April	13-7	1979	11-2	.846	1918
May	23-7	1978	21-6	.778	1946
June	21-8	1912	20-5	.800	1901
	21-13	1961			
July	25-9	1948	25-9	.735	1948
August	24-6	1950	24-6	.800	1950
	24-8	1949			
September	22-8	1977	20-7	.741	1915
October	8-2	1904	7-0	1.000	1905*

*7-0, 1905; 6-0, 1911; 3-0, 1964, 1976; 2-0, 1925, 1929; 1-0, 1950, 1967.

RED SOX WORST MONTHLY RECORDS

FEWEST WINS			WORST PCT.		
April	1-3	1903	2-10	.167	1925
May	4-22	1906	4-22	.154	1906
	4-21	1932			
June	4-24	1927	4-24	.143	1927
July	6-24	1925	6-24	.200	1925
August	7-19	1925	7-22	.241	1964
	7-22	1964			
September	4-18	1926	4-18	.182	1926
	1- 1*	1918			
October	0-3†	1921	0- 3	.000	1921†

*War shortened season
†5 years 0-2, 5 years 0-1

RED SOX MISCELLANEOUS YEARLY BATTING RECORDS

Most Hits	1665	1950
Most Doubles	310	1979
Most Triples	113	1903
Most Home Runs	213	1977
Most Walks	835	1949
Most Runs	1027	1950
Most Runs Against	921	1925
Most Stolen Bases	215	1909
Highest Batting Average	.302	1950
Fewest Hits	1175	1905
Fewest Doubles	116	1908
Fewest Triples	17	1968
Fewest Home Runs	12	1906
Fewest Walks	262	1903
Fewest Runs	463	1906
Fewest Runs Against	380	1918
Fewest Stolen Bases	18	1964
Lowest Batting Average	.234	1905, 1907

RED SOX MISCELLANEOUS YEARLY PITCHING RECORDS

Most Complete Games	148	1904
Most Innings Pitched	1473	1978
Most Hits Allowed	1615	1925
Most Walks Allowed	748	1950
Most Strikeouts	1094	1964
Most Shutouts	26	1918
Lowest Earned Run Average	2.12	1904
Fewest Complete Games	21	1964
Fewest Innings Pitched	1120	1918
Fewest Hits Allowed	931	1918
Fewest Walks Allowed	233	1904
Fewest Strikeouts	310	1925
Fewest Shutouts	2	1932
Highest Earned Run Average	5.02	1932

RED SOX PITCHERS
CONSECUTIVE COMPLETE GAME VICTORIES

10	Cy Young	1902
9	Joe Wood	1912
9	Joe Bush	1921

Red Sox Pitchers Consecutive Complete Game Victories (continued)

9	Dave Ferriss	1946†
8	Cy Young	1901
8	Jesse Tannehill	1905
8	Joe Wood	1912
8	Elmer Myers	1920#
8	Lefty Grove	1939
7	Allan Russell	1919*
7	Dave Ferriss	1945¢

†Pitched one complete game, relief appearance, 8 complete games.

*Relieved Herb Pennock with none out in the first inning. Counting this game he would have eight consecutive.

#Won his first game in 1921.

¢After 7 complete games pitched one inning of relief, then he had another complete game.

INDIVIDUAL SEASON RECORDS

BATTING

AT BATS
Left-handed, most .... 661, Roger Cramer, 1940
Right-handed, most .... 677, Jim Rice, 1978
BASES ON BALLS, most .... 162, Ted Williams, 1947 & 1949
BATTING AVERAGE
Left-handed, highest .... 406, Ted Williams, 1941
Right-handed, highest .... 360, Jimmie Foxx, 1939
.372, Dale Alexander, + 1932
DOUBLES, most .... 67‡, Earl Webb, 1931
EXTRA BASES ON LONG HITS .... 201, Jimmie Foxx, 1938
GAMES, most .... 163, Jim Rice, 1978
GROUNDED INTO DOUBLE PLAYS
Left-handed, most .... 30‡, Carl Yastrzemski, 1964
Right-handed, most .... 32‡, Jackie Jensen, 1954
Fewest .... 3, Tony Lupien, 1943
HIT BY PITCHER, most .... 17, Jack Barry, 1916
HITS, most .... 222, Tris Speaker, 1912
HITTING STREAKS, longest .... 34, Dom DiMaggio, 1949
Longest start of season .... 20, Eddie Bressoud, 1964
HOME RUNS, most .... 50, Jimmie Foxx, 1938
at home .... 35, Jimmie Foxx, 1938
by position
1b .... 50, Jimmie Foxx, 1938
2b .... 27, Bobby Doerr, 1948 & 1950
3b .... 30, Butch Hobson, 1977
ss .... 40*, Rico Petrocelli, 1969
lf .... 44, Carl Yastrzemski, 1967
cf .... 38, Fred Lynn,* 1979

+376 at bats   *Lynn hit 39 HR's, one as a DH.

Individual Season Records (continued)

```
rf ................................... 36, Tony Conigliaro, 1970
catcher......................... 26, Carlton Fisk, 1973 and 1977
des. hitter ................................ 31, Jim Rice, 1977
pitcher.................................... 7, Wes Ferrell, 1935
grand slams .................................... 4, Babe Ruth, 1919
on road .................................... 26, Ted Williams, 1957
                                          20, Ted Williams, 1949
one month ............................... 14, Jackie Jensen, 1958
```
LONG HITS, most .... 92, Jimmie Foxx, 1938
RUNS, most.................................... 150, Ted Williams, 1949
RUNS BATTED IN, most .... 175, Jimmie Foxx, 1938
SACRIFICES
```
most, including flies .......................... 54, Jack Barry, 1917
most, no flies .............................. 35, Fred Parent, 1905
most, flies ........................... 12, Jackie Jensen, 1955 & 1959
                                          12, Jim Piersall, 1956
```
SINGLES, most .... 172, Johnny Pesky, 1947
SLUGGING PERCENTAGE
```
left-handed, highest ......................... 735, Ted Williams, 1941
right-handed, highest ....................... 704, Jimmie Foxx, 1938
```
STOLEN BASES, most .... 54, Tommy Harper, 1973
```
most caught stealing ....................... 19, Mike Menosky, 1920
```
STRIKE OUTS
```
left-handed, most ....................... 96, Carl Yastrzemski, 1961
right-handed, most ....................... 162, Butch Hobson, 1977
fewest ....................................... 9, Stuffy McInnis, 1921
```
TOTAL BASES, most .... 406, Jim Rice, 1978
TRIPLES, most .... 22, Tris Speaker, 1913; Chick Stahl, 1904

PITCHING

BASES ON BALLS
```
Left-handed, most .......................... 134, Mel Parnell, 1949
Right-handed, most ......................... 121, Don Schwall, 1962
                                          121, Mike Torrez, 1979
```
BATTERS
```
Most retired without a hit ...................... 76, Cy Young, 1904
```
EARNED RUNS, most .... 139, Jack Russell, 1930
EARNED RUN AVERAGE, lowest .... 1.01‡, Dutch Leonard
                                          (223 innings), 1914
GAMES, most .... 79, Dick Radatz, 1964
```
complete, most........................... 41, Cy Young, 1902 & 1904
finished, most............................... 67, Dick Radatz, 1964
lost, most .................................. 25, Charley Ruffing, 1928
lost consecutively, most...................... 14, Joseph Harris, 1906
started, most................................. 43, Cy Young, 1902
winning percentage, highest .............. 882, Bob Stanely, (15-2), 1978
```

Individual Season Records (continued)

won, most . . . . 34, Joe Wood, 1912
won, most in relief . . . . 16, Dick Radatz, 1964
won consecutively, most . . . . 16**, Joe Wood, 1912
HIT BATSMEN, most . . . . 20, Howard Ehmke, 1923
HITS, most . . . . 350, Cy Young, 1902
HOME RUNS, most . . . . 37, Earl Wilson, 1964
INNINGS, most . . . . 385, Cy Young, 1902
consecutive hitless, most . . . . 25-1/3, Cy Young, 1904
consecutive scoreless, most . . . . 45-2/3, Cy Young, 1904
RUNS, most . . . . 162, Charley Ruffing, 1929
Jack Russell, 1930
SAVES, most . . . . 31, Bill Campbell, 1977
SHUTOUTS
Left-hander, most won . . . . 9*, Babe Ruth, 1916
right-hander, most won . . . . 10, Cy Young, 1904
Joe Wood, 1912
most lost . . . . 8, Joe Harris, 1906
won by 1-0, most . . . . 5**, Joe Bush, 1918
STRIKE OUTS, most . . . . 258, Joe Wood, 1912
WILD PITCHES, most . . . . 21**, Earl Wilson, 1963
‡major league record   *American League record   **tied for A.L. record

ROOKIE

BASES ON BALLS . . . . 107‡, Ted Williams, 1939
BATTING AVERAGE . . . . 342, Pat Dougherty, 1902
DOUBLES . . . . 47*, Fred Lynn, 1975
GAMES . . . . 162‡‡, George Scott, 1966
HITS . . . . 205, Johnny Pesky, 1942
HOME RUNS . . . . 34, Walt Dropo, 1950
LEAST STRIKEOUTS, ... 25*, Tom Oliver, 1930
MOST INT. WALKS . . . . 13*, George Scott, 1966
RUNS . . . . 131, Ted Williams, 1939
RUNS BATTED IN . . . . 145‡, Ted Williams, 1939
SLUGGING PERCENTAGE . . . . 609*, Ted Williams, 1939
STRIKEOUTS . . . . 152‡‡, George Scott, 1966
TOTAL BASES . . . . 344, Ted Williams, 1939
‡major league record   *American League record   ‡‡tied for major league record

INDIVIDUAL GAME, INNING RECORDS

BATTING, GAME

Most Times Faced Pitcher .... 8‡‡, Clyde Vollmer, June 8, 1950
Most Times Faced Pitcher, No At Bats.................. 6‡‡, Jimmie Foxx,
June 16, 1938, (6 walks)
Most Runs .... 6‡, Johnny Pesky, May 8, 1946
Most Hits .... 6**, Jimmy Piersall, June 10, 1953 (1 double, 5 singles)
6** Pete Runnels, Aug. 30, 1960, (1 double, 5 singles) (15 inng. game)
Most Singles............................. 5, Billy Goodman, June 4, 1952
Jimmy Piersall, June 10, 1953
Most Doubles .... 4‡‡, Billy Werber, June 17, 1935
Al Zarilla, June 8, 1950; Orlando Cepeda, August 8, 1973
Most Consecutive Doubles .... 4‡‡, Billy Werber, July 17, 1935
Most Triples................... 3‡‡, Patsy Dougherty, September 5, 1903
Most Home Runs ...... 3, Jim Tabor, July 4, 1939; Ted Williams, July 14, 1946
Bobby Doerr, June 8, 1950; Clyde Vollmer, July 26, 1951
Norm Zauchin, May 27, 1955; Ted Williams, May 8, 1957
Ted Williams, June 13, 1957; Ken Harrelson, June 14, 1968
Joe Lahoud, June 11, 1969; Fred Lynn, June 18, 1975
Carl Yastrzemski, May 19, 1976, Jim Rice, August 29, 1977
Most Consecutive Home Runs .... 3, Ken Harrelson, June 14, 1968
Most Grand Slam Home Runs.................. 2‡‡, Jim Tabor, July 4, 1939
Rudy York, July 27, 1946
Most Total Bases .... 16**, Fred Lynn, June 18, 1975
Most RBI .... 10, Rudy York, July 27, 1946
Norm Zauchin, May 27, 1955; Fred Lynn, June 18, 1975
Batting In All Club's Runs (Most)........... 7, Ken Harrelson, June 14, 1968
Most Walks .... 6‡‡, Jimmie Foxx, June 16, 1938
Most Intentional Walks .... 3, Carl Yastrzemski, April 17, 1968
Most Strikeouts (9 Innings) .... 5‡‡, Ray Jarvis, April 20, 1969
Most Strikeouts (Extra Innings) .... 6‡‡, Cecil Cooper, June 14, 1974
Most Sacrifices .... 4‡‡, Jack Barry, August 21, 1916
Most Sacrifice Flies for RBI .... 3‡‡, Russ Nixon, August 31, 1965

PITCHING, GAME

Least Hits Allowed First Game .. 1‡‡, Billy Rohr vs. New York, April 14, 1967
Most Strikeouts .... 17, Bill Monbouquette, May 12, 1961 (N)
Most Consecutive Strikeouts................ 6, Buck O'Brien, April 25, 1913
Ray Culp, May 11, 1970 (N)
Most Innings .... 24**, Joe Harris, Sept. 1, 1906 (L, 4-1)
20, Cy Young, July 4, 1905 (L, 4-2)
17, Mickey McDermott, July 13, 1951 (ND)

Individual Game, Inning Records (continued)

BATTING, INNING

Most Times Faced Pitcher . . . . 3‡‡, Ted Williams, July 4, 1948 (7th)
Sammy White, Gene Stephens, Tom Umphlett, Johnny Lipon and
George Kell, all on June 18, 1953 (7th)
Most Runs . . . . 3‡‡, Sammy White, June 18, 1953 (7th)
Most Hits . . . . 3‡‡, Gene Stephens, June 18, 1953 (7th)
Most Pinch-Hits . . . . 2‡‡, Russ Nixon, May 4, 1962 (4th)
Most Home Runs . . . . 2‡‡, Bill Regan, June 16, 1928 (4th)
Most RBI . . . . 6‡‡, Tom McBride, August 4, 1945 (4th)
Home Run, First Major League At Bat . . . . Lefty LeFebvre, June 10, 1938
Eddie Pellagrini, April 22, 1946

PITCHING, INNING

Most Batters, Faced . . . . 16‡‡, Merle Adkins, July 8, 1902 (6th)
Lefty O'Doul, July 7, 1923 (6th)
Howard Ehmke, September 28, 1923 (6th)
Most Hits Allowed . . . . 12‡, Merle Adkins, July 8, 1902 (6th)
Most Runs Allowed . . . . 13‡, Lefty O'Doul, July 7, 1923 (6th)
Most Walks Allowed . . . . 6, Lefty O'Doul, July 7, 1923 (6th)
‡M.L. record   ‡‡tied for M.L. record   *A.L. record   **tied for A.L. record

CLUB SEASON RECORDS

Most players . . . . 48 in 1952
Fewest players . . . . 18 in 1904
Most games . . . . 163 in 1961 and 1978
Most at-bats . . . . 5587 in 1978 (163 games)
Most runs . . . . 1027 in 1950 (154 games)
Fewest runs . . . . 463 in 1906 (155 games)
Most hits . . . . 1665 in 1950 (154 games)
Fewest hits . . . . 1175 in 1905 (153 games)
Most singles . . . . 1156 in 1950 (154 games)
Most doubles . . . . 310 in 1979 (160 games)
Most triples . . . . 113 in 1903 (141 games)
Most homers . . . . 213 in 1977 (161 games)
Most home runs with bases filled . . . . 9 in 1941, 1950
Most home runs by pinch-hitters, season . . . . 6 in 1953
Most times 5 or more HR, one game . . . . ‡8 in 1977 (161 games)
Most times 2 or more consecutive HR . . . . ‡16 in 1977 (161 games)
Most long hits . . . . 538 in 1979 (160 games)
Most extra bases on long hits . . . . 1009 in 1977 (161 games)
Most total bases . . . . 2560 in 1977 (161 games)
2557 in 1950 (154 games)
Most sacrifices . . . . (includes sacrifice flies)   310 in 1917 (157 games)
(no sacrifice flies)   142 in 1906 (155 games)

Club Season Records (continued)

Most stolen bases............................. 215 in 1909 (151 games)
Most bases on balls .... 835 in 1949 (155 games)
Most strikeouts .... 1020 in 1966 (162 games)
                                                 1020 in 1967 (162 games)
Fewest strikeouts .... 329 in 1921 (154 games)
Most hit by pitcher .... 46 in 1920 (154 games)
                                                 46 in 1924 (156 games)
Fewest hit by pitcher.......................... 11 in 1934 (153 games)
Most runs batted in .... 974 in 1950 (154 games)
Highest batting average .... .302 in 1950 (154 games)
Lowest batting average .... .234 in 1905 (153 games)
                                                 .234 in 1907 (155 games)
Highest slugging average .... .465 in 1977 (161 games)
Lowest slugging average .... .318 in 1916 (156 games)
                                                 .318 in 1917 (157 games)
Most grounded into double play................. 169 in 1949 (155 games)
                                                 169 in 1951 (154 games)
Fewest grounded into double play .... 94 in 1942 (152 games)
Most left on bases .... 1304 in 1948 (155 games)
Fewest left on bases .... 1015 in 1929 (155 games)
Most .300 hitters .... 9 in 1950
Most putouts .... 4418 in 1978 (163 games)
Fewest putouts .... 3949 in 1938 (150 games)
Most assists .... 2195 in 1907 (155 games)
Fewest assists .... 1555 in 1964 (162 games)
Most chances accepted....................... 6425 in 1907 (155 games)
Fewest chances accepted .... 5667 in 1938 (150 games)
Most errors................................. 373 in 1901 (137 games)
Fewest errors .... 111 in 1950 (154 games)
Most errorless games .... 86 in 1971 (162 games)
Most consecutive errorless games .... 9 in 1951, 1961
Most double plays .... 207 in 1949 (155 games)
Fewest double plays........................... 74 in 1913 (151 games)
Most consecutive games, one or more double plays
                                        ‡‡25 (38 double plays), 1951
Most double plays in consecutive games in which double plays were made —
                                        ‡‡38 (25 games), 1951
Most passed balls.............................. 24 in 1913 (151 games)
Fewest passed balls .... 3 in 1975 (160 G) and in 1933 (149 G)
Highest fielding average .... .981 in 1948, '50 and '71
Lowest fielding average......................... .942 in 1901 (137 games)
Most games won .... 105 in 1912
Most games lost................................ 111 in 1932
Highest percentage games won .... .691 in 1912 (Won 105, Lost 47)
Lowest percentage games won .... .279 in 1932 (Won 43, Lost 111)
Games won, league...................................... 6175 in 79 years
Games lost, league .... 5978 in 79 years
Most shutouts won, season .... 26 in 1918

Club Season Records (continued)

Most shutouts lost, season .... 28 in 1906
Most 1-0 games won .... 8 in 1918
Most 1-0 games lost .... 7 in 1909, 1914
Most consecutive games won, season .... 15 in 1946
Most consecutive games lost, season .... 20 in 1906
Most times finished first.. 9
Most times finished second 13
Most times finished last 10
Most consecutive games, one or more home runs .... 13 (21 homers), 1962
13 (26 homers), 1963
Most home runs in consecutive games in which home runs were made —
33 (10 games), 1977

‡M.L. record   ‡‡tied for M.L. record

CLUB GAME, INNING RECORDS

BATTING, GAME

Most Times Faced Pitcher .... 64*, vs. St. Louis, June 8, 1950
Most Runs, One Club .... Boston 29**, St. Louis 4, June 8, 1950
Most Runs, Both Clubs .... 36*, Boston 22, Philadelphia 14, June 29, 1950
Most Runs, Shutout .... Boston 19, Philadelphia 0, April 30, 1950
Most Runs by Opp. .... Cleveland 27, Boston 3, July 7, 1923
Most Runs, Shutout by Opp. .... Cleveland 19, Boston 0, May 18, 1955
Most Innings Scored, 9-Inning Game
8** vs. Cleveland, September 16, 1903, did not bat in 9th
8 vs. Milwaukee, Aug 5, 1979
Most Runs to Overcome and Win
11, down 1-12 vs. Cleveland, August 28, 1950, won 15-14
Most Spectacular Rally to Win .... down 5-12 vs. Washington,
one on and one out in 9th, June 18, 1961, won 13-12
Most Hits, One Club .... 28, vs. St. Louis, June 8, 1950
Most Hits, Both Clubs .... 45**, Philadelphia 27, Boston 18, July 8, 1902
Most Consecutive Hits, One Club ..... 10*, vs. Milw., June 2, 1901, 9th Inning
Most Players 4 Or More Hits............... 4**, vs. St. Louis, June 8, 1950
Most Singles, One Club ....24‡‡, vs. Detroit, June 18, 1953
Most Singles, Both Clubs ....36‡‡, Chicago 21, Boston 15, August 15, 1922
Most Home Runs .... 8‡‡, vs. Toronto, July 4, 1977
Most HR, Season Opener, One Club ......5‡‡, vs. Washington, April 12, 1965
Most HR, Season Opener, Both Clubs ‡‡7, Boston 5, Washington 2, April 12, 1965
Most Players 2 or More HR, One Club........ 3‡‡, vs. St. Louis, June 8, 1950
Most Players 1 or More HR, Both Clubs
9‡‡, Minnesota 5, Boston 4, May 25, 1965
Baltimore 7, Boston 2, May 17, 1967
Boston 5, Milwaukee 4, May 22, 1977

- 69 -

Club Game, Inning Records (continued)

Most HR, Start of Game ...2‡‡, vs. Minnesota, May 1, 1971 (Aparicio, Smith)
at Milwaukee, June 20, 1973 (Miller, Smith)
vs. N.Y., June 17, 1977 (Burleson, Lynn)
Most HR, 9 innings, none on .... ‡7, vs. Toronto, July 4, 1977
Most Grand Slams, One Club
2‡‡, vs. Chicago, May 13, 1934 (Bucky Walters, Ed Morgan)
vs. Philadelphia, June 4, 1939 (Jim Tabor 2)
vs. St. Louis, July 27, 1946 (Rudy York 2)
vs. Chicago, May 10, 1960 (Vic Wertz, Rip Repulski)
Most Total Bases .... 60‡, vs. St. Louis, June 8, 1950
Most Extra Base Hits .... 17‡, vs. St. Louis, June 8, 1950
Most RBI .... 29‡,vs. St. Louis, June 8, 1950
Most Strikeouts (Nine Innings) .... 19‡‡, vs. California, August 12, 1974

BATTING, INNING

Most Batters Facing Pitcher ....23‡, vs. Detroit, June 18, 1953 (7th)
Most Runs ....17*, vs. Detroit, June 18, 1953 (7th)
Most Runs With 2 Out .... 10, vs. Detroit, September 21, 1937 (5th)
Most Runs With 2 Out, None On ....9, vs. Milwaukee, June 2, 1901 (9th)
Most Hits ....14‡‡, vs. Detroit, June 18, 1953 (7th)
Most Consecutive Hits .... 10‡‡, vs. Milwaukee, June 2, 1901 (9th)
Most Batters Reaching First Base, Consecutive
12, vs. Detroit, June 23, 1952 (4th)
Most Batters Reaching First Base ....20‡, vs. Detroit, June 18, 1953 (7th)
Most Triples..........................4, vs. Detroit, May 6, 1934 (4th)
Most Home Runs .... 4, vs. Philadelphia, September 24, 1940 (6th)
vs. Cleveland, May 22, 1957 (6th)
vs. Kansas City, August 26, 1957 (7th)
vs. N.Y., June 17, 1977 (1st)
vs. Toronto, July 4, 1977 (8th)
Most Consecutive Home Runs ... 3, vs. Philadelphia, September 24, 1940 (6th)
vs. Philadelphia, April 19, 1948 (2nd)
vs. Detroit, June 6, 1948 (6th)
vs. New York, September 7, 1959 (7th)
vs. Toronto, July 4, 1977 (8th)
vs. Seattle, August 13, 1977 (6th)
Most Total Bases .... 25*, vs. Philadelphia, September 24, 1940 (6th)
Most Extra Base Hits .... 7‡‡, vs. Philadelphia, September 24, 1940 (6th)
‡M.L. record   ‡‡tied for M.L. record   * A.L. record   **tied for A.L. record

MISCELLANEOUS

Players named the Minor League Player of the Year who played with the Red Sox some time during their career.

1951 — Gene Conley (Boston Braves Organization)
1962 — Bob Bailey (Pittsburgh Pirate Organization)
1965 — Joe Foy
1974 — Jim Rice

Annual Man of the Year as selected by the Bosox Club:

1967 — Rico Petrocelli
1968 — Mike Andrews
1969 — Lee Stange
1970 — Gerry Moses
1971 — John Kennedy
1972 — Bob Montgomery
1973 — Tommy Harper

1974 — Rick Miller
1975 — Denny Doyle
1976 — Reggie Cleveland
1977 — Butch Hobson
1978 — Bill Campbell
1979 — Tom Burgmeier

JUNE 1977

One of the major league's most awesome displays of home run power was put on by the Red Sox during ten days in June 1977. The spree as it occurred is presented here.

Date	Opponent	Home Runs	Pitchers
6/14	Chicago	(3) George Scott 2, Bernie Carbo	Chris Knapp 2, Lerrin LaGrow 1
6/16	Chicago	(2) George Scott, Jim Rice	Steve Stone 2
6/17	New York	(6) Carlton Fisk 2, Rick Burleson, Fred Lynn, George Scott, Carl Yastrzemski	Catfish Hunter 4 Dick Tidrow 2
6/18	New York	(5) Bernie Carbo 2, Carl Yastrzemski 2, George Scott	Mike Torrez 3 Sparky Lyle 2
6/19	New York	(5) Denny Doyle, Bernie Carbo, Jim Rice, Carl Yastrzemski, George Scott	Ed Figueroa 1 Dick Tidrow 4
6/20	At Baltimore	(1) Butch Hobson	Rudy May 1
6/21	At Baltimore	(2) Jim Rice, George Scott	Dennis Martinez 2
6/22	At Baltimore	(5) Carlton Fisk 2, George Scott, Jim Rice, Butch Hobson	Jim Palmer 5
6/23	At Baltimore	(1) Butch Hobson	Mike Flanagan 1
6/24	At New York	(3) Carl Yastrzemski, Butch Hobson, George Scott	Catfish Hunter 3

The string of 33 home runs in 10 straight games was stopped by Mike Torrez on June 25 in New York.

MAJOR LEAGUE RECORDS SET DURING THE SPREE

Most home runs, three consecutive games, club 16, June 17-19
Most home runs, four consecutive games, club 18, June 16-19
Most home runs, five consecutive games, club 21, June 14-19

Miscellaneous (continued)

Most home runs, six consecutive games, club 24, June 17-22
Most home runs, seven consecutive games, club 26, June 16-22
Most home runs, eight consecutive games, club 29, June 14-22
Most home runs, nine consecutive games, club 30, June 14-23
Most home runs, ten consecutive games, club 33, June 14-24

MAJOR LEAGUE RECORD TIED

Most home runs, none on base, inning, club — 4 Boston vs. New York June 17 1st inning. (Accomplished again on July 4th vs. Toronto, 8th inning)

In addition the Red Sox set or tied other major league records during the 1977 season as follows:

MAJOR LEAGUE RECORDS SET

Most hits, consecutive, start of career — 6 Ted Cox, September 18-19.
Most seasons leading league, assists, outfielder — 7 Carl Yastrzemski.
Most runs, inning, both clubs, since 1900-19 Cleveland (13) vs. Boston (6) April 10 (8th inning).
Most runs, eighth inning, both clubs — 19 Cleveland (13) vs. Boston (6) April 10.
Most seasons, consecutive, 100 or more home runs club — 32 Boston.
Most home runs, none on base, game club — 7 Boston vs. Toronto, July 4.
Most games, 5 or more home runs, season, club — 8 Boston.
Most times, 2 or more home runs, consecutive, season, club — 16 Boston.

MAJOR LEAGUE RECORDS TIED

Most hits, first major league game — 4 Ted Cox, September 18.
Most hits, consecutive, first major league game — 4 Ted Cox, September 18.
Most home runs, game club — 8 Boston vs. Toronto, July 4.
Most home runs, game, both clubs — 11 Boston (6) vs. Milwaukee (5) May 23 first game.
Most players, 1 or more home runs, game, both clubs — 9 Boston (5) vs. Milwaukee (4) May 23 — first game.
Most home runs, none on base, inning, club — 4 Boston vs. New York June 17 (1st inning) and Boston vs. Toronto, July 4 (8th inning).
Most seasons 200 or more home runs, club — 2 Boston.

AMERICAN LEAGUE RECORDS SET

Longest game — 3 hours, 57 minutes Boston vs. Cleveland, April 10.

AMERICAN LEAGUE RECORDS TIED

Most players, 30 or more home runs, season, club — 3 Boston.

When the Red Sox play Carl Yastrzemski, Fred Lynn and Dwight Evans in the outfield, they have an entire outfield of players with the middle name of Michael.

Miscellaneous (continued)

RED SOX LONGEST GAMES

24 innings — Sept. 1, 1906 vs. Philadelphia at Boston — lost 4 to 1 (J. Harris)
20 innings — July 4, 1905 vs. Philadelphia at Boston — lost 4 to 2 (Young)
20 innings — Aug. 29, 1967 vs. New York at New York — lost 4 to 3 (Brandon)
20 innings — July 27, 1969 vs. Seattle at Seattle — won 5 to 3 (Lonborg)
19 innings — July 13, 1951 vs. Chicago at Chicago — lost 5 to 4 (Taylor)
18 innings — Sept. 5, 1927 vs. New York at Boston — won 12 to 11 (Wiltse)
18 innings — April 16, 1967 vs. New York at New York — lost 7 to 6 (Stange)
18 innings — Aug. 25, 1968 vs. Baltimore at Baltimore — lost 3 to 2 (Stephenson)
17 innings — July 9, 1902 vs. Philadelphia at Boston — lost 4 to 2 (Dineen)
17 innings — May 21, 1915 vs. Chicago at Chicago — lost 3 to 2 (Mays)
17 innings — July 14, 1916 vs. St. Louis at Boston — tie 0-0
17 innings — July 12, 1951 vs. Chicago at Chicago — won 5 to 4 (Kinder) 2nd game
17 innings — June 23, 1954 vs. Baltimore at Baltimore — lost 8 to 7 (Henry)
17 innings — July 20, 1954 vs. Cleveland at Boston — tie 5 to 5
17 innings — Aug. 3, 1978 vs. New York at New York — win 7 to 5 (Stanley)

RED SOX YEARLY HIGHS AND LOWS

Best Record:	Home	1946, 1949	61-16	.792
	Away	1912	48-27	.640
	Year	1912	105-47	.691
Worst Record:	Home	1906	22-54	.289
	Away	1932	16-61	.208
	Year	1932	43-111	.279

RED SOX MISCELLANEOUS WON-LOST RECORDS

Most Consecutive Years Winning Record At Home	20	1934-1953
Most Consecutive Years Winning Record On The Road	7	1911-1917
Most Consecutive Years Losing Record At Home	9	1925-1933
Most Consecutive Years Losing Record On The Road	21	1918-1938
Most Consecutive Years Over .500 For Season	13	1967-1979
Most Consecutive Years Under .500 For Season	15	1919-1933
Most Games Won Home Season	61	1946,1949
Most Games Won Away Season	48	1912,1975
Most Games Lost Home Season	54	1906
Most Games Lost Away Season	61	1932
Fewest Games Won Home Season	22	1906
Fewest Games Won Away Season	16	1932
Fewest Games Lost Home Season	16	1946,1949
Fewest Games Lost Away Season	27	1903,1912

Miscellaneous (continued)

RED SOX ONE-HITTERS 1950-79

Pitcher	Date	Opp.	Hitter	Hit	I	O	Score
McDermott	5/29/52	Washington	Hoderlein, M.	Single	4	1	1-0
*McDermott +Kinder	7/19/53	At Cleveland	Smith, A.	Single	4	0	2-0 1st game
Kemmerer	7/18/54	Baltimore	Mele, S.	Single	7	0	4-0 1st game
Susce	7/20/55	At Kansas City	Power, V.	Single	1	0	6-0
Monbouquette	5/7/60	Detroit	Chrisley, N.	Double	1	1	5-0
Morehead	5/12/63	Washington	Hinton, C.	HR	1	2	4-1 2nd game
‡Monbouquette	9/6/64	At Minnesota	Versalles, Z.	HR	6	2	1-2
Rohr	4/14/67	At New York	Howard, E.	Single	9	2	3-0
Culp	9/21/68	At New York	White, R.	Single	7	2	2-0
Siebert	7/31/70	At California	Johnstone, J.	Single	3	0	2-0
Pattin	7/11/72	At Oakland	Jackson, R.	Single	9	1	4-0
Moret	8/21/74	Chicago	Allen, D.	Single	7	1	4-0
Wise	6/14/76	At Minnesota	Terrell, J.	Single	3	1	5-0
Wise	6/29/76	Baltimore	Blair, P.	Single	6	0	2-0
**Renko	7/13/79	At Oakland	Henderson, R.	Single	9	1	2-0

*McDermott pitched 8 innings, relieved by Kinder in the 9th inning with no outs and a 2 and 0 count on the batter, Kinder retired the side in order.

‡Versalles two run homer wins game for Twins.

**Renko pitched 8-2/3 innings relieved by Campbell.

There were no one-hitters in 1950, 51, 56, 57, 58, 59, 61, 62, 65, 66, 69, 71, 73, 75, 77, 78.

RED SOX 20 RUN GAMES 1901-1979

Date	Opponent	Score	Boston Hits	Winning Pitcher
May 2, 1901	At Philadelphia	23-12	21	Parson Lewis
May 29, 1912	Washington (1st Game)	21-8	18	Joe Wood
Sept. 27, 1940	Washington	24-4	22	Fritz Ostermueller
June 24, 1949	St. Louis	21-2	25	Ellis Kinder
June 7, 1950	St. Louis	20-4x	23	Joe Dobson
June 8, 1950	St. Louis	29-4*x	28	Chuck Stobbs
June 29, 1950	At Philadelphia	22-14+	19	Al Papai
June 18, 1953	Detroit	23-3#	27	Ellis Kinder
May 31, 1954	Philadelphia (1st game)	20-10	18	Tom Herrin
Aug. 30, 1970	At Chicago (1st game)	21-11	22	Ken Brett
Sept. 6, 1975	At Milwaukee	20-6	24	Roger Moret

*Was American League Record For Runs Scored.

xAmerican League Record For Most Runs Scored — Two Consecutive Games

+Amreican League Record For Runs Scored By Both Clubs One Game (36)

#This Game Set Many Records Including Most Runs One Inning (17) And Most Hits One Inning (14)

Miscellaneous (continued)

BOSTON RED SOX ONE-HITTERS 1901-1949

Pitcher	Date	Opp.	Hitter	Hit	Score
Gibson	9/14/04	New York	Anderson	Single	1-1 (5 innings)
Winter	4/18/05	At Washington	Mullin	Single	0-1
Dineen	7/27/06	At St. Louis	O'Brien	Single	1-0
Young	5/30/08	Washington	Freeman	Single	6-0
Arellanes	9/4/08	Philadelphia (2nd game)	Nicholls	Home Run	10-1
Wood	10/3/08	At Philadelphia	Coombs	Single	5-0 (6 innings)
Hall	8/27/10	Cleveland	Koestner	Single	7-1
Collins	8/30/10	Chicago	Meloan	Single	4-0
Wood	5/8/11	At New York	Caldwell	Single	4-0 (6 innings)
Wood	7/7/11	At St. Louis	Shotten	Single	6-1
Wood	6/29/12	New York	Sterrett	Single	6-0 (7 innings)
Wood	8/7/15	Cleveland	Wambsganss	Single	2-0
Shore	9/9/15	Philadelphia	Walsh	Single	5-0
Ruth	7/11/17	At Detroit	Bush	Single	1-0
Foster	8/6/17	Cleveland	Harris	Double	0-2
Mays	4/16/18	Philadelphia	Dugan	Single	1-0
Bush	5/28/18	Chicago	Felsch	Single	1-0
Mays	6/21/18	Philadelphia	Munch	Single	13-0
Bush	8/1/21	St. Louis	Sisler	Single	2-0
Ehmke	9/11/23	At New York	Witt	Single	3-0
Ferriss	5/27/45	Chicago	Cuccinello	Single	7-0
Dobson	9/17/47	St. Louis	Judnich	Single	4-0

There were no one hitters in 1901, 02, 03, 07, 09, 13, 14, 16, 19, 20, 22, 24 to 44, 46, 48, 49.

RED SOX PITCHERS MOST SAVES

31	Bill Campbell	1977	25	Dick Radatz	1963
29	Dick Radatz	1964	24	Dick Radatz	1962
27	Ellis Kinder	1953	22	Dick Radatz	1965

BOSTON RED SOX PLAYING MANAGERS

Jack Barry	— 1917	(2B)
Lou Boudreau	— 1952-54	(SS-3B, '52)
Bill Carrigan	— 1913-16, 1927-29	(C, '13-'16)
Jimmy Collins	— 1901-06	(3B)
Joe Cronin	— 1935-47	(SS-1B-3B, '35-'45)
Deacon McGuire	— 1907-08	(C-1B)
Marty McManus	— 1932-33	(1B-2B-SS-3B)
Chick Stahl	— 1906	(OF)
Jake Stahl	— 1912-13	(1B)
Bob Unglaub	— 1907	(1B)
Cy Young	— 1907	(P)

Miscellaneous (continued)

RED SOX PITCHERS ONE GAME STRIKEOUTS

17	Bill Monbouquette	1961	14	Ellis Kinder	1949
15	Joe Wood	1911	13	Joe Wood	1911
15	Mickey McDermott	1951*	13	Joe Bush	1918
14	Joe Harris	1906+	13	Harry Harper	1920
14	Joe Wood	1914#	13	Earl Wilson	1965
14	Dutch Leonard	1915	13	Jim Lonborg	1967

*16 inning game   +24 inning game   #11 inning game

RED SOX PITCHERS WINNING STREAKS
OVER MORE THAN ONE SEASON

13	Ike Delock	1957-58	11	Joe Heving	1939-40
13	Roger Moret	1971-72-73	11	Mickey Harris	1941-46*
12	Jose Santiago	1967-68	9	Charlie Hall	1911-12
11	Sonny Siebert	1970-71	9	Lefty Grove	1937-38
11	Luis Tiant	1977-78	9	Lefty Grove	1935-36
11	Elmer Myers	1920-21			

*In The Military

RED SOX PITCHERS PITCHING A SHUTOUT
IN THEIR FIRST MAJOR LEAGUE GAME

Date	Vs.	Pitcher	Score	Hits
9/30/06	At St. Louis (2nd game)	Rube Kroh	2-0	2
10/5/08	New York	King Brady	4-0	8
7/6/09	Washington (2nd game)	Larry Pape	2-0	4
9/9/11	At Philadelphia	Buck O'Brien	2-0	6
4/13/14	At Washington	Adam Johnson	5-0	6
9/17/34	At St. Louis	George Hockette	3-0	2
4/29/45	At Philadelphia	Dave Ferriss	2-0	5
4/13/63	At Washington	Dave Morehead	3-0	5
4/14/67	At New York	Billy Rohr	3-0	1

RED SOX PITCHERS PITCHING A SHUTOUT
IN THEIR FIRST MAJOR LEAGUE START*

Date	Vs.	Pitcher	Score	Hits
8/5/53	St. Lous	Ben Flowers	5-0	8
7/18/54	Baltimore	Russ Kemmerer	4-0	1
5/6/78	Chicago (2nd game)	Jim Wright	3-0	7

*All appeared in relief roles earlier.

Miscellaneous (continued)

RED SOX CONSECUTIVE GAME HITTING STREAKS

34	Dom DiMaggio	1949	23	Del Pratt	1922
30	Tris Speaker	1912	23	George Burns	1922
27	Dom DiMaggio	1951	23	Ted Williams	1941
26	Buck Freeman	1902	22	Denny Doyle	1975
26	John Pesky	1947	22	Tris Speaker	1913
25	George Metkovich	1944	22	Dom DiMaggio	1942

RED SOX WINNING STREAKS

15 games 1946
13 games 1948
12 games 1937, 1939, 1946
11 games 1903, 1909, 1949, 1950, 1977
10 games 1912, 1917, 1951, 1967, 1975
 9 games 1901, 1910, 1912, 1919, 1942 (twice), 1944, 1948, 1978

RED SOX PITCHERS SEASON WIN STREAKS

16	Joe Wood	1912	10	Dick Radatz	1963
13	Ellis Kinder	1949	9	Cy Young	1903
12	Cy Young	1901	9	Jesse Tannehill	1905
12	Dutch Leonard	1914	9	Joe Wood	1915
12	Dave Ferriss	1946	9	George Foster	1916
11	Tex Hughson	1942	9	Elmer Myers	1920
11	Jack Kramer	1948	9	Joe Bush	1921
11	Roger Moret	1973*	9	Mel Parnell	1950
11	Bob Stanley	1978	9	Sonny Siebert	1971*
10	Cy Young	1902	9	Bill Monbouquette	1963
10	Dave Ferriss	1946*	9	Rick Wise	1975
10	Ike Delock	1958*			

*From Start Of The Season.

INTERESTING MISCELLANEOUS RED SOX RECORDS

Winning streaks of 9 or more games over two seasons:
   10   1940-41 (Last 5 games of 1940, first 5 of 1941)
    9   1911-12 (Last 6 games of 1911, first 3 of 1912)

Most wins, start of season — 6 in 1918

Most losses, start of season — 8 in 1945

Most wins, end of season — 8 in 1905 and 1978

Most consecutive wins over an opponent on the road — 18. Over New York at New York in 1911, 1912 and 1913. Last three games of 1911, ten straight in 1912 and the first 5 of 1913. This is the major league record.

Miscellaneous (continued)

Largest lead lost by the Red Sox — 9 runs (2)

August 2, 1936 second game at Chicago. Red Sox lead was 10 to 1 after 4-1/2 innings. Final score was Chicago 12, Boston 11 in 12 innings. The Red Sox made 22 hits in this game. (Road)

April 18, 1950 against New York at Fenway Park on Opening Day. Red Sox led 9 to 0 after 5 innings. Final score New York 15, Boston 10. (Home)

Most Extra Inning Games One Season — 31 in 1943. 15 wins, 14 losses, 2 ties. This is a major league record.

Pitchers with 10 or more strikeouts in a game — 3 or more times 1901-79.

Joe Wood	18	Bill Monbouquette	6
Jim Lonborg	10	Dutch Leonard	4
Ray Culp	10	Earl Wilson	4
Luis Tiant	9	Red Ruffing	3
Dave Morehead	9	Lefty Grove	3
Cy Young	8	Mickey McDermott	3

RED SOX CONSECUTIVE GAME WINS OVER OTHER CLUBS — MORE THAN ONE SEASON (13 OR MORE)

22 — Washington (Last 6-1903, First 16-1904)
18 — Philadelphia (Last 13-1940, First 5-1941)
17 — New York (Last 3-1911, First 14-1912)
15 — Seattle (Last 10-1977, First 5-1978)
13 — Philadelphia (Last Game 1936, First 12-1937)

RED SOX CONSECUTIVE GAME WINS OVER OTHER CLUBS — ONE SEASON (12 OR MORE)

16 — Washington (1904)
14 — New York (1912)
14 — Washington (1949)
13 — Philadlephia (1940)
12 — Philadelphia (1937)
12 — Philadelphia (1950)
12 — St. Louis (1950)

RED SOX CONSECUTIVE GAME WINS OVER OTHER CLUBS AT BOSTON

22 — Philadelphia (11 Games 1949, 11 Games 1950) (Major League Record)
20 — Washington (10 Games 1903, First 10 Games 1904)*

*This is two games better than the National League Record of 18 games by the Milwaukee-Atlanta Braves 1964-1966 over the New York Mets.

THE D.H.

Amid a wave of controversy the American League adopted the designated hitter rule for the 1973 season. While the arguments for it and against it had many valid points, it was nevertheless put into effect. Basically, what it did was take the bat out of the hands of the pitcher and put it into the hands of aging sluggers who were no longer able to perform in the field, but had still retained their batting eye. This has pretty much been the rule for most teams, although Boston has had a notable exception in their young power hitter Jim Rice. In Rice's case, he began his career more or less as the team's DH while working to improve his fielding skills.

Actually, the first ever major league DH appeared at Fenway Park with Boston's starting time ahead of the other 1973 season opening games on April 6 of that year. The Opening Day game with the New York Yankees found Ron Blomberg of New York becoming the first DH and he was walked by Boston pitcher Luis Tiant in his first at bat. Orlando Cepeda, going 0 for 6, was the first Sox DH. On April 8, Cepeda got the first Boston DH hit—a home run.

Presented here are the Red Sox team records for designated hitters. While Cepeda and Rice hold most of the records, due mainly to the number of games that they were used as the DH, the Red Sox also used others a number of times. Others of note making a number of appearances would include Ben Oglivie, Cecil Cooper, Bernie Carbo, Danny Cater, Tommy Harper, Juan Beniquez, Tony Conigliaro, Carl Yastrzemski, Bobby Darwin, Ted Cox, Tommy Helms, Butch Hobson, Bob Bailey, Garry Hancock, Jack Brohamer and Carlton Fisk.

DESIGNATED HITTING RECORDS — SEASON

Most games	—	142	— Orlando Cepeda (1973)
Most at bats	—	550	— Orlando Cepeda (1973)
Most runs	—	74	— Jim Rice (1977)
Most hits	—	159	— Orlando Cepeda (1973)
Most singles	—	114	— Orlando Cepeda (1973)
Most doubles	—	25	— Orlando Cepeda (1973)
Most triples	—	13	— Jim Rice (1977)
Most home runs	—	31	— Jim Rice (1977)
Most R.B.I.'s	—	87	— Jim Rice (1977)
Most base on balls	—	50	— Orlando Cepeda (1973)
Most strike outs	—	92	— Jim Rice (1977)
Most stolen bases	—	16	— Tommy Harper (1974)
Highest B.A. (100+AB's)	—	.318	— Cecil Cooper (1975)
Most players to D.H.	—	16	(1974, 1976)

PITCHING STREAKS

BOSTON RED SOX PITCHERS
LONGEST WINNING AND LOSING STREAKS — 1901-1979

(Numbers in parentheses indicate number of times)

	WINNING STREAK		LOSING STREAK	
1901	Cy Young	12	Ted Lewis	5
1902	Cy Young	10	Bill Dineen	5
1903	Cy Young	9	George Winter	4
1904	Jesse Tannehill	7	Bill Dineen	4
			Norwood Gibson	4
			Cy Young	4
1905	Jesse Tannehill	9	George Winter	5
1906	Jesse Tannehill	4	Joe Harris	14
1907	George Winter	5	Joe Harris	7
1908	Cy Young	5	George Winter	6
1909	Frank Arellanes	7	Frank Arellanes	4
			Cy Morgan	4
1910	Ed Karger	5	Frank Arellanes	4
			Joe Wood	4
1911	Joe Wood	5	Ed Cicotte	4(2)
			Ray Collins	4
			Charlie Hall	4
1912	Joe Wood	16	Ed Cicotte	3
			Buck O'Brien	3(3)
1913	Ray Collins	7(2)	Fred Anderson	6
	Earl Moseley	7	Dutch Leonard	6
1914	Dutch Leonard	12	Hugh Bedient	4
1915	Joe Wood	9	Ray Collins	4
			Babe Ruth	4
1916	George Foster	9	Ernie Shore	5
1917	Babe Ruth	8	Dutch Leonard	4
1918	Sam Jones	7	Joe Bush	5
1919	Al Russell	8	Sam Jones	6
1920	Elmer Myers	9	Harry Harper	10
1921	Joe Bush	9	Hank Thormahlen	7
1922	Rip Collins	6	Ben Karr	5
1923	Howard Ehmke	6	Bill Piercy	11
1924	Howard Ehmke	4	Alex Ferguson	9
	Alex Ferguson	4		
	Bill Piercy	4		
	Jack Quinn	4(2)		
1925	Howard Ehmke	4	Red Ruffing	9
	Jack Quinn	4		
	Ted Wingfield	4		
1926	Tony Welzer	3	Red Ruffing	6
	Ted Wingfield	3	Paul Zahniser	6

Boston Red Sox Pitchers Longest Winning and Losing Streaks (continued)

1927	Slim Harriss	6	Red Ruffing	6	
			Tony Welzer	6	
1928	Ed Morris	7	Dan MacFayden	9	
1929	Ed Morris	5	Red Ruffing	12	
1930	Dan MacFayden	5	Jack Russell	7	
			Ed Durham	7	
1931	Bob Kline	4	Milt Gaston	12	
	Dan MacFayden	4			
	Wilcy Moore	4			
1932	Ivy Andrews	4	Wilcy Moore	7	
1933	Gordon Rhodes	4	Ivy Andrews	4	
			Gordon Rhodes	4	
1934	John Welch	6	John Welch	7	
1935	Lefty Grove	6	Dusty Rhodes	9	
1936	Lefty Grove	5	Jack Wilson	5	
	Jim Henry	5			
1937	Lefty Grove	4(3)	Fritz Ostermueller	4	
	Footsie Marcum	4	Jack Wilson	4	
	Archie McKain	4			
1938	Lefty Grove	8	Jack Wilson	4	
1939	Lefty Grove	8	Fritz Ostermueller	4	
	Joe Heving	8			
1940	Jack Wilson	4	Jim Bagby	5	
1941	Joe Dobson	7	Mickey Harris	7	
1942	Tex Hughson	11	Heber Newsome	6	
1943	Mace Brown	6	Heber Newsome	6	
1944	Joe Bowman	5	Clem Hausmann	6	
	Tex Hughson	5	Emmett O'Neill	6	
	Mike Ryba	5	Yank Terry	6	
1945	Dave Ferriss	8(2)	Emmett O'Neill	7	
1946	Dave Ferriss	12	Dave Ferriss	3	
			Tex Hughson	3	
1947	Joe Dobson	5	Harry Dorish	4	
1948	Jack Kramer	11	Mickey Harris	7	
1949	Ellis Kinder	13	Jack Kramer	6	
1950	Mel Parnell	9	Mel Parnell	5	
1951	Ellis Kinder	5	Harry Taylor	6	
1952	Bill Henry	4	Ike Delock	6	
	Dizzy Trout	4			
1953	Hector Brown	7	Willard Nixon	7	
1954	Russ Kemmerer	4	Hector Brown	8	
	Ellis Kinder	4			
	Frank Sullivan	4(2)			
1955	Tom Hurd	8	Tom Brewer	6	
1956	Tom Brewer	8	Bob Porterfeld	5	
1957	Frank Sullivan	5	Willard Nixon	4	
			Dave Sisler	4	

Boston Red Sox Pitchers Longest Winning and Losing Streaks (continued)

1958	Ike Delock	10	Ike Delock	5
1959	Jerry Casale	5(2)	Ted Wills	6
	Ike Delock	5		
1960	Mike Fornieles	4	Jerry Casale	9
1961	Don Schwall	7	Bill Monbouquette	6
			Billy Muffett	6
1962	Bill Monbouquette	4	Don Schwall	5
	Dick Radatz	4		
1963	Dick Radatz	10	Dave Morehead	5
			Earl Wilson	5
1964	Earl Wilson	6	Earl Wilson	7
1965	Bill Monbouquette	4	Bill Monbouquette	7
	Dick Radatz	4		
1966	Jim Lonborg	5	Jerry Stephenson	5
1967	Jose Santiago	8	Bucky Brandon	4
			Lee Stange	4
1968	Ray Culp	7	Gary Waslewski	7
1969	Mike Nagy	7	Jim Lonborg	8
1970	Vicente Romo	6	Gary Peters	6
			Sparky Lyle	6
1971	Sonny Siebert	9	Luis Tiant	7
1972	Luis Tiant	7	Marty Pattin	5
1973	Roger Moret	11	Marty Pattin	6
1974	Luis Tiant	6(2)	Dick Drago	6
1975	Rick Wise	9	Dick Pole	4
1976	Luis Tiant	7	Jim Willoughby	8
1977	Jim Willoughby	6	Bob Stanley	4
1978	Bob Stanley	11	Bill Lee	7
1979	Dennis Eckersley	8	Dennis Eckersley	5

BOSTON RED SOX
LONGEST WINNING AND LOSING STREAKS BY SEASON

(Numbers in parenthesis indicate number of times streak was duplicated)

Year	Winning	Losing	Year	Winning	Losing
1901	9	5	1910	9	6(2)
1902	8	6	1911	6	7
1903	11	3(3)	1912	10	5
1904	8	6	1913	5	5(3)
1905	8	6(2)	1914	6(3)	5
1906	4	20	1915	8	5
1907	4	16	1916	7	4
1908	5	7	1917	10	4(2)
1909	11	6	1918	6(2)	6

Boston Red Sox Longest Winning and Losing Streaks by Season (continued)

Year	Winning	Losing	Year	Winning	Losing
1919	9	5(2)	1950	11	5
1920	6	5(2)	1951	10	9
1921	5(2)	8	1952	5(3)	7
1922	5	9	1953	6	8
1923	5	5(3)	1954	6	8
1924	6	9	1955	7	7
1925	3(2)	9	1956	6	5(2)
1926	5	17	1957	6	5
1927	6	15	1958	6(2)	8
1928	7	7	1959	5(2)	7
1929	4(2)	8	1960	7	10
1930	5	14	1961	6	6(2)
1931	5	8(2)	1962	5	8
1932	3(2)	11	1963	6	9
1933	6	9	1964	5	7
1934	5(2)	4(5)	1965	4	8
1935	4(5)	4(2)	1966	6	6
1936	5(2)	7(2)	1967	10	5
1937	12	5(3)	1968	8	4(2)
1938	8	6	1969	8	7
1939	12	6	1970	7	5(3)
1940	6(2)	8	1971	7	7
1941	8	5(2)	1972	7(2)	5
1942	9(2)	5	1973	8	4
1943	4(3)	8	1974	6	8
1944	9	10	1975	10	5
1945	5(2)	8	1976	7	10
1946	15	6	1977	11	9
1947	8	6	1978	9	5(2)
1948	13	5	1979	7	4
1949	11	8			

ON THE AIR WAVES

Here are the play by play announcers who have entered your homes via radio and TV over the years. How many do you remember? They are listed approximately in the order of their appearance.

FRED HOEY	DON GILLIS	KEN COLEMAN
FRANK FRISCH	BOB DELANEY	JOHN PESKY
LEO EGAN	BOB MURPHY	DAVE MARTIN
TOM HUSSEY	BILL CROWLEY	JIM WOODS
JIM BRITT	ART GLEESON	KEN HARRELSON
JIMMIE FOXX	NED MARTIN	DICK STOCKTON
CURT GOWDY	MEL PARNELL	RICO PETROCELLI

OPENING DAY LINEUPS

In this section you will find the opening day lineup for each year for the Boston club. Opening day has always been one of special interest to fans and players alike. There is always a certain amount of electricity in the air as hopes are born anew. In these lineups you may find some surprises. There are rookies who set a hot pace in spring training to gain a starting spot. Some survived the season, some went on to play for years, others were back in the minors by June 1st, never to appear again. You will find veterans who appear year after year with an occasional miss, due to an injury or illness. You will find some players at positions other than where they gained their fame. Substitutes that were made in the lineups have not been listed. In most cases, this is not the lineup which prevailed through the season and should not be used for that purpose.

As you read through them, I think you will find some surprises and settle some arguments.

OPENING DAY LINEUPS — 1901-1979

1901
LF	Tommy Dowd
RF	Charlie Hemphill
CF	Chick Stahl
3B	Jimmy Collins
1B	Buck Freeman
SS	Fred Parent
2B	Hobe Ferris
C	Lou Criger
P	Win Kellum

1902
SS	Fred Parent
CF	Chick Stahl
3B	Jimmy Collins
RF	Buck Freeman
LF	Charlie Hickman
1B	Candy LaChance
2B	Hobe Ferris
C	John Warner
P	Bill Dineen

1903
LF	Pat Dougherty
3B	Jimmy Collins
CF	Chick Stahl
RF	Buck Freeman
SS	Fred Parent
1B	Candy LaChance
2B	Hobe Ferris
C	Duke Farrell
P	George Winter

1904
LF	Pat Dougherty
3B	Jimmy Collins
CF	Chick Stahl
RF	Buck Freeman
SS	Fred Parent
1B	Candy LaChance
2B	Hobe Ferris
C	Lou Criger
P	Cy Young

1905
LF	Jesse Burkett
SS	Fred Parent
CF	Chick Stahl
3B	Jimmy Collins
RF	Buck Freeman
1B	Candy LaChance
2B	Hobe Ferris
C	Duke Farrell
P	Cy Young

1906
LF	Kip Selbach
3B	Jimmy Collins
CF	Chick Stahl
SS	Fred Parent
RF	Buck Freeman
1B	Moose Grimshaw
2B	John Godwin
C	Charlie Graham
P	Cy Young

1907
CF	Denny Sullivan
3B	Jimmy Collins
1B	Bob Unglaub
LF	John Hoey
RF	Buck Freeman
2B	Hobe Ferris
SS	Heinie Wagner
C	Lou Criger
P	Cy Young

1908
LF	Jack Thoney
3B	Harry Lord
CF	Jim McHale
RF	Doc Gessler
2B	Frank LaPorte
1B	Bob Unglaub
SS	Heinie Wagner
C	Lou Criger
P	Cy Young

1909
2B	Amby McConnell
3B	Harry Lord
1B	Jake Stahl
RF	Doc Gessler
CF	Tris Speaker
SS	Heinie Wagner
LF	Jack Thoney
C	Bill Carrigan
P	Frank Arellanes

1910
2B	Amby McConnell
3B	Harry Lord
CF	Tris Speaker
1B	Jake Stahl
SS	Heinie Wagner
RF	Harry Niles
LF	Harry Hooper
C	Bill Carrigan
P	Ed Cicotte

1911
2B	Larry Gardner
RF	Harry Hooper
CF	Tris Speaker
LF	Duffy Lewis
SS	Heinie Wagner
1B	Rip Williams
3B	Clyde Engle
C	Red Kleinow
P	Joe Wood

1912
RF	Harry Hooper
2B	Steve Yerkes
CF	Tris Speaker
1B	Jake Stahl
3B	Larry Gardner
LF	Duffy Lewis
SS	Heinie Wagner
C	Les Nunamaker
P	Joe Wood

Opening Day Lineups — 1901-1979 (continued)

1913

RF	Harry Hooper
2B	Steve Yerkes
CF	Tris Speaker
LF	Duffy Lewis
3B	Larry Gardner
1B	Hal Janvrin
SS	Heinie Wagner
C	Hick Cady
P	Charley Hall

1914

RF	Harry Hooper
1B	Clyde Engle
CF	Tris Speaker
LF	Duffy Lewis
3B	Larry Gardner
2B	Steve Yerkes
SS	Everett Scott
C	Bill Carriagn
P	Ray Collins

1915

RF	Harry Hooper
2B	Heinie Wagner
CF	Tris Speaker
LF	Duffy Lewis
1B	Dick Hoblitzell
SS	Everett Scott
3B	Larry Gardner
C	Hick Cady
P	Ernie Shore

1916

RF	Harry Hooper
SS	Everett Scott
1B	Dick Hoblitzell
CF	Tilly Walker
LF	Chick Shorten
3B	Larry Gardner
2B	Jack Barry
C	Pinch Thomas
P	Babe Ruth

1917

RF	Harry Hooper
2B	Jack Barry
1B	Dick Hoblitzell
LF	Duffy Lewis
CF	Tilly Walker
3B	Larry Gardner
SS	Everett Scott
C	Pinch Thomas
P	Babe Ruth

1918

RF	Harry Hooper
2B	Dave Shean
CF	Amos Strunk
1B	Dick Hoblitzell
3B	Stuffy McInnis
LF	George Whiteman
SS	Everett Scott
C	Sam Agnew
P	Babe Ruth

1919

RF	Harry Hooper
2B	Jack Barry
CF	Amos Strunk
LF	Babe Ruth
1B	Stuffy McInnis
3B	Oscar Vitt
SS	Everett Scott
C	Wally Schang
P	Carl Mays

1920

RF	Harry Hooper
2B	Mike McNally
LF	Mike Menosky
CF	Tim Hendryx
1B	Stuffy McInnis
3B	Ed Foster
SS	Everett Scott
C	Roxy Walters
P	Al Russell

1921

3B	Oscar Vitt
2B	Ed Foster
LF	Mike Menosky
RF	Tim Hendryx
1B	Stuffy McInnis
CF	Shano Collins
SS	Everett Scott
C	Muddy Ruel
P	Sam Jones

1922

CF	Mike Menosky
RF	Elmer Smith
2B	Del Pratt
LF	Joe Harris
1B	George Burns
3B	Clarke Pittenger
SS	Frank O'Rourke
C	Muddy Ruel
P	Jack Quinn

1923

SS	Chick Fewster
RF	Shano Collins
CF	Camp Skinner
LF	Joe Harris
1B	George Burns
2B	Norm McMillan
3B	Howard Shanks
C	Al DeVormer
P	Howard Ehmke

1924

CF	Ira Flagstead
2B	Bill Wambsganss
LF	Bobby Veach
1B	Joe Harris
RF	Ike Boone
3B	Howard Shanks
SS	Dud Lee
C	Steve O'Neill
P	Howard Ehmke

Opening Day Lineups — 1901-1979 (continued)

1925
CF	Ira Flagstead
3B	Doc Prothro
RF	Ike Boone
LF	Bobby Veach
1B	Joe Harris
SS	Ewell Gross
2B	Billy Rogell
C	Val Picinich
P	Alex Ferguson

1926
CF	Ira Flagstead
3B	Fred Haney
RF	Si Rosenthal
1B	Phil Todt
LF	Tut Jenkins
2B	Mike Herrera
SS	Dud Lee
C	Al Gaston
P	Howard Ehmke

1927
SS	Pee Wee Wanninger
3B	Fred Haney
RF	John Tobin
CF	Ira Flagstead
1B	Phil Todt
LF	Wally Shaner
2B	Bill Regan
C	Fred Hofmann
P	Slim Harriss

1928
SS	Jack Rothrock
1B	Phil Todt
CF	Ira Flagstead
LF	Ken Williams
3B	Buddy Myer
2B	Bill Regan
RF	Doug Taitt
C	Fred Hofmann
P	Danny MacFayden

1929
CF	Jack Rothrock
SS	Hal Rhyne
RF	Russ Scarritt
LF	Ira Flagstead
2B	Bill Regan
3B	Bob Reeves
1B	Phil Todt
C	Charles Berry
P	Red Ruffing

1930
RF	Jack Rothrock
3B	Otis Miller
CF	Tom Oliver
LF	Russ Scarritt
2B	Bill Regan
1B	Phil Todt
SS	Bill Narleski
C	John Heving
P	Dan MacFayden

1931
SS	Rabbit Warstler
LF	Russ Scarritt
1B	Bill Sweeney
RF	Earl Webb
3B	Jack Rothrock
2B	Bobby Reeves
CF	Tom Oliver
C	Charlie Berry
P	Wilcy Moore

1932
LF	Jack Rothrock
SS	Hal Rhyne
2B	Marty McManus
RF	Earl Webb
3B	Urbane Pickering
1B	Al Van Camp
CF	Tom Oliver
C	Charlie Berry
P	Dan MacFayden

1933
SS	Rabbit Warstler
3B	Marty McManus
CF	John Watwood
1B	Dale Alexander
LF	Smead Jolley
2B	John Hodapp
RF	Roy Johnson
C	Merv Shea
P	Ivy Andrews

1934
2B	Max Bishop
SS	Bill Werber
1B	Joe Judge
LF	Roy Johnson
CF	Carl Reynolds
RF	Moose Solters
C	Rick Ferrell
3B	Bucky Walters
P	Dusty Rhodes

1935
2B	Max Bishop
3B	Bill Werber
CF	Carl Reynolds
SS	Joe Cronin
C	Rick Ferrell
RF	Moose Solters
CF	Mel Almada
1B	Babe Dahlgren
P	Wes Ferrell

1936
RF	Bill Werber
CF	Doc Cramer
LF	Heine Manush
1B	Jimmie Foxx
SS	Joe Cronin
3B	Eric McNair
C	Rick Ferrell
2B	Oscar Melillo
P	Wes Ferrell

Opening Day Lineups — 1901-1979 (continued)

1937		1938		1939	
2B	Bobby Doerr	CF	Doc Cramer	CF	Doc Cramer
CF	Doc Cramer	LF	Joe Vosmik	LF	Joe Vosmik
RF	Fabian Gaffke	1B	Jimmie Foxx	1B	Jimmie Foxx
SS	Joe Cronin	SS	Joe Cronin	SS	Joe Cronin
3B	Pinky Higgins	3B	Pinky Higgins	3B	Jim Tabor
C	Rick Ferrell	RF	Ben Chapman	RF	Ted Williams
LF	Buster Mills	2B	Bobby Doerr	2B	Bobby Doerr
1B	Mel Almada	C	Gene Desautels	C	Gene Desautels
P	Wes Ferrell	P	Jim Bagby	P	Lefty Grove

1940		1941		1942	
RF	Dom DiMaggio	CF	Dom DiMaggio	SS	John Pesky
CF	Doc Cramer	RF	Lou Finney	CF	Dom DiMaggio
LF	Ted Williams	LF	Pete Fox	LF	Ted Williams
1B	Jimmie Foxx	1B	Jimmie Foxx	1B	Jimmie Foxx
SS	Joe Cronin	SS	Joe Cronin	3B	Jim Tabor
2B	Bobby Doerr	2B	Bobby Doerr	RF	Pete Fox
3B	Jim Tabor	3B	Jim Tabor	2B	Lamar Newsome
C	Gene Desautels	C	Frank Pytlak	C	John Peacock
P	Lefty Grove	P	Jack Wilson	P	Herber Newsome

1943		1944		1945	
SS	Eddie Lake	SS	Lamar Newsome	2B	Ben Steiner
RF	Pete Fox	1B	George Metkovich	1B	George Metkovich
2B	Bob Doerr	RF	Ford Garrison	RF	Pete Fox
LF	John Lazor	LF	Bob Johnson	LF	Bob Johnson
1B	Tony Lupien	2B	Bobby Doerr	3B	Joe Cronin
CF	Ford Garrison	3B	Jim Tabor	CF	Leon Culberson
3B	Lamar Newsome	CF	Leon Culberson	SS	Lamar Newsome
C	John Peacock	C	Roy Partee	C	Fred Walters
P	Tex Hughson	P	Yank Terry	P	Rex Cecil

1946		1947		1948	
CF	Dom DiMaggio	3B	Ed Pelligrini	CF	Dom DiMaggio
SS	John Pesky	SS	John Pesky	3B	John Pesky
LF	Ted Williams	CF	Dom DiMaggio	LF	Ted Williams
2B	Bobby Doerr	LF	Ted Williams	1B	Stan Spence
1B	Rudy York	2B	Bobby Doerr	SS	Vern Stephens
RF	George Metkovich	1B	Rudy York	2B	Bobby Doerr
3B	Ernie Andres	RF	Sam Mele	RF	Sam Mele
C	Hal Wagner	C	Hal Wagner	C	Birdie Tebbetts
P	Tex Hughson	P	Tex Hughson	P	Joe Dobson

Opening Day Lineups — 1901-1979 (continued)

1949		1950		1951	
CF	Dom DiMaggio	CF	Dom DiMaggio	CF	Dom DiMaggio
3B	John Pesky	3B	John Pesky	RF	Bill Goodman
LF	Ted Williams	LF	Ted Williams	LF	Ted Williams
SS	Vern Stephens	SS	Vern Stephens	3B	Vern Stephens
2B	Bobby Doerr	RF	Al Zarilla	1B	Walt Dropo
RF	Tom O'Brien	2B	Bobby Doerr	2B	Bobby Doerr
1B	Walt Dropo	1B	Bill Goodman	SS	Lou Boudreau
C	Birdie Tebbetts	C	Matt Batts	C	Buddy Rosar
P	Joe Dobson	P	Mel Parnell	P	Bill Wight

1952		1953		1954	
CF	Dom DiMaggio	2B	Bill Goodman	2B	Billy Consolo
3B	John Pesky	RF	Jim Piersall	CF	Jim Piersall
LF	Ted Williams	LF	Gene Stephens	RF	Jack Jensen
1B	Walt Dropo	1B	Dick Gernert	3B	George Kell
RF	Faye Thorneberry	3B	George Kell	LF	Bill Goodman
SS	Jim Piersall	C	Sam White	1B	Dick Gernert
P	Mel Parnell	CF	Tom Umphlett	C	Sam White
2B	Ted Lepcio	SS	Milt Bolling	SS	Ted Lepcio
C	Gus Niarhos	P	Mel Parnell	P	Mel Parnell

1955		1956		1957	
2B	Bill Goodman	2B	Bill Goodman	3B	Frank Malzone
SS	Ed Joost	3B	Frank Malzone	SS	Billy Klaus
LF	Faye Thorneberry	LF	Ted Williams	LF	Ted Williams
RF	Jack Jensen	RF	Jack Jensen	1B	Dick Gernert
C	Sam White	1B	Mickey Vernon	CF	Jim Piersall
1B	Norm Zauchin	CF	Jim Piersall	RF	Gene Stephens
3B	Ted Lepcio	SS	Don Buddin	2B	Gene Mauch
CF	Jim Piersall	C	Sam White	C	Sam White
P	Frank Sullivan	P	Frank Sullivan	P	Tom Brewer

1958		1959		1960	
SS	Don Buddin	SS	Don Buddin	2B	Pumpsie Green
1B	Pete Runnels	2B	Pete Runnels	1B	Pete Runnels
LF	Gene Stephens	CF	Gene Stephens	3B	Frank Malzone
RF	Jack Jensen	1B	Vic Wertz	RF	Gene Stephens
3B	Frank Malzone	RF	Jackie Jensen	LF	Ted Williams
CF	Jim Piersall	3B	Frank Malzone	CF	Gary Geiger
2B	Ken Aspromonte	LF	Gary Gieger	SS	Don Buddin
C	Pete Daley	C	Sammy White	C	Haywood Sullivan
P	Frank Sullivan	P	Tom Brewer	P	Frank Sullivan

Opening Day Lineups — 1901-1979 (continued)

1961
2B	Chuck Schilling
CF	Gary Geiger
1B	Vic Wertz
RF	Jack Jensen
LF	Carl Yastrzemski
3B	Pete Runnels
C	Russ Nixon
SS	Pumpsie Green
P	Bill Monbouquette

1962
1B	Pete Runnels
2B	Chuck Schilling
CF	Gary Geiger
LF	Carl Yastrzemski
3B	Frank Malzone
C	Russ Nixon
RF	Carroll Hardy
SS	Ed Bressoud
P	Don Schwall

1963
2B	Chuck Schilling
SS	Ed Bressoud
LF	Carl Yastrzemski
1B	Dick Stuart
CF	Roman Mejias
RF	Lou Clinton
3B	Frank Malzone
C	Bob Tillman
P	Bill Monbouquette

1964
2B	Chuck Schilling
SS	Ed Bressoud
LF	Carl Yastrzemski
3B	Frank Malzone
1B	Dick Stuart
RF	Lou Clinton
CF	Tony Conigliaro
C	Bob Tillman
P	Bill Monbouquette

1965
SS	Rico Petrocelli
CF	Lenny Green
LF	Carl Yastrzemski
RF	Tony Conigliaro
1B	Lee Thomas
2B	Felix Mantilla
3B	Frank Malzone
C	Bob Tillman
P	Bill Monbouquette

1966
2B	George Smith
CF	George Thomas
LF	Carl Yastrzemski
RF	Tony Conigliaro
3B	George Scott
1B	Tony Horton
SS	Rico Petrocelli
C	Mike Ryan
P	Earl Wilson

1967
CF	Jose Tartabull
3B	Joe Foy
LF	Carl Yastrzemski
RF	Tony Conigliaro
1B	George Scott
2B	Reggie Smith
SS	Rico Petrocelli
C	Mike Ryan
P	Jim Lonborg

1968
2B	Mike Andrews
3B	Dalton Jones
LF	Carl Yastrzemski
CF	Reggie Smith
1B	George Scott
RF	Joe Lahoud
SS	Rico Petrocelli
C	Elston Howard
P	Dick Ellsworth

1969
CF	Reggie Smith
2B	Mike Andrews
LF	Carl Yastrzemski
1B	Ken Harrelson
RF	Tony Conigliaro
3B	George Scott
SS	Rico Petrocelli
C	Russ Gibson
P	Jim Lonborg

1970
2B	Mike Andrews
CF	Reggie Smith
LF	Carl Yastrzemski
1B	George Scott
SS	Rico Petrocelli
RF	Tony Conigliaro
3B	Luis Alvarado
C	Jerry Moses
P	Gary Peters

1971
SS	Luis Aparicio
RF	Reggie Smith
LF	Carl Yastrzemski
3B	Rico Petrocelli
1B	George Scott
C	Duane Josephson
CF	Billy Conigliaro
2B	Doug Griffin
P	Ray Culp

1972
CF	Tommy Harper
SS	Luis Aparicio
LF	Carl Yastrzemski
CF	Reggie Smith
1B	Danny Cater
2B	Doug Griffin
C	Duane Josephson
P	Marty Pattin

Opening Day Lineups — 1901-1979 (continued)

1973
LF Tommy Harper
SS Luis Aparicio
1B Carl Yastrzemski
CF Reggie Smith
DH Orlando Cepeda
3B Rico Petrocelli
C   Carlton Fisk
2B Doug Griffin
RF Dwight Evans
P   Luis Tiant

1974
LF Tommy Harper
CF Rick Miller
DH Cecil Cooper
1B Carl Yastrzemski
C   Bob Montgomery
RF Bernie Carbo
2B Doug Griffin
3B Terry Hughes
SS Mario Guerrero
P   Luis Tiant

1975
LF Juan Beniquez
CF Fred Lynn
1B Carl Yastrzemski
DH Tony Conigliaro
3B Rico Petrocelli
RF Dwight Evans
C   Bob Montgomery
SS Rick Burleson
2B Doug Griffin
P   Luis Tiant

1976
DH Cecil Cooper
2B Denny Doyle
CF Fred Lynn
LF Jim Rice
1B Carl Yastrzemski
C   Carlton Fisk
RF Dwight Evans
3B Rico Petrocelli
SS Rick Burleson
P   Ferguson Jenkins

1977
SS Rick Burleson
2B Denny Doyle
LF Jim Rice
RF Carl Yastrzemski
CF Rick Miller
1B George Scott
DH Bernie Carbo
C   Carlton Fisk
3B Butch Hobson
P   Ferguson Jenkins

1978
2B Jerry Remy
SS Rick Burleson
DH Jim Rice
LF Carl Yastrzemski
C   Carlton Fisk
CF Fred Lynn
1B George Scott
RF Dwight Evans
3B Butch Hobson
P   Mike Torrez

1979
2B Jerry Remy
SS Rick Burleson
CF Fred Lynn
DH Jim Rice
LF Carl Yastrzemski
1B George Scott
3B Jack Brohamer
RF Dwight Evans
C   Bob Montgomery
P   Dennis Eckersley

FREE AGENTS SIGNED (Re-entry Draft)

1976 — Bill Campbell - P (Nov. 6, 1976)*
1977 — Jack Brohamer - IF (Nov. 30, 1977)*
       Dick Drago - P (Nov. 22, 1977)*
       Mike Torrez - P (Nov. 23, 1977)*
       Tom Burgmeier - P (Feb. 17, 1978)*
1978 — Steve Renko - P (Jan. 20, 1979)*
1979 — Tony Perez - 1B (Nov. 16, 1979)*
       Skip Lockwood - P (Nov. 27, 1979)*

*Date Signed

BOSTON RED SOX COACHES — 1942-1979

Del Baker	1945-48, 1954-60	Eddie Mayo	1951
Mace Brown	1965	Bill McKechnie	1952-53
Don Bryant	1974-76	Oscar Melillo	1952-53
Jack Burns	1955-59	Buster Mills	1954
Bill Burwell	1944	Leo Okrie	1961-62, 1965-66
Doug Camilli	1970-73	Steve O'Neill	1950
Tom Carey	1947	Mickey Owen	1956
Earl Combs	1948-53	John Pesky	1975-
Hazen Cuyler	1949-50	Eddie Popowski . . .	1967-74, 1976
Tom Daly	1942-46	Pete Runnels	1965-66
Bobby Doerr	1967-69	Paul Schreiber	1948-58
Harry Dorish	1963	John Schulte	1949-50
Dave Ferriss	1955-59	Frank Shellenback .	1942-44
Billy Gardner	1965-66	Lee Stange	1972-74
Harvey Haddix . . .	1971	George Susce	1951-54
Billy Herman	1960-64	Bob Turley	1964
Walt Hriniak	1977-	Charlie Wagner . . .	1970
Al Jackson	1977-79	Stan Williams	1975-76
Darrell Johnson . .	1968-69	Larry Woodall	1942-48
Al Lakeman	1963-64, 1967-69	Rudy York	1959-62
Don Lenhardt	1970-73	Eddie Yost	1977-
Sal Maglie	1960-62, 1966-67	Don Zimmer	1974-76
Harry Malmberg .	1963-64		

BOSTON RED SOX NO. 1 PICK IN THE BASEBALL DRAFT

1965 — Billy Conigliaro, outfielder
1966 — Ken Brett, left handed pitcher
1967 — Mike Garman, right handed pitcher
1968 — Tom Maggard, catcher
1969 — Noel Jenke, outfielder
1970 — Jimmie Lee Hacker, third baseman
1971 — Jim Rice, outfielder
1972 — Joel Bishop, infielder
1973 — Ted Cox, infielder
1974 — Eddie Ford, shortstop
1975 — Otis Foster, first baseman
1976 — Bruce Hurst, left handed pitcher
1977 — Andy Madden, right handed pitcher
1978 — Ed Connors, third baseman
1979 — Marc Sullivan, catcher

FORTY SEVEN YEARS OF RED SOX TRAINERS

1942-1947	Win Green	1951-1965	Jack Fadden	1975-		Charlie Moss
1948-1950	Ed Froelich	1966-1974	Buddy Leroux			

BOSTON PITCHERS PLAYING OTHER POSITIONS

1901	Fred Mitchell	P-17	2B-2	SS-1
	George Cuppy	P-13	OF-4	
	Charlie Beville	P-2	1B-1	
1902	Tom Hughes	P-9	OF-3	
1904	Jesse Tannehill	P-32	OF-5	
1906	Ralph Glaze	P-13	3B-1	
1910	Charles Hall	P-35	OF-3	
	Chris Mahoney	P-2	OF-1	
1913	Charles Hall	P-35	3B-1	
1916	Sam Jones	P-12	OF-1	
1918	George Ruth	P-20	OF-59	1B-13
	Walt Kinney	P-5	OF-1	
1919	George Ruth	P-17	OF-111	1B-4
1920	Joe Bush	P-35	OF-2	
1921	Joe Bush	P-37	OF-4	
1925	Joe Lucey	P-7	SS-3	
1928	Danny MacFayden	P-33	OF-1	
1929	Red Ruffing	P-35	OF-2	
1942	Mike Ryba	P-18	C-2	

BOSTON PLAYERS ALSO APPEARING AS PITCHERS

1902	Charles Hickman	OF-27	P-1					
1913	Duffy Lewis	OF-142	P-1					
	Harry Hooper	OF-147	P-1					
1914	Tris Speaker	OF-156	1B-1	P-1				
1920	Henry Eibel	OF-5	P-3	1B-1				
1924	Phil Todt	1B-18	OF-4	P-1				
1928	Doug Taitt	OF-139	P-1					
	Jack Rothrock	OF-53	3B-17	1B-16	SS-13	2B-2	C-1	P-1
1931	Robert Reeves	2B-29	P-1					
1938	Doc Cramer	OF-148	P-1					
1939	Jimmie Foxx	1B-123	P-1					
1940	Ted Williams	OF-143	P-1					
1944	Eddie Lake	SS-41	2B-3	3B-1	P-6			
1952	George Schmees	OF-38	1B-2	P-2				

BOSTON RED SOX PLAYERS WITH
SEVEN YEARS OF SERVICE OR MORE (Through 1979)

19
Ted Williams
Carl Yastrzemski

14
Bob Doerr

13
Rico Petrocelli

12
Harry Hooper

11
Heinie Wagner
Frank Malzone
Bill Goodman
Dom DiMaggio
Ike Delock
Joe Cronin

Boston Red Sox Players With Seven Years of Service or More (Through 1979) (continued)

10
Bill Carrigan
Carlton Fisk
Larry Gardner
Bill Lee
Bob Montgomery
Mel Parnell

9
Joe Dobson
Willard Nixon
George Scott
Tris Speaker
Sammy White

8
Tom Brewer
Lou Criger
Dwight Evans
Dick Gernert
Lefty Grove
Tex Hughson
Ellis Kinder

8 (continued)
Ted Lepcio
Duffy Lewis
Bill Monbouquette
Fred Parent
John Peacock
John Pesky
Herb Pennock
Jim Piersall
Jack Rothrock
Jack Russell
Everett Scott
Reggie Smith
Gene Stephens
Frank Sullivan
Luis Tiant
George Winter
Joe Wood
Cy Young

7
Jimmy Collins
Ray Collins

Tony Conigliaro
Billy Consolo
Hobe Ferris
Ira Flagstead
Mike Fornieles
Jimmie Foxx
Buck Freeman
Gary Geiger
Olaf Henriksen
Jackie Jensen
Earl Johnson
Jim Lonborg
Danny MacFayden
Rick Miller
Russ Nixon
Fritz Ostermueller
Red Ruffing
Jim Tabor
Phil Todt
Earl Wilson
Jack Wilson

SCOUTS

"THE UNSUNG"

It was a relatively cold February day at Fenway Park and up in the roof top dining room the final press conference before spring training was being held. As lunch was about to be served, I joined Red Sox scout Bill Enos and central scouting bureau scout and former Chicago Cub infielder Lennie Merullo. Conversation naturally got around to scouting and I soon realized little recognition had been given this dedicated group of men who, when you come right down to it, are the backbone of the organization. Perhaps with the advent of the draft and the central scouting bureau the role of the scout has changed, but after all they are the ones who actually check the prospects and make the recommendations. Bill mentioned that this group seldom gets recognized, so here is a listing of those dedicated unsung heroes who have toiled for the Red Sox over the past thirty five years.

35 YEARS OF RED SOX SCOUTS

John Barclay	1965-66	Ray Boone	1961-79
Bill Barrett	1947-50	Joe Brawley	1948
Joe Becker	1944, 1947-49	Wayne Britton	1979
Doc Bennett	1947-49	Joe Brown	1948
Milt Bolling	1965-79	Mace Brown	1947-64, 1966-78

35 Years of Red Sox Scouts (continued)

Jack Burns	1961-74	Felix Maldonado .	1971-79
Donie Bush	1953-55	Frank Malzone ...	1967-79
D.T. Campbell ...	1949	Conrado Marrero .	1960-61
Pete Cerrone	1971-72	Socko McCarey ...	1947-73
Jack Corbett	1947-48	Bill McCarren	1944, 1947-71
Dan Crowley	1950-51	Tommy McDonald	1974-79
Ray Culp	1974	Ted McGrew	1951-56
Tom Daly	1944-46	Sam Mele	1968-79
Paul Decker	1947-49	Oscar Melillo	1954
Maurice DeLoof ..	1947-73	Bob Murray	1966
George Digby	1947-79	John Murphy	1948
Billy Disch	1944, 1948-49	Ramon Naranjo ..	1977-79
Roy Dissinger ...	1948	Bots Nekola	1950-76
Bobby Doerr	1957-66	Charlie Niebergall	1944, 1947-54
Harry Dorish	1960-62	Willard Nixon ...	1960-64
Tom Downey	1952-60	Steve O'Neill	1950, 1952
Danny Doyle	1949-79	Jack Onslow	1952-60
Joe Dugan	1955-66	Willie Paffen	1971-79
Hugh Duffy	1947-54	Meade Palmer ...	1971-73
Hugh East	1950-51	Mel Parnell	1964
Jack Egan	1944-46	Dave Philley	1967-73
Bill Enos	1974-79	George Pipgras ..	1947-49
Frank Fahey	1970-73	Tony Ravish	1970-74
John Fedders	1970	Rod Rice	1949-73
Denny Galehouse .	1951-65	Paul Schreiber ...	1960-65
Billy Goodman ...	1966	Ed Scott	1962-79
Bill Harrell	1967	Matt Sczesny	1971-79
Jap Haskell	1948	Hank Severeid ...	1944-68
Bunn Hearn	1944-49	Clayton Sheedy ...	1949-51, 1961-67
Sid Hudson	1956-60	Marv Stendel	1971-73
Fred Hunter	1947-48	Joe Stephenson...	1950-79
Earl Johnson.....	1954-79	Bill Summers	1964-65
Ernie Johnson ...	1944-53	Paul Tavares	1979
Stan Johnson	1971-72	Larry Thomas....	1966-79
Bill Joyce	1954-58, 1962-66	Tommy Thomas .	1950-57, 1959,
Eddie Kasko	1974-77		1961-73
Chuck Koney	1950-79	Pedro Vazquez ...	1964-69
Don Lee	1974-76	Charlie Wagner ..	1961-69, 1971-79
Lefty Lefebvre ...	1966-79	Charlie Wallgren .	1945-63
Don Lenhardt....	1957-79	Larry Woodall ...	1955-63
Fred Maguire	1950-58, 1960-61	Ed Wopperer	1947
Neill Mahoney ...	1947-60	Glenn Wright....	1948-54, 1958-73
		Elmer Yoter	1948-54, 1962-66

THE BATS

It isn't often that the average baseball fan gets to look at his favorite player's bat close enough to know what it is really like. They vary in length, weight and style, each tailored to the player's individual taste. Some batters are more particular about their bats than others. It is said that Ted Williams knew his bats so well, he could tell if they were off by an ounce in weight. Players with long careers often changed the style of bat they used depending upon what felt comfortable to them at a particular stage of their career. Not only do bats vary in size, but they also vary in color. This is often caused by the way they treat the bat or the amount of pine tar is used by a particular batter. In recent years there has also been a return to a darker colored bat. The bats may all look the same from the grandstand, but if you could see them up close you would see many differences. Most of the players today have their bats custom made by the bat manufacturers to their own specifications and their names are usually stamped into the barrel end of the bat denoting the personalized model.

The author had the privilege of visiting a Red Sox farm team (Bristol Red Sox) in 1979 with Joe Wood, the famous pitcher of the early Red Sox, and discussing various aspects of the game with these players. In addition to the size of the gloves worn by the players of today, Mr. Wood was amazed at the bats which were much lighter in weight and had thinner handles than in his day. A good hitter himself, he felt that it should be easier to hit with today's bats but that with the emphasis on home runs and holding the bats all the way down at the knob the hitters of today were not using the bat to its best advantage. How often do you see a batter choking up or batting with his hands spread apart like the great Ty Cobb did when he could spray hits to all fields?

So that you can get an idea of what the bats of some of the Red Sox hitters were like over the years, I am listing them here. In some cases, where the hitter changed models the earliest model used is listed first.

LOU BOUDREAU — Medium long with a medium sized barrel tapered to a small handle and a large knob.

JOE CRONIN — Long with a small barrel with a straight taper to a medium handle and a small knob.

DOM DiMAGGIO — Medium large barrel with a medium length hitting space with a gradual taper to a very thin handle and a large knob.

WALTER DROPO — Barrel tapers gradually from medium size end to a very small handle with a very large knob.

BOBBY DOERR — (1) Medium large barrel with a long taper to a very small handle and a large knob.
(2) Large at extreme end, barrel tapers slightly below medium size, the handle is very small and tapers up quickly to a very large knob.

JIMMIE FOXX — (1) Medium long, large barrel tapered to a medium handle and a large knob.
(2) Medium large with a medium large barrel tapered to a very small handle with a large knob.

BILLY GOODMAN — Medium size at the end with a barrel that tapers gradually then drops very quickly into a medium handle and a very small knob.

KEN HARRELSON — A small sized handle which builds slowly into a small sized barrel. Knob is medium size.

GEORGE KELL — (1) Barrel medium large with a long taper to a very small handle and a large knob.
(2) Small near end, barrel tapering down slowly to slightly below medium size. Very small handle that builds up quickly to a large knob.

FRED LYNN — A medium barrel which tapers sharply to a small handle with a large knob.

JOHN PESKY — Small with a medium long barrel tapering to a long, small handle and a small knob.

RICO PETROCELLI — A long small barrel which tapers rapidly to a medium handle with a medium knob.

BABE RUTH	—	Medium large with a moderately short barrel with a long taper to a very small handle and a large knob.
VERN STEPHENS	—	Long barrel, medium size near end with little taper. Farther down, barrel tapers noticeably into extremely small handle. The handle builds up quickly to a large knob.
MICKEY VERNON	—	Medium size with a barrel of medium length, tapering gradually to a small handle with a large knob.
TED WILLIAMS	—	(1) Small barrel with a straight taper to a medium handle and a small knob. (2) Medium size large barrel with medium length hitting surface and a very small handle and a large knob. (3) Small barrel that tapers down to a very small handle which builds up sharply to a large knob.
CARL YASTRZEMSKI	—	Medium size barrel with a long small handle which builds up quickly into the barrel. Medium to large knob.
RUDY YORK	—	(1) Large barrel tapering very gradually to a small handle and a large knob. (2) Barrel of medium size and length, tapering to a small handle and a large knob.

THE HITTERS

Four of the greatest hitters to perform for the Red Sox were Babe Ruth, Tris Speaker, Jimmie Foxx and Ted Williams. Not many fans have been able to say they lived long enough to see each one of them play. Here for your mind's eye is a description of how each stood at the plate.

BABE RUTH: His batting style was as distinctive as the way he looked. He stood with his feet close together, his body turned so he was looking at the pitcher over his right shoulder. Feet four inches apart with his right foot about an inch closer to home plate than his left. He stood to the rear of the batter's box, but not necessarily deep, almost on a line with the plate. He took a big stride forward with his right foot, planted his back foot firmly, swinging forward on a level plane, snapping his wrists into the swing at the moment the bat hit the ball. He

The Hitters (continued)

held the bat long, the knob at the small end gripped in his right hand. When he missed the ball the force of his swing often sent him to the ground. Despite all his power, he was also a good bunter and place hitter.

TRIS SPEAKER: Speaker stood deep in the batter's box and batted from a semi-crouch. His right foot was about five inches in front of his left foot. His right foot was also two to four inches nearer to the plate. He used a full stride and held his bat rather low with his hands almost resting on his left hip. While at the plate he was continually moving the bat up and down with very slow motion. Later in his career he altered his stance to take advantage of pulling for the short fence in Cleveland's Dunn Field (League Park).

JIMMIE FOXX: A powerful hitter, he presented a menacing picture at the plate. He held the bat long and stood fairly deep in the batter's box, using a straddle stance with a full stride leading into the ball with his powerful arms. He used a full follow through. Foxx was a very awesome sight at the plate and may have well been the most powerful of all Sox hitters. As the pitch approached him, you could see his powerful muscles flexing, ready to hit the ball.

TED WILLIAMS: A careful study of the pitcher preceded his turn at bat. Who can forget Ted down on one knee in the on-deck circle watching every motion of the pitcher. At the plate only one word can describe him—loose. This tall and gangly batter, knees slightly bent, would take a few nervous swings of the bat, hands tightly wrapped around the handle. He stood fairly deep in the box, right foot closer to the plate than his left, which was about fifteen inches behind the right. He batted with his feet close together and took a long stride. In the latter part of his career he widened his stance and shortened his stride. His great eyesight and wrist action made him exceptional. He had a whiplash swing and a great sense of timing.

BOSTON AMERICAN LEAGUE FIRSTS

Since expansion arrived on the major league scene many of the new teams have published lists of the first this and the first that in their history. This is a relatively easy task for the recorders of team history for these new clubs. When the original teams in the American League got underway there was little emphasis on such records and even if there was they have disappeared over the years. Presented here are some of the firsts in the Boston American League team's history. You will find the various firsts broken down by general team records, batting, pitching, firsts at the two ball parks they have played in, the Huntington Avenue Grounds and Fenway Park, and World Series firsts. The author owes a thank you to Frank Williams, another Red Sox nut, who verified these various firsts for him.

No list of firsts would be complete without a little history of the first team. Bob Lindsay, a very devoted Red Sox historian, of State College, Pennsylvania has researched the comings and goings of this first club and has generously allowed the author to present it in this section The author has added a little background on the birth of the team to set the scene. Of course, the feats have been repeated many times, but somehow there is always something magical about who was the first to do something. So here they are — the firsts — many accomplished by long forgotten ball players of eras long past in the pages of history.

THE FIRST AMERICAN LEAGUE BOSTONIANS

When baseball pioneer Ban Johnson was formulating plans for a new baseball league, to be called the American League, his blueprint did not call for a team to be placed in Boston, Massachusetts. In January of 1901, Johnson learned that the American Association was planning to put a club in Boston and wishing to combat that move, he dropped his plan to put a club in Buffalo, New York and decided to establish a team in Boston instead. This was a risky move at best as Boston was a baseball hot bed for the National League Boston Red Stockings. (Later the Bees and Braves). Through some strange maneuvering on Johnson's part, Charles W. Somers became the owner of the new club and had the task of acquiring players to stock the roster. This was no easy task. Remember there was no draft in those days as has been the case with recent expansion teams. Contracts not withstanding, players moved from club to club, wherever the best deal arose. There was no reserve clause in existence. It was not unusual for players to take ads in the help wanted section of newspapers offering their services to various regions of the country where they were desirous of playing. An early so called war between the National and American Leagues broke out with the newer league raiding the older for players. These players who switched leagues were often referred to as "jumpers". Several years elapsed before a peace agreement was reached between leagues ending this migration of players.

Johnson had assembled a fine group of baseball wise men who became his "raiders". They included Charles Comiskey, Connie Mack, John McGraw, Clark Griffith and Hugh Duffy. They had placed the bait before the National League stars with the early raids aimed at the Philadelphia Nationals. With Boston now in the new venture they shifted their offers to the stars of the Boston Nationals who, under the guidance of Frank Selee, had been National League Champions in 1897 and 1898, a strong second in 1899 but had slid to fourth in 1900. Of Johnson's raiders, two were New Englanders, Mack and Duffy, and appeared to have the inside track of convincing the Boston players to make a move. Their big break came when they convinced third baseman Jimmy Collins to switch leagues and become playing manager of the American League's new team. Collins convinced teammates center-fielder Chick Stahl, right fielder Buck Freeman and pitcher Ed "Parson" Lewis to join him with dollars being the deciding factor.

The next big break for the Boston Americans was the capture of pitcher Cy Young from the St. Louis Cardinals. Young, of course, had much to do with early Boston American successes and went on to become one of baseball's immortals. Not only did Young join up, but he brought along his battery mate, catcher Lou Criger and pitcher George "Nig" Cuppy, who had gone from St. Louis to the Boston Nationals.

So with this as a core, let's take a look at the rest of that first team of 1901.

PITCHERS

CHARLIE BEVILLE   —   Came out of the Montana League to Detroit who sent him on to Boston for his first and only major league appearance. He went back to the minors during the 1901 season.

The First American League Bostonians (continued)

NIG CUPPY — Jumped from the Boston Nationals. He left the majors after the 1901 season.

FRANK FOREMAN — Came from minor league Buffalo and was released to Baltimore during the 1901 season.

WIN KELLUM — Came from Indianapolis to make his first major league appearance. Was released during 1901. Appeared in the National League in 1904-1905.

PARSON LEWIS — Jumped from the Boston Nationals. Left the majors after the 1901 season.

FRED MITCHELL — Made his first major league appearance and was sent to Philadelphia during the 1902 season.

DEACON MORRISSEY — Made his first major league appearance and wound up with the Chicago Nationals in 1902.

JAKE VOLZ — Made his first major league appearance and was released after 1901.

GEORGE PRENTISS — Made his first major league appearance. Was
(WILSON) — sent to Baltimore for the 1902 season.

GEORGE WINTER — Made his first major league appearance. Was sent to Detroit in 1908.

CY YOUNG — Jumped from the St. Louis Nationals. Sent to Cleveland after the 1908 season.

CATCHERS

LOU CRIGER — Jumped from the St. Louis Nationals. Sent to the St. Louis Browns after the 1908 season.

OSSEE SCHRECKENGOST — Came from minor league Buffalo, but had played in the majors with Louisville, Cleveland and St. Louis. Was sent to Cleveland for the 1902 season.

JACK SLATTERY — Made his first major league appearance. Released during 1901, but returned to the majors with Cleveland in 1903.

The First American League Bostonians (continued)

INFIELDERS

JIMMY COLLINS — Jumped from the Boston Nationals. Traded to Philadelphia in 1907.

HOBE FERRIS — Made his first major league appearance. Was traded to the St. Louis Browns via New York after the 1907 season.

BUCK FREEMAN — Jumped from the Boston Nationals. Sent to the minors in 1907.

HARRY GLEASON — Came from minor league Utica and was released after the 1902 season. Appeared with St. Louis in 1904.

LARRY McLEAN — Made his first major league appearance. Released in 1901, but appeared with the Chicago Nationals in 1903.

FRED PARENT — Came from Providence of the Eastern League. Had been with the St. Louis Cardinals in 1899. Sent to the Chicago Americans after the 1907 season.

OUTFIELDERS

TOM DOWD — Came from minor league Milwaukee. Released after the 1901 season.

CHARLIE HEMPHILL — Came from minor league Kansas City. Released to the Cleveland Americans after the 1901 season.

CHARLIE JONES — Came from minor league Detroit. Released after 1901 season. Appeared with the Chicago Americans in 1904.

CHICK STAHL — Jumped from the Boston Nationals. Died before the 1907 season.

FIRSTS IN BOSTON AMERICAN LEAGUE HISTORY

TEAM RECORDS

First Home Game .... May 8, 1901 - Philadelphia won 12 to 4
First Road Game .... April 26, 1901 - At Baltimore lost 10 to 6
First Win .... April 30, 1901 - At Philadelphia 8 to 6, 10 innings
First Loss .... April 26, 1901 - At Baltimore 10 to 6
First Win At Boston .... May 8, 1901 vs. Philadelphia 12 to 4
First Win On Road .... April 30, 1901 - At Philadelphia 8 to 6, 10 innings
First Loss At Boston .... May 11, 1901 vs. Washington 3 to 2
First Loss On Road .... April 26, 1901 at Baltimore 10 to 6
First Extra Inning Win At Home ..... August 13, 1901 vs. Philadelphia 4 to 3
13 innings
First Extra Inning Win On Road...... April 30, 1901 - At Philadelphia 8 to 6
10 innings
First Extra Inning Loss At Home .... May 17, 1902 vs. Philadelphia 7 to 5,
10 innings
First Extra Inning Loss On Road........ July 19, 1901 - At Cleveland 2 to 1,
10 innings
First Doubleheader Win At Home .. June 17, 1901 vs Chicago 11 to 1, 10 to 4
First Doubleheader Win On Road .. July 17, 1901 - At Cleveland 9 to 3, 10 to 2
First Doubleheader Loss At Home September 23, 1901 vs. Detroit 4 to 5, 2 to 9
First Doubleheader Loss On Road .... May 30, 1901 - At Chicago 8 to 3, 5 to 3
First Doubleheader Split At Home   August 9, 1901 vs Baltimore 9 to 11, 6 to 2
First Doubleheader Split On Road. August 5, 1901 - At Baltimore 3 to 1, 0 to 9
First Shutout Win At Home .... July 6, 1901 vs. Washington 7 to 0
First Shutout Loss At Home .... May 15, 1901 vs. Washington 4 to 0
First Shutout Win On Road .... May 25, 1901 - At Cleveland 5 to 0
First Shutout Loss On Road .... May 24, 1901 - At Detroit 3 to 0
First Tie Game At Home .... August 18, 1902 vs. Detroit 4 to 4, 11 innings
First Tie Game On Road .... August 31, 1901 - At Detroit 4 to 4
First Home Series Win .... May 8-9, 1901 vs. Philadelphia 2 games
First Home Series Loss .... May 11-15, 1901 vs. Washington 4 games
First Road Series Win ...... May 3-4, 6-7, 1901 - At Washington 3 games to 1
First Road Series Loss .... April 26-27, 1901 - At Baltimore 2 games

BATTING

First Player To Get A Hit .... Unknown
First Player to Hit A Double ,..... Jimmy Collins - April 26, 1901 At Baltimore
First Player To Hit A Triple .. Buck Freeman - April 29, 1901 At Philadelphia
First Player to Get A Home Run Buck Freeman - April 30, 1901 At Philadelphia
First Player To Get A Home Run At Home ..... Buck Freeman - May 8, 1901
First Player To Get Two Home Runs In A Game............ Buck Freeman
- June 1, 1901 At Chicago
First Player To Have Two Hits In A Game .... Jimmy Collins and Lou Criger,
April 26, 1901 At Baltimore

Firsts in Boston American League History (continued)

First Player To Have Three Hits In A Game .... Charlie Hemphill
- April 27, 1901 At Baltimore
First Player To Have Four Hits In A Game .... Jimmy Collins and Fred Parent
- May 2, 1901 At Philadelphia
First Player To Have Five Hits In A Game ...... Chick Stahl - August 7, 1901
First Game At Baltimore
First Player To Have Six Hits In A Game .... Jim Piersall - June 10, 1953
At St. Louis
First Player To Go Four For Four .... Tom Dowd - June 2, 1901 At Milwaukee
(4 singles)
First Player To Go Five For Five .... Chick Stahl - August 7, 1901
First Game At Baltimore (4 singles & Double)
First Player To Go Six For Six .... Jim Piersall - June 10, 1953
At St. Louis (1 double, 5 singles)
First Player To Get A Pinch Hit .. Larry McLean - April 26, 1901 At Baltimore
First Pitcher To Get A Hit .... Win Kellum - April 26, 1901
First Designated Hitter .... Orlando Cepeda - April 6, 1973
First Designated Hitter To Get A Hit .... Orlando Cepeda - April 8, 1973
First Player To Steal A Base .. Tommy Dowd - April 29, 1901 vs. Philadelphia
First Pitcher To Hit A Home Run .... George Winter - July 18, 1901
First Player To Get Three Home Runs In A Game ...... Jim Tabor - July 4, 1939
At Philadelphia 2nd Game
First Player To Have A Sacrifice Hit Ted Lewis - May 2, 1901 At Philadelphia
First Batter .... Tom Dowd - April 26, 1901 At Baltimore

PITCHING

First To Win A Home Game .... Cy Young - May 8, 1901 vs. Philadelphia
First To Lose A Home Game .... Ted Lewis - May 11, 1901 vs Washington
First To Win A Road Game .... Cy Young - April 30, 1901 At Philadelphia
First To Lose A Road Game ...... Win Kellum - April 26, 1901 At Baltimore
First To Win A Shutout .... Ted Lewis - May 25, 1901 At Cleveland 5 to 0
First To Win A Shutout At Home Cy Young - July 6, 1901 vs. Washington 7 to 0
First To Pitch A Complete Game .. Win Kellum - April 26, 1901 At Baltimore
First To Record A Strikeout .... Win Kellum - April 26, 1901 At Baltimore
First To Issue A Walk .... Win Kellum - April 26, 1901 At Baltimore
First To Give Up A Hit .... Win Kellum - April 26, 1901 At Baltimore
First To Strike Out 10 Batters In A Game Cy Young - May 17, 1901 vs. Baltimore
First To Win 10 Games .... Cy Young - June 17, 1901, 2nd game
First To Lose 10 Games .... Ted Lewis - July 27, 1901
First To Win 20 Games .... Cy Young - August 2, 1901
First To Win 30 Games .... Cy Young - September 14, 1901
First To Relieve A Starter .... Fred Mitchell - April 27, 1901 At Baltimore

Firsts in Boston American League History (continued)

FENWAY PARK FIRSTS

First Game .... April 20, 1912 - vs. New York
First Win .... April 20, 1912 - vs. New York 7 to 6, 11 innings
First Loss .... April 23, 1912 - vs. Washington 6 to 2
First Pitcher To Win A Game .... April 20, 1912 - Charley Hall
First Pitcher To Lose A Game .... April 23, 1912 - Joe Wood
First Multi-Run Game For Boston .... May 13, 1912 - vs St. Louis, 14 runs
First Shutout Game By Boston .... May 20, 1912 - 2 to 0 vs. Chicago
First Pitcher To Pitch A Shutout .. May 20, 1912 - Joe Wood vs. Chicago 2 to 0
First Shutout of Boston ..... May 30, 1912 - By Washington, Second Game 5 to 0
First Rain Out .... April 18, 1912 vs. New York
Most Runs, One Game, First Year .... May 29, 1912 - 21 vs. Washington
First Red Sox Single .... Unknown
First Red Sox Double .... April 20, 1912 - Steve Yerkes
First Red Sox Triple .... April 25, 1912 - Tris Speaker
First Red Sox Home Run .... April 26, 1912 - Hugh Bradley
First Red Sox Run .... April 20, 1912 - Steve Yerkes
First Red Sox Sacrifice Hit .... April 20, 1912 - Harry Hooper
First Red Sox Stolen Base .... April 20, 1912 - Duffy Lewis
First Red Sox Hit Batter .... April 20, 1912 - Les Nunamaker - By Quinn
First Red Sox Wild Pitch .... April 20, 1912 - Buck O'Brien
First Red Sox Batter .... April 20, 1912 - Harry Hooper
First Red Sox Pinch Hitter ...... April 20, 1912 - Olaf Henriksen - 5th inning
for Bucky O'Brien
First Red Sox Pitcher To Start A Game .... April 20, 1912 - Buck O'Brien
First Red Sox To Relieve A Starter .... April 20, 1912 - Charley Hall
First Red Sox Pitcher To Hit A Batter .... April 20, 1912 - Buck O'Brien
(Bert Daniels - New York)
First Red Sox Pitcher To Issue A Walk .... April 20, 1912 - Buck O'Brien
First Red Sox Pitcher To Record A Strike Out .. April 20, 1912 - Buck O'Brien
First Red Sox Pitcher To Commit A Balk ...... April 20, 1912 - Buck O'Brien
Umpires First Game .... Tom Connolly, Bill Hart
Time Of First Game .... 3 Hours, 10 Minutes
Attendance First Game 24,383
First Red Sox Winning Hit .... April 20, 1912 - Tris Speaker (11th inning,
single drove home Steve Yerkes)
The First Band To Appear .... The Letter Carriers Band

HUNTINGTON AVENUE GROUNDS FIRSTS

First Pilgrim Player To Get A Hit .... Unknown
First Pilgrim Player To Hit A Single .... Unknown
First Pilgrim Player To Hit A Double .... May 8, 1901 - Charlie Hemphill
First Pilgrim Player To Hit A Triple .... May 8, 1901 - Charlie Hemphill
First Pilgrim Player To Hit A Home Run .... May 8, 1901 - Buck Freeman
First Pilgrim Batter .... May 8, 1901 - Tom Dowd
First Pilgrim Pitcher To Start A Game .... May 8, 1901 - Cy Young

Firsts in Boston American League History (continued)

First Pilgrim Pitcher To Relieve . . . . July 10, 1901 - Fred Mitchell
(For Parson Lewis)
First Pilgrim Pitcher To Strike Out A Batter . . . . May 8, 1901 - Cy Young
First Pilgrim Pitcher To Walk A Batter . . . . May 11, 1901 - Parson Lewis
First Umpire . . . . John Haskell
Time Of First Game . . . . 2 hours, 5 minutes
Attendance Of First Game . . . . 14,000 - 11,025 Paid
First Pilgrim Player To Steal A Base . . . . May 8, 1901 - Cy Young
First Pilgrim Player To Get A Sacrifice Hit . . . . May 8, 1901 - Chick Stahl

BOSTON WORLD SERIES FIRSTS

First World Series Game . . . . October 1, 1903 vs. Pittsburgh at Boston
Forst World Series Loss . . . . October 1, 1903 vs. Pittsburgh at Boston
First World Series Win . . . . October 2, 1903 vs. Pittsburgh at Boston
First World Series Shutout Win October 2, 1903 vs. Pittsburgh at Boston, 3 to 0
First World Series Shutout Loss . . . . . September 10, 1918 vs. Chicago at Boston
First World Series Single . . . . Chick Stahl - October 1, 1903
First World Series Double . . . . Chick Stahl - October 2, 1903
First World Series Triple . . . . Buck Freeman - October 1, 1903
First World Series Home Run . . . . Pat Dougherty - October 2, 1903
First World Series Run . . . . Buck Freeman - October 1, 1903
First World Series Stolen Base . . . . Jimmy Collins - October 2, 1903
First World Series Strike Out . . . . Pat Dougherty - October 1, 1903
First World Series Walk . . . . Candy LaChance - October 2, 1903
First World Series Pinch Hitter . . . . Jack O'Brien - October 1, 1903
9th inning for Lou Criger
First World Series Hit Batter . . . . Hobe Ferris - October 1, 1903
First World Series Pitcher To Win . . . . Bill Dineen - October 2, 1903
First World Series Pitcher To Lose . . . . Cy Young - October 1, 1903
First World Series Pitcher To Pitcher A Shutout . . . . Bill Dineen
- October 2, 1903, 3 to 0
First World Series Pitcher To Pitch A Complete Game . . . . Cy Young
- October 1, 1903

HOW DO YOU SAY 'EM

Often misunderstood is the pronunciation of players names. An example of this would be the case of Red Sox catcher Forrest Cady. Should the last name be pronounced Caddy or Kay dee? To help clear up such misunderstandings the author has attempted to set forth here the correct pronunciations. In the case of Cady it required talking to his battery mate Joe Wood to be certain I had the right pronunciation. Others had to be obtained from fans, former employees or players of the era involved. So here is a list of some of the Red Sox players. Those with common names have not been listed. Some of the credit for this list must be given to Bill Gavin of South Weymouth, Massachusetts who was weaned on Boston baseball. Bill, whose family was employed by the earliest Boston American League teams, was himself a fixture around Fenway Park for many years.

HOW DO YOU SAY 'EM

AASE, DON	AH-SEE
ADAIR, JERRY	A-DARE
ALMADA, MEL	AL-MAH-DA
ALVARADO, LUIS	AL-VER-AH-DOUGH
ANDRES, ERNIE	AN-DRAYS
APARICIO, LUIS	AP-PAR-EACH-EE-OH
ARELLANES, FRANK	AIR-A-LANES
ASBJORNSON, BOB	AS-BA-JORN-SON
ASPROMONTE, KEN	AS-PRUH-MONN-TEE
AUKER, ELDON	AUK-HER
AVILA, BOBBY	A-VEAL-A
AVILES, RAMON	AH-VEAL-ESS
AZCUE, JOE	AS-KOO-EE

BAGBY, JIM	BAG-BEE
BARBARE, WALT	BAR-BAYER
BARBERICH, FRANK	BARBER-ICK
BARNA, HERB	BAR-NA
BATTS, MATT	BATS
BAUMANN, FRANK	B-OW-MAN
BAYNE, BILL	BAIN
BEDIENT, HUGH	BEAD-E-ENT
BENIQUEZ, JUAN	BEH-NEE-KEZ
BERBERET, LOU	BURR-BURR-ET
BEVAN, HAL	BEV-AN
BEVILLE, CHARLES	BEH-VIL
BIGELOW, ELLIOT	BIG-A-LOW
BLETHEN, CLARENCE	BLETH-EN
BLUHM, HARVEY	BLOOM
BOERNER, LARRY	BORN-ER
BOLIN, BOB	BO-LYNN
BOLLING, MILT	BOWLING
BOUDREAU, LOU	BOO-DROW
BOWMAN, JOE	BO-MAN
BOWSFIELD, ED	BOHS-FIELD
BRESSOUD, ED	BRUH-SOO
BRODOWSKI, DICK	BROO-DOW-SKI
BROHAMER, JACK	BRO-HAMMER
BUCHER, JIM	BEW-KER
BUDDIN, DON	BUD-IN
BURCHELL, FRED	BIRCH-EL
BURKETT, JESSE	BUR-KETT
BURLESON, RICK	BURL-SON
BUSHEY, FRANK	BUSH-EE
BYERLY, BUD	BUYER-LEE

How Do You Say 'Em (continued)

CADY, FOREST .... KAY-DEE
CAMILLI, DOLPH .... CAM-ILL-EE
CARBO, BERNIE .... CAR-BOW
CASALE, JERRY .... CAH-SALE
CATER, DANNY .... KAY-TER
CEPEDA, ORLANDO .... SE-PAY-DA
CHAKALES, BOB .... SCHACKLES
CHITTUM, NELSON .... CHIT-UM
CICOTTE, ED .... CY-COTT
CLEVENGER, TRUMAN .... CLEV-EN-GER
CONIGLIARO, BILL, TONY ...... CO-NIG-LEE-AH-RO
CONSOLO, BILLY .... CON-SO-LO
COUGHTRY, MARLAN .... COUGH-TREE
COUMBE, FRED .... COOMB
CRIGER, LOU .... CREE-GER

DAHLGREN, BABE .... DAWL-GRIN
DALLESSANDRO, DOM .... DEL-ES-SAND-ROW
DEMETER, DON .... DEM-A-TER
DESAUTELS, GENE............. DES-AU-TELS
DEUTSCH, MEL .... DOITCH
DIAZ, BO .... DEE-AZ
DIDIER, BOB .... DEE-DER
DIPIETRO, BOB .... DEE-PETE-ROW
DOERR, BOBBY .... DOOR
DRAGO, DICK .... DRAY-GO
DREISEWERD, CLEM .... DRIES-WIERD
DROPO, WALT .... DROO-PO
DUBUC, JEAN................. DO-BECK
DULIBA, BOB .... DO-LEE-BAH

ECKERSLEY, DENNIS .... ECK-ERZ-LEE
EHMKE, HOWARD .... EM-KEY
EIBEL, HANK .... EE-BELL

FIORE, MIKE.................. FEE-OR-EE
FORNIELES, MIKE .... FOUR-NEE-LEES
FRIBERG, BERNIE.............. FRY-BERG
FUHR, OSCAR .... FUR

GAFFKE, FABIAN .... GAF-KEY
GEIGER, GARY................. GUY-GER
GEYGAN, JIM .... GAY-GUN
GILE, DON .... GEE-LEE
GRILL, GUIDO .... GRILL-EE
GUERRA, FERMIN.............. GOO-WERA
GUERRERO, MARIO .... GOO-WER-EROW
GUINDON, BOB............... GIN-DON

How Do You Say 'Em (continued)

HANEY, FRED .... HAIN-EE
HARTENSTEIN, CHARLES .... HART-EN-STEEN
HAUSMANN, CLEM .... HOWZ-MAN
HEIMACH, FRED .... HY-MACK
HERRERA, MIKE .... HER-RAH-RA
HINRICHS, PAUL .... HIN-RIX
HISNER, HARLEY .... HY-SNER
HOBLITZEL, DICK .... HOBE-LIT-ZEL
HODERLEIN, MEL .... HOE-DER-LINE
HOEFT, BILLY .... HEFT

JABLONOWSKI, PETE .... JAB-LON-OW-SKI

KASKO, ED .... KASS-KO
KEMMERER, RUSS .... KEM-ER-ER
KEOUGH, MARTY .... KEE-OH
KIELY, LEO .... KI-LEE
KLAUS, BILLY .... KLOUSE
KRAUSSE, LEW .... KRA-OUSE
KOONCE, CAL .... KOONSE
KREUGER, RICK .... CREW-GER
KRUG, MARTY .... CREW-GH

LAHOUD, JOE .... LA-HUDE
LAMABE, JOHN .... LA-MAY-ABE
LAZOR, JOHN .... LAY-ZOR
LE FEBVRE, LEFTY .... LA-FEB
LEHENY, REGIS .... LA-HAIN-EE
LEHNER, PAUL .... LAY-NER
LEPCIO, TED .... LEP-SEE-OH
LOEPP, GEORGE .... LOPE
LUPIEN, TONY .... LOOP-E-EN
LYLE, ALBERT .... LIE-L

MAGRINI, PETE .... MA-GREEN-EE
MALZONE, FRANK .... MALZ-OWN
MANTILLA, FELIX .... MAN-TEE-YUH
MANUSH, HENRY .... MAN-OOSH
MARICHAL, JUAN .... MAR-EE-CHAHL
MATCHICK, JOHN .... MATCH-CHICK
MAUCH, GENE .... MOCK
MC AULIFFE, DICK .... MICK-ALL-IF
MC GLOTHEN, LYNN .... MC-GLOW-THEN
MEJIAS, ROMAN .... MUH-HEE-US
MELE, SAM .... ME-LEE
MELILLO, OSCAR .... MEL-ILL-O
MEOLA, EMILE .... ME-O-LA

How Do You Say 'Em (continued)

MINARCIN, RUDY .... MIN-ARR-SIN
MOFORD, HERB .... MO-FERD
MOLYNEAUX, VINCE .... MOLY-NEW
MONBOUQUETTE, BILL .... MON-BOO-KET
MONCEWICZ, FRED .... MON-SA-WITZ
MORET, ROGELIO .... MOR-ETT
MOSER, WALT .... MOS-HER
MOSKIMAN, BILL .... MOS-KA-MAN
MUFFETT, BILLY .... MUFF-IT
MUSER, TONY .... MEW-SIR
MUSTAIKIS, ALEX .... MUS-TAKE-US

NARLESKI, BILL .... NAR-LESS-KEY
NEITZKE, ERNIE............... NEET-SKEE
NEUBAUER, HAL .... NOO-BOWER
NEWHAUSER, DON .... NEW-HOUSER
NIARHOS, GUS .... NY-ER-HOS
NIEMIEC, AL................... NE-MICK
NIPPERT, MERLIN .... NIP-ERT
NONNENKAMP, LEO .... NON-EN-CAMP
NUNAMAKER, LES .... NUN-A-MAKER

OGLIVIE, BEN .... OGE-LI-VEE
OKRIE, LEN.................... OAK-REE
ORME, GEORGE .... ORR-ME
OSINSKI, DAN................. O-SIN-SKI
OSTDIEK, HENRY .... OST-DICK
OSTERMUELLER, FRED .... OS-TER-MULER
OSTROWSKI, TED .... OS-TROW-SKEE

PAGLIARONI, JIM............... PAG-LEE-AH-ROAN-EE
PAPAI, AL .... PAPIE
PAPE, LARRY .... PAPE (As in Paper)
PAPI, STAN .... PAP-EE
PARTEE, ROY.................. PARR-TEA
PARTENHEIMER, STAN .... PAR-TEN-HI-MER
PASCHAL, BEN .... PAS-KUL
PATTIN, MARTY .... PAT-IN
PAVLETICH, DON .... PAV-LICK
PELLAGRINI, EDDIE .... PELL-A-GREENIE
PENNOCK, HERB .... PEN-KNOCK
PERTICA, BILL .... PER-TEA-CA
PESKY, JOHN .... PES-KEY
PETROCELLI, RICO .... PET-ROW-CELL-EE
PICINICH, VAL .... PICK-IN-ICH
PIERSALL, JIM .... PEER-SAUL
PIPGRAS, GEORGE .... PIP-GRASS

How Do You Say 'Em (continued)

PITTENGER, CLARK	PIT-EN-GER
POQUETTE, TOM	PO-KET
POULSEN, KEN	POLE-SON
PROTHRO, DOC	PROTH-ROW
PRUIETT, CHARLES	PRU-IT
PYTLAK, FRANK	PIT-LACK
RADATZ, DICK	RA-DITS
REDER, JOHN	RAIDER
REHG, WALT	RAY-G
REMY, JERRY	REM-EE
RENNA, BILL	REN-NA
REPULSKI, RIP................	RE-PUL-SKEE
RHYNE, HAL	RINE
ROGELL, BILL	ROW-GEL
ROGGENBURK, GERRY	ROWE-GEN-BURK
ROHR, BILLY..................	ROAR
ROMO, VICENTE	ROW-MO
ROSAR, BUDDY	ROSE-ARE
RUEL, HEROLD	RULE
RYBA, DOMINIC	RHEE-BA
SADOWSKI, ED, BOB	SA-DOW-SKEE
SANTIAGO, JOSE...............	SAN-TEE-AH-GO
SATRIANO, TOM	SAT-REE-ANO
SAYLES, BILL	SAILS
SCARRITT, RUSS...............	SCARE-IT
SCHANZ, CHARLEY	SHAN-Z
SCHERBARTH, BOB	SHARE-BAR-TH
SCHLESINGER, BILL............	SCHLESS-IN-GER
SCHLITZER, VIC	SCHLIT-ZER
SCHMEES, JOHN	SH-MEES
SCHOFIELD, JOHN	SKO-FIELD
SCHRECKENGOST, OSSEE	SCHRECK-EN-GOST
SCHROLL, AL	SCROLL
SCHWALL, DON	SH-WALL
SEGUI, DIEGO.................	SEE-GEE
SHOFNER, PINKY	SHOF-NER
SIEBERN, NORM	SEE-BURN
SIEBERT, SONNY	SEE-BERT
SKOK, CRAIG	SKOAK
SOLTERS, MOOSE	SOLE-TERS
SPOGNARDI, ANDY	SPOG-NAR-DEE
STAHL, CHICK, JAKE	STALL
STANDAERT, JERRY	STAN-DART
STANGE, LEE	STANG
STEELE, ELMER	STEEL

How Do You Say 'Em (continued)

STURDIVANT, TOM	STUR-DI-VANT
SUCHECKI, JIM	SUCH-CHECK-EE
SUMNER, CARL	SUM-NER
SUSCE, GEORGE	SUE-SEE
SWORMSTEDT, LEN	SWORM-STAT
TABOR, JIM	TAY-BORE
TAITT, DOUG	TAIT
TARTABULL, JOSE	TAR-TA-BULL
TASBY, WILLIE	TAS-BEE
TATUM, KEN	TAY-TUM
TEBBETTS, BIRDIE	TEB-BETS
THIELMAN, JOHN	THI-L-MAN
THONEY, JOHN	THON-EE
THORMAHLEN, HERB	THOR-MAY-LEN
THRONEBERRY, FAYE	THROWN-BERRY
TIANT, LUIS	TEE-AHNT
TODT, PHIL	TOAT
UMPHLETT, TOM	UM-PLETT
UNGLAUB, BOB	UN-GLAUB
VACHE, ERNIE	VACH-E
VEALE, BOB	VEAL
VOLLMER, CLYDE	VOL-MER
VOLZ, JAKE	VOOLZ
WAMBSGANSS, BILL	WAM-B-S-GANS
WANNINGER, PAUL	WAN-IN-GER
WARSTLER, HAL	WAR-SLER
WASLEWSKI, GARY	WAAS-LOU-SKEE
WERLE, BILL	WHIRL
WERTZ, VIC	WERTS
WILHOTT, JOE	WILL-HOLT
WILLOUGHBY, JIM	WILL-O-BEE
WILTSE, HAL	WILT-SEE
WITTIG, JOHN	WHIT-IG
WYCKOFF, JOHN	Y-COUGH
YASTRZEMSKI, CARL	YAS-TREM-SKI
YERKES, STEVE	YERX

"UP FROM DOWN ON THE FARM"

The Red Sox take pride in pointing to the number of players on their major league roster who have progressed up through their farm system to the varsity. Not only are these players found on the Red Sox, but many other major league clubs. This is an outstanding tribute to Red Sox Vice President for Player Development Ed Kenney and his staff. Ed has been involved for a number of years in this department and certainly must take justifiable pride and satisfaction as he sees "his boys" develop and progress.

It would be impossible in a book of this size to list every player that has ever played in the farm system, but it should interest the reader to see who the present Sox played with while in the minors. As I travel around the minor league circuits, I find an increasingly large number of fans who want to reminisce about the clubs of the past and bring up names of players, many of whom have passed from the baseball scene and maybe have never been heard of by the average fan but to the minor league devotee they are as real and as great as if they were in the Hall of Fame. Let's go back for a few years and look at the lineups of the teams that at least the present Red Sox played on. In some cases players moved about the system and will appear on several rosters. No attempt is made to list averages or won or lost records. This is just a game of names. Among the names you'll find the Red Sox of the future.

This section is dedicated to people like Ben Mondor down in Pawtucket, a great booster of minor league ball. The 1979 rosters are the season opening rosters and do not reflect player changes. The only minor league teams listed are those which players on the current forty man roster played on, provided they were in the Red Sox system.

1979 **MINOR LEAGUE CLUBS**

PAWTUCKET — Manager Joe Morgan — AAA

Pitchers — Mike Burns, Joel Finch, John LaRose, Win Remmerswaal, Al Ripley, Steve Schneck, Burke Suter, John Tudor, Rich Waller.

Catchers — Roger LaFrancois, Andy Merchant.

Infield — Bucky Denton, Otis Foster, Glenn Hoffman, Buddy Hunter, Dave Koza, Dave Stapleton, Julio Valdez.

Outfield — Sam Bowen, Barry Butera, Garry Hancock, Ken Huizenga.

BRISTOL — Manager Tony Torchia — AA

Pitchers — Brian Denman, Al Faust, Frank Harris, Pete Ladd, Jerome King, Danny Parks, Keith MacWhorter, Mike Smithson, Kevin Stephenson.

Catchers — Rich Gedman, Dave Schmidt.

Infield — Rocky Alburtis, Wade Boggs, Ron Evans, Ed Jurak, Russ Laribee, Chico Walker.

Outfield — Ray Boyer, Mike Ongarato, Gary Purcell, Carl Steele, Jim Wilson.

WINTER HAVEN — Manager Rac Slider — A

Pitchers — Bruce Hurst, Dennis Burtt, Gary Givens, Bob Ojeda, Kevin Kane, Bob Sprowl, Clint Johnson, Steve Collins, Bill Davis, Paul Carlander.

Catchers — Dick Colbert, John Morgan, Tim Wadsworth.

Infield — Del Bender, Julio Colazzo, Frank Gill, Jim Fabiano, Ron Lee, Russ Quetti, Andy Schardt, Jack Wright.

Outfield — Lee Graham, Charlie Parker, Juan Pautt, Ken Young.

WINSTON-SALEM — Manager Bill Slack — A

Pitchers — Mark Baum, Steve Crawford, Mike Howard, Al Hulbert, Andy Madden, Keith Pecka, Marty Rivas, Dave Schoppee, Steve Shields, Dave Tyler, Dan Weppner.

Catchers — Ron Harrington, John Lickert, Len Thompson.

Infield — Erwin Bryant, Ed Connors, Mark Kaeterle, Jim Mugele, Noel Roman, Stan Smith, Miguel Tavera.

Outfield — Craig Brooks, Gene Gentile, Reid Nichols, Jack Sauer.

ELMIRA — Manager Dick Berardino — A

Pitchers — Bob Birrell, Tom DeSanto, Jay Fredlund, Scott Gering, Don Hayford, Tom McCarthy, Bill Moloney, Mark Saunders, Steve Schaefer, Wayne Tremblay.

Catchers — John Ackley, Tom Brummer, Dave Holt.

1979 **Minor League Clubs** (continued)

Infield — Glenn Eddins, Steve Fortune, Joaquin Gutierrez, Dan Huffstickler, Steve McQueen, Arturo Samaniego, Andy Serrano, Francisco Vasquez.

Outfield — Ed Berroa, Lloyd Bessard, Eddie Lee, Russ Pruitt, Gus Malespin.

SELECTED BOSTON MINOR LEAGUE CLUBS

Here are the basic lineups of the minor league clubs from which the 1979 Red Sox came. Space prohibits listing complete rosters, but I bet you will find some enjoyment and suprises as you browse through these lists of players. Can you find among the players their teammate or mates who were playing at Fenway Park in '79?

I am sure you will find some forgotten names here, some who have left the major league scene, some who never reached there, and some who will arrive in the next few years. Let's flash back to:

RALEIGH 1959
1B-Hal Holland 2B-Carl Yastrzemski 3B-Dick Hergenrader SS-Al Moran OF-Dean Robbins, Walt Napier, Tom Agosta C-Russ Gibson P-Bill Spanswick, Warren Hodgdon, Merlin Nippert, Bob Doig Mgr.-Ken Deal.

MINNEAPOLIS 1960
1B-Don Gile 2B-Chuck Schilling 3B-Shep Frazier SS-Jim Mahoney OF-Tom Umphlett, Carl Yastrzemski, Dave Mann C-Bob Tillman P-Hal Kolstad, Don Schwall, Galen Cisco, Al Worthington Mgr.-Ed Popowski.

OLEAN 1962
1B-Bob Guindon 2B-Hank Pascone 3B-John Bland SS-Mike Andrews OF-Vin Benedetto, Larry Thomas, Homer Green C-Dick Wohlmacher P-Patsy DeMaio, Mario Pagano, Arnold Rowland, Asa Small Mgr.-Hal Holland (George Scott-Utility).

WELLSVILLE 1963
1B-Bob Lawrence 2B-Dave Casey 3B-George Scott SS-Bob Grenda OF-Larry Thomas, John Maddox, Tony Conigliaro C-Jim Keagy P-Spence Hammons, Mario Pagano, Jim Krause, Bill Minkley Mgrs.-Bill Slack, Matt Sczesny.

WATERLOO 1963
1B-Tony Horton 2B-Mark Rosen 3B-Bob Montgomery SS-Mike Andrews OF-Chris Coletta, Bob Levingston, Mel Sanders C-Dick Rambo P-Gene King, Jim Thornton, Bill McMahon, Wayne Tatum Mgr.-Len Okrie.

SEATTLE 1964
1B-Bob Guindon 2B-Bill Gardner 3B-Tim Cullen SS-Rico Petrocelli OF-Felix Maldonado, Stan Johnson, Barry Shetrone C-Russ Gibson P-Wilbur Wood, Hal Kolstad, Bob Smith, Fred Holmes Mgr.-Ed Vanni. (Bob Montgomery-Team Member).

Selected Boston Minor League Clubs (continued)

WINSTON-SALEM 1964
1B-Tony Torchia 2B-Mark Rosen 3B-Jerry Fund SS-Al Lehrer OF-Mike Page, Chris Coletta, Harry Kalbaugh C-Dick Wohlmacher P-Mario Pagano, Steve Chamos, Spence Hammons, Bill Minkley Mgr.-Bill Slack (George Scott-Utility).

WATERLOO 1964
1B-Jerry Dorsch 2B-Dave Casey 3B-Reggie Smith SS-Al Montreuil OF-John Maddox, Len Patinsky, Jim Ferguson C-Bob Montgomery P-Luis Pellot, Bob Johnson, Dan Petz, Ron Klimkowski Mgr.-Matt Sczesny.

PITTSFIELD 1965
1B-Jim Russin 2B-Al Lehrer 3B-George Scott SS-Al Montreuil OF-Felix Maldonado, Reggie Smith, Chris Coletta C-Owen Johnson P-John Hawksin, John Thibdeau, Bill MacLeod, Fred Wenz, Pete Magrini Mgr.-Ed Popowski.

WINSTON-SALEM 1965
1B-Tony Torchia 2B-Dave Casey 3B-Bob Grenda SS-Dick Kratz OF-Jim Ferguson, Carmen Fanzone, Gage Naudain C-Bob Montgomery P-Bob Myer, Sparky Lyle, Paul Dowd, Bob Snow, Al McQueen, Ken Wright Mgr.-Bill Slack.

TORONTO 1966
1B-Tony Horton 2B-Mike Andrews 3B-Jim Russin SS-Al Lehrer OF-Reggie Smith, Mike Page, Stan Johnson C-Russ Gibson P-Gary Waslewski, Pete Magrini, Billy Rohr, Mickey Sinks Mgr.-Dick Williams (Bob Montgomery-Team Member).

PITTSFIELD 1966
1B-Tony Torchia 2B-Al Montreuil 3B-Carmen Fanzone SS-Dick Kratz OF*-Felix Maldonado, Tony Conigliaro, Chris Coletta, Bob Mitchell C*-Gerry Moses, Bob Montgomery P-Sparky Lyle, Ken Wright, Doug Gentry, Bob Myer, John Thibdeau Mgr.-Ed Popowski.
*Position shared as to games played.

TORONTO 1967
1B-Joe Calero 2B-Syd O'Brien 3B-John Ryan SS-Al Lehrer OF-Tony Torchia, Stan Johnson, Al Yates C-Jackie Moore P-Pete Magrini, Fred Wenz, Bob Myer, Jerry Hudgins Mgr.-Eddie Kasko (Bob Montgomery-Team Member).

LOUISVILLE 1968
1B-Jose Calero 2B-Syd O'Brien 3B-John Ryan SS-Al Lehrer OF-Al Yates, Bob Mitchell, Joe Lahoud C-Gerry Moses P-Fred Wenz, Bob Myer, Galen Cisco, John Thibdeau Mgr.-Eddie Kasko (Bob Montgomery-Team Member).

WATERLOO 1968
1B-Bill Brown 2B-Bob Schultz 3B-Jim Gruber SS-Walt Ransom OF-Mike Koritko, Charles Day, Neil Rivenberg C-Carlton Fisk P-Henry O'Reilly, Berny Linn, Charles Prediger, Bill Sandstedt Mgr.-Rac Slider.

Selected Boston Minor League Clubs (continued)

LOUISVILLE 1969

1B-Tony Muser 2B-Dick Kratz 3B-Don Fazio SS-Luis Alvardo OF-Tony Conigliaro, Al Yates, Chris Coletta C-Bob Montgomery P-Fred Wenz, Ed Phillips, Charles Pfeiffer, Jerry Janeski, Billy Farmer Mgr.-Eddie Kasko.

PITTSFIELD 1969

1B-Frank Austin 2B-Buddy Hunter 3B-John Mason SS-Kat Shitanishi OF-Don Dilly, Fred Wolcott, Dan Rudanovich C-Carlton Fisk P-Ivy Washington, Ken Wright, Tom Parsons, Jim Thornton Mgr.-Billy Gardner.

LOUISVILLE 1970

1B-Tony Muser 2B-John Mason 3B-Carmen Fanzone SS-Don Fazio OF-Al Yates, Joe Lahoud, Don Lock C-Bob Montgomery P-Dick Mills, Don Cook, Jay Ritchie, Charles Pfeiffer Mgr.-Billy Gardner.

GREENVILLE 1970

1B-Bill Brown 2B-Ken McCormick 3B-Tom Hanegan SS-Ramon Aviles Of-Dwight Evans, John Stephen, Scott Neat C-Jim Powers P-Craig Skok, Paul Sparkman, Jim Jackson, Keith Terry Mgr.-Rac Slider.

WINTER HAVEN 1970

1B-Steve Miller 2B-Mike Harvison 3B-Dave Coleman SS-Rick Burleson OF-John Klitsner, Curt Suchan, Vin Albury C-Chris Cross P-Frank Ward, Bob Remson, Leo Edge, Dick Gilman Mgr.-John Butler.

PAWTUCKET 1970

1B-Tony Torchia 2B-Buddy Hunter 3B-Manny Crespo SS-Jeff Grate OF-Rick Miller, Ben Oglivie, Don Dilly C-Carlton Fisk P-Roger Moret, Cecil Robinson, Glenn Lohfink, Jack Gaines Mgr.-Matt Sczesny.

LOUISVILLE 1971

1B-Jose Calero 2B-Buddy Hunter 3B-John Mason SS-Juan Beniquez OF-Rick Miller, Chris Coletta, Ben Oglivie C-Carlton Fisk P-John Curtis, Lynn McGlothen, Dan Murphy, Bob Snyder, Jose Santiago, Mgr.-Darrell Johnson.

WILLIAMSPORT 1971

1B-Jack Baker 2B-Bob Jablonski 3B-Milt Jefferson SS-Fred Seymour OF-Jim Rice, Tom Henner, Chet Lucas C-Mike Mooney P-Jim Vosk, Bill Todd, Steve Foran, Mark Bomback, Karl King Mgr.-Dick Berardino

WINSTON-SALEM 1971

1B-Bill Brown 2B-Joe McCullough 3B-Terry Stokes SS-Rick Burleson OF-Frank Mannerino, Dwight Evans, Mike Cummings C-Jim Powers P-Ken Watkins, Charles Pfeiffer, John Jones, Keith Terry, Phil Corddry Mgr.-Don Lock.

GREENVILLE 1971

1B-Efrain Vasquez 2B-Henry Garcia 3B-Tom Hanegan SS-Ramon Aviles OF-Scott Neat, Larry O'Brien, Gary Myers C-Steve Miller P-Sam Phillips, Jim Wright, Rick Kreuger, Dave Klastava Mgr.-Rac Slider (Rick Burleson-Team Member).

Selected Boston Minor League Clubs (continued)

LOUISVILLE 1972
1B-Cecil Cooper   2B-Buddy Hunter   3B-Bobby Pfeil   SS-Mario Guerrero   OF-Dwight Evans, Bob Gallagher, Chris Coletta   C-Vic Correll   P-Craig Skok, Mike Nagy, Mike Garman, Bob Snyder, Mike Neal   Mgr.-Darrell Johnson.

PAWTUCKET 1972
1B-Steve Miller   2B-Ramon Aviles   3B-Curt Suchan   SS-Rick Burleson   OF-Mike Koritko, Bob Cason, John Stephen, Curt Suchan   C-Tom Maggard   P-Jim Burton, Wayne Milam, Terry Williams, Charles Pfeiffer   Mgr.-Don Lock.

WINTER HAVEN 1972
1B-Jack Baker   2B-Al Ryan   3B-Brad Hanson   SS-Carlos Quinones   OF-Jim Rice, Tony McLin, Ted Frett   C-Sebastian Martinez   P-Mark Bomback, Jim Vosk, Bill Moran, Dale Bjerke   Mgr.-John Butler.

PAWTUCKET 1973
1B-Cecil Cooper   2B-John Mason   3B-Efrain Vasquez   SS-Rick Burleson   OF-Roger Nelson, Mike Cummings, Juan Beniquez   C-Vic Correll   P-Dick Pole, Mark Bomback, Lance Clemons, Ken Tatum   Mgr.-Darrell Johnson.

BRISTOL 1973
1B-Dave Coleman   2B-Manny Crespo   3B-Mike Koritko   SS-Ramon Aviles   OF-Jim Rice, Reggie Niles, Bob Cason   C-Tim Blackwell   P-Wayne Milan, Glenn Lohfink, Al Jackson, Ken Watkins   Mgr.-Rac Slider (Fred Lynn-Team Member).

WINSTON-SALEM 1973
1B-Jack Baker   2B-Al Ryan   3B-Milt Jefferson   SS-Steve Dillard   OF-Tony McLin, Henry Baker, Tony Leopaldi   C-Ernie Whitt   P-Dale Bjerke, Bill Moran, Jim Wright, Barry Sbragia   Mgr.-Bill Slack (Butch Hobson-Team Member).

ELMIRA 1973
1B-Jack Medick   2B-Charlie Meyers   3B-Ray McDonald   SS-Ted Cox   OF-Rick Berg, Herm Beras, Leo Sutten   C-Dan Roatche   P-Al Ripley, Tom Jones, Jim Metzler, Roswell Brayton   Mgr.-Dick Berardino.

PAWTUCKET 1974
1B-Dave Coleman   2B-Charlie Goggin   3B-John Kennedy   SS-Steve Dillard   OF-Jim Rice, Fred Lynn, Chris Coletta   C-Bob Didier   P-Craig Skok, Mark Bomback, Rick Kreuger, Lance Clemons   Mgr.-Joe Morgan.

WINSTON-SALEM 1974
1B-Dan Roatche   2B-Charlie Meyers   3B-Milt Jefferson   SS-Luddy Benedetti   OF-Mike Bennett, Butch Hobson, Joe Krsnich   C-Andy Merchant   P-Al Ripley, Don Aase, Jose Caldera, Roswell Brayton   Mgr.-Bill Slack.

ELMIRA 1974
1B-Ralph Russo   2B-Charlie Reilly   3B-Bill Fahey   SS-Eddie Ford   OF-Sam Bowen, Leo Sutten, Larry Morello   C-Jim Shankle   P-Joel Finch, Chuck Rainey, Bob Stanley, Ivan Polonio   Mgr.-Dick Berardino.

Selected Boston Minor League Clubs (continued)

BRISTOL 1975
1B-Dave Coleman   2B-Charlie Meyers   3B-Butch Hobson   SS-Eddie Ford
OF-Mike Bennett, Lanny Phillips, Frank Mannerino   C-Ernie Whitt   P-Tom
Farias, John LaRose, Jim Wright, Steve Foran, Mark Bomback   Mgr. Dick
McAuliffe, Bill Slack.

WINTER HAVEN 1975
1B-Otis Foster   2B-Mark Buba   3B-Ron Evans   SS-Luis DeLeon   OF-Ken
Huizenga, Dave Koza, Larry Morello   C-Mike O'Berry   P-Steve Burke, Joel Finch,
John Proctor, Win Remmerswaal, Bob Stanley   Mgr.-Rac Slider.

WINTSON-SALEM 1975
1B-Wayne Harer   2B-Charles Reilly   3B-Ted Cox   SS-Ed McMahon   OF-Rick
Berg, Joe Krsnich, Luis Delgado   C-Steve Tarbell   P-Luis Aponte, Chuck Rainey,
Al Ripley, Burke Suter, Jose Caldera   Mgr.-John Kennedy.

RHODE ISLAND 1976
1B-Jack Baker   2B-Buddy Hunter   3B-Butch Hobson   SS-Ramon Aviles   OF-
Dave Coleman, John Balaz, Dick Sharon   C-Ernie Whitt   P-Mark Barr, Jim
Burton, Tom Farias, Rick Kreuger   Mgr.-Joe Morgan (Al Ripley-Team Member).

BRISTOL 1976
1B-Wayne Harer   2B-Charlie Meyers   3B-Ted Cox   SS-Eddie Ford   OF-Sam
Bowen, Joe Krsnich, Lanny Phillips   C-Steve Tarbell   P-John Proctor, Chuck
Rainey, Al Ripley, Bob Stanley, Jim Vosk   Mgr.-John Kennedy (Gary Allenson-
Team Member).

WINSTON-SALEM 1976
1B-Otis Foster   2B-Dave Tyler   3B-Ron Evans   SS-Ed Jurak   OF-Luis Delgado,
Ken Huizenga, Matt Coletta   C-Mike O'Berry   P-Al Faust, Ron Herlihy, Phil
Welch, Breen Newcomer, Bruce Poole, Walt Bigos, John Tudor   Mgr. Tony
Torchia.

WINTER HAVEN 1976
1B-Dick McAlister   2B-Ed Rose   3B-Dave Stapleton   SS-Luis DeLeon   OF-
Gary Purcell, Ivan Rivera, Bob Hampton   C-Dave Schmidt   P-Win Remmerswaal, Gary Hardeman, Juan Agosto, Steve Burke   Mgr.-Rac Slider.

PAWTUCKET 1977
1B-John Doherty   2B-Buddy Hunter   3B-Ted Cox   SS-Ramon Aviles   Of-Luis
Delgado   Sam Bowen, Dave Coleman   C-Bo Diaz   P-Jim Vosk, Rick Kreuger,
Jim Burton, Jim Wright, Al Ripley   Mgr.-Joe Morgan (Chuck Rainey-Team
Member).

BRISTOL 1977
1B-Otis Foster   2B-Dave Stapleton   3B-Ron Evans   SS-Ed Jurak   OF-Ken
Huizenga, Gary Purcell, Dave Koza   C-Mike O'Berry   P-Joel Finch, Rich Waller,
John Tudor, Burke Suter, Jose Caldera, Breen Newcomer   Mgr.-John Kennedy.

Selected Boston Minor League Clubs (continued)

WINTER HAVEN 1977
1B-Mike Ongarato   2B-Ed Rose   3B-Dave Tyler   SS-Glenn Hoffman   OF-Jack Sauer, Carl Steele, Reid Nichols   C-Gary Allenson   P-Steve Schneck, Danny Parks, Phil Welch, Bob Sprowl, Dave Schoppee   Mgr.-Rac Slider.

PAWTUCKET 1978
1B-Wayne Harer   2B-Buddy Hunter   3B-Dave Stapleton   SS-Glenn Hoffman OF-Dave Coleman, Sam Bowen, Garry Hancock   C-Gary Allenson   P-Mike Burns, Joel Finch, Win Remmerswaal, Burke Suter, Rich Waller, John Tudor, Chuck Rainey, John LaRose   Mgr.-John Morgan.

BRISTOL 1978
1B-Otis Foster   2B-Bucky Denton   3B-Noel Roman   SS-Julio Valdez   OF-Gary Purcell, Carl Steele, Mike Ongarato   C-Mike O'Berry   P-Steve Schneck, Mike Smithson, Danny Parks, Tom Farias, Jose Caldera   Mgr.-Tony Torchia.

THE LAST FOUR YEARS DOWN ON THE FARM

1976

TEAM	RECORD W	L	FINISH	LEADING HITTER	AVG.	LEADING PITCHER	W-L	MANAGER
Rhode Island	68	70	5th	Dave Coleman	.278	Jim Burton	11-7	Joe Morgan
Bristol	74	60	2nd	Rick Berg	.321	Chuck Ross	11-5	John Kennedy
Winston-Salem	42	26	1st	Luis Delgado	.294	Breen Newcomer	14-6	Tony Torchia
Winter Haven	65	76	4th	Dave Stapleton	.288	Win Remmerswaal	7-6	Rac Slider
Elmira	26	11	1st	Mike Ongarato	.358	Danny Parks	6-3	Dick Berardino

1977

TEAM	RECORD W	L	FINISH	LEADING HITTER	AVG.	LEADING PITCHER	W-L	MANAGER
Pawtucket	80	60	1st	Wayne Harer	.350	Jim Wright	12-8	Joe Morgan
Bristol	72	67	4th	Gary Purcell	.299	Joel Finch	15-6	John Kennedy
Winston-Salem	27	45	4th	Wade Boggs	.352	Walt Bigos	11-7	Tony Torchia
Winter Haven	70	66	3rd	Mike Ongarato	.290	Danny Parks	10-11	Rac Slider
Elmira	32	37	3rd	Roland Alburtis	.301	Alvin Hulbert	5-2	Dick Berardino

1978

TEAM	RECORD W	L	FINISH	LEADING HITTER	AVG.	LEADING PITCHER	W-L	MANAGER
Pawtucket	81	59	2nd	Gary Allenson	.299	Chuck Rainey	12-7	Joe Morgan
Bristol	72	66	3rd	Wade Boggs	.311	Steve Schneck	15-7	Tony Torchia
Winston-Salem	55	77	6th	Roger LaFrancois	.311	Kevin Stephenson	11-10	Bill Slack
Winter Haven	82	56	2nd	Rich Gedman	.300	Brian Denman	16-5	Rac Slider
Elmira	21	48	5th	Steve Fortune	.287	Clint Johnson	4-1	Dick Berardino

1979

TEAM	RECORD W	L	FINISH	LEADING HITTER	AVG.	LEADING PITCHER	W-L	MANAGER
Pawtucket	66	74	5th	Garry Hancock	.325	Joel Finch	9-1	Joe Morgan
Bristol	73	65	3rd	Mike Schmidt	.328	Keith MacWhorter	11-10	Tony Torchia
Winston-Salem	85	54	1st	Reid Nichols	.293	Mike Howard	12-3	Bill Slack
Winter Haven	79	58	1st	Ken Young	.303	Bob Ojeda	15-7	Rac Slider
Elmira	33	26	2nd	Russ Pruitt	.316	Bill Moloney	6-1	Dick Berardino

DID YOU KNOW THAT. . . .

There are many interesting facts about the Red Sox that do not fit into a day by day section, usually because the story they tell relates to the season or seasons in which they occurred in general. Here I have broken them down into various categories. As you read through them in your mind, preface each statement with "Did You Know That. . . .". It will add to your enjoyment.

GENERAL

During the 1928 season Jack Rothrock appeared at all nine positions.

Buck Freeman led the American League in 1902 and 1903 in total bases.

Ted Williams led the American League six times in total bases (1939, 42, 46-47, 49, 51). The only others to accomplish this were Ty Cobb and Babe Ruth.

Ted Williams led the American League during three seasons in receiving intentional bases on balls. (1955, 56, 57).

Ted Williams holds the American League record for intentional walks, 33, set in 1957.

George Scott started in 162 games in his rookie year of 1966, a feat shared with three other American Leaguers.

Candy LaChance played 157 games at first base in 1904, the most ever by a Red Sox first baseman.

Only 18 players appeared for the 1904 Red Sox, including only 5 pitchers.

30 players appeared for the 1965 Red Sox, 12 were pitchers.

The 1957 Red Sox split only 2 doubleheaders.

The 1946 Red Sox won 14 doubleheaders.

The 1976 Red Sox played only 6 doubleheaders, the 1968 team only 10, the 1959 team only 11.

The 1977 Red Sox lost only 2 extra inning games.

The 1966 Red Sox lost 16 extra inning games.

The 1943 Red Sox won 15 extra inning games.

The 1943 Red Sox played 31 extra inning games.

The 1966 Red Sox won only 25 night games.

The 1962 Red Sox played only 66 night games.

The 1906 Chicago White Sox defeated Boston 8 times by shutouts.

The 1950 Red Sox lost only 11 one run games.

The Red Sox won the first five World Series they played in (1903, 12, 15, 16, 18) and have lost the last three. (1946, 67, 75).

Joe Cronin managed the Red Sox for 13 years (1935-47)

The Red Sox hold the major league record for most consecutive years without a tie game. The last tie was on June 8, 1961. (Through 1979).

The 1946 Red Sox won 15 consecutive games.

Tommy Harper holds the Red Sox record of 54 stolen bases in a season (1973).

Harry Hooper stole an even 300 bases as a Red Sox to lead teammate Tris Speaker (266) for the lifetime high.

General (continued)

When only 17 Red Sox were caught stealing in 1948 a new major league record was established.

Each member of the 1918 Worlds Champions were given only $890 for defeating the Chicago Cubs.

The 1949 team won its last 21 games at Fenway Park.

The 1949-50 Red Sox won 22 consecutive games from Philadelphia at Fenway during those years.

In 1950 an August home stand produced a 16-1 record.

The 1964 Red Sox played 73 consecutive games at Fenway Park without a post-ponement.

Some 5000 fans were standing in the outfield for a doubleheader with the New York Yankees in September of 1935.

Reggie Smith stole 5 bases in a twin bill with the Yankees in 1967.

The 1962 Red Sox used only 15 fielders but used 18 pitchers.

Between August 25 and 27, 1905 the Pilgrims lost three consecutive doubleheaders at Chicago.

The 1950 Red Sox might have won the pennant had they played all their games at night. Their won-lost percentage under the arcs was .700.

BATTING

During the 1938 season Jimmie Foxx hit nine home runs against the Cleveland Indians, a league record for home runs against one team during a season.

Babe Ruth hit four grand slam home runs during the 1919 season.

Jack Jensen led the American League batters in grounding into double plays in 1954, 56, and 57. His 32 in 1954 is a major league record.

During the 1943 season Joe Cronin batted in 25 runs as a pinch hitter.

Ted Williams' .609 slugging average in 1939 was the highest ever by an American League rookie.

Fred Lynn's 47 doubles in 1975 is the American League record for rookies.

Ted Williams' 145 RBI's in 1939 is the major league record for rookies.

Ted Williams' 107 walks in 1939 is the major league record for rookies.

George Scott's 13 intentional walks in 1966 is the American League record for rookies.

George Scott's 152 strikeouts in 1966 is the major league record for rookies.

Batting (continued)

The 1977 Red Sox had a team slugging percentage of .4646 and 2560 total bases, made 527 long hits including 213 home runs. They also had 828 team RBI's.

The 1962 Red Sox made 257 doubles.

In 1903 Red Sox made 113 triples while the 1968 team made only 17 triples.

In 1964 Red Sox made 8 grand slam home runs.

In 1964 Red Sox made 35 sacrifice hits.

In 1964 Red Sox stole only 18 bases.

In 1965 Red Sox grounded into 157 double plays.

The 1917 Red Sox had 310 sacrifice hits, a major league record.

When Ted Williams won the batting championship in 1958 he became the oldest batter to do so at 40 years 28 days.

When Tony Conigliaro won the home run championship in 1965 he became the youngest player to do so at 20 years 270 days.

Fred Lynn batted safely in 20 consecutive games in 1975 and in the same season Denny Doyle hit in 22 straight.

Dom DiMaggio batted safely in 34 consecutive games in 1949 and Tris Speaker in 30 in 1912, Red Sox highs.

The Fenway Park record for home runs in a season is 35 by Jimmie Foxx in 1938.

The Red Sox high for hitting home runs on the road is 26 by Ted Williams in 1957.

When 823 Sox walked during the 1948 season it established a major league record.

The 1963 Red Sox hit 171 home runs breaking the previous high of 161 made in 1950.

Jackie Jensen hit three bases loaded triples in 1956.

In 1921 the Red Sox put on a bunting show against the St. Louis Browns by bunting nine times in a game, five in succession.

In 1957 Ted Williams reached base 16 times in succession on six hits and ten walks.

Pinky Higgins was the first big league player to make 12 consecutive hits, accomplished in 1938.

Jim Piersall had a double and five singles in six at bats in 1953.

John Pesky had 11 consecutive hits in 1946.

Pitchers helping their own cause by hitting grand slam home runs were Lefty Grove in 1935, Wes Ferrell in 1936 and Ellis Kinder in 1950.

Jackie Jensen holds the Red Sox record for the most home runs in a month—14 in June 1958. Clyde Vollmer hit 13 in July 1951. Jimmie Foxx 13, July 1939, Jim Rice 13, May 1978.

Luis Aparicio, in 1971, went 11 games and 44 times at bat without a hit.

FIELDING

Bobby Doerr led American League second basemen in double plays in five years, 1938, 40, 43, 46 and 47.

Jim Tabor led American League third basemen in errors from 1939 to 1943.

Frank Malzone led American League third basemen in double plays from 1957 to 1961.

Carl Yastrzemski holds the major league record for the most seasons leading majors in outfield assists with 7. 1962-64, 66, 69, 71, 77.

Tris Speaker made double plays from the outfield in 1909 and 1914.

The 1913 Red Sox made only 74 double plays.

The Red Sox, from 1916 through 1921, led the American League in the fewest errors per season.

The Red Sox have led the American League in triple plays in 18 different seasons.

Carl Yastrzemski holds the seventh longest outfield consecutive errorless game streak in the American League — 167 games (7/28/76-4/7/78).

Dom DiMaggio set an American League record for putouts in a season by an outfielder at 503 in 1948. He also set the standard for chances accepted at 516.

The 1924 Red Sox made 3 triple plays equalling the major league record set by the 1911 Detroit Tigers and later tied by the 1964 Philadelphia Phillies, the 1965 Chicago Cubs, the 1979 Oakland A's and the 1979 Red Sox.

First baseman John "Stuffy" McInnis made only one error in 152 games in 1921.

The 1945 Red Sox made 198 double plays, a major league record at the time.

In 1945 Lamar "Skeeter" Newsome tied an American League record by making nine assists in a game.

The 1951 Red Sox made double plays in 25 consecutive games.

Catcher John Peacock lost his glove while chasing down a foul but caught it barehanded.

PITCHING

In 1904 pitcher Bill Dineen pitched 37 consecutive complete games.

For two consecutive years, Cy Young led the major leagues in shutouts 1903-04.

In 1916 Babe Ruth pitched nine shutouts.

In 1904 Cy Young shut out seven different clubs.

In 1916 pitcher Babe Ruth had an ERA of 1.75 for 324 innings pitched.

Pitcher Red Ruffing led the league in two consecutive seasons in runs and earned runs allowed, 1928-29.

Pitching (continued)

Pitcher Joe Wood won 16 consecutive games in 1912, pitcher Ellis Kinder 13 in 1949, pitcher Cy Young 12 in 1901, pitcher Dave Ferriss, 12 in 1946, pitcher Dutch Leonard 12 in 1914, while Red Ruffing lost 12 consecutively in 1929.

The 1976 Red Sox used 11 different pitchers.

In 1904 Red Sox pitchers made only 9 relief appearances and in 1974 only 139 appearances.

The Red Sox led the American League in balks in 1932, 38, 41, 44, 47, 55, 58, 60, 65.

In three seasons 1904, 16, 62, Red Sox pitchers pitched two no hitters.

In 1904 Boston pitchers set a major league record of pitching 148 complete games.

In 1930 Boston pitchers struck out only 356 batters.

The 1968 Red Sox pitching staff made 73 wild pitches.

The 1965 Red Sox pitching staff made 12 balks.

Bill Campbell recorded 31 saves in 1977, high for a Red Sox pitcher.

Bill Monbouquette struck out 17 batters in a game in 1961, a team high.

In three seasons a single Red Sox pitcher has won 30 or more games. Cy Young 33 in 1901, 32 in 1902, Joe Wood 34 in 1912.

Only three Red Sox pitchers have led the American League in strikeouts — Jim Lonborg-1967, Cy Young-1901 and Tex Hughson-1942.

The 1929 Red Sox finished last but their pitchers led the league in complete games with 84.

In 1945 Dave Ferriss set an American League record for rookie pitchers by pitching 23-1/3 consecutive scoreless innings.

In a 1934 doubleheader Sox pitchers walked Philadelphia's Max Bishop eight times.

In 1904 Cy Young walked only 29 batters in 380 innings pitched.

In 1948 two Mickey's—Harris and McDermott, combined to give the Cleveland Indians 18 walks.

A RED SOX POTPOURRI

Presented in this section is a collection of facts, interesting tales and trivia about the Red Sox down through the years. It is arranged in no special order and just wanders from year to year, back and forth. It is designed for the busy reader who wants to pick up a book, open to any page and find something of interest for a few minutes of reading. Here is guessing you will want to go right through it, front to back or back to front, finding a memory or long forgotten fact on each page. Keep a pencil handy to check that special item you want to remember. The little facts found here have gone into the building of the traditions which enrich the baseball history of the Boston American League club. Perhaps your favorite story isn't here, since they couldn't all be included, but I am sure you will enjoy what you find hidden away here.

A RED SOX POTPOURRI

Ever hear of a person being bitten by his own teeth? Well, it happened to a pitcher of little note named Clarence "Climax" Blethen who performed for the 1923 Bosox. It seems he carried his false chompers in his back pocket when on the ball field. One day while sliding into second base his teeth somehow became connected and nipped him. Imagine the headline writers' delight — "Blethen Nipped At Second". "Blethen Averts A Disaster" or "Blethen Steals In A Pinch".

When broadcaster Fred Hoey's voice went bad during the 1933 World Series, his physician told him to take a rest. He did by editing the Boston Garden Hockey Magazine.

Evidence of the Red Sox willingness to spend money during the early 30's to move the club from the second division team was apparent in the cash tossed in to obtain the following players: The Lefty Grove deal $150,000; Rick Ferrell $75,000; George Pipgras $50,000; Dusty Cooke $35,000; Fritz Ostermueller $25,000; Moose Solters $25,000; Fred Muller $10,000; Bucky Walters $10,000; Mel Almada $10,000; Carl Reynolds $15,000, and Gordie Hinkle $10,000. Not exactly chicken feed in those depression days.

A Red Sox pitcher of the early 30's was Pete Jablonowski who changed his name to Pete Appleton but really didn't go as far afield in doing so as one would be led to believe. Appleton could be considered a liberal translation of Jablonowski. The apple, in Polish, jablko, of course, grows on the apple tree, jablon, so the transition to the Americanization, Appleton was appropriate.

Tom Yawkey may have hurt his own cause in 1934 when he worked out a bonus system with his players if they would finish in the top three teams in the American League. The players grew overeager for the cash rewards causing team play to suffer.

Talk about being haunted by a traded away player consider what Moose Solters did to the Red Sox after they traded him off to the St. Louis Browns in 1935. In the first fourteen games he faced his former mates he had 28 hits, 15 singles, 8 doubles, 2 triples and 3 home runs for 52 total bases and a .467 average.

Perhaps adopting the theory that if you are out of the pennant fight you should start one of your own, Billy Werber told Babe Dahlgren he didn't like the way he handled the ball on a particular play during a game in the 1935 season. Heated words followed and Werber took a punch at Dahlgren and the Sox had their fight on the bench.

When catcher Rick Ferrell injured his hand in a 1933 Yankee series, the Albany Club of the International League 'loaned' cather Lou Legett to the Sox. The injury couldn't have lasted long, as Legett appeared in only two games.

In 1932 it was rumored that when a player was sold or traded to the Red Sox, he would wire his Congressman, but in 1933 things turned around and everyone wanted to go there. Such was the influence of the Yawkey coffers.

Did you know that in 1932 the major league rumor mill insisted that Babe Ruth would return to the Red Sox as the manager? Others mentioned were Tris Speaker, Ossie Vitt and Bert Niehoff.

In 1932 the Red Sox dealt left fielder Earl Webb to Detroit and it was said the move was made to prevent centerfielder Tom Oliver from running himself to a skeleton. Oliver had been playing center and covering right and left fields for the equally slow moving Webb and Smead Jolley.

The 1932 Red Sox (finishing last) had the second most costly outfield in the American League. Smead Jolley, Roy Johnson and John Watwood represented $120,000 plus a raft of players. The New York Yankees (finishing first) had a $155,000 outfield (tops in the league) Babe Ruth $100,000, Earl Combs $50,000 plus a $5,000 bonus to Ben Chapman.

Red Sox owner Bob Quinn once hired a specialist to look after the Red Sox players feet. The headline proclaimed "Expert hired by Quinn to Care For All Aching Dogs". One is led to wonder if this was a reference to the players on the last place Sox, their feet, or those of the canine variety which might have been found hanging around outside Fenway Park.

In 1931 Red Sox pinch hitters led the league with a .304 over all average. Perhaps several should have considered pinch hitting as a career. Listed first is their regular season average followed by their pinch hitting average—Jack Rothrock .281 - .474; Al VanCamp .275-.375; Tom Winsett .195-.275 and Urbane Pickering .253-.273.

Late in the 1931 season the Red Sox moved out of the American League basement for the first time in six years (since 1925).

Catcher Lou Legett (1933-35) a University of Tennessee graduate, practiced dentistry in Memphis and played semi pro baseball for four years before signing a contract.

In June 1931, that's right 1931, the Red Sox had all kinds of arguments against putting their home games on television. Owner Bob Quinn stated them in his early reply to a request by a TV company as follows: 1. It has rained every Sunday. 2. Our club is in last place. 3. And now you want me to let fans see the home games for free. Where are we going to get the money to pay the players? If you can furnish me with a substitute for money, please let me know immediately. My how times have changed or have they?

Some time after pitcher Red Ruffing was traded to the New York Yankees, sports writers claimed he was thriving on he scenery change. I wonder how they assessed the talent behind him?

Speaking of his trade to the Philadelphia Athletics, former Red Sox first baseman Phil Todt said "Then I was released to the A's which is just the same as being kicked upstairs".

At spring training in 1931 owner Bob Quinn gave a stern lecture to his players and ordered manager Shano Collins to draw up a set of strict rules, the lack of which he said had kept the team in the American League cellar for too many years. (It would seem a lack of talent might also have been a consideration).

During the winter of 1928-29 Red Sox owner Bob Quinn said he was thinking of closing down Fenway Park (what a loss for baseball that would have been) giving the impression and rise to rumors that the Red Sox would be co-tenants at Braves Field, home of the Boston National League entry.

In May of 1902 the city of Boston Board of Aldermen ordered the Pilgrims to widen the Huntington Avenue entrance to the "Boston American League Grounds". Seems the city has a long history of telling the Sox what to do.

If you think today's teams do all they can to curb expenses, especially by attempting to rid themselves of high priced no longer useful players it's nothing new. In Boston's second season (1902) they obtained pitcher Long Tom Hughes from Baltimore. The reason, to reduce expenses. This may be true today, but when was the last time you saw a club give the true reason for a release of this nature. Note: Maybe Baltimore knew something as Hughes was 7-5 with them and only 3-3 with the Pilgrims and wound up with a sore arm to boot.

Long time Boston outfielder Chick Stahl once decided to open a barber shop in Ft. Wayne, Indiana, thus making him the original barber until Sal Maglie arrived on the Boston scene. Can't you see it now—Stahl safe by a whisker; Stahl has a close shave while at bat; Stahl called to diagnose a hair line fracture; Stahl just the tonic Boston needs; Stahl missed the ball by a hair; Stahl cut down at home or Stahl razor sharp. Surely the folks at Gillette would have had him on the all star ballot. Whan an advertising campaign they could have had—"Use Gillette Blue Blades, don't **Stahl**, get your convenient dispenser today".

In October of 1902, pitcher Bert Husting announced he was retiring to become a laywer. Do you suppose he was the original club house lawyer?

Two of the Red Sox greatest players, roommates and good buddies were outfielder Tris Speaker and pitcher Joe Wood. They were the Boston heroes during the glory years of 1912 to 1915 and then during the 1915-16 winter storm clouds appeared above the Hub as problems arose with their heroes. In February of 1916 headlines appeared, "Seems Joe Wood Loses His Smoke". Manager Carrigan refused to disclose his plans for Wood and the Sox asked waivers on Smokey. Late in the same month Speaker signed his contract but Wood kicked about his.

When American League chief, Ban Johnson notified Boston owner Lannin that the Federal League had made pitcher Rankin Johnson (2-4 at Chicago and 7-11 with Baltimore) a free agent and he would revert to Boston, Lannin replied, "Why should I take Johnson when I can't use a man like Wood?" This certainly was a sign all was not well in the Boston camp. In early March the Sox again asked waivers on Wood among others. (Ray Collins, Pinch Thomas, Hick Cady). Johnson was sold by Boston in mid-March to Ft. Worth for $300.00.

As spring training arrived Cady, Thomas and Speaker reported to camp in Hot Springs, Arkansas. Speaker's arrival was not cordial as the other players openly admitted they wanted to show they could win without him. Then came the block buster deal on the eve of the 1916 season. Speaker was dealt to Cleveland where he continued to enjoy success and wound up as their manager in 1919. It was felt that Speaker's case would serve as a lesson for the players that no man is an absolute necessity to any ball club. Tris thought the Red Sox must meet his terms or perish. Now he knows better and it hurts.

Rumors of dissention on the Red Sox continued, but Sox officials said if there was discord, a lot of it had been removed by the sale of Speaker and the absence of Wood and that there was no need to comment on this further.

By late April and in early May, it was reported that Wood had notified Boston friends that he wanted to be sent to Cleveland where he could join Speaker. "Even a chance to play with the Yankees and shine on Broadway cannot overcome his desire to again be with Tris". By late July, it was rumored Wood would rejoin Boston, but the predicted signing did not materialize. He would not try out for the rest of the year and let his performance determine his 1917 contract based on what he accomplished. Some even suggested Wood's supposed arm miseries would show recovery as Boston was going into first place. Then there was a rumor Wood would be traded to Philadelphia for their ace pitcher Bullet Joe Bush. The 1916 season passed without Wood's appearance. New owner Harry Frazee took over in Boston and Wood was sold to Cleveland to join Speaker. Thus, two of Boston's greats were gone, both to new successes in Cleveland.

The author asked Joe Wood years later about all of this and was told that "my arm was so sore there was no way I could have pitched for anyone in 1916." Anyone who has suffered a sore arm knows of the agonies one goes through and can well understand Joe Wood's position as he went from doctor to doctor looking for a cure. As Wood is a good Christian man I can not help but believe him and all of the rumors were simply a smoke screen by Boston ownership to divert attention from their colossal mistake of selling Speaker to Cleveland.

Many pitchers have been hit by batted balls hit directly back at them and for many it has cost them their careers. The Sox have had their share but one was nearly fatal yet did not deter the pitcher involved. Pitcher Jim Wilson was a sensation in 1945 with a great promise for the future. He had beaten the great Detroit Tiger pitcher Hal Newhouser three times in that war year, a year that found the Tigers the top team. One day it all changed. Pitching against Detroit's Hank Greenberg, who had just returned from World War II, a batted ball came screaming back at him. He never saw it. There was a shattering crash and the ball thudded against the side of Wilson's head and he dropped like a shot, his skull crushed, he lay motionless at the mound. Brain surgeons were summoned to the Detroit hospital to save his life. Greenberg was a daily visitor. Wilson returned to pitch but was never the same and he carried a souvenir of the impact in his hand. The following spring he returned to pitch and before he could win or lose a game he was struck again. This time his leg was smashed from stopping a line drive. For most players that would have been enough, but he returned once more to the mound, not for the Red Sox, but an assortment of other teams.

Ted Williams came to the minor league San Diego club as a pitcher in 1936 but even the casual observer could see he was a natural hitter. The seventeen year-old was given a shot at the outfield when one of the regulars, Chick Shivers, quit baseball in the middle of August to accept a football coaching position.

Hall of Fame pitcher Cy Young reached a high of $4000 in salary during his major league career. In 1903 in the first World Series when Boston played Pittsburgh, Cy was up to a salary of $2400. Just before the final game a would be briber offered him $20,000 if he wouldn't "bear down". Cy rejected the offer telling the bribe offerer, "If you put any value at all on your money, you will bet it on me to win." The next day he went out and clinched the series for Boston, never giving a thought to the offer which was $17,600 higher than his yearly salary.

According to San Diego news sources at the time "the boy star" Ted Williams was as surprised as were the West Coast fans at his sale to the Red Sox.

In early 1938 Red Sox trainer Roland Logan quit the Red Sox to take a job at the University of Pittsburgh as head athletic trainer and physical education instructor. He had been with Boston for three years. Win Green was appointed to replace him.

Left hander Jennings Poindexter who pitched three games for the 1936 Red Sox earlier tied a Southern League strike out record while with Little Rock by fanning 17 Nashville batters.

Pitcher Bill Sayles, who appeared briefly with the 1939 Red Sox, was a pitcher at the University of Oregon when he signed with the Sox and had been a member of the Olympic baseball team that went to Berlin, Germany in 1936 for the Olympic Games.

On June 15, 1902 the Pilgrims signed a pitcher named Doc Adkins who must have suffered through his stay in Boston. By mid July, four games and a 1-1 record, he was gone but not before Manager Jimmy Collins had been told to run about thirty pounds off "fatty" Adkins. The reason given for his release — too wild (I assume in his pitching abilities and not his personal life) and not in playing condition. Did they expect him to lose 30 pounds in a month? This rocky start landed him, perhaps appropriately, to a club in Rockland, Massachusetts.

Oldtimers proclaimed that it was an impossible feat to drive a ball over the right field fence at the Huntington Avenue Grounds. In the Pilgrims' second season their first baseman Candy LaChance did the impossible off the servings of Cleveland's Earl Moore.

Right handed pitcher George Winter became ill in July 1902 with what was diagnosed as appendicitis, but a later diagnoses showed he had typhoid. He had already won 11 games for Boston. Perhaps his loss cost the pennant. This story has a happy ending. He recovered and was back on the mound in 1903.

Ace pitcher Bill Dineen entered Cornell for a course in Forestry during the 1902-03 off season. By the way, since he had taken the lumber out of the hands of opposing batters, perhaps he felt this would be a good way to learn what to do with it.

In recent years hitting backgrounds have been a topic for Red Sox players to grouse about. Remember what they did for Tony C. in centerfield at Fenway Park? Well, guess what the early Huntington Avenue Grounds players had to say. Right, advertising on the centerfield fence hurt their batting. They claimed a fence painted green is the best background for batting purposes. Wonder what they would have thought about the "Green Monster" of today?

Speaking of pressure, consider what Carl Yastrzemski was up against in his first year of spring training with the Red Sox: 1. He was trying to fill the shoes of the great Ted Williams. 2. He was the highest paid bonus player in the Sox system. 3. He was only 21 years old with only two years of minor league experience. 4. He was trying his third different position in three years.

In early June 1963, slugger Dick Stuart experimented with eye glasses wearing them during three games. What happened the day he abandoned them? He went hitless.

Pitcher Ike Delock, who at one time in his career became a 14 game winner as a relief pitcher, was also noted for his explosive temper which often got him into difficult situations. Often sailing along nicely in a ball game an error behind him or a mistake on his part would cause him to blow his top. Once he made an obscene gesture at Fenway Park. Fans booed him and he was fined by the Sox. In his last mound appearance for the Sox when manager Pesky went to the mound to take him out, Delock flipped the ball at the manager, a fact which hastened his departure from Boston.

During the 1963 American League season five American League managers had, only a few years earlier, played for the Red Sox. They were John Pesky (Boston), Mickey Vernon (Washington), Birdie Tebbetts (Cleveland), Billy Hitchcock (Baltimore), Sam Mele (Minnesota). It seemed like it was join the Red Sox and become a big league manager.

Lu or Lou Clinton? Seen both ways in the press, this popular Red Sox outfielder during the 60's signs his name Lou.

Over the years the Red Sox have made many mistakes in evaluating players. One of the early ones was a 5'8½" 155 lb. first baseman who was brushed off as too small in 1915 and sent to the Sox farm club in Buffalo, managed by Patsy Donovan. Donovan recommended this nimble, graceful player to Clark Griffith at Washington. The rookie who could run, throw and hit, joined the Senators late in 1915 and became and institution in the nation's capital where he played until 1931. His name, Joe Judge, rated by old timers as better than Lou Gehrig, Jimmie Foxx and Hank Greenberg.

In the late 1930's Sox catcher John Peacock returned to his room on the 27th floor of a Detroit hotel to find his roommate Eric McNair standing outside on the ledge. McNair, unhappy over the recent death of his wife, was talked back into the room by Peacock. The inducement — a highball.

Good roommates among ball players stick up for each other. Among the Sox two who stuck together were Dusty Cooke and Bill Werber. Anyone who wanted to fight Cooke could be sure he would also have to fight Werber.

Speaking of roomies, Tex Hughson's roommate Dave Ferriss said Tex talked in his sleep and if he had pitched that day he would recount every pitch — what he was thinking, what he threw or should have thrown.

Ted Williams usually roomed with either Charlie Wagner, Woody Rich or batting practice pitcher Paul Schreiber. Ted, an early riser, would be up practicing his swing in front of a mirror prompting the remark that he often had hit 25 homers even before he went to breakfast.

During the 1963 season relief pitcher Dick Radatz in two consecutive appearances, totaling 14 2/3 innings struck out 21 batters, walked two and allowed five singles.

In 1926 pitcher Red Ruffing signed his Red Sox contract supposedly without looking at the salary figure. He said he had enough confidence in owner Quinn to know he would get square deal. Imagine any player doing that today in this age of agents!

Long Tom Hughes, who pitched for the 1903 Pilgrims, was still around the baseball world in 1926 as in April of that year he signed as a free agent with Little Rock.

The Red Sox first baseman in 1926 was likeable Phil Todt who was known as a faithful, plodding athlete. It was said it would be a great thing if Phil would just go out and get excited about something. Certainly he characterized the Red Sox of his era, nothing to get excited about.

How about this for strange deals. In late 1903 Boston signed infielder Bob Unglaub with the provision the New York Highlanders could have him if they wanted him. Boston owner Harry C. Killilea said that "New York manager Clark Griffith will only have to say the word and we would be obligated to give him up." Griffith must have said the word as Unglaub appeared in five games for New York in 1904 before being sent to Boston for Pat Dougherty.

One of the first salary disputes for the Boston Americans occurred in early 1907 when infielder Bob Unglaub argued with owner Taylor. Unglaub had received $2,700 at Williamsport but wanted $4,500 from Taylor. He wound up playing 130 games at first base and managing the team for part of the 1907 season. Seems Taylor was going to get his money's worth.

A social item from 1911 — "Joe Wood, the Red Sox pitcher, was married recently to Miss May Perry of Boston. The ceremony was held in Philadelphia and they will make their home at Parkers Glenn, Pennsylvania where Joe's father lives. It was another romance of the diamond. Miss Perry was a fan and fell in love with Joe's pitching then with Joe himself."

In January 1912, the news was about the big outlay for salaries for the Red Sox, estimated to run $90,000 for the season. In today's market I wonder what it would be?

The Jersey City club bought pitcher Hugh Bedient from John I. Taylor for $750 and thought so little of him that they loaned him to Providence. Later they sold him back to Boston for a price said to be $10,000 cash. A pretty good investment.

Pitcher Fred Anderson once refused to join the Red Sox so he could finish a dentistry course. Several years later in 1913 he finally joined the club. He had made a reputation for himself by pitching Worcester to the New England League pennant.

A news item early in the 1912 season (Fenway Park's first) said that the reason for "the poor patronage at New Fenway Park" was "It's too big for fans to exchange pleasantries about the weather and they're used to going in another direction."

What do you suppose these players would be worth today? In 1912 they were World Champions. Their 1913 salaries are shown — Tris Speaker ($9000), Joe Wood ($7500 and he had won 34 games in 1912), Heinie Wagner ($6500), Larry Gardner ($6000), Jake Stahl ($10,000 — he was the manager), Duffy Lewis ($5000), Harry Hooper ($5000), Bill Carrigan ($4500). Entire payroll for all players amounted to $80,000.

A spring training series between the Red Sox and the Pittsburgh Pirates in 1913 was said to have hurt both teams as they each took it too seriously. Perhaps they were thinking back to that first World Series in 1903. At any rate, both clubs finished fourth in 1913.

Just before the 1913 season opened the Red Sox insured pitchers Joe Wood, and Hugh Bedient, outfielder Tris Speaker and third baseman Larry Gardner for $25,000 each. Pennant insurance?

Although pitcher Joe Wood has told the author that the 1912 World Champions were a team that got along well, battle lines may well have been formed during the World Series of that year. What seemed to appear, at least in the news media of 1913 were two factions: Carrigan and Wagner vs Speaker and Wood. Speaker and Wood stood behind manager Stahl while Carrigan reportedly held a grudge against Stahl for by-passing him in favor of Forrest Cady to do the catching in the 1912 World Series. This may cause some wondering among historians as the Sox fell to 4th in 1913 and midway through the season Carrigan replaced Stahl as manager.

In early 1914 former Red Sox manager Jake Stahl turned down an offer to manage the Brooklyn team in the Federal League. He said he was now in the banking business.

When the Federal League was forming in 1914 they tried to lure Tris Speaker, Clyde Engle, Steve Yerkes, George Foster, Hal Janvrin and Duffy Lewis from the Red Sox.

Infielder Heinie Wagner sat out the 1914 season because of rheumatism.

In 1914 there were rumors of a trade between Boston and Detroit — Tris Speaker for Ty Cobb.

Owner Joe Lannin not only released (they were actually fired first) second baseman Steve Yerkes and infielder Clyde Engle in 1914 but he also released the club announcer and the club mascot, Jerry McCarthy, a Boston feature for several seasons. It is not known what the popular McCarthy's offense was.

Released after the 1912 season to Denver, Red Sox pitcher Casey Hageman sued for a full year's salary from the Red Sox. He had been given a salary cut and refused to report to Denver, claiming Boston was bound by his contract to pay him full salary. He reported each day all season (1913) to the Boston park but was never used. The Players Fraternity took up his case and lost.

In 1915 pitcher George Foster worked on developing a knuckle ball and by adding it to his other pitches predicted that all the games he pitches would be shutouts.

Pitchers Ray Fisher of the New York Yankees and Ray Collins of the Red Sox had a strange rivalry. It started in high school, continued in college (Middlebury vs Vermont) and continued in the big leagues.

A news item in the Ft. Worth, Texas paper of March 16, 1915 said that Tris Speaker had sold 27 cows to a local livestock market for $1,517.80. Twenty six were heifers averaging 765 lbs. and selling at $7.35 per 100 weight, the other was a fat cow.

In May of 1915 pitcher Dutch Leonard was suspended by the Red Sox for failure to get into condition.

The 1917 Red Sox had their pitching woes going into spring training. Joe Wood had been sold to Cleveland to join his pal Tris Speaker. Dutch Leonard reportedly had typhoid fever and Rube Foster was holding out asking the Sox to guarantee his salary and pay his wife's transportation. Actually, all worked out well as Babe Ruth and Carl Mays each wound up as twenty game winners. Leonard (who had been pitching on the West Coast) made a quick and remarkable recovery to win 16 games. Foster settled his differences and chipped in eight wins.

In June of 1917 rain held up a game with the Chicago White Sox at Fenway Park. During the delay a gang of gamblers invaded the field and fought with the White Sox players in an attempt to prevent the game's resumption. White Sox players Buck Weaver and Fred McMullen were arrested on assault and battery charges. That wasn't the only fighting to take place that month as a week later Red Sox pitcher Babe Ruth was suspended for hitting umpire Brick Owens.

Another gambling incident surfaced in November of 1917. Red Sox pitcher Carl Mays was involved in a suit (which he won) to collect a "phantom" gambling debt. It seems that in 1915 he was advised to bet $500 that the Red Sox would *not* win the pennant. He let the proposition go without a word of acceptance. He stated he did not believe in betting against any club for which he is playing.

How time changes things. When owner Harry Frazee took over the Red Sox, he was welcomed as a hero by the fans and he gained their friendship by talking about the good times ahead for the team. Of course things changed and to this day he is despised by Red Sox fans for what he did to the team.

Owner Frazee moved in strange circles when it came to money. It is a familiar story of how he sold off his best players for large chunks of the New York Yankee's money in order to finance his theatrical productions. It is little remembered that the Chicago White Sox owner Charles Comiskey offered him $50,000 for pitcher Bullet Joe Bush and $30,000 for outfielder Amos Strunk which would have meant a $20,000 profit for him. Frazee was quoted, "Sell Bush to Commy for $50,000. I would sell him to Cleveland or New York for a little more than $50.000 maybe, but not to Commy even for $100,000 since the White Sox need right handed pitching." Later in 1918 he had to pay pitcher Casey Hageman his salary for 1912 and was cited for contempt for refusing to pay Hageman the $2,326 awarded him for back pay.

Early in 1918 there were rumors of Red Sox manager Ed Barrow being moved into the front office to run the business end with the Sox asking retired manager Bill Carrigan to return to take the helm. Sounds like a preview of the 1978-79 Yankee Lemon-Martin affair. Sometimes it seems like nothing is new.

The famous baseball writer Hugh Fullerton was once sued by Sox owner Frazee over some alleged slanderous criticism of Frazee by Fullerton in one of his articles. As later events proved perhaps Fullerton knew what he was writing about.

First baseman Dick Hoblitzell was appointed the Red Sox field captain in 1918 but after 19 games he entered military service as a dentist during World War I. Outfielder Harry Hooper succeeded him as field captain.

They speak of Babe Ruth's home run hitting ability, but in April of 1918 at Fenway Park in a game against the New York Yankees he hit a tremendous fly ball to right field that was caught by Frank Gilhooley. The Sox Everett Scott was on second base and scored on this fly ball.

In 1918 Babe Ruth became the first pitcher to ever hit ten home runs. Interestingly he was not only called Babe but *Honey*, something long forgotten today.

A sad note for the Red Sox in July 1918 former pitcher Larry Pape died of complications from an old injury he received from playing ball. Pape was only 35 years old.

Pitcher Bill Pertica found one Red Sox scout didn't recommend him because he used a spitter.

In the Red Sox early years their biggest rivals were the Detroit Tigers as not only the fans but the players rooted against each other due to a long standing grudge.

The Red Sox had little faith in pitcher Joe Wood after he sat out the 1916 season due to a sore arm, a story the Sox wouldn't believe. They dealt him off to the Cleveland Indians and how he proved them wrong. In 1918 he was the season's real surprise and it was said that he deserved the honor as the "Best Comeback In Baseball". He was certainly the find of the season and his comeback was hailed as the real sensation of baseball history. He switched from the mound to the outfield with appearances at first and second bases, batted .296 with a slugging percentage of .403 led the Indians in home runs, was second in hits, hit 22 doubles and 4 triples, led the team in RBI's and stole 8 bases. In addition he refused his pay until he made good. He insisted that he wanted to prove he could earn his money and even paid his own expenses.

By late 1918 Sox owner Frazee was talking of selling off his players for large sums. This loose talk caused Boston fans to turn against him. Boston was running true to form as Sox ownership had been a cause of controversy ever since the club entered the American League. He kept his word by sending the popular pitchers Dutch Leonard and Ernie Shore, along with the great outfielder Duffy Lewis to the New York Yankees.

In 1919 pitcher-outfielder Babe Ruth gave the Sox an ultimatum. He wanted more pay and must play only *one* position. Later in the season he said his ambition was to be the home run king of all time.

Owner Harry Frazee, in late 1918, put Red Sox on the market for $1,5000,000 but in early 1919 took them off the for sale list when no one was willing to meet his price.

When, in 1919, pitcher Carl Mays jumped the Red Sox the ownership said they would trade him for the best offer. The fans thought he should have been given a long suspension. Earlier in the season he had gotten into trouble in Philadelphia when he threw a baseball at a spectator and was fined $100 by American League President Ban Johnson, a fine he refused to pay but which was eventually paid by someone. Meanwhile the Yankees gave Frazee no rest in their efforts to land Mays. The Boston press made up alibis for Mays saying he had a disturbed mind when he quit the Sox. They intimated that matters outside of baseball made him irresponsible for his actions. There was also reference to his being hit on the head by a throw by catcher Wally Schang and that Mays had been found weeping in the clubhouse. Evidence was also piling up that he was a bean ball pitcher. The most damaging was that he had hit a young player named Thrasher in the head a few years earlier. (Note — Mays was the pitcher for New York when Cleveland Indian shortstop Ray Chapman was beaned and became the only major leaguer to be killed by a pitched ball).

In 1919 the Sox purchased a reserve outfielder named Joe Wilhoit from Wichita where he had established a baseball record of hitting in 69 consecutive games. In this stretch he had 151 hits in 299 at bats for a .505 average.

Babe Ruth once boasted he was going to beat up Ty Cobb on sight because of the Tiger Star's remarks about living up to contracts. Ruth had supposedly torn up a three year contract. There is no report that such a title fight ever took place.

In 1920 the Red Sox affairs were a mess under owner Frazee. Former owner Joe Lannin had not been paid, so he tied up Frazee with an injunction, which prevented any player sales but did allow the Sox to buy players.

Pittsburgh's Hall of Fame third baseman, Pie Traynor's sale by Portsmouth to the Pirates in 1920 was protested by the Red Sox. Manager Ed Barrow said he had sent Traynor to the Virginia Club on an option arrangement or "gentleman's agreement". What a loss for the Sox.

When pitcher Buck O'Brien's career ended he took up pitching in an independent league around Boston. Many other former Sox have followed in his footsteps.

By late 1920 the parade of great Boston baseball stars being sold to the New York Yankees prompted one New York newspaper to comment, "The wrecking of this once famous ball club (Boston) is a crime and somebody ought to put an end to such methods." I wonder what it did to the stock of the New York, New Haven and Hartford railroad? "Don't worry," said Frazee as he promises Boston a good baseball show if it will just wait as he is too busy with show biz just now.

On March 14, 1921 fomer Red Sox first baseman (1901) Larry McLean was shot to death in a Boston saloon, at the age of 39. Baseball never had a more famous character or drinker. He bounced around baseball for years at all levels often signing contracts that were contingent upon his staying sober. A terror when in "his cups" but even then a child could lead him if he was properly approached. He was described as a boy who never grew up. Many Red Sox fans will remember the famous picture of that first team — there is Larry stretched out on the floor in the front row.

During the 1921 spring training at Hot Springs, Arkansas the players were "cutting up" by throwing any object they could get their hands on through the open transoms at their hotel. Other guests naturally objected to this "innocent fun". Manager Hugh Duffy had to call a team meeting to halt the practice. I hope their aim was better than the fifth place they finished in.

By mid July 1921 Sox fans were showing their ill feeling toward owner Frazee and his bad deals, as for one game with Cleveland at Fenway Park only 500 showed up. Frazee had raised prices to a higher level than the National League Boston Braves by not absorbing the war tax. By December fans across the country (not only Boston) were demanding the Red Sox owner retire or be removed by the League.

A reserve shortstop, Chick Maynard, of the 1922 Red Sox was described as overrated and a thousand years away from being a major leaguer as waivers were asked on him. The Sox seem to have had a number of such individuals over the years.

Hugh Duffy, 1922 manager, ordered his players to stop playing golf in the morning adding "Too bad, it is the one game most of them can play well." Note — the 1922 Red Sox finished last, 33 games out of first place.

In late summer of 1922 Red Sox owner Harry Frazee was telling the Boston fans of his big plans for rebuilding the team. "They will be the wonders of 1923" he said. He claimed three minor leaguers had been already bought and there would be more. These three minor league phenoms turned out to be a pitcher from Memphis named Fowlkes, (cost $10.000) another pitcher from Rock Island named Stimpson (cost $2,500) and a first baseman from Evansville named Reichle (cost $5,000) After all the money he had raked in on his deals with New York this $17,500 represented a very small outlay.

It would seem the New York owners were also running the Red Sox in 1922. When Frazee made a deal with Detroit before he gave the Yankees full information on what he was doing the New Yorkers became quite "put out" with him and he got a good "calling down". After being put straight by the Yankees, Frazee tried to call off the Detroit deal, but it was too late because he had already cashed the $25,000 bonus check sent to him by Detroit.

An example of the way Frazee ran things would be the deal he pulled in 1922 of sending O'Rourke to Toronto, but Philadelphia claimed they had not passed the waivers on that player. Frazee then admitted that he had been a "little preliminary" by not waiting until waivers had been completed, all this after he had already received Toronto's check.

Rumors in late 1922 indicated that former star catcher Bill Carrigan wanted to buy the Red Sox, but management did not accept the deal and then named Frank Chance manager eliminating Carrigan from that job also. This upset the fans further as they felt they had been misled by Frazee, who had led them to believe Carrigan, a very popular figure in Boston, would be named as the new manager for 1923.

By late February 1923 Boston owner Harry Frazee was saying he was ready to sell out and it was said that the whole league was united in a movement to get him out of baseball. At this point the New York management must have felt that the supply of worthwhile players they could purchase from Frazee had been exhausted.

The team batting average of the Red Sox dropped from .283 in 1941 to .276 in 1942 but they still led the American League in batting for the third straight season.

Red Ruffing won 258 games in the American League mostly for the New York Yankees. While he pitched for the Red Sox his record against New York was 1 and 14.

Red Sox first baseman Tony Lupien captained the Harvard baseball team while a student there. His father worked his way through Harvard by playing semi-pro ball and was therefore ineligible for college competition.

In 1942, pitcher Bill Butland registered five putouts in one game. During the season he won seven games, one from each club and lost only one to St. Louis.

Tex Hughson led the majors in victories in his first complete major league season 1942. He was also the only pitcher in the majors to finish with a winning percentage against seven clubs.

Never before did a player dominate the major league scene as completely as Ted Williams did in 1942. Although his average dropped 50 points under his average for 1941 (.406-.356) he led both big leagues in batting, slugging, bases per hit, total bass, home runs, runs batted in, runs scored and bases on balls. In day games Ted batted .348 and had an astounding batting average of .485 in night games. The following comparision will point up how completely Williams dominated the major leagues.

	American League		National League	
Batting	Williams	.356	Ernie Lombardi	.330
Slugging	Williams	.648	John Mize	.521
Bases per hit	Williams	1.92	John Mize	1.71
Total Bases	Williams	338	Enos Slaughter	292
Home runs	Williams	36	Mel Ott	30
Runs batted in	Williams	137	John Mize	110
Runs scored	Williams	141	Mel Ott	118
Walks	Williams	145	Mel Ott	109

Should the Red Sox have been the 1942 American League champions? Consider what a 38 year old St. Louis Browns pitcher did to prevent it. John Niggeling, the veteran knuckle-baller started 6 games against Boston and beat them 5 times. He started 5 times against the champion New York Yankees and lost all five. That is a difference of ten games in the team standings. The Yankees finished nine games ahead of the second place Red Sox.

In 1942 Dom DiMaggio started seven double plays from his centerfield position and completed the only unassisted double play by an outfielder. On August 2, in a game against Detroit, he caught Doc Cramer's fly ball behind second base and tagged out Jimmy Bloodworth before he could return to first base.

An unusual coincidence in 1942 — Lenny Merullo of the Chicago Cubs led the National League in stolen bases. John Pesky of the Red Sox led the American League. Each had 22.

1943 marked Joe Cronin's eighth season as Red Sox manager making him the longest tenured Sox manager, surpassing Jimmy Collins' seven seasons.

Between June 7 and August 15, 1942, pitcher "Broadway Charlie" Wagner won six games, all by one run.

Washington Senator pitcher Walter Johnson struck out four Red Sox on April 15, 1911 in the fifth inning. The catcher missed the third strike on the third batter and he reached first safely. Johnson struck out the next batter.

Before major league expansion the longest jump was from Boston to St. Louis — 1,212 miles by rail, 1,113 by air.

Marty McManus, Red Sox manager in 1932-33, was manager of the Kenosha Comets of the All American Girls Professional Ball League during the mid 40's.

During World War II shortstop John Pesky and second baseman Tom Carey were 14th Naval District All Stars.

Pitcher Earl Johnson spent nearly four years in the Army during World War II and earned a battlefield promotion to lieutenant for action under fire in Germany.

Jimmie Foxx said New York Giant pitcher Carl Hubbell's screwball was the toughest pitch he ever swung at.

Consider this group of rookies who made their major league debut in 1925 — How many played for the Red Sox at one time or another? Lou Gehrig, Jimmie Foxx, Mel Ott, Joe Cronin, Mickey Cochrane, Red Ruffing, Bob Grove, Fred Fitzsimmons and Chick Hafey.

When Dave Ferriss attended Mississippi State College he played first base left handed and pitched right handed.

Despite constantly shifting combinations the 1945 Red Sox still managed to complete more double plays than any club had ever made before in the major leagues.

Shortstop Joe Cronin's playing career ended in 1945 when he severely fractured his ankle when he caught his spikes in the bag at second base in Yankee Stadium.

Outfielder Leon Culberson made an unassisted double play against St. Louis in 1945 by catching a short blooper in centerfield and tagging second base before the runner could return.

In a five game stretch in July 1945 shortstop Eddie Lake had 10 hits in 16 at bats for a .691 average.

To win his 20th game in 1945 pitcher Dave Ferriss had to double home the winning run in the 10th inning himself to gain a 4-3 win over Philadelphia.

In 1947, Johnny Pesky filed a petition in a Massachusetts court to have his name legally changed from Paveskovich to Pesky, the name he has used in professional baseball.

Dave Ferriss' shutout of the St. Louis Cardinals in the third game of the 1946 World Series was the fiftieth ever recorded in the fall classic.

Talk about being in a rut? On May 27, 28, 29, 1902 the Pilgrims (as the Red Sox were known then) defeated the St. Louis Browns at the Huntington Avenue Grounds in Boston by identical scores of 6 to 2.

Like so many Red Sox clubs the 1949 edition was strictly a home club. At home they boasted a 61-16, .792 record while on the road they were 35-42, .455. Had they been able to match their 1948 road record they would have finished the season with 102 games won and 52 lost for a percentage of .662.

Joe McCarthy, while managing the Red Sox said, "Too much importance is placed on the starting pitchers. It's much more important to have a finishing pitcher."

Ted Williams said, "There never was a .400 hitter who wasn't lucky."

Red Sox owner Bob Quinn was the first owner to popularize "Ladies Day" in baseball.

In late November 1935 the Hollywood club of the Pacific Coast League gave the Red Sox options on infielders Bobby Doerr and George Myatt for pitcher George Hockette and cash. Both made the majors in 1938 — Doerr with the Sox, Myatt with the New York Giants.

After many years in the second division the Red Sox were picked to win the American League pennant in 1936 only to have rumors crop up of them being "prima donnas". This rumor was denied by manager Joe Cronin who defended his stars and claimed his second line pitchers would bring a flag to Fenway. "Just one big, happy family these Red Sox millionaires." (Note — the Sox were eliminated by the Yankees on September 4 and finished 6th).

In early April 1936 the Red Sox played an exhibition game against Holy Cross College and were hard pressed to win 2 to 1. One of the Holy Cross pitchers was Bill "Lefty" Lefebvre who later (1938-39) pitched for the Red Sox.

All Red Sox fans know of Ted Williams gestures to the fans, but several years before Ted's antics pitcher Wes Ferrell was endearing himself to Hub fans by thumbing himself a ride (thumbed his nose) to the hoots and jeers of the Fenway faithful.

The Red Sox reached into the college ranks in May 1936 to sign the University of Richmond battery of pitcher Herb Hash and catcher George Lacy. Each received a $3,000 bonus and contracts which said they would be kept together. A month later another college twirler accompanied the Sox on a western trip — Emerson Dickman from Washington and Lee.

A young Chicago high school pitcher named Frank Dasso was signed by the Red Sox in June 1936 for supposedly more money than any high school player has ever received from a big league club.

Few players came directly from college campuses to big league mounds but Ted Olson was signed in June 1936 off the Dartmouth campus and joined the Red Sox for several weeks before he was optioned to Minneapolis. He did appear in 5 games for the '36 Sox, winning one and losing one.

In the midst of a New York Yankee rally in a game with the Red Sox in mid August 1936 pitcher Wes Ferrell walked off the mound, an act which doomed his Red Sox career. The Sox front office said they were fed up and planned a winter swap of the tempermental pitcher. It is believed Ferrell was the leader of a faction opposing manager Joe Cronin. Note-Ferrell won 20 games while losing 15 for the 6th place Sox of 1936, a fact which probably earned him another chance with the 1937 team for whom he won 3 and lost 6 before being traded to Washington.

In February 1937 an 18 year old outfielder who had made his minor league debut with San Diego (Pacific Coast League) in 1936 was graduated from a San Diego High School (Hoover) and was among the honor students. His name — Ted Williams.

The June 10, 1937 trade which sent the Ferrell brothers and Mel Almada to the Washington Senators was known as the "Harmony Deal" since the trouble makers on the Sox would be gone. However, it would seem that the players who arrived from Washington — Bobo Newsom and Ben Chapman — did little to restore peace in the clubhouse ("to solve the temperament problem"), while Boston fans did not take kindly to the loss of the popular and colorful Ferrells.

Leon Culberson came to the Red Sox as an outfielder but wound up at third base until a torrid smash by Joe DiMaggio off his finger put him out of action in 1946 and Rip Russell at third.

On July 25, 1941 pitcher Lefty Grove won his 300th game. After the game, manager Bill Barrett of Brattleboro of the Northern League appeared in the Red Sox clubhouse with a college boy from Mississippi and introduced him around. It was the first time the boy had ever been inside a major league ball park. He later went on to pitch for the Sox. His name — Dave Ferriss.

Pitcher Dave Ferriss won his first 10 games in 1946 and later won 12 straight and did not lose a game at Fenway Park. By the way, the 24th of the month played a big role in his life in 1945. On February 24, 1945 he was discharged from the service, on March 24th he reported to the Sox Louisville farm club and on April 24th he reported to the Red Sox.

The great Red Sox centerfielder Dom DiMaggio made his first big league appearance as a sub for Ted Williams in left field. Doc Cramer was in center that day and Lou Finney in right. Early in the game Williams and Cramer had collided with Ted being injured.

Pitcher Eldon Auker had a 9-10 record for the Red Sox in 1939, but what was unusual about it was that every game he won was on the road.

In the mid thirties there was a Sox outfielder known to the loyal followers as Smeederino Jolliani, but you won't find this name in the record books. You see his real name was Smead Jolley. Johnny Garro, sports editor of *"La Notizia"* a Boston Italian newspaper, invented the name for the Italian community desperate for a hero on the Boston roster.

In July 1946 Ted Williams hit 3 home runs in the first of two games against Cleveland prompting Indian manager Boudreau to use his unusual shift against Ted in the second game. Williams did an unusual thing himself between innings of the first game, so it is told. One inning instead of going to the bench he stepped into the scoreboard, stepped out a trap door into the street, ran (in uniform) to a nearby cafeteria and ordered a plate of ice cream, retraced his steps and arrived at his position in time for the next inning. A story this author finds hard to believe.

In 1945 outfielder John Lazor batted .310 and was five at bats short of qualifying for the American League batting championship.

The 1946 Red Sox participated in 27 doubleheaders sweeping 14 of them and splitting the balance. They swept 10 of 16 at Fenway Park and 4 of 11 on the road.

Eleven of twenty four players on the first New York Yankee World Championship team came from the Red Sox.

Red Sox Hall of Fame outfielder Harry Hooper once said he never remembered being booed in Boston. On his first return to Boston, after being traded to the Chicago White Sox, he was presented with many gifts and on his first at bat received a standing ovation as he stood at the plate with tears streaming down his face, ashamed to wipe them away.

Until 1934 there was an ordinance in Boston that prohibited Sunday baseball from being played within 1000 yards of a church. There was a Protestant Church within 1000 yards of Fenway Park. Lt. Governor Leverett Saltonstall went to talk with the minister and found he had no objection to baseball being played on Sunday, thus opening the way to Sunday baseball at Fenway Park.

The Boston Elevated Railroad owned the Huntington Avenue Grounds property and wanted to build a huge terminal there, but the company couldn't get zoning clearance. Daniel Prendergast, who was general manager of the railway, was convinced to lease the property to the ball club rather than let it stand idle.

When Red Sox owner Tom Yawkey renovated Fenway Park in 1934 he installed what was believed to be the first press room anywhere. The room was a place where the press could wind up their work after the game and quench their thirst. Yawkey was also the first to provide the scribes lunch between doubleheaders.

Centerfielder Dom DiMaggio had 503 put outs in 155 games in 1948.

In 1948 70,000 fans looked on at Cleveland as Manager Joe McCarthy kicked rookie catcher Matt Batts on the backside at home plate. The reason was Indian Lou Boudreau's steal of home. The real culprit may have been pitcher Mickey Harris who retreated to the mound when McCarthy, who was on the field arguing the call, proceeded to tell him off after the kick. McCarthy later denied the act.

1948 was a record breaking year for second baseman Bobby Doerr. When he set major league records by playing 73 consecutive games at second base without an error, he broke his record of 59 set in 1943 and by accepting 414 chances without an error he broke his record of 349 set during the 59 game streak.

Red Sox first baseman Jake Jones was a Navy fighter pilot during World War II with seven Japanese planes shot down to his credit.

In 1963 Dick Stuart hit 42 home runs and drove in 118 runs to become the first player in history to hit 30 home runs and drive in 100 runs in a season in both the American and National Leagues.

When the Red Sox used an outfield of Carl Yastrzemski in left, Fred Lynn in center and Dwight Evans in right they had in addition to a great defensive combination an outfield where all the fielders had the middle name of Michael.

On opening day in 1948, the Philadelphia A's started a rookie left hander against the Red Sox named Lou Brissie, whose left leg had been badly shattered by German shrapnel during the war. He was forced to wear a shinguard to protect the leg. Sox slugger Ted Williams hit a bullet like line drive which hit Brissie an inch above the plastic guard. The hurler fell in agony as the ball bounded sharply out of the infield. Brissie, after several minutes of rest and treatment, continued, earning a 4 to 2 victory.

Superstitious habits have long been known among baseball players and some of the Red Sox have not been exempted. Buck Freeman was one who always balked at being photographed when warming up. The great Lefty Grove was another who shooed away the camermen when taking his warm up tosses. Eddie Collins, who was once the Sox vice president and general manager, always parked his chewing gum on his cap button during his playing days, positive this custom brought him good luck.

The great Babe Ruth had a superstition about never lending one of his bats to a teammate. One day after the Sox had sold him to New York he made an exception and presented Joe Jackson of the Chicago White Sox with one of his warclubs, but insisted that Joe refrain from using the bat against the Yankees. The next day the White Sox moved on to Fenway Park and Jackson decided to use the gift bat and on his first trip to the plate hit one of the longest home runs ever seen in New England up until that time.

Outfielder Harry Hooper started his baseball career at St. Mary's College as a pitcher. That little college also sent Duffy Lewis and Dutch Leonard among others to the Red Sox. Speaking of Hooper and Lewis the third member of that great outfield, Tris Speaker, also started his baseball career as a pitcher for Cleburne, Texas of the North Texas League in 1906. Boston paid $400 to obtain "Spoke" who went on to a remarkable career as a great hitter and the greatest defensive outfielder the game has ever known.

Pitching hero of the early Red Sox and the first World Series was right-hander Bill Dineen. When his pitching days ended he turned to umpiring and for years was regarded as one of the American League's better judges of balls and strikes. Bill was also known as quite a chef in his spare moments and his hobby was baking pies.

Strange facts in baseball life of Joe Cronin. When Sox owner Tom Yawkey purchased him from Washington the man he replaced as Bosox manager was Bucky Harris. Where did Harris wind up? — as the Washington manager. Cronin was the youngest manager in the majors at the time. In October before coming to Boston, Cronin was married to the niece of the Senators owner, Clark Griffith. Griffith made a neat $260,000 by selling off his new relative. Cronin attended Sacred Heart College in California, a school that had educated the great boxer James J. Corbett and baseball great Harry Heilmann. A versatile athlete Joe once won a tennis championship for 14 year-olds in San Francisco. One of the teammates in high school was Wally Berger who became a star with the Boston Braves.

Fred Mitchell who was a right handed pitcher and infielder for the 1901 Pilgrims went on to become manager and president of the Chicago Cubs, manager and general manager of the Boston Braves, baseball coach at Harvard and played both pitcher and catcher, infield and outfield during his major league career. His 1918 Cubs won the National League championship.

Red Sox catcher Rick Ferrell during his younger days went in for boxing, but a kayo clout changed his mind and he pursued a baseball career.

Outfielder Carl Reynolds may have closely approached being a Frank Merriwell as he was known as "The One Man Track Team" while attending Southwestern University in Texas where he also excelled in baseball, football and basketball.

Outfielder Julius Solters is remembered by most fans as "Moose" Solters but early in his career he was known as "Lemons" because of his craving for the citrus fruit. His real name by the way was Soltesz. Solters was the erroneously spelled name which appeared in a box score of a game his brother Frank appeared in and "Moose" continued the error by using the spelling as his name.

Mel Almada, who patrolled the Sox outfield in the 30's, once as a minor leaguer beat out two regular bunts and two drag bunts in a single game for four hits against a southpaw hurler.

Catcher Doc Legett had a D.D.S. degree in dentistry when he played with the Red Sox.

Pitcher Hank Johnson came over to the Red Sox in 1933 from the New York Yankees where his best remembered accomplishment was beating Lefty Grove six straight times in 1928.

How would you like Herb Pennock, Lefty Grove and Rube Walberg as your pitching coaches? Well, Sox hurler, Spike Merena claimed that when he joined the Boston team in 1934 they all helped him tremendously.

When Robert McRoy, who was the first secretary under American League President Ban Johnson, left that post to become a Red Sox vice president, his job was taken by Will Harridge who later assumed the leadership of the Junior circuit.

That big black board out in centerfield is not an electronic scoreboard insist the Red Sox. It is a message board and it does not make weird noises, explode or produce various and sundry caricatures. It was introduced for the 1976 season.

As a rookie duo in 1939, Ted Williams and Jim Tabor knocked in more runs than any other major league rookie twosome — 240. Williams 145, Tabor 95. In 1975 Fred Lynn and Jim Rice had 207 RBI's, Lynn 105, Rice 102.

During the early 20's Sox owner Harry Frazee tried to get former manager Bill Carrigan to return as team manager.

Hall of Fame pitcher Cy Young, when with the Red Sox was known to take a few cups of his favorite rye, "Cascades" but never the night before he was scheduled to pitch.

In 1976 pitcher Bill Lee was told by American League president Lee MacPhail to write a letter promising that he would not retaliate against the Yankees for an injury suffered in a brawl at Yankee Stadium on May 20.

Long time Red Sox owner Tom Yawkey said he felt Carl Yastrzemski was the best all around player he ever had.

In 1976 Red Sox manager Don Zimmer in a rush to get onto the field from the dugout to protest an umpire's call tripped over first base and went sprawling on the ground.

During a game at Yankee Stadium in 1936 pitcher Wes Ferrell decided to remove himself from the mound and manager Cronin decided to remove $1000 from Wes' wallet and suspended the hurler as well.

There have been several father-son combos and brother acts on the Red Sox over the years, but as far as known only one brother-in-law act. Rick Miller and Carlton Fisk. Miller married Fisk's sister.

Ever see that picture of the 1912 Red Sox where pitcher Joe Wood is holding a little girl? That was his sister. Seems his mother and sister were attending the game that day and brotherly love dictated she would get into the act.

Pitcher Lefty Grove was once asked the secret of his success. "No secret. They tell me to pitch and I say gimme the ball."

Credit Sox manager Ed Barrow's informal advisory committee of Heinie Wagner, Everett Scott and leader Harry Hooper for convincing the manager to use his great left handed pitcher Babe Ruth in the outfield. Hooper pointed out to Barrow, not only did Boston fans come out to see the Babe pitch but also to hit. Barrow who had a $60,000 investment in the club quickly saw the light in drawing fans daily.

Speaking of Hooper, he was the first American League outfielder to use sunglasses, borrowing the idea from the National League's Fred Clarke.

One of the weakest positions on the Sox over the last forty years has been in the catching department, except for Rick Ferrell, Sammy White, Birdie Tebbetts and "Pudge" Fisk. Consider who has passed behind the plate at Fenway, in no special order: — Don Pavletich, Tom Satriano, Ed McGah, Merv Shea, Hal Wagner, Moe Berg, Gene Desautels, Les Moss, Gus Niarhos, Mickey Owen, Joe Glenn, Joe Azcue, John Peacock, Bob Tillman, Bill Conroy, Andy Merchant, Jim Pagliaroni, Buddy Rosar, Mike Guerra, Mike O'Berry, Bob Scherbath, Lou Berberet, Russ Gibson,

Gene Oliver, Del Wilber, Aaron Robinson, Elston Howard, (at the end of a great career), Mike Ryan, Jerry Moses, Bob Garbark, Roy Partee, Duane Josephson, Al Evans, Len Okrie, Frank Pytlak, Joe Ginsberg, Russ Nixon, and sundry others not mentioned here.

When manager Steve O'Neill suggested catcher Mike Guerra start doing some catching Mike replied "Me tired", which led to Guerra's suspension and ticket to far away places.

When Joe Glenn was catching for the Red Sox, which was rare, the former Yankee second stringer had a unique method of keeping his pitchers on their toes. He did little except endanger their lives with his low throws to second base.

Buddy Rosar drove trainer Win Green up his training room wall by putting his sore finger in the whirlpool. Green was quoted as saying, "Fifty gallons of water for a hangnail."

How would you like to have been in catcher Russ Nixon's shoes one day at Fenway? He caught a third strike in the dirt for what he thought was the third out and tossed the ball to the Yankee batter Pete Mikkelson who tossed the ball toward the mound and started running around the bases while the Red Sox were trotting off the field and wound up on second base before the Bosox figured out what was happening. He later scored on a single and poor Russ Nixon left an unforgettable memory for those who were there.

When Hall of Famer Cy Young pitched a no hitter on May 5, 1904 he was so intent on beating the Philadelphia A's and rival Rube Waddell, he didn't realize he had pitched a perfect game until his catcher Lou Criger rushed out to him after the final out.

Old time Red Sox fans will remember an embankment in left field at Fenway Park known as "Duffy's Cliff" after Duffy Lewis who played it so well, but how many will remember it was covered with cinders before they planted grass out there?

When left handed pitcher Mickey "Himself" Harris launched his big league career in 1940 he was attempting a big jump from A ball to the bigs and was hailed as the second coming of Lefty Grove. He had a 4 and 2 record for the Sox when suddenly he was returned to the minors "for more seasoning." At the time there was talk that the move was strictly a disciplinary measure. He bounced back in 1941 but could only win 8 with 14 losses before he was drafted and spent four years in Panama developing his arm.

When the great left-hander Herb Pennock pitched for the Red Sox his top salary was $3,000 and it took a season ending bonus of $500 from owner Harry Frazee to reach that figure.

Speaking of Pennock, he only hit four homers in his long major league career, but one came against the Yankees at Fenway Park, an inside-park job, and he stopped Babe Ruth, who had recently been sold to the New Yorkers for a Boston win.

Another early Red Sox pitching great, Carl Mays, claimed the 1915 and 1916 Red Sox were the best teams he played with and their manager Bill Carrigan was the best manager he ever had, which was quite a compliment, considering he also played under greats John McGraw, Miller Huggins, Jack Barry, Ed Barrow and Jack Hendricks.

Red Sox manager Bill Carrigan was known as "Rough" and if you were a pitcher and got knocked out in the early innings, it was no quick shower and out of the ball park, it was change your sweatshirt "and be quick about it" because you sit on the bench no matter how long the game went.

Carrigan showed no quarter. Once when the team was going bad owner Joe Lannin entered the clubhouse demanding to know why Bill wasn't using pitcher Dutch Leonard. Now Leonard, a great left-hander who could really throw when he felt like it, was also lazy and slow getting in shape this year with Carrigan refusing to use him. "Leonard is not in condition to pitch yet and I won't pitch him until he is. Does that answer your question?" he replied to Lannin and then proceeded to tell Lannin never to come into his clubhouse again. I wonder how today's owners would react!

Often major leaguers play side by side successfully without speaking to one another. Such occurred to the great Red Sox outfield of Lewis, Speaker and Hooper that performed together for six years which may be a record for outfields. Seems Duffy Lewis was quite self conscious about growing bald. One day when closing out a series in St. Louis the heat became so bad he had his head shaved. The team returned to Boston and while Duffy was taking batting practice Speaker sneaked up and grabbed Lewis's cap from his head exposing the shaved noggin for all to see. An infuriated Lewis tossed his bat at Speaker cracking him across the shins so hard Speaker fell to the ground in pain with Joe Wood and Larry Gardner having to help him off the field. The story has it that they never spoke again.

From 1966 until May 2, 1971 the Sox won only three 1 to 0 games at Fenway Park when on that date Ray Culp defeated Minnesota on a two hitter. Previously Lee Stange defeated Washington on July 4, 1966 and Ken Brett and Sonny Siebert combined for 14 inning victory over the Yankees on September 24, 1969. Strangely during this period they were also defeated three times by 1 to 0 scores (by the Angels, A's and Yankees).

One of the better trades in Red Sox history found pitcher Ray Culp coming to the Red Sox from the Chicago Cubs for minor league outfielder Bill Schlesinger and some of Tom Yawkey's cash in November of 1968. Pitchers seemed to always be involved in controversial Red Sox deals, two of which were with the New York Yankees — Sparky Lyle for Danny Cater and in 1930 Red Ruffing for one Cedric Durst, two of the all time worst Red Sox trades.

The granddaddy of all Fenway Park wild pitches occurred in April, 1978. In the seventh inning Len Barker of the Texas Rangers uncorked a pitch which hit the top of the screen behind home plate. Carlton Fisk who was on third base trotted home in disbelief.

In June 1958 Jackie Jensen hit 14 home runs in the month of June for a Red Sox record. Clyde Vollmer hit 13 in July 1951 and Jim Rice 13 in May of 1978.

In 1973 Carl Yastrzemski volunteered to play third base for the injured Rico Petrocelli and piled up 10 errors in his first 11 games.

The statistics compiled by Red Sox players in the 1948 and 1978 playoff were included in their regular season stats.

Ted Williams' famous number nine is the only uniform retired by the Red Sox.

Fenway Park has been the site of six World Series, but the Sox have played in only five of them — 1912, 1918, 1946, 1967 and 1975. The Boston Braves played their home series games at Fenway in 1914 and the Sox played theirs in 1915 and 1916 at Braves Field.

When New York Yankee Joe DiMaggio was hitting in 56 straight games in 1941 he compiled a batting average of .406. Boston's Ted Williams during the same period was batting at a .412 clip.

In 1946 Red Sox right fielder, Tom McBride, chased a bird in flight instead of a fly ball hit by Philadelphia's Sam Chapman.

Red Sox outfielder Jackie Jensen was the American League's MVP in 1958. He had also been an All American football player with California's Golden Bears.

Frankie Campbell who succumbed after a bad beating in a boxing fight with former world heavyweight champion Max Baer was the brother of Red Sox first baseman Dolph Camilli.

Jack Rothrock was a handy player to have around in 1928. He played all nine positions and was used as pinch hitter and pinch runner.

Pitcher Al Benton was the only man to pitch to both Babe Ruth and Mickey Mantle in a major league game. Against the Babe in 1934 while pitching for the Philadelphia Athletics and in 1952 against Mantle while with the Bosox.

Carroll Hardy is the only man to pinch hit for both Ted Williams (9/21/60) and Carl Yastrzemski (5/31/61).

Having lost four toes on one foot in a coal mine accident pitcher Red Ruffing had to wear a specially made shoe.

One of the most costly player collisions occurred for the Red Sox midway through the 1929 season. Converging on a blooper at full speed were shortstop Wally Gerber and outfielder Ken Williams. The two hit head on and remained unconscious on the field for some time. Gerber never played again and Williams labored through the season but never played another.

Do you realize a player getting 200 hits in a season would have to get a double every third hit to break Red Soxer Earl Webb's record of 67 doubles hit in 1931?

Red Sox catcher in the mid 30's George "Skeets" Dickey was the brother of Yankee great Bill Dickey, also a catcher.

In 1926 Red Sox outfielder Bill Jacobson played 7 consecutive games in which he did not make a putout or an assist.

Pitcher Ray Culp held the dubious Red Sox record of striking out eight times in eight consecutive plate appearances.

Early Boston American League teams used the nicknames "Somersets", "Pilgrims", "Puritans" and "Speed Boys" before they became the Red Sox in 1907, but these names were mostly dreamed up by the press while most opposing players preferred to call them "The Bostons".

When the "Boston Americans" went into business in 1901 five numbers of the "Boston Nationals" crossed over the railroad tracks separating the teams' ball parks to join up. They were third baseman Jimmy Collins, outfielder Chick Stahl, first baseman Buck Freeman and pitchers Ed "Parson" Lewis and George "Nig" Cuppy.

Infielder Hobe Ferris made 61 errors for the 1901 Boston's. Not too bad when you consider the lumps and bumps the infields were made of in those days. As friend Bill Gavin says, the ball parks featured disastroturf.

Down through the history of major league baseball left handed catchers are a real rarity, yet Tommy Doran performed from 1904-1906 for Boston.

Who was the first Boston switch hitter? — George "Candy" LaChance who joined the club in 1902.

Before the Yawkey era, lineups at Fenway Park were announced to the crowd by megaphone by a gentleman in a straw hat who circled the field announcing game lineups to the crowd. "Stonewall" Jackson called the earliest rolls, with a loud "who" from the crowd after each name was called. The portly Jack O'Brien succeeded him. Wonder how the present PA announcer Sherm Feller would feel about making his announcements that way?. In fact, the use of the megaphone to give information to the fans was introduced in Boston in 1901, with Wolfie Jacobs as the first announcer.

Al Schact while coaching at third base for the Red Sox was known as the "Whistling Coach" for the shrill whistles he was capable of.

Third baseman Jim Tabor found a major league career forced upon him in 1938. When regular third sacker Pinky Higgins had an injured leg,Tabor was called up from Minneapolis to replace him. When Higgins recovered the Sox tried to send Tabor back only to find out there was an AA rule that a player couldn't be returned from a big league club until 30 days had expired. The Sox had a little better luck with pitcher Al Baker who they wanted as a spot pitcher. He went from Dallas to Little

Rock to Boston. When he showed little, he was sent back to Little Rock. Baker had pitched for five years at Dallas (present day pitchers take notice).

When the Red Sox staff was battered around late in the 1938 season, outfielder Doc Cramer was pressed into service as a hurler. He survived but vowed to stick to outfielding in the future.

In one of their largest recalls of minor league players in their history 13 were recalled in late 1938. How many can you recall? They were named Williams, Gaffke, Henry, Wagner, LeFebvre, Poindexter, Sayles, Deal, Gonzales, Olson, Marcum, Dickey and Petrushkin.

Catcher John Peacock was selected as the catcher on the 1938 major league rookie All Star team.

In November 1938, baseball commissioner Judge Landis turned down a complaint by the Portland Club of the Pacific Coast League against the Red Sox for signing infielder John Pakeskovich, a former Portland bat boy despite his being a sand lot player. Landis held the transaction to be legal, inasmuch as Pakeskovich was signed to a Rocky Mount contract. Oh yes, you know this player as Johnny Pesky.

In early 1939 the Red Sox were denied travel by airplane. Earlier in the season they had chartered two planes to hop from St. Louis to Chicago, a plan that met with objection by several American League owners and their pleas were upheld by American League President Harridge. Denied use of the airways, Red Sox owner Tom Yawkey chartered a special train for the St. Louis to Chicago hop on the night of June 9th.

When first baseman Jimmie Foxx lost his appendix in early September 1939, it was said that the team felt the pain more than he did.

Bill Enos, now a popular New England area Red Sox scout, was named the most popular player on the 1939 Gloversville team in the Canadian American League.

It would seem former Red Sox owner Bob Quinn had his sights set on Fenway Park again when in January 1940 he suggested the ball park would be suitable for a Boston city stadium.

In early September 1940 the Red Sox recalled many of their optioned farm hands 14 players were affected (more than the 13 of 1938). Let's see how many of these you can remember! From Sacramento — Butland, Harris, LeFebvre and Rich: From Little Rock — Sayles, Brazle, Lupien and Sieling: From Newark — Nonnenkamp: From Louisville — Wagner, Lacy and P. Campbell: From San Francisco — Dasso and Powell.

In mid October of 1940 rumors were flying in Chicago that Ted Williams would be changing his Sox from Red to White with Chicago sending pitcher Johnny Rigney (14-18) and *maybe* outfielder Taft Wright (.337 and 5 home runs) to Boston. This was probably the result of Williams' August demands to be traded, saying he was under paid and that he didn't like Boston and preferred to play for the Detroit Tigers or the New York Yankees.

In September, 1935 one of the most unusual triple plays in major league history occurred at Fenway Park against the Red Sox by Cleveland. Trailing by two runs in the bottom of the ninth the Sox quickly loaded the bases with Dusty Cooke on third, Bill Werber at second and Mel Almada at first, no one out and Joe Cronin at bat. Indian manager Steve O'Neill, realizing Cronin was an excellent clutch hitter, brought in Oral Hildebrand to pitch to him. Cronin hit the first pitch like a bullet to third baseman Odell Hale, who lost sight of the ball and it caromed off the side of his head right into the hands of shortstop Bill Knickerbocker retiring Cronin. Knickerbocker threw to Roy Hughes at second to catch Werber. Hughes then threw to Hal Trosky at first to nail Almada. I guess you could say Hale was playing heads up ball or really used his head on that play!

In baseball a simple player status change or trade can create a host of changes. Consider the events in June of 1979:
1. Boston pitcher Jim Wright is placed on the disabled list.
2. Pawtucket pitcher Joel Finch is called up to replace Wright.
3. Winter Haven pitcher Bobby Sprowl is called up to Pawtucket to replace Finch.
4. Infielder Bob Watson is obtained from Houston for Bristol pitcher Peter Ladd and a player to be named later, who turned out to be pitcher Sprowl.
5. Winter Haven pitcher Bruce Hurst was sent to Bristol to replace Ladd.
6. Bristol pitcher Danny Parks was sent to Pawtucket to replace Sprowl.
7. Winston Salem pitcher Mark Baum was sent to Bristol to replace Parks.
8. Two rookie pitchers from the June draft would get a chance to replace Hurst and Baum.

So here we have two transactions somewhat related and eight players being affected. I am not sure what this proves, but it gives you an idea of the far reaching effects of changes, gives the airlines additional business and may have caused the New England gas shortage of the summer of 1979.

Until Ted Williams' rookie season of 1939 only five players had hit balls into the right field bleachers at Fenway Park since Tom Yawkey rebuilt the park in 1933-34. Think of some of the great left handed hitters in the league at that time — Babe Ruth, Lou Gehrig, Charlie Gehringer, Bill Dickey and Hal Trosky. In the first half of 1939 alone Ted hit seven baseballs into that sector. It was 402 feet to the front of those bleachers. One of Williams' hits, off Yankee Charlie Ruffing, landed half way up in the bleachers and was probably the longest ball ever hit up until then at Fenway Park, traveling fully 460 feet.

In 1918 Eusebio Gonzales became the first of many Red Sox players born in Latin America. The first to be born on the European Continent to play for the Sox was Otto "Pep" Deininger who was born in Germany.

Pitcher Lefty Grove's son, Bob Jr., pitched for the Red Sox second stringers in a charity game in July 1938 as a 16 year old. It was said he had his dad's speed and he hoped to follow his famous father into baseball after getting his education at Duke University.

In 1937 the Red Sox had a bat boy named Freddy Stack who, with some coaching from manager Joe Cronin, had hoped for a playing career, but his inability to add weight rendered him too small to pursue a playing career and he changed his hopes to a job as a conditioner.

When Ted Williams signed his first Red Sox contract, a two year deal, he received a $2,500 bonus. His parents were attempting to get part of his purchase price, "an attitude that didn't help the boy's cause any and may result in his being farmed out to an AA club earlier than otherwise would have been the case," it was reported.

In July, 1909 at Cleveland pitcher Smokey Joe Wood pitched the last four innings in relief and struck out ten batters in a 6 to 4 Boston win.

One of pitcher Joe Wood's biggest minor league thrills came on May 21, 1908 while pitching for Kansas City of the American Association, as he pitched Kansas City to a 1 to 0 victory over Milwaukee on a no hitter.

Before California's Nolan Ryan broke it Boston's Buck O'Brien held the American League record for consecutive strike outs at 6. He struck out the last batter of the first inning, all three batters in the second inning and the first two men in the third inning.

On the Fourth of July 1948 in a game at Fenway Park against the Philadelphia A's the Red Sox scored 14 times in the 7th inning to tie the then major league record.

The Red Sox set the American League record for long hits in a single game in September, 1940 in a game against Philadelphia at 14, including five doubles, three triples, and six home runs.

In the 4th inning of a game against Detroit on May 6, 1934 the Red Sox hit four consecutive triples, a feat which only the National League Brooklyn team had done before and that on August 23, 1902.

In 154 games in 1943 first baseman Tony Lupien grounded into only 3 double plays.

In 1949 second baseman Bobby Doerr grounded into 31 double plays.

In 1938 pitcher Lefty Grove led the American League in both won and lost percentage .778 and ERA at 3.07.

In 1943 shortstop manager Joe Cronin hit 5 pinch hit home runs.

During the 152 games he played in 1921 first baseman Stuffy McInnis made only one error. From May 31 of that year until June 2, 1922 he played 163 games without making an error.

In 138 games in 1948 second baseman Bobby Doerr fielded an amazing .9925.

Third baseman Jimmy Collins played 156 games at the hot corner in 1904.

When third baseman Frank Malzone made his major league debut in 1955 at Fenway Park against the Baltimore Orioles, he had six hits in the twin bill.

Pitcher George Prentiss, a pitcher with the 1901 Pilgrims, created quite a furor in the Connecticut and New York State Leagues in 1901. He had pitched for Waterbury in the Connecticut League in 1898-1900 under the name Prentiss. He became ill in 1900 (died in 1902) and Waterbury paid his hospital bills. Recovering he signed with Albany of the New York State League, using the name Wilson, and compiled a 16-10 record. Later he jumped the Albany team and signed with Boston. Not much gratitude among some old time ball players.

Joe Cronin had a between innings ritual when coaching third base for the Sox of kicking the bag and punching his fist into a glove. The players left their gloves on the field in those days.

During the 1946 season St. Louis Browns pitcher Jack Kramer became exasperated with his pitching, and his teammates' play and marched over just to the foul side of the first base line and fired the ball up over the roof and out of Fenway Park.

When Ted Williams hit his 500th home run, it marked the 47th time that one of his homers had provided the margin of victory and in 34 games he had saved the Sox from a shutout. Ted hit his 100th on May 21, 1942 at League Park in Cleveland off Joe Krakauskas, his 200th at Shibe Park in Philadelphia on April 29, 1948 off Bill McCahan. His 300th came at Fenway Park off Chicago White Sox hurler Howie Judson on May 15, 1951 and number 400 came on July 17, 1956 at Boston against Tom Gorman of the Athletics.

During the 1938 spring training a Newark catcher named Courtney made a remark to Red Sox manager Joe Cronin, "Why don't you make those fellows hustle?" Cronin taken back replied, "I don't want my players to hustle too much in the spring." Perhaps a little more hustle during the following season would have put them in first instead of second place. As it turned out in the early going heads up play by a couple of kids kept the Sox hustling at a better pace than had been seen in years. They were pitcher Jim Bagby and Bobby Doerr, the second baseman.

Manager Joe Cronin often tried players at positions other than their normal position. In one of his earliest he attempted to convert outfielder Fabe Gaffke to a catcher in 1938. Fabe appeared on July 26 as a catcher and showed a good arm and broke up a double steal.

Manager Joe Cronin had to censure Ted Williams many times during his tenure as Bosox field boss but the first time may have been in the spring of 1939 on the team's way north. During a game in Atlanta Ted missed a foul fly ball which he then picked up and flung over the grandstand roof, all of which resulted in his immediately being removed from the game and a fatherly talk from Cronin that night.

Speaking of long Williams' home runs at Detroit's Briggs Field, one went so high it landed on the right field roof at a point 360 feet from home plate where the roof was

120 feet from the ground. On his next turn at bat Williams hit one over that roof, the ball hitting the building across the street. In Sportsman's Park St. Louis during that same 1939 season Ted hit a ball clean over the right field pavilion and the ball bounced so high after it landed on Grand Avenue it was visible for the second time. Local St. Louis fans agreed it was as long as a 455 foot blast he uncorked in a pre-game hitting contest with Jim Foxx, Jim Tabor and George McQuinn. Several years later he hit one of the longest home runs ever hit at Washington's Griffith Stadium and several times hit drives deep into the third deck in New York Yankee Stadium's right field. Old League Park in Cleveland saw Ted hit one of the longest right field home runs ever there also. He also cleared the roof in deep right field in Chicago's Comiskey Park.

During Ted Williams' rookie year he had many nicknames — "Torrid Ted", "Kid Wonder", "Thumpin Teddy", "Timely Ted", "Titanic Ted", "Whizzer Williams" and "The Kid". The latter, along with "The Splendid Splinter", seemed to be the only ones that stuck.

The right field bleacher area at Fenway Park gained the name "Williamsburg" and was altered early in Ted Williams' career, so he and Jimmie Foxx could take advantage of it with their home run blasts. It wasn't, of course, a natural home run area for Foxx, but one he often took advantage of.

A couple of more Williams' stories? One day against Chicago Jimmie Foxx struck out. The next batter Ted Williams also struck out. Ted threw a tantrum, kicked the sod, tossed his bat skyward and punched the empty air, and as the Chicago fans hooted Ted lifted his cap and made an extravagant curtsy. The umpire was about to give Ted the heave-ho when manager Cronin hollered "Busher" and a lot of other uncomplimentary things at his young star, a scolding more to appease the umpire than reprimand Williams. Nothing happened. A little later, after a bad inning, Ted walked to his outfield position and instead of picking up his glove he gave it a mighty kick sending it fifty feet in the air. On another occasion as he walked past Detroit pitcher Buck Newsom, who was warming up, he said "I'm going to give yuh a goin' over." Buck replied "You rookie, you couldn't hit me with a banjo." His first time up he homered into the upper mezzanine and later doubled. Then he waggled his fingers at old Bobo. "Fresh busher" was Newsom's comment after the game with Williams claiming he would lead the league in homers by 1942, which he did.

Ted Williams established himself as the greatest freshman ever in 1939 for his feats on the field and possibly for some of his off-the-field doings and sayings. It started in spring training while talking to no one in particular he said, "I'm 3000 miles from home. I'm 1500 miles away from my girl friend. I'm in a hitting slump. And I'm happy. There must be something wrong with me."

It used to be the custom among Boston baseball writers to have sort of a game in which they claimed certain "boys" from the newcomers to spring training, most of course claiming the best prospects. One day Tom Yawkey, Red Sox owner, was present when a group began naming their boys — Woody Rich, Jim Tabor, Bobby Doerr and others were named. Then somebody named Ted Williams. "Just a minute fellows," interrupted Yawkey, "Haven't I got any rights at all?" "I want to take Williams for my boy." From then on he was Yawkey's favorite.

Bill Werber has granted permission to include the following stories which appeared in his book *"Circling The Bases"*. In 1936 it seems that the salary Tom Yawkey offered Werber was $2000 less than he felt he merited. He signed his contract but was not too happy about it, nevertheless determined to play his best. In an early season game he made a spectacular catch after falling flat on his back into the visiting New York Yankees dugout. After the game Mr. Yawkey requested Werber report to his office. Yawkey related how he knew Werber was unhappy and then called the catch the greatest he had ever seen and put the $2000 back in Werber's contract.

Werber also related how the 1934 club was enjoying a rare winning streak on a western swing during which Mr. Yawkey was accompaning the club. He was enjoying the firecrackers and horseplay as much as the players when the club arrived in Detroit. The high jinx continued until their stay at the Detroit hotel was in jeopardy and had attracted the attention of the Detroit police. The next day Mr. Yawkey called a team meeting and announced that anymore fireworks would be accompanied by a $500 fine. The firecrackers had been fun but not $500 worth.

Once in a game against Detroit Bill Werber received a walk and as he ran casually toward first base with an eye on the Detroit shortstop Bill Rogell and second baseman Charley Gehringer, both of whom were busy, he decided he could keep on going to second base, which he did. As the throw from the catcher went into centerfield he continued on safely to third base and scored the tying run on a sacrifice fly.

Two of Boston's better pitchers in the 30's were Lefty Grove and Wes Ferrell. If they had a fault it was their temper which was usually directed at themselves. When Grove would get upset he would never bother to unbutton his shirt when he reached the clubhouse. He would just take both hands and pull in opposite directions sending shirt buttons flying all over the clubhouse floor. Grove also had a habit after an unsuccessful outing of coming into the dugout and kicking the water bucket all over the place. Doc Woods, the trainer, got tired of replacing the broken buckets so he replaced it with a heavy duty one. Bill Werber decided, after a bad game, to vent his wrath on the bucket a la Grove. He did little damage to the bucket but fractured his big toe. Ferrell often did other strange things. One day in Cleveland after failing to survive the first inning he entered the dugout, got a pair of scissors, and began to cut his glove into small pieces. On another occasion in Philadelphia he had a 10 to 0 lead and gave up nine runs and was removed from the game. He sat on the bench and began to berate himself in the strongest possible language. All of a sudden he threw a right to his jaw and knocked his head against the concrete wall. When he recovered he threw a left hook to his jaw and banged his head a second time. By now manager Bucky Harris had pinioned his arms so he could do no further damage. On another occasion he had been the victim of a practical joke and before practice the next day he mounted a clubhouse chair and challenged the whole team collectively or individually.

There was a time when the Red Sox would accept telephone reservations for tickets. This all ended in early 1946 when their switchboard became so jammed with calls normal business could not be conducted. A special ad was taken in Boston newspapers asking the public to cooperate.

When the '46 Red Sox obtained third baseman Pinky Higgins from Detroit they gained their fifth starter at that position. Previously Ernie Andres, Ed Pellagrini, Leon Culberson and Glen Russell had performed there. In the author's travels this is one of the questions most frequently asked of him. Many think the '46 third baseman was Jim Tabor. For the record Jim was summering with the Philadelphia Phillies in the National League.

Sophomore sensation, pitcher Dave Ferriss, had pitched four shutouts by June 1 in 1946. His total number of walks issued for those games was three, never issuing more than one free pass in a game. His May 19, 4 to 0 blanking of Detroit was his first major league game in which he failed to issue a walk.

Asked to rate the 1946 Red Sox, Babe Ruth said he felt the 1915, 1916 and 1918 Red Sox pennant winners would have beaten Ted Williams and company. "Furthermore," the Babe said, "Bobby Doerr and not Ted Williams is the number 1 man of the Red Sox in my book."

When the Sox called up pitcher Mickey McDermott from Louisville in midseason 1949, he had a 6-4 record and had struck out 116 batters in 77 innings. On May 24th of that year in a game against St. Paul, he struck out 20 Saints, winning 3 to 1. He struck out the side in the 3rd, 5th, 6th, 8th and 9th innings and allowed only three hits. Some pitching on any level!

Speaking of 1949 and minor league pitchers, Ellis "Cot" Deal,who had been with the Red Sox in '47 and '48,pitched a complete 20 inning game for Columbus, topping his former Louisville mates 4 to 3.

Outfielder Bob Seeds, who played with 1933-34 Sox, hit four home runs in four consecutive innings (4-7) on May 6, 1938 while playing for Buffalo. The next day he hit three more. In two days he went 9 for 10, 7 home runs, 17 RBI-s.

Fans in Birmingham, Alabama will never forget the 1951 season Red Sox farm hand Jim Piersall had for their Barons. He hit .346 and fielded sensationally earning him his way to Boston.

Former Red Sox outfielder Joe Cicero led the Eastern League in base stealing for five consecutive years (1933-37) while with Scranton. He never returned to the Sox but did receive a brief trial with the Philadelphia A's in 1945 (12 games). He never stole a base in the big time.

In 1946 Sox farm hand, pitcher Tommy Fine, of Scranton in the Eastern League won 17 consecutive games. His season's record was 23-3. In 1947 he pitched in Boston, posting a 1-2 record, his only major league win.

One of Tommy Fine's pitching mates at Scranton during that 1946 season boasted a 13-4 record and established an Eastern League ERA record at 1.30. Who was he? Mel Parnell.

Ken "Hawk" Harrelson, Red Sox TV announcer, when a twenty year old and with the Eastern League Binghamton Club (his fourth year as a pro) hit 38 home runs and drove in 138 runs. That was in 1962.

In 1965 Pittsfield Red Sox pitcher Billy MacLeod won 18 consecutive games setting an Eastern League record, finished the season with an 18-0 mark and a 2.73 ERA.

In 1968 Carl Yastrzemski won the American League batting crown with an average of .301 and during that same season Pittsfield Red Sox outfielder Tony Torchia became the first man in the history of the Eastern League to win that league's batting crown with a sub .300 average when he hit .294. Pittsfield third sacker Carmen Fanzone placed second with a .270 mark. It must have been a pitcher's league. Tony later became a successful Sox minor league manager and his batting instructor is Sam Mele, another ex-Red Sox, who won the Eastern League batting crown with a .342 average while with Scranton in 1946. George Scott (1965 Pittsfield .319) and Jim Rice (1973 Bristol .317) were also Eastern League swat kings.

Pitcher Lou Lucier, a Sox farm hand at Canton, Ohio in 1941, led the Middle Atlantic League in pitching with a 23-5 record and a 1.51 ERA.

The Middle Atlantic League, one of the most successful Class C minor leagues sent the Red Sox some fine pitchers) Harry Dorish, Tex Hughson, Mel Parnell and Lou Lucier (from Canton, Ohio); Fritz Ostermueller (Wheeling, W.Va.); Mike Ryba and John Murphy (Scottdale, Pa.); and Denny Galehouse (Johnstown, Pa.).

In September 1974, Sox general manager Dick O'Connell was on a goodwill tour of Europe. He went to a Dutch Federation League game and saw a young pitcher named Wilhelmus Remmerswaal whom he signed. Five years later Remmerswaal was pitching for the Red Sox.

In his first spring in the U.S. Win Remmerswaal, the young Dutch pitcher, was asked if he thought he could make the majors. He didn't understand, saying he was here to pitch for Winston-Salem for a few years. He didn't know if he could make it to Boston. That was in 1974. Three years later the author became friendly with him and Win confided he felt he would soon be released. The author could see differently and told him so. It was only days later he was called to triple A Pawtucket where he pitched well in the International League playoffs. Seemed like a young man in a strange country needed a pat on the back. A few months later an envelope arrived in my mail box from Holland, a Christmas card which seemed to say it all. It was from my friend Win. Between the lines it said thanks when I needed it the most. Sitting in the bull pen before a game with pitcher Remmerswaal you may find him discussing anything from Holland's famous tulips to how Europeans sign autographs differently than we do. All business when he gets up to warm up: he is firing at full speed after only several pitches. Win made it to Boston in 1979.

During the spring training 1978 rookie pitcher Bobby Sprowl was wounded in the arm by a bullet while sleeping in bed. Seems the person in the next room of his motel accidentally discharged a firearm. It didn't seem to affect Sprowl as he pitched well for farm clubs at Bristol and Pawtucket and reached Fenway Park before the season ended.

Tris Speaker is number one in Red Sox history for streaks of consecutive hitting. Tris had four streaks of twenty consecutive games or more. Dom DiMaggio is second on the list with three streaks of twenty or more.

Former Red Sox personnel (players, managers, front office) Ike Boone, Joe McCarthy, Steve O'Neill, Herb Pennock, Dick Porter, Tommy Thomas, and George Toporcer are members of the International League Hall of Fame.

Following manager Chick Stahl's death during spring training in 1907, pitcher Cy Young was told by Boston president John I. Taylor to take charge of the team "until further notice." Cy replied that from the way he was going that spring, he felt he would have one of his best seasons and would not want the managers worries and felt he did not have the ability to manage. "I could not do justice to both positions," he said.

They called them "The Cardiac Kids" among other titles, that 1967 "Impossible Dream" Red Sox club. Few who lived through it will ever forget how they captured the hearts of millions as they climbed from ninth place in 1966 to win the American League Championship and came within a whisker of defeating the St. Louis Cardinals in the World Series. How many remember the honors that fell upon the stars of that club? Carl Yastrzemski won 21 major awards, pitcher Jim Lonborg won 5, manager Dick Williams won 5, general manager Dick O'Connell captured 3 and first baseman George Scott won 1.

Believe it or not, the slugging Red Sox shortstop Vern Stephens weighed only 98 pounds in his last year of high school, but by the time he reached his first year in pro ball (1938) he was up to 155 pounds.

Pitcher Bill Zuber picked up from the New York Yankees in 1946 made his first major league start against the Red Sox while he was pitching with the Cleveland Indians.

Sox outfielder Jackie Jensen performed as a football player in the Rose Bowl and the East-West Shrine football game and also appeared in the World Series and a major league All Star game.

Speaking of Jensen, while playing minor league ball for Oakland of the Pacific Coast League in 1949, Jensen hit .261 and got a sizeable bonus when called up by the New York Yankees. On that same Oakland club was a scrappy infielder who was a .290 hitter with a great double play record and was a throw in when Jensen went up to the majors; a little guy who even took a cut in pay from what the Oaks were paying him. Oh, yes, that throw-in was Billy Martin.

One time Red Sox catcher Sammy White was a basketball stand-out at the University of Washington.

In early June of his rookie year, Sammy White hit a grand slam home run off veteran pitcher Satchel Paige. As he rounded third base he dropped to his knees and crawled to home plate bowing his head reverently on the way.

Outfielder George Schmees, who threw a good left handed curve, served as the Red Sox batting practice pitcher on days when they were slated to face a southpaw.

Tris Speaker, who began his professional career as a pitcher, was switched to the outfield because of his hitting. When he first came up to the Red Sox the great pitcher Cy Young took a liking to him and would spend a half hour every day hitting Tris fungos to sharpen his fielding skills. Speaker credited Young for making him a great outfielder.

Once the Red Sox played a benefit game for the benefit of the widow of Boston sports writer Tim Murnane, and as a part of the activities Will Rogers put on a rope trick demonstration. When Rogers finished, Tris Speaker, a Texas cowboy himself, put on a better roping exhibition for the crowd than Rogers.

During the 1955 season relievers Ellis Kinder, Tom Hurd and Leo Kiely appeared in 104 of the team's first 135 games. Their combined record for this period was 16-8.

To get the Harry Agganis Memorial Foundation off on the right foot, Red Sox owner Tom Yawkey donated $25,000. Agganis was the first baseman of the Sox who died when his career was just getting started.

In the winter of 1955 Ted Williams made it clear that when the Red Sox were through with him he'd be through with baseball.

As director of the Red Sox minor league clubs, Billy Evans suggested the Sox buy the entire Louisville club so they could obtain shortstop Pee Wee Reese. Unfortunately, Reese got away and starred for years for the Brooklyn Dodgers.

Outfielder Jackie Jensen once suggested that major league players be given a week's vacation in addition to the All Star break.

Former Red Sox rookie (1955) Gordie Windhorn had never played a game of baseball when he went to a Giant's tryout school in Phoenix, Arizona and was signed to a contract. He had played softball, but track was his sport.

Although he wore number four on his uniform, the number six was big in Joe Cronin's life. There are 6 letters in each of his names — Joseph Edward Cronin. He was born in 1906, entered the majors with Pittsburgh in 1926, led the Red Sox to a pennant in 1946, voted into the Hall of Fame in 1956 and his boss had six letters in each of his names — Thomas Austin Yawkey.

Red Sox farm clubs at Bristol, Connecticut and Pawtucket, Rhode Island are known as the Brisox and the Pawsox, but perhaps the first to have a similar connotation was in the mid-fifties when the Sox had a farm club at San Jose, California. They were known as the Josox.

In 1956 pitcher Mel Parnell started his tenth season with the Red Sox, a new record for Bosox hurlers breaking the nine season record of Joe Dobson.

Red Sox third baseman Billy Klaus was not itching when Fenway fans saw him fishing inside his uniform jersey during a 1956 game. It seems a grounder hit by Detroit Tiger Bill Tuttle disappeared into Klaus's shirt when he went to field it.

The Red Sox farm club at Winston-Salem, N.C. plays it's home games at Ernie Shore Field, named for the former Red Sox pitching star.

Pitcher Tom Brewer turned down a Red Sox bonus offer so he could work his way up through the minor leagues. This was during the period when "Bonus Babies" had to go directly to the major league club signing them.

Pitcher "Sea Lion" Hall once said that the highlight of his career was when he relieved against the Detroit Tigers in the ninth inning and struck out Ty Cobb, Sam Crawford and Jim Delahanty in succession. Hall's real name was Carlos Clolo.

When Mel Parnell pitched a no hitter on July 14, 1956 against the Chicago White Sox, he was the oldest (34) pitcher to accomplish the feat in the lively ball era (since 1920).

When Ted Williams drew a $5000 fine for spitting in 1956 the story got more space in the Boston papers than the famed Brinks robbery of 1948.

In 1956 a restriction on beer sales was instituted at Fenway Park in an effort to curb rowdyism, but the real reason may have been to curb vicious personal attacks on Ted Williams by fans who had had a mite too much.

Yankee owner Dan Topping and Red Sox owner Tom Yawkey made an agreement to pay Mrs. Edward G. Barrow $1,000 a month for life. She was the widow of the late Yankee general manager and President and Sox manager. The idea was Yawkey's.

The late Red Sox owner Tom Yawkey was not only against interleague play but against promotional ideas to stimulate interest and attendance. He felt it was an admission that the product was not adequate. He felt you should spend money to improve your team.

The 1911 Red Sox trained at Redondo Beach near Los Angeles, California in a small ball park with a rough infield. After a week there, manager Patsy Donovan took the best players to San Francisco for some exhibition games. What they got were ten successive days of rain and ten postponements, but finally got to play the Fresno team at San Francisco, winning 6 to 4 behind Joe Wood and Ed Cicotte before 3,500. Finally the regulars were sent back to L.A. and the subs to San Francisco. They finally managed to play 17 games on the coast, losing only one.

Who will ever forget Gary Geiger tripling in what he thought was the winning run, only to find he had tied the game when he was tagged out as he headed for the dugout. There were no outs at the time.

> "I'd like to be a pitcher
> Amid the baseball fight,
> With Duffy Lewis out in left
> And Hooper out in right;
> With Speaker out in centerfield
> And with no fences near,
> I'd like to pitch upon that club
> For sixty cents a year."

One of the biggest batteries in the major leagues in the late fifties was six foot four inch catcher Haywood Sullivan and pitcher Frank Sullivan at six feet seven and one-half inches. Each weighed 215 pounds.

Rookie pitcher Russ Kemmerer thought he was going to get his release to the minors on July 18, 1954. Instead he got his first major league start from manager Lou Boudreau and proceeded to pitch a one hit 4 to 0 shut-out over the Baltimore Orioles in the first game of a doubleheader.

Doubleheaders, manangers claim, raise havoc with pitching rotations. Just imagine what manager Jimmy Collins faced in September 1905. He had doubleheaders to play on the 4th, 11th, 15th, 19th, 22nd, 23rd, 25th, 26th and 30th and closed out the season with another on October 7th.

It's unusual for sons of former major leaguers to reach the big time, but it is even more unusual for two of them to be brought up at the same time to the same club from the same team. It happened to the Bosox after the 1953 season with the players to report for 1954 spring training. Outfielder Allen Van Alstyne and catcher Guy Morton were acquired from Albany of the Eastern League. Allen's father, Clayton Van Alstyne, pitched for Washington in 1927-28 and Guy's father, Guy Morton, Sr., pitched for Cleveland from 1914 to 1924.

Del Wilber served as a pinch hitter for the 1953 Red Sox and on his first two tries he hit home runs both times on the first pitch made to him.

Tom Yawkey gave $10,000 to Childrens Hospital in Boston for a room at the hospital to be dedicated to former Red Sox second baseman Bobby Doerr. Doerr was held in high esteem by Yawkey for his exemplary character and sportsmanship.

When Red Sox pitcher George Susce, Jr. pitched a one hit 6 to 0 victory over Kansas City in early 1955, a K.C. coach must have had mixed emotions. You see, George Susce, Sr., a former major leaguer was one of the Athletics' coaches.

Ted Williams, in making a comeback from the service in 1955, hit for the cycle in his first three games. May 28, his first game against Washington, he singled in his first at bat for his only hit in four at bats. The next day he got a couple of hits—a double and a triple in four at bats. In his third appearance, first game of the Memorial Day doubleheader, he homered.

Pitcher Mel Parnell has said he expected to pitch that historic playoff game against

Cleveland in 1948. The usual routine was for the starting pitcher to refrain from outfield practice which he did and was as surprised as everyone when Denny Galehouse got the call.

Pitcher Dutch Leonard became a millionaire grape grower in California after his retirement from baseball. He laid the foundations for his fortune when pitching for the Red Sox as he would always send a good bit of salary home to his father.

The 1904 Boston Pilgrims used only 18 players during the entire season for an all-time major league record for fewest players used.

Slugger Jimmie Foxx established a record by hitting 30 or more home runs in 12 successive seasons — 1929 to 1940.

Who says the Red Sox need Fenway's left field wall to win games? In 1958 they defeated the Cleveland Indians 4 to 3, scoring the runs as follows: 1. a walk with the bases loaded. 2. two passed balls. 3. two sacrifice bunts. 4. a wild pitch.

In 1958 relief pitcher Murray Wall had won three games by May 26, equalling the total wins by Sox three top right-handed starters — Tom Brewer, Frank Sullivan and Willard Nixon.

Manager Bill Carrigan had a salary dispute with Sox owner Joe Lannin after two successive World Championships in 1915-16 and retired to his banking business in Lewiston, Maine, leaving infielder Jack Barry as the manager for 1917. Owner Bob Quinn lured him back as manager in 1927, but without good players Carrigan could not win and he returned to his bank in 1929.

In 1950 when it became apparent that Billy Goodman had a shot at the American League batting title, manager Steve O'Neill was faced with a problem. Goodman had been filling in for the injured Ted Williams in left field and upon the slugger's return where would Goodman play? In an unselfish move, third baseman John Pesky offered to step aside and allow Goodman to play third when Williams was ready to return. O'Neill's problem was solved.

Lolly Hopkins, long time Red Sox fan, took out a message on a sign board on a roof overlooking left field at Fenway Park in 1950. It said "Let's Go Sox." Commuting from her home in Providence, Rhode Island, she was for years a familiar figure at Fenway with her megaphone and candy bars she tossed on the field as rewards for individual achievements.

In 1959 rookie pitcher Jerry Casale performed a feat achieved by few rookies when he completed a cycle of having defeated each rival team.

The 1932 Red Sox finished 64 games out of first place, the 1927 team 59 behind, the 1930 club was 50 off the pace and the 1929 edition 48 behind.

In 1957 the Washington Senators swept a three game series from the Red Sox in mid-August in a humiliating fashion as the three winning pitchers were Red Sox cast-offs. It's possible that no club was beaten in such a manner. The three who were traded to the Senators were Chuck Stobbs, Russ Kemmerer and Truman Clevenger.

Ted Williams with the Red Sox in 1939 drew 107 walks for the best total of any player in his first major league season up until that time.

In 1951 when Bobby Doerr retired he had played in 1,865 games, more than any Red Sox at that time. He had a lifetime batting average of .289. Eight times he was voted an all-star. In six seasons he batted in over 100 runs, three times he batted over .300 and was a steady dependable, often sensational second baseman. He was a humble, soft spoken man who made more than 2000 hits, two of which cost Cleveland's Bob Feller no hitters. Periodic back problems caused his retirement.

In 1902 pitcher Cy Young, at the age of 35, completed 41 of 43 starts, winning 32 while losing 11.

The 1912 Red Sox had the best road record of any Boston team — 48 wins and 27 losses for a .640 percentage. Their home record of 57 and 20 wasn't bad either. They won 14 straight games over New York and 10 straight against St. Louis. The 19 and 2 advantage in a season series over New York was the worst series disadvantage the Yankees ever had. This was the second best season series advantage by a Red Sox team. The 20 to 2 advantage over the Washington Nationals in 1904 was their best ever.

While dogs, cats and pheasants have found ways to get free admission into Fenway and by the way delay games, who can ever forget the surprise of St. Louis pitcher Ellis Kinder in 1947 when a low flying bird dropped a smelt on the mound. Philadelphia's Hal Peck knocked down a pigeon on a return throw from the outfield and there were reports of Ted Williams with a shot gun stalking the same birds. A Detroit batter knocked one of these feathered friends out of the sky in 1974 with a foul fly and Billy Hunter of St. Louis did the same in batting practice. I wonder why so many visiting players were part of the act?

If Mel Parnell had not wild pitched with the bases loaded against Washington, allowing the Senators to gain a 2 to 1 victory with only three games left in 1949, might the Sox have been pennant winners?

Wind currents around Fenway Park have been a big factor in games won or lost and making outfielders look foolish. Fred Lynn noticed the change when the new scoreboard in centerfield was erected and had to adjust his play accordingly.

In October of the 1972 season Carl Yastrzemski hit what should have been a triple but Luis Aparicio, the preceeding runner, fell rounding third base and Yaz was caught between second and third. The game at Detroit (the eventual pennant winner) resulted in a 4 to 1 Tiger win. Had the Sox won they would have had a game 1 1/2 lead with two games left to play.

Tie games seldom find their way into baseball history, but on July 14, 1916 the Sox engaged the St. Louis Browns in a 17 inning 0-0 contest, at Fenway Park, the Sox longest. The shortest April 14, 1925, 0 to 0, five innings with Washington at Fenway Park.

In the 1935 opening game at New York, Yankee catching great Bill Dickey dropped a third strike, and while he was throwing out the runner at first, Billy Werber scampered home with the winning run in a Sox 1 to 0 victory.

In 1919 former Red Sox pitcher Dutch Leonard, by then with Detroit, had a yearning to pitch to his old teammate Babe Ruth, and with two out and a four run lead, walked a batter to get at "The Babe". You guessed it, a home run on the first pitch. Earlier "The Babe" had two doubles.

Ted Williams in a fit of anger once tossed his bat up on the screen at Fenway, which runs from the back stop up to the roof behind home plate, and Texas Ranger pitcher Len Barker in 1978 pitched a baseball up there.

Jim Rice is so strong he once held up on a swing only to have the bat break off in his hands. A line drive he hit to left once was caught, but it knocked the fielder backwards.

Pitcher Emmett O'Neill, a wartime hurler, walked ten Detroit Tigers one afternoon at Fenway Park, but won the game 7 to 1.

In 1978 Butch Hobson's pop up to second was dropped and thrown around the infield while Hobson circled the bases to score against the Cleveland Indians.

First baseman Jake Jones arrived from Chicago in a 1947 trade for Rudy York to win the first game of a twin bill from his former teammates, with a home run and in the ninth inning of the second game hit a two out grand slam homer for another Red Sox victory.

In 1949 John Pesky doubled with the bases loaded but was awarded a triple when it was ruled Cleveland outfielder Dale Mitchell threw his glove at the ball, a play not often seen in the big time.

In 1943 at Yankee Stadium, the Yankees swept the Sox in a four game series, winning by one run in each contest and in three of the games the winner came in the last of the ninth.

St. Louis Browns shortstop Billy Hunter once asked Sox outfielder Jim Piersall to adjust the second base bag, and as Piersall did so Hunter, who had the ball, tagged him out.

Two Red Sox pitchers, Fritz Ostermueller and Jim Wilson, didn't like to see Detroit's Hank Greenberg come to bat. Each had been hit in the face by line drives hit by him.

A strange and seldom seen play occurred in the 1915 World Series when Philadelphia Phillies first baseman Milt Stock was refused first base when hit by a George Foster pitch because he did not try hard enough to get out of the way.

The 1902 Pilgrims made 10 hits in a row, the 1929 Red Sox nine and the 1970 Sox eight.

Tom Oliver hit safely in the first 16 games of 1930, Elmer Smith in the first 18 of 1922 and Eddie Bressoud the first 20 of 1964.

The Sox won a 13 to 12 thriller from Washington at Fenway Park in 1961 as Senator Willie Tasby hit a grand slam home run in the top of the ninth, only to have the Sox Jim Pagliaroni duplicate the feat in the last of the ninth.

When Earl Wilson tossed his 2 to 0 no hitter over California in 1962 it was his home run that won the game for Boston. In the 1967 World Series another Red Sox pitcher showed his batting prowess. Jose Santiago drove a Bob Gibson pitch out of the park but the Cardinals won 2 to 1.

Just for the record, Roger Maris hit his 61st home run in 1961 off Boston Tracy Stallard in Yankee Stadium. It was good for a 1 to 0 Yankee win.

Three Red Sox have homered on their first official at bat in the majors — Lefty LeFebve, Eddie Pellagrini, and Bob Tillman.

Dick Stuart, known for his long home runs, hit an unusual inside-the-park one in 1963. It hit the Fenway wall, bounded off and hit Cleveland outfielder Vic Davalillo's head before bounding into the left field corner as Stuart ran around the bases.

Remember Fred "Fireball" Wenz? Once, in 1969, he gave up seven home runs in eleven innings. Cal McLish of Cleveland (May 22, 1957) allowed four of five Red Sox he faced to hit home runs on just 16 pitches.

Years ago if a player hit a home run with a runner or runners on base who represented the winning run the game ended when the game winner scored and the batter did not get credit for the homer. It happened to Harry Hooper in 1911.

Speaking of 1911, American League president Ban Johnson put into effect a new rule that year to speed up games that pitchers would not be allowed warm-up pitches before innings. Boston pitcher Ed Karger, while waiting for centerfielder Tris Speaker to take his position, lobbed a warm-up pitch to catcher Les Nunamaker which Philadelphia batter Stuffy McInnis hit into centerfield, and since no one chased the ball McInnis took off and rounded the bases unchallenged. The home run stood.

What Red Sox player appeared in official capacity at both Fenway Park and Braves Field on the same day? — Harry Agganis. He hit a home run at Fenway to win a game for the Sox and on the same day in 1954 received his degree from Boston University at graduation in Braves Field.

It was May 30, 1938 when a Yankee Stadium crowd of 80,000 plus jammed the Bronx ball park to see the New Yorkers and Bostonians do battle and battle they did. In the first of two games Lefty Grove was on the mound for Sox and very shortly in the shower replaced by Archie McKain who was greeted with two singles on his first two pitches. The next Yank batter was Jake Powell who took a pitch near his head. The next pitch hit him and Jake started out to the mound, only to be intercepted by

Sox shortstop Joe Cronin, both benches emptied and the fight was broken up with the two combatants ejected only to resume the warfare under the stands.

The 1933 Sox on their way north from spring training were involved in a serious train wreck in New Jersey. The first time a major league team had ever been in such a thing. Pitcher Bob Kline was the only Bosox hurt (a minor back problem), luckily for the club. I guess you could say they really trained that spring.

Before Bob Fothergill was traded to the Red Sox he played for Detroit. After a home run at Fenway Park one day he delighted the rival Sox fans by doing a graceful front flip without touching his hands to the ground and landed on the plate with both feet.

"Suitcase" Bob Seeds, a fairly decent outfielder, gained his nickname because of the large size of his feet. In 1934 he and his wife purchased the Amarillo club of the Class D Texas-Arizona League. While he was off playing, she successfuly ran the team.

Over the years the Sox have had many players with bad tempers (Grove, Werber, Williams) but one of the worst was pitcher Wes Ferrell. He once crushed his expensive watch with the heel of his foot, he tore up uniforms, gloves and caps, threw baseballs out of ball parks, knocked his head against walls, and turned over lockers, but he also won ball games with his arm and bat.

Catcher Moe Berg was a Phi Beta Kappa graduate of Princeton, a Rhodes Scholar, a lawyer, an avid reader of newspapers, could speak a number of languages and read many more.

When the Red Sox won the American League pennant in 1946 one of the radio announcers was former slugger Jimmie Foxx.

Speak of statisticians, and you must admire the job done by the present Red Sox statistician Dick Bresciani, as all those little tid bits you read in your daily newspaper and hear during radio or TV broadcasts come from him. Certainly Red Sox followers are among the best informed. To sit with Dick during a game is a treat as he is surrounded by all types of record books and books of his own making where every move on the field is recorded. He constantly keeps the press informed of the latest stats. A truly remarkable job well done.

Down on the farm at Pawtucket is another statistician who does an excellent job — Bill George. Anyone who has seen Bill's year-ending stat book would be truly amazed. Bill is also the official scorer in Pawtucket and while he doesn't make the road trips, he spends a lot of his own time compiling the stats of the Pawsox. Bill, by the way, is an attorney and does the Pawtucket job in addition to his own work. Care to guess which he enjoys the most?

If you live close enough and want a very enjoyable day or evening, drop into McCoy Stadium (just off the thruway) in Pawtucket, Rhode Island and see the Red Sox top farm hands in action. McCoy is a fine, clean ball park with excellent parking and seating. As you enter the stands you will wind your way past those beautiful murals of Pawsox who have gone on to Boston to play. Take time to admire them. As you enter you may find yourself being greeted by a congenial gentleman, owner Ben

Mondor. Ben is a great baseball man who has as his primary mission making sure his fans are happy and enjoying themselves. Once you have gone you are sure to return. Ben is assisted by an equally fine front office staff of General Manager Mike Tamburro and Vice President Chet Nichols (remember when he pitched in Boston?). The Pawtucket picture would not be complete without a tip of the hat to their fine public address announcer Mike Pappas.

A trip into the Connecticut countryside to Bristol, nestled among gently rolling hills in the central section of the state, will bring you to Muzzy Field where the Bristol Red Sox play. Here in a picturesque ball field you will enjoy the hospitality of Charlie Eshbach and his staff while seeing some more of the Sox farm hands battling their way to Fenway. A very worthwhile visit to see the excellent baseball played in the double A Eastern League.

The 1938 Red Sox were led by slugging Jimmie Foxx who cracked 50 home runs, but long forgotten is his sinus which plagued him for years. Leading the league in batting (.349) he won game after game for the Red Sox, while playing with this handicap.

1938 also led to the rejuvenation of the farm system which included such future stars as Dave Ferriss, Tex Hughson, John Pesky, Earl Johnson, Ted Williams and Mickey Harris. Billy Evans had a big hand in developing this sytem. He resigned in 1940 to become general manager of the pro football Cleveland Rams.

Whistling Jake Wade, a Sox pitcher of the late 30's had two claims to fame. He was the best whistler in baseball and while with Detroit in 1935 he defeated Cleveland ace Johnny Allen who had won 15 straight games.

The story goes that when rookie Ted Williams arrived at his first spring training camp, he was told what a great hitter Jimmie Foxx was and replied, "Wait until Foxx sees me hit." Actually, Williams had a lot of respect for Foxx and spent hours with him talking baseball.

Bill Daley operated the left field scoreboard at Fenway Park in the late 30's and early 40's. As it is today, it was connected to the press box by telephone, a fact which Ted Williams used to take advantage of by talking with Daley to get the up-to-the-minute news from around the baseball world.

Ted Williams, Navy doctors discovered, had eyes that occur six times in 100,000 cases. His depth perception was the sharpest they had ever seen. The coordination of eyes and muscles were the keys to Williams' success as a batter.

Not only was Tex Hughson a great pitcher, he was also tops at playing pin ball machines. He and Lefty Grove, in addition to expertise on the mound, shared a common love for cigars, and I am not sure why that is put in this book, except to please cigar smoking pin ball machine addicts.

It has been estimated that Tom Yawkey spent better than four million dollars, in addition to thousands, to purchase star players, develop a farm system and suffered numerous disappointments before a championship flag was raised at Fenway Park in 1946.

When Ted Williams, after a fielding mishap, tossed the ball out of the Atlanta ball park, it not only went over the right field fence, it went through a nearby store's plate glass window.

In a game against the New York Yankees one day, a pitching change was in order and Yankee lefty Tommy Byrne was brought in to face Ted Williams. As Byrne was warming up, the next two Red Sox batters, Williams and Mickey Vernon, were looking at his pitches much to his displeasure. His next pitch came right at the on-deck area which caused the Sox to duck and angered Williams so that he hit one right back through the middle when he got up.

Pitcher Wes Ferrell had a terrible spring training in 1935 but kept telling manager Cronin he wanted to pitch Opening Day against the Yankees. He couldn't get anyone out in the South, but beat the New Yorkers and Lefty Gomez 1 to 0 in the opener, justifying Cronin's faith in him.

Babe Ruth and Joe Wood may well have been the only players to play in one World Series as pitchers and another as outfielders.

"Can I throw harder than Joe Wood? Listen , my friend, there's no man alive who can throw harder than Smokey Joe Wood." This quote is from a 1912 interview with Hall of Fame pitcher Walter Johnson.

The 1979 Red Sox often had three MVP's batting in order in their line-up — Fred Lynn, Jim Rice and Carl Yastrzemski. What other team can make that claim?

We all know how our modern day Red Sox uniforms look, but how many remember the early years when they had little collars, often worn turned up, and the shirts were laced up at the top instead of zippered as they are today? It was also common in those early days that the shoes were higher than those of today.

There was a period when the front of the uniform bore a big red sock, or replica thereof, with the word Boston written on it.

American League players so admired the great pitcher Cy Young that in 1908 they presented him with a giant loving cup.

Young Ted Williams seemed to always have a bat in his possession. One evening he decided, while in his hotel room, to take a few practice swings with some new bats. What happened? No, he didn't break the mirror but he did a job on the bed upon which his roommate Charlie Wagner was resting.

Pitcher Jim Lonborg, hero of the 1967 Red Sox, pitched for an amateur team in Scituate, Massachusetts in the summer of 1979 after his release by the Philadelphia Phillies.

First baseman George Scott, after much griping and becoming the number one resident of manager Zimmer's dog house, was traded in June 1979 by the Sox to the Kansas City Royals. By late August he was released by K.C.

During the 1915 season the Detroit Tigers appeared to have a jinx on the Red Sox. When the team arrived in Detroit, manager Bill Carrigan asked his pitching staff for a volunteer to break the jinx. Right-hander Carl Mays volunteered, saying if he didn't win he would walk back to Boston. The Sox won 2 to 1 and Mays was able to ride home. Oh, yes, it was Mays' ninth inning base hit that won the game. I guess he was inspired.

A number of players have played with both the Boston Americans and Boston Nationals. Among them are: Cy Young, Parson Lewis, Babe Ruth, Stuffy McInnis, Danny MacFayden, Nig Cuppy, Jimmy Collins, Buck Freeman, Chick Stahl, Bill Dineen, Jake Volz, Frank Barberich, Dave Shean, Fred Lake, Joe Wilhoit, Rabbit Warstler, Bucky Walters, Roy Johnson, Al Simmons, Babe Dahlgren, Wes Ferrell, Woody Rich, Red Barrett, Andy Karl, Murray Wall, Chet Nichols, Gene Conley, and Jim Wilson.

Pitcher Ed "Parson" Lewis, after his baseball days were over, became president of the University of New Hampshire and a close friend of poet Robert Frost.

At the end of the 1908 season, Cy Young gave a dinner for his Red Sox teammates in the Student's Spa of the Putnam House of Boston. Unknown to Cy at the time, it was to be his last season in Boston, as he was soon to be traded to Cleveland. Each course of the meal and item on the menu was labeled after a particular player on the team.

It has been said one of the weaknesses of the 1951 Red Sox was too many good pitchers. How come you say? Good hurlers require regular work to stay that way and the Sox staff lost effectiveness, due to prolonged inactivity.

Look at the credentials of these rookie pitchers the 1952 Red Sox took to Sarasota with them: Jim Atkins 18-9, Ralph Brickner 15-9, Ike Delock 20-4, Ben Flowers 17-8 and Hershell Freeman 12-5. Quite a crop, but only Delock amounted to anything in the big time.

Billy Goodman, who won the 1950 American League batting championship while batting .354, really had no regular position and earned the title "one man bench".

The 1949 Red Sox led the American League in batting by a wide margin, yet left 1284 men on base, more than any other team. Doesn't seem possible, does it?

A quality that made John Pesky a highly respected player was his spirit. He was great at lifting a team's spirits, a fighter and a dangerous batter.

Outfielder John Lazor batted .310 for the 1945 Red Sox, a percentage high enough to win the league batting championship that year, but he failed to qualify because of the rule which required 400 at bats. He had only 335.

Late in 1940 pitcher Alex Mustaikis was sent to the Louisville Club for one John Barrett, an outfielder. Alex, upset at the move claimed he was mishandled and appealed to baseball czar Judge Landis. Landis ruled that the deal would stand. Actually the deal was completed with cash as Mustaikis' claim was based on the failure of the San Diego club, to which he was optioned by the Sox earlier in the year, to file official papers with Landis within the prescribed period.

Landis had another complaining Red Sox player in early 1941 when pitcher Ted Olson, who appeared briefly in 3 seasons with the Sox 1936-38, quit the Baltimore club in 1940 saying he did not want to report there claiming he had not been given a fair trial by the Red Sox. Landis did not agree and the deal stood.

Pitcher Jack Wilson started his career as an infielder in the Pacific Coast League appearing with Hollywood in 1930 and San Francisco in 1931 and 1932 before being converted to a pitcher at Portland in 1933.

In April of 1941 former Red Sox pitcher Joe Wood enjoyed a collegiate baseball game that is often referred to as the "Battle of the Woods". Smokey Joe was coaching at Yale and had his son Joe, Jr. as a pitcher. His other two sons, Steve and Bob were playing for Colgate and when the two schools met it was Joe, Jr. vs Steve with Bob playing first for Colgate. Yale won with Joe giving up 10 hits and Steve lasting seven innings. Bob went 1 for 4. Joe, Jr. later also pitched for the Red Sox.

Former Red Sox bat boy Freddy Stack was the public address announcer at Fenway Park in 1941, and a 19 year-old Mississippi State College pitcher threw batting practice for the Red Sox in September of that year — his name: Dave Ferriss.

The news out of New Haven, Connecticut was all good for the Wood family on June 17, 1941. The Yale alumni rallied to support baseball coach smokey Joe whose job was in jeopardy because of the possible need to cut the University coaching staff and Joe, Jr. was pitching and defeating Harvard 1 to 0 while striking out 13, walking 2 and allowing only 2 hits.

The son of another Red Sox pitching great (Lefty Grove) Bob Grove, Jr. was pitching for the Blolin, New Hampshire Red Sox of the Twin State League in 1941.

Future Red Sox third baseman Rip Russell was named the Texas League MVP in 1941. The same season found future shortstop Johnny Pesky the American Association MVP. Meanwhile the Pacific Coast League was naming pitcher Yank Terry their MVP. By the way, Terry was noted for making faces at the hitters to draw laughs, a trick which didn't seem to work for him in the majors. Anyway it was a great minor league year for future Red Sox.

Ted Williams not only took aim on Fenway Park's fences with his bat, but in 1941 "Two Gun Ted" did a one man Western when he shot out the scoreboard lights in a target practice drill of his own.

In June, 1913 with the score tied 5 to 5 in the 15th inning in a game with Cleveland, three Indians (Naps in those days) stole home in succession against Dutch Leonard. Perhaps the biggest Boston theft before the famous Brinks heist.

In June, 1911 at the Huntington Ave. Grounds, pitcher Smokey Joe Wood walked into a game against Chicago in the ninth inning, with Boston leading 5 to 4 and fanned pinch hitters Pat Dougherty, Fred Payne and Jimmy Block. Ed Karger was the Boston starter.

The foul strike rule was adopted by the American League in 1903.

Old timers say pitcher Fritz Ostermueller was never the same after a 1933 operation. This was prior to his coming to the Sox from the Cardinal system.

A master of many languages, catcher Moe Berg once suprised a group of touring Japanese who were attending a game at Fenway by autographing a baseball for them in Japanese.

Tom Daly, former Red Sox coach, once hit a home run before King George V while a member of the Chicago White Sox. It was said, "the King applauded roundly and then took time out for tea."

Lefty Grove made a turkey of many a batter but it is little remembered that he spent his winters hunting wild turkeys, which he stuffed with his special chestnut dressing.

Infielder Marv Owen had such large hands he could hold seven baseballs in one hand at a time.

Catcher Birdie Tebbetts was the number two catcher when he joined the Detroit Tigers. Who was number one? Rudy York. Later, of course, both played for the Sox, York as a first baseman.

Eldon Auker was a submarine ball pitcher.

Walter Johnson once said of Billy Rogell he was the equal of any shortstop in the league.

Pitcher Red Ruffing wanted to be an outfielder until a coal mine accident cost him a couple of toes. He was a rarity — a hitting pitcher who once held out for a larger bonus for his pinch hitting.

Outfielder Mel Almada was one of the few Mexicans to gain major league fame.

Oscar Melillo made a famous remark after hitting a triple to left center at Fenway. "It must be a lively ball if a squirt like me can hit a wall."

Outfielder Carl Reynolds may have been the first Nettles to play at Fenway. That was his middle name. He also was noted for his speed and his nickname, Sheeps.

Pitcher Bob Klinger was a cousin of Chicago Cub star Charlie Hollocher. Carlton Fisk is the brother-in-law of Rick Miller, formerly of the Sox, now with California and infielder Don Gutteridge was a cousin of Ray Mueller, a catcher with the Boston Bees. Lou Finney's brother Hal caught for the Pirates.

Infielder "Rabbit" Warstler got his nickname because he was only about five and a half feet tall.

Pitcher Danny MacFayden once struck out Babe Ruth, Lou Gehrig and Tony Lazzeri with the bases loaded.

The famous relief pitcher "Milkman Jim" Turner had a trial with the 1924 Red Sox but was cut loose, a tragic mistake.

Skeeter Newsome once switched from right to left handed hitting and in his first attempt went five for six. I wonder why he switched back?

Catcher Charlie Berry's father also played professional baseball for one year, 1884.

Infielder Bill Cissell was in the U.S. Army Cavalry in 1924 and 1925.

Outfielder Dom Dallessandro started out as a southpaw pitcher in the minors and once hurled a no hit game.

Do you think that Butch Hobson was the first University of Alabama football hero to play for the Red Sox? Wrong, pitcher Lee Rogers, a pitcher for the 1938 Red Sox, was a baseball and football star at Alabama.

While pitcher Wes Ferrell was known to take punches at water bottles, dugout walls and clubhouse lockers, his brother, catcher Rick, once contemplated a professional boxing career before turning to baseball.

Billy Werber tells how Wes Ferrell, mad at himself after a poor pitcher performance, returned to the dugout, got a pair of scissors and proceeded to cut his glove into little pieces.

In 1920 catcher Wally Schang handled eight assists in one game.

Infielder Odell Hale was of Indian descent and often called "Chief".

Pitcher Bill Zuber, although born in Iowa, could not speak English until 1931, five years before he reached the majors. His parents were members of a religious sect that had no contact with the outside world.

Pitcher Joe Cascarella might have made it big as a professional singer had he not turned to baseball. Wonder if he entertained while in the showers?

Pitcher Paul Trout was nicknamed Dizzy because of his speed and talkativeness.

The 1947 Red Sox had a string of games in July where 8 of 10 were decided by one run. At St. Louis July 18 lost 9 to 8, July 19 won 1 to 0, July 20 (two games) lost 3 to 4 and 6 to 7. Chicago at Boston July 22 won 3 to 2, July 23 won 8 to 7, July 24 won 8 to 2; St. Louis at Boston July 25 won 7 to 6, July 26 won 12 to 1, July 27 won 4 to 3. (Won 8, lost 2).

Dom DiMaggio was once quoted as saying if Ted Williams had played with the New York Yankees he would have broken Babe Ruth's home run record. A Boston sports writer later mentioned this to Yankee manager Joe McCarthy who replied, "Lou Gehrig didn't!"

Babe Ruth once said a player should retire when all the base lines appear to run uphill.

When Ted Williams first joined the Sox they sent him back to Minneapolis after a spring trial. As he left, the three regular outfielders kidded him by saying "Good-bye busher." Williams yelled back at them "I'll be back soon and I'll make more money than all three of you together." He did too.

Outfielder Smead Jolley was sent in to play left field at Fenway one day and when a deep fly was hit in his direction he went back for it and encountered "Duffy's Cliff", a sloping little hill, and fell flat on his face, the hit going for a triple. Upon returning to the dugout he was asked what happened. "Us outfielders have enough trouble without you putting trenches out there." "Don't worry," his manager said, "that's what our coaches are for, they will teach you how to play the cliff." For two weeks they worked with Jolley and he showed great improvement. Finally back in the lineup all went well for seven innings when another high fly ball headed his way. A wind was blowing in and Smead had to come down from the cliff for the ball which the wind had caught. Again he fell down — another triple. Upon his return to the dugout he was asked what his excuse was this time. "Great coaches we have; for two weeks they teach me how to go up that hill, but not one had the sense to tell me how to come down," Jolley replied.

One of the strangest quirks of all Red Sox players belonged to Dib Williams. For some reason he could not get off third base on a fly ball. Often pinch runners were put in for him if a run was needed.

Pitcher Cy Young and catcher Lou Criger paired together for 11 seasons and some 500 games as a battery. They began together in 1897 with Cleveland in the old National League, moved to St. Louis for two years and then on to Boston for eight years.

A DECADE OF RED SOX LEADERS

Annual averages have become an important part of baseball and are an integral factor in retaining fan interest and creating a continuing interest. The appeal of statistics is very much a part of the Red Sox picture and in this section are the Red Sox batting and pitching leaders in various major categories for the past ten years. For a complete list dating back to 1901, it is recommended that you consult "This Date In Boston Red Sox History". It is hoped you will find some memory joggers here.

BATTING

Batting Average

1970	Carl Yastrzemski	.329
1971	Reggie Smith	.283
1972	Carlton Fisk	.293
1973	Reggie Smith	.303
1974	Carl Yastrzemski	.301
1975	Fred Lynn	.331
1976	Fred Lynn	.314
1977	Jim Rice	.320
1978	Jim Rice	.315
1979	Fred Lynn	.333

Slugging Average

Carl Yastrzemski	.592
Reggie Smith	.489
Carlton Fisk	.538
Reggie Smith	.515
Carl Yastrzemski	.445
Fred Lynn	.566
Jim Rice	.482
Jim Rice	.593
Jim Rice	.600
Fred Lynn	.637

At Bats

1970	Mike Andrews	589
1971	Reggie Smith	618
1972	Tommy Harper	556
1973	Tommy Harper	566
1974	Carl Yastrzemski	515
1975	Rick Burleson	580
1976	Jim Rice	581
1977	Rick Burleson	663
1978	Jim Rice	677
1979	Rick Burleson	627

Hits

Carl Yastrzemski	186
Reggie Smith	175
Tommy Harper	141
Carl Yastrzemski	160
Carl Yastrzemski	155
Fred Lynn	175
Jim Rice	164
Jim Rice	206
Jim Rice	213
Jim Rice	201

Singles

1970	Carl Yastrzemski	117
1971	Reggie Smith	110
1972	Doug Griffin	107
1973	Luis Aparicio	117
1974	Carl Yastrzemski	113
1975	Jim Rice	119
1976	Rick Burleson	122
1977	Rick Burleson	148
1978	Jerry Remy	130
1979	Rick Burleson	132

Doubles

Reggie Smith	32
Reggie Smith	33
Tommy Harper	29
C. Yastrzemski, O. Cepeda	25
Carl Yastrzemski	25
Fred Lynn	47
Dwight Evans	34
Rick Burleson	36
Carlton Fisk	39
Fred Lynn	42

Triples

1970	Reggie Smith	7
1971	John Kennedy	5
1972	Carlton Fisk	9
1973	Rick Miller	7
1974	Dwight Evans	8
1975	Fred Lynn	7
1976	F. Lynn, J. Rice	8
1977	Jim Rice	15
1978	Jim Rice	15
1979	Butch Hobson	7

Home Runs

Carl Yastrzemski	40
Reggie Smith	30
Carlton Fisk	22
Carlton Fisk	26
R. Petrocelli, C. Yastrzemski	15
Jim Rice	22
Jim Rice	25
Jim Rice	39
Jim Rice	46
F. Lynn, J. Rice	39

A Decade of Red Sox Leaders — Batting (continued)

Research done by the author has uncovered evidence that outfielder Tris Speaker hit 10 home runs in 1912. This has been accepted by reliable sources and is now being used in The Sporting News books and the MacMillan Encyclopedia. It gave Speaker a tie for the American League leadership in home runs with Philadelphia's Franklin Baker.

RBI
1970	Tony Conigliaro	116
1971	Reggie Smith	96
1972	Rico Petrocelli	75
1973	Carl Yastrzemski	95
1974	Carl Yastrzemski	79
1975	Fred Lynn	105
1976	Carl Yastrzemski	102
1977	Jim Rice	114
1978	Jim Rice	139
1979	Jim Rice	130

Walks
Carl Yastrzemski	128
Carl Yastrzemski	105
Rico Petrocelli	78
Carl Yastrzemski	105
Carl Yastrzemski	104
Carl Yastrzemski	87
Carl Yastrzemski	80
Carlton Fisk	75
Carl Yastrzemski	76
Fred Lynn	82

Runs Scored
1970	Carl Yastrzemski	125
1971	Reggie Smith	85
1972	Tommy Harper	92
1973	Tommy Harper	92
1974	Carl Yastrzemski	93
1975	Fred Lynn	103
1976	C. Fisk, F. Lynn	76
1977	Carlton Fisk	106
1978	Jim Rice	121
1979	Jim Rice	117

Stolen Bases
Carl Yastrzemski	23
D. Griffin, R. Smith	11
Tommy Harper	25
Tommy Harper	54
Tommy Harper	28
F. Lynn, J. Rice	10
R. Burleson, F. Lynn	14
Rick Burleson	13
Jerry Remy	30
Jerry Remy	14

PITCHING

Wins
1970	Ray Culp	17-14
1971	Sonny Siebert	16-10
1972	Marty Pattin	17-13
1973	Luis Tiant	20-13
1974	Luis Tiant	22-13
1975	Rick Wise	19-12
1976	Luis Tiant	21-12
1977	Bill Campbell	13-9
1978	Dennis Eckersley	20-8
1979	Dennis Eckersley	17-10

Games Appeared In
Sparky Lyle	63
Bob Bolin	52
Bill Lee	47
Bob Bolin	39
Diego Segui	58
Bill Lee	41
Jim Willoughby	54
Bill Campbell	69
Bob Stanley	52
Dick Drago	53

A Decade of Red Sox Leaders — Pitching (continued)

ERA

1970	Ray Culp	3.04
1971	Sonny Siebert	2.91
1972	Luis Tiant	1.91
1973	Bill Lee	2.75
1974	Luis Tiant	2.92
1975	B. Lee, R. Wise	3.95
1976	Luis Tiant	3.06
1977	Ferguson Jenkins	3.68
1978	Dennis Eckersley	2.99
1979	Dennis Eckersley	2.99

Innings Pitched

Ray Culp	251
Ray Culp	242
Marty Pattin	253
Bill Lee	285
Luis Tiant	311
B. Lee, L. Tiant	260
Luis Tiant	279
Ferguson Jenkins	193
Dennis Eckersley	268
Mike Torrez	253-1/3

Games Started

1970	Gary Peters	34
1971	Ray Culp	32
1972	Marty Pattin	35
1973	Luis Tiant	35
1974	Luis Tiant	38
1975	R. Wise, L. Tiant	35
1976	Luis Tiant	38
1977	Luis Tiant	32
1978	Mike Torrez	36
1979	Mike Torrez	36

Complete Games

Ray Culp	15
R. Culp, S. Siebert	12
Marty Pattin	13
Luis Tiant	23
Luis Tiant	25
Luis Tiant	18
Luis Tiant	19
Ferguson Jenkins	11
Dennis Eckersley	16
Dennis Eckersley	17

Strike Outs

1970	Ray Culp	197
1971	Ray Culp	151
1972	Marty Pattin	168
1973	Luis Tiant	206
1974	Luis Tiant	176
1975	Luis Tiant	142
1976	Ferguson Jenkins	142
1977	Luis Tiant	124
1978	Dennis Eckersley	162
1979	Dennis Eckersley	150

Walks

Ray Culp	91
Gary Peters	70
M. Pattin, L. Tiant	65
John Curtis	83
Luis Tiant	82
Roger Moret	76
Luis Tiant	64
Bill Campbell	60
Mike Torrez	99
Mike Torrez	121

Shutouts

1970	Gary Peters	4
1971	Sonny Siebert	4
1972	Luis Tiant	6
1973	John Curtis	4
1974	Luis Tiant	7
1975	Bill Lee	4
1976	Rick Wise	4
1977	Luis Tiant	3
1978	Luis Tiant	5
1979	Bob Stanley	4

Hits Allowed

Gary Peters	221
Gary Peters	241
Marty Pattin	232
Bill Lee	275
Bill Lee	320
Bill Lee	274
Luis Tiant	274
Reggie Cleveland	211
Mike Torrez	272
Mike Torrez	254

BOSTON RED SOX ALL TIME FIELDING LEADERS

Pos.	Player	Yr.	G	PO	A	E	Ave.
1B	Stuffy McInnis	1921	152	1549	102	1	.999
2B	Bob Doerr	1948	138	366	430	6	.993
SS	Vern Stephens	1950	146	258	431	13	.981
	Rico Petrocelli	1969	153	269	466	14	.981
	Rick Burleson	1978	144	285	482	15	.981
3B	Grady Hatton	1955	111	97	225	8	.976
	Rico Petrocelli	1971	156	118	334	11	.976
OF	Ken Harrelson	1968	132	241	8	0	1.000
	Carl Yastrzemski	1977	140	287	16	0	1.000
C	Mike Ryan	1966	114	685	50	6	.992
P	Jack Russell	1929	35	15	69	0	1.000
	Dennis Eckersley	1978	35	19	29	0	1.000

RED SOX PLAYERS APPEARING IN THE 1978 PLAYOFF

Bob Bailey - PH
Jack Brohamer - 3B
Rick Burleson - SS
Dick Drago - P
Frank Duffy - 3B
Dwight Evans - PH
Carlton Fisk - C
Andy Hassler - P

Butch Hobson - DH
Fred Lynn - CF
Jerry Remy - 2B
Jim Rice - RF
George Scott - 1B
Bob Stanley - P
Mike Torrez - P
Carl Yastrzemski - LF

RED SOX HITTING MORE THAN
TWO HOME RUNS IN A GAME

1919 — Babe Ruth at Baltimore - 4*
1939 — Jim Tabor at Philadelphia - 3
1946 — Ted Williams at Boston - 3
1950 — Bobby Doerr at Boston - 3
1951 — Clyde Vollmer at Boston - 3
1955 — Norm Zauchin at Boston - 3
1957 — Ted Williams at Chicago - 3
1957 — Ted Williams at Cleveland - 3
1968 — Ken Harrelson at Cleveland - 3
1969 — Joe Lahoud at Minnesota - 3
1975 — Fred Lynn at Detroit - 3
1976 — Carl Yastrzemski at Detroit - 3
1977 — Jim Rice at Boston - 3
*Exhibition Game

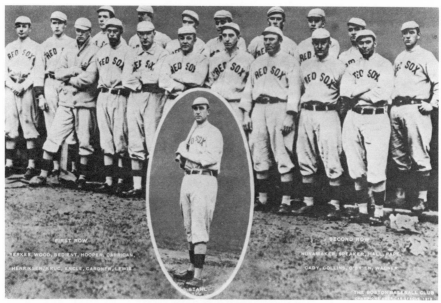

BOSTON RED SOX — 1912

Front Row: (L to R) Yerkes, Wood, Bedient, Hooper, Carrigan, Henrikson, Krug, Engle, Gardner, Lewis. Back Row: Nunamaker, Speaker, Hall, Pape, Cady, Collins, O'Brien, Wagner. Insert: Manager Stahl.

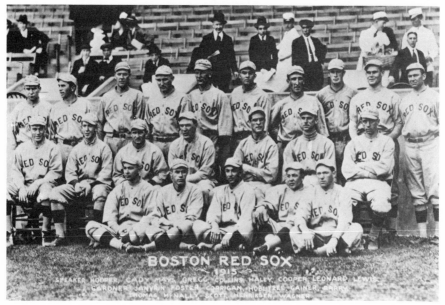

BOSTON RED SOX — 1915

Front Row: (L to R) Thomas, McNally, Scott, Henrikson, Wagner. Middle Row: Gardner, Janvrin, Foster, Carrigan, Hoblitzel, Gainor, Barry. Back Row: Speaker, Hooper, Cady, Mays, Gregg, Collins, Haley, Cooper, Leonard, Lewis.

BOSTON RED SOX — 1946

Front: Batboy Kelly. Front Row: (L to R) Traveling Secretary Dowd, Pesky, Doerr, Pellagrini, Coach Woodall, Manager Cronin, Coach Baker, Coach Carey, D. DiMaggio, C. Wagner, Gutteridge. Middle Row: Trainer Green, Brown, Ryba, Campbell, McGah, Lazor, Partee, Moses, H. Wagner, Harris, York, Higgins, Culberson, Clubhouse Attendant Orlando. Back Row: Klinger, McBride, Russell, Metkovich, Dreisewerd, Dobson, E. Johnson, Zuber, Bagby, Hughson, Ferriss, Schreiber, Williams.

BOSTON RED SOX — 1948

Front Row: (L to R) Spence, Batts, Schreiber, Coach; Combs, Coach; McCarthy, manager; Baker, Coach; Woodall, Coach; Parnell, DiMaggio, Doerr, Stephens, Dowd, Traveling Secretary. Middle Row: Orlando, Clubhouse Attendant; Hitchcock, Kramer, Kinder, Pesky, Wright, McCall, Martin, Tebbetts, Goodman, Mele, Moses, Froelich, Trainer. Back row: Harris, Jones, Ferriss, Hughson, Caldwell, Johnson, Dobson, Galehouse, Stobbs, Williams.

BOSTON RED SOX — 1949

Front Row: (L to R) Coach Combs, Kinder, Dorish, Tebbetts, Doerr, Parnell, DiMaggio, Manager McCarthy, Pesky, Goodman, Stephens, Zarilla, Coach Schulte. Middle Row: Trainer Froelich, Kramer, Wright, O'Brien, McDermott, Quinn, Batts, Stringer, M. Combs, Martin, Coach Cuyler, Property Man Orlando. Back Row: Stobbs, Hitchcock, Masterson, Coach Schreiber, Johnson, Dobson, Mueller, Williams, Hughson, Douglas, Ferriss, Traveling Secretary Dowd. Front: Batboy Donovan.

BOSTON RED SOX — 1967

Front: Batboys Rosenfield and Jackson. Front Row: (L to R) Yastrzemski, Foy, Conigliaro, Coach Popowski, Coach Doerr, Manager Williams, Coach Maglie, Coach Lakeman, Smith, Scott, Traveling Secretary Dowd, Trainer LeRoux. Middle Row: Equipment Managers Fitzpatrick and Orlando, Adair, Thomas, Fischer, Stange, Petrocelli, Tartabull, Osinski, Cisco, Andrews, Rohr, Ryan. Back Row: Landis, Gibson, Bennett, Bell, Jones, Tillman, Santiago, Brandon, Lonborg, Waslewski, Wyatt.

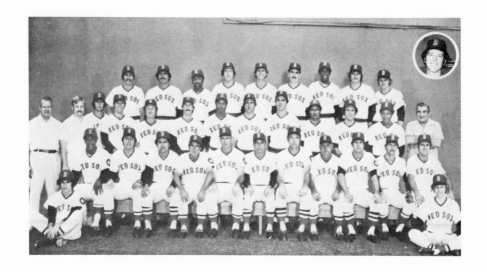

BOSTON RED SOX — 1975

Front: Batboys Naticchioni, Krall. Front Row: (L to R) Rice, Fisk, Petrocelli, Coach Pesky, Coach Bryant, Manager Johnson, Coach Williams, Coach Zimmer, Yastrzemski, Burleson, Lynn. Middle Row: Equipment Manager Cerrone, Trainer Moss, Griffin, Heise, Doyle, Blackwell, Cooper, Montgomery, Evans, Beniquez, Carbo, Segui, Equipment Manager Orlando. Back Row: Miller, Drago, Tiant, Wise, Lee, Burton, Moret, Pole, Cleveland. Inset: Willoughby.

BOSTON RED SOX — 1979

Front Row: (L to R) Burleson, Rice, Yastrzemski, Coach Pesky, Coach Hriniak, Manager Zimmer, Coach Jackson, Coach Yost, Fisk, Lynn, Remy. Middle Row: Fitzpatrick, Clubhouse; Trainer Moss, Brohamer, Wolfe, Montgomery, Hobson, Watson, Evans, O'Berry, Poquette, Allenson, Papi, Dwyer, Orlando, Clubhouse Attendant. Back Row: Rainey, Finch, Campbell, Renko, Eckersley, Torrez, Stanley, Wright, Drago, Burgmeier.

PAWTUCKET RED SOX

Front: (L to R) Batboys Al Riendeau, Peter Cassels. Front Row: Bobby Sprowl, Wayne Harer, Gary Allenson, Owner Ben Mondor, Manager Joe Morgan, Player Coach Buddy Hunter, General Manager Mike Tamburro, Glenn Hoffman, Otis Foster, Win Remmerswaal. Middle Row: Allen Ripley, Burke Suter, Rick Berg, Joel Finch, John LaRose, John Tudor, Ed Jurak, Trainer Dale Robertson. Back Row: Chuck Rainey, Andy Merchant, Dave Stapleton, Dave Coleman, Ken Huizenga, Mike Burns, Sam Bowen.

BRISTOL RED SOX — 1979

Front: Batboy Steve Kirschner. Front Row: (L to R) Bob Birrell, Ray Boyer, Wade Boggs, Manager Tony Torchia, Ed Jurak, Dave Schmidt, Rich Gedman. Middle Row: Trainer Dave Labossiere, Keith MacWhorter, Kevin Stephenson, Bruce Poole, Rocky Alburtis, Mike Smithson, Jerry King, Bruce Hurst, Mark Baum. Back Row: Mike Ongarato, Otis Foster, Chico Walker, Brian Denman, Ron Evans, Carl Steele, Russ Laribee. The Pawtucket and Bristol Red Sox, where the Red Sox top prospects perform. Can you spot any future big leaguers? (PHOTOS COURTESY OF THE PAWTUCKET AND BRISTOL RED SOX)

FENWAY PARK — An aerial view of that Grand Old Lady of Boston's Back Bay.

CHAIN O'LAKES PARK — The spring training site for the Bosox. Winter Haven, Florida.

Mike Higgins and Ted Williams watch batting practice at Fenway in 1955.

Recognize Dick Gernert, Pumpsie Green and Gary Geiger?

DUANE JOSEPHSON — Heart problems ended Duane Josephson's career.

TEX HUGHSON — A stint in the service and a sore arm prevented him from achieving even greater success as a Sox pitcher.

RAY CULP   **JIM LONBORG**

Fate delt a sore arm to Ray Culp and a bad knee to Jim Lonborg.

STARTERS OF 1969 — (L to R) George Thomas (OF), Tony Conigliaro (OF), Rico Petrocelli (SS), Reggie Smith (OF), Carl Yastrzemski (OF), Ken Harrelson (1B), Mike Andrews (2B), George Scott (3B), Russ Gibson (C).

An interesting group of Red Sox all in the twilight of their careers — (L to R): Ted Williams, Bobby Thomson, Vic Wertz, Frank Malzone and Gene Stephens.

CHUCK RAINEY

JOEL FINCH

JOHN TUDOR

GARY ALLENSON

Three of the "BOYS FROM PAWTUCKET" who hope to gain prominence on the mound at Fenway — Chuck Rainey, Joel Finch and John Tudor, and catcher Gary Allenson who attempted to replace the injured Carlton Fisk in 1979.

LUIS APARICIO — Whose best days were behind him when he arrived at Fenway. He once had a 1 for 55 slump and a message from President Nixon.

RICO PETROCELLI — A great Sox infielder whose career as a player ended abruptly, but later resumed in the radio booth.

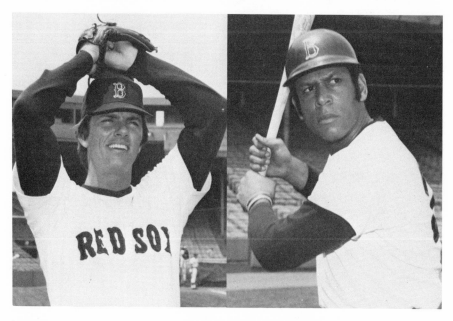

BILL LEE — You either hated or loved Bill Lee, whose antics and remarks never ceased to amaze Sox followers. He enjoyed many triumphs and brought on his own tragedies.

ORLANDO CEPEDA — The major league's and Red Sox first ever D.H. fell upon bad times after his career ended.

Surviving members of the 1912 World Champions gathered in reunion at Fenway Park 50 years later. That's Ray Collins (P) seated, joined by (L to R): Bill Carrigan (C), Hugh Bedient (P), Joe Wood (P), Larry Gardner (3B), Duffy Lewis (OF), Steve Yerkes (2B), Olaf Henriksen (OF), and Harry Hooper (OF).

A couple of pretty fair pitchers during a low period of Red Sox history were Rube Walberg and Herb Pennock

JOSE SANTIAGO — Helped the Sox to one pennant and appeared to be making a repeat performance when his arm suddenly failed him.

LUIS TIANT — The loss of Luis Tiant to the Yankees hurt.

MIKE TORREZ — Came over from the Yankees as a free agent and might have had a better 1979 record had he not been the victim of five shutouts.

BILL CAMPBELL — The once effective reliever has suffered arm and shoulder problems.

The very talented Red Sox outfield of Jim Rice, Fred Lynn and Dwight Evans.

One met with great success, the other with tragedy. Carl Yastrzemski (L) and Tony Conigliaro (R).

TOM BREWER — A brilliant righthander until arm problems slowed him down.

MICKEY McDERMOTT — The popular lefty the Sox pinned their hopes on during the late 40's and early 50's.

BILLY ROHR — Once came within one pitch of baseball immortality, but dreams of a brilliant future soon faded away.

FRANK SULLIVAN — One of the biggest hurlers ever to pitch for the Sox.

This Red Sox infield of 1950 all had their problems at one time or another. (L to R): Walt Dropo, Bobby Doerr, Lou Boudreau and Vern Stephens.

Red Sox pitching aces in the early 60's were Gene Conley, Bill Monbouquette and Earl Wilson. The latter two hurled no hitters for Boston.

Here is **TRIS SPEAKER** at the height of his Boston career before his tragic sale to Cleveland. That's Clyde Engle to the right.

JIM PIERSALL — Played both infield and outfield for the Red Sox. A tragic story with a happy ending.

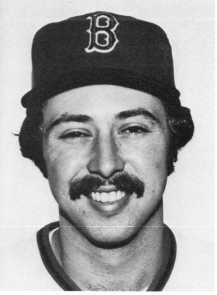

CARLTON FISK — Appears quite happy here, giving little indication of the many miseries, which have plagued his brilliant career.

JERRY REMY — The Red Sox hope this smile will return to the second baseman's face after the crippling knee injury suffered in 1979.

Old Timers will recognize a shot like this as the first sign of spring when, in early March, it appeared on your sports page. Why don't they pose like this anymore? Oh yes, at Sarasota in 1939 this trio is (L to R): Jim Tabor, Tom Carey and Boze Berger.

This 1935 photo shows Babe Ruth, then with the Boston Braves, posing with a group of Red Sox players. That's Billy Werber on the far right.

A reunion brought together a couple of pretty fair Red Sox pitchers, Bill Monbouquette and Smokey Joe Wood.

A young Carl Yastrzemski poses with two other great Red Sox outfielders, Harry Hooper (left) and Duffy Lewis (right).

Determination can be seen in Carl Yastrzemski's eyes. It all led to more years as a Bosox than any other player — 3000+ hits, 400+ home runs and awards by the carload.

Recognize this young Red Sox catcher? He is present executive vice president, Haywood Sullivan. Note the mourning band worn in respect for Harry Agganis.

Tommy Harper seems to be contemplating the feet which in 1973 stole 54 bases to break Tris Speaker's team record of 52 set in 1912.

Here are a couple of men from the broadcasting booth. Recognize Curt Gowdy seated and Bob Murphy?

WIN GREEN — Long time trainer

You will recognize Don Zimmer on the left and certainly you have heard, but seldom seen, the gentleman on the right. He is Sherm Feller, Fenway Park's public address announcer.

Three pretty fair Red Sox sluggers discuss batting grips. That's Jackie Jensen on the left, Frank Malzone in the middle watching Pete Runnels demonstrate his grip.

Sox V.P. Bill Crowley (with that ever-present pipe) points out something of interest to Ted Williams while Don Zimmer listens.

Both Jimmie Foxx (L) and Joe Cronin (R) enjoyed much success in Red Sox uniforms, but Foxx met a tragic end and Cronin took fan abuse for Sox failures of the 50's.

Yankee Killers All were these Boston favorites of the late 30's and early 40's. (L to R): Doc Cramer (OF), Ben Chapman (OF), and Bobby Doerr (2B).

This group of 1946 Sox played various roles in the Club's history. (L to R): Hal Wagner (C), Rip Russell (3B), Roy Partee (C), Pinky Higgins (3B).

Ted Williams upon acceptance into the Hall of Fame.

This couple is highly respected in the baseball world. Long time Red Sox owner, the late Thomas Yawkey and his widow, current Red Sox President Mrs. Jean R. Yawkey.

Doug Griffin, Press Box Steward Tommy McCarthy, Carl Yastrzemski and Pudge Fisk celebrate St. Patrick's Day.

MAJOR HONORS AWARDED RED SOX PERSONNEL

Associated Press
Male Athlete Of The Year
    1957 — Ted Williams
    1967 — Carl Yastrzemski
    1975 — Fred Lynn

Cy Young Memorial Award
    1967 — Jim Lonborg

Chalmers Award
    1912 — Tris Speaker

Most Valuable Player Award —
Baseball Writer's Association
    1938 — Jimmie Foxx
    1946 — Ted Williams
    1949 — Ted Williams
    1958 — Jack Jensen
    1967 — Carl Yastrzemski
    1975 — Fred Lynn
    1978 — Jim Rice

Rookie Of The Year —
Baseball Writer's Association
    1950 — Walt Dropo
    1961 — Don Schwall
    1972 — Carlton Fisk
    1975 — Fred Lynn

Most Valuable Player Award —
"The Sporting News"
    1938 — Jimmie Foxx
    1944 — Bobby Doerr

Player, Pitcher Of The Year —
"The Sporting News"
Player
    1949 — Ted Williams
    1957 — Ted Williams
    1958 — Jack Jensen
    1967 — Carl Yastrzemski
    1968 — Ken Harrelson
    1975 — Fred Lynn
    1978 — Jim Rice

Pitcher
    1949 — Ellis Kinder
    1967 — Jim Lonborg

Fireman Of The Year —
"The Sporting News"
    1960 — Mike Fornieles
    1962 — Dick Radatz
    1964 — Dick Radatz
    1977 — Bill Campbell

Rookie Award —
"The Sporting News"
    1961 — Don Schwall
    1969 — Mike Nagy
    1972 — Carlton Fisk
    1975 — Fred Lynn

Major League Executive —
"The Sporting News"
    1946 — Tom Yawkey
    1967 — Dick O'Connell
    1975 — Dick O'Connell

Major League Manager —
"The Sporting News"
    1967 — Dick Williams
    1975 — Darrell Johnson

Major League Player —
"The Sporting News"
    1941 — Ted Williams
    1942 — Ted Williams
    1947 — Ted Williams
    1949 — Ted Williams
    1957 — Ted Williams
    1967 — Carl Yastrzemski

"Baseball Digest"
Rookie All Star Team
    1971 — Doug Griffin - 2B
    1972 — Carlton Fisk - C
    1974 — Rick Burleson - 2B
    1975 — Jim Rice - LF
    1975 — Fred Lynn - RF
    1976 — Rick Jones - LHP

Outstanding Player —
Major League All Star Game
    1970 — Carl Yastrzemski

RED SOX PLAYERS NAMED TO SPORTING NEWS ALL STAR FIELDING TEAM

1957 — Frank Malzone - 3B
1958 — Frank Malzone - 3B
    Jim Piersall - CF
1959 — Frank Malzone - 3B
    Jack Jensen - RF
1963 — Carl Yastrzemski - OF
1965 — Carl Yastrzemski - OF
1967 — George Scott - 1B
    Carl Yastrzemski - OF
1968 — George Scott - 1B
    Carl Yastrzemski - OF
    Reggie Smith - OF

1969 — Carl Yastrzemski - OF
1971 — George Scott - 1B
    Carl Yastrzemski - OF
1972 — Carlton Fisk - C
    Doug Griffin - 2B
1975 — Fred Lynn - OF
1976 — Dwight Evans - OF
1977 — Carl Yastrzemski - OF
1978 — Dwight Evans - OF
    Fred Lynn - OF
1979 — Rick Burleson - SS
    Dwight Evans - OF
    Fred Lynn - OF

RED SOX PLAYERS NAMED TO SPORTING NEWS MAJOR LEAGUE ALL STAR TEAMS

1938 — Jim Foxx - 1B
    Joe Cronin - SS
1939 — Jim Foxx - 1B
    Joe Cronin - SS
    Ted Williams - OF
1940 — Ted Williams - OF
1941 — Ted Williams - OF
1942 — John Pesky - SS
    Ted Williams - OF
    Tex Hughson - P
1944 — Bob Doerr - 2B
1945 — Dave Ferriss - P
1946 — Bob Doerr - 2B
    John Pesky - SS
    Ted Williams - OF
    Dom DiMaggio - OF
    Dave Ferriss - P
1947 — Ted Williams - OF
1948 — Ted Williams - OF
    Birdie Tebbetts - C
1949 — Ted Williams - OF
    Mel Parnell - P
    Ellis Kinder - P
1950 — Walt Dropo - 1B
1951 — Ted Williams - OF
1952 — George Kell - 3B
1955 — Ted Williams - OF
1956 — Ted Williams - OF

1957 — Ted Williams - OF
1958 — Ted Williams - OF
1963 — Frank Malzone - 3B
    Carl Yastrzemski - OF
1964 — Dick Stuart - 1B
1965 — Carl Yastrzemski - LF
1967 — Carl Yastrzemski - LF
    Jim Lonborg - P
1968 — Ken Harrelson - OF
1969 — Rico Petrocelli - SS
1970 — Reggie Smith - OF
1972 — Luis Aparicio - S
    Carlton Fisk - C
1975 — Jim Rice - LF
    Fred Lynn - CF
1977 — Rick Burleson - SS
    Carlton Fisk - C
    Jim Rice - OF
1978 — Fred Lynn - OF
    Jim Rice - OF

RED SOX LEAGUE LEADING PITCHER
IN WINNING PERCENTAGE (15 wins or more)

1903	Cy Young	28-9	.757
1905	Jesse Tannehill	22-9	.710
1912	Joe Wood	34-5	.872
1915	Joe Wood	15-5	.750
1918	Sam Jones	16-5	.762
1939	Lefty Grove	15-4	.789
1944	Tex Hughson	18-5	.783
1946	Dave Ferriss	25-6	.806
1948	Jack Kramer	18-5	.783
1949	Ellis Kinder	23-6	.793

RED SOX LEAGUE LEADING PITCHER
EARNED RUN AVERAGE

1901	Cy Young	1.63
1914	Dutch Leonard	1.01
1915	Joe Wood	1.49
1916	Babe Ruth	1.75
1935	Lefty Grove	2.70
1936	Lefty Grove	2.81
1938	Lefty Grove	3.07
1939	Lefty Grove	2.54
1949	Mel Parnell	2.78
1972	Luis Tiant	1.91

RED SOX LEAGUE LEADING PITCHER IN STRIKEOUTS

1901	Cy Young	159
1942	Tex Hughson (Tied with Newsom of Washington)	113
1967	Jim Lonborg	246

RED SOX LEAGUE LEADER PITCHING SHUTOUTS

1901	Cy Young (Tied with Griffith of Chicago)	5
1903	Cy Young	7
1904	Cy Young	10
1912	Joe Wood	10
1916	Babe Ruth	9
1918	Carl Mays (Tied with Johnson of Washington)	8
1921	Sam Jones	5
1929	Dan MacFayden (Tied with three others)	4
1936	Lefty Grove	6
1949	Ellis Kinder (Tied with two others)	6
1974	Luis Tiant	7

RED SOX LEAGUE LEADERS - BATTING AVERAGE

1932	Dale Alexander*	.367
1938	Jimmie Foxx	.349
1941	Ted Williams	.406
1942	Ted Williams	.356
1947	Ted Williams	.343
1948	Ted Williams	.369
1950	Billy Goodman	.354
1957	Ted Williams	.388
1958	Ted Williams	.328
1960	Pete Runnels	.320
1962	Pete Runnels	.326
1963	Carl Yastrzemski	.321
1967	Carl Yastrzemski	.326
1968	Carl Yastrzemski	.301
1979	Fred Lynn	.333

*Also with the Detroit Tigers

RED SOX LEAGUE LEADERS - SLUGGING PERCENTAGE

1918	Babe Ruth	.555
1919	Babe Ruth	.657
1938	Jimmie Foxx	.704
1939	Jimmie Foxx	.694
1941	Ted Williams	.735
1942	Ted Williams	.648
1944	Bobby Doerr	.528
1946	Ted Williams	.667
1947	Ted Williams	.634
1948	Ted Williams	.615
1949	Ted Williams	.650
1951	Ted Williams	.556
1954	Ted Williams	.635
1957	Ted Williams	.731
1965	Carl Yastrzemski	.536
1967	Carl Yastrzemski	.622
1970	Carl Yastrzemski	.592
1975	Fred Lynn	.566
1977	Jim Rice	.593
1978	Jim Rice	.600
1979	Fred Lynn	.637

RED SOX LEAGUE LEADERS - RUNS SCORED

1903	Pat Dougherty	106
1904	Pat Dougherty*	113
1919	Babe Ruth	103
1940	Ted Williams	134
1941	Ted Williams	135
1942	Ted Williams	141
1946	Ted Williams	142
1947	Ted Williams	125
1949	Ted Williams	150
1950	Dom DiMaggio	131
1951	Dom DiMaggio	113
1967	Carl Yastrzemski	112
1970	Carl Yastrzemski	125
1974	Carl Yastrzemski	93
1975	Fred Lynn	103

*Also with New York

RED SOX LEAGUE LEADERS IN HITS

1903	Pat Dougherty	195
1914	Tris Speaker	193
1938	Joe Vosmik	201
1940	Doc Cramer	200
1942	John Pesky	205
1946	John Pesky	208
1947	John Pesky	207
1963	Carl Yastrzemski	183
1967	Carl Yastrzemski	189
1978	Jim Rice	213

RED SOX LEAGUE LEADERS - SINGLES

1903	Pat Dougherty 161		1942	John Pesky 165
1939	Doc Cramer 147		1946	John Pesky 159
1940	Doc Cramer 160		1947	John Pesky 172

RED SOX LEAGUE LEADERS - DOUBLES

1912	Tris Speaker 53		1963	Carl Yastrzemski 40
1914	Tris Speaker 46		1965	Carl Yastrzemski 45
1931	Earl Webb 67		1966	Carl Yastrzemski 39
1938	Joe Cronin 51		1968	Reggie Smith 37
1948	Ted Williams 44		1971	Reggie Smith 33
1949	Ted Williams 39		1975	Fred Lynn 47
1956	Jim Piersall 40			

RED SOX LEAGUE LEADERS - TRIPLES

1904	Chick Stahl 22		1956	Jack Jensen 11
1950	Dom DiMaggio 11		1972	Carlton Fisk 9
	Bobby Doerr 11		1978	Jim Rice 15

RED SOX LEAGUE LEADERS - HOME RUNS

1903	Buck Freeman 13		1942	Ted Williams 36
1910	Jake Stahl 10		1947	Ted Williams 32
1912	Tris Speaker* 10		1949	Ted Williams 43
1918	Babe Ruth** 11		1965	Tony Conigliaro 32
1919	Babe Ruth 29		1967	Carl Yastrzemski 44
1939	Jimmie Foxx 35		1977	Jim Rice 39
1941	Ted Williams 37		1978	Jim Rice 46

*Tied with Frank Baker — Phila.   **Tied with Tilly Walker — Phila.

RED SOX LEAGUE LEADERS - RUNS BATTED IN

1902	Buck Freeman 121		1950	Walt Dropo 144
1903	Buck Freeman 104			Vern Stephens 144
1919	Babe Ruth 112		1955	Jack Jensen* 116
1938	Jimmie Foxx 175		1958	Jack Jensen 122
1939	Ted Williams 145		1959	Jack Jensen 112
1942	Ted Williams 137		1963	Dick Stuart 118
1947	Ted Williams 114		1967	Carl Yastrzemski 121
1949	Ted Williams 159		1968	Ken Harrelson 109
	Vern Stephens 159		1978	Jim Rice 139

*Tied with Ray Boone - Detroit

RED SOX LEAGUE LEADERS - WALKS

1938	Jimmie Foxx*	119	1949	Ted Williams	162
1941	Ted Williams	145	1951	Ted Williams	143
1942	Ted Williams	145	1954	Ted Williams	136
1946	Ted Williams	156	1963	Carl Yastrzemski	95
1947	Ted Williams	162	1968	Carl Yastrzemski	119
1948	Ted Williams	126			

*Tied with Hank Greenberg - Detroit

RED SOX LEAGUE LEADERS - STRIKEOUTS

1918	Babe Ruth	58	1955	Norm Zauchin	105
1919	Maurice Shannon*	70	1966	George Scott	152
1936	Jimmie Foxx	119	1976	Jim Rice	123
1941	Jimmie Foxx	103			

*Also with the Philadelphia Athletics

RED SOX LEAGUE LEADERS - STOLEN BASES

1928	Buddy Myer	30	1950	Dom DiMaggio	15
1934	Billy Werber	40	1954	Jackie Jensen	22
1935	Billy Werber	29	1973	Tommy Harper	54
1937	Ben Chapman	35			

RED SOX LEAGUE LEADERS - TOTAL BASES

1902	Charles Hickman*	288	1949	Ted Williams	368
1903	Buck Freeman	281	1950	Walt Dropo	326
1914	Tris Speaker	287	1951	Ted Williams	295
1919	Babe Ruth	284	1963	Dick Stuart	319
1938	Jimmie Foxx	398	1967	Carl Yastrzemski	360
1939	Ted Williams	344	1970	Carl Yastrzemski	335
1942	Ted Williams	338	1971	Reggie Smith	302
1946	Ted Williams	343	1977	Jim Rice	382
1947	Ted Williams	335	1978	Jim Rice	406

*Also with Cleveland

RED SOX PLAYERS LEADING LEAGUE GROUNDING INTO MOST DOUBLE PLAYS (Since 1940)

1947	Bobby Doerr	25	1962	Carl Yastrzemski	27
1948	Vern Stephens	25	1963	Frank Malzone	24
1949	Bobby Doerr	31		Dick Stuart	24
1951	Vern Stephens	22	1964	Carl Yastrzemski	30
1954	Jack Jensen	32	1966	George Cott	25
1956	Jack Jensen	23	1973	Orlando Cepeda	24
1957	Jack Jensen	22			

RED SOX MAJOR LEAGUE ALL STAR GAME SELECTIONS
1956-1979

1956 — Tom Brewer - P
      Jim Piersall - OF
      Frank Sullivan - P
      Mickey Vernon - 1B
      Ted Williams - OF

1957 — Frank Malzone - 3B
      Ted Williams - OF

1958 — Jack Jensen - OF
      Frank Malzone - 3B
      Ted Williams - OF

1959 — Frank Malzone - 3B
      Pete Runnels - 2B
      Ted Williams - OF

1960 — Frank Malzone - 3B
      Bill Monbouquette - P
      Pete Runnels - 2B
      Ted Williams - OF

1961   **Mike Fornieles - P**
      Don Schwall - P
      Mike Higgins - Coach

1962 — Bill Monbouquette - P
      Pete Runnels - 1B

1963 — Frank Malzone - 3B
      Bill Monbouquette - P
      Dick Radatz - P
      Carl Yastrzemski - OF
      John Pesky - Coach

1964 — Ed Bressoud - SS
      Frank Malzone - 3B
      Dick Radatz - P

1965 — Felix Mantilla - 2B
      Carl Yastrzemski - OF

1966 — George Scott - 1B
      Carl Yastrzemski - OF

1967 — Tony Conigliaro - OF
      Jim Lonborg - P
      Rico Petrocelli - SS
      Carl Yastrzemski - OF

1968 — Gary Bell - P
      Ken Harrelson - OF
      Jose Santiago - P
      Carl Yastrzemski - OF
      Dick Williams - Manager

1969 — Mike Andrews - 2B
      Ray Culp - P
      Rico Petrocelli - SS
      Reggie Smith - OF
      Carl Yastrzemski - OF

1970 — Gerry Moses - C
      Carl Yastrzemski - OF

1971 — Luis Aparicio - SS
      Sonny Siebert - P
      Carl Yastrzemski - OF

1972 — Luis Aparicio - SS
      Carlton Fisk - C
      Reggie Smith - OF
      Carl Yastrzemski - OF

1973 — Carlton Fisk - C
      Bill Lee - P
      Carl Yastrzemski - OF

1974 — Carlton Fisk - C
      Luis Tiant - P
      Carl Yastrzemski - OF

1975 — Fred Lynn - OF
      Carl Yastrzemski - OF

1976 — Carlton Fisk - C
      Fred Lynn - OF
      Luis Tiant - P
      Carl Yastrzemski - OF
      Darrell Johnson - Manager
      Don Bryant - Coach

Red Sox Major League All Star Game Selections — 1956-1979 (continued)

1977 — Rick Burleson - SS
    Bill Campbell - P
    Carlton Fisk - C
    Fred Lynn - OF
    Jim Rice - OF
    Carl Yastrzemski - OF

1978 — Rick Burleson - SS
    Dwight Evans - OF
    Carlton Fisk - C
    Fred Lynn - OF

1978 — (continued)
    Jerry Remy - 2B
    Jim Rice - OF
    Carl Yastrzemski - OF
    Don Zimmer - Coach

1979 — Rick Burleson - SS
    Fred Lynn - OF
    Jim Rice - OF
    Bob Stanley - P
    Carl Yastrzemski - OF

RED SOX ALL TIME LEADERS — 1901-1979

BATTING

Games		At Bats		Runs	
Yastrzemski	2862	Yastrzemski	10,447	T. Williams	1798
T. Williams	2292	T. Williams	7,706	Yastrzemski	1640
Doerr	1865	Doerr	7,093	Doerr	1094
Hooper	1646	Hooper	6,269	DiMaggio	1046
Petrocelli	1553	DiMaggio	5,640	Hooper	988

Hits		Doubles		Triples	
Yastrzemski	3009	Yastrzemski	565	Hooper	130
T. Williams	2654	T. Williams	525	Speaker	106
Doerr	2042	Doerr	381	Freeman	91
Hooper	1707	DiMaggio	308	Doerr	89
DiMaggio	1680	Cronin	270	Gardner	87

Home Runs		RBI's		Average	
T. Williams	521	T. Williams	1839	T. Williams	.344
Yastrzemski	404	Yastrzemski	1613	Speaker	.337
Doerr	223	Doerr	1247	Foxx	.320
Foxx	222	Foxx	788	Runnels	.320
Petrocelli	210	Petrocelli	773	R. Johnson	.313
				Pesky	.313

PITCHING

Games		Innings		Games Started	
Kinder	365	Young	2728	Young	298
Young	327	Tiant	1774	Tiant	238
Delock	322	Parnell	1753	Parnell	232
Lee	321	Monbouquette	1622	Monbouquette	228
Parnell	289	Winter	1600	Brewer	217

Red Sox All-Time Leaders — 1901-1979 (continued)

Wins		Losses		Saves	
Young	193	Young	112	Radatz	104
Parnell	123	Winter	96	Kinder	91
Taint	122	Ruffing	96	Lyle	69
Wood	115	Russell	94	Fornieles	48
Dobson	106	Monbouquette	91	Campbell	44
		Dineen	86		

Strikeouts		Shutouts		Complete Games	
Young	1347	Young	39	Young	276
Taint	1075	Wood	28	Dineen	156
Wood	986	Tiant	26	Winter	141
Monbouquette	969	Leonard	24	Wood	121
F. Sullivan	821	Collins	20	Grove	119
		Parnell	20		

Winning Pct. (100 Dec.)		Walks	
Wood (115-56)	.673	Parnell	758
Ruth (89-46)	.659	Brewer	669
Hughson (96-54)	.640	Dobson	604
Young (193-112)	.633	J. Wilson	564
Grove (105-62)	.629	Nixon	530

On the night of May 12, 1961 pitcher Bill Monbouquette made hurling history when he broke the American League strike out record for night games and set the all time Red Sox high at 17. Interestingly he missed by a dropped foul third strike of tying the modern strikeout record held by Bob Feller and Sandy Koufax.

Here is how he did it and who his victims were:
    1st inning — Gene Woodling
    2nd inning — Dale Long and Lenny Green
    3rd inning — Jim Mahoney, Pete Burnside and Billy Klaus
    4th inning — Willie Tasby and Jim King
    5th inning — Pete Burnside
    6th inning — Billy Klaus and Willie Tasby
    7th inning — Lenny Green, Marty Keough (pinch hitter) and Billy Klaus
    8th inning — Willie Tasby
    9th inning — Dale Long and Inman Veal

RED SOX CONSECUTIVE GAME HITTING STREAKS AT THE START OF THE SEASON

1965 — Eddie Bressoud - 20		1962 — Eddie Bressoud - 14	
1922 — Elmer Smith -18		1902 — Jimmy Collins - 13	
1930 — Tom Oliver - 16		1940 — Jimmie Foxx - 12	
1923 — George Burns - 14			

Although not successful in two American League playoffs, the Red Sox won the coin toss to determine at whose field the games would be played in 1948, 1949 and 1978.

RED SOX HITLESS STREAK RECORD
AT THE START OF THE SEASON

George Metkovich   0-30
Frank Malzone   0-27

The 1946 Red Sox boasted a number of relatively long hitting streaks. Here they are:

11 games Dom DiMaggio - July 13-21   10 games Ted Williams - September 5-21
11 games John Pesky - July 17-27   10 games John Pesky - August 1-11
10 games Ted Williams - June 5-16   10 games Dom DiMaggio - August 8-17
10 games Ted Williams - July 14-21   10 games Leon Culberson- April 23-May 10

In the war shortened season of 1918 Red Sox pitchers tossed a team record of 26 shutouts. Despite most record books showing 25 below are the 26 which have been verified by 1918 box scores. A glance at the Red Sox yearly pitching records elsewhere in this book will show how amazing this record is. Only the 1914 and 1916 teams came close and that was in a regular length season.

1.	April 16	Philadelphia	1-0	Mays
2.	April 23	New York	1-0	Bush
3.	May 28	Chicago	1-0	Bush
4.	May 29	Washington	3-0	Jones (2nd Game)
5.	June 3	At Detroit	5-0	Leonard
6.	June 6	At Cleveland	1-0	Jones (10 innings)
7.	June 9	At Cleveland	2-0	Leonard
8.	June 10	At Chicago	1-0	Bush
9.	June 12	At Chicago	7-0	Mays
10.	June 13	At Chicago	6-0	Leonard
11.	June 17	At St. Louis	8-0	Mays
12.	June 20	Philadelphia	3-0	Molyneaux (W) in relief of Leonard (2nd Game)
13.	June 21	Philadelphia	13-0	Mays
14.	July 8	Cleveland	1-0	Jones (10 innings) (1st Game)
15.	July 9	Cleveland	1-0	Bush (12 innings)
16.	July 10	Cleveland	2-0	Bader
17.	July 11	Chicago	4-0	Mays
18.	July 17	St. Louis	7-0	Bush (Doubleheader)
19.	July 17	St. Louis	4-0	Ruth (Doubleheader)
20.	July 19	Detroit	5-0	Mays
21.	July 22	Detroit	1-0	Bush (Doubleheader (10 innings))
22.	July 22	Detroit	3-0	Mays (Doubleheader)
23.	August 16	Chicago	2-0	Bush
24.	August 19	Cleveland	6-0	Jones
25.	August 28	Detroit	3-0	Jones
26.	August 30	Philadelphia	12-0	Mays (1st Game)

RED SOX VS YANKEES
BASEBALL'S GREATEST RIVALRY

"Hey, I have tickets to the Yankees-Red Sox game." These words immediately make the speaker the envy of his friends. At one time it may have been Highlanders vs Pilgrims, but no matter the rivalry between the cities of New York and Boston has been intense for many an American League season. From the Delaware River up the Jersey Shore and the Hudson, across New England to the Maritime Provinces of Canada no sports event creates the interest generated as when these two teams meet. It has been a long and colorful series spiked with those memories which make baseball the national pastime. Entering the 1980 season, the Yankees hold a decisive edge in games won, 880 to Boston's 705. Forty-five times the Yanks have won the season series, while the Bosox have prevailed twenty-four times and in eight seasons they have ended their season's work against each other evenly.

When, in 1902, Wilbert Robinson's Baltimore Orioles dropped out of the American League and were replaced by the New York Highlanders, managed by Clark Griffith (later long-time Washington Senators owner), the rivalry was born — a natural between these two great eastern cities who are really not separated by that many miles. A rivalry which has developed to the point of being the greatest in baseball, certainly surpassing the great Brooklyn Dodger-New York Giant feuds. This year will be no different. When these two meet, their records at the time will mean little.

Let's take a look at the reasons behind the rivalry. The fact that the two have often been in the pennant fight right down to the wire is certainly one. The shift of a great many of the star players, who made Boston the powerhouse of the American League up until the early 20's, to New York is another. The fact that each club has boasted their share of the American League's better players since the 30's can not be overlooked. The proximity of the two cities with their overlapping areas of fan interest, especially in Connecticut is a contributing factor. Transplanted Bostonians who reside in the New York-New Jersey area, and New Yorkers living in or attending the many fine schools in the Boston area make their way to Fenway Park or Yankee Stadium annually in such numbers, it is often difficult to tell who the home team is. This year is no different. Tickets to the battles to be staged by these clubs are the most difficult to obtain. The battles between the two have been likened to the Hatfields and McCoys. (No reflection intended on Fred Hatfield, Boston infielder 1950-52).

Boston fans may admit that Red Ruffing and Babe Ruth, both of whom played for the Sox, or Joe DiMaggio (who could not out field his brother Dom according to some) and maybe Mickey Mantle were pretty fair country ball players. New York fans on the other hand will concede Ted Williams could hit (my, what he could have done if he played his home games in Yankee Stadium) or a Willard Nixon was a Yankee stopper, and maybe Carl Yastrzemski, who grew up in the fields of Long Island, were better than average ball players, but still neither will concede to the other. The Boston fan looks upon the New Yorker as less knowledgeable, one-sided due to press build-up, smug, greedy, flaunting, the big city con and they harbor a deep ingrown hatred of the Yankee pin stripe. New Yorkers look east to their Boston counterparts as complainers, who boast of overrated ball players, whose team plays in a match box ball park and whose press makes heroes out of bush leaguers. All of this results in one of the fiercest of battles between their favorites when they meet on the diamond with all else that is going on in the world taking a back seat.

Now that we have looked at the present day reasons for the rivalry let's, as has been a popular pastime lately, take a look at the roots of this series and develop it up through the present season.

Boston entered the American League in its initial season of 1901 and were known as the Somersets (after owner Charles Somers) and at various times up until 1907 as the Pilgrims, Puritans, Beaneaters and Speed Boys. When the Boston National League entry gave up their Red Stockings in 1907, the Boston American League owner, John I. Taylor, grabbed the name and modernized it to Red Sox. In the first several years, the Bostons boasted such great players as Hall of Famers Jimmy Collins (3B) and Cy Young (P), and other all-time favorites Fred Parent (SS), Buck Freeman (1B-OF), Lou Criger (C), Bill Dineen (P), George Winter (P), Chick Stahl (OF), Hobe Ferris (2B), Candy LaChance (1B), Patsy Dougherty (OF-IF) and Long Tom Hughes (P).

It wasn't until January 9, 1903 that Frank Farrell and Bill Devery purchased the Baltimore franchise and moved it to New York. The cost, $18,000. In March of that year the American League owners approved the sale and New York was officially an American League city. Overcoming problems of where they would be allowed to located their ball park and adopting the name Highlanders, because of the final location of that park, they played their first game on April 22, 1903 by losing to Washington 3 to 1 at the Nation's Capital. An ironic twist to this game was that Clark Griffith, who was the Yankee manager, would eventually become the longtime owner of the Washington franchise. Turning things around, they staged their home opener on April 30 at Hilltop Park (168th St. and Broadway) by beating Washington 6 to 2. They maintained the name Highlanders until April 1913 when they became the Yankees and moved from Hilltop Park to share the Polo Grounds with John McGraw's National League Giants. In May of 1922, they started the construction of Yankee Stadium where they moved in April of 1923, opening with the Red Sox (more on this later). Except for the 1974-75 seasons, when they played in the Mets' home at Shea Stadium while their Bronx playground was being rebuilt, they have been at home in Yankee Stadium. Those 1903 Highlanders brought few players over from Baltimore — Jimmy Williams, the second baseman, outfielder Herm McFarland, pitchers Barry Howell and Snake Wiltse being the most noteable. The others of note to perform for the initial issue New Yorkers were pitchers Jack Chesbro, Jesse Tannehill and Clark Griffith; outfielder Wee Willie Keeler; infielder Wid Conroy and catcher Monte Beville.

The first meeting between Boston and New York took place in Boston on May 7, 1903 at the Huntington Avenue Grounds, where the Boston entry played until moving to Fenway Park in 1912, with the Pilgrims winning 6 to 2 behind Big Bill Dineen who was caught by Lou Criger. Snake Wiltse took the loss for New York and was caught by Monte Beville. Chick Stahl had two triples and Hobe Ferris had a home run for the winners. The New Yorkers took the second game of the three game set 6 to 1 with Jack Chesbro besting George Winter. The third game went to Boston 12 to 5 but it marked the first of many rhubarbs to take place over the years when umpire Caruthers called a ball on New York pitcher Jesse Tannehill as he started to pitch and Boston batter Stahl hit the pitch for a double. The New York players in protest stormed to the plate with Tannehill and second baseman Williams being ejected from the game. The first meeting of the two teams in New York occurred on June 1, 1903 with Boston winning their 20th game of the season 8 to 2 as Long Tom Hughes defeated Chesbro with Buck Freeman of Boston hitting two home runs. Boston swept the three game series, winning by scores of 9 to 0 and 9 to 3 with Lou Criger homering in the second and Freeman again in the third game. Boston went on to win the league championship and to meet and defeat the Pittsburgh Pirates in the first modern World Series to become World Champions.

The 1904 season perhaps saw the birth of the great rivalry between these two teams and it has grown right down to today. Few fans are left who can go back to the events of 1904, but the roots of the competition of today's teams really took hold during that long ago summer. Going into late September of that season, not only Boston and New York had a shot at the pennant, but also Chicago, Cleveland and Philadelphia were in the running. The latter three teams finally fell by the wayside, leaving the Pilgrims and Highlanders to fight it out. New York's stocky thirty-year-old right-handed pitcher, Jack Chesbro, had pratically single handedly kept them in the pennant chase and wound up winning 41 games. On the Boston side of the ledger, a five man pitching staff kept them on a pennant course and they boasted three-twenty plus game winners, righties Cy Young (26-16) and Bill Dineen (23-14) and former Highlander left-hander Jesse Tannehill (21-11).

Going into the final week of play as the schedule would have it, New York and Boston were to meet on the last weekend of the season, an occurrence which would be repeated in years to come as we shall see. Manager Collins had his Pilgrims in first place from August 29 to September 3, when manager Griffith managed to get his Highlanders into first place. On September 5th, Boston regained the lead only to lost out to New York again a day later, a lead they held for three days. Boston was again setting the pace from the 9th through the 14th when New York took over for a day. The Pilgrims were again in the driver's seat on September 15th and 16th when New York took the lead and held on until September 29th, after which Boston spent three more days on top. This seesaw battle continued in the first week of October with the Highlanders winning the October 7th game 3 to 2 in New York (Chesbro beating Norwood Gibson for his 41st win) to lead by 1/2 game.

Boston now got a break as the October 8th doubleheader, originally scheduled for the Highlander Park, was transferred to Boston's Huntington Avenue Grounds because New York owner Frank Farrell, looking to make a few extra bucks, had earlier rented his park to Columbia University for a football game. Twenty thousand jammed the Huntington Avenue Grounds as Chesbro faced Dineen. It was Boston's day all the way as they won the first game 13 to 2, making fourteen hits including three each by Collins, Parent and Ferris and went back into first by half a game. The second game thus became of utmost importance. If Boston won they would be a game and one-half ahead. If New York prevailed, they would return to New York with their 1/2 game lead. Cy Young and Jack Powell hooked up in a pitching duel which, with excellent fielding support, saw Young and Boston emerge victorious 1 to 0 in a seven inning affair halted by darkness. The next day being a Sunday, a day on which baseball was not played in 1904, the teams traveled back to New York for another doubleheader on the 10th of October. A split would give Boston the flag, whereas New York had to win both games.

The stage was now set for what would forever remain a bitter memory for New York fans and a happy one for the several hundred Royal Rooters (a Boston fan club) led by "Nuf Ced" McGreevey, a prominent Boston saloon keeper. As game time arrived fans stood twelve to fifteen deep in the outfield of the little New York ball park. Big Bill Dineen was announced as the Boston starter while Happy Jack Chesbro was making his third start in as many games for New York. The Highlanders got to Dineen for two runs in the fifth inning, one being knocked in by former Boston favorite Pat Dougherty, and the other being forced in by a bases loaded walk. Some erratic fielding by New York in the seventh inning allowed Boston to score two runs and tie up the game. Then came the historic ninth. Lou Criger opened the Boston half with an infield single and was sacrificed to second by Dineen and on to third he went on Kip Selbach's out. Then came the play which has gone down in baseball history as one of the most written about and discussed plays of all time. While Chesbro was pitching to Fred Parent,one of his spitters took off over catcher Jack Kleinow's head for a wild pitch,and Criger scampered home with what proved to be the winning run and Boston's second American League Championship in as many years, forever known as "the pennant, won on a wild pitch". Dineen retired the Highlanders with ease in the bottom of the ninth. Both managers stuck with their first string line-ups in the second game which New York won in ten innings 1 to 0 with Ambrose Putnam out pitching George Winter. So it was a triumphant return to Boston with a final game-and-one-half lead and eight percentage points margin of victory. As has been told many times, much to the dismay of Bostonians, the owner of the National League champion New York Giants, John T. Brush, refused to accept the Americans' challenge to play a World Series. So ended the first of many great New York-Boston battles.

In 1905 both teams went backwards with Boston falling off to finish fourth, while the Highlanders slipped from second to sixth. One of the few high points of the season for the New Englanders were two May series victories over the New Yorkers of three games out of four at New York and again in Boston.

Probably no team in the history of baseball faded as fast as the Boston champions of 1903-04 when their 1906 edition finished dead last 45 1/2 games behind the pennant winning "Hitless Wonders" of Chicago. The Highlanders meanwhile moved up to second place and started the season off on the right foot by taking their first three games from the Pilgrims. The one bright light of the season for Boston came on April 30 when they visited New York and touched Chesbro and Doc Newton for twenty-three hits and a 13 to 4 victory. The next day the New Yorkers returned to shut them out 8 to 0, Brad Hogg besting Norwood Gibson in a game which marked the start of their downfall and foreshadowed events to come. Returning to the Huntington Avenue Grounds they dropped nineteen straight games before Jesse Tannehill managed to shut out the White Sox 3 to 0 on May 25. Despite the twenty consecutive defeats the loyalty of the Boston fan was demonstrated at that mid-week victory as 8,000 showed up (a good crowd for those days). A further testimony to fan loyalty was the twenty-five thousand who showed up several days later on Memorial Day for a twin bill with the Athletics and who were rewarded with two unexpected wins.

Although Boston moved out of the cellar in 1907, the most memorable events of the season were their adoption of the name Red Sox and the tragic death, during spring training, of their manager Chick Stahl. The thread that ran between the New York and Boston teams took a strange twist when Bob Unglaub, who had come up from New York in 1904 in an unpopular deal which saw Pat Dougherty go to the Highlanders, became the Sox manager. A couple of other Boston favorites passed from the scene when Bill Dineen was dealt to St. Louis and Jimmy Collins to Philadelphia. It was also a season when a new "Spoke" was added to the Boston machine. A young lad arrived from Texas in early September and went on to become one of baseball's all-time great centerfielders — Tris Speaker. He first appeared in the line-up on September 12.

In 1908 Boston continued their climb reaching fifth place while the Highlanders dropped to eighth. It did see another deal between New York and Boston when in mid-season Jake Stahl was regained by Boston and immediately took over the first base chores, giving them a very fine infield as he combined with Amby McConnell (2B), Heine Wagner (SS) and Harry Lord (3B). The most memorable of the games between the two clubs occurred on June 30 when forty-one year-old Cy Young hurled his third career no-hitter by beating New York 8 to 0 in New York. Cy and his long-time battery mate, Lou Criger, were rewarded by being traded during the winter, Criger going to St. Louis in December and Young to Cleveland in February as owner Taylor cleaned out the last of the '03-'04 World Champions.

Fred Lake, who assumed the Boston managerial post in the latter stages of the 1908 season, did an excellent job of handling the 1909 Red Sox and brought them home in third place while the New Yorkers rose out of the American League cellar under the guidance of manager George Stallings, who would later (1913-20) arrive in Boston to manage the Braves and gain everlasting fame as manager of the 1914 Miracle team. This 1909 Boston team, called the Speed Boys by owner Taylor, were typical of recent Red Sox clubs in that they were plagued by injuries. The speedy Jack Thoney was out most of the season with an ankle injury which signaled the end of what appeared to be a brilliant career. Thoney had come to Boston in 1908 but had been with New York in 1904. Players Stahl, McConnell, Lord and Wagner all were injured at crucial stages of the season. Jack Thoney, little known to today's fans, is spoken of in glowing terms by his teammates leading me to believe he was not only popular among the players of his era but also respected for his skills on the diamond. Boston won 13 of 22 games from New York in 1909 and only four times during that season did they score in double figures in single games and each time it was against New York. They did it in back-to-back games, April 28th and 29th, 12 to 2 and 10 to 4, at the Huntington Ave. Grounds, again 14 to 5 on June 23 in Boston and again on

September 6, 10 to 9 in the first of two games. Late in the season the great New York Highlander pitcher Jack Chesbro came to Boston from New York and made his only appearance as a Red Sox in the first game of a season-ending doubleheader against his former teammates and was the loser in a 6 to 5 New York win. Perhaps had owner Taylor kept Cy Young for one more year a pennant would have waved in Boston at the end of 1909. Owner Taylor and manager Lake had their differences during the campaign but under it all the foundations were being laid for the great Red Sox teams of the near future. Tris Speaker had come into his own; Harry Hooper arrived; Joe Wood became a winning pitcher; two young Vermonters, pitcher Ray Collins and third baseman Larry Gardner joined the team; pitcher Sea Lion Hall was obtained from St. Paul for pitcher Charlie Chech, thus the ground work for one of the most brilliant chapters in Red Sox history was started in 1909.

1910 saw the New Yorkers jump up to second place while a disappointing Red Sox team dropped back to fourth place under new manager Patsy Donovan. The season did see the Sox obtain two utility players from New York in catcher Red Kleinow and outfielder Clyde Engle. The New Yorkers reversed the 1909 season record by taking 13 of the 22 games the two clubs played, with all of the games relatively close in scores except for Joe Wood's 10 to 0 shutout of New York on May 9 at Boston and Ed Karger's 13 to 4 win in New York on July 7 and an 11 to 0 Highlander win at the Huntington Avenue Grounds on May 6. The two clubs opened the season on April 14 in New York by battling to a 4 to 4, 14 inning stand-off. This was the first season that the great Red Sox outfield of Duffy Lewis, Tris Speaker and Harry Hooper played together. When great outfield combinations are spoken of, this one ranks as the greatest despite the later-day Yankee outfield of Bob Meusel, Earl Combs and Babe Ruth which perhaps hit with more power but could not field as well as the Red Sox trio. The Highlander managerial reins passed from Stallings to their star first baseman Hal Chase during the season.

Despite Joe Wood's 23-17 record the 1911 season was as much of a disappointment for Bostonians as New York's was for them. The Sox slipped to fifth but the Highlanders fell all the way from second back to sixth, a game and one-half behind the New Englanders. Actually, Boston and Chicago (fourth place) were each 24 games behind Connie Mack's champion Philadelphia A's but Boston, even though they won one more game than Chicago (78 to 77) they lost one more (75 to 74). A familiar theme ran against this 1911 Boston club, which really wasn't that bad, injuries, injuries and more injuries affecting most every regular player. Five of Woods' 23 victories came at the expense of the New Yorkers, three of them being shutouts (2-0 May 4, 4-0 May 8, 7-0 October 3), all coming on New York's home grounds as Boston took the season series 12 to 10. Strangely, New York was 7 and 4 at Boston while Boston was 8 and 3 at New York. Maybe they should have switched fields! Joe Wood celebrated his 23rd win with a 7 to 0 shutout of the Highlanders at New York in the second game of a doubleheader sweep by sitting down 13 Yanks via stike outs.

1912 saw the Red Sox move into their new ball park, one of the finest in the country (Fenway Park); get a new manager (Jake Stahl); new owners (Jim McAleer and Bob McRoy); a pennant and world championship; a most valuable player (Tris Speaker) and a pitcher who would chalk up 34 victories, plus 3 more in the World Series (Joe

Wood). It was a year which saw them win more ball games than any Red Sox club to date (105-47), a truly remarkable team. The Highlanders meanwhile dumped Hal Chase as manager and brought in Harry Wolverton who had been a highly successful manager at Williamsport of the Tri-State League. His success did not follow him and he brought the New Yorkers home dead last 55 games behind the Boston champions. Stahl, who it later developed owned some stock in the new Red Sox ownership, gave up a successful banking job in Chicago to return to the big league wars as the first baseman-manager and what a job he did. His 48 road victories was tops for a Bosox club until the 1975 gang equalled it and his 27 road defeats matched the 1903 club's record and remains the best of any Red Sox team. His 57-20 home record ranks third in all of Sox history being topped only by the '46 and '49 clubs who each stood at 61-16 at the Fens. This was the year the Sox feasted on the Highlanders, at one point winning 14 straight from them, and it should be added 10 straight from the seventh place St. Louis Browns. The season series with New York wound up 19-2 to Boston's advantage and was the worst series disadvantage a New York American League club has ever had. It was the second best season series advantage by a Boston club being topped only by the 1904 club's 20-2 record over the Washington Nationals.

The link between Boston and New York grew greater in 1912 as it was the New Yorkers who helped Boston open Fenway Park losing 7 to 6 in eleven innings as spitballer Bucky O'Brien and Sea Lion Hall combined to defeat New York's big left-hander Jim Vaughn. Two facts stand out here; one, the Sox were to return the opening day favor by opening Yankee Stadium in 1923, and secondly, the loss by a left-hander seemed to set a precedent as Fenway Park has become a park notably tough for lefties to win in, a fact which can trace its roots back to this very first game. A good aggressive catcher, Hick Cady, made his appearance on the Boston scene in 1912, ironically he was acquired from Newark which in the Yankee haydays became their top farm club. The season also saw the Sox sweep a five game set at New York by scores reminiscent of the Yankee series in September of 1978 at Fenway Park. This series ran from June 19 to 22 with the Sox winning 5 to 2 behind Hugh Bedient; 15 to 8 Bucky O'Brien the winner; 12 to 3 as Joe Wood won his 14th; 13 to 2 behind Hall and finally 10 to 3 with Ray Collins the winner. A six game series in late June and early July at Fenway saw the Sox take five of the six behind the same pitchers with Sea Lion Hall chalking up two wins. Joe Wood's 33rd win of the season was recorded at New York on September 25 as he shut out New York 6 to 0 for the Bosox 100th win of the campaign. After all was said and done for the year the Sox had outscored the Highlanders 150 to 76 for their season series.

The Boston bubble burst quickly in 1913 as the Sox floundered around the second division until a late season surge pushed them up to fourth place where they settled. The reason for such a topple, that old bugaboo — injuries. As seems to happen with all great teams who take a tumble, managerial changes must take place and this became no exception in Boston as after 80 games Stahl was replaced by his catcher, Bill Carrigan, who proceeded to show his players he was in fact the boss. The Highlanders meanwhile were giving up their old Hilltop Park and moving into the Polo Grounds as tenants of the National League New York Giants. This in itself was a major move but the big news out of Gotham was the name change from

Highlanders to Yankees*. The Yanks moved up one notch from cellar to finish seventh in 1913. The Sox again took the season series, winning 14 games, while the Yankees copped 6.

In late October 1913 the Red Sox were sold to one Joe Lannin, a French Canadian with a good sense for business. While he was a Bostonian for years, he owned hotels not only in Massachusetts but in New York City and on Long Island. His Long Island holdings also included several golf courses. Again the Boston-New York tie-in raises its head. Carrigan became a miracle man in 1914 bringing the still injury-plagued Sox home in second place. This was particularly due to the arrival of a slick fielding shortstop, Everett Scott, who was later traded to New York. In a couple of deals between the clubs the catcher of the 1912 champions, Les Nunnamaker, was sent to New York and pitcher Guy Cooper came from New York and neither did much to distinguish themselves, although Nunnamaker pretty much split the catching chores in New York with Ed Sweeney.

Certain events were taking place now which were to shape the history of baseball and especially enhance the hatred between Boston and New York fans, although no one at the time could have in their wildest dreams envisioned that what was happening would have the effect it finally did. I do not want to get ahead of our story, but it is important to lay the groundwork for what will come later on. About the time Lannin purchased the Red Sox he also acquired the nearby Providence, Rhode Island club of the International League. With the outlaw Federal League raiding the International League clubs in 1914 for players Jack Dunn, the Baltimore club owner (yes, they were in the International League then), decided to break up his club. He offered as a package deal three of his young stars, a left-handed pitcher named George Herman Ruth, a giant (6'4 1/2") right-hander named Ernest Shore and their catcher Ben Egan. Dunn gave Philadelphia's Connie Mack first crack at buying the trio but money problems forced Mack to turn down the deal, so on July 18, 1914 Lannin purchased the group for $8,000. (Ruth's price was $2,900). Any serious student of baseball knows what Babe Ruth and Ernie Shore meant to the Red Sox. All were in the 1914 Red Sox line-up. Ruth posted a 2 and 1 record, Shore was 10 and 4 and Egan was dealt off to Cleveland with two pitchers for a sore-armed left-hander, Vean Gregg. Ruth won his first game for the Sox on July 11, a 4 to 3 victory over Cleveland at Fenway (a lefty winning at Fenway!) and lost his first game five days later 5 to 2 to Detroit. He was then shipped back to Providence where he helped them win the pennant, but returned later in the Sox season to defeat the Yankees 11 to 5 on October 2, again at Fenway. Shore gained a victory in his first Boston decision, a 2 to 1 win over Cleveland on July 14, and stayed on for the remainder of the season. The Yanks and Sox split their season series 11 and 11. We can see then that 1914 was the season which laid the groundwork for the growth of the rivalry between the two clubs which had been fairly dormant since 1904.

The 1915 season which culminated in a Red Sox championship actually found the New York nine led by Wild Bill Donovan in first place in mid-May, but Boston

---

*April 1913 official change of name. Many referred to them as the Yankees as early as 1911. The Spalding Guides start in 1911 referring to the Yankees. Called Yankees as early as 1904 in some sources.

moved into the lead on July 19 and never were headed, although second place Detroit fought them stubbornly. The fifth place Yankees gave the boys from Back Bay fits all year and wound up winning the season's series 12 games to 10. There were several Yankee-Red Sox firsts this season also. The Yankees wore their famous pin stripe uniforms for the first time and the young Red Sox pitcher Babe Ruth hit his first of many major league home runs off Yankee right-hander Jack Warhop on May 6 at New York's Polo Grounds, but lost the game to the Yanks 4 to 3 in 13 innings. The Yankees purchased pitcher Allan Russell from Jersey City He was destined to wind up in Boston.

The 1916 season started out on a sour note (was this a trend beginning for seasons following a championship — remember 1913 and 1979) as star outfielder Tris Speaker was traded to the Cleveland club for two players who were not exactly household names; pitcher Sad Sam Jones and infielder Fred Thomas. Jones, of course, developed into an outstanding pitcher (later sent to the Yanks) while Thomas did little except get farmed out not to return until 1918. Pitcher Joe Wood had such a painful arm he could not pitch at all and sat out the entire season. Down in New York, Yankee owners Ruppert and Huston, who were spending money anywhere they could to build up the franchise, were greatly upset by the deal which sent Speaker to Cleveland when they never got a chance to bid for the future Hall of Famer.

The Yankees finished fourth and the Red Sox, with everlasting credit to manager Carrigan's leadership skills, finished with their second consecutive American League crown. The Sox and Yanks alternated for the league lead in April but both later dropped off the pace with the Sox eventually returning to the top spot. The two met in New York in late April and the series was a wonderful one with the Sox taking the first and third games of three by one run margins 4 to 3 and 3 to 2, each a hard fought extra inning affair with Ruth winning his fourth consecutive game in the first encounter and Gregg copping the second for his first win of the season for the Crimson Hose. The second game was all Yankee as the New Yorkers dealt the Sox a 9 to 0 shut out. The teams staged a return engagement in Boston a week later and the Yankees prevailed in three of the four games, one being a 13 inning affair with Gregg losing two of the three games, including this extra inning one. On June 21 at Fenway Park, George Foster tossed a no-hitter at the Yankees, winning 2 to 0. In late September the two teams met in a four-game set at Boston with three of the games going ten innings. Another future Yankee, Carl Mays, won one and lost one while Dutch Leonard won the last game of the series, a ten inning 1 to 0 shut out. It was the second Sox shut out in a row as Babe Ruth won the third game 3 to 0. The season series again ended in an even split of 11 games each. The Sox duplicated the feat of the 1915 and later the 1967 team of dropping seven games back and coming on to win the pennant.

Sox owner, Joe Lannin, after two championships and a second place finish, decided he had had enough of baseball and in December of 1916 sold his holdings to two New York theatrical men, Harry Frazee and Hugh Ward. Little did the Boston or New York baseball worlds realize what this move would mean. As we shall see, it meant that the Boston days as the premier club in the American League would be coming to a drastic end, as the balance of power shifted to New York, the Yankees would begin a dynasty which would extend until today. This all certainly added to, if not cemented, the great Yankee-Red Sox rivalry. The Red Sox would suffer a series of humiliations which would last some thirty seasons, but that is getting ahead of our story. To Frazee's credit, in his first two seasons in Boston he attempted to help the club, but player demands for higher salaries certainly must have had him worried. The 1917 season series between New York and Boston produced a no hitter by New York's George Mogridge on April 24. Other than that, little excitement resulted although the Sox took four straight in late June at Fenway Park and won the season series 13 games to 9. Interestingly, the big four of manager Jack Barry's pitching staff were Babe Ruth (24 wins), Carl Mays (22 wins), Ernie Shore (13 wins) and Dutch Leonard (16 wins). In a few seasons the first three would be playing for the Yankees and Leonard would be earning his living in a Detroit uniform. For the record, the Sox finished second and the Yankees sixth.

One more pennant was to come Boston's way before they began their plunge into the American League's lower levels, that in the war-shortened 1918 season. As manager Barry joined the service, Ed Barrow was brought on to manage the Red Sox. He, of course, also plays a major role in the Red Sox-Yankee rivalry. Little remembered today as a Red Sox manager, he is better known as the Yankee general manager-president and builder of the great Yankee teams of the late 20's through the 1940's. Significantly, it was Barrow, on outfielder Harry Hooper's advice, who began the conversion of Babe Ruth from a pitcher to an outfielder in 1918. Perhaps an omen of things to come was the way the Yankees dominated the season series with Boston, winning 11 and losing six. The champion Red Sox enjoyed a wide series advantage over all other clubs, except for Washington and Cleveland who they played evenly. The first meeting of the two resulted in the Sox winning four of five games at Fenway. Of course, they could manage only two more victories the rest of the way with the Yankees sweeping two of the remaining four series and finishing fourth 13 1/2 games behind Boston.

What happened to the Red Sox in the years after the 1918 win has often been referred to as "The Rape of the Red Sox," first by the Boston sports writer Burt Whitman. Owner Frazee's theatrical interests were suffering and he needed money. It was available from Yankee owners Ruppert and Huston who wanted a winner at any cost. First to go to the hungry New Yorkers were pitching aces Ernie Shore and Dutch Leonard, along with outfielder Duffy Lewis. In return the Sox got four borderline players and Frazee got a check for $50,000. Leonard refused to report to the Yankees and was sent by them to Detroit. A few interesting things took place in the 1919 Red Sox-Yankee games. On June 28 at New York, Sox pitcher Carl Mays pitched both ends (complete games) of a doubleheader winning the first 2 to 0 and losing the second 4 to 1. A month later, after a dispute with Boston management, Mays would be pitching for the Yankees and Frazee would be $40,000 richer. The other notable attraction was the home run hitting of Babe Ruth who wound up setting a then American League record of 29 with number 28 coming off New York's Bob Shawkey on September 24 at the Polo Grounds. The Sox dropped back to sixth in the standings and the Yanks moved up to third and, although Boston took the season series between the two clubs (10 to 9), it would not be until 1946 they would again finish ahead of New York in the standings. Can you see how the frustration of the Boston fans must have grown, along with their hatred of the New Yorkers who had gathered up the bulk of Boston's diamond heroes? The crowning blow came in January, 1920 when it was announced that the Babe had been sold to New York. The rest of his career is a story perhaps too painful to repeat here in a book for the Red Sox fans. What was in New York and might have been in Boston is history and conjecture. It would have been nice to find out though! Damn Harry Frazee anyway. Harry made $125,000 on the deal and got Jake Ruppert to give another $350,000 loan against a mortgage on Fenway Park. Not a bad transaction for those days.

The 1920 season saw Ed Barrow swing a couple of deals which kept the Sox in fifth place while the Yanks, despite the imported Boston talent, remained in third. The Sox even swept the first series between the two clubs, taking a Patriots' Day twin bill! 6 to 0 and 8 to 3 and winning the next day 3 to 2. The three winning pitchers in that series — Waite Hoyt, Joe Bush and Herb Pennock — would all soon be traded to New York where they played major roles in pitching the Yankees to pennants and World Series victories. Before the year ended Hoyt, pitcher Harry Harper, infielder Mike McNally and catcher Wally Schang found their way to New York with second baseman Del Pratt, outfielder Sam Vick, catcher Muddy Ruel and pitcher Herb Thormahlen coming to Fenway. Perhaps of greater significance was the fact that Ed Barrow also said "so long" to Boston and would now be on the receiving end of his former bosses' deals. The Patriots' Day game set a Fenway Park attendance record (since broken). The attraction, of course, being the ex-Red Sox now playing for the Yankees, Babe Ruth.

1921 saw the Yankees win their first American League championship while the Red Sox again finished 5th and they would remain in the second division for 13 years. Actually, the Sox under new manager Hugh Duffy did quite well, despite the loss of pitchers Hoyt and Harper, by losing only four more games than they won (75-79). The leading Sox pitchers were Sad Sam Jones (23-16) and Bullet Joe Bush (16-9), a fact which did not escape the notice of the Yankee owners who in December obtained Bush, Jones and shortstop Everett Scott. Scott was in the process of setting an American League durability record for consecutive games played which stood until broken by the Yankee Hall of Famer Lou Gehrig years later. In exchange the Sox got shortstop Roger Peckinpaugh and pitchers Rip Collins and Jack Quinn. Collins and Quinn became the Sox leading pitchers in 1922, although Collins was foolishly shipped off to Detroit for the 1923 season. Peckinpaugh never played for the Sox, but was immediately sent off to Washington for third baseman "Jumping Joe" Dugan. Dugan was a good third baseman and after a fine start with Boston in 1922 he was traded along with outfielder Elmer Smith to whom else but the Yankees for outfielders Chick Fewster and Elmer Miller, shortstop Johnny Mitchell and a player to be named later who turned out to be Lefty O'Doul. Again New York got the better of the deal and Harry Frazee got another $50,000. The Yankees gained an eight game season series bulge, winning 15 while the Sox took 7.

The Red Sox seemed to find a home in 1922 as they fell into eighth place, a spot they had not been in since 1906, but a place they would remain in until 1933, except for a seventh place finish in 1924 and a 6th in 1931. This was their reward for all those Yankee trades. A once great Boston team now in utter discredit. The Yankees just barely nosed out the second place St. Louis Browns by one game for the American League pennant in 1922 and it was almost Boston who prevented it. For some reason the Yankee castoffs and misfits now wearing the Crimson Hose rose to the occasion when playing against New York, taking the season series 13 to 9 and winning the first two games of a season-ending three game series. The Yanks won the pennant on their final game of the year with the Sox 3 to 1. An unusual occurrence happened in the final Yankee-Red Sox series at the Polo Grounds in New York. In the first game of a Red Sox doubleheader win, Sox pitcher Herb Pennock gave up a home run to New York's Babe Ruth. This would prove to be the Babe's final home run at the Polo Grounds as the Yankees were to move into their new ball park, Yankee Stadium in 1923. What made it so unusual was that Pennock also gave up the Babe's first home run as a Yankee at the Polo Grounds on May 1, 1920. Oh, yes, in that last game in September, manager Duffy wanted to use Herb Pennock but Frazee, who was enjoying the plight of his benefactors, decided pitcher Alex Ferguson should be used. Fergie was knocked around for the three Yankee runs in the first inning and was relieved by Pennock who pitched seven effective innings before he was removed for a pinch hitter. You now have three guesses where Pennock would be pitching in 1923. He left Boston on January 30 and spent 11 successful seasons hurling for the Bronx Bombers before returning to Boston in 1934 to win two more games for Boston. The 1922 Yankees pitching staff consisted primarily of former Boston ace right-handers Mays, Hoyt, Bush and Jones. No wonder Boston fans hated New York.

To complete the rape of the Red Sox, the only player left with any promise was a young right-hander named George Pipgras who had been farmed out to Charleston, South Carolina for the 1922 season. He too was stolen away from the Sox (Jan. 3, 1923) and starred for the Yankees for eight and one-half seasons before being sent back to Boston in 1933. The ace of the 1923 Red Sox pitching staff was Howard Ehmke who managed 20 wins for the tail-end Sox. He also figured in two games of some note against the Yankees, who won the pennant for the third consecutive year. Ehmke had tossed a no-hitter at the Philadelphia A's on September 7 and on his next outing, September 11, he faced the Yankees at Yankee Stadium. On this occasion he hurled a brilliant one-hitter. The hit was made by the first Yankee batter of the game, Whitey Witt, and it was questionable. The ball was misplayed by third baseman Howard Shanks, but from then on Ehmke retired the next twenty-seven batters in order, thus barely missing becoming the first pitcher in history to toss back-to-back no-hitters. Ehmke suffered an unkind fate in the game of September 28 against the same Yankees. In the sixth inning of this game he faced 16 batters and in the six innings he pitched he allowed 17 runs and 21 hits as New York banged out 30 hits over all and won the game 24 to 4. Ehmke also was on the mound for the Sox on April 18 when they opened Yankee Stadium, losing 4 to 1. The big and happy news in 1923 for Boston fans was the sale of the club by Harry Frazee to Bob Quinn in mid-season. No tears were shed in Boston over this move.

Hopes rode high in 1924 for new manager Lee Fohl and despite an April four-game series loss at Yankee Stadium, the Sox spent May and half of June on the 1923 world champions' heels. On June 4 and June 9 the Red Sox were actually in first place and Bostonians were sure the drought was over. The joy was short-lived and by July 1 they had slipped to seventh place where they finished. The Yanks wound up in second place and winning 17 of 22 contests from the Sox.

For the next six years, 1925-1930, the Red Sox remained in the American League cellar taking their lumps from the Yankees who remained on or near the top of the American League with teams solidly built on a base supplied courtesy of the Red

Sox. Players continued to move from Back Bay to the Bronx during this distressing period. In December, 1924 infielder Howard Shanks and catcher Steve O'Neill found their way to New York. In May of 1925 outfielder Bobby Veach and pitcher Alex Ferguson moved on to New York. June of 1926 saw outfielder Roy Carlyle head south. In May of 1930 pitcher Red Ruffing was traded to New York and he continued to win pennants for them into the early 40's. The 1927 Yankees are considered by many as the greatest major league team ever assembled as they tore through every team in the league. Against Boston they won 18 games while losing just 4, as the Sox were no match whatsoever for the Yankees. They took three of four games of the first clash between the teams in April; swept a five-game series in Boston in mid-June and walked away with a four-game set June 29 to July 2 at New York. Perhaps the most exciting encounter was the first game of the September 5 twin bill at Fenway Park in which the Sox hung on to win 12 to 11 in 18 innings. They dropped the second game 5 to 0 in five innings with pitcher Hal "Hooks" Wiltse gaining both decisions. Bob Quinn, the hoped-for savior of the Red Sox, was beset with all types of bad luck and, in efforts to survive, sold his former ace pitcher Danny MacFayden to the Yankees in 1932 for a couple of pitchers and $50,000 and later in the same season pitcher Wilcey Moore took the same route. There were even rumors of pitcher Ed Morris going to New York for $100,000 before the big right-hander was fatally stabbed to death in the spring of 1932. So on and on it went, with the Yanks finishing ahead of the Sox and easily taking the season series year after year. Even in 1931 when Boston managed a sixth place finish, the Yankees had an easy time with them, winning 16 of their 22 meetings.

As 1933 approached, Quinn found himself owing $350,000 and in February of that year along came Thomas Austin Yawkey to buy out Quinn, and on the heels of a "I don't intend to mess around with a loser" statement, Boston's hopes were raised again. Until his death in 1976, Mr. Yawkey tried to live up to that statement, but the Yankee dominance was not over yet. In Mr. Yawkey's first season as the Sox owner they moved out of the American League cellar, a position they have not returned to since. In one of his first major deals he sent $100,000 to the Yankees for the pitcher who was once a promising Sox farm hand, George Pipgras and infielder Billy Werber. For the Red Sox to buy players from the Yankees was big news in Boston where for years they had seen them going the other way. These two players may well have meant the difference of the Sox moving out of last place. Pipgras pitched well until he injured his arm, and while he hung on until 1935, he was never the same again. Another former Yankee had a hand in Boston's baseball fortunes in 1933. Former Yankee trainer Doc Woods was engaged by Yawkey to administer to his players and it happened one day that slugging first baseman Dale Alexander (and Boston's first batting champion) hurt his leg and was given heat lamp therapy in the clubhouse while Woods went to the dugout to watch the game. A Red Sox rally held his interest while Alexander was being roasted. By the time Woods rescued his patient the leg was so damaged that Alexander was lost to the team for weeks. Actually, he never returned to his former self and was out of the big leagues after the season, a serious blow to the Red Sox hopes. An October 1 game with the Yanks found Babe Ruth returning to the mound to pitch a complete game victory 6 to 5 over his former team. His effectiveness might be questioned as the Yankees made 18 outfield put-outs in the game.

The 1934 season saw Boston move up to fourth place under new manager Bucky Harris, who would later manage the Yankees to a pennant in 1947. In May the Sox sent $20,000 and infielder Fred Muller to New York for infielder Lyn Lary. On

Sunday, August 12 some 48,000 jammed Fenway Park to give Babe Ruth a rousing ovation in his farewell Boston appearance as the Yanks and Sox split a doubleheader. The paid attendance was announced as 46,766 and it was estimated that another 15,000 were turned away, although many stayed and lingered outside the ball park fuming mad because they couldn't be admitted. It was the largest crowd to see the Sox play in Boston and it overflowed onto the playing field in a solid mass from the right field foul line to the center field flag pole. I should note that the 1979 Red Sox Media Guide lists this crowd at 41,766 as the largest Fenway crowd in history. I should further note that in my research I found reports of the August 19, 1934 game with Detroit as drawing 50,000 (46,995) as being reported as the largest crowd in Boston's American League history. I don't know why this game is not listed as Boston's largest, but somewhere in the sands of time it seems to have been overlooked. How they fit that many fans into Fenway Park is also a mystery. I bet the Boston fire marshal sat up and took notice.

Infielder Lyn Lary was sent packing off to Washington before the 1935 season, and in exchange, shortstop Joe Cronin came to Boston as manager and lasted in that capacity longer than any other Sox manager, 13 seasons. At the time and for years this deal with the $250,000 involved was baseball's biggest. Along with other players Yawkey was buying up, the Red Sox were now being called the "Millionaires" and "Gold Sox". 1935 saw pitchers Wes Ferrell win 25 games and Lefty Grove 20, but still the Yankess dominated the season series 12 to 9 with a three-game sweep in Boston in late September making the difference. The Sox still could not move out of fourth place but things appeared to be on the up-swing, although during most of the early Cronin years, the Yankees were unbeatable. The rivalry with the Yanks had now been fully revived and resulted in packed stands both in New York and Boston whenever the two clubs met. On June 2 the fans were treated to a rare occurrence during a 7 to 2 Yankee win in New York against their old pal George Pipgras. Six of the New Yorkers unloaded for home runs, all with no one on base.

In 1936 and 1937 there were disappointments in Boston. While the Yankees were winning pennants the Sox were finishing 6th one season and 5th the next. During these years one deal transpired between the clubs when first baseman Babe Dahlgren was sold to New York, no longer needed with the arrival of Jimmie Foxx in Boston. It was during these years that it became apparent that it was Yawkey's aim to catch and beat the Yankees. When talk got around to winning, it was not to take the American League championship but to beat the Yankees. This type of talk certainly set up priorities in the minds of the fans, all leading up to fueling the fires of the rivalry. Yawkey found that while the Yankee success was built upon buying star players from the Red Sox, that when he tried it by buying the Philadelphia heroes of Connie Mack, he did not meet with the same successes the Yankees had. Taking a close look at the baseball world, Yawkey saw that Branch Rickey had given the St. Louis Cardinals success by building a good solid farm system and he further saw that the old Red Sox manager, Ed Barrow, and George Weiss of the Yankees had done a great job of blending in players from the minors and a farm system of their own to carry along Yank successes. "That's the only way we can catch the Yankees" was the Yawkey battle cry as he set out to establish a farm system. It was during these seasons that some of the players first appeared who would finally become members of the 1946 team, which would finally beat out the hated Yanks. Mike Higgins (3rd base in 1946 and later to manage) came from Philadelphia in the winter of 1936 with the Sox giving up former Yankee Billy Werber to get him. Higgins later went to Detroit but returned in '46, and at the 1937 Sarasota spring training camp there was a young rookie named Bobby Doerr, who later would be a real nemesis for the Yankees. (Want to start an argument with a Yankee fan? Ask him who was better, Doerr or Joe Gordon.) The Yankees were not standing still and were developing a few players of their own. Foremost among the new Bronx men was a young man from San Francisco (Joe Cronin's home town); Joe DiMaggio, whose brother Dom would star in Boston, was his name. He celebrated his second season in the big time in 1937 by hitting his first major league grand slam home run in the 6th inning of a July 5th game off Boston's Rube Walberg and on October 3, he hit his third of the year off Boston's Joe Gonzales.

After the disappointments of '36 and '37, the Sox rose to heights in 1938 they had not attained since finishing first in 1918 (the longest twenty years they would ever go through) by finishing second to the champion Yankees. Actually, the Sox played ball at a .591 pace, the same as their championship year of 1916. Joy abounded in Boston in 1938, not only because of the heroics of slugger Jimmie Foxx, but wonder of wonders, the Sox split their 22 games with the Yankees. The Yanks were 9 1/2 games ahead in the standings but the Sox (perhaps it should have been socks) led the majors in batting with a .299 average, 25 points higher than New York, and the two clubs were the only ones in the majors to top 900 runs scored (New York 966, Boston 902). Despite Jimmie Foxx's 50 home runs, the Yanks out-homered Boston 174 to 98. Anyway, the Sox were happy and so were their fans. It so goes in major league circles that contending clubs usually do little swapping of players between them, and you will notice deals between the Yanks and Sox were growing fewer and fewer. However, in 1938 the Red Sox did steal a player from under the noses of the Yankees when they signed a native New Yorker, pitcher Mickey Harris, who would later help Boston win the American League crown. Before we leave the 1938 season, we should note that a Yankee Stadium attendance record for a doubleheader was established on May 30, which stands to this day. 81,841 fans jammed the Yankee ball yard that day to see the Red Sox and Yankees do battle in two games, one marked by a brawl between manager Joe Cronin and Yankee outfielder Jake Powell who had objected to a pitch made too close to him by the Sox twirler Archie McKain. Cronin was just defending his pitcher! The next day Jimmie Foxx hit the first of three grand slams he would hit that season by belting a pitch by Yankee right-hander Joe Beggs into the stands.

The Red Sox celebrated baseball's centennial year (1939) with another powerful squad again finishing second, this time 17 games behind the New Yorkers, but taking the season series 11 games to 8. In July the Sox had one of the finest hours in their history, long remembered and gloated upon by Red Sox fans, although I must admit what the Yankees did to our Sox in September of 1978 takes some of the luster from it. See how long Red Sox fans remember! In that long ago season the Sox were running up a sensational July twelve-game winning streak, which included a five-game sweep of the mighty Yanks at Yankee Stadium from July 7 to July 9. In this historic sweep the Sox won the opener on a steaming hot July afternoon 4 to 3 with Emerson Dickman besting Red Ruffing. In a doubleheader the next day they won 3 to 1 with Fritz Ostermueller beating Oral Hildebrand, and 3 to 2, with Denny Galehouse over Marius Russo. On the 9th there was another twin bill with Dickman gaining the win in relief of Lefty Grove over Monty Pearson, (4 to 3) and in the second game Jack Wilson completed the sweep by besting Bump Hadley 5 to 3. It was one of the worst humiliations suffered by the Yankees in their glory years under Marse Joe McCarthy. McCarthy was prompted to say "Just who the hell are supposed to be the World Champions, us or the Red Sox?" The winning streak of 12 ended when Detroit beat them 13 to 6 on July 17. The whole streak came on the road. Another important event happened in an April 20th Yankee-Red Sox encounter in New York. A brash young rookie named Ted Williams got his first major league hit, a double off the former Red Sox pitcher Red Ruffing.

The Yankees offered the Sox a golden opportunity in 1940 as the four-time consecutive world champions slumped to third place, but the same fate hit the Red Sox. With some of their stars starting to show their age, the Sox fell back to a fourth place tie with Chicago, and Boston again had a taste of disappointment. One of the bright spots for Boston was the introduction of a new outfielder, Dom DiMaggio, the younger brother of the Yankees' famous Joe DiMaggio. The Sox seemed to get off on the right foot by beating the Yanks on opening day when manager Cronin surprised the baseball world by naming young Jim Bagby, Jr. instead of one of his veterans to start the season. Bagby stopped the Yanks cold, but from then on it was all down hill.

In 1941 the Yankees again moved up to first place and, following their example, the Red Sox made it to second place and while they battled the Yanks closely for a good part of the season, they finally faltered and finished 17 games behind the winners. The season series was again in the Yankees' favor 13 to 9. It was a season that the older Boston heroes just about faded away while the Williamses, DiMaggios, Doerrs, Peskys and Hughsons were about to take their place. One of the oldtimers, Lefty Grove, had a history-making event occur to him against the Yankees on May 25. On that date he gave up a single to Joe DiMaggio, becoming the first pitcher to become a part of two of baseball's greatest feats — DiMaggio's 56-game hitting streak and Babe Ruth's 60 home runs. As a Philadelphia A's pitcher he had given up a home run to Babe Ruth during the Babe's streak in 1927. (Ted Lyons of the Chicago White Sox was the other pitcher involved in both records.) Speaking of DiMaggio's record, it was in a game against Boston on July 1 at Yankee Stadium that his single in the second game of a doubleheader off Jack Wilson tied Wee Willie Keeler's record of hitting in forty-four consecutive games. The next day Joe's home run off Heber Newsome broke the record. Of course, the highlight of the season as far as Boston was concerned was Ted Williams' batting .406. It was felt, in Boston at least, that Ted should be awarded the league's most valuable player award. "The Sporting News" named him Player of the Year, but when it came to MVP, DiMaggio and his 56 game streak won out. Resentment flared in Boston only adding more fuel to the rivalry between the two teams. After three unsuccessful attempts, the Fenway Faithful had seen Lefty Grove finally win his 300th major league game.

The Japanese attack on Pearl Harbor in December of 1941 had its effects on the 1942 season as many players began trading their baseball uniforms for the blue and khaki of Uncle Sam. Enough of the Red Sox and Yankee regulars remained to make both very legitimate and good ball clubs, however. The story remained the same, the Yankees again in first with the Sox trailing in second place by nine games. For awhile it seemed it might be a Boston year as at the All Star break they trailed New York by only four games. The Sox won 93 games. Not bad in most seasons, but the Yanks picked '42 to win 103. Even so, the Sox took 12 of 22 games with the New Yorkers. Boston fans, hoping for the best, turned out in record numbers setting a new Fenway attendance record which would stand for several years.

No team was hit any harder by players going into service than were the 1943 Red Sox. They had a good excuse for tumbling back to seventh place other than old age and player trades a la Frazee. The Yankees, with a mixture of war-time players and veterans not yet in the service, actually fielded a decent representative team and again won the league championship. Pitcher Tex Hughson did manage to defeat the Yankees on June 26 for his eighth consecutive victory over them in two years.

The war-time seasons of 1944 and 1945 saw both the Yankees and Sox play along with hit-and-miss lineups. In 1944 each team had a few genuine big leaguers, especially on the mound, but the story remained the same, the Sox finishing 4th — one step behind the Yanks. The 1945 Sox finished 7th with the Yanks 4th. There was some excitement in the games between the clubs. Thirty-nine-year-old Joe Cronin started the 1945 season opening series in Yankee Stadium for the Sox and actually got off to a decent beginning. In the third game of the series, as he was rounding second base, his spikes caught in the bag, his leg was fractured and his playing career was ended. The Sox not only lost that series but the season series to the New Yorks 16 to 6. As a matter of fact, they not only lost that opening three-game series but dropped five more before getting their first win of the year. The 1945 season will long be remembered as the season that a young man from Mississippi got his discharge from the service and joined the Red Sox mound corps. He turned in one of the most sensational freshman seasons of any rookie pitcher. Dave Ferriss not only won his first two games via shutouts, but he reeled off eight consecutive wins at the start of his career; had a second eight-game winning streak; won 21 games and defeated each team in the league the first time he faced them. That second straight shutout came at the expense of the Yankees during their first trip to Boston. Having chalked up his eight straight the Sox invaded Yankee Stadium for a four-game set in early June. This was one of the most ballyhooed series between the clubs in years. The first two games were split, and as a Sunday twinbill approached, Ferriss was billed as the main attraction. Could he make it nine straight? The day dawned with threatening skies and at game time a light rain was falling. With a big crowd on hand there was no way they were not going to play. The Yanks won the contest 3 to 2, mainly due to a run which resulted from Ferris slipping on the wet grass allowing a batter to reach base. From then on the Yanks owned Ferriss, defeating him four more times that season. Dave only dropped ten games that year but five of which were to New York.

The 1946 season found the major league clubs back to prewar strength for the most part and what a grand year it was for Boston. They finally finished ahead of the Yankees, winning the American League championship with New York finishing in 3rd place, 17 games off the pace. Mr. Ferriss, by the way, won all his games at Fenway Park and shut out the St. Louis Cardinals in the third game of the World Series, also at Fenway. Other grand things happened to the Red Sox in 1946. On May 10, despite Joe DiMaggio's fifth inning grand slam home run off Joe Dobson, the Sox defeated New York 5 to 4 for their fifteenth consecutive win. The streak stopped the next day at Yankee Stadium when Tiny Bonham shut them out 2 to 0 with Tex Hughson taking the loss. After years of no player transactions between the two clubs, the Sox purchased pitcher Bill Zuber from the Yanks. Zuber was helpful, picking up 5 wins against one loss. Boston won its season series from every club with a 14 to 8 advantage over New York. Looking back, there may well have been one series which turned the tide for Boston. On April 24 and 25 the Yanks invaded Fenway and walloped Tex Hughson and three relievers around for a 12 to 5 win. The next day behind Joe Dobson the Sox reversed the score and won 12 to 5. From then on the Sox seemed to hold no fear of their longtime tormentors. The Yankees were having managerial problems in 1946 as their longtime, very successful leader, Joe McCarthy, resigned and was replaced by former catching great Bill Dickey. In his first game after assuming command, the Red Sox defeated New York at Boston 7 to 4 with Dave Ferriss winning his seventh consecutive game with the Yankees ace Spud Chandler being knocked out for the first time.

The Sox did not have long to bask in their glory and although it was not even dreamed of at the time, it would be twenty-one seasons before they returned to the top rung. Along the way there were some exciting seasons and some very disappointing ones, but sadly for Red Sox rooters the Yanks were usually on top. In 1947 the Red Sox joy turned to tears as three of their top pitchers, Tex Hughson, Dave Ferriss and Mickey Harris all came up with sore arms resulting in a drop to third place while the Yanks jumped back into first on the bat of Joe DiMaggio and the arms of Allie Reynolds and Joe Page. On September 3 the Yankees banged out 18 hits against the Sox at Fenway, all of them being singles, but later in the month the baseball world was startled when the Red Sox announced the signing of Mr. Yankee, Joe McCarthy as their manager for 1948.

A new manager and two tremendous winter trades brought the best of the St. Louis Browns to Boston in the way the Sox formerly sent players to New York. Coming to Boston from St. Louis were pitchers Jack Kramer and Ellis Kinder, and infielders Vern Stephens and Billy Hitchcock which seemed certainly enough to insure the 1948 flag. The chase was on from the opening gun, a three-way battle between New York, Boston and Cleveland with the race going right down to the final Sunday of the season as the pitching of Kramer, Mel Parnell, Dobson, Kinder and Earl Johnson took up the slack of the loss of the sore arms. On that Sunday, October 3, the Red Sox beat the Yankees at Fenway 10 to 5 with Johnson getting the victory to go into a first place tie with Cleveland and force the first American League playoff, which Cleveland won 8 to 3. The Sox had a season advantage over every club except Cleveland and were 14 and 8 over New York.

The 1949, 50 and 51 seasons might easily have been Boston's had they been able to just develop one more pitcher. As it was they had to settle for a second and two-thirds in three of their most frustrating seasons. In '49 Red Sox fans had to swallow a pill even more bitter than the playoff loss of the previous October. That 1949 club may have been one of the best ever assembled in Boston. Again, it was Cleveland (14 wins, 8 losses) and the lads from the Bronx (13 to 9) who made the difference. The Fenway opening day crowd for a game with New York was the Sox largest opening day crowd until it was broken 20 years later. (New York won 5 to 3.) The Yanks had signed on a new manager, Casey Stengel, considered by many as a buffoon, yet he won his first of many pennants and went on to enter the Hall of Fame, on the same day, I might add, as Ted Williams. Not to get ahead of ourselves, but in the final series of the season the Sox needed to win only one game of two for the pennant and didn't. The season may actually have been lost on June 28, 29, 30 in what I like to call the "DiMaggio Series". The Sox lost three straight at Fenway Park, taking the loss so badly they went to Philadelphia, dropped three more in a row, skipped up to Yankee Stadium where they dropped two more before Mickey McDermott pitched them to a 4 to 2 win on July 5 to even their season record at 36-36. This streak came on the heels of a home stand where they had won 10 of 11. Back to the "DiMaggio Series", it was one never to be forgotten by those who saw it. A splendid athlete, Joe D. had one weakness; he was prone to injuries. In 1949 he missed spring training and half the season as the result of a bone spur on his right heel. He finally played an exhibition game against the Giants in New York and didn't decide until the last minute to make the Boston trip. He arrived at Fenway just prior to the game and in time to make the starting line-up. Now remember here was a man who had no seen real good pitching for eight months. His first time up on the 28th (this game set a Fenway Park record for attendance at a night game — 36,228), he singled; next time up he homered with Phil Rizzuto aboard, a blow that proved to provide a 5 to 4 Yankee win. Yankee fans rate this as one of their all-time thrills. The next night he hit two home runs, the first a three run blast. The second broke a 7 to 7 tie and led to a 9 to 7 Yankee win. In the third game he had another three run homer to give the Yanks a 6 to 3 victory. When the dust settled Joe had nine RBI's, four homers, a single and a .455 average for the three games, which certainly provided New York with plenty of inspiration for the rest of the season.

With two games left and a one game lead, the Sox arrived at Yankee Stadium needing only a split to win the pennant from the second place New Yorkers. In the first game they got off to a 4 to 0 lead but New York rallied to win 5 to 4, the big hit being John Lindell's homer. Now tied with one game left (shades of 1904) Ellis Kinder and New York's Vic Raschi battled for 8 innings with the Yanks leading 1 to 0. McCarthy pinch hit Tom Wright for Kinder in the 8th, but the Sox could not score. In the Yanks half of the inning they scored four times off Parnell and Hughson. The Red Sox scored three times in the ninth; too late, New York won 5 to 3 to become champions — perhaps their finest hour. Until this day folks wonder about McCarthy's decision to remove Kinder. Not much to look back on, but on July 4 the Yankees were 12 games ahead of Boston who tied them on September 25, a reverse of 1978. The Sox did set a new record for them in completing double plays. It came in a September 25 game against the Yanks. It was in this game that Bobby Doerr lay in pain having been taken out of a DP where he was told by McCarthy "C'mon Bobby, get up. You don't want all these people in the stands to think you are a Yankee, do you?"

1950 found the Yanks win as usual and Sox finish third four games off the pace. 1951 was a repeat, except the Sox were 11 games behind the winning Yankees. On April 18, 1950 the Sox blew a nine run lead while losing 15 to 10 to New York and equalled a record by using five pitchers in one inning. Late in 1950 Yankee Phil Rizzuto got a letter saying if he played in Boston he would be shot. Manager Casey Stengel had an answer. He gave Rizzuto's uniform to Billy Martin to wear during the game. Martin couldn't sit still all day. Rizzuto's only fear was that the Sox Jim Piersall might take a swing at him as he and Martin were always fighting. On Memorial Day, 1951 Red Sox pitchers were hot as they struck out budding Yankee slugger Mickey Mantle five consecutive times. This twin bill pretty much was a Ted Williams-Vern Stephens affair. Ted scored from second base on a sacrifice bunt, a rare play for anyone. In the first game his home run tied the score and Stephens' 15th inning homer won it. In the nitecap Ted doubled to tie matters up and Stephens singled to win the game. On July 1, 1951 Captain Bobby Doerr singled off Yankee pitcher Ed Lopat for his 2000th major league hit. Seven days later the Yanks set a record of sorts when for the 20th straight game they played at Fenway Park their starting pitcher failed to complete the game. On September 28, 1951 (1st game) at Yankee Stadium, Yankee Allie Reynolds pitched a no-hitter against the Sox winning 8 to 0. The suspense in the game, like all no-hitters, lasted right up to the final out. With two out the Red Sox batter was Ted Williams. He hit a high foul pop-up that Yankee catcher Yogi Berra dropped. Given a second chance, on the next pitch Ted fouled to the same spot. This time Yogi held the ball and Reynolds had his gem.

Things began to get worse for the Red Sox in 1952 as they slipped to sixth place while the Yankees remained on the top. Worse was still to come the Sox way. By now you must be getting the picture of how Boston fans frustrations and ill feeling toward their arch rivals, the Yankees, were growing again. A late August deal in 1952 saw pitcher Ray Scarborough sold to New York. 1953 was the first of four consecutive fourth place finishes while the Yankees were winning their fifth consecutive pennant. The New Yorkers finished second in 1954 then ran off four more first place championships, but we are getting ahead of our story again. By 1953 most of the old gang was gone from the Boston scene and manager Lou Boudreau was embarking upon a youth movement. On July 1, 1953 lefty Mel Parnell shut out the Yankees 4 to 0 at Fenway Park to record his 100th Red Sox career win. A lefty pitching a shut-out at Fenway Park was a rare feat in itself. He joined Cy Young, Joe Wood, Lefty Grove and Joe Dobson in the 100 win circle. On September 19, Mel shut out the Yankees 3 to 0 again in Boston. It was his fourth blanking of the Yanks for the season and he became the first pitcher to shut out an opponent four times in a single season since Hall of Famer Walter Johnson accomplished this feat in 1908 for Washington.

The 1954 Red Sox club did nothing to distinguish itself. It was in fourth place, an unbelievable 42 games off the pace set by the Cleveland Indians who led the second place Yankees by 8. Just for the record, Boston was 2 and 20 against Cleveland, one of the worst series disadvantages they ever suffered as injuries and sickness crippled Ted Williams and Mel Parnell suffered a broken arm. Little occurred in the 9 to 13 annual series loss to the Yanks. Only of passing interest was the June 30, 6 to 1 Boston win at Fenway when in the 3rd inning three Sox batters were plunked by pitched balls. In the second game of the September 6 doubleheader the Sox were down 7 to 0 to the Yanks and came back to win 8 to 7. It was a miserable season. In 1955 the Sox could move no higher but improved their games behind to 12 and the Yankees regained to top of the pile besting the Sox in 14 of their 22 encounters. The Sox did sweep a fourth of July doubleheader at New York as their pitchers Willard Nixon and Tommy Hurd struck out four Yankee pinch hitters. For the fourth consecutive year the Sox wound up 4th in 1956, 13 behind the usual Yankee winners who again took 14 games from the Sox. On August 7 some 36,350 jammed Fenway

Park to set a single day game record which stood until 1978. This was the game which cost Ted Williams $5,000 for his spitting performance and his famous bat throwing incident. He tossed his bat high into the air and spit in the direction of the press box. The Sox behind nemesis Willard Nixon won the game 1 to 0 in 11 innings. The September 21 game at Fenway Park produced a 13 to 7 Boston win, but it saw Yankee slugger Mickey Mantle hit a space shot home run off Frank Sullivan into the centerfield bleachers about 40 feet to the right of the flag pole, a blast that failed by a foot to clear the wall.

The 1957 and 1958 seasons passed into the record books with little excitement between the Red Sox and Yankees with each finishing in the same place in the standings on both occasions — Yanks first, Sox third. New York won the season series both times 14 to 8 and 13 to 9. The teams did play an unusual number of extra inning games in '57, which may or may not have meant something other than three more wins for the Yanks against one loss. On April 21, 1958 in a game at Yankee Stadium, it seems the Sox just didn't want to win. They were beaten 4 to 1, but in the process had sixteen runners on base. Their only run resulted from a Ted Williams homer. Of the 16 runners, 13 were stranded and two were eliminated on double plays.

In 1959 the Yankees championship run came to an end and they dropped back to third place, but the Sox dropped back to fifth while winning the season series for the first time in years, 13 to 9. This was due mainly to a five-game series the clubs played at Fenway Park July 9 to 13. The Sox got off to a bad start in '59 and General Manager Bucky Harris seized this opportunity to replace manager Pinky Higgins of whom he was none too fond anyway. Things began to happen under new manager Billy Jurges, who lasted less than a year, being replaced by Higgins again in 1960, and one was the five-game sweep of the New Yorkers by scores of 14-3, 8-5, 8-4, 7-3 and 13-3 with Frank Sullivan winning the first and last games. In the final game of the series Gene Stephens was sent in in the sixth inning to run for Ted Williams and the Sox proceeded to bat around bringing Stephens to bat and he delivered a grand slam home run. This sweep brought back memories of that famous 1939 sweep in New York for many Beantowners. Earlier in '59 the Sox Tom Brewer threw a shut-out at the Yanks at Fenway, winning 4 to 0 which was the first time the Sox were able to shut out New York over a 55 game stretch. In a September 7 game at Fenway Park the unlikely candidates Don Buddin, Jerry Casale and Pumpsie Green hit consecutive home runs against New York as Boston won 12 to 4. None of the three were noted sluggers and Casale, by the way, was the winning pitcher.

The seasons of 1960 to 1966 brought five more Yankee pennants and then, of all things, a sixth and tenth (expansion had arrived) place finish. For the Red Sox it brought a series of comical incidents, a few decent players, a series of comical ones, a succession of deep second division finishes, and in 1966 a ninth place finish at last put them ahead of the boys from Gotham; but really, what did it mean? 1960 saw Ted Williams leave the active ranks and 1961 saw the arrival of one Mr. Carl M. Yastrzemski. There was one 1961 game between the Sox and Yanks that will be remembered as long as baseball is discussed. It insured immortality for a Red Sox pitcher whenever trivia experts gather. Tracy Stallard, on October 1st, gave up home run number 61 to Yankee Roger Maris. In 1962 there was a player transaction between the two clubs when the Sox obtained infielder Billy Gardner for outfielder

Tom Umphlett who had been playing at the Sox farm club in Seattle. This was also the year of the Gene Conley-Pumpsie Green defection. On a hot July afternoon Conley was pitching at Yankee Stadium when Carl Yastrzemski, playing left field, lost a fly ball in the sun which led to the departure of Conley. Upset over the pounding, he took his frustration to the clubhouse. It only grew when the team bus got stuck in New York traffic on the way to the airport. Conley, requiring relief for the second time that day, left the bus with Green in tow. The nearest men's room was in a nearby tavern. Two days later Green rejoined the team in Washington and Conley had gone home. While in New York, they had decided to visit the Holy Land (perhaps they figured they needed all the help they could get), but lack of passports put an end to that plan. The hero of any success during this period against the Yankees was ace reliever Dick Radatz, but then there were few teams who had success against him. Then there was slugger Dick Stuart who had all kinds of trouble with ground balls hit his way. Who will ever forget one Sunday afternoon at Yankee Stadium after Mr. Stonefingers Stuart had messed up several grounders, a disgusted Earl Wilson standing on the mound flagging his arms at Stuart as if to say "get out of here, I give up with you." Finally, funny man Stuart was traded for a sore arm pitcher, Dennis Bennett, but neither the departure or arrival helped any. The 1966 editions of both the Yankees and Red Sox were terrible and the Sox nosed out the Yanks by 1/2 game for ninth place. However, the Sox were showing something noticeable to the careful baseball observer. They were miserable during the first half of '66, at one point losing 5 straight, but in the second half they had a 42-35 record but still manager Billy Herman felt the ax and Dick Williams was named as his replacement. What followed was one of the most successful eras in Red Sox history.

For any fans who lived through it, 1967 will always be remembered as "The Impossible Dream" year. One of the great years in baseball history, it saw the Sox march from ninth place to win the league championship by winning on the last day of the season. The Yanks moved up one spot to ninth, but the two were still battling each other as if it were they who were battling for the flag as in the late 40's. In late June things got rolling at Yankee Stadium when it appeared Yankee pitcher Thad Tillotson tossed a "wild pitch" at Sox third sacker Joe Foy, who had hit a grand slam homer the previous night. Foy was hit in the helmet. In the bottom of the inning Tillotson came to bat only to be plunked by a Jim Lonborg pitch. The benches emptied and a five minute brawl ensued led by the Yanks' Joe Pepitone and Boston's Rico Petrocelli with Petrocelli going several rounds with a number of Yankees. Following innings found Boston's Reggie Smith and New York's Dick Howser each being hit by pitches before things finally cooled down. It seemed every time the teams met that season the games were hard fought. Perhaps the reason was their first New York encounter when a Red Sox rookie named Billy Rohr took the mound and tossed a brilliant game, having a no-hitter going into the ninth with two out before Yankee catcher Elston Howard got a hit, the lone hit for New York. Before the season ended Howard was in the uniform of the Red Sox, a move which may have insured them the flag. Two days later the clubs were involved in an 18 inning game which saw a 7 to 6 Yankee win after 5 hours and 50 minutes of play. Five days after Howard arrived in Boston, Red Sox catcher Bob Tillman was sold to New York. Extra inning games between the clubs culminated in a granddaddy of a twi-night doubleheader on August 29. The first game went the normal nine, but the second became a marathon with the Bronx Bombers finally prevailing in 20 innings,

4 to 3. This made a total of 29 innings played for the evening and fears arose that the strain on the Sox might seriously hurt their pennant drive, but it did not.

The 1968-71 period was a continuation of what had gone on before, marked by hard-fought games with nothing of special interest occurring, except that on September 21, 1968 Sox pitcher Ray Culp pitched his third straight shut-out, completing 30 consecutive scoreless innings by tossing a one-hitter at the Yankees in Yankee Stadium. In most of those years the Sox finished ahead of the Yankees who were building for the future. In 1970 the Yanks managed a second place finish, one spot ahead of the Sox. Each club had their turmoils but were taking back seats to the Baltimore Orioles who were dominating the American League East.

A 9-9 split of the now reduced season series (since 1969 when the league split into two divisions) was not the big news of 1972. The Red Sox made what has been referred to as their worst trade when in March of that year they sent relief pitcher Sparky Lyle to New York for first baseman Danny Cater and shortstop Mario Guerrero. Lyle haunted the Red Sox and helped the Yankees regain their former dominance while the pair who came to Boston were soon gone and forgotten. The Sox managed a second place finish, still ahead of the fourth place Yankees.

Things began to heat up again in the 1973 season. The Sox started the season off by taking a three-game series at Boston, the first two games by the lopsided scores of 15 to 5 and 10 to 5, then went to New York where they split a pair. They took four more of five over the Fourth of July weekend in New York, all close, hard fought games. The tension and frustration between the clubs was mounting when an August 1-2 set was upon them. The Sox won both games, the first 3 to 2, the second 10 to 0. What happened in that first game served to heighten fan interest in the series for the next six seasons. In the ninth inning the Yankee batter was Gene Michael and with runner Thurman Munson on third, Michael attempted a bunt with Munson coming home. Michael missed and here came Munson toward the plate where Carlton Fisk was waiting with ball in hand. Munson came in with elbows high, ready to move the stone walled Fisk, who absorbed the full force of Munson and landed squarely on the snuff in his back pocket, but popped right up swinging. Fisk was attacked by both Munson and Michael, coming away with a bruised eye and scratches. Thus was born the famous Fisk-Munson brawl. Until Munson's untimely death in 1979 the confrontations between the two were anticipated by the fans as much as the games themselves. Upon Munson's death in an airplane crash, Fisk said that the bad blood between the two actually disappeared years before and what had occurred was a press build-up making more of an issue of the affair than actually was fact. Nevertheless, here were the two premier catchers in the American League. The careful observer would have noticed the good natured bantering between the two when either came to bat, but perhaps they were more interested in possible explosions. At any rate, it was a good year for the boys from the Hub as they took 14 of 18 games.

1974 saw the Sox continue where they left off by winning 11 of the 18 encounters. The Yanks jumped over the Sox, finishing second, while the injury plagued Sox dropped back to third. Boston had opened a big lead but the Yanks and Orioles would not give up. Injuries and suddenly silent Bosox bats started to drag them back and on September 9 they opened a crucial two-game series at Fenway Park. In the first game the Yanks prevailed 6 to 3 for their first win at Fenway in over a year, to move into first place. The second game promised to be another Red Sox-Yankee classic, Pat Dobson vs Luis Tiant. Tommy Harper got the Sox a run in the first inning which stood up until the ninth as Dobson was retiring 19 of 20 batters. Lou Piniella worked Looie for a walk and the speedy Larry Murray went in to run for him. Chambliss then hit a Tiant offering to right which a fan touched with Murray scoring and Chambliss going to third. Out popped Boston manager Johnson arguing a ground rule double saying Chambliss should remain at second and Murray at third. A raging ten minute argument resulted in Chambliss being sent back to second, but Murray was allowed to score as the umpires felt he would have anyway. A golden opportunity for the Sox came and went in the bottom of the inning when they loaded the bases but could not score. So the game went on into the 12th inning when Alex Johnson, obtained the day before, crushed one of reliever Diego Segui's pitches into the centerfield bleachers and another typical Sox-Yank game ended with that ex-teammate, Sparky Lyle, holding back the Sox in the bottom of the frame. Don Zimmer, current manager, didn't realize how big a rivalry this was until a game in '74 at Shea Stadium while Yankee Stadium was being rebuilt when he had to don a batting helmet for protection from the debris being tossed his way. Unfortunately, this has been a sad occurrence over the past few years of the rivalry. In 1977 Billy Martin threatened to pull his Yankees off the field at Fenway when his centerfielder, Mickey Rivers, became a target of the bleacherites. Bosox ace reliever, Bill Campbell, suffered a similar fate in the bullpen at Yankee Stadium. The fights in and around the ball parks reached their zenith in 1978 when a trip to a Yankee-Red Sox game resembled a Bowery brawl. Much of this brought about by the obscene chants of Yankee fans and subsequent rebuttals by Red Sox faithful. The fact that T-shirts, buttons and hats emblazened with the saying were quickly produced and sold outside the park did not help settle down the fights at all.

As always happens in this long series, the tables would turn and in 1975 it happened. The Yanks started the season as the favorites but the Sox, led by the two fantastic rookies, Jim Rice and Fred Lynn, got off in the lead. In late July the New Yorkers had a chance to catch up when the Sox invaded Shea Stadium for a four-game series. The Yanks took the opener 8 to 6 on Friday night. The second game shocked Yankee fans when the Sox scored three times in the ninth (an old Yankee trick) to pull out a 4 to 2 win. Sunday brought on a memorable twin bill. In the opener, Catfish Hunter and Bill Lee dueled pitch for pitch, a magnificent game before a turn-away crowd. With one out in the ninth, Fred Lynn reached on an error, Rice whiffed but Lynn surprised everyone by stealing second. Rick Miller got a hit to left center and Lynn scored. Sox 1, Yanks 0, only three Yankees needed to be put out. With one out up stepped Graig Nettles who promptly sent a long drive to left center between centerfielder Lynn and left fielder Rice with extra bases written all over it. Then came certainly one of the most remarkable catches in all of baseball history — a charging Fred Lynn, driving and rolling over, came up with the ball, holding it high for all to see while he was still lying on the ground. These great catches have become a Lynn trademark, but certainly never will such a catch be made again in such a crucial situation. Lee got the third out, a pop-up to third. The Yanks' backs were broken and soon their manager, Billy Virdon, would be gone to be replaced by Billy Martin. For the record, the Sox completed the doubleheader by shutting out the Yanks in the second game 6 to 0 behind Yankee killer Roger Moret and moved on to a pennant and World Series.

All kinds of bad news hit the Red Sox in 1976: owner Tom Yawkey's death, contract problems with several stars, cancelled deals with Oakland, etc., etc., etc. The favored Sox found themselves in the same circumstances as the '75 Yankees and the teams completed the similarity by swapping places in the standings: Sox 3rd, Yankees 1st. The first meeting of the two occurred on May 20 at Yankee Stadium and again fireworks prevailed. In the 6th inning the Yankees' Lou Piniella, attempting to score from second on a hit to right, was caught at the plate by a Dwight Evans to Carlton Fisk throw. In the resulting collision Piniella believed the ball had been dropped and he tried to kick the ball away, but instead inadvertently kicked Fisk. The upset Fisk saw red and tagged Piniella again, this time on the head. Lou's turn now and he grabbed Fisk by the chest protector and Fisk rapped him again with the ball, this time on the chin. That did it. The benches emptied and the war was on with Yaz leading the charge. Bill Lee joined the festivities only to have Graig Nettles put both arms around him to try to drag him away. Then Mickey Rivers jumped Lee from behind, put an arm around the pitcher's neck and began punching him. Lee was down and in obvious pain. Nettles, meanwhile, was trying to explain to a menacing group of Lee's teammates that he simply wanted to get Lee off the pile. By now Lee was up and charged Nettles with a verbal barrage. Nettles now blew his cool and socked Lee in the eye, knocking him to the ground. Finally, Red Sox trainer Charlie Moss escorted Lee away. Lee had injured his shoulder. It was weeks before he recovered. It was the fight for which the game is remembered, but overlooked is the fact that Carl Yastrzemski hit two home runs, making five in two games to tie a major league record.

Peace did not prevail in 1977 as the clubs again battled for the League Championship, but as has happened so often, the Yankees won it all and Boston was the runner-up, despite winning the season series 8 to 7. On June 17, the two met in Fenway Park and the Sox unloaded four home runs in the first inning (Burleson, Lynn, Fisk, Scott) to greet Catfish Hunter. Two days later the Sox completed the three-game sweep (9-4, 10-4, 11-1) as Doyle, Carbo, Rice, Yaz and Scott all homered, establishing a new major league record of hitting a total of 21 homers over 5 consecutive games. The Sox out-homered the Yanks 16 to 0 in this series. On June 24 at Yankee Stadium, the Yanks won 6 to 5, halting a seven-game Boston winning streak (actually the Yankees won the three-game series), but homers by Yaz, Hobson and Scott allowed them to set a major league record of 33 home runs in ten consecutive games. Boston's 6 to 3 win at Fenway Park on September 18 was marked by Carl Yastrzemski's eighth inning home run which was the Red Sox 200th of the year, making them only the fifth team to hit 200 or more home runs in a season twice.

The story of the 1978 Red Sox-Yankee chase has been told over and over and the details may be too painful to enter into again here for Red Sox fans. Certainly it was a great comeback by New York. The race appeared to be a runaway for the Bosox, who at one point led the Yanks by 14 games, but a faltering Red Sox machine struck by injuries saw their lead slowly disappear. Then came that fateful series in Boston — "The September Massacre", which found the clubs tied when the dust had settled. Sparing you the details, New York wins them all: September 7, 15-3, September 8, 13-2; September 9, 7-0; September 10, 7-4. It was the first time since 1943 that the Yanks took four straight at Fenway Park. The totals tell the story: Total runs, N.Y.

—42, Sox 9; Hits, N.Y. 67, Sox 21; Errors, N.Y. 5, Sox 12. From then until the last day of the season the two battled back and forth, the Sox slipping only to battle back. On the final day of the season, October 1, the Sox beat Toronto 5 to 0 while New York lost to Cleveland 9 to 2 resulting in the second ever American League tie, each club at 99 and 63. The two best teams in baseball would come down to one game, that at Fenway Park. The stage was set, Yank ace Ron Guidry vs ex-Yank Mike Torrez. A 39 year-old Carl Yastrzemski, playing like a youngster, put the Sox in lead by hitting his 17th home run in the second frame and later singled in another run. Rice got Burleson home in the sixth and the Sox went ahead 2 to 0. With two on in the seventh, ex-Yankee Torrez got himself in trouble. Two singles (Chambliss and White) put two on and up stepped the weak hitting Bucky Dent. He caught a Torrez pitch which just made the screen in left — Yanks 3, Sox 2. Paul Blair then doubled and Munson doubled him home, 4 to 2. In the 8th Reggie Jackson homered off relief pitcher Bob Stanley making it 5 to 2. Then Jerry Remy doubled in the 8th and Yaz singled him home; 5 to 3 Yanks. Fred Lynn then drove Yaz home; 5 to 4 Yanks. The Sox got two on in the last of the ninth, but Yankee reliever Rich Gossage got Yaz to pop up and the season ended with the Sox battling down to the last out with the tying run 90 feet away. The Sox had won 99 of 162, but they had lost 64 of 163. Perhaps the greatest game of all between the two had taken place. Those who could remember certainly must have thought back to 1904 and 1949.

The 1979 season saw the Yankees tumble from first to fourth place and the Red Sox drop back to third as injuries took their toll on both clubs. The new scheduling arrangement was taking its toll as the number of games between these two natural rivals dwindled to 13 with their first meeting not occurring until May 18. Again the two battled before turn-away crowds whenever they met. The Yankees took the year's play 8 to 5 and since both were out of the pennant race, although the Sox hung close until late July, not much occurred between the two except the usual fan excitement. Jim Beattie shut out the Sox 10 to 0 on May 18 and two days later Tommy John did likewise, 2 to 0, and the Sox Bob Stanley returned the favor on September 5, 5 to 0. You can be sure when tickets go on sale for 1980 at Fenway and Yankee Stadium, the first to be grabbed up will be those for games involving these clubs, with the fans getting them doing the bragging and their friends the envying.

So there you have it — the history of this great rivalry. As the future unfolds, more great chapters will be added. The fierce rivalry is certain to continue as they have played this way since 1903. The reasons why this grew to such a rivalry? Certainly the closeness of the two cities, the underdog vs the established club, the fact that they have both been closely involved in many pennant races, the fights and arguments, the good feelings fans on either side get when their boys win, the memories, take your pick or advance your own reasons, because fans and players alike feel the electricity. The feeling even gets down to the minor league level when their farm clubs meet. It's this type of thing that baseball is all about and makes it the great game it is. Got your tickets yet?

RED SOX TRAGEDIES

In drama, tragedy can be defined as the conflict of man with fate or the gods with a resulting unhappy ending, usually brought about by some weakness or error by the central character. In baseball the same can be said to be true. Surely the fate that befalls a player with a sore arm or one who is hit squarely by a batted or thrown ball, shortening a career or ending a promising one, falls within the realm of the unhappy. The batted ball which hits a pebble in the infield and bounces over the fielder's head or the error committed at a crucial moment are all sad fates which are beyond the control of the player. The team with only three solid starting pitchers demonstrates a weakness which is often tragic, especially if the balance of the team is better than average. Then there are the events which easily can be called a tragedy by one team, and luck, skill or a great play by the other club. Bucky Dent's home run in the 1978 Red Sox-Yankees play-off game certainly was a tragedy for the Red Sox hopes but in the New York camp it would be looked upon in a different light. The list of such events in Red Sox history could be, and is indeed long, but here we will not look at them as much as the players who have met with some unexpected or sudden event which not only curtailed or ended their careers but also had an effect upon the Boston team as a whole.

Baseball, by its very nature, lends itself to injuries often serious enough to render a player unable to continue. They say just throwing a baseball with the velocity that is required of professionals is unnatural in itself, and combined with the arm motion and twists required to throw a variety of pitches it is a wonder the arm can hold up at all. Baseball tragedies come in all sizes and shapes; some get sore arms, some pulled muscles, some lose their reflexes, some their sight, some succumb to John Barley Corn, fast women and high living. If the player makes it to the majors we often hear about his tragedy, but stop for a moment and think about all of those stories of the local hero who sets out for a career in baseball only to find it abruptly ending in the minor leagues. Sometimes it ends when they start throwing curve balls, yet for others it ends in a variety of other ways. Who hears about these misfortunes which are no less tragic to the one involved than to the established major leaguer who suffers some twist of fate? Who among us hasn't said, "Hey, see that guy over there, he could have been in the big leagues if only he hadn't _____." It would probably take volumes to discuss all of those promising players who were at one time or another in the Boston farm system whose careers ended permaturely. Here we will only touch on several of them. We will look more closely at those on the major league level.

I suppose you could say that the very first club was a tragedy of sorts. Maybe not to the new American League fans but certainly to the fans in the cities from which that first crew came to join the Boston Americans. Certainly the Boston Nationals were crippled by the defecting players who crossed over to the other side of the New Haven railroad tracks to play in the new Huntington Avenue Grounds. The fates of illness and injuries have plagued the Sox almost since their birth. A good right handed pitcher in those early years was George Winter and in the very second season of Red Sox existence he became ill and that combined with injuries to their best hitters, Pat Dougherty, Jimmy Collins and Chick Stahl, who were all out for long periods, certainly cost them the American League pennant. Interestingly, tragedy seemed to stalk all of these 1902 Bostons. Winter never really had another great year, although he hung around until 1908 when he was sent to Detroit and drifted out of baseball. Dougherty recovered to become a popular Boston hero until he was suddenly traded to New York in 1904. Collins and Stahl are interesting studies in tragedy. Collins, the first Boston manager, Hall of Famer and local hero fell into disfavor with owner John I. Taylor who believed Jimmy was retreating to the dugout too often in an effort to escape the wrath of the fans who were on his back, and not performing in the field where he was needed. Collins had hurt a knee but when the club physician stated he felt Collins could play he countered that his nerves were shot and placed the club in Stahl's hands, while he took an unauthorized trip to a nearby beach. The Pilgrims, as the Sox were known then, suspended Collins, and toward the end of the 1906 season he was relieved as manager, primarily because of his differences with owner Taylor, a tragic end to an early Boston Hero of both National and American League fame. The irony hadn't ended yet. Chick Stahl was named the new manager and finished up the 1906 season with a poor 5-13 record in the spot held by his pal and roommate Collins who was now cast in a player role. After forty-one games in 1907 the popular third baseman was sent packing to Philadelphia. That 1907 spring training season held in store for Bostonians their first real tragedy of a major magnitude.

The team was training in Hot Springs, Arkansas and on the way back to Boston the club stopped at a place, soon to be well known to the folks back in the Hub, West Baden Springs, Indiana. It was here that the very popular manager-player Chick Stahl committed suicide by swallowing carbolic acid. He had been given the acid by a doctor in Hot Springs for external treatment of a slow healing bone bruise suffered in training. At the time there was little to explain such an act by the man who was most popular among his fellow players and fans alike. He had been married less than a year and apparently quite happily. A friend of mine, Bill Gavin, now of South Weymouth, Massachusetts, remembers Stahl's family well. The Gavins were neighbors of Miss Julia Harmon, Stahl's bride, and got to know Chick well also. Both were happy and very popular members of their community and the manager's death was keenly felt back in Boston, according to Bill. It was later learned that Stahl had tried to resign as manager several days prior to his death, but had been convinced by owner Taylor to stay on for awhile and to retain the team captaincy. Several of his teammates reported that they felt that Stahl had been considering such an act for several days, but at the time they did not consider it a threat. On the day of his death he was up early and spoke with his roommate, Jimmy Collins, regarding what a fine day it would be for practice. He dressed and went to breakfast, apparently in good spirits. An hour later he returned to his room and complained to Collins that he was not feeling well. He appeared chilled and was having an effort speaking. The alarmed Collins called in several players who gathered around the bed where Stahl had by now fallen. Stahl, obviously trying to suppress the pain he was feeling, was now muttering to himself, finally addressing the assembled players, "Boys, I couldn't help it. It drove me to it." Those were the last words he spoke. A moment later he was dead. No one present knew what his final words referred to. It is assumed the pressure of managing had gotten to him. Boston American League baseball had lost one of its most well-liked and popular players.

The sadness evoked by Stahl's death was to be followed by two more bizarre events. Fred O'Connell, the reporter who had written of Stahl's death, followed him within the month as pneumonia struck him down, also in West Baden Springs. The coincidences didn't end here. A year later Stahl's widow was found dead back in Boston under some mysterious circumstances. Found in an alley doorway, she had been assumed murdered for her expensive jewelry. There were reports that she had died of natural causes, probably exhaustion brought on by the use of drugs and alcohol. At any rate, this was a strange chapter in Boston baseball.

In 1903 Boston was having catching problems which appeared solved when they picked up a National League jumper from the Brooklyn club, one Charles "Duke" Farrell, who despite his thirty-seven years was considered an excellent catcher and a dangerous hitter. Unfortunately, he broke a leg in an early season game and was lost for the year and never again played a full major league season. There was another strange set of circumstances surrounding Farrell's injury. The only remaining catcher was Lou Criger, who had been ill all spring. This fact caused manager Collins to seek another catcher, and he signed Garland "Jake" Stahl, who would later become the manager of the great 1912 Red Sox team. Here was a tragedy whose circumstances led to a move which later helped the club, and perhaps would never have taken place except for Farrell's busted leg.

In 1905 the Red Sox had a rookie pitcher named Joe Harris who, in one full season and two partial campaigns, won a grand total of three games while dropping thirty. In '06 he was 2-21 but he did manage one memorable game. He pitched a 24 inning game against Philadelphia, but as luck would have it, he lost but gained everlasting fame. After the game he was praised and it was predicted he would now have a brilliant future. It was his last good game in the majors as the next season he fell ill and was released. His opponent that day was a young Jack Coombs who went on to become one of the greatest pitchers in the game.

That brings to mind another Red Sox rookie who burst on to the major league scene in a grand fashion. In 1967 a young Billy Rohr started an early season game against the hard-hitting New York Yankees, and for eight and two-thirds innings held the Bronx Bombers hitless before Yankee catcher Elston Howard managed a single. The Red Sox won the game amid predictions of a brilliant future for Rohr who became the toast of Boston. Unknown at the time, that was the end of Rohr. He won but one more game for Boston while dropping three. The next season he popped up in Cleveland and won a game for the Indians and has not been heard from since.

One of Rohr's pitching mates in 1967 was Jim Lonborg who had finally reached his pitching potential and almost single-handedly pitched Boston to the American

League championship. "Gentleman Jim" took the baseball world by storm, sure to be a great pitcher for years to come. After a fine World Series, Jim felt like a little skiing out west around the holiday season. A fall off the slopes, an injured leg and the end of a promising career were all he got for his venture. Attempted comebacks were only partially successful. After four more seasons with Boston, shunting between the majors and minors in an effort to regain his former brilliance, he was dispatched to Milwaukee and then to the Philadelphia Phillies for six seasons, in a couple of which he performed fairly well. His loss was a hard pill for Boston to swallow, and destroyed their hopes for future pennants, a major tragedy.

The great pitcher, Cy Young, picked another way to end his stay in Boston. Good living and the inability to push away from the table, along with the delights of good Kentucky whiskey developed quite a bay window on Cy's front side. This fact did not go unnoticed by enemy batters who began bunting on Young, realizing he would have trouble stooping over to make the required fielding play. this was the beginning of the end for the Hall of Famer, who years later would have the major pitching award in baseball bear his name.

In 1908, a player joined the club by the name of Jack Thoney, little known or even remembered by today's fans. Ask any of the players who served with him and they will extol upon how he gained his nickname, "Bullet Jack". One of the fastest runners in the league, Thoney was very popular with his teammates. In 1909, in an early season game, Jack injured his ankle and appeared in only a few games for Boston that summer. His speed gone, never to return, Thoney didn't make the 1910 squad, appeared in a few games in 1911 and was out of baseball for good, with the promise of a great future gone. Ironically, owner Taylor loved to refer to that 1909 club as his "Speed Boys", a name the press adopted for the team for a short period. Perhaps the speediest of them all, Jack Thoney, hardly appeared at all.

Another speedster appeared about the same time as Thoney. This man set the team record for stolen bases until it was broken sixty-one years later by the current Red Sox coach, Tommy Harper. Although the tragedy involving Tris Speaker was not a great blow to him personally, it was to the Boston baseball world. For nine seasons in Boston, Tris had done everything expected of him and more. He made the move from the Huntington Avenue Grounds to Fenway Park and led the Sox to World Championships in 1912 and 1915. Then came that fatal Opening Day announcement in 1916. Speaker had been sold to Cleveland for $50,000 and two Cleveland rookies, pitcher Sad Sam Jones (who later developed into a great pitcher) and infielder Fred Thomas. Speaker had been a hold-out all spring and although he did play in the exhibition games, he was not under contract. Speaker, of course, went on to star at Cleveland for many seasons, while Boston's baseball fortunes began to sink despite pennants in 1916 and 1918. This trade,next to the Babe Ruth trade to New York in early 1920, certainly ranks as one of the great mistakes in Red Sox history.

Tris Speaker's roommate and good friend during his Boston years was pitcher Smokey Joe Wood. Perhaps the fastest pitcher baseball has ever seen, Joe Wood was also tied into this 1916 Speaker trade as we shall see. Wood in his prime may have been the best pitcher ever to perform for the Red Sox. He joined the Sox in 1908 and won only one game in his first season, but what progress he made after that. Eleven wins, then 12, then 23 until he led the 1912 team with an incredible 34 wins, including 16 straight at one point, and added three more wins in the World Series against the powerful New York Giants. What a pitcher he was that season. In an 1912 interview, the future Hall of Famer and great pitcher Walter Johnson was asked if he could throw harder than Joe Wood. Now remember, Johnson was known as one of the all-time hard throwers. "Can I throw harder than Joe Wood? Listen, my friend, there's no man alive who can throw harder than Smokey Joe Wood," was Johnson's reply. Wood would do everything in 1912. If the game was close and a relief pitcher might be needed, his teammates would come over and say, "How about it, Woodie," and usually manager Stahl would say "Okay, go down to the corner (as they called the bullpen in those days)." Joe would go and start throwing, just in case he was needed. As Wood would tell the author years later, "You see, no one would head down to the bullpen before the game like they do today. Back then, no one would go down there until the middle of the game. You started and you relieved, it made no difference."

So here he was, not yet twenty-three years old and the toast of the baseball world. It appeared that a bright future would be his for a long time. Joe had minor tragedies such as Speaker accidentally slamming a door on him and breaking a toe, and being hit by a ball in batting practice that caused a bloot clot in his leg which had to be operated on. These were nothing compared to what happened in the spring of 1913. Joe went to field a ground ball on wet grass and slipped, falling on his thumb, which he broke. It was the thumb on his pitching hand and it was placed in a cast for several weeks. Whether he tried to pitch too soon after the mishap or not, something happened to his shoulder and he was never again able to pitch without a terrific amount of pain in his right shoulder. The author can attest that, to this day (1979), Joe Wood has trouble lifting that right arm much above his waist. Despite the end to a spectacular career, Joe Wood remains to this day one of the finest gentlemen I have met in this game of baseball. Not a bit bitter about the fate which befell him, he did win 10 games in 1913 and 9 in 1914 adding 15 more in 1915, but was never the same.

Now in 1916, the year Wood's lifelong pal, Speaker, was traded to Cleveland, Joe was also listed as a holdout and did not appear at the training camp. It was reported that Wood, along with others, had been upset when owner Lannin had forced salary cuts upon them. Not so, says Joe, "My shoulder was so sore I couldn't pitch in 1916 and laid off for the season." At any rate, in 1917 Joe wound up in Cleveland with Tris Speaker, never to win another game on the mound, but to star in the Cleveland outfield as a hitter. Another tragic tale in Boston history, but at least a fairly pleasant ending for a fine player and person.

Another pitching story came to a sad conclusion at the end of the 1917 season when George "Rube" Foster, who had pitched very well for the Sox for five years, announced that, due to illness along with a sore arm and back which had bothered him every time he tried to pitch, would retire to his Oklahoma ranch. Another brilliant pitching career came to an early and tragic end. Actually, Foster had announced his retirement a year earlier but had returned to give it one more try.

The Boston front office has not been without its share of tragedy. When Bob Quinn purchased the Red Sox from Harry Frazee in 1923 he installed Jim Price as the club's secretary. Price had a long history as a sports writer and minor league club president and was well known in baseball circles of the day. In January, 1929 Price committed suicide by slashing his wrists with a razor blade. This was the second tragedy for Quinn in his early years as Red Sox owner. When he purchased the club he had as his biggest backer Palmer Winslow, a glassworks millionaire from Indiana. Less than two years after Quinn purchased the club, Winslow was stricken with illness in 1926 and died leaving Bob alone to run the club in the middle of the depression and without the funds Winslow had brought to the deal. Actually, Winslow's health had been failing since shortly after the purchase of the club and Quinn received little in the way of advice or cash from him. Add to this the fact that the third base bleachers at Fenway Park burned down in May, 1926 and many of Quinn's Sunday and holiday dates were rained out and you have a tragic reign for the Boston front office.

As Quinn's ownership was coming to an end, another tragedy hit him, this time in the player ranks. Big Ed Morris, a pitcher of some promise, was stabbed at a farewell fish fry given by some of his friends in Brewton, Alabama on the eve of his departure for spring training and he died two days later, March 3, 1932, in a Century, Florida hospital. Morris was known for his smoking fast ball which won him 19 games with the 1928 last place Red Sox. Despite several off seasons, due to a sore arm, he was still considered a fine prospect at the time of his tragic death. It seems that a fight broke out at the going-away party between Morris and Joe White, a local gasoline station operator, and a knife was plunged several times into the big right-hander's chest. There has been a question in my mind for several years now as to the reasons for Big Ed's poor showing in the 1930 and 1931 seasons, especially since Bill Gavin has explained to me that for three years one of his prime obligations was to find two pints of very sour milk and have it ready for Big Ed the minute he entered the park. Billy Rogell, an infielder during Morris' 19 win season, would often hide the milk with Morris threatening to leave the park if it were not produced. Such antics have long been typical clubhouse scenes.

In the last year of Bob Quinn's ownership he made a trade with the Detroit Tigers that brought a big but sluggish fielding first baseman to the Red Sox who proceeded to win the first American League batting championship by a Boston player. Dale Alexander, a Tennessee farmer, won the batting crown with a .372 average. He played again for the Sox in 1933, but an unfortunate clubhouse accident ended his career after that season. The Sox had engaged the former Yankee trainer Doc Woods, who decided that a leg injury suffered by Alexander might best be treated by heat therapy. So one day he placed Dale under the heat lamp and left him for a few minutes to stroll out to the dugout to check on the progress of the game. He became so interested in the game that he forgot all about Alexander and, by the time he did, Alexander was extremely well done. It was weeks before Dale returned to action and it was this "treatment" which was later the cause of his passing form the major league scene.

George Pipgras, a former American League umpire and Red Sox scout, was obtained from the New York Yankees in 1933 after several very good years on the mound in New York. He was considered an excellent purchase and to be the pitcher who would lead the Sox out of a series of second division finishes. His future as the Red Sox savior ended abruptly when he injured his elbow. He remained with Boston until 1935 but could not manage another win in just five appearances in the two years.

Another pitcher who was obtained in a trade between the 1933-34 season was the former ace of the Philadelphia A's staff, Lefty Grove. Mose had won 24 games in the "City of Brotherly Love" in 1933, his seventh twenty-plus win season in succession. The 1934 spring training season at Sarasota, Florida was only a few days old when something happened to that famous left arm and the speed was gone. Lefty managed only eight victories for the '34 Sox. This story had a happier ending than some of the tragedies as Grove recovered to win 20 in 1935 and added four more good seasons, winning 17, 17, 14 and 15 before he found himself struggling through two seasons, striving for his 300th major league win.

Grove's manager in those days was Joe Cronin. Joe had had many good years before World War II came along, and as many Bosox marched off to war, Joe lingered on as an active player and successful pinch hitter until one early season game in 1945. In this game Joe's career as an active player came to a sudden and tragic end. Rounding second base in New York's Yankee Stadium, Cronin's spikes caught in the bag and down he went with a fractured right leg, ending a great playing career.

No mention of Joe Cronin can be dismissed without referring to a tragic, yet somewhat comical play that Joe once started. It was in the 1935 season during a game at Fenway Park that Joe hit a hard line drive which hit Cleveland Indian third baseman Odell "Bad News" Hale in the head. The Sox down 5 to 1 at the start of the fateful inning, were in the midst of a big rally, having already scored two runs and having the bases loaded. The ball which hit Hale caromed over to shortstop Billy Knickerbocker who caught it on the fly, tossed it to Roy Hughes at second base who retired Billy Werber before he could return to the bag, and Hughes relayed it to first baseman Hal Trosky, who completed the triple play by retiring Mel Almada. A tragic, but laughable triple play.

Cronin's second base partner for many years was the very popular Boston captain, Bobby Doerr. Doerr enjoyed many fine seasons as a player at Fenway Park until he began to be bothered with headaches and back problems. Finally his ills became so painful he decided to call it a career late in the 1951 season. Although Boston fans surmised the gentleman from Oregon was nearing the end of the trail, they were not prepared for the sudden September announcement that Bobby would wind up his career before the season's end. Hurried plans were made to honor Doerr before he left the club, and it was a grey Sunday he bid his adieu to the Boston fans. There were few dry eyes or throats without lumps in them that afternoon at Fenway Park when a career that might have stretched out a few more years ended. The author knows, as he was one of them. Doerr did return later as a coach but never again did anyone see the fielding magic or hitting wizardry of this popular Red Sox.

On the opposite ends of that Cronin-Doerr infield were two hard playing (both on and off the field) Red Sox heroes. At first base was the slugging Jimmie Foxx and at third the talented Jim Tabor. Father time was edging up on "Old Double X" in the early 40's and he presented a rather sad figure of what he had once been as aging legs were winning the battle of time. Gallantly trying to help the Sox to another win, it was tragic to watch him out there at first base. Finally, while helping out by pitching batting practice, a Tony Lupien line drive broke several of his ribs and his Boston days were over. With a heart of gold, Jimmie had given away most of his fortune to those with tales of woe who would approach him. After several bouts with the bottle and several business failures, Foxx bounced from job to job after his retirement, this in itself a tragedy. On the night of July 21, 1967 in Miami, Florida, while eating dinner, Jimmy choked to death when a piece of meat became lodged in his throat.

As for third baseman Jim Tabor, he would thrill Red Sox fans with his fielding and scatter those seated in back of first base with his throws. He could hit and appeared to have settled any third base problems the Sox might have had, but he too had a problem. His was that he frequently took manager Cronin's training regulations quite lightly, and as a result, after a year in military service he was sold to the Philadelphia Phillies where he lasted a season and a half.

Tabor's job was up for grabs in 1946 and a whole parade of candidates lined up for a try at third base and the winner appeared to be Leon Culberson, that is until Joe DiMaggio's line drive knocked him out of the job and Pinky Higgins had to be obtained in a trade with Detroit to settle the problem. Culberson, of course, wound up in the outfield (remember the 1946 World Series — Enos Slaughter and Johnny Pesky do!), but his career never really materialized.

The early Yawkey years were marked with a number of tragic trades and the early forties were no exception. In a deal with Washington, a promising outfielder, Stan Spence, and a Boston favorite, pitcher "Black Jack" Wilson were sent to the Senators for outfielder Johnny Welaj and a pitcher who was to save the franchise, one Kendall Chase. Welaj never got into the game with the Sox and Chase immediately came up with a sore arm. Wilson never did much for the Senators and was traded off to Detroit, but Spence starred for several years as one of the league's top hitters before he was traded back to Boston.

The 1946 Red Sox came up with three fine pitchers — Tex Hughson, Mickey Harris and Dave Ferriss, and it appeared that they might ride to pennant after pennant on the fine arms of this trio. All had pitched for the Sox prior to '46 but all blossomed together that season bringing the first pennant to Boston since 1918. In this tragic tale we must treat the three as one, as they all suffered arm problems in 1947 and in several seasons were all gone, leaving a gaping hole in the Red Sox mound corps. Ferriss, 25 and 6 in '46, won 12 in '47, and in three more seasons won only 7 games before he went back to his gas station in Mississippi. He did return as a coach some years later. Harris, 17 and 9 in '46, won only 14 games over the next two and one-half seasons before he was traded to Washington where his former winning ways never returned. Hughson was 20 and 11 in '46, slipped to 12 and 11 in 1947, and in two more seasons won only seven games for Boston. Who will ever forget the tragic figure of Tex out on the Fenway mound trying gallantly to regain his former magic? He even took a tour in the minors hoping to regain his winning ways. In 1949 he retired to his ranch in Kyle, Texas, with thoughts of what might have been.

The regular centerfielder for the Red Sox in the 40's and early 50's was "The Little

Professor," Dominic DiMaggio, who may well have been one of the slickest to ever perform in that position for Boston. Arguments raged between Red Sox and Yankee fans as to who was better, Dom or his brother Joe. Most conceded the hitting to Joe and the fielding to Dom. In 1952 Lou Boudreau took over as Boston's manager and for some reason seemed to lean away from using Dom and decided to go with rookie Tommy Umphlett in centerfield for the 1953 season as part of his youth movement. Early in 1953 there were rumors that Dom, who wore glasses, was having an eye problem, but in reality, it was Boudreau who was his problem and the rookie who was named to replace him. On May 12 DiMaggio issued a statement to the press indicating as of that day he was voluntarily retiring. A sad day for the Sox fans who saw another one of their 1946 pennant heroes fade away under less than favorable conditions. Dom went on to say, "I want it perfectly understood there is nothing wrong with my right eye. My vision is better than 20-20 in both eyes with glasses. I believe I could have played at least one more year of good baseball, but under the circumstances, I prefer to turn my interests elsewhere rather than be a hanger-on." DiMaggio went on to become a successful executive and rose to a position where he was able to make an offer to buy the Red Sox from the Yawkey estate.

Another tragedy the Red Sox have had to face up to, especially in the early Yawkey years, was their handling of a host of young pitchers. It seems strange indeed that many of them came up with sore arms or for one reason or another were traded away before they reached full stride. Not many teams have seen players with such promise come along only to meet with disaster. The sore arms of Woody Rich and the Canadian Oscar Judd and Frank Quinn; the lack of control by Jack Wilson, Emmett O'Neill and Fitz Ostermueller; the uncontrollable appetite of Pinky Woods; the career delays forced on Charlie Wagner and Bill Butland; the trades of Denny Galehouse, Nelson Potter and minor-leaguer Al Brazle, all rank high on the list of pitchers lost.

There was one rookie infielder who the Red Sox let get by them that may well have cost them many championships. He was shortstop Pee Wee Reese, who was at the Sox farm club in Louisville when he was sold to the Brooklyn Dodgers whom he led to a number of pennants. The Sox once thought so highly of Reese they purchased the Louisville club to get the rights to him. Why did they sell him? Much of the blame, whether true or not, has been laid at the feet of Joe Cronin. Cronin, the Red Sox shortstop and manager at the time, may have been fearful of his job. After seeing Reese play, Cronin was quoted as saying "He's too small. He'll never hit." What a tragic mistake the Red Sox made!

Once one of the best hitters in the minor leagues, Ty LaForest, was called up to play for the 1945 Red Sox and broke in sensationally by making six hits in two successive doubleheaders. His batting cooled off and he was returned to the Louisville farm club in 1946. Pneumonia hit him during the 1946-47 winter and left him weak. In the spring of 1947 he reported to the San Antonio club of the Texas League, and after three days of training he collapsed on the field. He never recovered and died several months later in an Arlington, Massachusetts hospital.

Speaking of some of the highly regarded rookies who didn't make it, perhaps one of the most tragic cases was that of infielder Chuck Koney of the Louisville Colonels farm club. A sore arm had put him on the disabled list in 1948, but the Sox still had high hopes for the twenty-two year-old second baseman who had been on their roster at one point. He had been preparing to play at Louisville and on his way he made a trip to his home in Chicago to visit his wife and two week old daughter. He went into the cellar to see a new hot water heater his father had installed. His father had been burning refuse in the old heater and a pressure build-up caused it to explode and Koney's right leg was shattered and cut by jagged metal, his left leg fractured and his nose and jaw broken. Physicians had hoped there might be a slim chance to save the right leg, but finally an operation to amputate became necessary and a promising career was ended. Red Sox owner, Tom Yawkey, hired the young infielder as a scout and now, 31 years later, Charles Koney is still a midwestern talent hunter for Boston.

Another infielder who had great potential and seemed headed for stardom was third baseman, Joe Foy, who had a good season with the 1967 champions. He had a remarkable appetite and that became his downfall. Failure to keep his weight down, he lost his job and passed from the big leagues after only a few seasons. On the receiving end of Foy's tosses across the infield was George Scott who fought the same weight problems. Scott had several chances with the Sox but weight was always a problem, although he did enjoy several good seasons.

As mentioned at the start of this story, John Barley Corn has claimed a number of Red Sox over the years and contributed highly to their departure from Boston. We have touched on several already, but rather than go into details, suffice it to say Vern Stephens, Jack Quinn, Hick Cady, Ellis Kinder, Roy Johnson, Earl Webb and Billy Cissell were among the victims.

Michael "Pinky" Higgins spent many years in the Red Sox organization as a player, manager, general manager and vice president. Most of them were controversial, especially those spent as general manager as he was blamed for many of the ills which prevailed at Fenway Park in the sixties and no purpose will be served here by bringing them up again. They finally led to his firing very unceremoniously in September of 1965 on the day Dave Morehead pitched his no-hitter. Success did not follow Mike and he died of a heart attack in 1969, two days after his release from the Louisiana State Prison where he had served two months of a four year term for negligent homicide growing out of an accident in which his car ran into a group of highway workers, killing one and injuring three. Mike had been accused of drinking at the time.

About the same time Mike Higgins had his heart attack, former outfielder Jackie Jensen suffered a serious heart attack of his own. Jensen, who played the outfield for the Red Sox, had appeared in the 1948 Rose Bowl game as a football player for the University of California. Ten years later he was the American League's most valuable player. Truly the "Golden Boy", he was married to a famous woman athlete, had appeared in a World Series and All Star game and was certainly the All American boy. There was one crack in the armor — Jackie had a fear of flying. Often he spent sleepless nights worrying about upcoming flights. Often he would travel from city to city by train or car while the rest of the team flew. With expansion these feats became harder to pull off and were taking their toll on Jensen. Several times he retired out of this fear of flying. He sat out the 1960 season, but returned for a final fling in 1961, another career cut short tragically.

Mike Higgins' having served a prison term brings to mind the case of Orlando Cepeda who played for the 1973 Red Sox and holds the bulk of their designated hitting records. Cepeda got involved in and was accused of selling drugs and until recently was serving a prison term.

Another Latin American player was the right handed Jose Santiago who joined the Red Sox in 1966, coming over from Kansas City, and perhaps more than any other pitcher (although he does not get credit for it) was responsible for the 1967 Red Sox championship. He won several key games going down the stretch. Who will ever forget his home run in the opening game 2 to 1 loss to the Cardinals in the '67 series? Santiago was off to a great start in 1968 as were the Sox, and fans hoped another pennant was in the offing. At the halfway point Jose had nine wins and was the most effective starter on the staff. Then it was arm miseries that put him on the disabled list and he would never win another game for Boston.

In recent years there were other pitchers on the Red Sox scene who had some excellent years only to have their careers come to a drastic halt because of sudden arm problems. Not only did their careers end, but Red Sox hopes for winning seasons vanished and the hunt for replacements was on. I guess this proves the old baseball adage, "You never have enough pitching." Remember Tom Brewer, Gene Conley, Ray Culp, Don Newhauser, Gary Peters, Ken Brett, Mike Nagy, Gary Wagner, Gary Bell, Gary Waslewski, Jerry Stephenson, Dick Ellsworth and Lee Strange?

Then there was Dick Pole who took a line drive in the head and second baseman Doug Griffin who was hit by a pitch, and Gary Geiger whose illness cut short a fine career and Duane Josephson who had a heart condition end his catching career. The popular outfielder and present Red Sox TV announcer, Ken Harrelson, was traded to Cleveland and a promising golf career led to his retirement. Then there was the fine pitching prospect, Bobby Sprowl, who in one season (1978) advanced from A ball to Fenway Park and the next spring couldn't find home plate and was traded to Houston. Two members of the 1979 staff whose futures are clouded are relief ace Bill Campbell and rookie Jim Wright, both suffering shoulder and arm problems. What will be the final story on third baseman Butch Hobson's arm, or will Dwight Evans recover from his beaning? You see, as long as there are Red Sox, there will be these tragic stories. Remember that left-hander who seemed to come up with a big win when needed — Roger Moret? He had numerous problems with the Red Sox, including an auto accident, but they did not compare with his recent mental problems while with Texas.

In recent years tragedy has hit native born New England baseball players rather hard. Catcher Carlton Fisk has suffered through a whole series of injuries — a broken arm, a severly injured knee, groin injuries and broken ribs, but has always battled back. He perhaps has had more serious injuries than any Red Sox player in the history of the team. The mysterious injury he suffered in 1979 may be the worst of them all, simply because there seems to be no answer as to what is wrong with his arm. It will be a sad day if one of the best catchers in baseball will have to be shifted to another position. It could well be years before the resulting catching problem can be solved.

Another New Englander was the late Harry Agganis. This fine young man was a football hero at Lynn Classical High School and later at Boston University where he was not only rated as a great quarterback, punter and runner, but also a great defensive player. Harry was also a fine baseball player and when he finally arrived at Fenway Park it appeared their first base problems would be solved for years. He had a fine first season in the Red Sox uniform. In 1955 Harry was batting .300 when he ws stricken with pneumonia in mid-May and spent ten days in the hospital. Within hours of his release from the hospital he was out at Fenway Park working out. His desire may have actually hastened his untimely death. He returned to first base and raised his batting average to .313. The team arrived in Kansas City on June 4 and he was complaining of chest pains and fever. When it was realized how sick he was, he was sent back to a Boston hospital. It was realized that his illness was severe, but was not believed to be fatal. He had been making a satisfactory recovery from a severe pulmonary infection complicated by phlebitis, when suddenly he died of a massive pulmonary embolism. The Red Sox and the baseball world were stunned and saddened by his death. Agganis was the key to the Red Sox future, and an example for the players and all the youth of the country to emulate.

Then there was the young right fielder who was struck down by a Jack Hamilton fast ball, putting him out of action for the latter part of the 1967 pennant drive. Tony Conigliaro was this New Englander who became a victim of the tragedy jinx. He went down like a shot, and for awhile it was not certain whether he was alive or not. Then the fears shifted to whether or not he would lose his eyesight. His future did not appear bright. Actually, this beaning was the beginning of the end of the career for this promising young player. He suffered from eye problems for the balance of his career. He thought about returning as a pitcher at one point but this never materialized. Tony made a spectacular return in 1969 after sitting out the 1968 season. He played again in 1970 for Boston, but was traded to California in 1971 where he played one season before retiring. He came out of retirement in 1975 and made the Sox again, playing 21 games before he retired for good. What had started out as a promising career ended with one pitch on that August evening in 1967. The outfield of Carl Yastrzemski, Reggie Smith and Tony Conigliaro was rated as one of the best, but they were unable to play together long enough to establish how great they might have become.

The final of our native New England Red Sox whose career was marked with tragedy was Connecticut's Jim Piersall. Jim was up for a cup of coffee in 1950 and then it was back to the minors. In 1952 he arrived as a shortstop, but after 30 games was switched to the outfield where he remained for the rest of his career. So unusual was his career, a book was written about it and a movie made about it, a movie which has a way of appearing now and then on television, usually around the opening of a new season. Jim appeared for the Red Sox until after the 1958 season when he was traded to Cleveland. He was an outstanding outfielder with great ability. His problem appeared to be handling the pressures of major league baseball. A worrier, he was never sure of his abilities. This fact manifested itself on the field and in the clubhouse. He had arguments with umpires, fights with teammates, clowning antics on the field which delighted the fans and enraged his manager and teammates, resulting in a trip back to the minors. Pushed by his father into a major league career until the tensions drove him into a mental hospital, he overcame his problems to return to become a successful player. His story should be an inspiration to those with similar problems. It was a tragic problem for the Red Sox to handle, but one which they did not turn their backs on.

There may be other tragic careers in Red Sox history, but you have seen here the more well known. Add to them the hundreds you never hear about in the farm system and you can see that a life in baseball does not always turn out to be a success story in all cases. Nevertheless, I bet there isn't a player among the group who would not do it all over again, if given the chance.

A TRIBUTE TO YAZ

He burst upon the Boston scene in 1961 as the left field replacement for the great Ted Williams. Nineteen seasons later he drew even with Williams as the two players who had played the most seasons in the uniform of the Red Sox. In 1980 he will stand alone as tops for a Red Sox player at 20 summers in Fenway Park. Those nineteen seasons have been dotted with ups and downs, heroics and disappointments, but despite all that has happened, Carl Michael Yastrzemski has emerged as one of the all time greats to ever perform for the Bosox. He has played left field without an equal. He has sacrificed for the sake of the team by playing third base when no one else was available. He has performed exceptionally well at first base and as a designated hitter despite a series of unfortunate injuries, aches and pains. In the spring of 1979 he assured Red Sox followers of a few more seasons when he had his contract extended for three more years past its 1980 expiration date. His batting eye remains sharp, his fielding abilities are still up to Gold Glove standards, so there is no reason to assume his leaving the Fenway scene soon. Quite a tribute to this ageless forty year old who is 1979 achieved his 3000th hit and his 400th home run as a major leaguer, a feat accomplished by no other American Leaguer and only three National Leaguers — Stan Musial, Willie Mays and Hank Aaron.

For the man with the gentle Long Island accent, baseball began as a youngster in that part of New York State as a member of the family team in Bridgehampton where the Yastrzemskis owned a potato farm. His dad started him at a young age playing make believe games against the line-ups of the heroes of the day, usually Boston vs New York. Born in 1939, Yaz arrived when the Yankee-Red Sox rivalry was being revived in earnest and certainly these little games between father and son were in keeping with the times. From hitting small rocks and potatoes Yaz moved into Little League baseball as most boys of his age do. Then it was on to Babe Ruth League baseball where he continued playing shortstop and pitching. His teams boasted winning records for the coach, who was often his dad, making sure his son got as much experience as possible. Not a bad pitcher, Yaz once hurled a no-hitter in a Babe Ruth League game. As a freshman he made his high school team at shortstop. The mold was cast and the form beginning to take shape. It wasn't hard to see the boy had the tools. Summers found him playing alongside his dad and uncles with that now famous family team. At one point, as so often happens in youth league baseball, no catcher was available and Yaz stepped in to try his hand behind the plate. By now the baseball scouts had heard of the boy from Long Island and from all over the major leagues they came. With his dad as his advisor it was decided that he might have an advantage by going to a college with a good baseball program. To play ball and get an education was the course they decided to follow with the colleges chipping in the scholarships. Many offers came in, but in the end it was Notre Dame in South Bend, Indiana that won out.

First it was the New York Yankees who invited Yaz over to the stadium for a look and to make an offer. Imagine the thrill it must have been for the young lad from Long Island. Again it was his dad who prevailed and said "no". Certainly the senior Yastrzemski knew he had a valuable commodity in tow. He also had fourteen major league teams interested, all but the Pittsburgh Pirates and the Cleveland Indians who probably figured their bank account was not large enough to afford a bid. The offers continued to roll in, from the Milwaukee Braves and the San Francisco Giants, just recently moved from New York. In the meanwhile young Yaz was working hard, building up his strength for the day that would certainly soon come his way. Every day and every night Carl was working hard to build himself up, and this dedication was something that would in future years serve him well. For a man of forty to play as Yaz does today, it takes a lot of hard work and dedication, something he works at during and in between seasons. How many times he is out at the ball park early in the day, or staying on after the game has ended, to take a few extra licks at bat? How many winters does he devote to keeping in playing condition? Perhaps it was Carl Sr., playing long after most men of his age have laid aside all thoughts of playing a boy's game, that has inspired Yaz. Perhaps it is pride. No matter what it is that lives inside that body, it is a tribute to him and an example that perhaps more players should follow. Certainly, the rewards of such a program that have come to this wonder of a man are more than most will ever enjoy. Sure, some have been monetary, but others have been something no amount of money could ever buy.

Starting in 1959, the major leagues put into effect a new rule limiting signing bonuses to $4000. Knowing that Carl could get a six figure bonus for signing, the decision was made that the young Notre Dame sophomore should consider such a move and hope he could complete his degree requirements in the off-season. Next, the Philadelphia Phillies made an offer to Carl and his father, but the result was rejection and they fell by the wayside, but not before they made a second offer which included college tuition to the University of Delaware. Next it was the Detroit Tigers who dropped out of the race, then the Cincinnati Reds, and on it went. The Red Sox scout in the New York area was Bots Nekola, who was one of the best salesmen the Sox ever had, bringing many players into the Boston system. The Yastrzemskis had become friendly with this likeable gentleman, a fact which would go a long way in favor of the Boston organization. Johnny Murphy, the then Red Sox farm director, was another person well liked by the Yastrzemskis, and it was he who would be talking for Tom Yawkey's Red Sox when Carl and his father-advisor would visit Boston. First offer $100,000, counter demand $125,000, the first day of the Boston visit ends at a stand-off. It was now the day before Thanksgiving 1958 and traces of snow lay on the diamond on Jersey Street. Later the demand dropped to $115,000 and the offer came back at a reported $108,000, plus college tuition and a triple A contract. Offer accepted and Yaz was on his way from the gold dome at South Bend to a summer at Raleigh in the Carolina League, where he would win the batting championship and be named the league's MVP. Next stop was to the triple A Minneapolis Millers of the American Association where he would hit a career high 193 hits, be converted to an outfielder but lose the batting championship on the final day of the season, but most importantly, receive a promotion to the parent Red Sox.

That first spring (1961) the Red Sox were training in Scottsdale, Arizona under manager Pinky Higgins and the highly touted rookie was put in the position of having to replace the future Hall of Famer, Ted Williams, and overcoming the reputation of being a spoiled brat. After a fine spring, he was chosen to open the season for the Sox. A lot has happened since that cloudy, chilled April afternoon when he took his place beside the likes of his friend and second baseman, Chuck Schilling, centerfielder Gary Geiger, first baseman Vic Wertz, right fielder Jack Jensen, third baseman Pete Runnels, catcher Russ Nixon, second baseman Pumpsie Green and pitcher Bill Monbouquette. Yaz batted fifth in that lineup and had a single off Kansas City's Ray Herbert, a fast ball that he hit sharply for his only hit in a 5 to 2 Red Sox loss. A catcher with that Kansas City club was Haywood Sullivan, now one of the Sox owners. That hit was the first and by 1966 when he stroked his 1000th, he had won many honors including several Gold Gloves and All Star team selections and an American League batting championship in 1963 (.321).

The road, however, was not without its bumps. The fans, for some reason, seemed to resent him and he would often hear their boos. He was hard to get to know, had his problems with manager Johnny Pesky, and became known as owner Yawkey's pet. They said he got managers fired and hired, all of which was untrue. He was benched for various reasons and gained a reputation of being hard to get along with. In 1967 Chicago White Sox manager Eddie Stanky called him "an all star from the neck down". That perhaps was the turning point, as the fans began to side with him. Forgotten were the arguments with manager Billy Herman over Rico Petrocelli and Yaz's criticism of his manager, his slow start in 1964 and his unsuccessful switch to centerfield; for in 1967, under new manager Dick Williams, he had one of the finest years a player could hope for. "The Impossible Dream" could be applied not only to the Red Sox but to Yaz who went on to win a triple crown and the league's MVP. He personally carried the Sox to the championship with his bat, glove and base running. Pressure seemed to only bring out his best. During the last two weeks of that season he went 23 for 44, including five home runs. In the last two games of the season against the Minnesota Twins he went 7 for 8, with a game-winning three run homer. In the World Series he hit .400 and finally he had won the acceptance of Boston fans.

He repeated his batting championship in 1968 with a great final month. Problems developed with manager Williams who took exception to Yaz's play in Oakland one night. Williams was soon gone and Yaz's relations with Eddie Kasko, Darrell Johnson and Don Zimmer have been good. There have been, however, other problems. In 1971 he became involved with the brothers Conigliaro when Billy claimed it was Yaz who got Tony traded to the Angels. Then there was the 1972 player strike when he was called "a union buster", as he indicated he wanted to get the season started. The same year rookie catcher Carlton Fisk charged that Yaz, along with outfielder Reggie Smith, had failed to provide the team with leadership through their indifferent play. It was about this time, after seeing his batting average slip, that he began the demanding off-season conditioning program he has followed until this day. Despite all of this, he was a favorite player around the league. Honors continued to come his way — MVP in the All Star game, fielding honors, a dangerous batter, he was always among the league leaders.

His 2000th came in 1973. Durability continued to be the key as Yaz often played while hurt. In all his 19 seasons, only once has he been on the disabled list. Only one other Red Sox player has performed for 19 years with Boston; the man Yaz replaced — Ted Williams — and next season Yaz will replace him as number one in service to the Sox. In every game he plays, Yaz moves up on the all time lists of major league accomplishments and he surpasses one after another the Hall of Fame members whose stats were better than his, insuring that one day a plaque of his own will hang in the Cooperstown shrine. Yaz has slowly gained the respect of fans everywhere. The boos, which once caused him to stuff cotton in his ears, have changed to cheers. Perhaps Ted Williams' prediction back in 1961, that young Carl would one day make Boston fans forget him, is coming true. A whole generation has grown up knowing only Yaz as the Red Sox leader and captain, left fielder, sometime first baseman and designated hitter. Married when he came to the Sox, his family has grown, his wife is well known to the fans, he has moved from Lynnfield, Massachusetts to Highland Beach in Florida and received his degree from Merrimack College. Among the heroics that he has produced along the way, the one that occurred on September 12, 1979 gained the most national attention.

The pressure had been on for days, you could feel it, the players could feel it, and certainly Yaz felt it. Day after day fans crowded the ball park, hoping to see the 3000th hit. Standing ovation after standing ovation had rolled down from the stands to embrace Yaz. The press box was as crowded as if it were the World Series. Sox publicity director, Dick Bresciani, estimated over 100 media people were there watching day after day, twice the usual crowd. Then it happened after 13 futile trips to the plate at 9:39 P.M., September 12, 1979; New York pitcher Jim Beattie delivered a pitch which Yaz hit cleanly to right field, past the out-stretched glove of second baseman Willie Randolph, and first base coach Johnny Pesky and umpire Ron Luciano became airborne in their joy. Teammates rushed onto the field and the Yankees, led by manager Billy Martin, marched across the field, all joining in the congratulations. Right fielder Reggie Jackson rushed in to present Yaz with the ball. Red Sox vice president for public relations, Bill Crowley, was soon on the field with a microphone and was introducing Yaz to the fans. In a short emotional speech, Yaz, with his father and son at his side, thanked the fans, teammates, his family and expressed a wish that his mother and Mr. Yawkey could have been present. (Both had passed away during the past couple of years). Handsome awards were presented to him by his teammates and the American League. At last the "Yaz Watch" was over and all that was really left of the season had ended. Yaz had become the 15th major leaguer to get 3000 hits.

Other honors awaited Yaz, the city of Boston would acclaim him, President Carter would honor him, one public appearance after another. All wanted to pay tribute to the gentleman ball player. From all walks of life they came to offer their congratulations to this man from Long Island who had led the Red Sox and sacrificed for the good of the team while still gaining his share of personal triumphs. The magic mark had been reached. Yaz agreed it was great, but typically, he added he would have to get down to work as a World's Championship would be better. That is the beauty of Carl Yastrzemski. Basically he has never changed. He accepted the challenge to be a hitter as a young player and made it all come true, picking up leadership qualities and respect along the way. Truly an ageless wonder, it will be a sad day when he hangs up his glove. Fenway Park will not seem the same. If 1967 was the "Impossible Dream Year" and "The Year of the Yaz", what was 1979 for Carl Michael Yastrezemski?

DOWN THE TRAIL WITH YAZ

— 1958 —

November 28, 1958 — Signed to a Red Sox contract by Boston scout "Bots" Nekola off the campus of Notre Dame as a shortstop. Received a reported $100,000 bonus.

— 1959 —

Plays his first professional baseball with the Red Sox farm club at Raleigh of the Carolina League. Named Carolina League MVP.

Lead the Carolina League in hitting (.377), hits (170), doubles (34) and putouts (255) as a second baseman-shortstop.

— 1960 —

Promoted to the Red Sox triple A American Association team at Minneapolis where he is converted to an outfielder. Loses the batting championship on the final day of the season.

— 1961 —

Replaces Ted Williams as the Red Sox left fielder. After a poor start raises his batting average 34 points to .266 in the second half of the season. Makes his first major league hit in his first time at bat — April 11. First home run May 9.

— 1962 —

Proves himself as one of the coming stars of baseball by hitting .296 as he leads the Red Sox in hits (191), runs (99), doubles (43) and total bases (303). Second to Frank Malzone with 19 home runs. Led league in outfield assists (15).

— 1963 —

Named to his first American League All-Star team as he wins his first American League batting championship while leading the league in hits (183), doubles (40) and walks (95). Wins a Gold Glove as he leads league in outfield assists (18).

— 1964 —

Makes a switch from left to center field. Leads the league in outfield assists (24). Makes first major league appearance at third base.

— 1965 —

Named to American League All Star team. Leads the league in slugging percentage (.536) and doubles (45). Wins fielding Gold Glove Award. Returned to left field. Hits for the cycle May 14 against Detroit.

— 1966 —

Named to American League All Star team. Elected as the Red Sox official captain. Receives college degree from Merrimack College. Leads the league in outfield assists (15). Gets his 1000th major league hit September 15.

— 1967 —

Perhaps his finest year. This season could easily be called the "Year of the Yaz" as he leads the Red Sox to the American League championship. Won the Triple Crown and American League MVP. His clutch hits, fantastic catches and strong throws make him a complete player in every sense of the word. Named The Sporting News Player of the Year and number 1 Major League Player, won a Gold Glove, led the league in slugging (.622), total bases (360), runs (112), hits (189), home runs (44), RBI's (121), batting (.326). American League All Star Team. The Sporting News All Star Team. Associated Press Male Athlete of the Year; UPI Major League All Star Team; Sport Magazine Man of the Year and top performer in baseball; Sports Illustrated Sportsman of the Year; UPI Comeback of the Year; Academy of Sports Man of the Year in pro sports; Van Heusen Award for outstanding achievements; S. Rae Hickok Belt Professional Athlete of the Year; Babe Ruth Crown for tops in sports (Baltimore, Maryland); Sid Mercer Award and Hutch Award-New York Chapter BBWAA; Ty Cobb Award-Atlanta Chapter BBWAA and BBWAA awards from Washington, D.C. and Minnesota Chapters. Hits his 100th major league home run May 16. Had 3 home runs in the World Series and batted .400.

— 1968 —

Wins American League batting championship with the lowest average ever (.301). Won Gold Glove. Had 17 game winning hits. Led the league in walks (119). Named to the American League All Star team. Led major leagues in total times on base. Plays first base for the first time in the majors.

— 1969 —

Wins fifth Gold Glove award. Led league in games played (162). Named to the All Star team. Hits his 200th major league home run September 23.

— 1970 —

Leads American League in runs (125). Named to American League All Star team. Leads league in slugging (.592) and total bases (335). Selected as the outstanding player in the All Star game. Named Red Sox MVP. Lost American League batting crown to Alex Johnson of California by .0003 of a point (.329). Led Red Sox in stolen bases (23). For several years he has been an associate in a Boston investing firm, director of a bank and now has his own automobile dealership.

— 1971 —

Hampered by a hand injury has a poor season (hit only .254), but still won his sixth Gold Glove award. Set a major league record for outfielders as 16 assists tops the American League for an unprecedented sixth time. Respect from rival pitchers is indicated by his 454 walks in the past four years high for the league. Did drug education work in New England schools. Tied for league lead in double plays by an outfielder with 4. Named to the All Star team.

— 1972 —

Was on the disabled list from May 9 to June 9 with an injured knee. Took over the first base job late in the season. In September he hit .306 with 8 homers and 24 RBI's. Cited by President Nixon for his work in drug education. Continues his activities for the Children's Cancer Research Foundation (The Jimmy Fund). Selected to the All Star team. Led the league in sacrifice flies.

— 1973 —

Makes his 2000th major league hit on June 9th. Volunteers to play third base when Rico Petrocelli injures his right elbow. Makes 12 of his 18 seasonal errors at third base. Named to All Star team but had to be replaced when he injured his wrist. The wrist injury bothered him all season, yet he managed to bat .371 over his last 57 games.

— 1974 —

Hits his 300th major league home run. Named to the All Star team. Led the league in runs (93). Named MVP by the Boston baseball writers. Appeared in more games at first base (84) than in the outfield (63).

— 1975 —

Named for the 12th time to the American League All Star team. Helped lead the Red Sox to the American League Championship. Batted .310 in the World Series to lead Red Sox batters. Hit .455 in the championship series with Oakland as he was Mister Everything in that series.

— 1976 —

Gets his 2,500th major league hit on July 26. Now leads all active players in the major leagues in doubles, walks and extra base hits and is second in games played. On July 28 starts an errorless game streak in the outfield which will extend 167 games and into the 1978 season. Named to the All Star team. Hits three home runs in one game on May 19 against Detroit. Red Sox MVP by the Boston writers. Had

— 1976 (continued) —

his best year since 1970. Received the Tom Yawkey Memorial Award. Ties an American League record for five home runs in two games.

— 1977 —

Now leads all active major leaguers in RBI's and games played in addition to walks, total bases and extra base hits. Leads all American League every day players in years of service. Now in his 17th season with the Red Sox, he has more longevity with the club as a home grown player than any previous player. (Ted Williams came in a trade). Won a Gold Glove for the seventh time. Led league's outfielders in assists (16) to extend his major league mark to seven seasons. Tied a major league record for the highest fielding average by an oufielder playing 100 or more games (1.000).

— 1978 —

Performance curtailed in the final two months by back and wrist injuries. Played left and center fields as well as first base and designated hitter. Chosen for the All Star team for the 15th time. On April 7 concludes 167 consecutive games (354 chances) without an error. The streak began in 1976.

— 1979 —

Chosen for the American League All Star team. Ties Ted Williams for the most seasons played for the Red Sox at 19. Reaches 40 years old. Hits his 400th major league home run on July 24 against Mike Morgan of Oakland in Boston. On September 12 his single against Jim Beattie of New York at Fenway Park is his 3000th major league hit.

YAZ VS THE RECORD BOOK*

	Total	All Time Rank	Active Rank	Red Sox Rank
Games	2862	6th	1st	1st
At Bats	10447	7th	2nd +	1st
Runs	1640	23rd	2nd +	2nd
Hits	3009	13th	3rd a	1st
Doubles	565	10th	2nd +	1st
Home Runs	404	18th	3rd b	2nd
Walks	1639	5th	1st	2nd
Total Bases	4858	13th	1st	2nd
Extra Base Hits	1025	12th	1st	2nd
RBI's	1613	13th	1st	2nd

* Through 1979 season
+ Behind Pete Rose
a Behind Pete Rose & Lou Brock
b Behind Willie McCovey & Willie Stargell

YASTRZEMSKI, Carl Michael (Yaz) #8   OUTFIELDER - 1B

Age: 40, Turns 41 Aug. 22; Born: August 22, 1939, Southampton, L.I., N.Y. Ht.: 5'11"; Wt.: 185 lbs. Brown eyes, Brown hair. Bats: Left; Throws: Right. Home: Highland Beach, Florida. Signed by Scout "Bots" Nekola, November 28, 1958. Married Carolann Casper. Children: Mary Ann 9/21/60, C. Michael Jr. 8/16/61, Suzann 6/15/66, Carolyn 4/15/69.

Year	Club	G	AB	R	H	2B	3B	HR	RBI	AVE.	BB	SO	E	SB
1959	Raleigh	120	451	87	170*	34*	6	15	100	.377*	78	49	45*	16
1960	Minneapolis	148	570	84	193*	36	8	7	69	.339	47	65	5	16
1961	Boston	148	583	71	155	31	6	11	80	.266	50	96	10	6
1962	Boston	160	646	99	191	43	6	19	94	.296	66	82	11*	7
1963	Boston	151	570	91	183*	40*	3	14	68	.321*	95*	72	6	8
1964	Boston	151	567	77	164	29	9	15	67	.289	75	90	11	6
1965	Boston	133	494	78	154	45●	3	20	72	.312	70	58	3	7
1966	Boston	160	594	81	165	39*	2	16	80	.278	84	60	5	8
1967	Boston	161	579	112*	189*	31	4	44●	121*	.326*	91	69	7	10
1968	Boston	157	539	90	162	32	2	23	74	.301*	119*	90	3	13
1969	Boston	162●	603	96	154	28	2	40	111	.255	101	91	6	15
1970	Boston	161	566	125*	186	29	0	40	102	.329	128	66	14	23
1971	Boston	148	508	75	129	21	2	15	70	.254	106	60	2	8
1972	Boston-a	125	455	70	120	18	2	12	68	.264	67	44	8	5
1973	Boston	152	540	82	160	25	4	19	95	.296	105	58	18	9
1974	Boston	148	515	93*	155	25	2	15	79	.301	104	48	6	12
1975	Boston	149	543	91	146	30	1	14	60	.269	87	67	5	8
1976	Boston	155	546	71	146	23	2	21	102	.267	80	67	4	5
1977	Boston	150	558	99	165	27	3	28	102	.296	73	40	0	11
1978	Boston	144	523	70	145	21	2	17	81	.277	76	44	5	4
1979	Boston	147	518	69	140	28	1	21	87	.270	62	46	4	3
Major Lg. Totals		2862	10447	1640	3009	565	56	404	1613	.288	1639	1248	128	168

a-On Disabled List May 9 to June 9, 1972 with injured right knee.

CHAMPIONSHIP SERIES RECORD

Year	Club	G	AB	R	H	2B	3B	HR	RBI	AVE.	BB	SO	E
1975	Boston	3	11	4	5	1	0	1	2	.455	1	1	0

WORLD SERIES RECORD

Year	Club	G	AB	R	H	2B	3B	HR	RBI	AVE.	BB	SO	E
1967	Boston	7	25	4	10	2	0	3	5	.400	4	1	0
1975	Boston	7	29	7	9	0	0	0	4	.310	4	1	0
World Series Tot.		14	54	11	19	2	0	3	9	.352	8	2	0

ALL STAR GAME RECORD

Year	League	Pos.	AB	R	H	2B	3B	HR	RBI	AVE.	BB	SO	E
1963	American	LF	2	0	0	0	0	0	0	.000	0	1	0
1967	American	LF	4	0	3	1	0	0	0	.750	2	1	0
1968	American	CF - LF	4	0	0	0	0	0	0	.000	0	2	0
1969	American	LF	1	0	0	0	0	0	0	.000	0	0	0
1970	American	CF - 1B	6	1	4	1	0	0	1	.667	0	0	0
1971	American	LF	3	0	0	0	0	0	0	.000	1	0	0
1972	American	LF	3	0	0	0	0	0	0	.000	0	1	0
1974	American	1B	1	0	0	0	0	0	0	.000	1	0	0
1975	American	PH	1	1	1	0	0	1	3	1.000	0	0	0
1976	American	LF	2	0	0	0	0	0	0	.000	0	0	0
1977	American	CF	2	0	0	0	0	0	0	.000	0	1	0
1979	American	1B	3	0	2	0	0	0	1	.667	0	0	0
All Star Game Tot.			32	2	10	2	0	1	5	.312	4	6	0

Member of 1966 American League team but did not play.
Named to 1965 American League team but replaced due to injury.
Named to 1973 American League team but replaced due to injury.
Named to 1978 American League team but replaced due to injury.

* led league   ● tied for league lead

FENWAY PARK

The city of Boston is a center of culture that treasures its historic monuments and shrines as no other city in the world. A great many of these are of national historic importance and are recognized across this nation of ours by students everywhere. Boston, sometimes known as the Hub of the Universe, is also the home of a monument, a shrine if you will, to Red Sox followers, a Mecca which draws them in like no other sports palace in the world. This place of hallowed ground is known as Fenway Park, home of the Boston Red Sox. This unique old ball field stands by itself among today's new and spacious characterless ball fields and along with the Chicago Cubs' Wrigley Field and Detroit's Tiger Stadium serves as a remaining link between an era when ball parks had character and the new era of cement monsters which often leave the fan cold and with a feeling of sameness which fails to generate the love for the ball park that those of thiry or forty years ago did. The long ago era is rapidly disappearing from the American scene, but it is here at Fenway Park where the fan of today can associate with the past, where he can look around and relive in his mind's eye the thrills and plays of decades past, where comparisons are made of Tris Speaker, Ted Williams, Dom DiMaggio, Tom Oliver, Bobby Doerr and so many others, where he can take his children or grandchildren and point out spots where he saw his hero past make that special play or hit that special hit.

Speak of Jersey Street, Lansdowne Street, Van Ness, Yawkey Way, the Green Monster, the Fens or Brookline Avenue and any Red Sox fan worth his salt will immediately understand what you mean. It wasn't always that way. When Boston entered the American League in 1901 they played in a ball park on Huntington Avenue, now the site of Northeastern University, known as The Huntington Avenue Grounds. They remained at Huntington Avenue for ten years with their players living down the Avenue at Putnam's Hotel (known as "Puts"), near the site of the Boston Conservatory of Music, until the 1912 season when they moved over to their new concrete and steel park on Jersey Street, known as Fenway Park.

John I. Taylor, who had become the owner of the Boston Club in 1904, selected the site for the new park, but during the winter of 1911-12 Taylor sold the club to James R. McAleer. The 1911 edition of the Red Sox had finished in the second division, losing fourth place to the Chicago White Sox by a tenth of a point, mainly because Chicago had played two less games. This fifth place team had been plagued by injuries and showed none of the promise which was to bloom in 1912 to make them one of the all time great Red Sox teams. Few of the fans who attended the Fenway opener could have envisioned what the 1912 season would hold in store for them. It is speculated that the majority came out to see the new ball park more than the almost same team which had represented Boston during the 1911 season, but we are getting ahead of our story.

As early as 1910 it was known that the Taylors (father and son owners) were looking around for a new site for the Red Sox to play and to get away from the Huntington Avenue field where space was limited and sparks from the coal burning railroad engines which ran in back of the first base side of the park presented a fire hazard to the wooden grandstand. After considering several sites the land bounded by Lansdowne and Jersey Streets, then a good residential area close by the Charles River and not far from the original ball grounds, was selected. It was a good business deal for the Taylors as they were large stockholders in the Fenway Realty Company who owned the land. Construction was started in 1911 and announcement was made that Boston would have the finest ball park in the country. Getting away from the old wooden stands concept, the park was to be constructed of concrete and steel, joining the recently completed ball parks in Philadelphia (Shibe Park), Pittsburgh (Forbes Field) and New York (Polo Grounds). The grandstand would swing around from behind first base to a point beyond third base. Joining the grandstand down the right field line was a covered pavillion which reached down along the foul line well into right field. A large wooden bleacher would run from the right field corner into center field, and wooden bleachers would be found down the left field foul line to the fence in left field. There was a ten foot embankment in left field, which for years became known as "Duffy's Cliff" out of respect to the fielding abilities of the original tenant of left field, Duffy Lewis.

Before any Red Sox would hit or field a ball in Fenway, a lot was to happen to the club. In late fall 1911, the park was taking shape and would certainly be ready for Opening Day 1912. An unexpected announcement in late December 1911 revealed that the Taylors had sold 50% of their club to James McAleer, who had managed the Washington team in 1911, and to Bob McRoy, secretary of the American League. The announcement further stated that Jake Stahl would return to the team as first baseman and manager, replacing the 1911 field boss, Pat Donovan. It was later revealed that Stahl owned some of the team also. Stahl was also to bring with him Joe Quirk as trainer. It was rumored that American League President Ban Johnson had engineered the whole deal because he was tired of running to Boston to solve John I. Taylor's problems. When the smoke had cleared McAleer had been elected president, John I. Taylor vice president and McRoy treasurer. So the stage was set for opening the new season, in a new ball park, with a new owner, a new manager, a new trainer and a new pennant to be won, and a new world championship to reside in Boston.

Rain was to plague the early season of 1912. The Sox trained that year at Hot Springs, Arkansas but the start of spring training was delayed by rain which also delayed their departure at the end of their stay there. After playing two exhibition games at Cincinnati rain again greeted the team upon their return to Boston. Fans were to get their first view of Fenway Park on April 9, 1912 when the Sox played an exhibition game, shortened to six and one-half innings by a snow storm, against Harvard University, which they won. Then they were off to New York to open the season with a three game series and on to Philadelphia for a two game series. They swept New York and split with the A's and returned to Boston with a 4-1 record to open the season with the Yankees on April 17 with Buck O'Brien to oppose New York's Ray Caldwell.

Rain took a hand again causing postponement of the April 17 scheduled opener, the game of the 18th and the Patriots Day doubleheader of the 19th. Finally, on Saturday, April 20, the Red Sox got a break from Mother Nature and before 27,000 fans defeated the New York Yankees in eleven innings 7 to 6 behind spitballer O'Brien and Sea Lion Charlie Hall who picked up his second win of the young season, having previously defeated the New Yorkers in New York 8 to 4. Big Jim Vaughn, a lefty, took the loss in relief of John Quinn who had relieved starter Caldwell for New York. It is rather ironic that the first loss at Fenway was by a left hander, as to this day it is supposed to be a tough park for lefties, although there have been notable exceptions such as Mel Parnell.

That long ago opening day crowd saw a ball park which was not quite completed, probably due to the bad weather earlier that spring. As a matter of fact the field was muddy that day, a fact which undoubtedly led to seven errors by the Sox fielders and two by their counterparts from New York. New York right fielder Harry Wolter became the first casualty at the park as he broke his leg sliding into second base. Mayor John F. Fitzgerald (Honey Fitz) threw out the first ball. He was the grandfather of President John F. Kennedy. The famous umpire Tom Connolly called balls and strikes and the Letter Carriers band entertained between innings. Successive singles by Steve Yerkes and Tris Speaker gave the home team the victory.

An official and formal dedication date was set for May 17 when flag raising was held and presentations were made before dignitaries, headed by League President Ban Johnson. This gala event was spoiled when the Chicago White Sox, scoring four runs in the 9th inning against Larry Pape, defeated the Sox 5 to 2 to bring the Sox record to 16-9. The Sox went on to romp to the pennant by 14 games. Its 105 victories stood as a league record until the 1927 New York Yankees won 110 games. The Sox team lost only 47 games. The first shutout at Fenway Park occurred several days later on May 20 against the same Chicago White Sox, with the Red Sox winning 2 to 0 behind Smokey Joe Wood who ran his record to 7-2. Two days later (May 22) Hall ran his record to 5-0 by shutting out Cleveland 9 to 0. The first shutout against the Sox occurred in the second game of the May 30 doubleheader with Washington as the Capital City boys beat Bucky O'Brien 5 to 0. In the meanwhile, on April 26 first baseman Hugh Bradley became the first batter to put the ball over the left field wall as Boston, behind Hugh Bedient, was defeating Philadelphia 7 to 6.

World Championship flags flew over Fenway not only in 1912 but again in 1915, 1916 and 1918. Then came the long drought. It was not until 1946 that another World Series would take place at Fenway and there were subsequent series in 1967 and 1975, none of which resulted in World Championships. No matter what year, Fenway Park was never a dull place to be around. Many mysterious things took place behind the closed front office doors in the executive suite, deep in the confines of the clubhouse and out on the field between the base lines.

While there have been many player comings and goings, perhaps three of the most unusual took place just before the era of the Roaring Twenties, an era which saw the Sox mired for the most part in the second division. Attendance at the Park on Jersey Street dropped to its lowest depths in years, although the trend continued into the mid thirties when a young Tom Yawkey came upon the scene to turn things around. As much as third baseman-manager Jimmy Collins and pitcher Cy Young had dominated the years at the old Huntington Avenue Grounds, centerfielder Tris Speaker, pitcher Joe Wood and pitcher-outfielder Babe Ruth dominated the early years at Fenway Park. Actually, Speaker and Wood were links between both parks as they joined the Boston club at the older ball park and were part of the move to the new facility. As the 1916 spring training sessions opened in Hot Springs, Arkansas, Speaker was in attendance but not under contract and Wood refused to show up. During the preceding winter, the major leagues had made peace with the rival Federal League and as a result salaries of the star players were being cut. In Speaker's case he had been dropped to $9,000 which was half of what he had commanded in 1915. Though he trained with the club and took part in the exhibition games, he never signed his contract. For Wood, taking a cut to $5,000, he just refused to play for that amount and wound up sitting out the whole season. A few days (April 12) before the Sox opened their home season, Boston fans opened their morning newspapers to find, much to their surprise, that their favorite Tris Speaker had been sold to the Cleveland Indians for two rookies, pitcher Sad Sam Jones and infielder Fred Thomas with $50,000 tossed in to sweeten Joe Lannin's coffers. It was again American League President Ban Johnson pulling the strings behind the scenes who engineered the deal. Spoke's pal Wood sat out the entire season and on February 24, 1917, he also was sold to Cleveland for $15,000 where he pitched for awhile before joining Speaker in the outfield where he performed for five years.

The third of these unusual transactions took place, (at least it was officially announced, although proof exists that the deal was made earlier) on January 5, 1920 This deal involved the young pitcher who had arrived on the Fenway scene in 1914 and had through his pitching and hitting carried the Sox to the 1915, 1916 and 1918 World Championships. George Herman "Babe" Ruth had been sold to the New York Yankees for $125,000, plus a $350,000 mortgage on Fenway Park held by Yankee owner Col. Jacob Ruppert, the beer baron. The Sox were now owned by one Harry Frazee, a New York theatrical man whose name still makes Red Sox fans' blood pressure rise by its mere mention. Once "The Babe" had left Fenway everything was down hill for the next eighteen years. His departure and the ensuing mortgage can not be overlooked in any history of the grand old ball park.

Over the next thirteen years (until 1933) Fenway Park remained in a decline. The team became a second division fixture finishing dead last in nine of those years, six of them (1925-30) in succession. Mixed in were two 5th place finishes (1920-21), one 6th (1931) and two 7th (1924, 1933). Duffy's Cliff remained in left field. Players, managers, and owners came and went without much success. Pitcher Sad Sam Jones managed twenty-three wins in 1921 and Howard Ehmke garnered an even twenty in 1923, but other than them no pitcher was outstanding. The batters and fielders of that dark era in Fenway's history enjoyed moderate success and numbered among their ranks such long forgotten heroes as Ike Boone, Ira Flagstead, Buddy Myer, Earl Webb, Jack Rothrock, Dale Alexander, Phil Todt, Smead Jolley, Roy Johnson, Del Pratt, Muddy Ruel, George Burns, Mike Menosky, Bill Regan and Hal Rhyne.

When the park originally opened, the right field corner was only 313 feet 6 inches down the line. During the 20's it was moved back to 358 feet as a new bleacher section was built on an open lot behind the original one. The most well known feature of this park is the left field wall affectionately known as the "Green Monster". When manager Jake Stahl sent his players out in the field in the spring of 1912, it measured 320 feet 6 inches down the left field line to this most famous of all Boston landmarks. During the ensuing years, due to the shifting of home plate, it is now officially listed as 315 feet away straight down the line. There have been various attempts in recent years to prove that it is even closer than that, but the Sox have never confirmed that it is. Certainly there are a number of members in the pitching fraternity who will swear "the wall" is located somewhere just the other side of shortstop. Nevertheless, it remains the most striking part of Fenway, and Boston fans have for years been treated to an endless succession of baseballs sailing over its uppermost reaches into or over the nets which were placed atop the wall to cut down on the number of broken windows in the business establishments on the opposite side of Landsdowne Street. For the record, the wall stands thirty-seven feet high, with the nets extending up another twenty-three feet. Over the years a succession of Sox left fielders have attempted to master the tricky rebounds of balls hit off the wall. None have been as successful as Ted Williams and most recently Carl Yastrzemski. Visiting left fielders have often given up in disgust trying to figure it out. Originally the wall was wooden. Later it was covered with tin and several years ago it was resurfaced with the effect of deadening balls hit off it. This caused the rebounding balls to take on entirely different characteristics and meant that Yaz had to reevaluate his former fielding abilities.

The prevailing winds at Fenway Park have also had their effects on fly balls hit to the outfield area. These winds change during the season but most of the outfielders have been able to compensate for the changes. The erection of the new scoreboard in the centerfield area shifted the wind currents in the park so that the fly balls responded differently. Centerfielder Fred Lynn was one of the first to encounter this change.

On February 25, 1933 Thomas A. Yawkey became owner of the Red Sox, purchasing the team from Bob Quinn, although the deal was not finalized until April 20. His goal was to get the club out of the cellar and in the process not only did he start bringing in new ball players, he also started a face lifting of Fenway, a process he continued until his death in 1976. With the arrival of Yawkey the fans who had been staying away also began to return. In one of his first moves Yawkey rebuilt the entire park at a cost estimated to be anywhere in the neighborhood of $750,000 to two million.

Shortly after the 1933 season the wooden centerfield bleachers burned down and with this a factor, Yawkey tore down the remaining wooden stands in left field and the old pavilion in right field, replacing them with steel and cement stands. The days of fans standing behind roped off outfield areas was over. The opening behind the grandstand in left field, where bleachers had been erected, was gone and the grandstand now extended to the famous left field wall. It should be mentioned that a fire in 1926 had once destroyed these left field bleachers. The grandstand was enlarged enabling more box seats to be added and was extended down the right field line and swung around into the outfield area. This shortened the right field line from its 358 feet to its present 302 feet in the corner, but it curves sharply to 380 feet in deep right field. Duffy's Cliff was leveled and the old wooden left field fence replaced by the sheet metal wall. The grandstand now boasted 6,000 additional seats. The center field bleachers were reconstructed completing the first overhaul of the park. While the construction was reaching the halfway point, January 5, 1934, a four alarm fire broke out and destroyed a good portion of the new bleachers and it required the Boston Fire Department better than five hours to bring the fire under control. Yawkey, determined not to be seriously set back, hired extra men to complete the task. Opening Day was scheduled for April 17, 1934 and with Boston Mayor James Curley among those on hand, the Sox bowed to Joe Cronin's Washington Senators by a 6 to 5 score. The rededication, like the original dedication, turned out to be another eleven inning affair. The exterior of Fenway Park, especially that section facing Yawkey Way (formerly Jersey Street), has remained basically the same over the years since 1912. Sure there are air conditioners protruding from the windows of the executive offices and two plaques mounted on either side of the door leading to these offices, one dedicated to Eddie Collins and the other to Tom Yawkey, but there still can be seen the words "Fenway Park 1912" in red on white cement high above these windows and the entrance to the stands on the tree-lined Yawkey Way side of the park.

The next major change occurred in1936 when the net was erected atop the left field wall to save the windows on the opposite side of Lansdowne Street which runs parallel to the wall. It is out where the wall joins the center field bleachers that the bleacher entrance is located. Even the casual fans has seen the pictures of people lined up along the outside of the wall at this point waiting for the bleacher gate to open. Other than the addition of the nets and occasional changes in the advertisements on the left field wall, about the only construction that took place in the 30's were the repairs necessary to correct the damage inflicted on the dugouts and clubhouse by the likes of Wes Ferrell and Lefty Grove who were often known to break things up when their pitching didn't work out right for them out on the mound.

With the arrival in 1939 of a young outfielder named Ted Williams who began hitting home runs at an unheard of rate into the right field bleachers primarily on the road, it was decided that some remodeling could be done in the Fenway right field area which had now become known as "Williamsburg". These changes were considered for several reasons, one being that the poor home record was due to the far away right field fence. Secondly, it would shorten the range for Ted Williams and his home run blasts. Strange as it may seem to today's "Fenway Faithful", on July 31, 1939 when the first mention of these possible changes were seen in the press, the Sox were 22-21 at home and 34-13 on the road. Also little remembered today was the fact that Jimmie Foxx, a right handed batter, hit many home runs to right field on the road that were just long outs in the deep right field at Fenway. So it was in the latter stages of the 1939 campaign that plans were announced to reduce the right field foul line from 332 feet to 302 feet and the right field bleacher wall from 402 feet to 380 feet for the 1940 season. The eighty-five cent pavilion would be eliminated and the sections starting at the grandstand and extending around the right field bend to the passageway to the center field bleachers would be filled with reserved seats. Additional box seats would be added in right and left fields. The bullpens would be moved to centerfield in front of the bleachers separated by a three-foot wall. New wider reserve seats would eat up the space to be gained by the moves, thus preventing any increase in seating capacity. Construction was scheduled to start right after the football season during which Boston College used the field. The result would be that the right field wall would be twenty feet closer to home plate, a fact which would please Williams and set Boston fans dreaming of more homers to right.

Except for elimination of advertising from the left field wall things remained just about the same at Fenway until just after the 1975 World Series. At a cost of $1.5 million an electronic message board was constructed atop the center field bleachers. The left field scoreboard was reduced in size and centered, the press box was enclosed and air conditioned, the left field wall resurfaced and the lower portions padded. With the arrival of the message board advertising again appeared in Fenway Park. For years this privilege was reserved for a sign on top of the right field grandstand plugging the Jimmy Fund. Now certain short commercials appear on this new board and on either side of the electronic portion of the message section on a more or less permanent basis. Old time fans will remember back to the Harry Frazee days when posters ballyhooing his theatrical productions adorned the outside walls near the entrances to the park. Anyone who has been to the park will also remember the sign boards outside the ball field atop nearby buildings which advertise petroleum products, liquor and printing services. Certainly with the rising costs of maintaining a ball park, the advertising within the ball park itself helps take care of some of these costs. For years Fenway has been known as one of the best maintained parks on the majors. Its carefully manicured infield and outfield are, according to the players, a joy to play on. An outfield drainage system installed a few years ago makes that area quite playable shortly after rain storms. Grass no longer extends to the base of the walls, but running completely around the playing area is a dirt warning track which serves as a warning for fielders as they approach the walls.

The charm and beautiful confines of the park have over the years drawn many capacity crowds. The record crowd at Fenway was drawn in the year of Tom Yawkey's original overhaul in 1934. 41,766 fans jammed the park on August 12 of that year to see the Sox and their arch rivals, the New York Yankees, play a doubleheader and to bid farewell to Babe Ruth. Thousands of fans had to be turned away as the Sox and Yankees split the twin bill. The aisles were filled and ropes stretched across the outfield to contain the fans. Opening day has always been a big draw and on April 14, 1969, 35,343 turned out to see the Sox play the Baltimore Orioles as Tony Conigliaro made his first Fenway appearance since being beaned in 1967. It was on June 28, 1949 that 36,228 fans were packed in for a record night game crowd with the New York Yankees again supplying the opposition to start a three game series sweep in which Joe DiMaggio's homers won all the games. It should also be mentioned that for a night game on May 31, 1976, again with the Yankees, 35,939 fans showed up. A single day game with the Yankees on August 7, 1956 drew 36,350 fans, a record for a Fenway day game. This game turned out to be a dandy, the Sox winning in 11 innings 1 to 0 as a bases loaded walk to Ted Williams forced in the winning run. The 1946 season was the first which saw the Red Sox draw over a million into the little ball field and in 1977 for the first time they surpassed the two million mark, a remarkable record when all is considered. The high water mark for a season prior to the Yawkey era was way back in 1912, the first at Fenway, when 597,096 passed through the turnstiles. The smallest season's attendance occurred during the depression year of 1932 when only 182,150 fans came out to Fenway. This 1932 mark was also the all time low as even at the smaller Huntington Avenue Grounds attendance topped this figure. In six years, 1967, 69, 70, 71, 74 and 75 the Red Sox led the league in home attendance.

Basically a baseball park, it has been the scene of many football games. During the late thirties and early forties it served as the home of Boston College football and the professional football Boston Yanks. In later years the Boston Patriots, now the New England Patriots, appeared at Fenway. For these games bleachers were erected in front of the left field wall and the football field ran from the left field foul line out into the area in front of the present right field bullpens.

The major league All Star game which has been held annually since 1933, except for the war year of 1945 has been staged twice at Fenway Park, once in 1946 and again in 1961. The 1946 game held on July 9 saw most of the major leaguers returning from service in time to participate. The American League led by Boston's own Ted Williams overwhelmed the Nationals 12 to 0. Williams put on one of the most dramatic shows in All Star history, hitting two home runs, two singles and drawing a walk in five trips to the plate. He also scored four runs and drove in five. His first homer, off Brooklyn Dodger pitcher Kirby Higbe, was a long smash into the centerfield bleachers and his second landed in the right field bullpen and came off a Rip Sewell blooper pitch. Sewell, of the Pittsburgh Pirates, was famous for the high lofted pitch which required the batter to supply the power to drive it anywhere. Other than Williams, Red Sox players who appeared in this game included catcher Hal Wagner, first baseman Rudy York, second baseman Bobby Doerr, shortstop John Pesky and centerfielder Dom DiMaggio. 34,906 fans were in attendance.

In 1961 the majors had adopted a two All Star game system. That year the first game had been played in San Francisco with the National League prevailing 5 to 4 in ten innings. The second game was staged at Fenway on July 31 and resulted in the game being called after nine innings due to rain, with the score all even at one run apiece. The only Red Sox to appear in the game was pitcher Don Schwall off whom the one National League run was scored. Playing an important part in the scoring of that one run was a shortstop from the Cincinnati Reds, later to become a Red Sox player, manager and director of player procurement — Eddie Kasko.

The longest home run ever hit at Fenway Park? This has been a question asked many times over the years. While it may be a subject for debate the late Red Sox owner Tom Yawkey said the longest he had ever seen was the shot Jim Rice hit over the centerfield wall to the right of the flagpole on July 18, 1975. Five other batters have hit balls out of the present park in the centerfield area: In 1937 Hank Greenberg of Detroit on May 22 and Jimmie Foxx on August 12; twenty years later, on April 20 in 1957, Bill Skowron of the New York Yankees; on May 16, 1970 Carl Yastrzemski; and on September 29, 1973 former Red Sox farm hand Bobby Mitchell then playing with Milwaukee did it. Many home runs have been hit over the wall in left field and in left center, but it is anyone's guess as to which went the farthest, but certainly shots by Jimmie Foxx and Hank Greenberg were among those traveling significant distances. Mickey Mantle's blast off Frank Sullivan on September 21, 1956 to centerfield is another long remembered home run. On September 6, 1927 Babe Ruth hit a tape measure job over the centerfield fence that at the time was called the longest hit ever at Fenway Park. Ted Williams, in 1939, hit what might have been the longest drive to right field off New York Yankee Red Ruffing and later almost matched that drive by hitting another off St. Louis Brown pitcher Ellis Kinder. Oddly Ruffing had been a Red Sox and Kinder was later to become one.

Four Red Sox have hit three home runs in one game at Fenway Park; Ted Williams in 1946, Bobby Doerr in 1950, Clyde Vollmer in 1951 and Norm Zauchin in 1955. When Jimmie Foxx hit 50 home runs during the 1938 season 35 of them left Fenway.

Home runs have not been the only thing to fly around Fenway Park. There have been a number of incidents there involving things that fly — namely pigeons. Who will ever forget Philadelphia Athletic right fielder Hal Peck chasing down Skeeter Newsome's double and throwing the ball back in only to conk a pigeon who happened to by flying by? Or the startled look on St. Louis Brown (later a Red Sox) pitcher Ellis Kinder's face when a passing seagull dropped a smelt in front of him on the mound? Or St. Louis' Bill Hunter batting practice line drive knocking a pigeon out of the air in the outfield? Or Detroit's Willie Horton's foul ball beaning another one near home plate? Then there was the time shots were heard coming from inside the ball yard. It was only Ted Williams trying to reduce the pigeon population with a shot gun. Several years ago there was a pheasant who flew in for a ball game and demanded a seat on the field and grown men spent several anxious moments chasing it around before it decided it would use the field as a runway to take off and fly away. Somehow on several occasions dogs have appeared on the field at Fenway (no pun intended for some of the poorer teams playing there) but on Easter Sunday, 1965 one jumped out of the right field seats and fielded a hit ball before a fielder could get to it and jumped back into the stands with the ball. Naturally the dog was a retriever.

A number of no hitters have been pitched at Fenway. Red Sox who performed this feat were George Foster vs New York on June 21, 1916, Dutch Leonard vs St. Louis on August 30, 1916, Ernie Shore vs Washington on June 23, 1917, Mel Parnell vs Chicago on July 14, 1956, Earl Wilson vs Los Angeles on June 26, 1962 (a night game) and Dave Morehead vs Cleveland on September 16, 1965. Visiting hurlers who turned in no hitters at Fenway were: George Mogridge of New York — April 24, 1917; Walter Johnson of Washington — July 1, 1920, Ted Lyons of Chicago — August 21, 1926; and Jim Bunning of Detroit — July 20, 1958.

There has been a long line of high scoring games at Fenway Park, but the granddaddy of them all occurred on June 8, 1950 when the Sox defeated the St. Louis Browns 29-4. Numerous records were established in this game which saw the Sox set a record for the most runs scored by one team. This record was later equalled by the Chicago White Sox. St. Louis had arrived at Fenway for a three game series and the opener on June 7 saw them lose to the Sox 20 to 4, then came the 29-4 game and on June 9 St. Louis pitchers gave up seven more runs, but the Brownies managed to pull out a 12 to 7 victory. Late in the 1940 season the Sox took the measure of the

Washington Senators 24 to 4 at Fenway and on June 18, 1953 they again won by a twenty run margin over the Detroit Tigers 23 to 3. In this game they scored seventeen runs in the seventh inning, had 27 hits in the game and broke or tied seventeen major league records. Back on September 28, 1923 the tables were turned on the Sox by their old rivals, the New York Yankees, who pounded out a 24 to 4 win and on May 31, 1970 the Chicago White Sox beat the locals 22 to 13. The Cleveland Indians also had a hand in the high scoring Fenway games when a young rookie, Herb Score, shut out the Sox 19 to 0 in 1955 in his first start at the Fens. First baseman Norm Zauchin hit three homers and knocked in ten runs on May 27 that same year as Tom Brewer shut out Washington for a 16 to 0 Sox win.

One of baseball's most memorable games took place at Fenway Park during its initial season. Two of the game's greatest pitchers met in baseball's greatest pitching match up — Washington's Walter Johnson and Boston's Smokey Joe Wood. Johnson had started a winning streak on July 3, 1912 which reached 16 before it ended on August 26. Meanwhile Joe Wood had started a winning streak on July 8, which was running concurrently with Johnson's and finally ended, after he too had won 16 straight, on September 20 in Detroit. The fact that these two pitchers were so unbeatable in that season gave rise to the natural match up the baseball public was demanding. The owners not wanting to lose the gate that such a pitching duel would insure, arranged that when Washington visited Boston in early September the two should meet. So on September 6 the day arrived with Johnson the record holder set to meet the challenger Wood, who by now had reeled off 13 straight victories. The crowd jammed Fenway so that it overflowed on to the field, the player benches were moved out along the foul lines so that fans could be packed in behind them, in the outfield, ropes were strung to contain the fans standing there. So crowded was the field, Wood found it hard to find room to warm up. The two put on a magnificent show with Boston and Wood winning 1 to 0 on Tris Speaker's sixth inning ground rule double into the crowd and a follow up double by Duffy Lewis, driving home Speaker. So Joe Wood had his fourteenth win and he went on to win two more to tie Johnson at 16 consecutive wins before the loss in Detroit. What a great year Smokey Joe had finishing with a league leading 34 wins and five losses and 258 strikeouts second only to Johnson's 303 strikeouts.

In recalling this great event in Fenway's first season one must surely lead the mind to recall the thrills provided by the World Series, many of whose games have taken place on Fenway turf. The very first season saw the Red Sox meet and defeat the New York Giants four games to three with a tie game thrown in for good measure. The tie occurred at Fenway on a raw, cloudy day (October 9) which saw Mayor Fitzgerald present manager Stahl with an auto and shortstop Heinie Wagner with a silver bat. The game went eleven innings and resulted in a 6 to 6 score. The Sox took the final game on October 16, 3 to 2 in ten innings at Fenway to clinch the World Championship. The next World Series at Fenway was in 1914 when the Sox loaned their ball yard, with its larger seating capacity, to George Stalling's "miracle" Boston Braves who met and defeated, 4 games to none, Connie Mack's Philadelphia Athletics. The final game was again at Fenway with the Braves winning 3 to 1 on October 13.

In 1915, the Red Sox replaced the Athletics as the American League Champions and

Bill Carrigan's gang turned on the Philadelphia Phillies of Pat Moran to win the series 4 games to 1. This time the clincher again coming on October 13, but in Philadelphia. This year the Boston end of the series was not played at Fenway, but was shifted to the newly constructed National League Braves Field where seating capacity was larger. The first game played in Boston did draw a record attendance, for that time, of 42,300.

The Sox won the American League pennant again in 1916 and again prevailed upon their National League neighbors to play their home games at Braves Field because of the larger seating capacity. The Sox won the series 4 games to 1 over the Brooklyn Dodgers with the final game coming on Columbus Day and setting a new attendance record of 42,620. In the war time shortened season of 1918 the Red Sox again became World Champions with a four game to two win over the Chicago Cubs — their fifth World Championship without a setback. This time it was the Cubs who shifted their home games to the larger Chicago American League Park — Comiskey Park — to take advantage of the larger seating capacity. The Red Sox decided to stay at Fenway Park for their games, where on September 11 they won the championship with a 2 to 1 victory over the Cubs.

It would be twenty-eight years before another World Series game would be played in Boston. The long drought ended in 1946 when a powerful Red Sox nine rewarded their long suffering owner Tom Yawkey with his first American League Championship. This time it was the St. Louis Cardinals who prevailed in the series 4 games to 3. The clincher came on October 15 at Sportsman's Park in St. Louis with a 4 to 3 Cardinal win made famous by Enos Slaughter's eighth inning dash around bases on Harry Walker's hit to slide home safely, much to the surprise of the Red Sox. While it looked like another Red Sox dynasty was about to begin in 1946, the closest the Sox could come in the next 21 years to hosting another series was in 1948 when they finished in a first place tie with the Cleveland Indians, but lost a one game playoff to Lou Boudreau's squad at Fenway Park 8 to 3 on October 4. This was the first American League playoff game ever and it saw Gene Bearden defeat Denny Galehouse on a five hitter behind two Boudreau home runs.

In 1967 the "Impossible Dream" Red Sox led by the "Cardiac Kids" came within one victory of defeating the St. Louis Cardinals in the World Series as the Cards won 4 games to 3 in a fine series. It was the Cardinals 7 to 2 victory at Fenway on Columbus Day over an overworked Jim Lonborg which returned the World Championship to St. Louis. Eight years later in a World Series which will go down in history as one of the most exciting ever the Cincinnati Reds won a hard fought 4 games to 3 victory over Boston. Again, the final game was at Fenway Park — a 4 to 3 win for the Reds on October 22. This series produced thrill after thrill and will never be forgotten by those who saw it. The claimed interference call by the Sox, the base running of Luis Tiant, the hitting of Pete Rose, the Tony Perez slump, the four day delay as rainstorms battered New England, Fred Lynn crashing into the centerfield wall, the sensational catches of Dwight Evans, the Joe Morgan hit in the final and on and on. Perhaps the most memorable of all events in World Series history occurred in the last of the twelfth inning of game 6. Boston catcher Carlton Fisk, the first man up, hit a long blast that caromed off the left field foul pole for a home run to end the four hour and one minute game at 12:33 A.M. For those that were there, plus the millions watching on television, none will ever forget this young man motioning with both hands as the ball was in flight as if attempting to guide it fair, his unexhibited joy as he loped and jumped around the bases and then ran into the outfield signalling that joy to the crowd — one of the great moments in baseball history. This whole series, with all its excitement and dramatics, went a long way to restore a somewhat sagging interest in baseball and to restoring it as the national pastime.

To reach the 1975 series the Sox had to win the American League Championship Series against the Western Champion Oakland Athletics. The first two games of this series were played in Fenway Park on October 4 and 5, with Boston winning both. The third game, also won by the Red Sox, was played at Oakland.

When memorable Fenway Park games are discussed, one cannot neglect the second ever American League playoff game. After a great start the 1978 edition of the Red Sox ran into a series of player injuries which saw their seemingly secure league lead dwindle and with only two weeks of the regular season left found them 3 1/2 games off the pace. They rebounded from this deficit to gain a tie with their old friends from New York at the end of the regular season. An eight game winning streak over the final games of the season found them in a tie with the Yankees who dropped their final game to the Cleveland Indians, while the Sox behind Looie Tiant were topping the Toronto Blue Jays at Fenway Park on that final Sunday to finish with identical 99-63 records. The Red Sox club held a ten game lead over second place Milwaukee Brewers on July 8 and as late as July 18 lead the eventual champion Yankees by 14 games. They could manage to win only 4 of 17 games from August 30 through September 16th while to the credit of the Yankees was a great second half season which saw them win 52 of 73 games from July 19 on to gain a season ending tie.

The playoff game for the American League East championship was played at Fenway Park on October 2, 1978 before 32,925 fans. The unlikely hero was the Yankees' weak hitting shortstop Bucky Dent. Trailing 2 to 0 in the seventh inning Dent, with runners on base, put the Yankees in the lead 3 to 2 by popping a Mike Torrez pitch up into the left field net. The Yanks went on to add two more runs and a Red Sox eighth inning rally added two more to their scoring column. The Sox threatened again in the ninth inning, but in the end it was the New Yorkers who prevailed 5 to 4. The second American league playoff, both of which involved the Red Sox, ended in the same way — a Red Sox loss.

Ladies Day, Family Day, Bat Day, Jacket Day, Nuns Day and various state days are among the special days that have been held at Fenway Park. These special days, actually ways of increasing attendance, are rarely needed at the park now. The uniqueness and friendly atmosphere are enough to draw the baseball fan into its confines. It wasn't always this way though. When big league baseball was born it was a game to be played in the daylight. In the mid thirties at Cincinnati the first major league night game was played with Brooklyn, Philadelphia, Cleveland and the Chicago White Sox following in the late thirties. The early forties found most other teams following with the Chicago Cubs and the Red Sox holding out. The Sox finally gave in during the 1947 season while the Cubs are still holding out. Fenway Park saw its first night game on June 13, 1947 with the Chicago White Sox the guests. The home team Sox came away the winners by a 5 to 3 score.

Tom Yawkey, the owner at the time, while claiming he thought baseball was a game to be played under the sun, said he thought enough of Boston fans to yield to their demands for at least 14 night games a year, a far cry from today's standards when most all the games are played under the arcs. Even on the day the lights were dedicated Yawkey was saying, "I've been around this game for a long time or ever since early boyhood, and I still think it should be played in the daytime." Nevertheless many letters from fans and the fact that the rival Boston Braves were enjoying much success with their lights were facts of life which could not be ignored Yawkey admitted. So the fans who could not make the afternoon games were accomodated. There were also rumors that the demand for night football in the fall also influenced the Red Sox decision. The popular Boston College eleven had left Fenway for the lights of Braves Field a year earlier. So at a cost estimated between 200 and 250 thousand the arcs were installed on seven light towers, a move which left only Detroit's Briggs Stadium in the American League without lights. In the initial season of night games at Fenway, 14 games were scheduled, two with each visiting club. The seven towers carried 1,120 lights and the 160 lights per tower was the largest assembly of lights ever mounted on a standing pole. The lighting system has been updated on several occasions since 1947.

So there you have it, the ups and downs, highs and lows, firsts and so on's of Fenway Park past. Prior to the 1979 season the new owners made and have pledged to continue to make significant improvements to the grand old lady. The offices, rarely seen by the average fan, are modern and comfortable, comparable to any modern office. A computer is used not only for scoreboard updates but every day business transactions. Rest room facilities have been improved and enlarged, a new first aid station installed, concession stands improved, new ticket booths built, the advanced sale ticket area renovated. The radio and press sections are clean and spacious. The clubhouse facilities have been improved greatly over the years. The dining room atop the roof, while not open to the general public, is spacious, clean and appropriately decorated with paintings of Red Sox and American League heroes — an ideal place for media people to gather. The magic of Fenway continues during the off season with many out of town visitors asking to take a peek at its unique features.

Fenway Park, a name which symbolizes exciting baseball, is a great place to watch a game, something New Englanders have known and come to appreciate over the years. The special thrill of this ball yard, steeped in a rich heritage has continued down through the years from 1912 and Tris Speaker and Joe Wood to today with Yaz, Fred Lynn and Jim Rice. Let's hope it never ends.

FENWAY FACTS

Attendance

Record attendance (also doubleheader record) — 46,995 August 19, 1934 vs Detroit.*

Single Game Attendance — 36,388   April 22, 1978 vs Cleveland
Night Game Attendance — 36,228   June 28, 1949 vs New York
Opening Day Attendance — 35,343   April 14, 1969 vs Baltimore

Distance To Fences

Left field foul line   — 315 ft.
Right field foul line   — 302 ft.
Center field   — 390 ft.
Deep center field   — 420 ft.
Left center field   — 379 ft.
Right center field   — 380 ft.

Height of Fences

Left field wall   — 37 ft. (screen extends upward 23 ft.)
Center field wall   — 17 ft.
Right field wall   — 3 to 5 ft.
Bullpen wall   — 5 ft.

*It should be noted that the Red Sox list the Fenway Park record crowd as 41,766 on August 12, 1934 for two games against New York (see page 249), but later research by the author has found reference to this August 19th game and all evidence appears to make this the correct date and figure.

A BOSTON RED SOX BASEBALL QUIZ

Over the years baseball fans have enjoyed displaying their knowledge of the game by quizzing one another on baseball trivia. It proves to be an excellent way of increasing one's knowledge of the game and perhaps gives the questioner a feeling of satisfaction when he can display some knowledge of his favorite team. It can lead to arguments, laughs or be just a good way to while away the hours. When baseball fans get together it is guaranteed to stir up interest and conversation. So with this in mind, here are a few questions to get you started. I am sure you can add some of your own. Actually, this little quiz started between myself and my friend and fellow Red Sox fan, Mr. Bill Gavin of South Weymouth, Massachusetts so many of the questions originated with Bill and I take no credit for them. We had some fun with them. I hope you will.

A Boston Red Sox Baseball Quiz

1. In 1912 the New York Giants met the Red Sox in the World Series, but what happened to their opposite league home   town counterparts the Braves and Yankees?

2. What Red Sox first baseman captained Harvard's baseball team and his dad worked his way through Harvard playing semi-pro ball?

3. In 1942, a 38 year old pitcher with the St. Louis Browns prevented the Sox from winning the pennant. Starting six times against the Sox he beat them five times. Starting five times against the 1st place Yankees he lost all five. That adds up to a difference of ten games and the Yanks won by nine games. Who was he?

4. In 1942 this slugger led both leagues in home runs (36), yet didn't hit more than two off any pitcher?

5. Pitcher Bill Butland posted a 7 and 1 record in 1942 but what was unusual about it?

6. Lenny Merullo of the Chicago Cubs led the National League with stolen bases in 1942 with 22 while a Red Sox player matched that total while leading the American League noted more for his hitting. Who was he?

7. In 1928 this Red Sox had 8 total bases in one inning, tying the league record?

8. In 1938 this Red Sox third sacker had 12 hits in succession?

9. During the 1919 season Babe Ruth tied an unusual major league record especially for that time?

10. In 1916 this Red Sox tied the major league record for four sacrifice hits in a game?

11. 1921 was a great fielding year for Boston first basemen as both Boston teams' players led their leagues in fielding while setting major league records. Walt Holke was the Braves first baseman (.997). Who for the Sox?

12. This poor second baseman committed 61 errors at that position in 1901.

13. In 1938 he made four errors in one game at third base.

14. In 1933 this catcher split his season between Boston and St. Louis, but accepted 409 chances without an error.

15. In 1920 this well known Sox catcher had 8 assists in a game.

16. It's unusual for a pitcher to have any number of put outs in a game and for years the major league record was four held by a number of pitchers. Do you know who the first Red Sox were to accomplish this?

17. In 1925 a Red Sox pitcher set an AL record for the most errors in a game (4). Who was he?

18. In 1904 "Big Bill" Dineen set an AL record for consecutive complete games pitched. How many?

19. In 1913 this Sox pitcher struck out six consecutive batters in one game.

20. Between June 7 and August 15, 1942 this Boston pitcher won six games all by one run.

21. A Red Sox Hall of Famer caught his spikes in the bag at second base at Yankee Stadium in early 1945 severly fracturing his ankle and putting an end to his playing. Who was he?

22. On April 17, 1945 a Red Sox first baseman set an AL record by making three errors at first base in the 7th inning. Who was he?

23. While attending Mississippi State College this future Red Sox played first base left handed and pitched right handed.

24. 1925 was a vintage year for rookies to make their debut. Among the group were Lou Gehrig, Mel Ott, Mickey Cochrane, Fred Fitzsimmons and Chick Hafey and four other greats, who spent part of their careers with the Sox, also started their major league careers that year not necessarily with Boston. Who were they?

25. Care to guess what pitch Jimmie Foxx claimed to be the toughest he ever swung against?

26. In 1946 Harry Brecheen became the 9th pitcher in World Series history to win three games. What two Sox pitchers had done it previously?

27. Not many major leaguers have been born outside the U.S. but in the 1940's the Sox had a pitcher who was. Who was he?

28. In 1947 a Red Sox shortstop petitioned a Massachusetts court to have his name legally changed. Who was he?

29. He recorded the fiftieth ever World Series shut out. Hint — 1946, third game vs Cardinals.

30. He pitched the longest game in World Series history (14 innings) against Brooklyn on October 9, 1916.

31. On July 18, 1947 Ted Williams achieved a first in his major league career. What was it?

32. He was the AL leading pitcher on won and lost percentage in 1948.

33. This Red Sox infielder once hit .376 while playing third base with the Mission club in the coast league (1933) and later gained fame as a pitcher at Cincinnati.

34. The first owner to popularize "Ladies Day"?

35. In the days of two major league clubs in many cities only two never had a subway series. What were the cities?

36. For real experts — when Joe Cronin played at Sacred Heart College in San Francisco he had an unusual nickname.

37. On August 19, 1949 the Sox defeated Washington 8 to 4, but the losing pitcher, Mickey Haefner, was pitching for Chicago. How come?

38. The 1907 Red Sox just managed to finish 7th but boasted a 22 game winning pitcher. Who was he?

39. In 1949 he pitched six shutouts?

40. Birds other than the Baltimore and Toronto type have played roles in the lore of Fenway Park. Who were the players involved when: a smelt dropped by a bird landed on the mound; a foul hit and killed a pigeon; an outfielder's return throw hit a bird; an outfielder armed with a shotgun spent his off days hunting pigeons?

41. The first sunglasses ever used in baseball were purchased from Lloyds of Boston by what Boston rightfielder?

42. For years a season ticket holder commuted from Providence to *her* box seat with her ever present megaphone to root on her favorite Sox Bobby Doerr. Remember her name?

43. He wanted to buy himself a 30th birthday present, so he bought the Sox.

44. Princeton graduate, catcher, spy for his country, speaking in any of twelve languages, delivering lectures to relief pitchers. Who is he?

45. Although the season ended a month early, the Sox won the pennant. What season?

46. One of the most exclusive clubs major leaguers can belong to is "The Four Decades Club" open to those who performed during four different decades. There are 14 members of this club. Name the Sox members.

47. Name the Red Sox half of a father-son team to appear in a World Series.

48. In 1943 this Red Sox established an American League record by hitting five pinch hit home runs?

49. He had a career total of 2,285 hits in regular season play better than 1/3 of which were for extra bases. Who was he?

50. During his playing career he was known as "The Gray Eagle"?

51. At 39 he became the oldest player to win a batting title in major league history.

52. The only Red Sox to hit three home runs in a game three times.

53. In the 1967 World Series this Red Sox pitcher joined Ed Reulback (1906), Claude Passeau (1945) and Floyd Bevens (1947) in an unusual feat. What was it and who was he?

54. In the fourth inning of game six, 1967 World Series, the Sox established a record for the most home runs in a single inning at three. Who hit them?

55. When Ted Williams became a regular who did he replace in the outfield?

56. Prior to Tommy Harper stealing the most bases in a single season, who held the Sox record?

57. Name the top Red Sox pitcher for the most wins in a single season.

58. This player won the league's MVP with the Sox, but prior to that had won it twice with another team, the only American Leaguer to win it with two AL clubs.

59. He popped up into a DP pinch hitting for a famous slugger, the only player to ever do so.

60. On April 6, 1973 history was made at Fenway Park. What happened?

61. He is the only player (modern) to lead his league in hits in each of his first three seasons.

62. In their last year in the minors, with Minneapolis, each of these Red Sox had the same number of hits (193) and each went on to win league batting championships. Who are they?

63. Cleveland pitcher Bob Feller saw this Sox break up two possible no hitters and get the only hit against him in these games. Who is he?

64. Only one Red Sox uniform number is officially retired. What number and who wore it?

65. In late 1951 a St. Louis Brown rookie, Bob Neiman, hit home runs in his first two at bats in the majors over Fenway's left field wall. Who was the Red Sox pitcher?

66. The oldest pitcher to toss a no hitter in the majors was 41 years old and pitched for the Red Sox. Who was he?

67. In 1960 the Red Sox made one of the "biggest" trades the major leagues have ever seen. Who was involved?

68. Name the Red Sox pitcher who threw left and right handed in the minors.

69. In 1906 he pitched 321 innings and walked only 21, but 1908 he pitched 380 innings walking only 29 batters.

70. In 1923 Cleveland defeated the Sox 27 to 3. By what name has this game become known?

71. In the history of the majors only two pitchers have pitched 22 consecutive years. Both pitched for the Sox during these remarkable strings.

72. The only left handed catcher to play for the Sox?

73. Two Sox catchers who each caught three no hitters?

74. In 1963 this first baseman set a record by assisting on all three outs in the first inning of a game against the Yankees.

75. Pitcher who gave up the first ever World Series hit (a single) and home run?

76. Who played for the Boston Bruins, Celtics and Red Sox all in the same year?

77. In 1916 he set the A.L. record for shut outs by a left hander at 9 (tied in 1978 by Ron Guidry)?

78. Three times Red Sox captured league batting championships with averages under .325. Who were they?

79. In three seasons the Sox have won 100+ games. Name them.

80. Dom DiMaggio may have been the Sox best known Italian heritage outfielder, but Red Sox fans of the mid thirties will remember Smeederino Jolliani. You say you can't find him in the record book? Well, then who is he?

81. Ted Williams was sometimes noted for his gestures to the fans and often in the Red Sox dog house, but in the mid thirties a brash young pitcher thumbed his nose at Boston's fans in May, walked off the field at Fenway

during a game with Washington in August, was warned not to repeat the performance, but did it again four days later in Yankee Stadium, leading to his departure from the Sox. Who was he?

82. On July 14, 1946 Ted Williams hit three home runs in the first game of two against Cleveland, prompting Indian manager Boudreau to use his famous Williams' shift in the second game. Between innings of the first game Ted did another unusual thing. Remember what it was?

83. Eldon Auker helped Detroit to pennants in 1934 and 1935 and later pitched well for the Browns, but while he was with the Sox he was 9-10. What was unusual about that?

84. The first major league infielder to wear glasses was a shortstop of some note with the St. Louis Cardinals. He later headed up the Red Sox farm system. Who was he?

85. So you think rookie outfielder Dom DiMaggio got his start by replacing Doc Cramer in centerfield? Wrong — who did he replace?

86. In 1940 the Sox gave up a promising young pitcher (the story of the franchise) to obtain veteran Mike Ryba. This youngster went on to some good years with the St. Louis Cardinals, losing his fifth game of the '46 series to Job Dobson and his four hitter. Remember him?

87. On July 25, 1941 Lefty Grove finally won his 300th game. After the game, manager Bill Barrett of Brattleboro of the Northern League appeared in the Sox clubhouse with a big, handsome college boy from Mississippi and introduced him around. It was the first time the youngster had ever been inside a major league ball park. Know who he was? He later pitched for the Sox.

88. This right handed pitcher also played first base left handed in the minors, gained valuable experience under former stars Heinie Manush and Bibb Falk in the minors and fell in love with the 24th of the month, as on February 24, 1945 he was discharged from service. On March 24th reported to Louisville farm and April 24th to the Sox. Who was he?

89. In 1946 he won his first ten games and later in the same year won 12 straight.

90. He came to the Sox as an outfielder, wound up at third base until a torrid smash by Joe DiMaggio off his finger drove him out of action and Rip Russell replaced him. The year 1946, the player?

91. Who was the Red Sox catcher in the middle 30's whose brother was also a catcher and made the Hall of Fame?

92. Who was the youngest playing member on a Red Sox ball club?

93. On August 24, 1940, during a laugher with Detroit, Joe Cronin sent Ted Williams in to pitch the last 2 innings. Who replaced the big guy in left field?

94. Two Red Sox players have hit 2 bases-filled home runs in 1 game. Both were also famous for actions on and off the field. Name them.

95. On June 9, 1934, a Red Sox pitcher set an American League record by giving up 6 doubles in 1 inning. His other records are in the Hall of Fame. Who is he?

96. In 1934, the Red Sox were no-hitted for 9 2/3 innings before Roy Johnson got the only hit driving in the winning run against which St. Louis Browns pitcher?

97. In 1901, "The Huntington Avenue Grounds" became the 1st home field for the new American League's Boston baseball club. Name the 2 Hall of Famers who located the site, and the 3rd Hall of Famer who leased the property under Ban Johnson's directions.

98. Why could they not play this country's National Anthem at Fenway and other major league parks prior to the 1931 season?

99. In 1907, Boston owner John I. Taylor proclaimed that his club was to be known as the Boston "Red Sox". New red striped stockings were issued to the players. What color were the stockings that they replaced?

100. Baseball has been subjected to many changes during its long history. Some were ludicrous, many were lucrative, several were laudatory. One that failed to get out of the starter's box was the dream of an early Red Sox manager. He made an official recommendation, before the 1909 season, that all outfielders be required to play within 240 feet of home plate until the bat met the ball. Who was this smitten innovator?

101. Where, within Fenway Park's fair ball territory, were the names Tom and Jean made evident in Morse code?

102. Don Zimmer played for 5 National League teams, but only 1 American League Club. Name that club.

103. Name the ex-Red Sox pitcher, sold without Bill Lee's approval in April, 1978, who collects government checks each time there is a monetary settlement for lands once occupied by the Pottawatomie Indians.

104. Who threw the granddaddy of all wild pitches in the 7th inning of an April 16, 1978 game between Texas and Boston? Who scored on the eye-popping heave?

105. Against Milwaukee, on April 17, 1978, a Red Sox player had two base hits

in the 1st inning at Fenway Park Sans Hoopla. Who was he?

106. Who was the pitcher who presented the Red Sox manager Don Zimmer with a single red rose and then proceeded to gain credit for an 8 hit win against his former teammates and manager?

107. Who holds the Red Sox record for home runs hit in one month. Pick him out of these: Jimmie Foxx, Clyde Vollmer, Jim Rice, Jack Jensen, Ted Williams and Butch Hobson.

108. Are the statistics for the 1978 Red Sox-Yankees playoff game to be included in the regular season player and team totals?

109. Name the sweet swinging Red Sox player who now lives in the home that formerly belonged to the man reputed to have "the sweetest swing" in golf.

110. Who was the man, later a Red Sox pitcher, who caught Hank Aaron's 715th home run in the Atlanta bullpen?

111. One of the present Red Sox players hit a home run in his 1st at bat as a starter. Which one?

112. Mr. Thomas A. Yawkey was the president of the Boston Red Sox when they finished 2nd in 1978. Which Red Sox farm club did win its World Series under woman president Hilary Buzas and vice president Frank Sinatra, Jr.?

113. Has Jim Rice hit a home run in every American League Park in which he has played?

114. Right field was a Red Sox problem spot in the 1967 series against the St. Louis Cardinals. 2 men played it most of the time. 2 others saw action in short stints. The group contributed 4 hits in 31 at bats for a .129 average. They were?

115. The pitcher with the season record for home runs by Red Sox pitchers.

116. What Red Sox President later served in the same capacity for the Boston Braves and the Boston Bees?

117. How can the Red Sox make 6 hits in one inning without scoring a run? It seems to happen a lot, but it doesn't. It could though.

118. With no foul balls involved, how can a Red Sox hitter look at 11 pitches, in one official time at bat, without taking the bat off his shoulder, as they say in the trade?

119. The Red Sox had a pitcher in the middle 30's who holds a little known major league pitching record. He pitched 6 opening day ball games and won

them all. Who was this man who won 193 games in 15 years with Cleveland, the Red Sox, Washington, the Yankees, the Dodgers and the Boston Braves?

120. How many World Series were played at Fenway Park and how many did the Red Sox participate in?

121. Ted Williams has been roasted for going 4 for 20 in his only World Series. Several Hall of Famers have had little series success. A reputed "Clutch Hitter" batted 101 times at a .171 clip during his 1st 23 series games. He batted .195 in 15 All Star games and went hitless in 9 of those. Who was this Hall of Famer?

122. Name the former member of the Red Sox who is the only former All American football player to win the MVP award in baseball?

123. Which pitcher, who ended his career with the Red Sox in 1952, is the only man ever to pitch against Babe Ruth and Mickey Mantle in major league games?

124. One Red Sox player is the only one ever to get 6 hits in a 9 inning game. He was known as a fielder. Who is he?

125. A Red Sox player is the only one to play all 9 positions, pinch hit, and pinch run in the same season. Years later he was a member of Frisch's "Gas House Gang". Name him.

ANSWERS

1. Each finished last in their league
2. Tony Lupien
3. Veteran knuckle baller John Niggeling
4. Ted Williams
5. Each victory came over a different club, as he defeated each team in the league once.
6. John Pesky
7. Bill Regan (two HR's)
8. Mike Higgins
9. Four grand slam home runs. First time in the A.L., done once in the N.L. (Frank Schulte — Chicago Cubs).
10. Jack Barry
11. Stuffy McInnins (.999)
12. Hobe Ferris
13. Pinky Higgins
14. Merv Shea
15. Wally Schang

Boston Red Sox Baseball Quiz Answers (continued)

16. Elmer Steele (1908) Joe Wood (1912)
17. Chet Ross
18. 37
19. Buck O'Brien
20. Charles Wagner
21. Joe Cronin
22. George Metkovich
23. Dave Ferriss
24. Red Ruffing, Lefty Grove, Joe Cronin and Jimmie Foxx
25. Carl Hubbell's screwball
26. Bill Dineen (1903), Joe Wood (1912)
27. Oscar Judd — London, Ontario, Canada
28. John (Paveskovich) Pesky
29. Dave Ferriss
30. Babe Ruth. Allowing 6 hits, winning 2 to 1
31. Went 5 for 5 and hit 2 homers for the 10th time in his career
32. Jack Kramer
33. Bucky Walters
34. Bob Quinn
35. Philadelphia and Boston
36. "Fuzzy"
37. The game actually started July 7 and Haefner, then with Washington, gave up five first inning runs and the game was called after six innings, with Boston ahead 8 to 3. American League President Harridge ordered the game finished later. Washington owner Griffith incensed with Haefner sold him to the White Sox in the meanwhile.
38. Cy Young
39. Ellis Kinder
40. (1) Ellis Kinder pitching for St. Louis, (2) Willie Horton batting for Detroit, (3) Hal Peck throwing in for Philadelphia, (4) Ted Williams hunting for himself.
41. Harry Hooper
42. Lolly Hopkins
43. Tom Yawkey
44. Moe Berg
45. 1918, due to W.W.I
46. Mickey Vernon, Ted Williams, Bobo Newsom, Deacon Jim McGuire, Nick Altrock and Jack Quinn
47. Jim Bagby, Jr. (1946). His father Jim, Sr. appeared with Cleveland in 1920
48. Joe Cronin
49. Joe Cronin
50. Tris Speaker
51. Ted Williams
52. Ted Williams
53. Pitching a World Series one hitter, Jim Lonborg
54. Carl Yastrzemski, Reggie Smith, Rico Petrocelli
55. Ben Chapman

Boston Red Sox Baseball Quiz Answers (continued)

56. Tris Speaker
57. Joe Wood (34-1912)
58. Jim Foxx (Sox 1938, A's 1932, 1933)
59. Carroll Hardy for Ted Williams
60. The first designated hitter (Ron Blomberg-NYY)
61. John Pesky
62. Ted Williams, Carl Yastrzemski
63. Bobby Doerr
64. 9 — Ted Williams
65. Mickey McDermott
66. Cy Young, June 30, 1908 a 8 to 0 victory over New York
67. Pitcher Frank Sullivan of the Sox to the Philadelphia Phillies for Gene Conley. Sullivan was 6'7", Conley 6'8"
68. Dave Ferriss
69. Cy Young
70. "The Indian Massacre"
71. Cy Young, Sam Jones
72. Tom Doran (1904-06)
73. Lou Criger, Bill Carrigan
74. Dick Stuart
75. Boston's Cy Young (1903)
76. John Kiely (organist)
77. Babe Ruth
78. Pete Runnels 1960 — .320, Carl Yastrzemski 1963 — .321, 1968 — .301
79. 1912 (105), 1946 (104), 1915 (101)
80. Johnny Garro, sports editor of "La Notizia" Boston Italian newspaper, invented the name for the Italian community desperate for a hero on Boston's roster — Oh, yes, he was Smead Jolley.
81. Wes Ferrell
82. Instead of going to the bench he stepped into the scoreboard, stepped out a trap door into the street, ran (in uniform) to a nearby cafeteria and ordered a plate of ice cream, retraced his steps and arrived at his position in time for the next inning. A tale often told but hard to believe.
83. Every game he won was on the road. He didn't win a single game at Fenway.
84. George Toporcer
85. His first major league appearance was for Ted Williams in left field (Lou Finney was in right, Cramer in center that day) Williams and Cramer collided with Williams being injured and replaced by Dom.
86. Alpha Brazle
87. Dave Ferriss
88. Dave Ferriss
89. Dave Ferriss. (He didn't lose a single game at Fenway in 1946.)
90. Leon Culberson
91. George "Skeets" Dickey was a brother of Yankee catcher Bill Dickey. The resemblance was purely facial.
92. Joe "Dode" Cicero, an 18 year old outfielder, played in 10 games for the

Boston Red Sox Baseball Quiz Answers (continued)

1929 team. Other 18 year olders played for the Sox, but, as in the case of Joe Wood, were a few months older in their 1st playing season.

93. Pitcher Jim Bagby, who could hit better than Ted could pitch, was the assigned left fielder.

94. Jim Tabor celebrated July 4, 1939 by hitting grand slams in the 3rd and 6th innings of a doubleheader's number 2 game. Rudy York chose the 2nd and 5th innings in a July 27, 1946 game to drive in 8 with 2 swings.

95. Robert Moses Grove chose the 8th inning on that date to wear out his outfielders.

96. September 18th was the day. The luckless pitcher was Bobo Newsom.

97. Hughie Duffy and Tommy McCarthy scouted the area and chose the site. Connie Mack leased the property and Johnson's new league had a field for its Boston entry.

98. Because a national anthem was non-existent until March 3, 1931. On that date Congress designated the Star Spangled Banner as the official National Anthem of the United States.

99. Black, and infrequently washed.

100. Bob Unglaub, a 28 game manager of the Sox in 1907, formally provided the idea for 1909. It was formally declined.

101. On the left field wall. Specifically, Mr. Yawkey had the personal touch applied to the score board in vertical alignment where it was least likely to be noticed.

102. Zim spent 3 years with the Washington Senators before signing to play for the Toei "Flyers" in Japan.

103. Jim Willoughby, whose ancestry included a great aunt who acted as a Washington lobbyist for the tribe's descendants.

104. Len Barker of the Rangers went for distance and hit the top of the screen behind home plate. Pudge Fisk trotted home from third as the Fenway faithful looked skyward in disbelief.

105. 2nd baseman Jerry Remy and he failed to get a standing ovation. 25 years earlier, on June 18, Sox outfielder Gene Stephens planted the modern record with 2 singles and a double in a Fenway Park stretch inning against the Tigers.

106. Ex-Red Soxer Fergie Jenkins turned both tricks on July 14, 1978. It bears mentioning that another Zimmer discard, Reggie Cleveland did his thing by blanking the Sox in the ninth of the same game.

107. "The Golden Boy", Jackie Jensen banged out 14 during the month of June, 1958. Vollmer hit 13 in July of 1951. Rice hit 13 in May of 1978 and is a good bet to rearrange this order in the near future. Jimmie Foxx hit 13 in July 1939.

108. Yes. For statistical purposes the playoff game is considered a part of the regular season.

109. Carl Yastrzemski's home in Boca Raton, Florida, bears the former address of golfing great Sam Snead.

110. On April 8, 1974, Tom House

111. In 1974, Freddie Lynn golfed one out of the park in the 1st time at bat in his 1st time starting role.

Boston Red Sox Baseball Quiz Answers (continued)

112. Bristol, Connecticut, Boston's double A farm club in the Eastern League, defeated the Reading Phillies behind the fine pitching of parent club hopefuls Steve Schneck and Danny Parks.

113. He sure has. He completed the feat on April 9, 1978, when he unloaded a Wilbur Wood pitch into the upper deck at Comiskey Park in Chicago.

114. Ken Harrelson, 1 for 13, Jose Tartabull, 2 for 13, George Thomas, 0 for 2, Norm Siebern, 1 for 3 (a pinch hit)

115. Wes Ferrell hit 7 in 1934.

116. Bob Quinn was the Red Sox honcho, with little dinero, from 1923 until 1933. In 1935, he took over as president of the Boston Braves of the National League and held a fan poll which renamed them the Boston Bees. The "Three Little Steam Shovels", Perini, Rugo and Maney purchased the club in 1940. Quinn was retained but "The Bees" again became "The Braves". Bob's son John took on the president's duties before the 1945 season.

117. The 1st 3 batters single. The men on 2nd and 3rd are picked off. The next 2 hitters single reloading the bases. The 6th batter hits a ground ball, which in turn hits a runner. He is credited with a base hit, the 6th of the inning. The hit runner is called out making it 3 outs, 6 hits, and no runs.

118. He looks, all the way, at a 3 and 2 count with 2 outs. He then looks at the runner being caught off 2nd to end the inning. He is still charged with the 1 official time at bat when he looks at another 3 and 2 count to start off the next inning. When he looks at the next pitch, he has looked at 11 in 1 official time at bat.

119. Right hander Wes Ferrell who had back to back seasons of 20 and 25 wins as a Red Sox hurler who threw smoke as well as tantrums.

120. Of the 6 series played, 5 involved the Red Sox. They played series home games in 1912, 1918, 1946, 1967 and 1975. The Boston Braves played their series home games at Fenway in 1914. A total of 6. The Sox also won pennants in 1915 and 1916, but played those World Series home games at Braves Field.

121. Lawrence "Yogi" Berra

122. Jackie Jensen, chosen MVP while with the Sox in 1958, had been a football All American with California's Golden Bears.

123. Al Benton, with the Philadelphia A's in 1934, faced Ruth in his final year as an American Leaguer. With the Red Sox in 1952, Al pitched to Mantle, the Yankee sophomore switcher.

124. Jim Piersall did it in the first game of a doubleheader on June 10, 1953. Pete Runnels went 6 for 7 in a 1960 game that lasted 15 long innings.

125. Jack Rothrock did it all during 117 games in 1928.

SELECTED ARTICLES

In this section you will find some articles, several of which have appeared in the official Red Sox Scorebook at Fenway Park. They all should help you catch the fever of the Red Sox story.

"The Strange Saga Of The 1904 Pilgrims" (written in 1979)
"Hitting For The Cycle" (updated through 1979)
"Boston's First World Champions" — 1903 (Written in 1978)
"Boston's Last World Championship" — 1918 (Written in 1978)
"Were The 49ers The Best" (The 1949 Red Sox)
"Joseph Wood — Pitcher"
"Remembering Joe McCarthy"
"The Batboy" (The story of a minor league batboy)
"Remembering The Four Seasons — 1978" (A nostalgic trip)

THE STRANGE SAGA OF THE 1904 PILGRIMS

This season will mark seventy-five years since the second league championship pennant flew from a Boston American League flagpole. Back in those days the Red Sox were known as the Pilgrims and the story of their championship season and the after effects is a strange saga at best. A good team, the 1904 edition, repeated their American League championship of 1903 by winning ninety-five games while losing fifty-nine and finishing a game and one-half in front of the second place New York Highlanders (Yankees). They presented an almost identical lineup as the one they had while winning the 1903 American League flag and their subsequent 5 game to 3 victory over the Pittsburg Pirates in the first modern World Series. All told they used only thirteen players and five pitchers during that 1904 season, the smallest Red Sox squad ever. Their basic lineup was Candy LaChance—first base; Hobe Ferris — second base; Fred Parent — shortstop and manager Jimmy Collins at third. In the outfield they had Buck Freeman, Chick Stahl and newcomer Kip Selbach. The catcher was Lou Criger and the pitchers were, the immortal Cy Young, Big Bill Dineen, Jesse Tannehill, Norwood Gibson and George Winter. With such a small pitching staff it was inevitable that there would be several twenty game winners, and so there were, with Young winning 26, Dineen 23 and Tannehill 21. Gibson won 17, a fine number by today's standards, while Winter won 8. They turned in 40, 37, 30, 29 and 12 complete games respectively, not much need for relievers in those days. Remarkably for a pennant winner they boasted no 300 hitters. Chick Stahl at .297 and little Freddy Parent at .291 were as close as they could come.

While there wasn't a great deal of change in player personnel for 1904 the Boston fans did greet a new owner, John I. Taylor, whose father, General Charles Taylor, had purchased the club from Henry Killilea with some behind the scenes maneuvering by league President Ban Johnson. A new seven year lease had been signed for the use of the Huntington Avenue Grounds as their home field, located on the present site of Northeastern University.

Boston opened the season in New York losing the opener to the Highlanders but copping the remaining two games of the three game set. Opening their home season on April 18th, Jesse Tannehill shut out Washington 5 to 0 as Taylor assumed the ownership reins. The following day, April 19, a morning-afternoon Patriots Day twin bill was staged with George Winter tossing a second straight shut out, 1 to 0, over the Senators and Cy Young winning a close 3 to 2 afternoon game. 28,000 loyal Pilgrim rooters passed through the turnstiles that day. As April ended, manager Jimmy Collins had his Pilgrims in first place with a nifty 10 and 2 record, and a Memorial Day doubleheader victory over Washington found them with a 25 and 10 record as May ended with Big Bill Dineen sporting an 8 and 1 pitching record.

It was one of the grandest of all American League races that season. Connie Mack's Philadelphia Athletics were the early challengers to Boston but they dropped off the pace in late May as the Cleveland Naps challenged for awhile, only to fall back in mid summer when the New Yorkers and Chicago alternated as challengers until August 4 when the Naps bested Boston 11 to 1 and Chicago went into first place. New York and Chicago each took turns in the lead until August 17, when,before a then record crowd of 30,178 at Chicago, Boston's left handed ace Jesse Tannehill hurled a brilliant 6 to 0 no hitter allowing only two runners to reach first base and shooting Boston back into the lead.

Earlier in the season (May 2) Philadelphia's Hall of Famer Rube Waddell had tossed a brilliant one hitter against Boston and Tannehill at the Huntington Avenue Grounds allowing only two batters to reach base. Waddell made great sport in bragging of his feat taunting Boston's great Cy Young to face him and meet the same fate as Tannehill. The four game series was to end on May 5 and the two future Hall of Famers were the scheduled mound opponents for the day. Young, irritated by Waddell's earlier remarks, rose to the occasion by not only pitching the first ever Boston no hitter but retiring all twenty-seven Athletics who faced him for a perfect game, reversing the score of Waddell's earlier victory, 3 to 0 this time for Boston. When the game ended it was Young's turn to taunt Waddell and he was quoted as hollering over to Rube "How did you like that one, you hayseed?"

Young, of course, went on to twenty-six victories, but along the way he performed another feat as rare as his perfect game. On September 10 at Philadelphia's Columbia Park, he was involved in a pitching duel with Eddie Plank, a 13 inning 1 to 0 affair, which he lost eventually but in one inning late in the game Cy struck out three consecutive A's on just nine pitches. They were all swinging strikes, not a foul ball or called strike among them.

Tannehill was the first to win twenty games, posting a 3 to 1 victory in the second game of a doubleheader at Washington on September 8. He might have won it even earlier except for an unfortunate incident earlier in the season. In a game with Phladelphia, while attempting to brush back the popular A's outfielder Danny Hoffman, a pitch got away from him and struck Hoffman just below the right eye. Hoffman went down like a bullet, his eye dangling from its socket and narrowly escaping death. For weeks Tannehill's pitching was affected as he would not throw a fast inside pitch. Young was brilliant down the stretch, winning his twentieth game on September 16 with a 4 to 2 victory over New York, and except for a 3 to 1 loss at Cleveland won his remaining games.

The Highlanders and Pilgrims exchanged first place all through September and into October as the other contenders fell back. As the schedule would have it, the two were to meet in the final five games of the season. New York beat Gibson 3 to 2 at Hilltop Park in New York on October 7 in the first of the five games to take a half game lead as spitballer Jack Chesbro won his 41st game of the year, quite a feat. Boston now got a break in that New York owner, Frank Farrell, had rented out his ball park to Columbia University for a football game on October 8 and the scheduled doubleheader had to be moved to Boston. Boston banged out fourteen hits and beat Chesbro 13 to 2 behind Bill Dineen to regain first place. The vital second game found Cy Young besting Jack Powell 1 to 0 in a 7 inning game called because of darkness and gaining a game and one-half lead. The next day being Sunday there was no game as Sunday ball was not played in those days, but the teams returned to New York for a doubleheader on Monday the 10th. Boston needed a split to win and New York needed a sweep. Boston, complete with their "Royal Rooters" crowded into the ball park, saw New York take an early 2 to 0 lead as former Boston hero, Pat Dougherty, (traded to New York earlier in the season on June 19 for utility man Bob Unglaub, a very unpopular trade which led to Kip Selbach's purchase from Washington) singled home a run. Dineen then walked in a run but recovered with the bases loaded to put out the fire. Boston tied the score at two all in the seventh on a couple of singles, a sacrifice and wild throw which allowed the two runs to score. In the ninth inning catcher Criger, not a fast man, beat out an infield roller, moved to second on a sacrifice, to third on an out and scored when a Chesbro spitter went for a wild pitch. There it was, a 3 to 2 Boston pennant victory on a wild pitch, one of the most famous plays in baseball history. Bill Dineen won his 23rd game. With the race over one would assume the second game would be just playing out the string affair. Instead, it was a battle with New York winning 1 to 0 in ten innings.

The defending World Champions issued a challenge after the doubleheader of the tenth to the National League champion New York Giants of John McGraw, but Giant owner John T. Brush refused to accept owner Taylor's offer contending his team "was content to rest on its laurels". Brush had no love for the new American League and resented its having put a team in New York and its making peace with the older league in 1903. To save face with regard to earlier statements in the New York press about not playing the American League when it appeared that the Highlanders, his New York competition, would win the Junior Circuit pennant, he could not back down now although he had nothing against Taylor and the Pilgrims. There was much criticism heaped upon Brush and his Giants by fans and press alike, but his decision stood even though the Giant players wanted to augment their low salaries by playing the series. The baseball bible, "The Sporting News", declared the 1904 Boston Americans "Worlds Champions by default". So ended the strange saga of the 1904 Boston Pilgrims, the only Boston American League Champions not to play in a World Series and the only American League Champions not to appear since the advent of the modern World Series seventy-six seasons ago.

HITTING FOR THE CYCLE

One of the rarest feats that can be performed by a major league baseball player is hitting for the cycle (single, double, triple, home run) in one game. Since 1901, when the Red Sox were born, their pitchers have thrown 14 no hitters, yet their batters have only hit for the cycle 13 times. One, Bobby Doerr, did it twice and one, Joe Cronin, did it once for another team (Washington Senators 1929). When you consider that since 1901 the Red Sox have played better than 12,000 games (12,238 through 1979) you can readily see how rare this feat is. Hitting for the cycle is something a batter can't think about in advance. It just happens. Admittedly there must be some luck, possibly some speed, some power and usually a wild type of a game involved. It is a feat which can never be forgotten for the accomplisher.

The ball park is also a factor. Fenway Park is a doubles park for right handed hitters who don't hit the ball high enough to reach the left field screen. Among those Red Sox to turn the cycle power hitters who hit to all fields predominate. Carl Yastrzemski, who did it in 1965, is the ideal type batter to perform the feat. Artificial turf has not been a factor for any of the Sox batters who have hit for the cycle, but it should be pointed out that there are fewer doubles when the hit goes directly to the outfielder preventing a batter from taking an extra base, but the possibility for a triple on artificial turf is greater.

Let's look at each of the Red Sox cycles. Certainly one of the most unique accomplishments in baseball. They were accomplished on:

June 21, 1903	Buck Freeman
July 29, 1903	Pat Dougherty
June 9, 1912	Tris Speaker
August 19, 1934	Julius Solters
August 2, 1940	Joe Cronin
July 3, 1943	Leon Culberson
May 17, 1944	Bob Doerr
July 6, 1944	Bob Johnson
July 21, 1946	Ted Williams
May 13, 1947	Bob Doerr
July 13, 1962	Lou Clinton
May 14, 1965	Carl Yastrzemski
September 15, 1979	Bob Watson

June 21, 1903 — Perhaps the major topic of discussion among the population of Boston was the collision of the Battleship Massachusetts with a schooner loaded with lumber near the Boston light ship. Or maybe it was the relief of knowing that the great stike of workers at nearby Lowell's textile mills had finally ended as 17,000 workers returned to mills which had been shut for three weeks, having been struck on March 30 but manned by supervisory personnel in the meanwhile. Commander Robert E. Peary was talking about another expedition in search of the North Pole but baseball diehards may have had none of this as their left fielder Buck Freeman was the topic of their conversations.

The Boston Pilgrims were playing in Canton, Ohio (yes, that's right the game was transferred from Cleveland) against their American League counterparts from Cleveland. Boston came away with an easy 12 to 7 win and found themselves in a first place tie with the Philadelphia Athletics and a 32-20 record. Long Tom Hughes was the pitcher that day for Boston with Lou Criger the catcher. Freeman had a grand day with two singles, a double, a triple and a home run becoming the first Boston American League player to hit for the cycle and fourth ever in the American League. (Harry Davis, Eddie Murphy and Nap Lajoie all of Philadelphia having done it in 1901.) Buck came to bat six times getting his five hits good for six RBI's while scoring three runs. His hits came off Cleveland pitchers Ed Walker and Gus Dorner, whose catcher was Harry Bemis.

July 29, 1903 — There were no earth shattering events taking place on this day. Oh, down in Washington they were talking about the need for new stables at the White House and there was talk of a trans Alaska-Siberian railroad to Russia via a tunnel to be built under the Bering Strait. At the Huntington Avenue Grounds ball park in Boston left fielder Pat Dougherty was becoming the second player in Boston American League history to accomplish the cycle.

The Pilgrims were playing the New York Highlanders, and in a heavy hitting contest the New Yorkers prevailed 15-14, although they had been shut out in the two previous games of the series. The immortal Cy Young pitched the complete game for Boston losing his fifth of the year against 18 wins. Jack Chesbro (to win 41 games in 1904) was the New York starter but was relieved by Harry Howell in the 6th. The fielding in the game was quite indifferent as Boston made 8 errors and New York 3. Only six New York runs were earned while eight of Boston's were. Dougherty was the lead-off man for Boston and had plenty of company in each of his hitting categories. Along with his double, second baseman Hobe Ferris had two, centerfielder Jack O'Brien had a triple, along with right fielder Buck Freeman as did Jake Stahl who pinch hit for Young in the 9th. O'Brien joined Dougherty in a home run. Dougherty also stole a base after his single and scored three runs in the game. On the Highlander side the famous Wee Willie Keeler had four hits and scored four runs and a future Boston pitching star, Jesse Tannehill, made a rare left field appearance.

June 9, 1912 — While the Red Sox were playing in St. Louis, back in Boston night service on the Boston Elevated was being cancelled after a bomb had been set off shattering a trolley in the Back Bay section in strike related violence. In the suburbs strike mobs were attacking the Boston street cars. In St. Louis the American League's leading batter, Tris Speaker, was attacking Brownie pitcher

Roy Mitchell by hitting for the cycle for what would turn out to be the only time in his long career he would do so. Speaker, batting third in the line-up and playing centerfield, had four hits in five at bats, scoring two runs in leading Boston to a 9 to 2 victory, strengthening their hold on second place. Rookie right hander Hugh Bedient pitched all the way for the Sox to garner the win. Second baseman Marty Krug chipped in with three hits in four tries and left fielder Duffy Lewis contributed a home run.

August 19, 1934 — The nation was beginning to show signs of recovery from the great depression when a crowd of 50,000 (46,995 paid), the largest in Boston American League history up to then, saw the Detroit Tigers defeat the Red Sox in a twin bill 8 to 6 and 4 to 3. Batting fifth in the line-up and playing centerfield that day was the colorful Julius "Moose" Solters who achieved his cycle in the first game. In five at bats the right hand hitting "Moose" had four hits and tallied two runs. All of his hits came off the veteran twirler Alvin "General" Crowder who had joined the Tigers earlier in the season coming over from the Washington Senators. The big rookie batter went 0 for 4 in the second game, but he had had his day in the sun. The Sox were in fourth place that day and a couple of pretty fair hurlers pitched for them in that first game — Lefty Grove, Henry Johnson and Herb Pennock.

August 2, 1940 — Troubles which were brewing in Europe seemed a long way away on this pleasant Saturday afternoon in Detroit which saw the Sox down the Tigers 12 to 9 while pounding out 14 hits. Shortstop manager Joe Cronin, batting third in the lineup, had four hits in five at bats in hitting for the cycle. His eighth inning homer, off Archie McKain, following a Doc Cramer triple put the game safely away for the Sox. The first place Tigers sent a parade of pitchers against the third place Red Sox, including Bobo Newsom, Tom Seats, Dizzy Trout, Clay Smith and McKain. Newsom, having lost to the A's the previous Sunday ending his personal 13 game winning streak, was attempting to start another streak. This time Seats wound up the loser. The Sox countered with rookie Earl Johnson, Jack Wilson (the winner) and Joe Heving with Jimmie Foxx handling the catching. In addition to Cronin's homer, Dom DiMaggio and Jimmie Foxx homered. For Foxx it was his 23rd of the season. In the fourth inning the Sox outstanding rookie, Ted Williams, pinch hit for Johnson and walked. It is interesting to note that the Tiger lineup contained three players who in a few years would play vital roles for the Red Sox — catcher Birdie Tebbetts, right fielder Pete Fox and first baseman Rudy York.

July 3, 1943 — World War II was beginning to swing in favor of the Allies. The Navy was driving the Japanese from Rendova and bombing Rabaul in the Pacific, while in Europe continued bombing of German bases in Italy was forcing their retreat. In Cleveland Red Sox rookie centerfielder Leon Culberson was doing some bombing of his own as he hit for the cycle while leading the Red Sox past the Indians 12 to 4 in a rare night game. Leon had four hits in five at bats and added a walk which forced in a run. The Sox had 13 hits in the game with their first three batters contributing nine of them. Lead-off man Culberson had four, the second batter, right fielder Pete Fox had three and the third batter, first baseman Tony Lupien had two. Victims of this attack were

Indian pitchers Chubby Dean, Mike Naymick, Pete Center and Al Milnar with Naymick taking the loss. Mike Ryba was the winner in relief of Joe Dobson. Forty-one year old future Hall of Famer Al Simmons pinch hit for Dobson in the 6th inning, while back in Boston the old veteran Red Sox pitcher Danny MacFayden was signing to pitch for the Braves. He had broken in with the Sox in 1926. All signs of the times for war time baseball.

May 17, 1944 — In Europe, the U.S. 8th Army had moved the Germans out of Cassino, in the Pacific the Navy was bombing New Guinea and General Stillwell was winning the battle of Burma. In Boston Tex Hughson was throwing a four hitter at the St. Louis Browns in the first game of a doubleheader winning 5 to 1. The second game of the pair was a wild affair with the Sox knocking out 15 hits to St. Louis' 14, yet the Browns won 12 to 8. It was in this second game that second baseman Bobby Doerr hit for the cycle, garnering four hits in five at bats off Brown pitchers Sig Jakucki and George Caster. The loss left the Sox in last place, 6 games behind the league leading Yankees with the Browns in second place 1/2 game off the pace. Doerr's infield partner, Skeeter Newsome, had a big day going 2 for 3 in the opener and 3 for 4 in the nitecap. Interestingly, the parade of Sox pitchers in that second game included a two inning stint on the mound by infielder Eddie Lake. The others were Emmett O'Neil (the loser), Pinky Woods, Lou Lucier and Clem Hausman. Jakucki picked up the win.

July 6, 1944 — For those New Englanders old enough to remember July 6, 1944 it will not be remembered as the day left fielder Bob Johnson hit for the cycle. In Washington President Roosevelt was greeting France's General DeGaulle. Across the Atlantic Winston Churchill was announcing that 2700 Londoners had died since June 15 as a result of German flying bombs. Down the road in Hartford, Connecticut one of New England's greatest tragedies was taking place as 139 adults and children lost their lives as the Ringling Brothers, Barnum and Bailey Circus tent burned to the ground. Overshadowed by these events was the fact that the eleven year American League veteran, Indian Bob Johnson was hitting for the cycle at Fenway Park as the Sox were blasting three Detroit Tiger hurlers for 20 hits and gaining a 13 to 3 victory behind Tex Hughson. The score matched the tall right hander's record of 13-3. Every Sox batter managed at least one hit off the offerings of Rufus Gentry, Jake Mooty and Boom Boom Beck. The aging Johnson was so tired after completing his cycle in the 7th inning that he gave up his left field spot to rookie Tom McBride. Bobby Doerr played a big part in the win by driving in 5 runs with a triple, double, and two singles in four trips to the plate. Johnson scored four runs himself, getting his four hits in five at bats. The win enabled the Sox to hold on to second place, 2 1/2 games behind the St. Louis Browns. At the time three Red Sox were among the top five American League batters. Doerr at .339 and Pete Fox at .333 were behind Chicago's Thurman Tucker's .346 and Johnson at .314 was 5th behind the A's Dick Siebert at .318

July 21, 1946 — In Asia the Chinese were still fighting the Communists. In Bolivia an uprising resulted in that country's President's death. Generally things on the baseball scene were great as the war was over and the genuine major leaguers were returning to the ball yards. Out at Fenway Park the home team was putting on quite a show by sweeping a doubleheader from the St. Louis Browns 5 to 0 and 7 to 4. In the opener, pitcher Dave Ferriss won his 15th game of the season with a neat five hit shut out, his fifth of the campaign. Ted Williams was giving a hint of things to come by going 3 for 4 off the offerings of Tex Shirley, Stan Ferins, Ellis Kinder and Frank Biscan.

In the second game Ted got things going in the second inning by smashing a 1 and 1 pitch 400 feet into the right field stands for his 27th home run of the year. In the third his sinking line drive bounced off the bullpen wall in right center and caromed off Brownie centerfielder Walt Judnick's thigh as Ted steamed into third with a triple. The fourth hit of the 5th inning was Ted's single. Later in the game he added a double and the cycle was his. Left fielder Williams was hitting fourth that day against Brown pitchers Cliff Fannin (the loser), Nelson Potter and Sam Zoldak. Joe Dobson pitched and won for Boston with relief help from Bob Klinger.

May 13, 1947 — Perhaps overshadowing Bobby Doerr becoming the first Red Sox player to twice hit for the cycle was the performance put on by Ted Williams at Fenway Park as the Red Sox downed the Chicago White Sox 19 to 6. Williams for the first time in his career hit two home runs into the left field screen, his first homers in Boston during that season. In 1946 Lou Boudreau had devised the "Williams Shift" primarily because of the slugger's aversion to hitting to left field. The score was 5 to 5 in the 7th when Ted sent a long towering smash to deep left center off Earl Harrist igniting a 5 run inning. His second homer was lined into the screen near the left field foul pole on the first pitch by lefty Ed Smith in the 8th inning. These were the first two homers he hit to left field at Fenway Park. There is a story behind these homers which has been lost in the passage of time. Earlier in the day Williams and pitcher Joe Dobson visited an eleven year old boy in a Malden hospital. The boy, who had recently lost both legs, asked Ted to hit him a homer. Ted said he would try. This was the second time in the young season Ted had done this. On the way north, from spring training at Sarasota, Ted had made a similar promise to an ailing youth at a Chattanooga, Tennessee hospital and had delivered that day against the Cincinnati Reds. Getting back to Doerr, who was playing second base and batting 5th, he started his cycle by homering in the 4th off John Rigney, tripled off Harrist in the 7th and chipped in with a single and a double in the 8th off Edgar Smith and Joe Haynes when he batted twice in the 9 run eighth inning. All the Sox in the lineup that day had hits except catcher Hal Wagner, who walked twice, and relief pitcher Bill Zuber who sacrificed. Dave Ferriss started the game, but it was Zuber who got the win. Harrist took the loss. It was quite a day not only for Doerr who had his four hits in six at bats, scoring three runs, but for Williams and that youngster in the Malden hospital.

July 13, 1962 — President Kennedy was delaying a tax cut decision, Eastern Air Lines was on strike, down in Texas Billie Sol Estes was declared bankrupt and over in Great Britain Prime Minister MacMillan was dropping seven cabinet members. Out in Kansas City the Red Sox were winning a 15 inning contest 11 to 10 as Lou Clinton was hitting for the cycle. It was Lou's 15th inning single which won the game, his second single of the game. Clinton was playing right field that day and batting sixth and in his seven at bats he had five hits, scored four runs and knocked in four more. The Sox made 21 hits that day to K.C.'s 20, certainly no pitchers battle. The two teams were both deep in the standings with Boston 8th, 6 1/2 behind while K.C. was 9th, 8 1/2 behind the league leaders. Dick Radatz picked up the win, evening his record at 4 and 4, while Ed Rakow was the loser. Bill Monbouquette was the starter followed by Chet Nichols, Hal Kolstad and Mike Fornieles for Boston. There were some interesting names in the K.C. lineup that day. Their catcher was a fellow named Haywood Sullivan, now a well known name in Boston. Incidentally, he went 4 for 4 and scored two runs before he gave way to a pinch runner in the 10th. His replacement was Joe Azcue, another name remembered in Boston. There were more of the 1967 "Impossible Dream" Red Sox in the K.C. lineup than the Boston lineup that day as Jose Tartabull was in centerfield, Norm Siebern at 1st base and John Wyatt pitched. The only Red Sox in their own lineup that would be around in 1967 were outfielder Carl Yastrzemski and catcher Bob Tillman.

May 14, 1965 — Frances Perkins, the first woman cabinet member under President Roosevelt died at 83, the United States had ordered a pause in bombing raids on North Vietnam and Bobby Hull of hockey's Chicago Black Hawks was named winner of the Lady Byng trophy. The Red Sox were resting in seventh place, 6 1/2 games behind the league leading Chicago White Sox, and were engaged in a Friday night opening game of a weekend series with the Detroit Tigers at Fenway Park. The game turned out to be a ten inning affair with the Tigers victorious 12 to 8. Boston's left fielder and third batter in the lineup was Carl Yastrzemski. He not only hit for the cycle but went 5 for 5 including his fifth and sixth home runs of the young season. He scored two runs himself and knocked in five more. As a matter of fact it was a big night for left fielders as Detroit's Willie Horton chipped in two homers for the Tiger cause.

Pitching for Boston that day were old friends Dennis Bennett, Bob Heffner, Jack Lamabe, Jay Ritchie and their ace fireman, who wound up the loser, Dick Radatz. Mike Ryan handled the catching. Detroit started Denny McLain, followed by Ed Rakow, Larry Sherry and the eventual winner Terry Fox. For Fox it was his third consecutive win.

Boston had taken an early 5 run lead only to see Detroit get 5 runs to tie in the third and add 3 more in the sixth to take an 8 to 6 lead, the Sox having scored a lone run in the 5th. Two Sox runs in the 7th knotted the score at 8 all. Jerry Lumpe got things going for Detroit in the 10th with a triple, scoring on Don Demeter's double to trigger a 4 run inning and carry Detroit to the 12 to 8 victory. Despite all of these heroics, it was Yaz's single, double, triple, and two home runs which were the highlight of the evening.

September 15, 1979 — An exhausted President Jimmy Carter had to drop out of a Maryland road race on doctor's orders. The troubled Chrysler auto company had asked for a $1.2 billion federal loan but was turned down by the government who declared the auto maker was asking for too much aid. Major oil firms were being pressured to ease their credit terms on home heating fuel. The Boston mayoral contest was entering its final week before the primary election and the Red Sox were in Baltimore for a contest with the Orioles who were headed for the American League East Championship.

Boston won the night contest by a 10 to 2 score behind starter Steve Renko and reliever Dick Drago. The big news of the game, however, was Bob Watson's four hits in five at bats for the cycle. Hitting for the cycle in itself is an unusual feat, but Watson chose the most unusual and extremely rare way of doing it.

Playing first base and batting in the sixth position, the big right hand hitting Watson singled to right in the second inning, doubled down the third base line in the fourth, reached on a fielder's choice in the sixth, tripled to right in the eighth and homered to left in the ninth.

There are very few players who can say they hit for the cycle, but even fewer who got the four hits in order — single, double, triple, home run — Bob Watson is one who can claim the honor.

"BOSTON'S FIRST WORLD CHAMPIONS"

The 1978 baseball season marked the 75th anniversary of Boston's first American League Championship team and of the first World Series of the modern era. That long ago season of 1903 marked many milestones in baseball history. The disastrous two year war between the National and American leagues ended with the Cincinnati peace pact in January of that year. The American League finally won recognition as a full major league despite the wounds left by several seasons of player raids by teams of both leagues. There was still an uneasy feeling between the leagues caused by the two earlier full seasons of bickering, and each league still had its personnel who wanted nothing to do with the other side.

One of the first to relent was Barney Dreyfuss, owner of the Pittsburgh Pirates. He had been successful in keeping the American League out of Pittsburgh and finally the newer league proclaimed it would place a team in New York. Although he lost two of his great pitchers, Jack Chesbro and Jesse Tannehill, to the new New York entry in the American League, his 1903 Pirates won their third of three straight pennants by seven games over John McGraw's New York Giants.

The Boston American League team, then known as the Pilgrims or the Puritans, were winning their first pennant by fouteen and one-half games over the Philadelphia Athletics. As Pittsburgh and Boston moved into late August, it appeared both would win their league's pennants so Pittsburgh owner Dreyfuss made overtures to Boston President Henry J. Killilea about playing a post season championship series. Killilea, unsure of how American League President Ban Johnson would feel about such an arrangement, went to Chicago to sound out Johnson about such an arrangement. Johnson asked Killilea if he felt his New Englanders could beat Pittsburgh and upon learning manager Collins felt his Boston nine could, he gave his blessing to proceed. In early September, Killilea and Dreyfuss met in Pittsburgh and drew up plans for the first World Series. It was Dreyfuss who suggested the winner be the first to win five games which meant the series could go a maximum of nine games. The owners agreed to split the gate receipts an both agreed to use no player who was not on the roster as of September 1st, an agreement which continues today. They further agreed to make their own financial arrangements with their players. This almost led to the cancellation of the first series. The Pittsburgh players were under contract until October 15, while the Boston contracts expired on September 30. This led to a threatened strike by the Boston players, unless they were given Boston's entire share of the gate. Owner Killilea appeased his players by giving them two weeks extra pay plus a share of his receipts.

The World Series was played in two relatively small ball parks — The Huntington Avenue Grounds in Boston (now the site of Northeastern University athletic facilities) and Exposition Park in Pittsburgh (abandoned in 1909). The size of these fields caused both clubs to put up ropes in the outfield to restrain the crowds. Hits into these crowds were ground rule triples and the four games in Pittsburgh resulted in seventeen triples, twelve by the Pilgrims.

There were a number of interesting side lights to this first series. There was the famed Boston Royal Rooters, an organization of Hub fans who had switched their allegiance from the Boston National League entry, who followed the Pilgrims from Boston to Pittsburgh and back again encouraging the locals on to victory while singing their victory song "Tessie". This group was led by Mike Regan, a famous fan of that period, and "Nuff Ced" McGreevey, a local saloon keeper whose business establishment was a player watering hole with walls covered with baseball pictures. These pictures are now part of collections of the Boston Public Library and the Baseball Hall of Fame in Cooperstown, New York. The first World Series scandal occurred during the game of October 3 in Boston and haunted the club for most of the following winter. On that date, an unruly crowd on the field often made play difficult. Many out-of-towners arriving for the game barged into the seats reserved for home town customers and refused to move when the ticket holders of the reserved seats arrived. Joe Smart, the Boston secretary, had an inadequate number of ushers on hand to handle the situation and the Boston police refused to step into the problem. Smart was criticized, after the series, along with owner Killilea for their tightwad methods which included making the Pittsburgh owner, owners of the Boston Nationals and sports writers from cities other than Pittsburgh and Boston pay their way into the Huntington Avenue Grounds. This along with the seating problems at the October 3rd game and the rhubarb over the way tickets were sold, many finding their way into the hands of speculators, caused continuing problems during the 03-04 off season.

American League President Ban Johnson, fearful of a bad reaction by Boston fandom, eased Joe Smart out of office and replaced him with a Chicago baseball writer Carl Green. To complete the overhaul, just prior to the start of the 1904 season, Ban struck a deal whereby Killilea sold the club to Charles Taylor, owner of the Boston Globe newspaper and his son John I. Taylor, who was named president of the club.

The Boston champions of 1903 presented a formidable lineup led by Hall of Famer, manager and captain Jimmy Collins at third base. His infield mates included Fred Parent at shortstop, Hobe Ferris at second and Candy LaChance at first. The outfield boasted three left handed batters led by Pat Dougherty, the team's leading batter at .331 in left field, Chick Stahl in center field and Buck Freeman, the leading home run hitter with 13 in right. The catching was handled for the most part by a very able Lou Criger, although they opened the season with Duke Farrell behind the plate, until an April injury limited him to only 17 games. Jack O'Brien, a favorite with the Boston fans, kept the team in the running after Chick Stahl was injured. Jack appeared in 71 games as an outfielder with an occasional tour in the infield. The pitching corps was made up of right handers Cy Young, winner of 28 games; Bill Dineen who captured 21 victories; Long Tom Hughes 20 wins; Norwood Gibson and George Winter. The lone lefty on the staff was Nick Altrock who stayed around only long enough to lose one game before he moved on to star for Chicago. There were also four utility players besides O'Brien. They were Jake Stahl, Aleck Smith, George Stone and Harry Gleason. This team won 91 games, while dropping 47 for a .659 percentage. The Pittsburgh team was led by left fielder Fred Clarke who teamed with Ginger Beaumont in center field and Jimmy Sebring in right. The fancy fielding Kitty Bransfield was at first, Claude Ritchey at second, Hall of Famer and all time great Honus Wagner at shortstop and little Tommy Leach at third. Eddie Phelps handled the catching along with Harry Smith. The pitching staff was headed by twenty-five game winner Sam Leever and twenty-four game winner Deacon Phillippe, backed up by Ed Doheny, Bill "Brickyard" Kennedy, Fred "Bucky" Vail and lesser lights Wilhelm, Thompson and Falkenberg.

Significant milestones for Boston during the season were:

1903 JANUARY

January 4 Chairman Herrmann of Cincinnati, head of the National League Peace Committee says his committee has full power to negotiate with the American League

January 6 The National League says its committee may meet with the American League before the week is out to settle difficulties between the leagues.

January 7 The American League, hoping to place a team in New York, is denied rental of grounds in that city by the Rapid Transit Company. Nevertheless, League President Ban Johnson says a team will open in that city against Washington on April 25.

January 11 The baseball war ends in a surprise move as the joint American League-National League conference ends. The American League gains a moral victory with their theme "Two clubs for New York and a lesson to contract jumpers."

March 1 Baseball rules committee chairman Tom Loftus of Washington announces that the pitcher's box must not be more than 15 inches higher than the base lines and home plate.

March 4 The American League meets at the 5th Avenue Hotel in New York. The major issue is to find a playing site for the New York entry.

March 6 Owner H.J. Killilea represents Boston at the American League meetings where the foul strike rule is the big issue. The delegates all oppose it, but out of consideration to the rules committee, agree to it.

March 10 A representative from Boston is elected to the American League Board of Directors. His name to be announced later.

April 20 Opening Day and Patriots Day (the holiday was celebrated on Monday the 20th as the 19th was a Sunday) doubleheader found 8,376 fans at a morning game and 27,658 at the afternoon contest with the Philadelphia Athletics. The Pilgrims won the opener 9 to 4 behind Winter and Dineen with Rube Waddell the loser. The Athletics won the second game 10 to 7 with Eddie Plank and

Chief Bender (making his American League debut) besting Cy Young and Long Tom Hughes.

April 22 Formal American League opening game with Philadelphia beating Boston 6 to 1, Waddell beating Dineen before 13,578 at Philadelphia, including American League President Ban Johnson who presented the 1902 championship pennant to the A's.

April 24 Outfielder Chick Stahl injured sliding into base in a game at Philadelphia.

April 27 Catcher Duke Farrell fractures his leg stealing second base in the second inning in a game in Washington.

April 29 In a 9 to 5 defeat at the hands of Washington, Boston pitcher Norwood Gibson walks nine and has eight bases stolen against him.

May 9 Umpire Caruthers calls a ball on New York pitcher Tannehill as he starts to pitch and Stahl hits it for a double. The New York players storm the plate with Tannehill and second baseman Williams being put out of the game. Boston won 12 to 5 at home.

May 11 In a game at Cleveland, seven of Cleveland's twelve hits are doubles or better. Score, Cleveland 6, Boston 5.

May 15 Detroit defeats Boston 8 to 6 at Detroit making five triples and two home runs. Boston outfielder Pat Dougherty misjudged many long hits.

May 16 Despite six errors, Boston beats Detroit 9 to 6.

May 19 Boston beats Detroit 3 to 2 at Detroit. Nineteen players struck out in this game.

May 20 In losing to St. Louis 4 to 3, Boston breaks St. Louis pitcher Willie Sudhoff's three consecutive game shut out streak.

May 24 Defeating the Chicago White Sox at Chicago 7 to 0, Boston makes 14 hits.

June 1 Buck Freeman hits two home runs at New York as Boston wins 8 to 2.

June 5 Hobe Ferris hits a grand slam home run at the Huntington Avenue Grounds, as Boston defeats Chicago 10 to 8.

June 6 Boston wins their 25th game of the season, beating Chicago 10 to 2, marking the third day in a row they have scored 10 runs. Special ground rules were in effect as a crowd of 10,000 jams the ball park.

June 8 A 6 to 1 win over Detroit at Boston is marked by Boston pitcher Tom Hughes four consecutive base on balls. This game was a 5 1/2 inning affair and was Boston's eleventh consecutive victory.

June 21 A game with Cleveland is transferred to and played in Canton, Ohio. Boston behind Hughes wins 12 to 7.

June 28 Estimated attendance for a doubleheader at St. Louis is 20,000 as Boston wins 1 to 0, Cy Young over Red Donahue, and 3 to 0, Tom Hughes over Jack Powell. In each game St. Louis had only five hits.

June 30 In a game at Chicago, the White Sox score eight runs in the first inning on three walks, a triple, and six singles, all off Nick Altrock who pitches the complete game (his only one ever for Boston). Final score Chicago 10, Boston 3.

July 1 Cy Young bats in the winning run to win his own game in the 10th inning at Chicago. Boston wins 1 to 0.

July 2 Pitcher Nick Altrock sold to the Chicago Americans.

July 4 With a doubleheader sweep of St. Louis at Boston 4 to 1 and 2 to 0, Boston is in first place with a 41-23 record.

July 8 Now pitching for Chicago, Nick Altrock loses to his old team 6 to 1 at Boston.

July 11 Jimmy Collins has three singles, a triple and a home run as Boston defeats Chicago at Boston 8 to 5 for their 45th win of the season.

July 15 With ground rules limiting hits to three bases, Cy Young's hit into the crowd scores Lou Criger for a 4 to 3 ten inning win over Cleveland and Addie Joss in the first of two games in Boston.

July 16 Four of Boston's seven runs in the first inning scored after the umpire disallowed a third out because he turned to the bench to demand new baseballs. The game at Boston resulted in an 11 to 4 victory over Cleveland.

July 23 Boston gains their 50th victory of the season by defeating New York in the first game of a doubleheader at New York 6 to 1 behind Cy Young. It was an interesting twin bill, as the first game lasted only one hour and thirty-five minutes, and the second game lasted only one hour and twenty-five minutes. New York won the second game 4 to 2.

July 25 In beating New York at New York 7 to 5, Boston batters hit seven doubles. Freeman and Parent two each and Dougherty, Collins and Ferris one each.

July 29 New York defeats Boston 15 to 14 at Boston. The game lasted two hours and ten minutes with Cy Young pitching all the way for Boston. Boston made eight errors and New York three.

August 6 A game at Philadelphia is called after eight innings because it became very cloudy. 9,661 attended and manager Collins protested the call. The A's won 4 to 3.

August 10 Before a large crowd of 10,378 at the Huntington Avenue Grounds, Cy Young pitches hitless ball for seven innings as Boston defeats Philadelphia 7 to 2.

August 11 One of the largest regular season crowds, 10,600 in Boston see the Pilgrims and Tom Hughes defeat the A's and Rube Waddell 5 to 1.

August 18 Boston stops an eight game Cleveland winning streak by beating them 10 to 2 at Cleveland.

August 20 Buck Freeman breaks a field record at Chicago by hitting the first ball ever over the right field score board. Boston lost 9 to 5.

August 21 Chicago left fielder Ducky Holmes sets a record with four outfield assists, despite Boston's 11 to 3 victory.

August 23 In the second game of a double header at St. Louis, Boston makes a triple play. Boston swept the games 5 to 3 and 4 to 2 before 21,300, an extremely large crowd for the times.

August 27 In a game at Philadelphia, pitcher Long Tom Hughes wins his own game with a home run over the left field fence. Boston 4, Philadelphia 2. It was Boston's 70th win of the season.

September 5 In a Boston 12 to 1, 8 inning win over Philadelphia at Boston, Pat Dougherty in five at bats has three triples and two singles.

September 16 Boston scores a run in each of the eight innings they bat and make twenty-three hits against Cleveland at Boston. Boston wins the game 14 to 7. Cleveland had twelve hits.
Formal agreement is signed between Pittsburgh and Boston to play a post season series.

September 17 Behind George Winter's pitching and home runs by Hobe Ferris and Jimmy Collins, Boston defeats Cleveland at Boston 14 to 3 to win the American League championship. They also completed a string of scoring in seventeen consecutive innings.

September 25 Pittsburgh owner Barney Dreyfuss announces, despite rumors to the contrary, the Boston-Pittsburgh world's championship will be played as originally scheduled. Pittsburgh and a party of rooters will leave for Boston on September 28.

October 1 The first modern World Series game took place at Boston's Huntington Avenue Grounds with Pittsburgh the winner 7 to 3, Deacon Phillippe besting Cy Young. Jim Sebring had four hits for the winners, including the first World Series home run. His first inning single driving in two runs was all the Pirates needed to win. On the Boston side, Fred Parent and Buck Freeman each had a triple and a single. Tommy Leach had four hits for the winners.

October 2 The first World Series shut out game resulted in a 3 to 0 Boston win. Bill Dineen was the winner over Pittsburgh ace Sam Leever. Pat Dougherty's first inning home run was all Dineen needed to insure the win. Dougherty also had a home run in the sixth inning and three hits over all. Big Bill struck out eleven Pirate batters while allowing only three hits, and manager Collins stole two bases.

October 3 Deacon Phillippe repeated his first game mastery over Boston by beating them again 4 to 2 before the largest crowd of the series, as 18,801 jammed into the Huntington Avenue Grounds. Jim Sebring again was the offensive hero for the Pirates, as his third inning fielders choice play allowed Leach to score from third, while the Pilgrims were trying to retire Honus Wagner at third base. Long Tom Hughes was the loser, while manager Jimmy Collins had half of Boston's four hits, a single and a double.

October 6 The series switched to Pittsburgh's Exposition Park for the next four games with the Pirates taking a 3 to 1 lead in the games won by beating Boston 5 to 4, despite a gallant 3 run ninth inning Boston rally. Phillippe won his third game of the series while Bill Dineen took the loss. Beaumont and Wagner had three hits for Pittsburgh, with Wagner's seventh inning single driving in the winning run. Chick Stahl and Candy LaChance each had two hits for Boston.

October 7 Behind the six hit pitching of Cy Young, Boston defeats Pittsburgh and Bill Kennedy 11 to 2. Pat Dougherty had three hits for the winners, including two triples and a single. Young, Parent, Freeman and Collins also had two hits each for Boston. Collins and Stahl had triples.

October 8 A 6 to 3 victory tied up the series at three games apiece. Bill Dineen was the winner over Sam Leever. Chick Stahl and Hobe Ferris had two hits each for Boston. Pittsburgh's Clarence Beaumont had four hits for the losers.

October 9 The World Series was postponed due to cold weather.

October 10 With Cy Young beating Deacon Phillippe 7 to 3, Boston took a 4 to 3 lead in the series. Boston took advantage of a ground rule which allowed balls hit into the crowd to be triples, as five of their eleven hits were to come in this manner — Collins, Stahl, Freeman, Parent and Ferris were the recipients. Bransfield had three hits for Pittsburgh.

October 13 The series returned to Boston and after an idle Sunday and a rainy Monday, the Pilgrims prevailed to become the winners of the first World Series Championship 3 to 0, as Bill Dineen won his third game of the series, defeating the overworked Deacon Phillippe. 7,458, the poorest turnout of the series, attended the game. Hobe Ferris' fourth inning single drove in the first of two runs that inning, enough to win the game. Freeman and LaChance had triples and Ferris and Criger had two hits each.

What the small crowd lacked in numbers, it made up in enthusiasm as the Royal Rooters continued celebrating well into the night.

BOSTON'S LAST WORLD CHAMPIONSHIP

It has been sixty years since a World Championship of baseball has come to the city of Boston. That's right, the last World Championship pennant to fly over Fenway Park was during the 1919 season and that was won by the wartime squad of manager Ed Barrow in 1918. The 1946, 1967 and 1975 Red Sox had a crack at it, but despite gallant efforts in the fall classic by these clubs, each carrying the series to a full seven games, they could not return the flag to Fenway. The National League Braves had a chance at it in 1948 but lost 4 games to 2 to the Cleveland Indians. Looking back at that 1918 club which posted a 75-51 record in a shortened season, we can see it was an unusual season, series and team at the least. In 1917 the Sox finished second to the Chicago White Sox by nine games and in 1919 they dropped to sixth, a whopping 20 1/2 games behind the Chisox again.

The first of the Red Sox to accept terms in 1918 was Babe Ruth who signed his contract on January 15 for seven thousand dollars, a fact which raises eyebrows in today's world of multi-million dollar contracts. Several other players were holdouts because of proposed salary cuts intended to prepare the club in case of hard times which might be encountered due to the war. Eventually all came into the fold, but the club was short-handed due to players entering the armed forces. One of the first to depart was manager-second baseman Jack Barry. He was followed by such regulars as outfielders Duffy Lewis, Chick Shorten and Del Gainor; infielders Hal Janvrin and Mike McNally; catcher Pinch Thomas, pitchers Herb Pennock and Ernie Shore and several other reserve players. Shore, by the way, became the only major leaguer to win a commission in the Navy during the war. Once the season began, first baseman Dick Hoblitzel, after 19 games, left for the Army and won his captain's bars. Pitcher Dutch Leonard appeared in sixteen games before entering the Navy, and third baseman Fred Thomas also left for service after 42 games.

In 1917 the Red Sox had a new owner, Harry Frazee, who is best remembered in Boston as the man who broke up the champions, but in this 1918 season he was the buyer of players, a necessity as those mentioned above were marching off to war. To fill the managerial post he picked one Edward Grant Barrow, a veteran with major and minor league experience who had managed at Detroit, Toronto, Montreal, Indianapolis and Paterson, New Jersey. Most recently he had been president of the International League, but a slash in salary, due to the war, made him jump at Frazee's offer. Barrow later went on to build the great Yankee teams of the 20's, 30's and 40's as their General Manager and President. It was during the start of this era that he was successful in getting Yankee owner Ruppert to finance Frazee in his theatrical interests by buying the best of Boston's players to form a foundation on which the Yankee teams were built.

Barrow was not especially liked by those who worked for him and was not above challenging and winning arguments with his players behind closed doors. He ruled with an iron hand and terror was his best management method. The best of his players, of course, was Babe Ruth. The two really never got along and had many a dispute during their years together, both on the Sox and later the Yankees. Despite this lack of admiration, it is to the everlasting credit of Barrow that he saw the possibilities in the Babe's bat and it was on this 1918 team that he took advantage of this by allowing his ace pitcher to play outfield so as to get his bat in the lineup more often. It should be noted that even when Ruth pitched, he batted fourth, the clean-up position. Barrow also gained another credit while in Boston and that was that he stopped the ushers at Fenway Park from fighting with fans over the custody of baseballs hit into the stands.

With so many of his regulars going to war, Frazee opened his coffers and bought from Connie Mack at Philadelphia the only players of any caliber the A's had left from their championship years (1910-11, 13-14). What a fine group they turned out to be in Boston too. First baseman Stuffy McInnis, centerfielder Amos Strunk, catcher Wally Schang and pitcher Joe Bush all will long be remembered by Bostonians. To get Bush, Schang and Strunk, he gave up pitcher Vean Gregg, catcher Chet Thomas and outfielder Merlin Kopp and $60,000. To get first baseman McInnis, Frazee had to part with popular third baseman Larry Gardner, outfielder Tilly Walker and catcher Forrest Cady. McInnis, a native of nearby Gloucester, became especially popular with the Fenway faithful. To replace Barry at second base, pitcher George Foster was sent to the Cincinnati Reds for an Arlington, Massachusetts native, Dave Shean. To replace Duffy Lewis, a minor league outfielder was purchased from Toronto by the name of George Whiteman. He was to become a World Series hero, something which was little suspected at the time of his purchase. The irony in this deal is compounded by the fact that Whiteman had at one time been Boston property, as he was purchased along with Hall of Famer Tris Speaker from Houston in 1907, but later released.

The Red Sox got underway with spring training in Hot Springs, Arkansas that year and when they returned to Boston for the season's start they presented a pitching staff built around Ruth, Carl Mays, Sad Sam Jones, Bullet Joe Bush and Dutch Leonard (who later entered the service). At first base was Stuffy McInnis, Dave Shean was at second, and the veteran Everett Scott was at shortstop. Third base was a problem spot with many taking a turn at the hot corner vacated by the trade of Gardner, but it was Fred Thomas who appeared there most often. The outfield consisted of the popular Harry Hooper, Amos Strunk, with the third spot shared by pitcher Babe Ruth and George Whiteman. The catcher for the most part was Sam Agnew. Pitcher-outfielder Babe Ruth not only led the team in batting (an even .300) but he also won 13 games on the mound and played 13 games at first base, a pretty versatile ball player!

The Boston boys showed the way through most of the season as they took the league lead on April 20 and held it until May 9 when Cleveland took over for three days. It is interesting that the Cleveland manager was Lee Fohl, who later was to manage the Sox and their catcher was Steve O'Neill, also later to manage the Sox. The leading players at Cleveland were the former Red Sox Tris Speaker and converted outfielder Joe Wood. Later in the season the Indians would be hurt by the suspension of

Speaker who assaulted umpire Tom Connolly over a dispute on a play at the plate in Philadelphia.

The Sox eventually beat out Cleveland by two and one-half games. The Sox regained the lead on May 12 and remained there until June 25 when Cleveland and New York both enjoyed short periods in the lead spot. The Sox regained first place on July 6 and were there the rest of the way, clinching the pennant on August 31 behind pitcher Babe Ruth by defeating the Philadelphia Athletics 6 to 1 in the first game of a doubleheader. The Sox had winning records at home over every club except New York with whom they split eight games. Their home record was 49-21. On the road they were 26-30, giving them a 75-51 record overall. Their record against the other clubs was: Philadelphia 13-6, Washington 7-7, New York 6-11, Chicago 12-7, Cleveland 10-10, Detroit 13-5 and St. Louis 14-5.

On June 3 pitcher Dutch Leonard pitched a no-hitter against the Detroit Tigers, winning 5 to 0. He allowed only one man to reach first base, that on a walk. He was helped out offensively by Babe Ruth, who had replaced Amos Strunk in centerfield when the Babe homered into the right field bleachers. Another unusual pitching feat occurred on August 30 when Carl Mays pitched both ends of a twin bill against Philadelphia, winning both by the scores of 12 to 0 and 4 to 1.

The team overall lacked batting strength, but made up for it with an airtight defense and great pitching. The final figures showed them first in fielding, second in ERA and a lowly sixth in batting. The pitchers showed the following final won and lost records: Carl Mays 21-13, Sam Jones 16-5, Joe Bush 15-15, Babe Ruth 13-7, and Dutch Leonard 8-6. As previously mentioned Ruth led the batters at .300. The only other batting averages of note were Harry Hooper at .289 and Stuffy McInnis at .272. Babe Ruth was tied for the league lead in home runs with his former teammate traded to Philadelphia, Tilly Walker with eleven. Of the Babe's 11 home runs all were hit before July 1 and while he was hitting the 11, his teammates could only hit 5 and the league as a whole hit only 100. On July 8 against Cleveland, Babe hit a ball into Boston's right field bleachers with a man on base (Strunk) in the bottom of the tenth inning and as Strunk's run won the game the homer was recorded forever as a triple, under the scoring rules of that era.

Old-timers will long remember the 1918 season as the one cut short by the war and ending on Labor Day, September 2. The early curtailment of the season occurred as a result of an order by Secretary of War, Newton Baker and his draft director, General Enoch Day that the major leagues shut down on Labor Day or be subject to their "Work or Fight" order. This order meant that professional athletes either had better go to work in the war plants or don the military uniform of the Army or Navy. The order issued on July 19 sent the major leagues into a panic as to what steps should be taken to resolve the problem with some owners offering alternate plans and others saying they would comply. The Red Sox were affected as season attendance dipped to an all time low up to that point of 249,513, even less than had been attracted to the smaller Huntington Avenue Grounds in their early years. Only two years in their history, 1923 and 1932, have fewer fans passed through their turnstiles.

The "Work or Fight" order also presented the owners with a unique problem which under today's conditions makes one wonder what havoc might have been wrought. The players had been signed to contracts running to the normal end of the season in late September or early October and now faced with paying them without benefit of income from the games, the owners had a new dilemma. Fearlessly, they released all the players from their contracts, making them all free agents! Wow, what would happen in today's market? The owners solved the problem by agreeing not to tamper with each others' players, thus saving themselves money and still keeping their players. Such was the way of patriotic duty during war time.

It looked for awhile as if the 1918 World Series might become a war casualty until Garry Herrmann, chairman of the National Commission (there was no commissioner then) wrote to Secretary of War Baker asking permission to play the series, indicating a share of the receipts would go to war charities. Permission was granted and it was agreed to start the series in Chicago on September 4, the Cubs being the National League champions. The Cubs transferred their games to Comiskey Park, home of the White Sox, because of the greater capacity which suited the Red Sox because they would be more at home there than the Cubs. Manager Fred Mitchell's (former Red Sox pitcher in 1901) Cubs presented the following lineup: Fred Merkle at first base, and the Charlies — Pick at second, Hollocher at short, and Deal at third while Max Flack, Dode Paskert and Les Mann patrolled the outfield. The catching was in the capable hands of Bill Killefer. The pitching staff was headed by Hippo Vaughn (22-10) and Claude Hendrix (20-7) supported by Lefty George Tyler (19-8) and Phil Douglas (10-9) a spitballer of some renown. As it turned out, Mitchell stuck pretty much with his lefties Vaughn and Tyler in an effort to combat the left handed hitting Babe Ruth. Many of these Cubs had been with other teams and faced the Red Sox in prior World Series.

Wartime travel conditions prompted that the first three games be played in Chicago with the remainder to take place in Boston's Fenway Park. Boston received a break at the start of the series when the Navy granted a furlough to Fred Thomas so he could play third base, the one weak spot in the Red Sox lineup. The Cubs were nevertheless the pre-series favorite.

Rain washed out the first game scheduled for September 4 and delayed the start of the game the next day which was won by the Sox 1 to 0 behind the six hit pitching of Babe Ruth. Boston won on only five hits, two of them by the utility outfielder George Whiteman. One of these hits was all the Sox needed, a single that moved Dave Shean from first to third from where he scored on a McInnis single. Cub pitcher Vaughn was so frustrated that he cursed Red Sox coach Heinie Wagner who then invaded the Cub dugout bent on revenge and fought the whole Cub roster until he was forced out, dripping water, mud and blood.

The Cubs took the second game 3 to 1 behind George Tyler, the old Boston Brave pitcher who defeated Joe Bush. Boston had but six hits, including triples by Strunk and Whiteman.

The third game, and the last at Chicago, saw Boston take the series lead with a 2 to 1 victory behind the pitching of Carl Mays. Vaughn again started and lost for Chicago. Each team made seven hits, with catcher Wally Schang collecting two for the Sox, while Les Mann and Charlie Pick had two for the losers. This game was played before the largest crowd of the series' 27,954. Boston scored twice in the fourth inning as George Whiteman again was hit by a pitch and scored on successive singles by McInnis and Schang. McInnis scored on Scott's single and that was enough for the victory.

A day off for travel found the players grousing about losing the revenue from not scheduling a Sunday game in Chicago, which surely would have drawn well. Part of their gripes stemmed from the fact that for the first time all the first division teams would share in the series' revenues. At this point, the Red Sox selected Harry Hooper and the Cubs Les Mann to represent them in a request to the National Commission to wait until peace time to put into effect this revenue splitting plan and let the contending players share the entire players pool as had been the custom. The commission refused their request and with the players grumbling, the fourth game was played at Fenway and won by the locals 3 to 2, with Ruth and Bush beating Tyler and Douglas and Boston gaining a 3 to 1 edge in the series. The Babe made his first World Series hit ever in this game, a triple, and also picked up the win as the pitcher. Two runners (Whiteman and McInnis) scored on the triple and the third run, scored later on pitcher Douglas' wild toss to first, which wound up in right field. Babe Ruth had pitched 13 1/3 scoreless innings in the 1916 World Series, and that combined with nine innings in the first game, plus 7 1/3 in this game gave him a total of 29 2/3 consecutive scoreless innings of World Series pitching, a record which stood until New York Yankee Whitey Ford topped it in 1961. The game was attended by forty wounded soldiers who had returned from France just two days before. The soldiers had caused a scene at the hospital to get the doctors to let them attend and the Red Cross was called upon to transport them to the ball park.

The fifth game scheduled for September 10 at Fenway was delayed at the start by a player strike. The players of both clubs hearing that each share of the players' pool would be less than $1000, refused to take the field. Hooper and Mann met with the commission in hopes of settling the affair, stating that the winners wanted $1500, the losers $1000. Since this and other proposals were rejected, Hooper suggested all money go to the Red Cross. At this point, American League President Ban Johnson, who had had a bit too much to drink, entered the room and demanded to know why the players were not on the field. Realizing Johnson was in no shape to talk and getting no concessions from the other members of the commission, the players agreed to get on with the game with the promise of no reprisals against them. This became an unhonored promise and the players never received their World Championship emblems as a fine for their actions. Despite efforts in later years to have the decision reversed, to this day they have never been rewarded. The eventual share for each winning Red Sox was $890, while the Cubs took home $535, both all time lows for series participants.

The fifth game went to Chicago 3 and 0 as Vaughn tossed the shutout and Sad Sam Jones wound up the loser, despite a good effort. Boston could muster only five hits to the Cubs seven.

The sixth and final game came the next day as Carl Mays and the Sox won the championship 2 to 1 on a fine three hitter over George Tyler and Claude Hendrix who limited the Sox to only five hits, two by Amos Strunk. A muffed fly ball by Max Flack, the Cub right fielder, in the third inning led to the two Boston runs.

Before we put this series to bed, let's look at some of the results. Boston won all of its four games by one run. They sparkled defensively and pitching wise but batted only .186. The Cubs only did slightly better, batting .210. There were no home runs in the series, the Sox managed only 5 extra base hits, the Cubs 6. Boston pitchers had an ERA of 1.70, the Cubs a better 1.04. The Cubs scored 10 runs to Boston's 9, truly a pitcher's series with the Sox having the better of the defense. the series hero was the thirty-two year old wartime ball player from Toronto, George Whiteman, who did well at bat and fielded brilliantly. Wally Schang, the Boston catcher, led all batters with a .444 average, although only at bat 9 times. The acknowledged leaders were George Whiteman and Stuffy McInnis at .250. Cub second baseman Charlie Pick led them all with a .389 average. The player strike, the pitching of Babe Ruth, the earliest series in history and the effects of the war all combined to make it a most unusual show. It was the Red Sox fifth World Series victory without a setback and it was the last time that a World Championship would come to Boston for many years, something no one anticipated on that long ago autumn afternoon.

"WERE THE 49ERS THE BEST?"

Thirty baseball seasons have passed since the team which many consider to be the best ever put forth by the Boston American League entry took the field at Fenway Park. They say history repeats itself and the 1979 Red Sox bore several similarities to that 1949 club. Both clubs had tied for the American League lead the year before, both meeting the same fate in a one game play-off. The boys of '48 losing to Lou Boudreau's Cleveland Indians 8 to 3 at Fenway Park and our boys of '78, of course, dropping a one game decision to Bob Lemon's New York Yankees 5 to 4 again at Fenway Park. Interesting that both rival managers are Hall of Famers who gained their laurels while playing for Cleveland.

There are those who will argue that the Red Sox champions of 1912 or 1915, 1946 or 1967 or maybe 1975 were greater, but even though the '49ers didn't win the pennant they certainly boasted one of the finest casts of players to perform together at the ball yard on Yawkey Way. No less authority than the late Casey Stengel named the 1949 Red Sox as one of the best teams he had ever seen despite the fact that it was his New York Yankees who beat them out on the final day of the season. What did the "Old Professor" say about the Sox — just one word — "awesome".

The 1949 Sox presented a lineup pretty much the same as they had in 1948 when they defeated the Yankees 10 to 5 on the last day of the season while Detroit's Hal Newhouser was checking Cleveland 7 to 1 on a five hitter to force a first ever American League playoff. Until the Indians won that game on October 4 the possibility of an all Boston World Series existed as Boston's National League entry, the Braves, had captured that league's flag by a 6 1/2 game margin over the St. Louis Cardinals.

The loss in the playoff was a bitter pill to swallow for the Boston fans and club owner Tom Yawkey. In an effort to strengthen the Red Sox organization for the future, Yawkey began a wholesale house cleaning late in '48 when the Sox farm system managers and business managers were summoned to Boston and told to start producing if they wished to retain their jobs. Longtime farm system manager Nemo Leibold had quit at Louisville and Sox assistant general manager Phil Troy and farm system chief George Toporcer had been relieved of their duties. Dick O'Connell had been brought in from Lynn to succeed Troy, and former Yankee pitching ace Johnny Murphy had been placed in charge of the farm system. There was even speculation as to whether manager Joe McCarthy would be back. Perhaps the one event which brought the inadequacy of the Red Sox system into the limelight was when second baseman Bobby Doerr was injured and his backup, Billy Hitchcock, also became sidelined, the system could produce no replacement and Lou Stringer had to be purchased from Hollywood. Late in the season when the pitching staff was hurting, the farm system again failed to produce and an aging veteran reliever, Earl Caldwell, was picked up on waivers from the Chicago White Sox. He did not distinguish himself at all on the Fenway mound. Not being able to conceal his disappointment at the Sox inept performance the lumberman, Yawkey, began to swing the axe. Popular coach Del Baker was dismissed and Kiki Cuyler hired to replace him. Farm team managers Fred Walters and Pinky Higgins were promoted to fill vacancies. Rumors persisted that the Sox would like to obtain Washington Senator pitching ace Ray Scarborough and the axe swinging continued with even the Fenway bartender being discharged and veteran outfielder Wally Moses being released.

One thing was certain as the 1949 spring training season approached, there would be fewer bachelors in camp as veterans Dom DiMaggio and Dave Ferriss were followed to the altar by rookie Sam Mele amid rumors Birdie Tebbitts was not far behind. From the Everglades, where he was fishing, Ted Williams revealed his '49 pact would call for a "little more pay". He reportedly drew between $70-75,000 in '48, a far cry from today's standards. Dom DiMaggio, on a visit to Boston, was predicting the Sox would win in '49 due mainly to better pitching built around rookies Maurice McDermott, Frank Quinn and Fritz Dorish and the return to form of Dave Ferriss and Tex Hughson. The annual Boston Baseball Writers dinner honored series managers Boudreau and Southworth, Sox manager McCarthy, new Detroit manager Red Rolfe, and Boston rookies Bill Goodman of the Sox and Al Dark of the Braves. Braves' pitcher John Sain received the James C. O'Leary Memorial trophy. Manager McCarthy revealed he would take 37 players to training at Sarasota with 19 being pitchers. Continuing his longtime policy of one a day workouts his emphasis would be in solving his biggest problem — pitching, with rookies Quinn, Mike Palm and Willard Nixon to receive his attention. Rookie first baseman Walt Dropo would get a thorough trial with Billy Goodman going back to the outfield.

As spring training opened at Payne Field in Sarasota, McCarthy was raving about his corps of big rookie hurlers Frank Quinn, Mike Palm and John Hofmann, with hopes that one of them would join his probable starters Jack Kramer, Joe Dobson and Mel Parnell, while praising the excellent condition of veterans Earl Johnson and Mickey Harris. As training moved along, pitcher Tex Hughson was impressive, but Ferriss was not, rookie outfielder George Wilson also was impressive to Eddie Popowski, coaching rookies at the minor league camp. John Pesky was rumored as going to the St. Louis Browns for Bob Dillinger, Dropo impressed as did McDermott and Billy Goodman. The first cuts found infielders Chuck Koney and George Strickland and pitcher Hampton Coleman being released to Louisville, and an experiment with Stan Spence at first base ended as he returned to the outfield. The backup catcher Matt Batts (what an ideal name for baseball) seemed to solve the catching problem. McCarthy stirred up a rhubarb with the Philadelphia Phillies when he failed to play his regulars against them. Finally, the Sox won the city series with the Braves as rookie John Antonelli walked in the winning run with the bases loaded at Fenway Park for a 4 to 3 win as rookies Stobbs and McCall pitched for the winners.

As the season opener drew near the Sox were established as the pennant favorites with the pitching being judged as adequate but vulnerable, the catching better than

'48, the infield and outfield as the American League's best.

As the season got underway the Sox presented an infield of Walt Dropo — 1B, Bobby Doerr — 2B, Vern Stephens — SS and John Pesky — 3B. The outfield was comprised of Ted Williams, Dom DiMaggio and Billy Goodman. Birdie Tebbetts was catching and the starting mound corps consisted of Joe Dobson, Mel Parnell, Tex Hughson, Jack Kramer and a surprising Ellis Kinder who had an impressive spring training. Just prior to the start of the season the Braves accused broadcaster Jim Britt, who did both Red Sox and Braves home games, as favoring the Red Sox although Britt denied the charge. It would seem history again repeats itself in the radio booth. The Sox closed out April with a 5 and 6 record. The young lefthander, Mel Parnell, who was to emerge as the ace of the staff, was off to a brilliant start by pitching shutouts in his first two starts. The opening series at home was with the Yankees and the three game set drew an even 100,000 fans, including the largest opening day crowd at Fenway Park up to that year 31,367. Batters were singing praises for Tex Hughson's pitching as the 33 year old was attempting a comeback after pitching for the Class B Austin team of the Big State League for part of the '48 season.

For the month of May, the Sox showed a 15-10 record but were still four games over the .500 mark at 20-16 overall. There were some good signs and bad though. Ted Williams, with 12 home runs, had his best monthly total since returning from war service and Al Zarilla, obtained from the St. Louis Browns for Stan Spence and $100,000, was appearing more often in right field. On the minus side, pitcher Jack Kramer was sidelined with a persistent sore shoulder, pitcher Joe Dobson was plagued with a bad back and veteran pitcher Denny Galehouse was released. Rumors had Tom Yawkey attempting to bolster his pitching corps by trying to buy the Browns ace pitcher Ned Garver or, if that failed, any one of several other of the league's better hurlers. On the minor league front, pitcher Maury McDermott was off to a good start at Louisville and the Sox acquired, for 1950 delivery, Seattle's sensational rookie catcher Sammy White to the tune of five players and some cash. Other factors in the Sox improved May showing was the play of Pesky at third base, Dom DiMaggio's steady outfield play and Goodman's return to first base when rookie Walt Dropo failed to hit and was optioned to Sacramento. Mel Parnell had posted seven wins by the month's end and Ted Williams was leading the league in hitting (.331), RBI's (41), and homers (12) and DiMaggio had 48 hits, 29 runs and 18 RBI's in 35 games.

As June arrived, second baseman Bobby Doerr was sidelined with a recurring back problem and it was obvious the sagging hill staff was in need of help. In an effort to help, pitcher McDermott was recalled from the minors and combined with another rookie, Chuck Stobbs, for several good outings. Outfielder Sam Mele and pitcher Mickey Harris were sent to the Washington Senators for pitcher Walt Masterson and 35 year old hurler John Wittig was picked up from Baltimore, then in the International League. As the end of June was in sight the Sox found themselves riding a six game winning streak and trailing the Yankees by five games, but all this disappeared when the Bronx Bombers along with Joe DiMaggio arrived at Fenway Park. The streak which had the Sox winning 10 of 11 games had revived World Series talk among proper Bostonians. Unfortunately, for the Sox, Joe

DiMaggio had recovered from an ailing heel and started to make up for lost time at their expense. Celebrating his return DiMaggio hit a two run blast in the first game to lead the Yanks to victory as 36,228 fans showed up for the largest night game crowd in Bosox history. In the second game, the Sox jumped to an early six run lead but with DiMaggio socking a three run homer the Yanks tied the score and later he hit his third homer in two days to garner another New York victory. The Jolter gave the Sox more of the same in the third and final game when his three run homer was the margin of victory in a 6 to 3 Yank win, giving the Sox an even 15-15 record for the month.

Birdie Tebbetts led the All Star balloting for catcher and Ted Williams led all players with more than 2 million plus votes. Teammates Mel Parnell, Billy Goodman, and Vern Stephens joined them on the American League Dream Team which posted an 11 to 7 victory over the Nationals at Brooklyn's old Ebbets Field.

The Sox, who were a disappointment to their followers during the first half of the season, climaxed an eight game losing streak on the Fourth of July by dropping a twin bill at Yankee Stadium as the Yankees were performing the way the Sox had been expected to. The halfway point of the season found the Sox mired in fifth place, twelve games off the pace. From this point on the Sox began to jell and close in on the Yanks. When July ended the Sox showed an 18-12 mark for the month. Ted Williams continued his torrid hitting. Bobby Doerr returned to the lineup and joined six regulars in batting over .300, (Williams, Tebbetts, Goodman, Pesky, DiMaggio and Stephens). Stephens took over the league lead in homers (23) and RBI's (96) by late July only to be surpassed later by Williams.

During August the Sox set a torrid pace by winning 24 games, while dropping only 8. Record performances were the byword in August. On the third, Ellis Kinder struck out 14 Browns in posting a 9 to 3 win, four short of Bob Feller's American League record and one short of Smokey Joe Wood's Boston record set back in 1911. On August 9, Dom DiMaggio ended a 34 consecutive game hitting streak, a Boston record. By a quirk of fate it was his brother Joe who pulled down his hit to deep centerfield for Boston's final out of the game and end the streak. Large crowds were becoming the rule at Fenway as DiMaggio, Williams, Stephens and Parnell were pacing the Sox run at first place. The only sad note seemed to be the decline of former pitching ace Dave Ferriss who had been relegated to the bullpen. The Sox and Senators set a record on August 12 for the longest nine-inning game in American League history, a 3 hour, 14 minute contest. Down at Louisville Tom Wright was leading the American Association in batting.

Heading down the home stretch in September, Mel Parnell picked up his 22nd win on the 10th with a 9 to 1 victory in Philadelphia. Bobby Doerr hit at a .422 pace for 15 games since late August. Ted Williams was batting at a .385 clip since July 5 (with 18 homers and 63 RBI's) when the Sox started to roll, but more importantly he had hit .636 at home and .429 away against the Yankees for a .556 combined average. Add the great pitching of Kinder, the hitting of Stephens and Zarilla, and Pesky's play at 3rd, and by September 18 the Sox had closed in on first place, only 2 1/2 games behind. On the 26th the Sox defeated the Yankees 7 to 6 and moved into first place — a comeback to rival that of the '78 Yankees. Kinder had joined the ranks of

20 game winners on September 14, a day which saw Ted Williams equal his previous home run high of 38 and RBI high of 145. On the 20th Parnell won his 24th game, which tied the high for a Sox lefty, Babe Ruth's 24 wins of 1917. On the 27th the Sox won their eleventh straight game with a victory over Washington. Nine of those wins were part of a 21 game streak still intact at Fenway Park. Their final September mark was 19-5. General Manager Joe Cronin declared the Sox were better than the '46 team, mainly because of Stephens and Pesky. With the pennant race so close the possibility of a playoff existed, so on September 29 a coin toss took place with the Sox winning the right to stage a one game playoff at Boston on October 3.

The Yankees tied for first place on September 28, but by the 30th the Sox were a game in front again. This meant the Sox needed only win one of a two game season-ending series with the Yanks in New York. On October 1st the Yankees overcame a 4 to 0 deficit to win 5 to 4 and deadlock the race. For the final game both clubs pitched their aces, Vic Raschi and Ellis Kinder. Trailing 1 to 0 in the eighth, manager McCarthy pulled Kinder for a pinch hitter. Parnell came on to pitch, giving up a homer and a single and was replaced by Hughson who gave up three more runs for a 5 to 0 Yankee lead. The Sox ninth inning, three run rally fell short and the Yankees won the pennant 5 to 3. The Sox ended with a 96-58 record, a phenomenal 61-16 record at Fenway but a losing 35-42 road record.

Ted Williams was the league's MVP and also won "The Sporting News" player of the year award. He lost the batting crown to Detroit's George Kell .3429 to .3427. Parnell won 25 games and Kinder 23 while Doerr, Pesky and DiMaggio all batted over 300. Williams and Stephens each batted in 159 runs, Doerr 109. Williams scored 150 runs, had 194 hits, including 39 doubles and 43 home runs. Dobson posted 14 wins and Stobbs 11. Winning only 19 of 40 one run games may have cost the Sox the pennant. During the Sox stretch run (after July 4), Kinder was 16-2, Parnell 15-2. Before July 4 Kinder was 7-4, Parnell 10-5. Kinder was named the American League's outstanding pitcher.

So there it is, the story of what many consider to be the best of the Red Sox teams. After the previous season's let down, a shaky start, a great stretch run and a disappointing finish by many of the greatest players to perform at Fenway Park, a fine season was concluded. Unfortunately, the 1979 team, while close for a while, faded in the stretch and finished a distant third, the only saving grace being that the Yankees finished fourth in the division.

JOSEPH WOOD — PITCHER

The 1912 season brought many surprises to Boston. It was the Red Sox first in their brand new ball park — Fenway Park. The team won the American League championship and went on to defeat the New York Giants four games to three in the World Series, with a tie game thrown in for good measure. With a club which had finished fifth the year before and was certainly not picked to win, it went on to prove the experts wrong. Blessed with perhaps the most potent lineup of any Sox aggregation, and with a suddenly strong pitching staff they proceeded to win 105 ball games, the most ever by any Bosox team Plagued by bad weather all season long, the Sox grabbed an early lead and played steady baseball all the way, winning by 14 games over second place Washington. Many factors were significant in the win. Freedom from serious injuries all year, the expertise of new manager Jake Stahl, a powerful offense, great defense in the infield and outfield and steady pitching were all plusses.

Individual factors influencing the championship were the superb catching of Carrigan and Cady, brilliant fielding by infielders Wagner and Gardner and the defense and hitting of outfielders Lewis, Speaker and Hooper. But perhaps the most significant factor was the wonderful pitching of Smokey Joe Wood.

The year 1912 which saw New York Giant pitcher Rube Marquard win 19 games in a row to set the National League standard, and the American League's Washington Senator Hall of Famer Walter Johnson set that league's mark at 16 straight, only to have young Wood come along to tie that mark. Not to be overlooked also were Boston moundsmen Bucky O'Brien, Hugh Bedient, Sea Lion Hall and Ray Collins, all of whom played important roles in the Red Sox success.

It was Joe Wood, however, whose work was largely instrumental in winning the pennant. In addition to his 16 consecutive wins, he posted 34 victories (most ever by a Red Sox pitcher) against only 5 losses. He started 38 games, completing 35 of them, hurling 344 innings, allowing 267 hits, striking out 258 batters while walking only 82, posting 10 shutouts and having an ERA of 1.91.

Twenty-two year old Wood was born in Kansas City, Missouri, on October 25, 1889 and started his ball playing at Ouray, Colorado where his family had moved. His first taste of professional ball was with a traveling Bloomer Girl team and at 17 he signed on with the Hutchinson, Kansas team of the Western Association, playing with them in 1907 and Kansas City in 1908 until July of the latter year when Boston purchased him. From the outset he was a success in Boston. He possessed a blinding fast ball, fine control and was an excellent hitter. Right handed all the way, he later followed his roommate of many years, Tris Speaker, to Cleveland where his hitting helped win him a job as an outfielder. Along with Cy Young, he ranks as an all time great among Red Sox pitchers with 1912 being not only his greatest season but the greatest season put together by any Red Sox pitcher, and one of the finest put together by any pitcher in major league history. It is only fitting that his record be presented here. Here it is with a title richly earned — "Smokey" Joe Wood — Pitcher.

JOE WOOD — PITCHING RECORD — 1912 BOSTON RED SOX

Date	Team	Bst.	Opp.	W/L	H	SO	BB	
April 11	At New York	5	3	1-0	7	2	3	
April 16	At Philadelphia	9	2	2-0	13	11	1	
April 23	Washington	2	6	2-1	8	7	7	
April 27	Philadelphia	6	5	3-1	7	6	1	
May 1	At Washington	1	2	3-2	6	7	4	
May 7	Detroit	5	4	4-2	11	1	1	
May 11	St. Louis	8	1	5-2	3	11	2	
May 15	St. Louis	2	1	6-2	5	5	1	
May 20	Chicago	2	0	7-2	5	8	1	
May 23	Cleveland (Relief)	6	5	8-2	2	1	0 - 10 inn	
May 25	Philadelphia	2	8	8-3	9	4	5	
May 29	Washington	21	8	9-3	11	4	0	
June 2	At Cleveland	5	4	10-3	7	6	3 - 10 inn	
June 5	At Detroit (Relief)			————	4	3	1	
June 8	At Detroit	8	3	11-3	6	4	3	
June 12	At St. Louis	5	3	12-3	6	6	1	
June 16	At Chicago	6	4	13-3	5	5	3	
June 21	At New York	12	3	14-3	9	6	2	
June 26	At Washington	3	0	15-3	3	9	1	
June 29	New York	6	0	16-3	1	4	2	
July 4	At Philadelphia	3	4	16-4	8	2	2	
July 8	St. Louis	5	1	17-4	7	8	2	
July 12	Detroit	1	0	18-4	5	10	1 - 11 inn	
July 15	Detroit (Relief)			————	0	1	0	
July 17	Chicago	7	3	19-4	6	8	2	
July 23	Cleveland	6	3	20-4	9	7	2	
July 28	At Chicago	5	4	21-4	6	6	2	
August 2	At St. Louis	9	0	22-4	3	5	3	
August 6	At Cleveland	5	4	23-4	13	5	0 - 11 inn	
August 10	At Detroit	4	1	24-4	7	10	2	
August 14	St. Louis	8	0	25-4	4	9	3	
August 16	St. Louis (Relief)			————	0	4	1	
August 17	Detroit (Relief)		1	————	2	0	0	
August 20	Detroit	6	2	26-4	6	3	1	
August 24	Cleveland	8	4	27-4	7	8	2	
August 28	Chicago	3	0	28-4	6	8	0	
September 2	At New York	1	0	29-4	8	8	3	
September 6	Washington	1	0	30-4	6	9	3	
September 10	At Chicago	5	4	31-4	12	5	1	
September 15	At St. Louis	2	1	32-4	7	8	2	
September 20	At Detroit	4	6	32-5	7	8	5	
September 25	New York	6	0	33-5	2	10	1	
October 3	At Philadelphia	17	5	34-5	8	6	2	
					267	258	82	

WORLD SERIES — 1912

October 8	At New York Giants	4	3	1-0	8	11	2	
October 11	At New York Giants	3	1	2-0	9	8	0	
October 15	New York Giants	4	11	2-1	7	0	0	
October 16	New York Giants	3	2	3-1	3	2	1	10 inn.
					27	21	3	

	G	W	L	Pct.	ERA	IP	K's	C.G.	WP	BK	HB
Final Totals	43	34*	5	.872*	1.91	344	258	35*	7	0	12

Defeated:

Walter Johnson   June 26   3-0

                 Sept. 6   1-0

	Won	Lost
Extra Innings	* 4	0
One Run Games	*12	2
Shutouts	*10	0
Two Run Games	4	1
1-0 Games	* 3	0
Home	*18	2
Away	*16	3

*Led League

Won 16 Straight

	Home		Away		Total	
	Won	Lost	Won	Lost	Won	Lost
Vs Washington	2	1	1	1	3	2
Philadelphia	1	1	2	1	3	2
Detroit	3	0	2	1	5	1
Cleveland	3	0	2	0	5	0
New York	2	0	3	0	5	0
Chicago	3	0	3	0	6	0
St. Louis	4	0	3	0	7	0
	18	2	16	3	34	5

Record as a starter	33 wins	5 losses
Record in relief	1 win	0 losses
Complete games	35	
Saves	1 (August 17)	
Balks	none	

REMEMBERING JOE McCARTHY

In January of 1978 the man known as Marse Joe McCarthy died at the age of 90. He never played a game in the major leagues, but spent some twenty summers toiling in the minors. He learned his lessons well and broke into the big time as manager of the Chicago Cubs, leading them to the National League crown in 1929. Midway through the 1930 season he was fired by the Cubs and in 1931 took over the managerial duties of the New York Yankees. He led the Yankees to a World Series victory in 1932 and added four consecutive world championships from 1936 through 1939. He added three more flags from 1941 to 1943, including two more World titles.

In 1948 he joined the Red Sox as their manager, breaking the long reign of Joe Cronin, who moved into the front office. He stayed at the helm until mid-1950 when he resigned for health reasons and was replaced by Steve O'Neill. As he joined, the Sox speculation rose as to how he and Red Sox star Ted Williams would get along, especially considering Ted's aversion to wearing a tie and Marse Joe's well known strict dress codes. The answer came on the first day of Spring training when Joe appeared in a Sarasota, Florida hotel with an open neck shirt. From that day on a fine relationship developed between star and manager with Ted exclaiming, "McCarthy was the best manager I ever worked for. The man knew what he was doing and knew the right moves."

Rated as one of the all time great managers, along with Connie Mack, Casey Stengel and John McGraw, he led two of the all time great Red Sox teams to near misses at the American League Championship. His 1948 edition won 96 games, finishing in a flat footed tie with the Cleveland Indians for first place. The first ever American League play-off resulted in a Cleveland victory and eliminated a possible all-Boston World Series. In 1949 his Boston Club also turned in 96 victories again and finished one game behind the pennant winning New York Yankees, battling right down to the final game of the season. In addition to Williams such Sox stalwarts as Mel Parnell, Ellis Kinder, Vern Stephens, Bill Goodman, Dom DiMaggio, Al Zarilla, John Pesky, Bobby Doerr, Sam Mele, Joe Dobson, Birdie Tebbetts and Jack Kramer performed for Joe. Certainly the Boston fans of that era will never forget the thrills he and his player personnel brought them.

In 1957 Joe was voted into Baseball's Hall of Fame, a nitch he richly deserved and an enormous thrill for him. Never one to name a favorite player among all the greats which came under his tutelage, he was known to maintain his interest in baseball right up until his death. Alarmed at the changes he saw, he would never rap the sport. He noted that present day players were faster than in his day, use larger gloves, receive bigger salaries and make too many one-handed catches.

So one of the all time baseball greats is gone, and while he only spent a little better than two seasons in the Fenway dugout, he certainly was among the more brilliant and well respected men ever to manage the Sox.

"THE BATBOY"

They all wore number 4 — Butch Hobson, Joe Cronin and Steve Kirschner. You say, "Okay, I know Hobson and Cronin, but who the heck is Kirschner?" Sounds like someone who runs a rock concert on late night TV. Our Kirschner is an important part of the Red Sox organization, but you will have to look hard to find his name. Many of the Red Sox rookies can tell you who he is. Ask Joel Finch, Win Remmerswaal, John Tudor, Mike O'Berry or Steve Schneck. They all know. Ok, he may never crack the Fenway starting line-up, but many who some day will can tell you without hesitation who Steve is. He is the envy of his friends as he rubs shoulders with the future stars. You see, Steve Kirschner is the Bristol Red Sox batboy.

A chat with Steve will give you an idea how seriously he takes his job, and well he should. What chaos would reign if he were not about to do his job. "I've been lucky, I never got in the way of a play around home plate while picking up bats." "One time I couldn't make one of the games and a friend of mine ("I am not mentioning any names") was serving as batboy and he got in the way as a runner was coming in from third and the ball got by the catcher." "It gave Bristol a run." "I've been hit by foul balls several times, but as I said, I have been lucky so far."

Steve is starting his third year as Brisox batboy having served many players, two managers (John Kennedy, 1977 and Tony Torchia, 1978-79) and is ever faithful to his boss, team trainer Dave Labossiere. It was Labossiere who gave Steve his first crack at batboy. While out at Muzzy Field one day, Steve approached the friendly trainer and asked if he needed any help with the bats. He did and the job has been Steve's ever since. Bats aren't the only problem for the thirteen year old honor student. In addition to the bats, he must get the other equipment ready for the game. The weighted bat, the pine tar rag, ice, water cooler, helmets, towels and the trainer's bag must all be in place. A fresh supply of baseballs must be ever ready for the umpires, while chasing foul balls and running errands for the players are added duties. "Sometimes a player forgets his Skoal or wants a towel and I must go to the clubhouse to get them." Busy is the word for this young man setting up for the game and then lugging the equipment back to the clubhouse after the game. Sometimes he must serve the visiting team as well.

The Eastern League, of which Bristol is a member, has some relatively short road trips where the team does not have to make overnight stays. Steve is on the bus with the squad on these short hops — Waterbury, West Haven and Holyoke. He doesn't make the road trips to Reading and Buffalo, but would like to. "Do you sleep on the bus?" he was asked. "Well, maybe sometimes going to the game, but on the way home I am too hyped up," he replies. "I have no specific duties when we return from a trip. The clubhouse boy (Mike Caron) has to see that the uniforms and towels are washed and the shoes are shined."

How does Steve manage his homework and tend to his duties early in the season while school is on? "Well, I come right home from school and study and I get home from the ball park between nine-thirty and ten o'clock when we play at home and usually by eleven when we are on the road, so I can brush up a little then also," said the Immanuel Lutheran School student. Most of Steve's classmates are New York Yankee fans and he takes some good natured ribbing when the parent Boston Red Sox have an off day on the ball field. "The kids don't bug me for tickets because they know I can't get them, but they are always after used equipment, but again I can't get them that either."

"At the games if a bat is cracked and the player doesn't want it, I am faced with a gang of kids who want it. All I can do is just hold it up to the crowd around the dugout and let them grab and fight over it." Steve says his uniform and cap are his responsibility, just like the players. He wears the official uniform cut down and tailored to his size by Bristol General Manager Charlie Eshbach's mother. The players do chip in by giving him used equipment. This evening he had on garters given him by outfielder Ray Boyer and a baseball undershirt given him by pitcher Steve Schneck. SCHNECK was still lettered in magic marker across the back.

You can see a fine relationship has developed between the players and Steve. The mutual admiration society formed between catcher Rich Gedman, who lives with the Kirschners', and Steve is evident in both their eyes. It's Rich who gives him a ride from home to Muzzy and back. The Brisox are a Kirschner family affair as Mom runs the concession stand, along with sister Karen, and Dad is the public address announcer. A short talk with these parents and you will soon realize the understandable pride they take in their son. They are fine folks doing what they love and helping make players away from home feel a little more comfortable while they are stopping at Bristol on their way up the minor league ladder. Dad works for the State of Connecticut, but somehow I feel he enjoys his baseball duties more. Mrs. K., a charming woman, says she loves meeting the people at ball games and I am sure likes working alongside Mr. K and son Steve.

Steve, who loves his job, says the best thing about it is meeting the players. He says he has no special favorites but mention Joel Finch and Joe Krsnich from the 1977 club, Barry Butera and Steve Schneck from '78 or Rich Gedman from this year's team and watch his eyes light up. Butera and Schneck, who are the best of friends, were constant visitors to the Kirschner household last year for a post-game card session, a meal,or to take Steve to a movie or out to eat.

Three seasons with the team and Steve wants more. "No, I am not training a replacement yet." "If I quit there are lots of guys who want my job." The bespeckled bat boy has thoughts of going on to college, but is undecided between becoming a sports writer, a lawyer or a minister—all good choices. If he pursues these as he does his duties in the Bristol dugout, success should come his way. Steve has one problem which he would love to have an answer for. His duties keep him from playing as much baseball as he would like . He did somehow manage to find time to pitch for his school team. A keen observer, he has learned many valuable lessons in playing techniques from the players, manager Torchia and Red Sox special coaches Sam Mele and Johnny Podres. "That's where I get my playing tips." Certainly he has learned more than most young men his age. Although Steve was too modest to say so, his coach often asks for advice from him as do his teammates at school.

His biggest thrill, other than just going to the ball park, was when his friend Butera smacked a home run that gave Bristol the first half league championship in 1978. Does he have a favorite player on the Boston Red Sox? "Yes, I do, ever since I was a kid I liked Yaz."

When our interview started, I asked Steve if I could ask him a few questions and he replied, "Sure, but hold on, I have to finish a few charts," and off he darts into the dugout. Ten minutes later, after running to the clubhouse, he breathlessly returns. "Do you normally prepare the charts?" he was asked. "No, but Tony (manager Tony Torchia) forgot them at Muzzy tonight." As our interview is about to conclude Steve says, "There are the umpires, I better get going." Off he goes only to emerge seconds later, bats under arm, pine tar rag and towels in the opposite hand. First baseman Otis Foster, who had joined us for the last part of our interview and was now finishing signing autographs for a group of youngsters herded his way by some eye-popping fathers. He looked over and said, "Hey, I gotta go now, catch you later," and with a quick nod in Steve's direction, "Quite a kid, eh?" I'll say he is.

So there you have the life of a typical minor league batboy. In this case, a fine young gentleman, a delight to know, and not a bit affected by his enviable position. It's not a boring job at all. Sure the duties may seem routine, but each game is different, the benefits enormous, the relationships with these fine Red Sox ball players will last a lifetime and should serve well in future years for young Steve Kirschner — batboy.

REMEMBERING THE FOUR
SEASONS — 1978

A short remembrance, typical of any year, of what thoughts run through the minds of baseball fans. These were based on the Boston Red Sox 1978 year, but with slight changes here and there could apply to any year. As you read them, let your mind run back. You will find memories slowly drifting into your thoughts or perhaps gain an insight into a scene you never thought about. How many of us ever think about Fenway Park on a cold snowy wintry day?

THE DAYS OF WINTER

The college bowl games will soon be over. Ahead lies the Super Bowl, the hockey games, the Stanley Cup, the Celtics, the basketball playoffs and tournaments, the ski trips and the many other winter sports attractions which occupy and satisfy the winter appetites of the sports fans. Deep down in their hearts the thoughts of a new year, a new baseball season, dawn hopefully on the Red Sox fan. Ahead lies the worst of the cold and snow, yet beneath it all a faint flame issues forth the warmth that sustains the true baseball fan during this seemingly never to end period. Soon the hot stove league will be going full blast, the banquets which will honor our heroes past and give us the first glimpse of our heroes to come will be upon us. We can hardly wait for the news item, tucked away beneath the Bruins' score, that the Red Sox van is being readied with equipment for the trek to Florida which will surely signal the start of "the summer game".

As the holidays end, activity in the offices at Fenway Park begins to perk up. Arrangements are rapidly being completed to insure a successful training period at Winter Haven, Florida. The ticket office is making plans for the coming rush of applications. Press Guides are being prepared, rosters have been issued, news releases for the coming flood of baseball magazines are readied, advertising is secured, concession plans made, repairs to the park are proceeding, contracts are sent out, travel arrangements made and the millions of details associated with the necessities to insure a pleasant summer for all are beginning to mesh behind the closed doors of 24 Yawkey Way.

Outside, staid old Fenway Park, the crowds of summer are gone, the trees are bare and one can walk up Yawkey Way unhindered. The warmth of the sun feels good, the cool of the shadows doesn't. From inside comes the rat tat tat of a jack hammer, breaking up concrete soon to be replaced. Tall poles support the screen over the seats behind home plate so as to keep it in place so the snows which are to come will not send it crashing down. The wind whistles over the Monster and through the girders of the grandstand, the scoreboard looms over it all with a stark black glare.

The smiling face of the Jimmy Fund boy beams down from the roof in right field on grass now turned winter brown. It gives one an eerie feeling to stand amidst all this, only to realize in what will seem like an eternity, the stands will be full and our heroes will be romping again on the Fenway turf amid the thunder arising from all points of the field.

These days of winter would soon bring the "Blizzard of 78" with snow swirling down the exit ramps, only to drift under the stands. It will pile into the dugouts and the bullpens, drift against the outfield walls, bury the mound and home plate and linger until late March or early April when it will have to be shoveled into the sun and hosed down to remove it from the box seats.

The preparation during these days of winter lays the groundwork and is the foundation of the season to come. What many fans fail to realize is that baseball is a full-time profession, especially for manager, coaching staff, scouts and executives.

These are just a few of the thoughts the author reflected upon, during a winter visit to Fenway Park.

THE DAYS OF SPRING

The arrangements have been made and spring training is underway at Winter Haven. The players will soon all be assembled to work out the kinks of winter. The warm Florida sun will be working its wonders: oranges, palm trees; the announcements of signings; the first pictures appearing in the papers; the intra squad games; the exhibition season; the Grapefruit League; the battles for a spot on the squad; the rookie phenoms; the anticipation and finally the trip north, only to find the last vestiges of winter will still be lingering in the corners of Fenway. It matters not, for the rebirth is about to begin, the agonies of '77 are history. Bring on the season is the cry heard throughout New England.

The first true sign of spring, the robin to many, is in reality that picture of the equipment man loading the van that appeared in your newspaper one cold morning. Then came the word that the advanced guard had arrived. (A few veterans working off the weight of the banquet circuit and a few rookies hoping to impress.) Then came the pitchers and catchers — Looie arrived early as we can see by pictures of him running around without his hat and cigar, and under that wonderful uniform with RED SOX across the chest, a heavy windbreaker. We know it has begun again. The extra few from the farm system who are always "invited" are there. Then comes the rest of the squad, always minus those delayed because of transportation, a wife about to give birth, or for just plain "personal reasons", and granted permission (by someone) to report late. Sometimes there are the hold-outs hanging around, but not this year. It seems all can hardly wait to go.

Soon we will hear that the pitchers are ahead of the batters and we will all feel a sense of security when one of the pitchers goes more than three innings. Shortly will come the first cuts with the rookies first, going over to the minor league complex. Then sooner or later the old veteran will secure his release. Maybe there will be a minor trade or two, all so orderly, spring after spring.

Years ago there were the traditional trips north with stops in such places as New Orleans, Jacksonville, Charleston, Macon, Spartanburg, Rocky Mount, High Point, Louisville, Braves Field, etc. Now it's Winter Haven one day, Fenway the next. I suppose easier on the players and the bank roll, but somehow the oldsters miss the annual spring love affair with such stops.

The concept of spring training, I have a feeling, was originally designed as a drying out period for the many players who had spent the off season drinking up their salaries. Now the players interrupt attending the local community college, selling stocks and bonds, working in the home office or just hunting or fishing. For the fans, what better excuse for a southern vacation, and how they will come this season! Sunbathed parks, swaying palms, suddenly .230 hitters and pitchers are the second coming of Babe Ruth or a Walter Johnson. Is spring training a publicity gimmick? Who knows, who cares; it is wonderful and it makes the dead of winter move.

Now they arrive at Logan, get ready to open the bleachers, is the press box ready? Are the politicians' arms in shape? Will they reach the catcher? Ah, soon we will see the flag raising, listen to the National Anthem, and hear the traditional cries "peanuts"," popcorn", "ice cold tonic", "beea heah", "get your skaw-cod line-up, heah!"

It's off to the Fens, the glory of our times, and the pursuit of the pennant is here. Out of the subway at Kenmore, up Brookline Avenue, over the expressway, past Lansdowne Street and the wall, past the hawkers, ice cream and peanut vendors, the mounted police, carried by the crowd through the turnstiles and into the dark under-the-stands area, past the souvenir and refreshment stands, up the ramp and into the sunlight, which temporarily blinds us, and then there it is, the lush green of the outfield, the brown of the infield with those ever so white bases in their proper place. Hey, there's Yaz and Dewey and Pudge. Where is the starting pitcher warming up? Look at the newly painted seats. I hope that bunting, all red, white and blue, will be here in October. Wow, look how white those uniforms are, how red the caps and, ah yes, the red socks with those white stripes, and all topped off by blue, and the big red numbers. Sure, they still have the peculiar RED SOX lettering across the front. Do they call it Old English? Does it really matter? All is beautiful. Let's PLAY BALL.

And so it starts on these cool, sometimes cold, spring days. So, come on, let's move along. Summer is coming to the land of the bean and the cod.

THE DAYS OF SUMMER

Radios blare out the voices of Jim Woods and Ned Martin along the now warm sandy beaches from Long Island Sound to the maritime provinces, into the Berkshires, down in Southie, in the farmlands, up in the White Mountains, and all New England is awake to the sound. Vacations are being planned around the Red Sox schedule — "Dad, who will be there when we go?" New heroes are emerging every week. First, it's Butch, then Fred, then Jim. In front of the corner candy store two dungaree-clad kids with Sox hats are heard saying, "Hey, trade you a Munson for five Fisks." Walk up a quiet summer street, and drifting out of the parlors and living rooms come the voices of "The Hawk" and Dick; go past the corner pub and the same thing can be heard, oh maybe a few more cheers and clanking glasses and a few profanities, but the countryside seems to be suffering from the same ailment — Red Sox fever.

And so it goes through the beautiful days of June, into the heat of July and August. The days of summer are here. The cares of the world center around Fenway Park, never mind the aggravation of getting there, the parking and the crowded subway. All will be forgotten when we settle into our seats. So our clothes stick to the seats when we attempt to get up. So we feel like we went through a wringer when we leave; bring on the Sox. Buy some peanuts and tonic, have a beer, chase it down with a three-flavored ice cream. It's all part of the fun. Get a scorecard, watch the scoreboard with all its fancy lights, see the glow in the distance from the light towers, dream about taking that road trip with the team — well maybe I can sneak down to Yankee Stadium for a game. Summer without the Sox is like a summer without the sun.

Young players across the nation will be drafted and start their way into the "bigs". The predictions based on the Fourth of July standings will be in. The All Star balloting and selection — "who will be named as pitchers?" along with the game itself, will take place. The summer slump will occur. "What's the matter with George or Tom or Bill?" will be everyday conversation, and so it will go until before we know it, thoughts of school and maybe an occasional glance at the football predictions will ever so vaguely creep into the corners of our minds. Got to think who I can get series tickets from is our primary concern, but that can wait for awhile. Let's open up that lead, maybe we can sneak in a few more games before the summer ends.

The neighborhood softball teams give us a chance to emulate our heroes, and oh how they are all managed by budding Don Zimmers. I wonder if I could get a tryout with a minor league team is a dream which crosses our thoughts. Suddenly we wonder about the kids at Pawtucket, Bristol or maybe even down in Winston-Salem, how are they doing? Who will be called up? Who will the next heroes be? Better get *The Sporting News* and take a look!

The lawn can wait. Doggone, I have to pick up the kids at camp. The city kids cool off under the open hydrant or in the park, or up on the roof, still a dominant theme threads its way into the picture. It's the Red Sox, Red Sox, Red Sox. Mothers tire of hearing it; fathers, never! On and on it goes with our hopes rising with each win and falling with each loss. The time of the year for New Englanders to be alive is at hand. No matter where you go, you see and feel it — at the gas station, the supermarket, the toll booth, the golf course, at the beach, in the car, the drive-in movie, the restaurant, the bar, and lo and behold, even at the ball park itself. You just can't escape it.

So, let's journey down the paths of summer and enjoy ourselves along the way, for soon the nights will turn cool and the leaves of fall will start to appear.

THE DAYS OF FALL

Now the shadows begin to grow longer at the ball parks and the days suddenly grow shorter. There is a certain feeling in the air, something you can't quite put your finger on, but it's there. Things don't seem quite as bright. Oh, sure, there are still signs of summer, but somehow it is all winding down. Something triggers inside of us and we know it won't be long now before another season will be upon us. The Little League fields are empty, the school yards full, where a few short days ago beer-bellied men hit softballs, kids are now tossing footballs. Slowly, baseball is being edged off the sports pages and football nudges in and even an occasional hockey notice appears. Suddenly we are awakened by the crack of the bat, back to the reality that the summer game is still with us. We are not making as many trips to the beach. The kids are headed back to school. What happened, why so suddenly, why can't it last just awhile longer? There are short-lived thoughts as we return to the race down to the wire. When will we clinch? The Fall Classic will soon be with us. A joyful, yet sad time. A signaling of the end. Soon the trees will turn to their brilliant fall display. Soon the very leaves we saw arrive last spring on Yawkey Way will wither and die and scurry up and down the street before a chilled wind,catching every now and then to linger against the Fenway steps. Soon the crowds will come no more and the old ball park will settle down for the winter to the echoes of the summer throngs. These things we know and even if we don't want them to arrive, we are powerless to stop them.

But first there is the unfinished business fall must bring us. The results will soon be in. A new batting champion, a new leader here and there and a repeating champion tossed in for good measure. A division winner, a championship series, players are now covering bronzed arms with blue sweat shirts, a fall mist hangs over the field at night, we feel a chill in the stands and the wind blows in heavier than it did just a few weeks ago. How nice and warm it looks out there on that green field, how white the uniforms, where did this chill come from? Will we make the series? Will we see our boys bring us the glory we yearn for? Will Fenway be decked out in that red, white and blue bunting? Will we have warm memories to get us through the cold white days ahead until the cry "play ball" is heard again? So many things must soon be settled. We feel the excitement, the thrills to come and we anticipate the memories of events which will never dull in our minds. Pennant fever time is here in its fullest. Where a few weeks ago we said "so we lost — there will be a better tomorrow," the tomorrows are fewer and fewer, and optimism is no longer a luxury. It's now or never. So, come on Yaz, Pudge, Rooster and Boomer. Let's get us moving for the season grows short. Come on, hurry up before all is football, hockey, basketball and skiing. Warm our fall for us, give us fuel for the winter. The days of fall are here, glorious and yet interwoven with a fine thread of sadness as unescapable as the feeling that will follow when all is put away for another year. As much as we will miss it all, we still have a few more days in the sun, so let's move on down through those days.

1978 AND 1979 REVISITED

Here is a review of the 1978 and 1979 seasons. I almost said for your enjoyment, but no Boston fan would fine them enjoyable. Great seasons, great memories, but not great endings. Some of the ups and downs are highlighted along with the final stats. They may serve you well in your memory bank and for the future may serve as some historical background.

"1978 — A SEASON TO REMEMBER"

"This is a great ball club, great athletes, great competitors, great guys. They have given it everything they had over the past two weeks and done a fantastic job. They knew what they had to do to gain a tie and they did it. These players are a credit to the Boston Red Sox".

Captain Carl Yastrzemski

Thus spoke Captain Carl in early October 1978 and perhaps he said it all about this chapter in Red Sox history. Let's take a close look at some of the highlights and events that shaped this team and took place during the year. The winter months prior to spring training brought little news to Red Sox loyalists. In early January the Sox did announce that lower bleacher seats would be sold in advance when all other sections of the ball park had been sold out. The big news in New England was the severe winter storm which brought the six state area to a stand still. Fenway Park was under 23.6 inches of snow. There were the usual announcements of player signings and an announcement that Hall of Famer Ted Williams would join in spring training as a special instructor. Just prior to the opening of the camp in Winter Haven, Florida twenty five year veteran physician Dr. Thomas Tierney resigned, and Dr. Arthur M. Pappas replaced him.

A look at the club on Opening Day showed perhaps the strongest set lineup in baseball. The pitchers were to be the veterans Bill Lee and Luis Tiant, joined by free agent pick up Mike Torrez and newcomer Dennis Eckersley. Bill Campbell, Bob Stanley, Tom Burgmeier and Dick Drago would operate out of the bullpen. The infield had George Scott at first, Jerry Remy at second, Rick Burleson at shortstop, and Butch Hobson at third. Carlton Fisk would catch and Carl Yastrzemski and Jim Rice alternate between left field and D.H. with Fred Lynn in center and Dwight Evans in right. It appeared to be a team well set with a pennant winning combination of pitching, hitting, fielding, and something new for the Sox, a player (Remy) who had base stealing abilities.

This, the most set of all lineups, would wind up playing only 38 games all season as a unit. They got off to a big lead and were playing .700 ball (51 wins, 21 losses at one point) while their main opposition for the American League East crown, the New York Yankees were suffering from a string of injuries. By early July they enjoyed a 10 game lead over second place Milwaukee. As late as July 18 they still led the Yankees by 14 games. At this point, injuries were beginning, not only to mount up, but take their toll on the Sox. Jim Rice among the regulars was to play every game. Rice took full advantage of his good health to have the best year of any major league player in three decades. At twenty five years old, Rice gained the American League M.V.P. award, an honor he richly deserved. He wound up leading the major leagues in hits (213) home runs (46) triples (15) and RBI's (139) all topped off by a slugging average of .600. To show his true value consider thirty of his forty six home runs, either tied the score or put the Sox into the lead.

The Red Sox machine moved in full gear until the All Star break. The downfall seemed to begin just before this half way point when shortstop Rick Burleson was injured. The players who it was felt were adequate in the early going did not prove to be so. When Remy also had to leave the lineup things went from bad to worse with Frank Duffy, Fred Kendall and Jack Brohamer seemingly unable to carry the load. Their record was 57-26 at the mid point, then they lost nine of ten games in late July and their lead shrank to 4 1/2 games. Late August found them still 8 1/2 games ahead of New York and Milwaukee, who were tied for second place. The slide continued with the Yankees taking a September four game series at Fenway Park and in all took seven of their final eight games with Boston, including the fateful playoff game.

The 1978 Boston Red Sox will forever be remembered in baseball history as perhaps the best of all teams to collapse after what seemed like a sure bet for a run away. Entering the season they were variously picked to finish first or second in their division. These picks were certainly based upon the 1977 edition which, except for two long losing streaks, seemed like a winner with their awesome home run power, which seemed to be missing during '78. They had the best reliever in baseball in Bill Campbell in '77 but he was hampered all this season by arm and shoulder woes. His role was assumed in '78 by Bob Stanley, an unlikely candidate when the season started. Stanley finished with an excellent 15-2 record. A stopper (other than Luis Tiant) was the cry following the '77 season, so the Sox entered the free agent market and came home with the Yankee hero, pitcher Mike Torrez. Torrez, hero of Yankee play off and World Series victories a year ago, was built up to be a sure 20 game winner, something he accomplished only once in 1975 with Baltimore. He finished with 16 wins, only one of which came during the September pennant drive. Look closely at his record — now with his sixth major league team, not really a consistent winner, a good journeyman pitcher who capitalized on his late season heroics in '77.

What about the rest of the '77 mound corps? Many were victims of the housecleaning of new owners, Haywood Sullivan and Buddy LeRoux. Gone were Jim Burton, Don Aase, Reggie Cleveland, Jim Willoughby, Rick Wise, Mike Paxton, Ferguson Jenkins, Tom Murphy, Tom House, Ramon Hernandez and Rick Kreuger. Replacing them were Dick Drago, Torrez, Al Ripley, Dennis Eckersley, Tom Burgmeier, Jim Wright, Andy Hassler, Bob Sprowl and John LaRose. Of the newcomers Drago rejoined the Sox as a reliever and spot starter picked up in the free agent draft. Burgmeier was also picked up for the same reasons and to aid the shortage of left handers. Andy Hassler, another lefty, was obtained from Kansas City in July when rookie Allen Ripley couldn't seem to fill the bill. Jim Wright, after a long stint on the Red Sox farm, performed ably winning 8 and losing 4. Sprowl, after a meteoric rise through the farm system, did little as a late season arrival as did LaRose, another rookie. Dennis Eckersley proved to be the gem of the pitching staff, a twenty game winner, and the stopper the Sox were looking for. To get Eck the Sox had to give up promising rookies Ted Cox, Mike Paxton and Bo Diaz, plus veteran Rick Wise. Paxton finished 12-11 and Wise 9-19 with Cleveland. Cox never won a starting role and Diaz suffered an injury early in the season. Jenkins (18-8) and Cleveland (5-8) summered in Texas and their value in Boston is questionable. Willoughby (1-6) with the Chicago White Sox seemed to be little missed. Aase, a most promising rookie with a doubtful history of arm problems finished 11-8 with

California but was a necessary sacrifice to obtain a much needed second baseman to replace the slowing Denny Doyle.

This brings us to the infield. Doyle's replacement appeared to be Jack Brohamer, who was also picked up in the free agent draft. After his signing Aase left for California with Jerry Remy coming east to play second base. This put Brohamer on the bench, a position from which he often appeared at second or third and at times showed some brilliance — a valuable addition. Pitcher Kreuger was sent packing for infielder Frank Duffy and Fred Kendall was picked up for spare parts at catcher, but appeared more often at first base for George Scott who had a poor year. Duffy tried to fill in for the injured Rick Burleson at shortstop in mid season and could not fill the bill. This among all injuries hurt the chances. Gone from the infield were Tommy Helms, Ramon Aviles, Doug Griffin, Steve Dillard, Jack Baker, Cox and Doyle. At third base was Butch Hobson, who in the early going seemed to carry the team. Bone chips in the arm and shoulder and leg problems slowed Hobson, who with 43 errors finally wound up as the D.H. Reserve Bob Bailey failed to perform as predicted.

The catching was almost exclusively Carlton Fisk, with Bob Montgomery and Fred Kendall making only token appearances. Perhaps Fisk, who had a brilliant season, should have been rested more.

In the outfield among the missing were Dave Coleman, Bobby Darwin and Rick Miller. Missed the most was Miller (lost in the free agent draft) who is a brilliant fielder and seemed to make the '77 Sox go when he got into the line up. Jim Rice had an exceptional season, leading the major leagues in virtually every hitting department except average. He had 46 home runs, 139 runs batted in, 213 hits, 15 triples, 121 runs scored and .315 average. He played in all the Sox 163 games. Injuries plagued the others — Yaz, Fred Lynn and Dwight Evans. Rookie Sam Bowen was alternated between Pawtucket and Fenway, mainly for his glove and rookie Garry Hancock appeared in 38 games with fair success. It was Captain Yaz, though, who came through game after game to keep the Sox in contention.

So what happened to the team that moved into first place in May, opened a ten game lead in early July and led the winning Yankees by 14 games at one point? They were figured to be a shoo-in even if they played 500 ball from July on. They did just that, but no one figured the Yankees would play .700 ball. It was the Yanks who humiliated them in Fenway in September, beat them in Yankee Stadium and beat them in the play off, the Yanks who were bickering and injured in the early going. One of the reasons for the Red Sox collapse had to be injuries. In only some 37 games were they able to field their first string. There were 34 different injuries, a loss of 209 player days to 17 players during the season.

Fred Lynn suffered seven different injuries, Jim Rice had eye problems in the early season, Jerry Remy had several serious injuries, Rick Burleson three injuries including a three week absence at one point, Luis Tiant suffered muscle injuries, Mike Torrez had a numb hand and Carl Yastrzemski had a bad back. Add to these the arm troubles of Campbell and Hobson, Dwight Evans' dizzy spells after a serious beaning, Carlton Fisk's cracked ribs, and anyone can sympathize with their troubles.

Despite all of this, the Sox would not use injuries as an excuse, yet all played hurt and the effect certainly was noticeable.

Perhaps manager Zimmer was at fault according to some. "No Way" said the front office. A new contract seems to sum up the feeling on Zim. The second half of the season stats will show the players will have to share in the blame, but what part did the injuries play here? The front office? They made attempts in September to pick up help only to be blocked by other teams via the waiver route.

There were other factors — the early success of pitcher Bill Lee (10-3) who finished 10 and 10 and never appeared after early September. What effect did Lee's one day defection after the Carbo sale have on him? What about Bob Bailey's inability to produce, Duffy's failure at shortstop filling in for the injured Burleson, or Jim Rice's reaction to a magazine article with racist overtones — one homer in nearly six weeks? George Scott had two horrendous streaks, going 0 for 36 and 2 for 72 at bat. The loss of six of seven late season games to the Yankees was critical, Torrez suffered through a winless streak of eight starts, six of which he lost.

Attendance climbed to record heights (2,320,643) the largest capacity percentage in history. Thrills, come from behind wins, individual heroics, pitching masterpieces, heartbreaks, exceeded expectations, let downs, injuries, all part of this season. Any team that manages 99 victories can't be all bad. Stanley, Eckersley, Rice, Yastrzemski, Hobson, Burleson and Fisk were heroes all.

The boys of '78 in the starting lineup, exclusive of the pitchers were all products of the farms with the exception of Remy and when you put Stanley on the mound eight of the nine starters came up through the system.

Let's look at some of the important dates and games along the way.

RED SOX, TORREZ OFF TO A BAD START

April 7 — Opening the season in Chicago's Comiskey Park before a record opening day crowd of 50,754, the Sox hopes rode on the $2.8 million dollar arm of Mike Torrez. Mike was touched for ten hits and four runs before he left the scene. It was an exciting game with the White Sox winning it in the last of the ninth 6 to 5 when Wayne Nordhagen dumped a bloop double into short center field to score Chet Lemon all the way from first. Losing pitcher Dick Drago (who had relieved Torrez) was replaced by Bill Campbell, after giving up a ninth inning game tying home run to Ron Blomberg, and a single to Lemon. Campbell then came on to get Soderholm to fly to Evans followed by Nordhagen's game winning hit. Carl Yastrzemski, who had two singles, marked his 11st straight year of having hit safely on opening day.

BOSTON   — 002 002 010 = 5
CHICAGO — 000 211 002 = 6

Torrez (6), Drago (2 1/3), Campbell (1/3) and Fisk; Stone (7)
LaGrow (2) and Nordhagen
WP — LaGrow (1-0), LP — Drago (0-1) HR — Blomberg (1)

April 13 — In preparation for tomorrow's home opener, the Sox held a workout in the friendly confines of Fenway Park. The most encouraging news item of the day was Luis Tiant's announcement that he feels he is ready to start serious pitching again. The 37 year old right hander had the first finger of his throwing hand dislocated when hit by a line drive back on March 17 in a game against Detroit at Winter Haven. When Tiant comes off the disabled list someone will have to be cut to enable the Sox to keep their roster at 25. It will probably be a pitcher.

Two items of serious concern also surfaced on this first day home. First, relief ace Bill Campbell had his ailing elbow examined and it was found he was suffering from an inflammation in the upper elbow which is particularly sensitive when he attempts to throw breaking balls. Campbell will not be allowed to pitch until this sensitivity disappears. The second concern centers on the throwing arm of third basement Butch Hobson. It seems there are some floating calcium chips in that right elbow that now not only pains Hobson when he throws, but when he is hitting as well. "There's nothing I can do but keep taking treatments and hope", said Hobson.

HOME SWEET HOME!

April 14 — In weather more suited for football than baseball, a home opening day crowd of 34,747 (fourth largest in Red Sox history) saw the Sox score a come from behind 5 to 4 ten inning victory over the Texas Rangers. Starter Dennis Eckersley making his first home start as a Red Sox received a thunderous ovation from the fans as he left the mound in the 10th inning with two Rangers on base and two out and the game tied. He had done an excellent job and they wanted to show their appreciation. Dick Drago came on to retire Toby Harrah to end the inning. With two outs in the bottom of the tenth and Butch Hobson on third base, Jim Rice broke up the first extra inning game of the year with a 395 foot single to the base of the right field wall scoring Hobson. Thus the Sox reached the .500 mark for the first time this season. While Rice was the offensive hero, the Red Sox, who left 15 runners on base in the 3 hour and 11 minute game, also were paced by Hobson and Fred Lynn, each of whom homered. Hobson had three hits while Rice, Lynn, Pudge Fisk, Jerry Remy and George Scott each had a pair. It was Carl Yastrzemski's 18th home opener. Remy and Rice have had hits in each game so far.

TEXAS — 011 000 110 0 = 4
BOSTON — 000 101 020 1 = 5

Alexander (6), Barker (3 2/3) and Sundberg; Eckersley (9 2/3),

Drago (1/3) and Fisk

WP — Drago (1-1) LP — Barker (0-1) HR — Sundberg (1), Lynn (2), Hargrove (1), Hobson (1)

A WISE GUY ENDS THE STREAK

April 22 — Rick Wise, with the help of Andre Thornton (who hit for the cycle), made his return to Boston a triumphant one as the Cleveland Indians stopped the Red Sox eight game winning streak with a 13 to 4 victory at Fenway Park. Wise, who was traded to the Indians in the final week of spring training, checked the Sox on six hits and one run for seven innings before being relieved by another ex-Sox, Rick Kreuger. George Scott hit a three run homer in the eighth inning and Dwight Evans had a three hit day for the Red Sox. Carlton Fisk enjoyed a fine day by throwing out three runners at second base. 36,005 fans attended the game, which was the fourth largest crowd in Fenway Park history. In the eight dates during the current homestand, the Sox have attracted 198,186 fans which is more than they drew during the entire 1932 season (182,150). It was also reported that Carl Yastrzemski has signed a contract through the 1979 season. This leaves only five Boston players who can become free agents at the end of the season — Bailey, Carbo, Kendall, Montgomery and Tiant.

CLEVELAND — 510 000 160 = 13
BOSTON   — 000 010 030 = 4

Wise (7), Kreuger (2), and Pruitt; Ripley (0), Stanley (5), Wright (2), Burgmeier (2) and Fisk.

WP — Wise (1-2) LP — Ripley (0-1) HR — Thornton (4), Horton (1), Grubb (2), Scott (2)

AMERICAN LEAGUE EAST STANDINGS
Monday, May 1

	W	L	Pct.	GB
Detroit	13	5	.722	——
Boston	11	9	.550	3
New York	10	9	.526	3-1/2
Milwaukee	9	11	.450	5
Baltimore	8	11	.421	5-1/2
Cleveland	8	11	.421	5-1/2
Toronto	8	13	.381	6-1/2

THE RICE SHIFT

May 8 — It was the seventh inning with Boston leading 5 to 4. Kansas City Royals manager Whitey Herzog orders an intentional walk to Jim Rice to pitch to Carl Yastrzemski. Bernie Carbo, who had walked prior to

Rice, was on second with two out when Yaz rammed his second homer of the season into the Royals bullpen and an 8 to 4 Red Sox lead which stood up for the remainder of the game. The Fenway faithful would not let the game resume until Yaz had waived from the dugout.

It was a game which saw the Jim Rice shift for the first time and Luis Tiant get injured, plus the Yastrzemski home run. The Rice shift was employed to thwart the American League's leading power hitter. In the third inning when the streaking Rice came to bat (he had earlier doubled) Herzog put four men in the outfield and left a hole at second base. Rice lined out but his next time up he singled against the shift. Tiant had to leave the game in the third inning when he pulled a hamstring muscle in his right leg while attempting to field a Jerry Terrill bunt. The injury is not considered serious. Bob Stanley came on to pitch the rest of the way to notch the Sox sixth straight victory.

Two awards were announced for Red Sox players. Jim Rice was named the "American League Player of the Week". He was an unanimous choice. Pitcher Bill Lee was named the "Champion Spark Plug Player of the Month".

KANSAS CITY — 003 001 000 = 4
BOSTON   — 400 100 30x = 8

Leonard (6 2/3), Hrabosky (1 1/3) and Porter; Tiant (2), Stanley (7) and Fisk
WP — Stanley (3-1) LP — Leonard (3-5) HR — Lynn (4) Yastrzemski (2)

BACK ON THE TRACK

May 11 — A two run homer by Jim Rice, his 11th of the season and sixth in the last eleven games, led Boston to a 5 to 4 victory over Baltimore. Rice's homer followed a Jerry Remy single in the third inning and it represented his 19th RBI while hitting safely in 10 of his last 11 games. Fred Lynn was going for the cycle, as he had a single, double and triple, but could not get the homer. Bill Lee continued to be the winningest Sox pitcher as he ran his record to 5-0, although he needed relief help from Stanley, Burgmeier and Drago. For Lee it was his 300th major league appearance, only the fifth hurler in Red Sox history to make that many appearances. The Orioles loaded the bases in the bottom of the ninth, but Dick Drago worked out of the jam getting his third save of the season.

BOSTON   — 012 000 002 = 5
BALTIMORE — 010 000 102 = 4

Lee (6 1/3), Stanley (1 2/3), Burgmeier (1/3), Drago (2/3) and Fisk; D. Martinez (8 1/3), Stanhouse (2/3) and Skaggs.
WP — Lee (5-0) LP — D. Martinez (3-3) HR — Rice (11)

FIRST PLACE!

May 13 — Behind the pitching of Mike Torrez and Tom Burgmeier and the hitting of Fred Lynn, the Red Sox moved into sole possession of first place for the first time this season as they defeated the Minnesota Twins 4 to 2. For Torrez, who won his third straight game, it was a five strike out, one walk game, with relief from Burgmeier in the ninth after Rod Carew led off with a single. Lynn gave the Sox a 3 to 1 lead in the fourth when he drove a 420 foot homer, his fifth of the season, into the dead center field stands. The Twins nearly tied the game in the eighth when Willie Norwood was thrown out at home after hitting a long fly ball to center, which Lynn dropped for an error. Lynn recovered the ball throwing it to second baseman Jerry Remy who relayed the ball to catcher Calton Fisk in time to nip the sliding Norwood at the plate.

Some concern must be expressed over Butch Hobson, who had to leave the game in the seventh inning with a sore arm — more than the chips in his elbow. Hobson is hoping warmer weather will solve the problem.

```
BOSTON      — 020 100 001 = 4
MINNESOTA — 100 000 100 = 2
```

Torrez (8), Burgmeier (1) and Fisk; Zahn (8), T. Johnson (1) and Wynegar
WP — Torrez (5-1) LP — Zahn (2-2) HR — Lynn (5), Cubbage (2)

LEE AND THE HR'S

May 26 — Dwight Evans slammed a pair of solo home runs and Jim Rice blasted his 16th of the season as the Sox opened the home stand and an important series with Detroit by beating the Tigers 6 to 3. Bill Lee went the route on the mound to pick up his seventh win of the season. He has lost just one. Despite Rice's homer in the first with Remy aboard and Evans' leadoff shots in the 5th and 8th, it was a single by Rick Burleson in the sixth which broke a 3-3 tie and set up Lee for the win. All of Detroit's runs were the result of homers — Rusty Staub in the fourth and Jason Thompson in the sixth, with a mate on base. In the sixth inning Jim Rice was trying to duck out of the way of an inside pitch when it hit his bat, splitting it into three pieces. The ball dribbled to pitcher Wilcox, who threw him out.

George Scott has had the cast removed from his broken middle finger and will start taking batting practice. The victory was Bill Lee's 91st win as a Red Sox and moved him into a ninth place tie on the all-time Sox winning list with Tom Brewer. Lee is now 46 and 25 at Fenway Park, not bad for a leftie in a ball park which is supposedly a graveyard for portsiders.

DETROIT — 000 102 000 = 3
BOSTON — 200 012 01x = 6

Wilcox and Parrish; Lee and Fisk
WP — Lee (7-1) LP — Wilcox (3-2) HR — Rice (16), Staub (5),
Evans 2 (8), Thompson (12)

AMERICAN LEAGUE EAST STANDINGS
Monday, June 5

	W	L	Pct.	GB
Boston	36	17	.679	——
New York	30	20	.600	4-1/2
Detroit	28	22	.560	6-1/2
Baltimore	27	25	.519	8-1/2
Milwaukee	25	25	.500	9-1/2
Cleveland	23	26	.469	11
Toronto	19	32	.373	16

RICE AND YAZ AGAIN

June 15 — For the second day in a row it was Jim Rice and Carl Yastrzemski who powered the Red Sox over the Oakland A's at Fenway Park, this time by a 7 to 3 count. Rice knocked in four of the runs with his twenty first home run of the year and a triple, while Yaz belted a two-run homer, his fifth of the season. For the slumping Oakland A's it was their eighth loss in a row, for Boston their seventh straight victory. Mike Torrez pitched the distance for the Bosox to gain his tenth win of the year, although he gave up twelve hits. The Sox trailed 3 to 1 entering the seventh inning when Jerry Remy walked to open the inning and Jim Rice followed with him home run into the left field nets to knot the score at 3 all. The Bostonians wrapped it up in the eighth as Butch Hobson started things off with a double, followed by a walk to Rick Burleson, then Rice tripled and scored on Yastrzemski's homer. The win gave the Sox a 26 and 4 record at home.

Just before the trading deadline at midnight, the Red Sox sold popular outfielder Bernie Carbo to the Cleveland Indians.

OAKLAND — 000 300 000 = 3
BOSTON — 010 000 24x = 7

Renko (6 1/3), Lacey (1 2/3) and Essian; Torrez and Fisk
WP — Torrez (10-2) LP — Lacey (5-3) HR — Rice (21),
Yastrzemski (5)

LYNN AND FISK DOUBLE, LEE WALKS

June 16 — After seeing the Seattle Mariners tie the game at 3 apiece in the top of the eighth, Fred Lynn's two out double drove in two runs in the bottom of the inning as the Sox struggled to their eighth straight victory 6 to 3 at Fenway Park. Seattle had tied the score with three unearned runs before Lynn, who had driven in Boston's first run with a second inning single, unloaded his double, and took third on second baseman Julio Cruz's wild relay throw and then scored on a throwing error by shortstop Craig Reynolds. Former Red Sox pitcher Dick Pole allowed just seven hits, while suffering his eighth loss of the season as his teammates went down to their ninth loss in a row.

Carlton Fisk continued his torrid hitting as for the fourth day in a row he had two hits, this time both doubles. He has had six doubles in the last four games and eleven hits in his last six games.

In a bizarre incident, veteran southpaw hurler Bill Lee cleaned out his Fenway Park locker and announced he was quitting the Red Sox. Manager Don Zimmer learned of the defection early in the afternoon, but declined any comment. Sox co-owner and general manager Haywood Sullivan said he was making every effort to contact Lee who reportedly was on his way to Maine. Earlier in the day Lee had made a public appearance at a Boston department store to demonstrate his cooking ability, preparing a spinach lasagna and then paid a visit to a sick boy at a local hospital. From there he went to the ball park and packed his gear and appeared to be irate over yesterday's sale of his buddy Bernie Carbo to the Cleveland Indians. One report stated that Lee cried for nearly forty minutes when he learned of his pal's sale. He was quoted as saying, "Today just cost us the pennant", in reference to Carbo's sale. Lee was off to his best start in several years (7 and 3) until tendonitis of the shoulder started to bother him. There had been rumors earlier this season that he and manager Zimmer weren't getting along after another of Lee's buddies, pitcher Jim Willoughby, had been dealt to Chicago. Zimmer vehemently denied there were any problems between himself and his ace southpaw. Willoughby, contacted in Chicago, was not shocked by the news.

There were a group of players on the Sox the press referred to as "The Outlaws", who for reasons real or imagined, considered themselves in disfavor with the Sox management and manager Zimmer, and all now have been dealt away or have left the Sox. In addition to Lee, they included Carbo, and pitchers Jim Willoughby, Ferguson Jenkins, Rick Wise and Reggie Cleveland.

The incident is not without precedent in the annals of Red Sox history. Back in 1919, pitcher Carl Mays left a game in Chicago after several errors had been made by his teammates behind him, and declared he would never pitch another game for the Red Sox. In 1962, pitcher

Gene Conley and infielder Pumpsie Green jumped the Red Sox in New York amid rumors they were headed for Israel. Another pitcher who toiled for the Sox in the late 60's and early 70's, Vicente Romo, would often turn up missing whereabouts unknown.

Outfielder Sam Bowen was called up from Pawtucket to replace Carbo.

SEATTLE — 000 000 030 = 3
BOSTON — 021 000 03x = 6

Pole and Stinson; Eckersley (7 2/3), Campbell (1 1/3) and Fisk
WP — Campbell (4-4) LP — Pole (4-8)

STREAK TO NINE — LEE RETURNS

June 17 — Carl Yastrzemski's bases loaded single through a drawn in infield capped a two run, ninth inning rally as the Bosox edged the Seattle Mariners 5 ro 4 extending their winning steak to nine, their longest of the season to date. The win boosted their Fenway Park record against their American League West rivals to 16 and 0. The loss was the 10th in a row for manager Darrell Johnson's Seattle club. For the Sox it was their 34th win in their last 44 starts, giving them an overall record of 45 wins against 19 losses, the best in the major leagues. They boosted their home record to 29 and 4.

Trailing 4 to 3 and entering the last of the ninth inning, Butch Hobson stroked a single to left center, pinch hitter Fisk lined out, but Rick Burleson singled sending Hobson to third with the tying run. Remy grounded to Julio Cruz who threw to the plate in an attempt to get Hobson, but the throw was wide. Hobson scored and Burleson took third while the speedy Remy wound up on second. With first base opened, Rice was intentionally walked — filling the bases, setting the stage for Yastrzemski's game winning hit.

Dwight Evans hit his 15th homer of the season in the sixth, a tremendous shot over the left field wall, screen and all.

Pitcher Bill Lee ended his disappearing act and returned to the Red Sox indicating he was returning because Bernie Carbo had asked him to. Perhaps the whole affair could be summed up by a tee shirt Lee was wearing which said "Friendship First, Competition Second." Lee claimed that the Red Sox management won't tell the real story of why Carbo was sold to Cleveland. Supposedly the reason for Lee's leaving the club was in protest of Carbo's sale. Lee was fined for his actions and while the amount of the fine was not revealed, it was assumed it was a day's pay which in Lee's case amounts to about $700. Lee is scheduled to pitch next Friday (June 23) against Baltimore.

SEATTLE — 003 000 010 = 4
BOSTON — 110 001 002 = 5

Colborn (5 1/3), Montague (3) and Stinson; Ripley (8), Stanley (1) and Montgomery
WP — Stanley (5-1) LP — Montague (0-3) HR — Roberts (8), Evans (15)

YANKEES NET RED SOX

June 27 — New York Yankee third baseman Graig Nettles cracked a two run home run in the 14th inning, to break a 4 to 4 tie and give the Yanks a 6 to 4 win and a series split with the Red Sox. It was Nettles' 13th home run of the year and came off Sox reliever and loser Dick Drago. The four hour and eight minute game produced twenty seven hits between the two teams, with the Sox getting fourteen of them. Rookie Jim Wright was the Boston starter and when he faltered in the third inning, manager Zimmer emptied his bull pen using Burgmeier, Stanley, Campbell and Drago in relief over the last eleven innings.

The Yankees started their ace Ron Guidry who was looking for his thirteenth win of the season against no losses. The fastballer lasted six innings and had been touched for eight hits. Former Bosox Sparky Lyle was the winner in relief. Every Red Sox in the line up had at least one hit with Rick Burleson getting three and Remy and Evans getting two each.

BOSTON   — 000 002 200 000 00 = 4
NEW YORK — 012 000 010 000 02 = 6

Wright (2 2/3), Burgmeier (4 2/3), Stanley (0), Campbell (1 2/3), Drago (4 1/3) and Fisk; Guidry (6), Gossage (5), Lyle (3) and Munson
WP — Lyle (6-1) LP — Drago (2-2) HR — Nettles (13)

AMERICAN LEAGUE EAST STANDINGS
Monday, July 3

	W	L	Pct.	GB
Boston	52	24	.684	——
Milwaukee	45	32	.584	7-1/2
New York	45	33	.577	8
Baltimore	42	35	.545	10-1/2
Detroit	37	40	.481	15-1/2
Cleveland	36	41	.468	16-1/2
Toronto	28	49	.364	24-1/2

ANOTHER MILESTONE FOR YAZ

July 3 — Carl Yastrzemski reached another milestone in his brilliant career when he hit a run scoring double in the third inning against the New

York Yankees. It was the 2800th career hit for the Red Sox captain. There are only 29 players in the history of baseball who have had more hits and before the season is over Yaz should move well up on that list. The double was only one of a barrage of extra base hits which powered the Sox over the Yankees at Fenway by a 9 to 5 count to give Dennis Eckersley his ninth win of the season.

Yaz added two singles to his evening's work and joined Carlton Fisk in driving in three runs. The Yankees touched Eckersley for three home runs accounting for most of their runs. The win, a fruitful one, allowed the Sox to pick up a game on the now second place Milwaukee Brewers who were losing to the Minnesota Twins and, of course, a game on the Yanks and also a full game on the Baltimore Orioles who were being shut out by the Cleveland Indians and old friend Mike Paxton.

In addition to Yaz's double, Jerry Remy, Jack Brohamer, Carlton Fisk and Dwight Evans all had doubles and George Scott had two. Jim Rice added an opposite field triple to Boston's twelve hit attack.

NEW YORK — 101 100 020 = 5
BOSTON   — 102 321 00x = 9

Figueroa (3 2/3), Lyle (1 1/3), Kammeyer (3) and Munson and C. Johnson; Eckersley (8), Burgmeier (1) and Fisk.
WP — Eckersley (9-2) LP — Figueroa (7-6) HR — Nettles (15), Thomasson (8), Dent (3)

YAZ AND LYNN AGAIN

July 6 — Carl Yastrzemski's first inning, three run home run staked Luis Tiant to an early lead, but the Chicago White Sox rallied in the ninth inning to tie the game at 6 to 6. This set the stage for Fred Lynn's tenth inning home run which gave the Red Sox a 7 to 6 victory over the White Sox at Comiskey Park. Lynn's homer, his 13th of the season and third in the two game Chicago series, came off former Red Sox hurler Jim Willoughby. Bill Campbell, in relief, picked up the win despite giving up the ninth inning game tying homer to Bill Nahorodny in the bottom of that inning. Lamar Johnson's homer in the eighth pulled Chicago within a run of the Red Sox. Frank Duffy, filling in for Jerry Remy at second base, had three hits in four at bats. Lynn also had a single and a double and extended to nine straight games which he has hit safely. Carl Yastrzemski has had seven hits in his last three games.

Yaz was named to the American League All Star team, but will not play because of back spasms which have bothered him lately. Also named were shortstop Rick Burleson and outfielder Fred Lynn. The Sox players were calling the All Star team a joke as they felt second baseman Jerry Remy should also have been named along with several American League players from other clubs.

BOSTON   — 301 001 100 1 = 7
CHICAGO — 200 001 111 0 = 6

Tiant (5), Burgmeier (2 1/3), Campbell (2 2/3) and Fisk; Wood (5),
Proly (2), Willoughby (3) and Nahorodny
WP — Campbell (5-4) LP — Willoughby (1-6) HR — Yastrzemski
(7), Fisk (10), L. Johnson (6), Nahorodny (8), Lynn (13)

July 10 — As the Red Sox take the annual All Star break they stand first in the
American League East with a nine game lead over the second place
Milwaukee Brewers. Their .687 percentage gives them the best record
in the major leagues. The club has compiled a 57 win against a 26 loss
mark which breaks down to 34-6 record at home and 23-20 record on
the road. They own a winning record over every team in the American
League with the exception of the Texas Rangers, with whom they are
3-3, and the Cleveland Indians with whom they have a 5-5 record.
While the All Star break is usually considered the half way point in the
season, the Sox actually arrived at the mid point of their season after
the first game of the July 8 twi-night doubleheader at Cleveland and
had a 56-25 record. In 1977 at the All Star break, the Red Sox record
was 51-38 and they were a half game behind the first place Baltimore
Orioles.

Shortstop Rick Burleson arrived in San Diego to play in the All Star
game, but had to withdraw when the badley bruised ankle he suffered
yesterday at Cleveland acted up. He was replaced on the American
League squad by teammate Jerry Remy. It is now expected that
Burleson will be out of action for at least two weeks.

July 12 — The statistics for the Red Sox at the mid point in the season stack up
this way.

BATTING

Games:	Rice - 83	Doubles:	Fisk - 26
	Burleson - 81		Burleson - 20
At Bats:	Rice - 347	Triples:	Rice - 13*
	Burleson - 347		Remy - 4
Runs:	Rice - 62	Home Runs:	Rice - 23*
	Fisk - 54		Evans - 16
Hits:	Rice - 112*	Strike Outs:	Evans - 62
	Lynn - 92		Rice - 61
RBI:	Rice - 74*	Stolen Bases:	Remy - 17
	Yastrzemski - 52		Evans - 7
Average:	Lynn - .331	Walks:	Yastrzemski - 48
	Rice .323		Evans - 43

*League Leader

PITCHING

Appearances:	Stanley - 26 Burgmeier - 23	Earned Runs:	Torrez - 57 Eckersley - 51
Wins:	Torrez - 11 Eckersley - 10	Walks:	Torrez - 46 Lee - 38
Losses:	Campbell - 5 Ripley - 5	Strike Outs:	Torrez - 64 Tiant - 49
ERA:	Stanley - 2.73 Lee - 2.84	Home Runs:	Eckersley - 19 Lee - 11 Torrez - 11
Innings Pitched:	Eckersley - 138 Torrez - 131 1/3	Saves:	Drago - 6 Stanley - 5
Hits:	Torrez - 149 Eckersley - 145	Complete Games:	Lee - 6 Torrez - 6

TEAM RECORDS

	W	L		W	L
Home	34	6	One Run Games	19	12
Away	23	20	Extra Innings	4	6
Day	26	10	Against Righties	42	19
Night	31	16	Against Lefties	15	7

Boston leads the American League in batting with a .283 average and is third in pitching behind Oakland and Texas with a 3.46 ERA.

Jim Rice leads the league in slugging at .628 and Fred Lynn is fourth at .543.

Upon learning that a member of the media had come down with hepatitis over the past weekend, Dr. Arthur L. Pappas administered hepatitis shots to the Red Sox players and club personnel. The team also held a ninety minute work out at Fenway Park.

CONTROVERSY PAYS OFF

July 19 — With the Milwaukee Brewers holding a two run lead, the Red Sox pushed across four runs in the top of the seventh inning, scored four more in the eighth and defeated the Brewers 8 to 2 in a night game at Milwaukee. The win increased their lead to nine games over the second place Brewers.

The seventh inning started with Larry Sorenson throwing a two hitter at the Sox, but Jim Rice and Carl Yastrzemski singled with Rice scoring on Fisk's infield out and Yaz moving to third on George Scott's single and scoring on Butch Hobson's single. Then the fun began.

With Scott on second base and Hobson on first, Frank Duffy singled to left and Scott dashed home sliding across the plate on a close play. Brewer catcher Charlie Moore, arguing the call, rushed plate umpire Rich Garcia neglecting to call time out and Hobson came all the way around from first to score the fourth run, while the argument raged. Meanwhile Duffy was attempting to go to third but the startled Brewers finally realized what was happening and threw him out there.

Hobson was making his first appearance in weeks, having been sidelined by a pulled hamstring muscle. In the eighth Dwight Evans came home from third on Bob McClure's balk and Carlton Fisk accounted for the other three runs with his 13th home run of the year.

BOSTON   — 000 000 440 = 8
MILWAUKEE — 002 000 000 = 2

Torrez and Fisk; Sorenson (7 1/3), McClure (2/3), Castro (1) and Moore.
WP — Torrez (12-5) LP — Sorenson (12-6) HR — Hisle (21), Fisk (13)

FISK GIVES SOX A SPLIT

July 24 — The Red Sox gained a split of a doubleheader at Minnesota, losing the first game to the Twins 5 to 4, extending their longest losing streak of the season to five games, but captured the nitecap 4 to 2 as the result of Carlton Fisk's three run home run. Earlier in the day the Sox announced they had sent rookie pitcher Allen Ripley to the Pawtucket Red Sox and purchased left handed pitcher Andy Hassler from the Kansas City Royals for a minor league player to be named later. Ripley's record stood at 2 wins and 5 defeats while Hassler had won 1 and lost 4 for the Royals.

In the opener of the twinbill, it was Tom Burgmeier (making his first start in ten years) against his former teammates and he was able to pitch long enough to enjoy a 3 to 2 lead before being relieved by Dick Drago. It was Drago who took the loss after Rod Carew's pinch hit, two run double in the sixth inning putting the Twins in the lead 5 to 3. A top of the ninth Boston rally could produce only one run and the fifth straight loss was in the books. In the night half of the twi-night doubleheader the Sox scored four runs in the sixth inning, enough to give them the 4 to 2 win. Fred Lynn walked to start the inning and reached third on Twin third baseman Larry Wolfe's error on a Jim Rice grounder. Carl Yastrzemski followed with a single driving in Lynn for

Yaz's 1500th career RBI. He became the 21st man in major league history to accomplish this feat. This set the stage for Carlton Fisk's 15th home run of the season, a 400 foot shot into the left field bleachers, and a two run Boston lead. The win went to Andy Hassler in relief of Bill Campbell, Hassler having reported earlier in the day from the Royals.

Mike Torrez, the starter in the second game, was ejected in the first inning when he argued vehemently on a balk call that scored the Twins first run.

BOSTON   — 200 010 001 = 4
MINNESOTA — 020 012 00x = 5

Burgmeier (4 2/3), Drago (3 1/3) and Montgomery; D. Jackson (7 1/3), Marshall (1 2/3) and Borgman.
WP — D. Jackson (3-3) LP — Drago (2-4) HR — Borgman (2)

BOSTON   — 000 004 000 = 4
MINNESOTA — 100 100 000 = 2

Torrez (2/3), Campbell (3 1/3), Hassler (3 1/3), Stanley (1 2/3) and Fisk; Zahn and Wynegar.
WP — Hassler (2-4) LP — Zahn (8-9) HR — Fisk (15)

AMERICAN LEAGUE EAST STANDINGS
Monday, July 31

	W	L	Pct.	GB
Boston	64	38	.627	—
Milwaukee	59	42	.584	4 1/2
Baltimore	57	46	.553	7 1/2
New York	57	46	.553	7 1/2
Detroit	55	48	.534	9 1/2
Cleveland	48	54	.471	16
Toronto	38	66	.365	27

FINALLY!

July 31 — The Red Sox, who had scored only five runs in their last six games, finally broke out of their slump and their bats came alive to help them gain a 9 to 2 victory over the Chicago White Sox at Fenway Park. The Red Sox were led to their third victory in their last thirteen games by pitcher Dennis Eckersley who scattered six hits and Jim Rice and George Scott who broke out of slumps. The recently returned Rick Burleson had three hits in the Red Sox twelve hit attack, knocking in three with his bases loaded double in the eighth. He also had another double and a single. Jerry Remy, Fred Lynn and Rice also chipped in with two hits apiece.

The slump was so bad that the first run they scored was only their fourth in 50 innings and the nine runs were the most they had made in a game since July 8 when they routed the Cleveland Indians 12 to 5 in the first game of a doubleheader.

For Eckersley it was his 12th victory of the year and he went the distance striking out seven and walking only two. Eckersley now leads the pitching staff in strike outs with 90.

The Red Sox fans began chanting from the start of the game in hopes of inspiring the club to break their slump. The fans were especially encouraging to George Scott who is suffering through one of his worst slumps.

CHICAGO — 000 001 001 = 2
BOSTON   — 000 102 24x = 9

Kravec (6 1/3) LaGrow (2/3), Hinton (1) and Colbern; Eckersley and Fisk
WP — Eckersley (12-4) LP — Kravec (7-10) HR — Soderholm (15)

SUSPENDED SUSPENSE

August   2 — The Red Sox and the New York Yankees battled to a 5 to 5 tie at Yankee Stadium in a suspended rain delayed game called after 14 innings at 1:16 A.M. in accordance with an American League curfew rule, which states that no inning may begin after 1:00 A.M. The game will be resumed on August 3 at the 15th inning prior to the regularly scheduled contest for that evening.

The Sox, at one point, trailed in the game 5 to 0, but managed to tie it up at five all in the eighth inning. Scoring four runs earlier, the Sox tied the game in the eighth on Jim Rice's double, a wild pitch and Carl Yastrzemski's sacrifice fly. Relievers Rich Gossage and Bill Campbell matched performances in relief of starters Dick Tidrow and Andy Hassler, by allowing only two hits during their appearances. Two Red Sox runs came as the result of bases loaded walks by Gossage. Sparky Lyle and Dick Drago were the pitchers when the game was called. The game was twice interrupted by rain, for 35 minutes in the eighth inning and 18 minutes at the end of the 12th inning.

WORTH THE WAIT

August   3 — The wait was worth it to the Red Sox as they gained two victories over the New York Yankees in New York. First, the completion of the suspended fourteen inning game with a 7 to 5 win in seventeen innings and then an 8 to 1 win in a rain shortened game of six and one-half innings.

Run scoring singles by Rick Burleson and Jim Rice in the 17th inning of the suspended game sent the Yankees down to defeat. The Yanks failed to score in the last 14 innings of that game against the Boston relief corps of Tom Burgmeier, Bill Campbell, Dick Drago and the eventual winner Bob Stanley.

Jim Rice, who had only one home run in his last 33 games drove in three runs against Yankee loser Jim Beattie, with an infield hit and a two run homer. Fred Lynn had a three run homer in the seventh inning and Bob Bailey followed that with a long drive that struck the facade of Yankee Stadium's rarely reached upper left field stands just inside the foul pole. Pitcher Paul Lindblad, who was recently acquired from Texas, gave up the Lynn and Bailey homers. Mike Torrez gained his first career win over his former teammates.

The win allowed the Sox, who had lost 11 of their previous 14 games to gain ground on all of the American League East contenders. They now have a six game lead over the second place Milwaukee Brewers.

BOSTON   — 000 202 010 000 000 02 = 7
NEW YORK — 041 000 000 000 000 00 = 5

Hassler (1 2/3), Burgmeier (4 2/3), Campbell (5 2/3), Drago (2), Stanley (3) and Fisk; Tidrow (5), Gossage (7), Lyle (2), Clay (3) and Johnson
WP — Stanley (6-1) LP — Clay (2-5)

BOSTON   — 002 020 4 = 8
NEW YORK — 000 001 x = 1

Torrez and Fisk; Beattie (4 2/3), Lindblad (2 1/3) and Munson
WP — Torrez (13-6) LP — Beattie (2-6) HR — Rice (25), Lynn (18), Bailey (4)

THE HOBSON HUSTLE

August 10 — You can watch baseball games for a lifetime and never see a play such as the one Butch Hobson pulled off in this game which was eventually won by the Red Sox over the Cleveland Indians 6 to 5 in a 13 inning four hour and 38 minute game.

Cleveland had broken a 4 to 4 tie in the top of the thirteenth inning by scoring a run and this set the stage for the bizarre play in the bottom of the inning.

Hobson, who had been struggling at the plate and in the field because of a bad knee and arm, put on an unbelievable show of hustle. As the lead-off batter in the 13th, Butch hit a high pop-up toward second base which Duane Kuiper got under, but appeared to be having trouble with the ball in the sun and by now first baseman Andre Thornton moved over to help out. While all this was happening Hobson was racing into second base. Now Kuiper picked up the ball again and bumped into Thornton who was hit by the ball which rolled over toward first base and was picked up by catcher Bo Diaz. Now Hobson was on his way to third base and Diaz overthrew third, the ball hitting the wall and bouncing into left field where it was retrieved by left fielder John Grubb. Hobson who had slid into third scrambled to his feet and headed home, amazed to see Diaz had time to return to the home plate area waiting for the throw from Grubb, who was having trouble getting the ball out of his glove. A belly flop slide across home plate ahead of the throw and Hobson had tied the game. An amazing play, never to be forgotten by those who saw it.

Garry Hancock, on deck to bat for George Scott, was called back and Scotty immediately doubled down the left field line. Hancock entered the game to run for Scott. Rick Burleson drilled a hit past third and the game was won. Hobson, who earlier had been presented with the "Big Brother of the Year Award" had proven that hustle can and does win ball games.

CLEVELAND — 010 012 000 000 1 = 5
BOSTON   — 000 102 100 000 2 = 6

Paxton (6 1/3), Monge (1/3), Kern (2 1/3), Hood (1/3), Spillner (3) and Alexander and Diaz; Eckersley (5 2/3), Drago (4 1/3), Stanley (3) and Kendall and Fisk.
WP — Stanley (8-1) LP — Spillner (2-1) HR — Norris (2), Lynn (19)

UMPS OUT — SOX HOME

August 25 — The major league umpires went on a walk out today or was it a strike? Whatever, both terms seem appropriate for action by umpires. The Red Sox, along with other clubs, brought in a group of fill-in umpires who did a commendable job as the Sox behind Dennis Eckersley turned back the American League West leaders, the California Angels, 6 to 0. Eckersley, in command all the way, limited the Angels to just four safeties and ran his Fenway Park record to 8 and 0 and 15 and 5 overall, the most games he has ever won in a major league season. He was helped by Jim Rice's 32nd homer of the season in the third inning off former teammate Don Aase.

Eckersley, on his way to his second shutout of the season, retired 11 straight batters at one point in the middle innings. Rice had three hits in five trips while Butch Hobson had three hits in three official at bats, two of which were doubles. The victory may have been a costly one for the Bosox as second baseman Jerry Remy chipped a bone in his left hand in the first inning when Rick Miller slid into him while stealing second. Remy will be limited to pinch running chores for a week to ten days.

CALIFORNIA — 000 000 000 = 0
BOSTON   — 101 102 01x = 6

Aase (5), D. Miller (3) and Downing; Eckersley and Fisk
WP — Eckersley (15-5) LP — Aase (8-8) HR — Rice (32)

ANOTHER PULLED OUT

August 28 — Trailing 9 to 7 in the ninth inning, the Red Sox rallied for a come from behind victory for the second day in a row to defeat the Seattle Mariners 10 to 9. The game was a real slugfest and included among sixteen extra base hits was Jim Rice's 34th home run of the season. In the home half of the ninth, Fred Lynn singled, his fifth hit of the game, and moved to second on Garry Hancock's single and scored when Seattle first baseman Dan Meyer threw George Scott's sacrifice bunt past third base. Butch Hobson then came through with a double which brought in Hancock and Scott with the tying and winning runs. All of these heroics made a winner of Bob Stanley, whose record rose to 12-1.

Boston's right fielder Dwight Evans was beaned in the seventh inning by a Mike Parrott pitch and was taken to a hospital after regaining consciousness in the clubhouse. X-rays later showed no sign of a fracture.

SEATTLE — 103 000 131 = 9
BOSTON — 032 010 103 = 10

Abbott (2), Todd (2), Parrott (2 1/3), Romo (1 2/3) and Plummer and Pasley; Torrez (2 2/3), Lee (4 1/3), Campbell (1 1/3), Stanley (2/3) and Fisk
WP — Stanley (12-1) LP — Romo (10-6) HR — Rice (34)

AMERICAN LEAGUE EAST STANDINGS
Monday, September 4

	W	L	Pct.	GB
Boston	85	50	.630	-
New York	79	55	.590	5 1/2
Milwaukee	78	58	.574	7 1/2
Baltimore	76	61	.555	10
Detroit	74	61	.548	11
Cleveland	58	78	.426	28
Toronto	55	83	.399	31 1/2

O's DUMP SOX, LEAD AT FOUR

September 5 — Pinch hitter Terry Crowley's two run double in the eighth inning and the pitching of Jim Palmer was all the Baltimore Orioles needed to defeat the Red Sox at Memorial Stadium in Baltimore by the score of 4 to 1. While the Sox were losing their closest rivals, the New York Yankees, were defeating the Detroit Tigers 4 to 2 to cut the Sox lead to just four games.

The Baltimore win spoiled the major league debut of Red Sox rookie pitcher Bob Sprowl, although the young left hander did a very creditable job. The use of Sprowl seems to indicate the plight of the Sox pitching staff at this point of the season when you must bring in a rookie, even if he boasts the very fine credentials that Sprowl brought with him. In just a year and one-half he had progressed from A ball at Winter Haven, to double A at Bristol and to triple A at Pawtucket. The youngster pitched seven fine innings, allowing only five hits, while striking out five.

Carlton Fisk scored on Dwight Evans' double in the second inning to give the Sox a temporary lead. In the Oriole seventh, Lee May homered and another run scored as the result of a Hobson error. In the Orioles' eighth a walk, a single, a Sprowl departure, a Drago relieving, two out and Crowley's double led to two runs and an Orioles' win.

```
BOSTON     — 010 000 000 = 1
BALTIMORE — 000 000 220 = 4
```

Sprowl (7), Drago (1) and Fisk; Palmer (8), Stanhouse (1) and Dempsey.
WP — Palmer (18-12) LP — Sprowl (0-1) HR — May (22)

HUMILIATED 15-3

September 7 — Bombing four Red Sox pitchers for 15 runs and 21 hits, the New York Yankees routed the Sox 15 to 3 at Fenway Park. The win put the Bronx Bombers within 3 games of the league leading Red Sox. The Yankees have won 13 of their last 15 games.

Sox third baseman Butch Hobson set the tone for things to come when he threw away a routine Willie Randolph grounder in the first inning leading to two quick Yankee runs. By the bottom of the fourth inning, when the Red Sox scored their first two runs, the Yankees had disposed of starter Mike Torrez and built a 12 to 0 lead. The two fourth inning runs resulted from a Yastrzemski triple, followed by a Carlton Fisk home run. Sox relievers Hassler, Drago and Campbell were all hit hard.

Yankee starter Catfish Hunter had to leave the game in the fourth inning with a pulled groin muscle suffered while pitching to Yaz. The batting hero for the Yanks was Randolph who had three hits and five RBI's including a bases clearing double. The 15 runs were the most scored against the Sox in a single game this season, topping the 13 Cleveland scored on April 22. Yankee catcher Thurman Munson was felled by a Dick Drago pitch in the seventh inning, but was able to leave the field under his own power. The Yankees out hit the Sox 21 to 8 with Randolph, Munson and White each contributing 3 hits.

NEW YORK — 232 501 020 = 15
BOSTON　　 — 000 200 100 = 3

Hunter (3), Clay (6) and Munson and Heath; Torrez (1), Hassler (2), Drago (4), Campbell (2) and Fisk.
WP — Clay (3-4) LP — Torrez (15-9) HR — Fisk (20)

AGAIN, 13-2

September 8 — The New York Yankees continued their assault on the Red Sox at Fenway Park this time by a 13-2 count. The Sox by giving up 28 runs and 38 hits and making nine errors in two games saw the league lead drop to two games. Seven Bosox errors led to seven Yankee unearned runs. Lost in the parade of Yankee runs was Reggie Jackson's three run homer, his 21st of the season. Lou Piniella also homered. The Sox were outhit 17 to 6.

Rookie pitcher Jim Beattie had the Sox shutout with two out in the ninth when his catcher Mike Heath dropped Carlton Fisk's foul pop. Given a new life Fisk singled driving home Rick Burleson, and Jim Rice scored when Jack Brohamer followed with another single. Mickey Rivers and Lou Piniella with three hits apiece led the Yankee attack. Piniella had a double, a triple and a home run.

Holding an 8 to 0 lead after two innings, the Yanks coasted to victory as Beattie retired 18 Sox in order at one point and had a three hitter entering the ninth inning.

Fisk made two errors on throws to second, mainly due to his injured ribs and Dwight Evans made two errors as problems from his recent beaning seem to be affecting him. These two are among Boston's best defensive players.

NEW YORK — 260 021 020 = 13
BOSTON　　 — 000 000 002 = 2

Beattie (8 2/3), Davis (1/3) and Munson and Heath; Wright

(1 1/3), Burgmeier (2/3), Lee (7) and Fisk
WP — Beattie (4-7) LP — Wright (8-3) HR — Jackson (21),
Piniella (5)

BOSTON MASSACRE CONTINUES, 7-0

September 9 — A seven run, fourth inning sent the Bosox down to a 7-0 defeat at
the hands of the New York Yankees at Fenway Park, as the New
Yorkers cut the Sox lead to one game. Dennis Eckersley was the
victim this time around as the American League's premier
pitcher Ron Guidry tossed a brilliant two hit shutout at the league
leaders. (Burleson and Rice had the only Sox hits, both singles.)

It was again Lou Piniella whose bloop double keyed the two out,
seven run rally. Actually on a very windy day the wind played a big
part in the double which dropped between Lynn, Burleson, Rice
and Duffy. For Guidry it was his 21st win, seventh shutout and
13th complete game of the season. The seven run outburst saw
the Yanks send 12 batters to the plate, giving them their 20th
victory in 25 games. On July 19, the Yankees trailed the Sox by 14
games, a margin now cut by 13 games. Guidry's shutout was the
first for a left hander over Boston since Oakland's Ken Holtzman
did it on August 5, 1974.

Carl Yastrzemski, playing despite torn ligaments in his right
hand and a constant back pain, made the defensive gem of the
game, a diving back hand catch to rob Munson of extra bases. The
Milwaukee Brewers' win over Minnesota moved them to within
4 1/2 games of the top.

Catcher Carlton Fisk received the annual 10th player award, (a
new auto), given to the player who most exceeds preseason
expectations.

The Sox passed the 2 million home attendance mark for the
second time in their history.

NEW YORK — 000 700 000 = 7
BOSTON   — 000 000 000 = 0

Guidry and Munson; Eckersley (3 2/3), Burgmeier (5 1/3) and
Fisk
WP — Guidry (21-2) LP — Eckersley (16-7)

YANKS SWEEP

September 10 — The New York Yankees completed the four-game series sweep
of the Red Sox at Fenway Park with a 7 to 4 win behind Ed
Figueroa and Rich Gossage who combined to four hit the Sox.

The win enabled the Yankees to tie the Sox for the American League East lead. The Yanks again out hit the Sox, this time 18 to 5 as Graig Nettles, Roy White, Thurman Munson and Bucky Dent all had 3 hits apiece. It was the sixth straight New York win.

Boston gambled by starting rookie Bob Sprowl who failed to last the first inning as the Yanks picked up 3 runs. Sprowl allowed only one hit but his nervousness was apparent as he walked three. Fred Lynn hit his 21st home run of the season.

It was the first time since 1943 that the Yankees took four in a row at Fenway Park. The four game totals were runs — N.Y. — 42, Sox—9; hits—N.Y.—67, Sox—21; Errors—N.Y.—5, Sox — 12, as the Sox 109 day stay in first place ended. Each team has 20 games remaining. Boston has won only two of their last eleven games.

NEW YORK — 320 100 100 = 7
BOSTON   — 000 201 100 = 4

Figueroa (6), Gossage (3) and Munson; Sprowl (2/3), Stanley (3), Hassler (2 2/3), Drago (1/3), Lee (2 1/3) and Fisk.
WP — Figueroa (16-9) LP — Sprowl (0-2) HR — Lynn (21)

AMERICAN LEAGUE EAST STANDINGS
Monday, September 11

	W	L	Pct.	GB
Boston	86	56	.606	-
New York	86	56	.606	-
Milwaukee	82	61	.573	4 1/2
Baltimore	80	62	.563	6
Detroit	77	65	.542	9
Cleveland	61	80	.433	24 1/2
Toronto	56	88	.389	31

DERAILED AGAIN

September 15 — New York Yankee pitching ace Ron Guidry fired a brilliant two hitter at the Red Sox in Yankee Stadium as the Yanks won 4 to 0. Chris Chambliss and Graig Nettles slammed successive home runs as the Yanks bunched all their runs off loser Luis Tiant in the fourth inning. Rick Burleson had a double and Fred Lynn a single for the only Sox hits. Actually, Andy Hassler who relieved Tiant only allowed two Yank hits the rest of the way, both by Roy White — a single and a double.

Mickey Rivers and Willie Randolph led off the fourth with

singles, then Lou Piniella hit a ground ball to Butch Hobson at third who went for the double play which worked, but allowed Rivers to go to third which he rounded and started home before deciding to return. First baseman Carl Yastrzemski noticed this and fired the ball to Hobson for what should have been a triple play, but the throw was wild and Rivers went home with the lead run. Reggie Jackson then walked and the home runs followed. A walk to White followed by Dent's double saw Tiant depart and Hassler came on. Fred Lynn hurt his ankle attempting to catch Chambliss' home run and limped noticeably throughout the remainder of the game.

The win was New York's 9th in 10 games and its fifth straight over Boston. The loss was Boston's fourth in a row, but despite this advertisements appeared in Boston papers on ticket application procedures for the Championship Series.

BOSTON   — 000 000 000 = 0
NEW YORK — 000 400 00x = 4

Tiant (3 2/3), Hassler (4 1/3) and Fisk; Guidry and Heath
WP — Guidry (22-2) LP — Tiant (10-8) HR — Chambliss (11)
   Nettles (26)

BOSTON MASSACRE PART II?

September 16 — Mickey Rivers tripled with one out in the ninth inning and scored on Thurman Munson's sacrifice fly and the New York Yankees again took the measure of the Red Sox this time 3 to 2 at Yankee Stadium. Pitchers Catfish Hunter and Mike Torrez went the distance, each pitching fine games. Hunter won his tenth game while Torrez was losing his fifth straight and eleventh of the year. The loss dimmed the Sox pennant hopes as the Yanks moved 3 1/2 games ahead of them. It was Boston's fifth straight setback.

Manager Zimmer was quoted after the game as saying "We're in tough shape." "We put ourselves almost in a spot where we have to win tomorrow and then about eight straight." Jim Rice's two run homer in the first inning gave the Sox their first lead against the Yankees in their last six meetings. It was Rice's 41st homer, tops in the major leagues. New York countered with a run in their half of the first and tied the game on Reggie Jackson's two out, two strike homer in the fifth.

Fred Lynn, who reinjured his ankle, was available only for pinch hitting duty.

BOSTON   — 200 000 000 = 2
NEW YORK — 100 010 001 = 3

Torrez and Fisk, Hunter and Munson
WP — Hunter (10-5) LP — Torrez (15-11) HR — Rice (41), Jackson (23)

FINALLY!

September 17 — The Red Sox finally won a game from the New York Yankees, after losing six straight to the Bronx Bombers, by a 7 to 3 count at Yankee Stadium. The win moved the Bosox to within 2 1/2 games of the league leading Yanks. A loss in this game would have left them 4 1/2 games behind and just about ended any hope of a pennant. Now they still have a life but must be dependent upon other teams to defeat New York while they must keep winning. Hoping to win two of three games with the Yanks they had to settle for one.

Dennis Eckersley, now the ace of the staff, and Bob Stanley combined to pitch a four hitter. Two Boston errors in the eighth inning, including Butch Hobson's second of the game and forty-second of the season, allowed a pair of unearned runs to score. Eckersley pitching with only three days rest, was lifted in the seventh with two outs and runners on first and second, but received credit for his 17th win of the year. Stanley did an excellent job again in relief. Eckersley has defeated New York four times this year against one loss.

George Scott, who had been benched for two games because of his lack of hitting, had a double and drove in a run to spark a three run eighth inning. Scott had been hitless in 36 trips to the plate.

Carl Yastrzemski, playing centerfield in place of the injured Fred Lynn, hit a ninth inning home run (his 14th of the season and the 380th of his career) into the right field grandstand.

Three players reported to the Sox from their Pawtucket farm club, which lost out in the final game of the International League Championship. They were catcher Gary Allenson, pitcher John LaRose and outfielder Sam Bowen.

BOSTON   — 001 010 131 = 7
NEW YORK — 000 000 120 = 3

Eckersley (6 2/3), Stanley (2 1/3) and Fisk; Beattie (7), Lyle (0), Clay (2) and Munson
WP — Eckersley (17-8) LP — Beattie (5-8) HR — Yastrzemski (14)

AMERICAN LEAGUE EAST STANDINGS
Monday, September 18

	W	L	Pct.	GB
New York	90	58	.608	-
Boston	88	61	.591	2 1/2
Milwaukee	85	65	.567	6
Baltimore	84	65	.564	6 1/2
Detroit	80	68	.541	10
Cleveland	65	83	.439	25
Toronto	57	92	.383	33 1/2

CLOBBERED

September 20 — The Red Sox were helpless against the pitching of Dave Rozema, getting only six hits and losing to the Detroit Tigers, who garnered 15 hits, 12 to 2 at Detroit. For Rozema it was his 3rd straight win, for Boston's starter Mike Torrez, it was his 6th straight loss. Rozema was backed by three run homers by Rusty Staub and Lou Whitaker. Staub also singled in a run as the Tigers clobbered four Bosox twirlers. A ninth inning single by Jerry Remy followed by Jim Rice's 42nd home run of the season led to Boston's only runs of the contest. Remy had four hits for the evening's work.

The loss, coupled with New York's doubleheader split in Toronto, dropped the Red Sox to two games behind the front running Yankees in the American League East with just ten games to go.

Rookie pitcher John LaRose made his major league debut in relieving Torrez in the fifth inning and was the victim of Whitaker's three run blast in the sixth. LaRose, Jim Wright and Tom Burgmeier allowed two runs each in Detroit's 6 run seventh.

Carl Yastrzemski has announced that he will play at least through the 1981 season. He had indicated last spring he might play only two more seasons retiring after the 1979 season.

BOSTON — 000 000 002 = 2
DETROIT — 100 203 60x = 12

Torrez (4), LaRose (2), Wright (2/3), Burgmeier (1 1/3) and Fisk; Rozema and M. May.
WP — Rozema (9-10) LP — Torrez (15-12) HR — Rice (42), Whitaker (3), Staub (23)

AMERICAN LEAGUE EAST STANDINGS
Monday, September 25

	W	L	Pct.	GB
New York	94	62	.603	-
Boston	93	63	.596	1
Milwaukee	90	67	.572	4 1/2
Baltimore	86	69	.555	7 1/2
Detroit	84	72	.538	10
Cleveland	68	85	.444	24 1/2
Toronto	59	96	.381	34 1/2

September 25 — The Red Sox had a very welcomed day off as did the New York Yankees. Each team opens up a six game home stand tomorrow which will complete the regular season for both clubs.

ECK WINS 19TH

September 26 — The Red Sox defeated the Detroit Tigers 6 to 0 at Fenway Park, but the New York Yankees defeated the Toronto Blue Jays at Yankee Stadium 4 to 1 to maintain their one game lead in the American League East. In Boston it was a battle of the aces, Dennis Eckersley going all the way for his 19th win of the season and Detroit's ace Dave Rozema suffering his 11th loss of the season. The win raised Eckersley's record at Fenway Park to 10 and 1 as he scattered seven hits for his third shut out of the year.

Jim Rice powered his 44th home run of the season in the fifth inning with Jerry Remy aboard. This represents the most home runs by a Red Sox batter since Carl Yastrzemski's 44 in 1967 and ties him for second place for the most by a Red Sox player in a single season since Jimmie Foxx hit 50 in 1938. It also gives Rice a lifetime total of 131 in just four full seasons to move him into a tenth place tie with Frank Malzone on the Red Sox all time homer list. Rice also has 135 RBI's, the most by a Red Sox since Vern Stephens and Walt Dropo each had 144 in 1950.

The Sox backed Eckersley's pitching with a 14 hit attack that included, in addition to Rice's home run, a two run double by Fred Lynn and three hits by Jerry Remy. Five games remain in the season.

DETROIT — 000 000 000 = 0
BOSTON — 300 021 00x = 6

Rozema (5 2/3), Tobik (2 1/3) and May; Eckersley and Fisk
WP — Eckersley (19-8) LP — Rozema (9-11) HR — Rice (44)

NO GAIN

September 27 — A three run first inning highlighted by Carlton Fisk's two run triple enabled the Red Sox to come out winners over the Detroit Tigers 5 to 2 at Fenway Park. While the Sox were taking their game the New York Yankees were continuing their winning ways by topping the Toronto Blue Jays 5 to 1 under the lights at Yankee Stadium. With each team winning, the standings at the top of the American League East remained the same — Yankees up by one. The win for the Red Sox was their 95th of the year.

George Scott got his first home run in almost a month and two singles good for two RBI's. The first RBI represented the 1000th of George's career. With two out in the first inning and Jerry Remy and Carl Yastrzemski on base via walks, Fisk drilled a triple into the right field corner, left unguarded as he rarely hits that way, scoring both runners. Fred Lynn then bounced a seeing eye single up the middle and the Sox went ahead 3 to 1 offsetting Detroit's Rusty Staub's earlier home run. Detroit's second run came as a result of Ron LeFlore's sixth inning homer.

The old veteran, Luis Tiant, collected his 203rd major league win, although he had to leave the game after six innings with a slight muscle pull behind his left knee. Tiant, Andy Hassler and Bob Stanley combined for a five hitter with Stanley picking up his 10th save of the season and making his 50th appearance. The remarkable Tiant lifted his overall Red Sox record to 27-12 in the months of September and October. The win was also his 27th career victory over the Tigers, the most by any active American League hurler.

DETROIT — 100 001 000 = 2
BOSTON — 310 000 01x = 5

Wilcox (7 2/3), Hiller (1/3) and May; Tiant (6), Hassler (2 1/3), Stanley (2/3) and Fisk.
WP — Tiant (12-8) LP — Wilcox (13-12) HR — Staub (24), Scott (12), LeFlore (12)

WAITING FOR HELP

September 28 — For the first time in more than five weeks (August 18) right hander Mike Torrez won a ball game, a brilliant three hit shut out over the Detroit Tigers at Fenway Park 1 to 0. The lone Sox tally came on Jim Rice's 45th round tripper of the season. When all the heroics had ended, the Red Sox were still trailing the league leading New York Yankees by one game as down in New York the Yanks were victorious over the Toronto Blue Jays by a 3 to 1 count behind lefty Ron Guidry. Guidry was becoming the single season Yankee strike out king as he bested Jack Chesbro's season strike out record of 239 with 243, a record set in 1904 when the Yanks, nee Highlanders, were engaged in another down-to-the-wire battle with the Red Sox, nee Pilgrims.

The Red Sox, to a man, were echoing "we've just gotta keep winning." Sharing the heroes' role with Torrez and Rice was Fred Lynn who made a bullet-like throw cutting down a runner at the plate. Captain Carl Yastrzemski sent three tremendous smashes to center which a strong crosswind cut down to three long outs which could have easily been three homers otherwise.

Torrez, not World Series sharp, issued seven walks but his infield teammates did not let him down as they turned four double plays led by second baseman Jerry Remy. A tribute to Torrez' pitching was the fact that there were only two (Lynn and Rice) outfield put outs.

Of Rice's blast, which landed four rows up in the center field bleachers, retiring Detroit manager Ralph Houk said, "He's just about the strongest guy I've ever seen with a bat."

The win was the fifth in a row for the Sox and ninth in their last eleven games.

Rice's 45th home run represents the most ever by a Red Sox slugger in a season except by Jimmie Foxx in '38.

DETROIT — 000 000 000 = 0
BOSTON   — 000 100 00x = 1

Young and May; Torrez and Fisk
WP — Torrez (16-12) LP — Young (6-7) HR — Rice (45)

HAIL — JIM RICE — 400 TB'S

September 29 — For the third time this season the Sox got back to back shutouts (May 6 & 7 vs Chicago, June 13-14 vs California and Oakland) as they defeated the Toronto Blue Jays at Fenway 11 to 0. Right hander Bob Stanley came out of the bullpen to make his third start of the season and came through in sensational fashion, allowing just two hits (both in the 6th) before retiring in the seventh in favor of Dick Drago who preserved the win allowing just one hit, as for the second day in a row the hill staff allowed the opposition just three safeties.

The win still kept the Sox close to the league lead. The

Yankees, losing 1 to 0 to the Cleveland Indians in the eighth, came up with three runs to ice a come from behind 3 to 1 victory and retain first place with just two games remaining.

Stanley and Drago weren't the only aces in the Sox victory. Fred Lynn, attempting to push his average back over the .300 mark, hit in his eighth straight game getting three hits good for five RBI's. Designated hitter Butch Hobson also had three hits, including two doubles and Jim Rice had a double and a single to become the first American Leaguer to collect 400 total bases in 41 years. New York Yankee Joe DiMaggio was the last to do it way back in 1937. Hank Aaron was the last major leaguer to do it when he had an even 400 in 1959. Rice received a standing ovation for his feat and the ball, his bat and first base were removed from the game and sent to the Baseball Hall of Fame in Cooperstown, New York.

Stanley had a perfect game going until he walked Willie Upshaw with two out in the fifth but kept his no hitter until one was out in the sixth and Gomez singled to center. The two other Jay hits were garnered by their fine rookie centerfielder, Rick Bosetti.

Rice's first inning double, giving him 399 total bases, broke a 40 year old Red Sox record for total bases (398) set by Jimmie Foxx. The win for Stanley was his 15th in 17 decisions as he threw just 69 pitches. He volunteered to come out while still twirling a no-hitter and the Sox ahead 8 to 0, so that he might be available for relief Sunday or hopefully during the league playoffs.

```
TORONTO — 000 000 000 = 0
BOSTON   — 332 000 03x = 11
```

Clancy (1 2/3), Wiley (2/3), Garvin (2 2/3), Lemanczyk (3) and Ashby; Stanley (7), Drago (2) and Fisk
WP — Stanley (15-2) LP — Clancy (10-12)

ECK WINS 20TH SOX ALIVE

September 30 — With Dennis Eckersley pitching a five hitter for his 20th victory of the season the Red Sox defeated the Toronto Blue Jays at Fenway Park 5 to 1. Meanwhile the New York Yankees were defeating the Cleveland Indians 7 to 0 behind Ed Figueroa, who also won his 20th game to clinch at least a tie for first place in the American League East. Now it all comes down to the final game of the year. For a tie, the Yankees must lose and the Red Sox must win tomorrow. Should they both lose the Yankees will be the champions.

The Sox, after falling behind 1 to 0 on Roy Howell's first inning home run, scored four times in their half of the first off loser Jesse Jefferson. Eckersley held the Jays in check the rest of the way getting his 16th complete game. In the first,lead off hitter Rick Burleson reached base on Howell's error and moved to third when Jerry Remy doubled. Jim Rice walked,loading the bases, and when Carl Yastrzemski grounded to first Burleson scored. Carlton Fisk then singled and two more runs scored. Fred Lynn singled and Fisk moved up and scored on Butch Hobson's sacrifice fly. Fisk scored an insurance run in the third after beating out a bunt, moving to third on a Lynn single and scoring as Hobson hit into a double play. Lynn, with three hits, moved his average back up to the .300 mark.

Eckersley became the 22nd Red Sox pitcher to win twenty or more games in a season, although a number have done it more than once, and the first since Luis Tiant won 21 in 1976. Eck's record at Fenway Park this season is 11 and 1. In his last four starts, all wins,he has allowed just three earned runs. The trade which brought him to the Red Sox looks very good. The win was the Sox seventh straight and 11th in their last 13 games. The win, number 98, surpassed the 97 they won last year and the team became the 4th winningest of all Sox teams, being surpassed only by the 1912 (105), 1946 (104) and 1915 (101) teams.

TORONTO — 100 000 000 = 1
BOSTON   — 401 000 00x = 5

Jefferson and Ashby; Eckersley and Fisk
WP — Eckersley (20-8) LP — Jefferson (7-16) HR — Howell (8)

A CHANCE

October 1 — The Red Sox defeated the Toronto Blue Jays 5 to 0 while the New York Yankees were losing to the Cleveland Indians 9 to 2 and so after 162 games the New Yorkers and the Sox were in a flat-footed tie for first place in the American League East as the curtain came down on the 1978 season. For the second time in American League history a play-off game will be necessary to decide the champion. The Red Sox have been involved in both, losing to the Cleveland Indians in 1948 by an 8 to 3 score in a bid for an all Boston Series as their National League counterparts, the Braves, had won that league's championship. The play-off will be in Boston, as decided by a flip of a coin several weeks ago.

Since closing within a game of the Yanks a week ago, the Sox have been trying to accomplish what the old pro Luis Tiant did for them as he fired a two hit shutout at the Jays, his fifth of the season and 48th of his career. Two unearned runs in the fifth, a two run homer by Rick Burleson in the seventh, and a solo shot by Jim Rice, his 46th of the year, in the eighth was all "Looie" needed.

"This has to be one of the biggest games I've ever pitched" said Tiant as he puffed on one of his big cigars after the game and well it was, as the only hits Toronto got were two harmless singles. So with Jack Brohamer taking Roy Howell's high foul fly for the final out the Sox headed for the second ever tie breaker in American League history.

TORONTO — 000 000 000 = 0
BOSTON   — 000 020 21x = 5

Kirkwood and Cerone; Tiant and Fisk
WP — Tiant (13-8) LP — Kirkwood (4-5) HR — Burleson (5), Rice (46)

AMERICAN LEAGUE EAST STANDINGS
Monday, October 2, 1978

	W	L	Pct.	GB
Boston	99	63	.611	-
New York	99	63	.611	-
Milwaukee	93	69	.597	6
Baltimore	90	71	.599	8 1/2
Detroit	86	76	.531	13
Cleveland	69	90	.434	28 1/2
Toronto	59	102	.366	39 1/2

DENTED
THE COMEBACK THAT FELL SHORT

October 2 — It came down to one game — a game of sudden death — the second ever American League play-off. Half of the teams were different, the location the same. In 1948 it was the Cleveland Indians, this time the New York Yankees against the Red Sox at Fenway Park. The Sox and Yanks finished the season in a tie after 162 games. Each had won 99 and lost 63. the Yanks were sending their ace, Ron Guidry against their former teammate Mike Torrez in the show down. As Yankee owner George Steinbrenner said, "It's too bad that the best two teams in baseball had to play in this game." Excitement was so high that the atmosphere was certainly that of a seventh game of a World Series. It could possibly be that the upcoming play-offs and World Series will have to take a back seat to what was to unfold upon the Fenway diamond. When the dust had settled the New York Yankees reigned as American League East Champions by virtue of one run, defeating the Sox 5 to 4.

Boston's 39 year old captain and inspirational leader, Carl Yastrzemski, put the Sox in the lead with his 17th home run of the season in the second inning. Yaz later singled in another run but in the bottom of the ninth could not produce another miracle with the tying run at third and the winning run at first. In the sixth inning Rick Burleson doubled and Jerry Remy sacrificed him to third. Jim Rice then singled with "The Rooster" coming home. The Sox picture looked good with a 2 to 0 lead.

It was not to be as Torrez ran into seventh inning trouble as with one out Chris Chambliss and Roy White singled for the Yankees. Pinch hitter Jim Spencer flied out and up stepped the fairly weak hitting Yank shortstop, Bucky Dent. Dent caught one of Torrez's pitches and sent a high fly toward left field which at first appeared that Yaz was under but the ball just made the screen atop the famous left field wall for a homer and suddenly the Yanks had a 3 to 2 lead. Paul Blair then batted for Mickey Rivers and walked, then stole second. Catcher Thurman Munson then doubled sending Blair home and the Yanks led 4 to 2. Things looked bad for Boston. How easy it would have been to quit then. Things got worse in the eighth as Reggie Jackson led off the Yankee eighth with a solid homer to the center field bleachers off reliever Bob Stanley. This, as it turned out, was the game winner.

But the Red Sox, who had battled for eight straight wins, were not about to give up. Remy led off the Sox eighth with a double and scored on Yaz's single, 5 to 3, Fred Lynn then singled, sending Yaz home, 5 to 4. Lynn almost won the game for the Sox in the sixth only to see Yankee right fielder, Lou Piniella, use his defensive prowess to make a fine running catch to deprive Lynn of a hit which would have scored two runs and given the Sox a 4 to 0 lead. This had to be the key play of the game.

Then came the Red Sox ninth. Burleson drew a one out walk. Remy came through again with a single to right, moving Burleson to second. Right fielder Piniella lost the ball in the sun and when it took a high hop after dropping in front of him, it seemed to pop right into his glove instead of getting by him. Had it gone by him, Burleson may have scored or certainly would have wound up at third base. Jim Rice then sent a fly deep to right with Burleson tagging and moving to third base. Up stepped Captain Carl to challenge the fast ball of Rich Gossage, but swinging at the first pitch — a fast ball which rose upward and inward — the Captain sent a foul pop-up off third and it settled in third baseman Nettle's glove to end the game and the season.

So ended a great game between two equal teams with drama to the very end. Certainly there could be no joy in Boston, but there had to be admiration for this gallant team the way they fought back over the last fifteen days. Words can not explain how it played its heart out and certainly the most diehard Red Sox fan had to admire the display of skill and ability shown by the defending World Champion Yankees. After 162 games all tied they battled the 163rd right down to the final out. The Red Sox had nothing to be ashamed of. Perhaps as Carlton Fisk said, "these are the two best teams in baseball." It seems they were no more than 90 feet apart.

Boston's Dennis Eckersley and New York's Ed Figueroa, both of whom gained their 20th victories last week, were named joint players of the week in the American League.

NEW YORK — 000 000 410 = 5
BOSTON   — 010 001 020 = 4

Guidry (6 1/3), Gossage (2 2/3) and Munson; Torrez (6 2/3), Stanley (1/3), Hassler (1 2/3), Drago and Fisk
WP — Guidry (25-3) LP — Torrez (16-13) HR — Yastrzemski (17), Dent (5), Jackson (27)

POSTSCRIPT

As I sit here, the old ball park that is Fenway is dark, the throngs have left, the lights are out, the field is bare, the "ifs", "maybe's", and "could have beens" have been put away for another year. The old cliches are hung out — "always a bridesmaid, never a bride", "we gave it our best shot", "wait 'till next year". For those guys from New York, they have once again done in our Red Sox. What can be said? I wish it were spring.

What will the playoffs and World Series mean? Four other, then two other teams fighting for something we thought would surely be ours this season. What will we have left? — refunds for our unused ducats emblazened with those beautiful *Red Sox* superimposed on that white baseball which were meant for the playoffs; refunds for our series tickets all blue and white with the same emblems and "75th World Series" artfully stamped across them. Sure, these will be our rewards but there will be others which can not be taken away. The memory of a season that is surely one to remember. One which saw the Red Sox off to a great start, a start which faded like the leaves on Yawkey Way until one gray October Sunday afternoon all came alive again and hopes rose on high, only to be dashed away under a beautiful blue sky a day later. Even nature seemed to have her moods reduced. A loss which was hard to take, especially since all was there for a last of the ninth victory.

No matter really, our boys gave us ninety-nine victories and when all is considered that's not bad. It took a superior effort on the part of the New York Yankees to overcome a fourteen game deficit — perhaps they deser_____ I just can't say that, but certainly it must be great to be a Yankee fan tonight.

That '78 Red Sox bunch. How great they were, how well they meshed, what a beautiful summer they gave us. Sure all Red Sox fans must be a bit down now, but as sure as another season will arrive they will be ready for that first game early next April. To be a Red Sox fan is to have been through this before. The true fan will never quit, no matter how battered we may be. Think of the effort the team gave you. The inspiration of Yaz, the tough pitching of Looie, the sensational season the kid from Alabama gave you — hurting all the way, and Pudge playing with those bad ribs, Jim Ed smashing records and heading toward more, the Eck, Fred Lynn climbing the wall at Yankee Stadium only to hurt his ankle again, the Rooster — how he made the team go, and Bob Stanley — on and on it can go.

Sure the winter will be long, but it will pass and the farther this team slips into history the more it will be appreciated and here will be your remembrance of it. Tell your grandchildren, brag a little because 1978 was a season that will not soon be forgotten.

The lights at Fenway are out now, the turnstiles still, winter will soon descend but for the Fenway faithful hope will again return, so it has been for generation upon generation. So bring on '79, let's go!

1979 HOME STANDS AND ROAD TRIPS

Home	W	L		Road	W	L
4/14-4/23	8	2		4/7-4/12	2	3
5/1-5/9	8	1		4/25-4/30	1	4
5/26-5/31	6	1		5/10-5/25	9	5
6/12-6/25	11	2		6/2-6/11	5	3
7/3	1	0		6/26-7/1	2	3
7/13-7/17	4	2		7/5-7/9	4	2
7/28-8/1	2	3		7/19-7/27	2	8
8/8-8/14	5	3		8/2-8/6	4	1
8/25-9/3	7	3		8/15-8/23	4	4
9/7-9/12	1	5		9/4-9/6	1	2
9/26-10/1	6	0		9/13-9/24	6	6
10/2	0	1				
	59	23			40	41

MISCELLANEOUS WON AND LOST RECORDS

	W	L			W	L
Home	59	23		One run games	32	25
Away	40	41		Two run games	17	12
Day	43	19		Extra Innings	11	7
Night	56	45		Shutouts	15	5

WINNING STREAKS

9 — 6/9-6/17
8 — 4/12-4/21
8 — 5/24-5/30
8 — 9/23-10/1
7 — 5/3-5/9

LOSING STREAKS

5 — 7/20-7/24
5 — 9/12-9/16
4 — 4/26-4/30
4 — 7/25-7/28
4 — 9/7-9/10

1978 MONTH BY MONTH

April	11	9	.550
May	23	7	.767
June	18	7	.720
July	13	15	.464
August	19	10	.655
September	14	15	.483
October	1	1	.500
	99	64	.607

Record 1st Half of Season	56-25	.691
Record 2nd Half of Season	43-39	.524
	99-64	.607

Double Plays — Boston — 172, Opponents — 168
Attendance — Home: 2,320,643   Away: 2,183,109   Total: 4,503,752

1978 TEAM PITCHING LEADERS

ERA .... D. Eckersley 2.99
Won .... D. Eckersley 20
Lost .... M. Torrez 13
Games ...... R. Stanley 52
Com. Games . D. Eckersley 16
Inns. Pitched   D. Eckersely 268.1
Hits .... M. Torrez 272

Runs .... M. Torrez 122
Earned Runs . M. Torrez 110
Walks ...... M. Torrez 99
Strikeouts ... D. Eckersley 162
Saves .... R. Stanley 10
Shutouts .... L. Tiant 5
Home Runs . D. Eckersley 30

PITCHER	ERA	W	L	AP	GS	CG	SV	SHO	IP	H	R	ER	HR	BB	SO	HB	WP
Burgmeier	4.40	2	1	35	1	0	4	0	61.1	74	33	30	7	23	24	3	0
Campbell	3.91	7	5	29	0	0	4	0	50.2	62	25	22	3	17	47	0	1
Drago	3.03	4	4	37	1	0	7	0	77.1	71	30	26	5	32	42	4	2
Eckersley	2.99	20	8	35	35	16	0	3	268.1	258	99	89	30	71	162	7	3
Hassler	3.00	2	1	13	2	0	1	0	30.0	38	13	10	0	13	23	0	1
Hassler T	3.87	3	5	24	11	1	1	0	88.1	114	49	38	1	37	49	2	4
LaRose	22.50	0	0	1	0	0	0	0	2.0	3	5	5	1	3	0	0	0
Lee	3.46	10	10	28	24	8	0	1	177.0	198	89	68	20	59	44	2	0
Sprowl	6.39	0	2	3	3	0	0	0	12.2	12	10	9	3	10	10	0	0
Stanley	2.60	15	2	52	3	0	10	0	141.2	142	50	41	5	34	38	1	0
Tiant	3.31	13	8	32	31	12	0	5	212.1	185	80	78	26	57	114	5	0
Torrez	3.96	16	13	36	36	15	0	2	250.0	272	122	110	19	99	120	3	7
Wright	3.57	8	4	24	16	5	0	3	116.0	122	51	46	8	24	56	7	0
Others	5.52	2	6	16	11	1	0	0	73.1	93	50	45	10	22	26	3	2
TOTALS	3.54	99	64	341	163	57	26	15	1472.2	1530	657	579	137	464	706	35	16

PITCHERS LONGEST LOSING STREAKS

Bill Lee	7	Bob Sprowl	2
Mike Torrez	6	Jim Wright	2
Luis Tiant	4	Bob Stanley	1 (twice)
Dick Drago	3	Tom Burgmeier	1
Dennis Eckersley	3	Andy Hassler	1
Al Ripley	3	Reggie Cleveland	1
Bill Campbell	2		

PITCHING

1978 SHUTOUT GAMES

	For Boston	WP		For Boston	WP
4/9	At Chicago	5-0 Lee	8/6	At Milwaukee	4-0 Tiant
5/6	Chicago	3-0 Wright	8/25	California	6-0 Eckersley
5/7	Chicago	4-0 Torrez	9/6	At Baltimore	2-0 Tiant
5/27	Detroit	1-0 Tiant	9/26	Detroit	6-0 Eckersley
5/30	Toronto	4-0 Eckersley	9/28	Detroit	1-0 Torrez
6/13	California	5-0 Wright	9/29	Toronto	11-0 Stanley
6/14	Oakland	9-0 Tiant	10/1	Toronto	5-0 Tiant
7/29	Kansas City	1-0 Wright			

1978 Shutout Games (continued)

	Against Boston	LP			Against Boston	LP
7/21	At Kansas City	0-9 Eckersley		9/9	New York	0-7 Eckersley
7/26	At Texas	0-2 Eckersley		9/15	At New York	0-4 Tiant
7/28	Kansas City	0-4 Torrez				

PITCHERS LONGEST WINNING STREAKS

Bob Stanley	11	Jim Wright	3	(twice)
Luis Tiant	7	Dick Drago	2	(twice)
Dennis Eckersley	6	Andy Hassler	2	
Bill Lee	6	Tom Burgmeier	1	(twice)
Mike Torrez	5	Al Ripley	1	(twice)
Bill Campbell	3			

BOSTON VS A.L. EAST

	Home		Road		Total	
	W	L	W	L	W	L
BALTIMORE	5	2	3	5	8	7
BOSTON	0	0	0	0	0	0
CLEVELAND	4	3	3	5	7	8
DETROIT	7	0	5	3	12	3
MILWAUKEE	6	2	4	3	10	5
NEW YORK	3	6	4	3	7	9
TORONTO	6	2	5	2	11	4
TOTALS	31	15	24	21	55	36

BOSTON VS A.L. WEST

	Home		Road		Total	
	W	L	W	L	W	L
CALIFORNIA	5	0	4	2	9	2
CHICAGO	4	1	3	2	7	3
KANSAS CITY	3	2	1	4	4	6
MINNESOTA	6	0	3	2	9	2
OAKLAND	3	2	2	3	5	5
SEATTLE	4	1	3	2	7	3
TEXAS	3	2	0	5	3	7
TOTALS	28	8	16	20	44	28
GRAND TOT	59	23	40	41	99	64

ATTENDANCE

	Home	Road
TOTAL	2320643	2183109
AVE.	30138	27989
DATES	77	78
GAMES	82	81

	BOS	OPP		WON	LOST
ERRORS	146	147	DAY	43	19
DOUBLE PLAY	172	168	NIGHT	56	45
COMP GAMES	57	47	SHO-INDV	14	5
STOLEN BASE	74	114	SHO-TEAM	15	5
CAUGHT STLG	51	55	1-RUN GM	32	25
DOUBLES	270	258	2-RUN GM	17	12
TRIPLES	46	18	EXTRA INN	11	7
HOMERS-HOME	94	72	VS RIGHT	78	45
HOMERS-ROAD	78	65	VS LEFT	21	19
HOMERS-TOT	172	137	DBL-HDR	4	0
LF ON BASE	1155	1200	SPLIT	4	
			STARTERS	70	50
			RELIEF	29	14
			STREAKS	9	5

BATTING

CONSECUTIVE GAME HITTING STREAK — LONGEST PER PLAYER

Jerry Remy	—	19	7/28-7/15
Rick Burleson	—	17	7/9-8/12
Fred Lynn	—	15	6/24-7/14
Jim Rice	—	13	8/8-8/19
Jack Brohamer	—	12	5/24-6/14
George Scott	—	11	8/22-9/2
Carl Yastrzemski	—	11	5/3-5/14
Butch Hobson	—	10	4/14-4/23
Dwight Evans	—	8	4/15-4/23
Carlton Fisk	—	6	6/10-6/16, 6/21-6/27, 9/3-9/8, 9/21-9/27
Bernie Carbo	—	4	4/30-5/3
Bob Bailey	—	2	5/25-5/28, 7/8 (2 games)
Frank Duffy	—	2	7/6-7/8, 7/13-7/14, 7/23-7/24, 8/30-9/4
Garry Hancock	—	2	7/28-7/29, 9/7-9/8
Fred Kendall	—	2	5/25-5/26

1978 TEAM BATTING LEADERS

Average	— Jim Rice	.315	Home Runs	— Jim Rice	46*
Games	— Jim Rice	163+	RBI	— Jim Rice	139*
At Bats	— Jim Rice	677+	Walks	— Carl Yastrzemski	76
Runs	— Jim Rice	121	Strike Outs	— Jim Rice	126
Hits	— Jim Rice	213*	Stolen Bases	— Jerry Remy	30
Singles	— Jerry Remy	130	Errors	— Butch Hobson	43
Doubles	— Carlton Fisk	39	Total Bases	— Jim Rice	406*
Triples	— Jim Rice	15*	Slugging Pct.	— Jim Rice	.600*

* Led Major Leagues
+ Led American League

BOSTON BATTERS

BATTER	PCT	G	AB	R	H	2B	3B	HR	RBI	BB	SO	SH-SF	HP	SB-CS	E
BAILEY	.191	43	94	12	18	3	0	4	9	19	19	0 2	1	2 1	0
BOWEN	.143	6	7	3	1	0	0	1	1	1	2	0 0	0	0 0	0
BROHAMER	.234	81	244	34	57	14	1	1	25	25	13	4 4	0	1 3	5
BURLESON	.248	145	626	75	155	32	5	5	49	40	71	10 5	4	8 8	15
DUFFY	.260	64	104	12	27	5	0	0	4	6	11	6 0	1	1 1	8
EVANS	.247	147	497	75	123	24	2	24	63	65	119	6 2	2	8 5	6
FISK	.284	157	571	94	162	39	5	20	88	71	83	3 6	7	7 2	17
HANCOCK	.225	38	80	10	18	3	0	0	4	1	12	4 1	0	0 0	0
HOBSON	.250	147	512	65	128	26	2	17	80	50	122	4 8	0	1 0	43
KENDALL	.195	20	41	3	8	1	0	0	4	1	2	0 2	0	0 0	2
LYNN	.298	150	541	75	161	33	3	22	82	75	50	4 6	1	3 6	7
MONTGOMERY	.241	10	29	2	7	1	1	0	5	2	12	1 0	0	0 0	1
REMY	.278	148	583	87	162	24	6	2	44	40	55	14 6	0	30 13	13
RICE	.315	163	677	121	213	25	15	46	139	58	126	1 5	5	7 5	3
SCOTT	.233	120	412	51	96	16	4	12	54	44	86	7 3	0	1 1	10
YASTRZEMSKI	.277	144	523	70	145	21	2	17	81	76	44	1 8	3	4 5	5
DH HITTERS	.251		613	88	154	24	7	19	73	71	96	4 6	3	10 5	0
PH HITTERS	.217		46	5	10	1	0	0	0	7	5	2 0	1	0 0	0
OTHERS	.261		46	7	12	3	0	1	6	8	8	0 0	0	1 1	11
TOTALS	.267		5587	796	1493	270	46	172	738	582	835	65 58	24	74 51	146

HOME RUNS ON THE ROAD

WEST

At California	—Hobson (2), Lynn, Rice	4
At Chicago	—Lynn (3), Yastrzemski (2), Burleson, Fisk, Rice	8
At Kansas City	—Evans (2), Lynn, Rice	4
At Minnesota	—Fisk (2), Lynn (2)	4
At Oakland	—Fisk (2), Rice (2), Evans, Hobson, Remy	7
At Seattle	—Evans (2), Scott (2), Burleson, Fisk, Scott	7
At Texas	—Bowen, Hobson	2

EAST

At Baltimore	—Rice (2), Evans, Lynn, Scott, Yastrzemski	6
At Cleveland	—Fisk (2), Yastrzemski (2), Lynn, Rice	6
At Detroit	—Evans (3), Rice (3), Bailey, Lynn, Yastrzemski	9
At Milwaukee	—Fisk (2), Evans, Remy, Yastrzemski	5
At New York	—Rice (3), Bailey, Fisk, Lynn, Yastrzemski	7
At Toronto	—Rice (3), Yastrzemski (2), Brohamer, Evans, Fisk, Hobson	9

HOME RUNS AT BOSTON

Vs Baltimore	—Rice (4), Hobson (3), Fisk (2), Burleson, Yastrzemski	11
Vs Cleveland	—Rice (4), Fisk (2), Hobson (2), Scott (2), Evans, Lynn	12
Vs Detroit	—Rice (5), Evans (3), Scott	9
Vs Milwaukee	—Hobson (2), Evans, Lynn, Fisk, Rice	6
Vs New York	—Hobson (2), Lynn (2), Fisk, Scott, Yastrzemski	7
Vs Toronto	—Rice (3), Burleson (2), Evans (2), Bailey	8

Home Runs at Boston (continued)

Vs California	—Lynn (2), Rice (2), Scott (2), Evans, Hobson	8
Vs Chicago	—Evans (2), Rice (2), Yastrzemski	5
Vs Kansas City	—Lynn, Rice, Yastrzemski	3
Vs Minnesota	—Bailey, Lynn, Scott, Yastrzemski	4
Vs Oakland	—Rice (3), Yastrzemski (2)	5
Vs Seattle	—Rice (2), Evans, Fisk, Scott	5
Vs Texas	—Lynn (3), Evans (2), Hobson (2), Carbo, Fisk, Scott, Rice	11

	Sox	Opponent
Home Runs At Boston	94	72
Home Runs Away	78	64
Stolen Bases	74	114
Left On Base	1155	1198
Errors	146	146
Double Plays	172	167
Complete Games	57	47
Saves	26	20

FIVE HITS — ONE GAME

Lynn   — 8/28 vs Seattle

FOUR HITS — ONE GAME

Brohamer	— 4/18 vs Milwaukee	Rice	— 8/8 vs Cleveland
	8/28 vs Seattle		9/12 vs Milwaukee
Burleson	— 6/17 vs Seattle		8/18 at Oakland
	9/21 vs Seattle	Scott	— 4/23 vs Cleveland
Lynn	— 4/20 vs Milwaukee		(2nd Game)
Montgomery	— 5/21 at Detroit	Yastrzemski	— 8/27 vs California
Remy	— 4/12 at Cleveland		
	9/20 at Detroit		

THREE HITS — ONE GAME

Bailey	— 5/19 at Detroit	Carbo	— 4/15 vs Texas
Brohamer	— 6/12 vs California	Duffy	—7/6 at Chicago
Burleson	— 4/20 vs Milwaukee	Evans	— 4/22 vs Cleveland
	5/26 vs Detroit		6/10 at Seattle
	6/10 at Seattle		7/22 at Kansas City
	6/23 vs Baltimore		7/27 at Texas
	6/27 at New York		8/5 at Milwaukee
	6/30 at Baltimore	Fisk	— 4/20 vs Milwaukee
	7/31 vs Chicago		7/8 at Cleveland
	8/10 vs Cleveland		7/13 vs Texas
	9/24 vs Toronto		7/20 at Milwaukee

Three Hits — One Game (continued)

Fisk   —   7/24 at Minnesota
     (2nd Game)
     7/25 at Minnesota
     7/28 vs Kansas City
     8/8 vs Cleveland

Hancock   —   8/17 at California

Hobson   —   4/14 vs Texas
     4/15 vs Texas
     5/21 at Detroit
     (2nd Game)
     8/25 vs California
     9/29 vs Toronto

Kendall   —   5/25 at Toronto

Lynn   —   4/7 at Chicago
     5/3 vs Minnesota
     5/11 at Baltimore
     6/11 at Seattle
     6/30 at Baltimore
     7/6 at Chicago
     9/29 vs Toronto
     9/30 vs Toronto

Remy   —   5/6 vs Chicago
     6/15 vs Oakland
     7/7 at Cleveland
     7/14 vs Texas
     8/2 at New York
     8/10 vs Cleveland
     9/26 vs Detroit

Rice   —   4/9 at Chicago
     4/15 vs Texas
     4/25 at Milwaukee
     5/1 vs Baltimore
     5/6 vs Chicago
     5/20 at Detroit
     6/5 at Oakland
     6/18 vs Seattle
     6/23 vs Baltimore
     7/7 at Cleveland
     7/16 vs Minnesota
     (1st Game)
     7/20 at Milwaukee
     8/14 vs Milwaukee
     8/25 vs California
     8/30 vs Toronto
     (2nd Game)
     9/2 vs Oakland
     9/3 vs Oakland
     9/11 vs Baltimore

Yastrzemski   —   4/16 vs Texas
     5/14 at Minnesota
     5/28 vs Detroit
     6/11 at Seattle
     7/3 vs New York
     7/15 vs Minnesota
     7/16 vs Minnesota
     (1st Game)
     7/17 vs Minnesota
     8/5 at Milwaukee
     9/24 at Toronto

TWO HOME RUNS — ONE GAME

Evans   —   5/26 vs Detroit
     7/14 vs Texas

Lynn   —   7/5 at Chicago

Rice   —   5/1 vs Baltimore
     8/8 vs Cleveland
     8/30 vs Toronto (2nd Game)
     9/11 vs Baltimore

THE DAZE OF SPRING 1979

As the Red Sox opened spring training 1979, many questions presented themselves for answering. Manager Zimmer and his staff of coaches had no easy task ahead of them. What would be the overall effect of the '78 playoff loss to the Yankees? Who would replace defected pitcher Luis Tiant and traded pitcher Bill Lee? Would third baseman Butch Hobson's arm and pitcher Andy Hassler's hand respond to winter surgery? Could ace reliever Bill Campbell recover from nagging shoulder and arm problems? Where would a back up catcher for Carlton Fisk be found? Could a good hitting back up outfielder be traded for? What would be the status of first baseman George Scott? Strength was needed for the bench which proved dramatically inadequate in '78.

The winter brought very little to the Sox from the trade and free agent market. Controversial pitcher Bill Lee was sent packing off to Montreal for reserve infielder Stan Papi, a move which was not popular with Red Sox followers. Papi no sooner arrived at Winter Haven when he injured his knee and was sent back to Boston for surgery. Outfielder Mike Easler was acquired from the Pittsburgh Pirates after leading the International League with a .330 batting average at Columbus. After singing his praises, Manager Zimmer found Mike had trouble catching the baseball and he was shipped back to Pittsburgh in trade for two minor leaguers. Free agent pitcher Steve Renko was signed in late January and brought with him nine plus years of major league travel and a bunch of statistics which were not much to get excited about. Third baseman Larry Wolfe was acquired from Minnesota for Pawtucket infielder-outfielder Dave Coleman.

Gone from the '78 edition of the Red Sox were Bob Bailey and Fred Kendall, neither of whom did anything to distinguish themselves while summering in Boston. The pitching staff lost the afore mentioned Lee and Luis Tiant, who after a brilliant career in Boston where he was a tremendous crowd favorite and one who could be counted upon to "win the big one", went the free agent route and was drafted by and signed with, of all teams, the arch rival New York Yankees. The year before, much to the joy of Red Sox fans, Mike Torrez went the same route only in the opposite direction, Tiant's move was unpopular with the same fans. Some blamed Looie, others shifted the blame to the front office forces of Sullivan and LeRoux. No matter, the deed was done and the first pictures from the Yankee camp showed Tiant, an early arrival, in the hated pin stripes — a sad day in Boston. The effects of this defection might not only be felt on the mound, because it was Luis who kept the team loose in the clubhouse and on those long plane flights. As for Lee, the continual center of the hurricane and long time resident of Zim's dog house, mixed reactions arose from his departure. There was no middle ground. You either disliked or loved this free spirit. Feeling generally was that more could have been obtained for him than someone named Stan Papi. Time will tell. Lee was soon off and running in Montreal, announcing he had used marijuana, although not at the ball park. This sparked an investigation by Baseball Commissioner Bowie Kuhn who later absolved Lee from any wrong doing. There were also rampant rumors that Lee had said he might some day return to Boston as their manager. A colorful part of recent Boston baseball history was now gone to the National League, where it appears his act will go on north of the border.

If the future did not lie in trades, where would it come from? It would seem it was arriving from two New England hamlets named Pawtucket and Bristol where the kiddie Sox had performed excellently during the summer of '78. Up from Pawtucket was the International League MVP catcher Gary Allenson and the highly touted infielder Glenn Hoffman, along with assorted pitchers of some promise Joel Finch, Chuck Rainey, Burke Suter, John Tudor and Win Remmerswaal. From the same club returning for another shot were the left handed pitching sensation Bobby Sprowl, pitcher Allen Ripley, who managed to get into Zimmer's dog house a year ago but was now promising to have turned a new leaf, reliever John LaRose and outfielders Sam Bowen and Garry Hancock, both of whom carried big gloves and little bats. From Bristol (and probably to wind up in Pawtucket) were the weak hitting but excellent fielding catcher Mike O'Berry, highly rated pitcher Steve Schneck and a slick fielding switch hitting shortstop Julio Valdez. In this lot could possibly lie the answers to the Red Sox quest for another try at the annual fall classic.

The spring task then had to be not only to find answers to these questions, but to blend the newcomers into a fairly well established starting line up of outfielders Carl Yastrzemski, Fred Lynn, Dwight Evans and Jim Rice; infielders George Scott, Jerry Remy, Rick Burleson and Butch Hobson, catcher Carlton Fisk and pitchers Dennis Eckersley, Mike Torrez, Bob Stanley, Jim Wright, Andy Hassler, Dick Drago, Bill Campbell and Tom Burgmeier.

Late winter rumors had rookie pitcher Joel Finch going to Cleveland for outfielder Jim Norris, but that rumor disappeared when Finch had a good winter in the Puerto Rican League ended by reports of possible arm trouble and Cleveland decided to take a longer look at Norris. Stories also made their way back to Boston that Win Remmerswaal was impressive as a reliever in Puerto Rico, adding fuel to the hot stove league fires.

As training opened, it was obvious that Campbell's arm was not what it once was. Easler couldn't make the grade. The rookie twirlers might not be as advanced as had been hoped for. Bobby Sprowl couldn't locate home plate for some unexplained reason. Butch Hobson wasn't throwing the way he should, although time was on his side and most alarming of all was the sore arm of all star catcher Fisk. As usual, veteran catcher Bob Montgomery was named as the first to make the squad, but who would back him up — O'Berry or Allenson? Jim Dwyer was picked up from San Francisco as a spare outfielder which seemed to assure Bowen and Hancock a spot on the Pawtucket roster. On the plus side veteran Carl Yastrzemski showed up on time, despite his threats not to show up at all unless contract difficulties could be resolved. Jim Rice and outfield cohorts Fred Lynn and Dwight Evans all started hitting as expected. Evans was apparently over that late season beaning which had left him with dizzy spells the previous fall. A new slim in shape model George Scott appeared, intent upon making up for lost ground during an injury riddled '78 season. Except for some remarks about the motives of the front office (profit or pennant) on the part of Rick Burleson, the keystone combo of Burleson and Remy seemed better than ever. In the early going the pitching was, except for Eckersley, suspect. As is typical of any spring training, there were good outings mixed with questionable ones, no one laying claim to that up for grabs fourth spot. The bench seemed to lack the strength it was assumed was present a year ago. Perhaps this was merely a reflection of the collapse of both ends of this splintery board of a year earlier. Speaking of splinters, a now not-so-thin "Splendid Splinter" Ted Williams was in Winter Haven to assist the batters. With the injury to Papi, it appeared the bench would have the same members again — Jack Brohamer, Frank Duffy and newcomers Larry Wolfe and Jim Dwyer, along with Monty and whoever wins the third catching job. Not much to scare the opposition, but then again the departed Bailey and Kendall didn't exactly cause waves of fear among the enemy.

As the annual trek to Chain O'Lakes Park reached the half way point rumors were surfacing about a pitcher or two being obtained, preferably one of the starting kind and one of the relieving kind with that kindly, financially hurting, gentleman from Oakland Charles O. Finley supposedly supplying the talent and old friend and hero of the 1967 Impossible Dream Red Sox, Jim Lonborg, making it known around the Philadelphia Phillie camp he would like to return to his first love — Fenway Park. Haywood Sullivan showed little interest in playing cupid.

As the second half of the training period began, the picture of the 1979 Red Sox began to clear a little bit but still a cloud of uncertainty hung over Winter Haven. Fred Lynn came up with a reinjured knee; Jim Wright reported a sore shoulder; Dwight Evans appeared to be having problems at the plate; but perhaps most serious of all was the nagging arm problem of catcher Fisk. Back up catcher Bob Montgomery had a sore back and a flip of the coin might decide who among the rookie backstops would claim the job. One day it would be Mike O'Berry looking like the best, the next it would be Gary Allenson.

Newcomers Wolfe and Dwyer performed better than expected and a slight ray of hope for a better bench prevailed. Both could prove genuine assets as Hobson's arm was taking a long time to come around and Wolfe was filling in well. With Lynn and Evans battling problems Dwyer's stock kept rising along with his batting average. It was decided although rookie shortstop Julio Valdez had performed well and hit better than expected, he needed the every day playing experience he would get at Pawtucket. He was joined by Glenn Hoffman on his trip to the minor league complex. Should any problem arise with Rick Burleson, Valdez might quickly be summoned back to Fenway. Speaking of Burleson, he was moved to the second spot in the batting order and was replaced by Jerry Remy at the top, a move which seemed to pay dividends and perhaps should have been made a year earlier.

Meanwhile, on the mound, rookies Chuck Rainey and John Tudor were turning in good performances in their bid for a spot in the rotation. Bobby Sprowl's unexplainable wildness earned him a trip back to the bushes with hopes he might turn things around. Joel Finch, after several impressive outings, was returned to

Pawtucket along with other promising rookies John LaRose, Win Remmerswaal, Burke Suter and Steve Schneck. All of these but Schneck, who needs experience, could well appear at Fenway Park before 1979 is over. Bob Stanley turned in enough impressive performances to win a starter's job, while the other returnees Eckersley, and Torrez both showed enough to retain their spots. Young Allen Ripley was even more impressive than a year ago when he won a spot and it appears he will get a second chance along with veterans Andy Hassler and Steve Renko.

Surprise of the camp was the hitting and fielding of George Scott who appeared as a new slimmed down version of what he had been. His work and that of pitcher Stanley were the brightest hopes for a good season.

Then suddenly the six week Florida stay was over, the van packed, the final game was in the books. The trek north to Fenway was a reality. When it all started there were many questions, injuries and hopes. Now that it was over there still questions, injuries and hopes. Six weeks in the sun brought a 15-11 record, and two newcomers from the farms, Rainey from Pawtucket and O'Berry from Bristol. Allenson was returning after a brief fall engagement, along with newcomers from other major league fields, Renko, Wolfe and Dwyer. The final cut saw pitchers John Tudor, Allen Ripley and outfielder Garry Hancock heading for Pawtucket. Pitcher Jim Wright joined infielder Stan Papi on the disabled list.

The twenty five man squad looked like this: Pitchers Tom Burgmeier, Bill Campbell, Dick Drago, Dennis Eckersley, Andy Hassler, Chuck Rainey, Steve Renko, Bob Stanley and Mike Torrez. Catchers Gary Allenson, Carlton Fisk, Bob Montgomery and Mike O'Berry. Infielders Jack Brohamer, Rick Burleson, Frank Duffy, Butch Hobson, Jerry Remy, George Scott and Larry Wolfe. Outfielders Jim Dwyer, Dwight Evans, Fred Lynn, Jim Rice and Carl Yastrzemski.

The opener was scheduled for Thursday, April 5 against the Cleveland Indians, with the Sox going to Cleveland for the weekend (4/7 & 8). The announced pitchers presented a strange quirk of fate as two former Red Sox would be on the mound for Cleveland, Rick Wise and Mike Paxton and the third Indian pitcher would be Rick Waits, who was the pitcher on that final day of the '78 season defeating the New York Yankees to force the historic playoff. Manager Don Zimmer said he would start his ace Dennis Eckersley followed by Mike Torrez and Bob Stanley.

So now the camp is over and on the eve of the new season Red Sox loyalists are faced with many questions. One of the first they will be faced with upon arrival in the general area of Fenway Park is written in the graffiti artists script on the neighborhood walls and bridges — "Who Is Stan Papi?". It appears everywhere from the Lansdowne Street side of the left field wall to the fence surrounding the players parking lot. Some are even signed by the supposed author Bill Lee. Read deeper into its meaning, my friends. It may say more about the entire Sox picture than it does about one transplanted infielder from Montreal named Stanley Gerard Papi. At the time of opening day at Fenway for 1979, here is the way the Red Sox looked, player by player. We will begin with the analysis of the pitching staff.

TOM BURGMEIER — A valuable commodity because he throws from the portside. He did little except against the Yankees, a fact which in itself might be enough to keep him around. The question is can he be of help at 36?

BILL CAMPBELL — Ace of the 1977 bullpen, is he still carrying his '78 sore shoulder and arm? Little can be expected of him in the early going, especially on those cold spring evenings. Sox chances probably rest in his shoes. A recovery from his problems of last year will solve a big problem for the Sox, but keep someone in Pawtucket for the summer.

DICK DRAGO — A key member of last season's bullpen staff. He will need to repeat his '78 performance. At 34 will he be able to do it? He may be counted on for an occasional start, something which has been rare in recent years. Could well be the work horse this year.

DENNIS ECKERSLEY — Ace of the 1978 staff. Can he repeat again in '79? A strong finish brought Eck into the magic circle of twenty game winners. He will have to provide a strong start and finish if the Sox are to emerge winners this year. A popular addition when he came over from Cleveland just before the '78 season began. This control pitcher must shoulder the pitching burden this season.

ANDY HASSLER — A valuable mid season (July 24) addition to the '78 staff, this lefthander will be counted upon to better his 2-1 record of a year ago. A severe cut on his pitching hand cost him his spot on the Kansas City Royal staff and subsequent sale to the Sox. Hopefully an operation on the hand over the winter has corrected the problems of last season. He can be a key contributor, if the operation proves successful, both as a spot starter and a reliever. As the season starts he remains a question mark.

CHUCK RAINEY — A five year veteran of the Red Sox farm system, this right hander hopes to repeat the recent successes of Bob Stanley, Don Aase and Mike Paxton by stepping directly into a starting role. A very popular player with his teammates, his excellent work in Florida caught manager Zimmer's eye and he becomes a member of the staff. How successful he will be only time will tell.

STEVE RENKO — Signed as a free agent in January, Renko started his

RENKO (cont'd)

career in the New York Mets system as a first baseman. A right hander who has pitched for Montreal, the Chicago White Sox and Cubs and the Oakland A's. A nine year veteran, he brings a 89-107 record with him and at 34 the peak of his career may be behind him. Hopefully there will be a few good starts left in his arm. A question mark.

BOB STANLEY —

A product of the Sox farm system, he arrived in Boston for the 1977 season. Used as a spot starter and reliever, he posted an 8-7 record in his first year. Last season he blossomed into the premier relief pitcher of the staff and turned in a very fine 15-2 record. The work horse of last year's staff, he will have to duplicate his fine work again this year, a task which will not be easy to do.

MIKE TORREZ —

This much traveled major league veteran was the Yankee hero of the 1977 championship series and the World Series. Signed as a free agent with Boston and turned a 16-13 in '78. A right handed thrower, who can be either very good or very bad, can be the key to this year's staff. He cannot afford to have a prolonged losing streak as he did in 1978 if the Sox are to win.

JIM WRIGHT —

This right hander started with the Sox system in 1969 toiling from one farm to another until last season. A good showing in Florida put him on the Fenway mound where he became the rookie pitcher of the year with an 8 and 4 record, including many fine efforts. A shoulder problem puts him on the disabled list out of spring training, so he becomes a big question mark for the season.

THE REST

JOEL FINCH —

Several good appearances in spring training failed to earn him a ticket to Boston. Rumored as trade bait, he was sent to Pawtucket where a good first half season may find him ready to move on to Fenway. He is probably better getting the work in the minors than riding the bull pen in Boston. The big right hander may be heard from before September.

JOHN LA ROSE —

Like Finch, this native of Pawtucket returns to his home town to take up relief chores for Joe Morgan. Should anything happen to the relievers in Boston,

LA ROSE (cont'd)   La Rose may be the first to return. He appeared in one game last fall during the pennant fight with New York.

WIN REMMERSWAAL —   This native of Holland received many rave notices in the off season but has returned to Pawtucket to gain this concentration which he needs to go along with his fast ball. Another righty, he will fight it out with La Rose for the Pawsox top reliever. The winner will be the first into the Fenway bull pen. Could be ready by mid season if needed.

ALLEN RIPLEY —   Rookie hero for Boston a year ago and son of a former Red Sox pitcher, he fell upon bad times and into Zimmer's dog house and was shipped back to Pawtucket in 1978. Displaying a new attitude in this year's Winter Haven camp, he boasts more major league experience than any other Pawtucket twirler, a fact which could help his recall should any Red Sox starter falter.

STEVE SCHNECK —   The right handed pitching hero of last season championship Bristol Red Sox, he was only a long shot to win a spot on the varsity mound staff. He will summer in Pawtucket and attempt to make his mark next spring in Florida. Experience and an improved fast ball are his needs.

BOBBY SPROWL —   One of the top left handers in the Red Sox system, he jumped from A ball to the majors in less than two years. Despite an 0-2 record last fall while with Boston, he was the big hope for the future. A mysterious streak of wildness in spring training had the Red Sox brass wondering what had happened. Left behind in Winter Haven where he will start over again for the Sox A league farm club, with hopes that he might regain his former effectiveness, he had been counted upon to be a starter in Fenway this season.

BURKE SUTER —   A variety of good pitches gave Suter his best minor league season in 1978. This big right hander seems to need more experience before he is ready to appear at Fenway Park. He will start the season in Pawtucket. Where he will end it is anyone's guess.

JOHN TUDOR —   A left hander from Peabody, Mass. he had a very fine spring and impressed the Red Sox management to the point where he survived to the final cut.

TUDOR (cont'd)   A good start at Pawtucket coupled with his spring showing may earn him a spot in Boston should the need arise.

The catching staff coming out of spring training was made up of the best catcher in the majors, an aging veteran and two untried rookies. Let's take a look at them:

CARLTON FISK —   The top catcher in the majors for the past several seasons, he has appeared in more games the last two seasons than should be expected of any catcher. They may have taken their toll as elbow and arm problems idled this popular hero during the spring. As the season opened, he was going from doctor to doctor looking for a cure. His loss for the season or any part of it could be a very serious blow to any pennant hopes. There are those who believe without him there is no hope for a championship.

GARY ALLENSON —   The International League's most valuable player last season, was called up at the end of the season and made little impression and raised suspicions about his throwing abilities. Spring training did little to erase this feeling, although with Fisk's problems he appeared to win a spot on the team. The job is his if he can prove he can handle it. He comes to Boston with a reputation as a hitter. How he will handle the pitchers and throw will probably soon become evident.

BOB MONTGOMERY —   Has had a home with the Red Sox since 1970 and has been a very capable fill in for Fisk for short periods during those years. At 35 he may not be capable of a full season behind the plate and will compete in the early going with rookies Allenson and O'Berry. The Sox can rest fairly comfortably in the fact that they have a veteran of Monty's capabilities to call upon until Fisk's fate is determined.

MIKE O'BERRY —   Jumping up from double A Bristol to the Red Sox for a catcher with questionable hitting ability is no easy task, but OB is a fighter who will handle the challenge. This rookie probably would have been in Pawtucket except for Carlton Fisk's arm. Now he will get his chance. He may still be in Pawtucket before the season ends but he will have his chance first in Boston.

The infield coming out of Winter Haven was almost identical to the one that finished the previous season at Fenway Park. Hobson, who did the bulk of the third basing until the latter stages of '78, was not at third base, but only because he was recovering from the off season elbow surgery he had. It appeared he would regain his spot when he fully recovered. So here are the infield crew:

JACK BROHAMER — The late season fill in at third base for Butch Hobson, the smallest man on the team proved to be a valuable utility man at second and third bases. He did and will see action as a DH and pinch hitter. Offensively Jack enjoyed a good first half season in '78 but his hitting fell off in the second half. Defensively he showed dependability all year. He will be expected again to prove his worth in the field and at bat. Could easily qualify for the unsung hero award.

RICK BURLESON — Many claim the ankle injury he suffered in '78 was the downfall of the team last season. One of the league's best defensive shortstops, he had an off year, for him, offensively. He must remain healthy and improve at the plate if the Sox are to win in '79. A valuable part of the infield he appears ready for a big year.

FRANK DUFFY — A utility infielder, he couldn't carry the burden for Burleson during his injury in '78. Filling in at all the infield positions except first base, he represented the back up hopes a year ago. He will have to improve in this role this season if the Sox are to make a fight of it. It would appear he can do this for short periods of time.

BUTCH HOBSON — Recurring elbow problems on his throwing arm caused his removal from the third base spot late in the '78 season. The results of surgery over the winter were tested in Winter Haven and some doubts remained. Given more time to adjust, he did not open the season at third, but it is hoped only a short period of working out the kinks will find him back at the hot corner. His bat will be missed until his return.

STAN PAPI — This utility infielder came in the trade of Bill Lee. A knee injury and subsequent surgery put him on the disabled list for the season's start. He will return in mid May with a big question mark. Let's hope he turns out to be more than a graffiti name.

JERRY REMY — Stellar second baseman whose injured hand didn't help the '78 team any. Appears to be healthy and should be more than adequate at the keystone corner and at the plate. Key member of the infield with speed on the bases he will be moved to the lead off spot which should help the offense go.

GEORGE SCOTT — Perhaps the most pleasant surprise of the spring. He appeared in Winter Haven minus the excess weight he carried a year ago. Appears to be over the back problems and injured hand which contributed to his poor showing in 1978. Things look good for a big year from the man who has appeared at first base more than any other Red Sox.

LARRY WOLFE — A good utility infielder obtained in the late winter as infield insurance for the questionable condition of Butch Hobson. He will be counted upon to carry the burden at third base until Hobson's return with occasional relief work for Butch during the season. A good fielder and hitter, he will be heavily relied upon.

OTHERS

There were two other infielders in Winter Haven who may soon be heard from and should be mentioned here, although both were sent to Pawtucket.

GLENN HOFFMAN — A very talented infielder who has made an impressive record during his three years in the Sox farm system. Jumped from A ball to triple A successfully. He has been a steady shortstop who may spend the season learning what third base is all about. Should any need arise on the left side of the Sox infield he may find himself at Fenway.

JULIO VALDEZ — One of the best young infield prospects in the Sox system he will be the Pawtucket shortstop this year. Lacks only needed experience. He has fantastic range and can come in on a ball as fast as anyone in the business. This switch hitting young man from the Dominican Republic may one day wear the Boston uniform.

The outfield except for the addition of Jim Dwyer remains just the same as 1978. Jim Rice or Carl Yastrzemski, Fred Lynn and Dwight Evans.

JIM DWYER — After a winter long search for a reliable back up outfielder the Red Sox picked up Jim from San Francisco. His value at this point is, of course,

DWYER (cont'd)

unknown, but based on his past performances he should be an excellent choice as a fill in both with his bat and glove whenever the need arises.

DWIGHT EVANS —

This Gold Glove winner possesses one of the finest arms in the big leagues in addition to his fielding abilities. Victim of a late season beaning which benched him, it is hoped he has fully recovered and will be able to assume his right field duties. Dewey remains a question mark in the field and at bat, one which will need a quick answer.

FRED LYNN —

Injury plagued since his sensational rookie season. Fred is nevertheless one of the best outfielders in the majors. An off season conditioning program hopefully will pay dividends, both in the field, at bat, and in fewer injuries. The consistency which has been his trademark will be needed again if the Sox are to make a run at the pennant. The hope is for an injury free season.

JIM RICE —

The American League's Most Valuable Player in 1978. A repeat of this fine year will be a decided plus. Used in left field and as a designated hitter his value to the Sox is irreplaceable and coming out of spring training all seems to be go for the space shot home runs which are his trademark.

CARL YASTRZEMSKI —

There has never been any question about Yaz's value in the Red Sox picture. Player of the left field wall like no one else, home run hitter, first baseman — you name it, he can do it. Now after 18 years of doing it all the question of age appears on the horizon. Can he continue at 40 (on August 22) to be Mr. Red Sox? Hopefully, the answer will be yes. A vital key, as always, to the Red Sox pennant hopes.

THE OTHERS

SAM BOWEN and GARRY HANCOCK, both better glove men then hitters have been sent to Pawtucket. Available if needed, they have both filled in for short periods in the past.

So there they are, the Red Sox who came north from spring training, full of hopes and questions, the answers to which will become apparent as the season moves along.

THE FIRST HALF

Opening day at Fenway Park found the Sox 7 to 1 winners over the Cleveland Indians and old friend Rick Wise with Dennis Eckersley taking up where he left off a year earlier. Then it was off to the mid west for a short road trip to Cleveland and Milwaukee and a split of four games. The opener on the road found the two pitchers who played big roles in the pennant chase of the previous autumn gaining their initial decisions of 1979. They also took up where they left off with Rick Waits of Cleveland shutting out the Sox 3 to 0 on a one hitter with Mike Torrez taking the loss. Returning home for a nine game home stand the Sox finished by winning four straight, including three over the reigning Western Division champion Kansas City Royals. Hitting the road again they ran the string to seven wins in a row with three straight victories at Seattle before the California Angels stopped them behind Mark Clear with Andy Hassler taking the loss. Putting together one of the best April records in their history (13-7), the month came to a close with the Red Sox in first place in the American League East by one and one half games over a pesky Baltimore Oriole nine.

Certain early season trends were beginning to develop. Shutouts which were few in the early going in '78 suddenly numbered six in April. Three were turned in by Sox hurlers, Torrez, Stanley and Renko and three were hurled against them by Cleveland's Waits, Milwaukee's Caldwell and California's Frost. Dick Drago was the man out of the bullpen as Bill Campbell seemed to be fighting off and on again arm problems. Rookie Rainey looked good in four appearances. Jerry Remy's switch to the lead off spot made him a better hitter and helped Rick Burleson run off a ten game hitting streak. Fred Lynn looked like the Lynn of '75 reeling off an eleven game hitting streak and eight home runs in April. Lynn's streak along with Hobson's of eleven were first half highs. Jim Rice seemed to be taking over in left field with Yaz becoming the first baseman — DH Carlton Fisk remained plagued by arm miseries, but surprisingly good catching was coming from three men named Montgomery, Allenson and O'Berry. May saw the Red Sox drop into second place as Earl Weaver's surprisingly good team from Baltimore pulled into the league leader's spot and held on to leads of mostly a game to two games. This trend continued until the season's mid point with the Orioles showing a 5 1/2 game bulge on July 2.

The season reached the half way point on July 7 and it found Boston with a 51-30 mark. May brought a 14-12 record, but June was good to the Crimson Hose at 20 and 8. Several roster changes occurred in the first half of the season. Pitcher Andy Hassler was sent to the New York Mets on June 15th. Jim Wright went on the disabled list and was replaced by Joel Finch, up from Pawtucket. Finch turned in several good performances and appeared headed for better things after an excellent start at Pawtucket. Allen Ripley, who also was off to a great start at Pawtucket, arrived at Fenway Park in early July to bolster the relief corps. Pudge Fisk caught only six games and parts of two others and was used mainly as a DH as his arm failed to respond. Nevertheless Montgomery proved an adequate fill in. Surprisingly good catching was turned in by Gary Allenson who turned out to be a real plus for the club. Mike O'Berry also handled the catching chores at times, but lack of consistent hitting found him being sent to Pawtucket in late June for further seasoning.

Infielder Frank Duffy was released in mid May and George Scott got his wish on June 13 by being traded to Kansas City for outfielder Tom Poquette. On the same day a deal was made with the Houston Astros, which was a great one for the rest of the season. The hard hitting first baseman Bob Watson was obtained for minor league pitcher Peter Ladd, some cash and player to be named later who turned out to be the highly regarded pitcher Bobby Sprowl.

At the mythical midway point, the All Star break, the Sox had the second best record in the majors 56-32 for .636 and were only two games behind the best record Baltimore Orioles 59-31 at .656. There were many things to look back on besides those already touched upon. Fred Lynn already had a career high 24 homers for the American League lead. He also led the league in doubles at 26 and was second in RBI's at 75. Jim Rice had 21 homers and was near the top in most offensive departments including flattening umpires. Pitcher Steve Renko at 8 and 3, with two near no hitters, was justifying manager Zimmer's faith in him. Zim kept saying his pitching would be good and so it was. Dick Drago, with whom Zim had words after some remarks Drago made, was 7 and 3. Torrez had chipped in 9 wins as had Eckersley. Bob Stanley stood at 11-6, while Rookie Rainey had 5 victories. Burgmeier and Campbell had been off again on again out of the pen with 4 victories between them, all of which prompted manager Zimmer to predict 95 to 100 wins if the mound men hold up for the second half. Remarkably the pitching had held the Sox close, as in only eight of 88 games have the Sox been more than 3 runs behind going into the eighth inning. So some of the questions concerning the staff have been answered and at this point the following ones were being asked by Red Sox fans. Will Renko hold up? Will Torrez supply his usual strong finish (despite people named Dent)? Can Ripley continue to help? Eckersley and Stanley must remain steady. Is Joel Finch ready? Will Rainey overcome a shoulder problem? Will Jim Wright ever return? Will Campbell get stronger? Positive answers may spell PENNANT.

The most important thing which happened in the first half was the arrival of Watson and Poquette. This gave the Sox a reliable first baseman — DH and strengthened the bench, a fact which has allowed injured players a chance to fully recover before returning to the line up. Jack Brohamer has filled in at third base for injured Butch Hobson and at second for the hurt Jerry Remy, both key factors. Larry Wolfe and Stan Papi have filled in at short and second giving Rick Burleson needed time off. Jim Dwyer has played at first as has Yaz when not the DH with Dwyer also appearing in the outfield along with Tom Poquette. As stated before, Allenson and Montgomery have carried the catching load. As with the pitching, the fans were also asking these questions. Will Monty's age catch up with him (no pun intended) with the arrival of the dog days? Would Fisk be ready to return? Will the slight hurts to Yaz and Lynn go away? Although injuries to front liners will hurt, would the bench be adequate? While Jim Rice was not having the season he had in '78, he still was probably the biggest factor in the Sox pennant drive.

Just for the record Fred Lynn, Jim Rice, Carl Yastrzemski, Rick Burleson and Bob Stanley were named to the All Star team. A record of sorts was set when the fans selected an all Boston (Rice, Lynn and Yaz) starting outfield, although Yaz was installed at first base when an Achilles tendon started to bother him.

The Sox showed a 32-10 home record and a 24-22 road slate at All Star time and an excellent 18-8 record in one run games and 10-7 in two runners with a 7-5 record in overtime games. They were third in team batting and second in pitching.

The key questions seemed to lie with Yaz, Remy, Fisk and the pitching and what developed with the other teams in the race. It was clear that the opposition could come from Baltimore, Milwaukee and possibly New York right to the wire.

THE SECOND HALF OF 1979

The second half of the season got off to a good start and saw the Sox gain ground on the first place Baltimore Orioles. Through the middle of July the Sox hung only two games behind the leaders, the closest they were to the league lead since mid-June. From this point on things began to collapse. Jerry Remy never seemed to recover from a leg injury he sustained in an early July game at Yankee Stadium. Remy's replacement, Jack Brohamer, was doing an excellent fill in job until he too suffered a leg injury and from then on second base became a problem. With George Scott traded to Kansas City, Bob Watson was spending more time at first base but again nagging minor injuries to him affected his fielding abilities and he spent many days as the DH. Yaz filled in at first and alternated as the DH but again aching legs were limiting his use in the field. Jim Dwyer's appearances at first became more frequent and by September he was playing first base regularly. When shortstop Rick Burleson suffered a bruised hand in a game at Texas in late July the team had already begun its second successive seasonal slide, and as July ended, the Orioles lead had increased to five. Burleson recovered and gamely played in 153 games, second only to Jim Rice's 158. The "Rooster" had a fine season and much of the success the Sox enjoyed was a direct result of his aggressive play. Butch Hobson, apparently recovered from his winter surgery, played his usual steady third base while showing some of his old power at the plate. His 28 homers were high for the team behind the leaders Fred Lynn and Jim Rice at 39. On July 24 at Fenway Park in a game against the Oakland A's Carl Yastrzemski hit his 400th major league home run. The watch which started before the season actually got underway was for Yaz to get his 3000th major league hit. There were many who had hoped the 400th home run would also be his 3000th hit, but such dramatics were not to be. The suspense began to build as to when the 3000th hit would finally come. The Boston newspapers carried daily reminders of the count down on the front pages of their daily editions, adding to the suspense. The fact that the team was slipping further behind first place almost seemed to take on secondary importance and crowds jammed the ball parks hoping to be in attendance when the hit occurred. The pressure seemed to take its toll, not only on Yaz but the team itself. The Sox returned from a road trip on August 29 for a short four game home stand with Texas. Yaz had four hits in the series and needed only six as the team headed for New York. While Sox followers wished him well, secretly they were hoping for the hit to come at Fenway when the team would return to face Baltimore who was now opening their largest lead of the season over the Sox and the Milwaukee Brewers who had now slipped into second place. Yaz had one hit in the New York series and needed five as the Bosox returned to Fenway. The first game on September 7 saw Yas go three for four. Now the tension reached its height.

Fans came to the ball park on Yawkey Way for only one thing, to say they were there when the hit came. No hits on the 8th, then one the 9th, one to go. Four at bats on the 10th, but no hits as Baltimore left town with three wins out of the four games and Boston in third place, 14 1/2 games off the pace, the farthest behind they would be all year. Into Fenway came the New York Yankees for three games. Yankee-Red Sox series traditionally are sell outs as the two old rivals do battle, but now with both teams out of the pennant chase the turn away crowds no longer had as their primary concern who would win. Forgotten was the playoff heroics of a year ago. Now it was strictly Yaz. In the first game of the series he was not successful. Playing in pain with seriously hurting Achilles tendons, so bad Yaz said he could not feel his feet on the ground when he went to the plate, he struggled on. It was now a matter of everyone, players and fans alike, hoping it would end. Hopes were let it be a home run. No cheap questionable hit possibly decided by some official scorer, all wanted at least a clean hit. Then it happened! In the eighth inning of the September 12th game, with Jim Beattie on the mound for the Yankees, Yaz hit a ground single to right, just out of the reach of second baseman Willie Randolph, and the waiting was over. The long sought milestone had become a reality and Yaz became only the second American Leaguer since 1925 to get 3000 hits and the first ever in the 78 year history of the American League to reach the 3000 hit, 400 home run plateau. Only three other major leaguers had accomplished the feat — All National Leaguers — Hank Aaron, Willie Mays and Stan Musial. An emotional ceremony followed the hit, with speeches, awards, and congratulations from both teams. Yaz said, "There's nothing as great as winning the pennant. I have one goal left, winning another pennant and then winning the World Series." So twelve hitless appearances had finally ended for Yaz and for the Sox the season had also ended, as the remaining games were only playing out the string.

For the record, the Sox finished third at 91-69 and 11 1/2 games behind the champion Baltimore Orioles. It was the third year in a row that Boston had won better than 90 games, the first time that they had done that since the 1948, '49, '50 teams had all turned in 90 plus. 1914, '15, '16, '17 is the longest stretch of ninety plus seasons in Red Sox history, a record the 1980 edition has a chance to tie.

We have discussed the infield, now let's look at the rest of the club before we end our review of '79. The catching was split three ways with Gary Allenson handling the bulk. Injuries hampered the veteran back up man Bob Montgomery, and he appeared only 32 times and may have reached the end of the line. Young Mike O'Berry returned on September 1st from Pawtucket where he had been sent in late June and did most of the September catching. It seemed someone gave up on Allenson, who will play winter ball in hopes of regaining the abilities he had in the minors and with O'Berry having trouble at the plate, it would seem catching may be a problem for years ahead at Fenway, if regular catcher Carlton Fisk can't make a successful return from arm problems. Fisk caught in only eight games during the first half of the season and did manage thirty one in the second half, but from the end of August appeared only in the DH and pinch hitting roles. The loss of Fisk was probably the most damaging jolt to the Red Sox chase of the pennant and the future may well rest on his arm.

The outfielding was a plus for the Sox. Except for a few defensive lapses by Jim Rice in left field, the outfield may have been the best in the majors with Fred Lynn in center and Dewey Evans in right. Lynn and Rice tied for the team lead in home runs at 39 and Lynn became the American League batting champion with a .333 average. Rice, the American League's 1978 MVP, actually had another fine year batting .325 (third best in the league) and he had 201 hits becoming the 17th player in major league history to do it three straight years. Evans continued to display his fine defensive skills. Rice played more games than any other Sox in '79, despite nagging hand injuries. The real story was Fred Lynn who had a grand year and was as steady at the end as he had been in the beginning. An off season conditioning program paid dividends for Lynn individually and for the Red Sox in general as it was Lynn who carried the team most of the season despite some nagging injuries brought on by his hustling outfield play and daring base running. Lynn broke Carl Yastrzemski's Fenway Park record for home runs by a lefty hitter, hitting his 28th there on September 27. Tom Poquette, who came from K.C. for Scott, proved to be a capable back up outfielder and hitter.

Of the others, Stan Papi had his problems at the plate and in the infield as did Larry Wolfe who made few appearances late in the season. Ted Sizemore, who was obtained from the Chicago Cubs in mid August as a fill in at second base for the injured Remy and Brohamer, did his share of hitting but had his problems with Zimmer and some of his teammates.

The pitching which manager Zimmer predicted would be among the best he had had since coming to Boston actually did not turn out to be that bad. Except for Dennis Eckersley, there were no genuine stoppers and the Eck had his problems after reeling off eight consecutive wins at the start of the second half (7 complete games) when his arm became tired and he dropped five straight before winning his final appearance of the year for his 17th victory. Mike Torrez managed 16 wins and may have won more except he was the victim of five of the ten shutouts hurled against the Sox. Bob Stanley, used both in relief and as a starter, matched Torrez's 16 wins and proved his rookie year was no fluke. After a decent start, Chuck Rainey developed arm problems and was sent back to Pawtucket to straighten out. He returned on September 1 and appeared to have recovered, taking three of four decisions. There were a group of young pitchers up from Pawtucket who became known as the "Boys from Pawtucket" — Joe Finch, Win Remmerswaal, John Tudor, and Al Ripley. None were too successful but may hold the keys to the future in their arms. The relief chores were handled primarily by Dick Drago (10-6) and Tom Burgmeier (3-2). Bill Campbell, the former ace out of the pen, made 41 appearances but still appeared to be having his problems. Surprise of the staff may have been free agent Steve Renko who was 11 and 9. Jim Wright, who in 1978 had shown signs of promise, suffered from a sore arm and did not appear in the second half of the season. Pitcher Andy Hassler was sold to the New York mets on June 15.

At the conclusion of the last home stand, it was announced that pitching coach, the popular Al Jackson, would not return next season and would be replaced by minor league pitching coach Johnny Podres. Don Zimmer would return as manager. In other coaching changes it was announced that John Pesky would assist Zim in the dugout and the popular Tommy Harper would coach first base. The removal of Jackson was not all that popular with the pitchers.

So there it is, the end of the journey that started last February in Winter Haven. A lot happened on the way, some good, some bad. Disappointment in not winning but not a bad season for a club to win 91 games. Individually it was history making for Yaz and rewarding for Fred Lynn. Where will they go before they return to Fenway in April is anyone's guess. The questions which ended the first half of the 1979 season remain. Can Yaz continue, will Remy recover, what about Fisk and will pitching help be obtained? Left handed pitching is a big need, a back up or first string catcher is another. The free agent market and or trades, the answers will come before the spring training camp opens. 1979 is history, records in the book, it's been fun, but let's move on into the future.

The first major development for the 1980 season is the loss of free agent Bob Watson to the Yankees. To replace him, the Sox signed veteran slugging first baseman Tony Perez to a multi-year contract. Rookie catcher Mike O'Berry was sent to the Chicago Cubs to complete the Sizemore Deal, catcher Bob Montgomery tested the free agent market without much success. Right handed relief pitcher Skip Lockwood was signed from the free agent market with hopes of bolstering the bullpen crew.

The following is a statistical recap of the 1979 season.

1979 HOME STANDS AND ROAD TRIPS

Home	W	L	Road	W	L
4/5	1	0	4/7-4/12	2	2
4/14-4/22	6	2	4/24-5/2	5	4
5/4-5/20	10	6	5/22-6/1	5	6
6/4-6/10	6	1	6/11-6/17	3	3
6/18-6/24	6	1	6/26-7/2	3	4
7/3-7/5	3	0	7/6-7/15	6	3
7/19-7/26	4	4	7/27-8/5	7	5
8/7-8/19	8	5	8/20-8/29	2	6
8/30-9/2	1	3	9/3-9/5	1	2
9/7-9/13	2	5	9/14-9/20	4	4
9/21-9/27	4	2	9/28-9/30	2	1
	51	29		40	40

WINNING STREAKS

7 — April 19-26
5 — June 7-11
5 — June 20-24
5 — July 11-19

LOSING STREAKS

4 — Sept. 1-4
3 — May 23-26
3 — July 30-31
3 — Aug. 24-26
3 — Sept. 7-9

MISCELLANEOUS WON AND LOST RECORDS

	W	L		W	L
Home	51	29	One Run Games	28	19
Away	40	40	Two Run Games	14	13
Day	31	25	Extra Innings	8	9
Night	60	44	Shutouts	11	10

1979 MONTH BY MONTH

	W	L	Pct.
April	13	7	.650
May	14	12	.538
June	20	8	.714
July	15	13	.536
August	16	13	.551
September	13	16	.448
	91	69	.569
Record 1st Half of Season	51	30	.630
Record 2nd Half of Season	40	39	.506
	91	69	.569

Double Plays — Boston 164, Opponents 187
Attendance — Home: 2,353,114   Away: 2,132,768   Total 4,485,882

1979 TEAM PITCHING LEADERS

ERA	— Dennis Eckersley	2.99	Runs	— Mike Torrez	144
Won	— Dennis Eckersley	17	Earned Runs	— Mike Torrez	126
Lost	— Mike Torrez	13	Walks	— Mike Torrez	121
Games	— Dick Drago	53	Strikeouts	— Dennis Eckersley	150
Complete Games	— Dennis Eckersley	17	Saves	— Dick Drago	13
Innings Pitched	— Mike Torrez	252.1	Shutouts	— Bob Stanley	4
Hits	— Mike Torrez	254	Home Runs	— Dennis Eckersley	29

PITCHING RECORDS

PITCHER	ERA	W	L	AP	GS	CG	SV	SHO	IP	H	R	ER	HR	BB	SO	HB	WP
BURGMEIER	2.74	3	2	44	0	0	4	0	88.2	89	32	27	8	16	60	4	1
CAMPBELL	4.28	3	4	41	0	0	9	0	54.2	55	28	26	5	23	25	1	7
DRAGO	3.03	10	6	53	1	0	13	0	89.0	85	33	30	6	21	67	3	4
ECKERSLEY	2.99	17	10	33	33	17	0	2	246.2	234	89	82	29	59	150	6	1
FINCH	4.87	0	3	15	7	0	0	0	57.1	65	31	31	5	25	25	1	2
RAINEY	3.82	8	5	20	16	4	1	1	103.2	97	47	44	7	41	41	3	3
REMMERSWAAL	7.08	1	0	8	0	0	0	0	20.1	26	16	16	1	12	16	1	0
RENKO	4.11	9	9	27	27	4	0	1	171.0	174	86	78	22	53	99	2	3
RIPLEY	5.15	3	1	16	3	0	1	0	64.2	77	42	37	9	25	34	3	3
STANLEY	3.99	16	12	40	30	9	1	4	216.2	250	110	96	14	44	56	4	0
TORREZ	4.49	16	13	36	36	12	0	1	252.1	254	144	126	20	121	125	5	6
TUDOR	6.43	1	2	6	6	1	0	0	28.0	39	23	20	2	9	11	0	0
WRIGHT	5.09	1	0	11	1	0	0	0	23.0	19	13	13	5	7	15	3	0
OTHERS	8.80	1	2	8	0	0	0	0	15.1	23	17	15	0	7	7	1	1
TOTALS	4.03	69		160		29			1431.1		711		133		731		31
			91		358		47	11		1487		641		463		37	

PITCHERS LONGEST LOSING STREAKS

Dennis Eckersley	5		Bill Campbell	2
Steve Renko	4		Andy Hassler	2
Dick Drago	3		Chuck Rainey	2
Joel Finch	3		John Tudor	2
Bob Stanley	3		Tom Burgmeier	1
Mike Torrez	3 (twice)		Al Ripley	1

PITCHERS LONGEST WINNING STREAKS

Dennis Eckersley	8		Tom Burgmeier	2
Dick Drago	5		Bill Campbell	2
Bob Stanley	4		Andy Hassler	1
Mike Torrez	4 (twice)		Win Remmerswaal	1
Chuck Rainey	3		John Tudor	1
Steve Renko	3 (twice)		Jim Wright	1
Al Ripley	3			

PITCHING

1979 SHUTOUT GAMES

For Boston	WP	Against Boston	LP
4/22 Kansas City	6-0 Torres	4/7 At Cleveland	0-3 Torrez
4/26 At Seattle	2-0 Stanley	4/10 At Milwaukee	0-3 Eckersley
4/29 At California	2-0 Renko*	4/28 At California	0-5 Rainey
5/27 At Toronto	1-0 Rainey	5/18 New York	0-10 Torrez
6/10 Minnesota	5-0 Eckersley	5/20 New York	0-2 Eckersley
6/11 At Kansas City	4-0 Stanley	7/9 At California	0-6 Torrez
7/3 Kansas City	10-0 Renko	7/20 Seattle	0-8 Torrez
7/13 At Oakland	2-0 Renko*	7/31 At Cleveland	0-3 Finch
7/28 At Texas	1-0 Eckersley	8/25 At Kansas City	0-1 Torrez
9/5 At New York	5-0 Stanley	8/30 Texas	0-6 Eckersley
9/19 At Toronto	8-0 Stanley		

*Not A Complete Game

BOSTON VS A.L. EAST

	Home		Road		Total	
	W	L	W	L	W	L
BALTIMORE	3	4	2	4	5	8
BOSTON	0	0	0	0	0	0
CLEVELAND	4	3	2	4	6	7
DETROIT	5	2	3	3	8	5
MILWAUKEE	3	2	5	2	8	4
NEW YORK	2	4	3	4	5	8
TORONTO	5	1	4	3	9	4
TOTALS	22	16	19	20	41	36

BOSTON VS A.L. WEST

	Home		Road		Total	
	W	L	W	L	W	L
CALIFORNIA	3	3	2	4	5	7
CHICAGO	3	3	2	3	5	6
KANS. CITY	6	0	2	4	8	4
MINNESOTA	6	0	3	3	9	3
OAKLAND	5	1	4	2	9	3
SEATTLE	3	3	5	1	8	4
TEXAS	3	3	3	3	6	6
TOTALS	29	13	21	20	50	33
GRAND TOT	51	29	40	40	91	69

	BOS	OPP
ERRORS	142	118
DOUBLE PLAY	165	185
COMP GAMES	47	41
STOLEN BASE	60	116
CAUGHT STLG	43	40
DOUBLES	310	266
TRIPLES	34	40
HOMERS-HOME	121	59
HOMERS-ROAD	73	74
HOMERS-TOT	194	133
LF ON BASE	1087	1114

	WON	LOST
DAY	31	25
NIGHT	60	44
SHO-INDV	9	9
SHO-TEAM	11	10
1-RUN GM	28	19
2-RUN GM	14	13
EXTRA INN	8	9
VS RIGHT	67	49
VS LEFT	24	20
DBL-HDR	1	1
SPLIT	2	
STARTERS	68	54
RELIEF	23	15
STREAKS	7	4

ATTENDANCE

	HOME	ROAD
TOTAL	2353114	2132768
AVE.	29786	27698
DATES	79	77
GAMES	80	80

BATTING

CONSECUTIVE GAME HITTING STREAK
LONGEST PER PLAYER

Fred Lynn	—	20	7/30-8/18	Dwight Evans	— 7	9/8-9/14
Jim Rice	—	13	8/4-8/16	Tom Poquette	— 7	8/1-8/10
Butch Hobson	—	11	6/1-6/11	George Scott	— 6	5/10-5/16
Jerry Remy	—	10	5/7-5/17, 5/19-5/31	Gary Allenson	— 5	6/22-6/27
				Stan Papi	— 5	8/24-8/28
Rick Burleson	—	10	4/17-4/27	Bob Montgomery	— 4	4/26-5/1
Carlton Fisk	—	9	6/2-6/10	Jim Dwyer	— 3	9/27-9/29
Bob Watson	—	9	7/19-7/27	Mike O'Berry	— 3	9/12-9/14
Carl Yastrzemski	—	9	6/2-6/10	Larry Wolfe	— 3	7/29-7/31
Jack Brohamer	—	7	8/15-9/19	Ted Sizemore	— 3	9/5-9/8

1979 TEAM BATTING LEADERS

Average	— Fred Lynn	.333	Home Runs	— F. Lynn, J. Rice	39
Games	— Jim Rice	158	RBI	— Jim Rice	130
At Bats	— Rick Burleson	627	Walks	— Fred Lynn	82
Runs	— Jim Rice	117	Stike Outs	— Jim Rice	97
Hits	— Jim Rice	201	Stolen Bases	— Jerry Remy	14
Singles	— Rick Burleson	132	Errors	— Butch Hobson	25
Doubles	— Fred Lynn	42	Total Bases	— Jim Rice	369
Triples	— Butch Hobson	7	Slugging Pct.	— Fred Lynn	.637

BATTER	PCT	G	AB	R	H	2B	3B	HR	RBI	BB	SO	SH-SF	HP	SB-CS	E	RB
ALLENSON	.203	108	241	27	49	10	2	3	22	20	42	6	3	1 1	1	9 0
BROHAMER	.266	64	192	25	51	7	1	1	11	15	15	1	2	0 0	3	5 2
BURLESON	.278	153	627	93	174	32	5	5	60	35	54	9	8	3 9	5	16 5
DWYER	.265	76	113	19	30	7	0	2	14	17	9	0	2	1 3	1	4 4
EVANS	.274	152	489	69	134	24	1	21	58	69	76	3	1	1 6	9	4 4
FISK	.272	91	320	49	87	23	2	10	42	10	38	1	3	6 3	0	3 8
HOBSON	.261	146	528	74	138	26	7	28	93	30	78	6	6	0 3	2	25 8
LYNN	.333	147	531	116	177	42	1	39	122	82	79	0	5	4 2	2	5 13
MONTGOMERY	.349	32	86	13	30	4	1	0	7	4	24	1	1	0 1	0	2 0
OBERRY	.169	43	59	8	10	1	0	1	4	5	16	2	1	1 0	0	5 0
PAPI	.188	50	117	9	22	8	0	1	6	5	20	4	0	0 0	0	3 1
POQUETTE	.331	63	154	14	51	9	0	2	23	8	7	0	5	3 2	2	4 2
POQUETTE T.	.311	84	180	15	56	9	0	2	26	9	11	0	6	3 2	2	4 2
REMY	.297	80	306	49	91	11	2	0	29	26	25	6	2	0 14	9	11 5
RICE	.325	158	619	117	201	39	6	39	130	57	97	0	8	4 9	4	4 12
SIZEMORE	.261	26	88	12	23	7	0	1	6	4	5	0	0	1 1	0	1 0
WATSON	.337	84	312	48	105	19	4	13	53	29	33	0	1	5 3	2	7 11
WOLFE	.244	47	78	12	19	4	0	3	15	17	21	2	2	1 0	0	5 2
YASTRZEMSKI	.270	147	518	69	140	28	1	21	87	62	46	0	8	2 3	3	4 10
DH HITTERS	.279		614	94	171	36	5	26	104	59	74	1	6	9 6	4	0 13
PH HITTERS	.247		93	10	23	5	0	0	12	11	11	1	4	2 0	0	0 3
OTHERS	.219		160	18	35	9	1	4	23	17	23	1	1	0 0	0	25 2
TOTALS	.283		5538	841	1567	310	34	194	805	512	708	42	59	33 60	43	142 89

1979 HOME RUNS ON THE ROAD

At California	— Hobson	1
At Chicago	— Rice (2), Burleson, Evans, Fisk, O'Berry	6
At Kansas City	— Wolfe (2), Allenson, Evans, Papi, Yastrzemski	6
At Minnesota	— Hobson (2), Allenson	3
At Oakland	— Evans (2), Hobson	3
At Seattle	— Lynn (3), Fisk (2), Rice (2), Evans, Hobson, Scott, Watson, Yastrzemski	12
At Texas	— Rice, Watson	2

EAST

At Baltimore	— Lynn, Watson	2
At Cleveland	— Lynn (3), Rice (3), Watson	7
At Detroit	— Fisk, Yastrzemski	2

Home Runs on the Road (continued)

At Milwaukee	— Evans (3), Hobson (3), Lynn (2), Watson (2), Yastrzemski (2), Fisk, Scott	14
At New York	— Hobson (3), Rice (2), Watson (2), Brohamer, Lynn, Sizemore, Yastrzemski	11
At Toronto	— Hobson (3), Rice (2), Evans, Lynn	7

1979 HOME RUNS AT BOSTON

Vs Baltimore	— Rice (3), Burleson, Hobson, Yastrzemski	6
Vs Cleveland	— Lynn (5), Rice (3), Allenson, Evans, Fisk	11
Vs Detroit	— Evans (2), Dwyer, Hobson, Lynn, Rice, Watson, Yastrzemski	8
Vs Milwaukee	— Lynn (2), Burleson, Dwyer, Hobson, Poquette, Rice, Yastrzemski	8
Vs New York	— Lynn, Rice	2
Vs Toronto	— Lynn (3), Rice (2), Watson (2), Yastrzemski (2), Fisk, Hobson	11
Vs California	— Rice (3), Evans (2), Hobson (2), Lynn (2), Yastrzemski	10
Vs Chicago	— Rice (3), Lynn (2), Watson (2), Evans, Hobson	9
Vs Kansas City	— Evans (3), Lynn (3), Rice (2), Burleson, Yastrzemski	10
Vs Minnesota	— Lynn (4), Rice (3), Yastrzemski (3), Fisk (2), Hobson (2), Evans	15
Vs Oakland	— Evans (2), Hobson (2), Rice (2), Scott (2), Fisk, Lynn, Yastrzemski	11
Vs Seattle	— Lynn (3), Hobson (2), Rice, Wolfe, Yastrzemski	8
Vs Texas	— Yastrzemski (3), Rice (2), Burleson, Hobson, Lynn, Poquette	9

	Sox	Opponent
Home Runs At Boston	121	59
Home Runs Away	73	74
Stolen Bases	60	116
Left On Base	1089	1114
Errors	143	114
Double Plays	164	187
Complete Games	47	40
Saves	29	28

FIVE HITS — ONE GAME

Remy   — 5/12 vs Oakland

FOUR HITS — ONE GAME

Brohamer	— 7/15 at Oakland	Papi	— 8/5 at Mil. (2nd game)
Evans	— 6/7 vs Chicago	Rice	— 4/20 vs Kansas
Fisk	— 6/6 vs Chicago	Watson	— 7/5 vs Kansas City
	— 8/5 at Mil. (2nd game)		— 9/15 at Baltimore (cycle)
Lynn	— 7/11 at California	Yastrzemski	— 4/12 at Milwaukee

THREE HITS — ONE GAME

Burleson	— 4/8 at Cleveland		7/30 at Cleveland
	4/20 vs Kansas City		8/14 vs Minnesota
	5/1 at Oakland		8/20 at Minnesota
	6/13 at Kansas City		8/31 vs Texas
	6/17 at Chicago		9/10 vs Baltimore
	6/18 vs Detroit	Montgomery —	4/5 vs Cleveland
	6/19 vs Detroit		4/30 at Oakland
	6/29 at New York		6/29 at New York
	7/7 at Seattle	Poquette —	7/9 at California
	7/11 at California		8/5 at Milwaukee
	8/2 at Milwaukee		8/10 vs Milwaukee
	8/5 at Mil. (2nd game)		9/28 at Detroit
	8/15 vs Minnesota	Remy —	4/26 at Seattle
	9/15 at Baltimore		4/27 at California
	9/19 at Toronto		5/23 at Baltimore
	9/29 at Detroit		6/18 vs Detroit
Brohamer	— 9/16 at Baltimore	Rice —	4/12 at Milwaukee
Evans	— 5/12 vs Oakland		4/21 vs Kansas City
	7/8 at Seattle		5/5 vs Seattle
	8/2 at Milwaukee		5/7 vs California
	8/5 at Mil. (2nd game)		5/13 vs Oakland
Fisk	— 6/5 vs Texas		6/4 vs Texas
	6/9 vs Minnesota		6/7 vs Chicago
	6/13 at Kansas City		6/9 vs Minnesota
	7/13 at Oakland		6/22 vs Toronto
	8/14 vs Minnesota		7/7 at Seattle
	9/27 vs Toronto		7/11 at California
Hobson	— 5/11 vs Oakland		7/25 vs Oakland
	5/13 vs Oakland		8/5 at Mil. (2nd game)
	6/20 vs Detroit		8/10 vs Milwaukee
	7/5 vs Kansas City		8/14 vs Minnesota
	8/8 vs Cleveland		8/18 vs Chicago
	8/14 vs Minnesota		9/12 vs New York
	8/16 vs Chicago		9/21 vs Detroit
	9/29 at Detroit	Scott —	4/12 at Milwaukee
Lynn	— 4/22 vs Kansas City		5/5 vs Seattle
	5/9 vs California		5/12 vs Oakland
	5/19 vs New York	Sizemore —	8/18 vs Chicago
	5/28 at Texas		9/28 at Detroit
	5/30 at Texas	Watson —	6/19 vs Detroit
	6/4 vs Texas		6/20 vs Detroit
	6/18 vs Detroit		6/30 at New York
	6/22 vs Toronto		7/25 vs Oakland
	6/24 vs Toronto		8/2 at Milwaukee
	7/3 vs Kansas City		8/27 at Chicago
	7/5 vs Kansas City	Wolfe —	7/31 at Cleve. (1st game)
	7/7 at Seattle	Yastrzemski —	4/20 vs Kansas City
	7/22 vs California		5/1 at Oakland

Three Hits — One Game (continued)

Yastrzemski — 5/24 at Baltimore   8/1 at Cleveland
                6/24 vs Toronto   9/7 vs Baltimore
                6/30 at New York

TWO HOME RUNS — ONE GAME

Wolfe   — 6/13 at Kansas City
Evans   — 8/2 at Milwaukee
Watson   — 7/3 vs Kansas City
            8/2 at Milwaukee
Fisk   — 7/8 at Seattle
Lynn   — 4/8 at Cleveland
            5/9 vs California
            7/7 at Seattle
            8/14 vs Minnesota
Rice   — 6/7 vs Chicago
            6/22 vs Toronto
            7/6 at Seattle
            7/25 vs Oakland
            8/1 at Cleveland

As we go to press with this volume of Red Sox history, we can only hope for a bright future for our beloved heroes. Being a Red Sox fan is truly a unique experience, harrowing at times, but one a royal rooter would never trade.